THE BASICS OF
INVESTING
Fifth Edition

BENTON E. GUP
The University of Alabama

JOHN WILEY & SONS, INC.
New York • Chichester • Brisbane • Toronto • Singapore

to Jean, Lincoln, Andy, and Jeremy

Acquisitions Editor	Whitney Blake
Production Manager	Joe Ford
Designer	Laura Nicholls
Production Supervisor	Charlotte Hyland
Manufacturing Manager	Lorraine Fumoso
Copy Editor	Elizabeth Swain
Illustration	Edward Starr

Recognizing the importance of preserving what has been written, it is a policy of John Wiley & Sons, Inc. to have books of enduring value published in the United States printed on acid-free paper, and we exert our best efforts to that end.

Library of Congress Cataloging in Publication Data:

Gup, Benton E.
    The Basics of investing / Benton E. Gup.
        p. cm.
    Includes index.
    ISBN 0-471-54853-7 (cloth)
    1. Investments.   I. Title.
    HG4521.G86   1992
    332.6'78 — dc20   91-39159
                        CIP

Printed in the United States of America

10 9 8 7 6 5 4 3 2

Printed and bound by R.R. Donnelley & Sons, Inc.

PREFACE

While the fifth edition of *The Basics of Investing* was being written, the economy was in a recession, hundreds of banks and savings and loan associations failed, Eastern Airlines and other debt-laden corporations unable to meet their financial obligations went out of business, Germany was reunited, there was war in the Middle East, and there was political unrest in the Soviet Union. As these and other events unfolded, investors learned that investments are risky — the prices of securities, commodities, and real estate (including homes) go both up and down. Stock and bond prices surged upward when the news was good and plunged sharply when the news was bad. While these events are history, future events will have a similar impact on the prices of securities, commodities, and real estate. That leaves you, as an investor, with a major problem. What is a good investment? Money market funds? Common stocks, futures, or options? Perhaps real estate, diamonds, or gold?

This edition of *The Basics of Investing* examines some of the major changes that will affect you as investors and explains how to take advantage of them. One major change is *globalization* — the expanded international scope of investments. The text will help you to find out more about how to invest in companies doing business in the Orient and Europe, as those markets for goods and services expand. Another major change concerns the increased debt burdens of some large companies. Because of their high levels of debt, it is imperative that you know how to analyze them properly. World events and the financial markets are so complex that many investors turn to "experts" for investment advice. This book explains how to evaluate your own needs and what to expect from brokers, financial planners, and investment advisers.

The Basics of Investing contains important information that you should know *before* investing your funds. It was written for those who have little or no knowledge of investing, but also for those who are already investors and want to improve their performance. This book provides basic information to familiarize readers with investments in securities, options, commodities, tax shelters, works of art, and more. It explains proven methods for analyzing investment opportunities, whether in stocks, oil wells, or diamonds in the rough. However, knowing *what* to buy is only part of the story. Knowing *when* to buy is equally important, and that is explained, too.

The Basics of Investing blends traditional and modern approaches to investment decision making. The traditional approach is largely descriptive, while the modern approach emphasizes quantitative techniques. When qualitative techniques are presented, the emphasis is placed on understanding the underlying concepts

rather than on mathematics. Readers who are not proficient in math should find this book easy to read and understand.

For your convenience, a glossary of terms is available at the back of the book. A glossary is useful if you forget the meaning of naked options, yield-to-maturity, or one of the dozens of other terms used in connection with investments. There is also an appendix of useful equations that lists the most important equations used in the book. Finally, a present value table and a present value of an annuity table are available for those who want to calculate stock and bond prices.

Writing a book about the art and science of investing is a challenging task that requires the efforts of many people. I want to express my gratitude to the following individuals whose comments, suggestions, and materials are incorporated in this book. They are Roger Ashamy, Robert Bondi, Dale Brown, Gary P. Cain, Myles Delano, Bill Dukes, John Emery, Eric Emory, Gene L. Finn, Jack B. Goddard, Patrick Hennessee, Michael Hopewell, Ray Jones, Claudia Kelley, Tom Kloess, Philip U. Lee, Ben Luna, Robert McElreath, Linda Mitchusson, Joe Narun, Donald W. Park, Harold Perl, Nelda Ray, Robert W. Rittenhouse, William D. Samson, Don Sandlin, M. Serna, Louis Sofer, John Swiger, Lyle Turner, Marguerite H. VanLandingham, John Wolkowski, Bernard J. Winger, Bill Wood, Gail Zumpano. I would also like to add a special thanks to Phil Lee, who wrote the Instructors Manual.

Benton E. Gup

ABOUT THE AUTHOR

Dr. Benton E. Gup has a broad background in economics, finance, and the securities markets. After receiving an undergraduate degree in economics from the University of Cincinnati, he was a stockbroker for a large Midwestern stockbrokerage firm, where he gained firsthand knowledge of the securities markets and the needs of investors. After returning to the University of Cincinnati to earn an MBA and doctorate in economics, Dr. Gup joined the Federal Reserve Bank of Cleveland and specialized in capital markets—stocks, bonds, mortgages, and interest rates. At present he holds the Chair of Banking at the University of Alabama, and he has also held banking chairs at the University of Virginia and the University of Tulsa.

Dr. Gup is the author of *Commercial Bank Management* (with Fraser and Kolari), *Management of Financial Institutions, Cases in Bank Management* (with Meiburg), *Financial Intermediaries, Bank Mergers, Bank Fraud: Exposing the Hidden Threat to Financial Institutions, Principles of Financial Management, Guide to Strategic Planning,* and *Personal Investing: A Complete Guide.* His articles on financial subjects have appeared in *The Journal of Finance, The Journal of Financial and Quantitative Analysis, The Journal of Money, Credit, and Banking, Financial Management, Financial Analysts Journal,* and elsewhere. Dr. Gup is a nationally known lecturer in executive development programs and seminars and has served as a consultant to government and industry.

CONTENTS

PART ONE

INVESTING IN SECURITIES AND OTHER ASSETS

Choices of Investments
Explains Various Investment Alternatives

S hould I invest in the stock market or antiques? How can I invest my money and take no risks? Would I be better off in bonds or gold instead of stocks? These are typical questions that investors ask. The first four chapters of this book provide some answers to such questions. Chapter 1 explains the advantages and disadvantages of investing in securities, limited partnerships, and real assets. Securities range from stocks and money market funds to nonmarketable bank deposits. Limited partnerships are widely used in real estate and oil ventures. Real assets include real estate as well as gold, diamonds, and works of art. Chapters 2 and 3 explain the basic types of securities in detail. These include equity securities — stocks — that represent ownership in a corporation, as well as debt securities that represent borrowed funds of business and government. Bonds and certificates of deposit are examples of debt securities. The final chapter of this part explains the risks of investing and the potential rewards that investors hope to gain. We will see that, although investors expect higher rewards for higher risks, it does not always work out that way.

–

AN OVERVIEW OF INVESTMENT ALTERNATIVES

S uppose your rich uncle dies and leaves $500,000 for you to invest within the next month, and you will receive the entire proceeds five years from now. You visit a stockbroker, and when she explains different types of investments from which you may choose—common and preferred stocks, convertibles, puts and calls, and others—you don't understand a word she is saying. That's all right. Nobody does before they learn about the basics of investing.

This chapter introduces various investment alternatives so that you will be familiar with them when we examine them in depth in latter chapters. After reading this chapter you will understand the difference between stocks, mutual funds, options, and other types of investments. The process of deciding which investments to make will be covered in later chapters.

The term **investment** means committing funds for the purchase of **securities** or **real assets** in order to receive some benefit such as profit, interest income, or

reduction in income tax payments. Securities are claims that organizations sell in order to finance their needs. For example, a group of individuals may form a partnership to invest in a large shopping center complex. To raise funds to buy the property, they may sell each individual in the group a **limited partnership,** which allows them to invest in the project and receive some of the benefits of ownership without becoming involved in the management of it.

Similarly, corporations sell stocks and bonds to finance plant and equipment, inventories, and their day-to-day operations. And federal, state, and local governments sell bonds and notes to finance schools, roads, and other capital projects.

Investors holding securities issued by business and government are entitled to collect cash dividends, interest income, principal, and certain tax benefits, depending on the type of securities held. Equally important, certain types of securities can appreciate in value. Consider the case of Robert Scheller, a research fellow at the California Institute of Technology, who became an instant millionaire when 15,000 shares of Genentech stock he owned soared from $35 per share at 10:25 A.M. on October 14, 1980, to $89 per share 20 minutes later when the stock began to be publicly traded for the first time.[1] Until this time, Genentech had been a privately held company and the stock was not traded. Scheller received the shares when he worked for Genentech, a firm that specializes in contract research for health-care companies. However, most investors at that time associated Genentech with high-technology research involving genetic engineering — the commercial application of DNA (deoxyribonucleic acid), "gene-splicing," and human growth hormones. Scheller's holdings increased in value from $525,000 to $1,335,000 within 20 minutes. Today Genentech is a major pharmaceutical company.[2]

There are instant losers too. On October 19, 1987, the stock market crashed. The Dow Jones Average, a popular measure of stock market activity, plunged 508 points, or 22.6 percent. This was far greater than the 12.8 percent decline that the crash on October 28, 1929 produced, marking the beginning of the Great Depression.[3] Genentech, which had reached a 52-week high of 65\frac{1}{4}$, closed at 30\frac{1}{2}$, off 34\frac{3}{4}$. International Business Machines (IBM) closed at 103\frac{1}{4}$, off 31\frac{3}{4}$ per share from the previous day's close. But it was by no means the biggest loser. Berkshire Hathaway went from $3890 per share to $3170, off $720 from its previous day's close.

On October 19, 1987, record declines in stock prices also occurred on stock exchanges in Frankfurt, London, Paris, Hong Kong, Tokyo, Sydney, and Singapore. These declines demonstrate how the international financial markets are linked to each other. Other declines in world stock prices occurred in October 1989 and in October 1990. We live in a global financial market where events in distant places affect us and vice versa.

---

[1] Hal Lancaster, "Instant Millionaire," *The Wall Street Journal,* October 15, 1980, 31.

[2] "Biotech's First Superstar," *BusinessWeek,* April 14, 1986, 68–72.

[3] "Stocks Plummet 508 Amid Panicky Selling," *The Wall Street Journal,* October 19, 1987, 1, 22.

The instant increase in wealth for Scheller and the abrupt decline in stock prices in the Crash of 87 provide two important lessons concerning investments. The first lesson is that what goes up can come down. Equally important, values can change abruptly. The stock price changes mentioned earlier occurred within a few hours. This suggests that investors should monitor their investments on a regular basis to take advantage of investment opportunities and to cut their losses.

The second lesson is that investments in risky marketable securities are not for the fainthearted. These two "lessons" apply to other types of investments as well. For example, the price of one-carat D-Flawless (investment grade) diamonds soared from $6700 in 1976 to $60,000 in 1980, and then plunged to less than $16,000.

Investments in real assets have some advantages over investments in securities. Real assets consist of tangible items such as real estate, works of art, antiques, gems, and precious metals. In addition to their investment value, some real assets have aesthetic value because one can appreciate antiques, wear gems, and enjoy looking at works of art. Moreover, one can live in an apartment that was bought as an investment. And in war-ravaged countries, jewels are popular investments because they are small and easy to hide if the owners have to make a quick departure from their homes.

Selling real assets is a different matter. There are auction markets for antiques, works of art, and other items such as automobiles. In addition, there are flea markets and antique shows where selected types of real assets can be bought or sold. In spite of the existence of such limited markets, it may be very difficult to sell some real assets. Suppose that I want to sell my house, which has an appraised value of $150,000. If I had to sell it today, I might get an offer of, say, $90,000 or less. It might take weeks or months before anyone would be willing to offer the appraised value. The point is that there are definite advantages to being able to sell an asset on short notice without having to take a loss from its appraised value.

MARKETABLE SECURITIES

Table 1-1 lists the marketable securities that will be examined in subsequent chapters. A brief introduction to these securities is in order before examining the benefits of organized securities markets where they are traded.

Stocks

Common Stock

Common stock represents ownership of a corporation. If a corporation has 2 million shares of common stock outstanding and one investor owns 500 shares, that investor owns 0.025 percent (500/2,000,000 = 0.00025) of that firm. It is the most popular form of investment as well as the riskiest form of ownership. It is risky because the shares can decline in value, and the shareholders may not receive any cash dividends. But as Robert Scheller discovered, common stock can

TABLE 1-1 Marketable Securities

Stocks
- Common ⎫
- Preferred ⎭ Represents ownership

Bonds, notes, and other debt instruments
- Corporate ⎫
- Government ⎭ Evidence of borrowed funds

Investment companies
- Mutual funds ⎫
- Money market funds ⎭ Monies pooled by investors

Equity/nonequity options
- Puts ⎫
- Calls ⎪ Equity options are contracts to sell or buy stocks, which represent potential ownership
- Rights ⎬ Nonequity options are contracts on stock indexes, interest
- Warrants ⎭ rates, foreign currencies, and commodities

Futures contracts
- Commodities ⎫
- Financial futures ⎭ Contracts to buy or sell commodities

also be very rewarding. The shares can appreciate in price, and many companies pay cash dividends. Thus, there is a tradeoff between risks and rewards.

Preferred Stock

Preferred stock also represents ownership of a corporation; however, preferred stockholders have a "preference" over common stockholders. Preferred stocks generally have a fixed cash dividend, such as $5 per share, which must be paid before common stockholders receive any cash dividends. In addition, preferred stockholders have priority over common stockholders in claims on the assets of the company if it has to be liquidated. Investors generally buy preferred stock for the income it provides and in some cases for price appreciation. More is said about common and preferred stock in Chapter 2.

American Depository Receipts and Foreign Securities

American Depository Receipts (ADRs) are negotiable receipts of a domestic bank representing title to a specified number of foreign (non-U.S.) shares held in safekeeping in the firm's home country. Banks, such as Citibank or Morgan, register the securities with the Securities Exchange Commission and get paid a fee for their services. If and when the domestic bank receives cash dividends from the firm (less applicable foreign taxes), it distributes them to the holders. The advantages of ADRs are that they are traded like other stocks in the United States, and by trading ADRs, some of the problems of dealing with foreign securities are eliminated. These problems include delays in the delivery and settlement of foreign securities, different transaction costs, liquidity, foreign currency risks, and

THE MIDAS TOUCH

Joe had the Midas Touch for awhile. He worked for Proctor & Gamble loading boxes of soap on pallets. His pay was based on the number of boxes he loaded, and he was fast. Joe was so fast that he accumulated a tidy sum of money in a short period of time. He listened to his brother, Bud, talk about his success in the stock market and Joe thought that he would take a flyer. Joe called Bud's stockbroker and explained that he was single, had some extra money to invest, and wanted to make a fortune in the stock market. The stockbroker gave Joe a list of several securities his firm recommended. Syntex — one of the first companies to produce a birth control pill — looked good to Joe. He talked it over with the stockbroker who suggested investing in options. Joe invested $1,500 and within one week the value of the options increased to $5,200! Joe was so excited about this easy way to make money that he invested more money. In less than one month, Joe made $23,000, and that convinced him he knew how to play the market.

A friend told Joe how he made money by selling short. He said, "You can't lose if the market goes down and if it goes up, protect yourself with stops." Not wanting to appear ignorant, Joe nodded his head at the appropriate times suggesting that he knew what *selling short* and *stops* meant. After all, he dealt in options and still did not know what options were, only that they made him richer. So Joe sold short and the value of his investment increased to $27,000. He thought he could not lose — but he was wrong.

The next time Joe sold short he lost. Within a few weeks, he went from rags to riches and back to rags again. He snatched defeat from the jaws of victory. His ego and his wealth were deflated. Joe knew now that the winning streak was luck, but he believed he could do it again, and he did. However, this time Joe tried a different approach. He realized that he had to walk before he could run, so he took the time to learn something about the various types of securities and the different ways to invest.

sovereign risk — the risk that a foreign government may take some action, such as expropriation, that will adversely affect investors' interests.

More than 100 firms' ADRs are actively traded. These include such familiar names as Sony, Volvo, Honda Motor Company, Ltd., British Petroleum Company, Rueters Holdings PLC, and De Beers Consolidated Mines.

Other foreign stocks — not ADRs — are traded in the United States. For example, KLM Royal Dutch Airlines, Royal Dutch Petroleum (Netherlands), and Shell Transport and Trading Company, Ltd. (United Kingdom) are listed on the New York Stock Exchange. Similarly, some foreign bonds are also actively traded in the U.S.

Debt Securities

The following listing of debt instruments is not complete. But it is sufficient to give the reader a starting point and a frame of reference for more detailed explanations given in other chapters.

Bonds

Bonds are long-term IOUs issued by corporations and federal, state, and local governments when they borrow funds. Most bonds have an initial maturity of 15 years or more.

Most bonds pay interest twice each year for the life of the bond, and the principal amount is repaid when it matures. They are secured by the financial strength of the borrower as well as by certain assets that are used as collateral and by the taxing power of state and local governments.

Although bonds are frequently bought for income, they are an exciting investment vehicle that can provide a lot of price action. Bonds are discussed in Chapters 3 and 20.

Notes

Notes are intermediate-term debt obligations issued by corporations and governments. They generally have an initial maturity of one to seven years. Like bonds, they are backed by the financial strength of the issuer.

Treasury Bills

Treasury bills are issued by the U.S. Department of the Treasury to borrow funds for one year or less. Most Treasury bills have a maturity of three or six months. They are issued in denominations of $10,000 or more, which precludes some investors from buying them directly. The large denominations and high market interest rates have contributed to the development of money market funds, a subject that is explained shortly.

Commercial Paper

Commercial paper is a short-term unsecured promissory note issued by leading business and financial concerns. Commercial paper generally has a maturity of 90 days or less and is issued in denominations of $25,000 or more.

Investment Companies

Mutual Funds

Investors can pool their funds in an **investment company** and have professional managers invest their funds for them at a nominal cost.

Mutual funds are one such pool of funds. There are many different types of mutual funds to meet the different needs of investors. For example, some specialize in growth stocks, others in income, foreign stocks, and so on.

Money Market Funds

This specialized type of pool is an investment in short-term securities, such as Treasury bills and commercial paper. The return on money market funds varies with the returns of the securities held in their portfolios. The initial investment in some **money market funds** is relatively low, $1000 or less, so that small investors can invest indirectly in large-denomination securities that they could not afford otherwise. In addition, investors can write "checks" against their balances in the money market funds, which makes it like an interest-bearing checking account. More is said about these and mutual funds in Chapter 2.

Options

Equity options are contracts to buy or sell stocks. **Nonequity options** are contracts to buy or sell other assets including options on stock market indexes (e.g., the Dow Jones Industrials, so investors can sepculate on the stock market as a whole), options on interest rates (e.g., Treasury bills), and options on foreign currency (e.g., the Japanese yen). Understand how to buy or sell options and it will be easy to understand how they may be used to your advantage. For example, you will learn how to profit from stock prices going up or down without ever buying the underlying security.

Calls

Call options are contracts to buy a specified number of shares of stock (or some other asset) at a set price on or before a certain date. Naturally, the holder has to pay the seller a fee for the contract. The contract gives the holder the right to buy the stock if it is profitable to do so. Such call options have value and are actively traded in the securities markets.

Puts

Similarly, put options are contracts to sell stocks at a set price if it is profitable to do so. Both puts and calls can be used to speculate, or they can be used to protect existing profits or minimize losses. In addition, they can be used to replicate the behavior of other securities. More will be said about them in Chapter 19.

Rights

Rights are issued to common stockholders when a corporation sells additional shares of common stock to the public. The purpose of issuing rights is to permit common stockholders to buy additional shares in order to maintain their proportionate share of ownership. Thus, a right is an option given to common shareholders to buy additional common stock.

Rights have value and are actively traded during their short life span, which is typically 90 days or less. Not all companies issue rights to their shareholders. A detailed examination of rights and warrants is presented in Chapter 20.

Warrants

Warrants are long-term options to buy a specified number of shares of common stock at a stated price. Some warrants expire in one or two years, while others are perpetual—they never expire. Tri-Continental Corporation has a perpetual warrant. It entitles the holder to buy 8.14 shares of common stock at $2.76 per share.

Most companies issue warrants that are attached to other securities such as stocks or bonds. They are issued as a "sweetener," to make the stock or bond more attractive to prospective investors. At some point in time, warrants can be detached from other securities and traded on their own.

Futures Contracts

Commodities

Commodities, such as wheat, pork bellies, and gold, fluctuate in price. The price changes give headaches to manufacturers and processors who want stable prices, but they present wonderful opportunities to speculators who hope to profit from them. **Futures contracts**—contracts to buy and sell commodities at some future date—are traded in the commodities markets. The value of the contracts changes when expectations about commodity prices in the future change. Thus, the forecast for a wet summer may affect wheat prices six months from now, and the threat of political instability in some other part of the world can affect the demand for gold.

Financial Futures

Traditionally, the term **commodities** applied to grains and other farm products. In recent years the term has been expanded to include foreign currencies as well as financial instruments and indexes that represent the movements of the stock market. Thus, investors can trade financial futures contracts to buy and sell commercial paper, Treasury bills, Treasury bonds, or stock market indexes. One popular stock market index is the Standard & Poor's 500 futures contract (S&P 500), which is based on the stock prices of 500 firms that account for 80 percent of the value of all stocks traded on the New York Stock Exchange. It is a proxy of a portfolio of large blue-chip stocks. **Blue-chip** companies are those with a history of sound management and reasonable dividend returns.

Investors who believe that such stocks are going to increase in value can invest in the index instead of buying shares of individual companies. The commodities and futures markets offer ample opportunity for profits. However, if you are a speculator, be prepared to lose money. Read more about commodities and futures contracts in Chapter 21 before you take the plunge.

ORGANIZED MARKETS
Global Markets

Stocks and bonds, options, and futures contracts are traded on securities exchanges throughout the world. There are organized securities markets in Australia, Brazil, Canada, France, Hong Kong, Japan, New Zealand, the United Kingdom, Germany, and elsewhere. As previously mentioned, individual investors dealing in foreign markets may encounter impediments, such as difficulties delivery of securities, foreign investor restrictions, and sovereign risk. Nevertheless, investors can deal in foreign securities traded in the United States without encountering such problems by buying shares of investment companies that specialize in overseas markets or investing in U.S. companies that have overseas operations. For example, IBM, Exxon, Mobil, and Coca-Cola deal extensively in Japan.[4] Because the practices and regulations of foreign securities markets are substantially different from ours, the discussion on securities exchanges in this book is limited to domestic markets.

Domestic Stock Exchanges

Organized securities markets in the United States are divided into **stock exchanges** and the **over-the-counter markets.** Stock exchanges are marketplaces that were organized so that buyers and sellers of securities could gather at a specific time and place. Nine active securities exchanges are registered with the Securities and Exchange Commission. As shown in Table 1-2, the New York Stock Exchange (NYSE) is the largest and accounts for most (83 percent) of the total volume of stocks, warrants, and rights. The two next largest stock exchanges, the American (AMEX) and Midwest, each account for less than 6 percent of the share volume. The table also shows that the Chicago Board Options Exchange is the most active in terms of options, followed by AMEX. Because the NYSE dominates stock trading activity on the U.S. securities exchanges, discussions of exchange practices here and in later chapters deal primarily with those of the NYSE.

Table 1-2 also shows the volume of trading securities in recent years. During the 1982–1987 period, the total number of equity and option securities traded increased dramatically, reflecting the increased trading activity of financial institutions and nonfinancial corporations.

Figure 1-1 provides a global perspective of trading activity. It shows that trading volume in Tokyo dwarfs the NYSE and other major exchanges in the world. It also shows that the National Association of Securities Dealers Automatic Quotation System (NASDAQ), which is discussed next, accounts for the third largest trading volume.

---

[4] "You Can Make Money in Japan," *Fortune,* February 12, 1990, 85–92.

TABLE 1-2 Volume of Equity/Options Sales on U.S. Securities Exchanges (data in thousands)[a]

	Stocks[c] (Shares)	Warrants (Units)	Rights (Units)	Equity Options		Non-Equity Options[e,f] (Contracts)
				Traded (Contracts)	Exercised[d] (Contracts)	
All Registered Exchanges For Past Six Years						
Calendar year: 1982	22,423,023	56,053	21,500	137,266	9,202	41
1983	30,146,335	157,942	11,737	134,286[b]	13,629	14,399
1984	30,456,010	77,452	13,924	118,925	11,917	77,512
1985	37,046,010	108,111	33,547	118,553	10,512	114,190
1986	48,337,694	195,501	47,329	141,931	14,545	147,234
1987	63,770,625	238,357	74,014	164,432	17,020	140,698
Breakdown of 1987 Data by Registered Exchange[g]						
* American Stock Exchange	2,496,326	69,400	2,092	52,771	5,188	18,179
* Boston Stock Exchange	819,833	0	0	0	0	0
* Cincinnati Stock Exchange	194,429	0	0	0	0	0
Midwest Stock Exchange	3,329,056	0	0	0	0	0
* New York Stock Exchange	53,037,522	134,364	71,515	1,306	157	2,193
Pacific Stock Exchange	2,033,856	32,996	407	18,952	2,106	459
* Philadelphia Stock Exchange	834,588	1,597	0	18,088	1,932	11,067
Spokane Stock Exchange	25,015	0	0	0	0	0
* Chicago Board Options[b]	0	0	0	73,315	7,637	108,799

Source: U.S. Securities and Exchange Commission.

Figures may not sum due to rounding.

N.A. = Not available.

* Data of those exchanges marked with an asterisk cover transactions cleared during the calendar month; clearance usually occurs within five days of the execution of a trade. Data of other exchanges cover transactions with effective trade dates falling within the reporting month.

[a] Data on the value and volume of equity security sales are reported in connection with fees paid under Section 31 of the Securities Exchange Act of 1934 as amended by the Securities Acts Amendments of 1975. They cover odd-lot as well as round-lot transactions.

[b] Data for June 1, 2, and 3, 1983, are not included.

[c] Includes voting trust certificates, certificates of deposit for stocks, and American Depositary Receipts for stocks, but excludes rights and warrants.

[d] Exercised contracts do not include January and February 1985 data.

[e] Includes all exchange trades of call and put options in stock indices, interest rates and foreign currencies.

[f] Trading in non-equity options began October 22, 1982.

[g] Total market value for individual exchanges does not include data for equity options exercised.

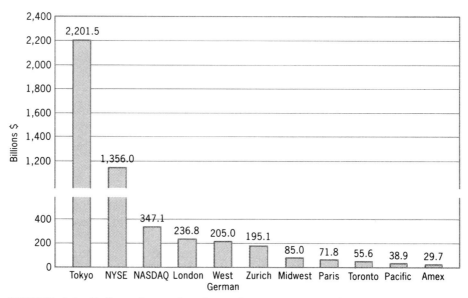

FIGURE I-I   Dollar volume of equity trading in major world markets, 1988. *Source:* NASD

Over-the-Counter Market

The over-the-counter market (OTC) consists of **brokers** and **dealers** located throughout the world who communicate with each other by telephone, teletype, or by other means. In the United States, brokers and dealers in the OTC market are regulated by the **Securities and Exchange Commission (SEC)** and the **National Association of Securities Dealers (NASD).** The SEC is a government agency, and the NASD is the self-regulatory organization responsible for regulating the OTC securities market in the United States. In 1938, the Maloney Act amendment to the Securities Exchange Act of 1934 authorized the establishment of the NASD, under SEC oversight (1) to promote the investment banking and securities business, (2) to standardize practices and principles, and (3) to promote high commercial standards and observance of federal and state securities laws by its members. Almost 7000 broker–dealer firms are members of the NASD, and over 450,000 persons are registered with the NASD as sales representatives and principals of member firms.

Brokers and Dealers

The difference between brokers and dealers is that brokers act only as agents for their customers, since they do not own the stocks they are trading. Brokers receive a commission for bringing the buyer and seller together. Such orders are called **agency orders.** In contrast, dealers own the stocks they trade. They are called **market makers** and they make a market (take a position) in selected stocks. Their

income comes from buying stocks at low prices and selling them at higher prices. Many firms are both brokers and dealers, but they do not act in both capacities in the same transaction.

Suppose you tell your broker to sell 100 shares of Apple Computer, Inc., at the best price available at that time — the **market price.** The order may be handled in two ways. If the firm makes a market in Apple, it can sell stock from its own inventory based on the best offer price available on the **National Association of Securities Dealers Automatic Quotation System (NASDAQ;** pronounced *naz-dak*). It is a computerized system that provides price quotation information on over 5700 domestic and foreign securities. The firm will trade the stock with a markup or markdown that is equivalent to a commission. In this case the firm is acting as a dealer and charging a markup. This type of transaction is called an **internalized order** because it is accomplished within the firm.

There are three levels of NASDAQ service. Level 1 service provides only price and quotation information, but does not identify the market makers. It can be used to obtain the best bid and offer or "**firm quotes**" — the prices at which the highest bidding market maker will buy or the lowest offering the market maker will sell stock. The Level 1 service is distributed through terminals leased by investors from private vendors such as Reuters and Quotron. Some vendors provide additional information about the stocks, including news announcements. NASDAQ Level 2 service, which is provided on NASDAQ-owned terminals, as well as through vendor- and investor-owned terminals, gives price information, volume, and other market summary information. NASDAQ Level 3 service contains the same information as Level 2, but it also allows registered market makers to enter price quotations, last sale prices, and sizes of orders into the system, and to report the stock's trading activity.

The alternative is for your broker to get the price from other market makers in Apple using NASDAQ's Level 2 or 3 service. On average, there are about eight market makers for every stock. Some have as many as 50 market makers, and others as few as two. Two is the minimum for the system to display price quotes. Your broker's terminal screen will display the best bid and best asked prices of the market makers. Bid and offer quotations must be firm for at least 100 shares to assure execution-quality quotations. **Best bid** is the highest price dealers (market makers) will pay for stock you want to sell, and **best asked (or offered)** is the lowest price they will sell stock to you. For example, Apple is quoted at $39 bid – 39\frac{1}{4}$ asked. This means you can sell Apple at $39 per share or buy additional shares of it at 39\frac{1}{4}$ per share. The difference between the bid and asked prices is called the **bid/ask spread.** In this case the spread is $0.25 ($39$\frac{1}{4}$ − $39 = $0.25).

If you are willing to buy Apple at 39\frac{1}{4}$ and instruct your broker to do so, the trade can be *locked in,* which means that you bought the stock.[5]

Market makers participate in NASD's **Small Order Execution System**

---

[5] The term **locked in** is used in connection with the Automated Confirmation Transaction (ACT) service. Locked-in transactions are sent to clearing corporations to be processed at the end of each ACT cycle. Locked-in trades can occur as a result of positive actions taken by the order entry firm, when orders are matched by the computer, or when no contra action was taken during the ACT cycles.

(SOES), which guarantees execution of agency orders at the best price for small orders (1000 shares or less in National Market Systems stocks [see following section] and 500 shares in others). Your broker may sell your Apple using SOES or deal directly with a market maker. The broker must get a "firm quote" and trade the stock at the best price available unless some price limit was specified. Brokers representing their customers may negotiate with market makers to determine the actual price at which the trade will be consummated.

One important difference between the OTC market and stock exchanges is that the OTC is primarily a **negotiated dealer principal market,** while the stock exchanges are **quasiauction markets** (less dealers and more broker or agency transactions). In an exchange market, the stocks are traded among all interested parties on the floor of the stock exchanges, and through a special type of broker–dealer called the specialist (which will be discussed in Chapter 7). Years ago OTC transactions were negotiated by brokers and dealers who communicated by telephone and teletype. Today computers are matching many buy and sell orders with best quotes. However, there are many OTC securities that are not currently part of the NASDAQ. Prices on such securities are listed in the interdealer **Pink sheets** (stocks), **Yellow sheets** (corporate bonds), and the **Blue List** (municipal securities). Transactions for such securities are negotiated.

National Market System

The **NASDAQ National Market System (NASDAQ/NMS)** is that segment of the NASDAQ market covered by real-time last-sale reporting. More than 3000 of the larger, more active securities are in this group. There may be 15 market makers competing for transactions in a particular stock. Transactions are reported to the NASDAQ data center within 90 seconds following execution of the order. As noted in the last section, price information including the best bid and offer prices — the **inside market** — is available on NASDAQ securities.

The **Intermarket Trading System (ITS)** links the NASD's **Computer Assisted Execution System (CAES)** with seven stock exchanges: New York, American, Boston, Cincinnati, Midwest, Pacific, and Philadelphia. CAES automatically executes transactions and creates a paper record for the buyer and seller. In 1982, the NASD joined the ITS, which permits exchange member firms to make markets away from any stock exchange trading floor. Some exchanges have obtained unlisted trading privileges in NASDAQ listed stocks through a NASDAQ system linkage. The NASD has also established a satellite link with financial markets in London and Singapore that permits real-time quotations on securities in those markets.

Table 1-3 lists the share volume and number of companies traded on NAS-DAQ, NYSE, and AMEX over a ten-year period. There was dramatic growth in both the share volume and number of companies traded on NASDAQ in comparison to the two stock exchanges. One reason for NASDAQ's growth is the difference in requirements for listing a stock on NASDAQ and on the exchanges. For example, for firms to list on NASDAQ they must have net tangible assets

TABLE 1-3 Share Volume/Number of Companies NASDAQ, NYSE, and AMEX Comparison Chart 1978–1988

	NASDAQ	NYSE	AMEX
1978	2,762,499,000	7,205,059,000	988,599,000
	2475	1581	1004
1979	3,651,214,000	8,155,914,000	1,100,264,000
	2543	1565	931
1980	6,691,631,000	11,352,294,000	1,626,073,000
	2894	1570	892
1981	7,823,410,000	11,853,741,000	1,343,400,000
	3353	1565	867
1982	8,432,275,000	16,458,037,000	1,337,725,000
	3264	1526	834
1983	15,908,547,000	21,589,577,000	2,080,922,000
	3901	1550	882
1984	15,158,823,000	23,071,031,000	1,545,010,000
	4097	1543	792
1985	20,699,146,000	27,510,706,000	2,100,815,000
	4136	1540	783
1986	28,736,561,000	35,680,016,000	2,978,612,000
	4417	1573	796
1987	37,890,006,000	47,801,309,000	3,505,955,000
	4706	1647	869
1988	31,070,103,000	40,849,537,000	2,515,025,000
	4451	1681	896
Percentage increase in share volume over last 10 years	1025%	467%	154%
Percentage change in number of companies over last 10 years	+ 80%	+ 6%	− 11%
Average daily volume in 1988	122,807,000	161,461,000	9,941,000

Source: NASD.

(total assets less goodwill and total liabilities) of at least $2 million and at least 100,000 publicly held shares. For firms to list on the NYSE they must have net tangible assets of at least $18 million and a minimum of 1,100,000 publicly held shares with a minimum market value of $18 million. There are many small firms that qualify for listing on NASDAQ that do not qualify for the NYSE. The fact that there are more small firms than large ones helps to explain the unprecedented growth of OTC listings and trading activity.

Continuous Markets

Under normal circumstances, stock exchanges and the NASDAQ system provide a **continuous market**—a market that has frequent trading activity and continuous real-time execution-quality quotation prices. Some stocks may trade once a

year, while others trade thousands of shares per day. The aggregate volume of trading on the NYSE and NASDAQ is one indicator of a continuous market, but it may be misleading. The volume on the NYSE was 604.3 million shares when the stock market panicked on Monday, October 19, 1987 (Black Monday), almost twice the prior record volume of 338.5 million the previous Friday. To put these numbers in perspective, the average daily trading activity on the NYSE in 1986 was 141 million shares. However, the volume on Black Monday and the following Tuesday was so heavy that IBM and Merck could not be traded at times because market makers were overwhelmed with unfilled sell orders.[6] This, of course, was the exception rather than the rule.

A continuous market has five attributes: frequency of sales, narrow bid/ask spreads, small price changes, prompt execution, and liquidity.

Frequency of Sales

Stocks can be bought or sold at any time when the market is open for trading.

Narrow Bid/Ask Spreads

A relatively small spread is desirable between the bid and asked price. For example, a $1 spread on a $20 stock and a $5 spread on a $100 stock are not unreasonable.

A recent study revealed that 85 percent of NASDAQ volume occurs in stocks with a $\frac{1}{4}$ point or less inside spread, and 50 percent of the NASDAQ/NMS volume had an inside spread of $\frac{1}{4}$ point or more. The average spread on the NYSE in 78 percent of quotes was $\frac{1}{4}$ point or less.[7]

Small Price Changes

When the spread is small in actively traded stocks, price changes between transactions tend to be relatively small. In the previous example, if a trade occurred at $19\frac{1}{2}$, the next trades could have been at $19\frac{5}{8}$ and $19\frac{3}{4}$. Price changes of less than $\frac{1}{2}$ are quite common. However, in stocks that are not actively traded, or in higher priced stocks, spreads tend to be wider and price changes greater. To observe the size of price changes during a day of trading, examine the transactions that appear daily in most local newspapers for various markets.

Prompt Execution

Orders are executed promptly in a continuous market. It takes seconds for an order to be executed at the market price on the NYSE. The NASDAQ system has reduced the time required to execute orders on the stocks that are covered by it to a few seconds also.

---

[6] James B. Stewart, "Terrible Tuesday: How the Stock Market Almost Disintegrated a Day after the Crash," *The Wall Street Journal*, October 20, 1987, 25.

[7] New York Stock Exchange, *Fact Book 1989*, 1989, 16; and NASD, *Quality of Markets*, 1988, 29.

Liquidity

The term **liquidity** refers to an investor's ability to convert assets into cash on short notice with little or no loss in current value. Frequency of sales, small spreads and price changes, and prompt execution all add up to increased liquidity for investments. To illustrate the advantage of liquidity, assume that at 11:00 A.M. you decide that you want to sell 100 of your shares of McDonald's Corporation. All you have to do is make one telephone call to your stockbroker and within a few seconds the order will be executed. Compare this to the sale of a parcel of real estate where the transaction would take months, or compare it to the sale of an automobile. It would be very unusual to sell a car within minutes or seconds at fair market value. Certainly, liquidity is a highly desirable attribute.

Information

Another advantage of investing in securities is that information about the market prices of securities is readily available. The prices of securities listed on major stock exchanges and the prices of NASDAQ securities are published daily in newspapers, and up-to-the-minute quotes can be obtained from stockbrokers or on home computers when investors subscribe to quotation services. Thus, investors are able to monitor the current value of their securities.

Information about many of the companies listed on stock exchanges and traded on the NASDAQ market is also available through various investment services such as Standard & Poor's and Moody's and through reports from stockbrokerage firms. The exchanges and NASDAQ require listed companies to give their stockholders periodic reports on earnings and any other information that may affect the value of the security. The Securities and Exchange Commission requires all companies registered with it to make periodic reports. Moreover, periodicals such as *The Wall Street Journal, USA Today, Forbes, BusinessWeek,* and *Fortune* contain articles about many companies.

Size of Transactions

Investors in the securities market can make transactions of almost any size. One can invest $50 or $50 million, just as one can buy one share or thousands of shares. The minimum denomination of some securities, such as bonds, keeps some investors from buying them. Corporate bonds usually have a minimum denomination of $1000, and some U.S. government notes have a minimum denomination of $10,000. However, the value of stocks can range from pennies to thousands of dollars per share. A typical stock on the NYSE sells for $10 to $40. A typical stock on NASDAQ/NMS sells for $8 to $12.

Low Commission Costs

When compared with commission costs for the sale of most real assets, commissions in the securities market are low. Commission charges are competitive among stockbrokerage firms. Those firms that offer a wide range of services to

their customers generally charge a higher commission fee than so-called discount stockbrokerage firms that specialize in executing orders, but do not offer the same variety of services as some other firms. For example, assume that you wanted to purchase 100 shares of stock at $40 per share, which amounts to $4000. The commission at a major stockbrokerage firm may be $81.80 (2.0 percent), while the same transaction at a discount firm may cost only $30.00 (0.75 percent). You have to decide whether the services, such as investment advice and recommendations, are worth the extra $51.80. By way of comparison, commissions on real estate are commonly 7 percent or more, and markups on jewelry are commonly 100 percent or more.

Insured Accounts

Investors in securities are also protected by the **Securities Investor Protection Corporation (SIPC),** which was created by Congress in 1970 to protect customers of SIPC member firms from certain financial losses should the firms fail. With a few exceptions, all broker–dealers registered with the Securities and Exchange Commission and all members of national stock exchanges are required to be members of SIPC. Currently, the limits of protection are $500,000 per customer, except that claims for cash are limited to $100,000 per customer. However, it should be noted that SIPC does *not* protect an investor from losses arising from fluctuations in the stock market or any other investment medium.

Regulation

The investor is further protected by regulation of the securities industry, both by government and by organizations within the industry. Interstate transactions and some intrastate transactions of securities are subject to certain federal laws and to regulation by the Securities and Exchange Commission. Securities must be registered with the SEC, and stockbrokers, dealers, and stock exchanges are also required to register with the SEC. In addition, their personnel are required to pass tests concerning knowledge of the securities business and security laws.

The Commodities Futures Trading Commission (CFTC) regulates the trading of commodities futures contracts on U.S. futures exchanges.

The Securities Investors Protection Corporation (SIPC) provides financial protection for the customers of brokers. Although it is not a regulatory agency, it cooperates with the SEC, NASD, and law enforcement authorities on matters dealing with violations of laws and actions where SIPC customer protection proceedings have been initiated. More will be said about the SEC, CFTC, and SIPC in Chapter 5.

The Board of Governors of the Federal Reserve System regulates the amount of credit that can be extended when buying securities on credit, which is called *margin,* or when borrowing and using securities as collateral for a loan.

The Department of Justice also gets involved in the approval of large corporate mergers.

State laws commonly called **Blue Sky Laws** require state registration of securities, dealers, and salespersons. The term *blue sky* is believed to have originated when a judge ruled that a particular stock had about the same value as a patch of blue sky.

Stockbrokers and dealers are also regulated by NASD. This organization has developed standards of quality and operating rules for members firms and their representatives.

Finally, the stock exchanges have their own rules. For example, New York Stock Exchange has certain minimum financial standards for stockbrokers and member firms. Generally, the rules and regulations of the federal and state governments and the industry attempt to protect the investing public from fraud and to ensure high-quality standards for the industry.

NONMARKETABLE SECURITIES

Deposit-Type Securities

A variety of nonmarketable, deposit-type securities are offered by financial institutions such as commercial banks, savings and loan associations, mutual savings banks, and credit unions. These securities are called by many names: time and savings accounts, passbook savings, share accounts, Christmas club accounts, golden age accounts, and so on. Although such securities are not marketable, they have certain desirable features: (1) some accounts are insured, (2) they provide liquidity, (3) they have a known rate of return, and (4) their market value does not fluctuate.

Insured Accounts

Several government agencies as well as some private insurance companies insure accounts at many, but not all, financial institutions. For example, the **Federal Deposit Insurance Corporation (FDIC)** insures accounts in the majority of commercial banks, savings and loans, and mutual savings banks. Each account in institutions that are members of the FDIC is insured for amounts up to $100,000. Similarly, the National Credit Union Administration insures accounts at member credit unions.

Federally insured accounts are safe. If a financial institution should become insolvent, depositors with insured accounts are protected up to the insured amount of $100,000. As previously mentioned, some financial institutions have neither federal nor private deposit insurance. If an uninsured institution should fail, depositors might lose their total investment. Recognizing this risk, uninsured financial institutions frequently pay higher interest rates on their deposits than insured institutions.

Liquidity

In addition to the safety provided by insurance, most types of savings accounts are relatively liquid. Investors can generally withdraw their funds at any time with no loss in principal. However, certain time deposits stipulate that if depositors withdraw their funds before an interest crediting period, they may lose some of the interest accrued on their accounts. **Time deposits** are funds that have been deposited for a specific period such as 90 days, 6 months, 1 year, or longer. Time accounts typically pay higher rates of interest than regular savings accounts. Investors can also withdraw their principal amount from time accounts, but an early withdrawal means they will not earn the higher interest rates.

Rate of Return

Financial institutions offer a wide variety of transaction accounts, and time and savings deposits with different denominations, interest rates, and maturities. **Transaction accounts** refer to accounts that can be used to pay your bills by check, by having the financial institution pay it for you, or by some other means. Demand deposits, or checking accounts as they are commonly called, are one type of transaction account. Some institutions pay interest on such accounts if they are sufficiently large. Money market funds are another popular type of transaction account. Unlike transaction accounts at commercial banks, accounts at money market funds are not insured by an agency of the federal government, except for those at brokerage firms, which are covered by the SIPC. Accounts that are uninsured by the federal government are considered riskier than insured accounts.

Time deposits, also called **certificates of deposit (CDs),** are issued by commercial banks and other types of financial institutions in a variety of amounts, interest rates, and maturities. They are called time deposits because the funds must be left on deposit for an agreed time, such as six months, to collect the promised interest. There is a penalty — you get less interest — for premature withdrawal of funds. Large CDs of $100,000 or more are negotiable securities. Small CDs pay higher interest rates than savings deposits. There is usually a minimum denomination for small CDs, such as $100, $500, and so on. There is no minimum denomination for **savings accounts,** and funds can be withdrawn at any time. Savings accounts earn less interest than time deposits.

United States Savings Bonds

The Treasury promotes the sale of savings bonds, particularly through payroll deductions, as part of its debt management program. It offers two types of savings bonds, series EE and HH. Both series are replacements for series E and H bonds, which are no longer issued.

The series EE bonds are sold at 50 percent of their face value in denominations of $50 to $10,000. If they are held to maturity (11 years), their accrued interest

provides investors with a minimum 6-percent return if held five years or more. After five years, a market-based rate is used to determine the redemption value. The bonds are registered in the name of the holder and cannot be used as collateral for a loan.

The series HH bonds provide current income. They are sold at face value in denominations of $500 to $10,000. Equal semiannual payments made over the 10-year life of these bonds provide investors with a 6-percent return.

LIMITED PARTNERSHIPS

Limited partnerships offer investors an intermediate position between owning securities and owning real assets such as real estate, oil and gas properties, railroad cars, cable television stations, and other enterprises. Limited partnerships give "small investors" the opportunity to "own" a portion of a real asset such as an oil well. The limited partners invest a large part of the capital required for such projects, and they get to share in the revenues and other benefits from that project. The general partners may or may not invest some of their own funds. Nevertheless, they also share in the revenues and benefits for operating the project and putting the deal together. The extent to which the general partners share in the revenues varies widely from partnership to partnership and is something to consider carefully before investing in one. More information about limited partnerships is presented in Chapter 17.

REAL ASSETS

You can invest in real assets that range from antiques to xylophones and make a lot of money, if you know what you are doing and you are lucky. The knowledge required to invest in some real assets tends to be more specialized than the knowledge required to invest in securities. For example, the knowledge required to invest in Chinese or French porcelain is substantially different from the knowledge required to invest in sports cars or airplanes. In contrast, someone who is familiar with security analysis, a subject that is examined in considerable detail in Chapter 9 – 14, should be able to analyze companies in virtually any industry with little or no difficulty. Thus, the scope of real assets covered in this book is limited to those that tend to be popular investments such as real estate and diamonds. These are examined in Chapters 17 and 18.

ORGANIZATION OF THE BOOK

This book is organized to help you make intelligent investment decisions. If you use the various techniques suggested in this book, you may gain the substantial rewards that all investors desire.

Learning about investments is fun, but it also involves a substantial amount of work. You must know some definitions and basic information in order to be an intelligent investor. Most investors want to be rich, not knowledgeable, but investors greatly increase their chances of becoming rich if they make intelligent decisions.

Choices of Investments

This book is divided into five parts. As shown in Table 1-4, the first part is about "choices." As mentioned in this chapter, you have unlimited investment opportunities in securities and real assets. This part of the book examines the two principal types of securities that you should become familiar with—stocks and bonds.

The *value* of securities is also introduced in this section. After all, you do not want to buy a stock for more than it is worth. Moreover, if a stock is so good, why are other people willing to sell it to you? Many investors fail to consider these points when they purchase a stock.

In addition, the first part of this book indicates the average return that can be expected from investing in stocks and bonds.

Although it is hard to believe, one method of stock selection advocated by some academicians is throwing darts at the stock quotation page of *The Wall Street Journal.* These academicians think they can do as well with this method of stock selection as professional investment advisors can do by making "intelligent" investment decisions. They claim that stock prices follow a random walk and that current prices fully reflect all available knowledge about the stock. Do not take sides on this issue yet, since it is not as farfetched as it may initially seem. Wait until you read more about the dart method before laughing at it.

Mechanics of Investing

Part 2 of this book examines how the securities markets function. It gives basic information about stockbrokerage firms that you should know before you invest.

TABLE I-4 Organization of Book

Part 1 • **Investing in Securities and Other Assets**
Choices of Investments: Explains various investment alternatives

Part 2 • **The Securities Business**
Mechanics of Investing: Examines how the securities markets function

Part 3 • **Analyzing Securities**
Analysis of Investment Opportunities: How to analyze investment opportunities

Part 4 • **Investment Administration**
Decisions: Which Investments to Choose: Managing your investments

Part 5 • **Special Situations**
High Flyers: Speculative investments

Remember Joe in Box 1-1, "The Midas Touch"? He did not really understand what selling short and stop orders meant. All that and more are covered in this part. By the way, Joe could have saved virtually all of his money if he had made correct use of stop orders or put options.

Analysis of Investment Opportunities

Part 3 is the fun part. After you learn what stocks and bonds are and how to buy and sell them, the important question becomes which ones should be bought and sold? Figuring out which securities to buy or sell is like a game. The objective of the game is to be the first one to determine which securities are going up or down. If other people figure that out first, they will be the big winners and you may only get a small part of the money to be made through buying and selling a certain security.

There are several ways that skillful investors determine the securities they think will be winners. Some people make detailed studies of financial and economic data; others draw pretty pictures and call themselves chartists. Allegedly, these charts are very accurate in predicting stock price movements. Still others throw darts.

Recently, I was on a long airline flight and was glancing through the magazine that was in the seat pocket in front of me. In the magazine was an advertisement for a device that measured body cycles — biorhythms. The ad stated that the device could be used by commodities traders to make better timing decisions and by stock options professionals to select the best days for speculative moves. Who knows, maybe there is a little bit of validity in all of these methods!

Decisions: Which Investments to Choose?

You may recall the child's rhyme, "This Is the House That Jack Built." It starts with the malt that lay in the house that Jack built. Then the rat eats the malt; and the cat kills the rat that ate the malt; and the dog worries the cat that killed the rat that ate the malt, and so on. This book is organized in that same building-block fashion. Having learned what stocks and bonds are, how to buy and sell them, and which ones to buy and sell, you are ready to ask how many should be bought and sold and when they should be bought and sold. Part 4, Investment Administration, deals with these questions. After reading this part of the book, people frequently say, "Why didn't you tell me that before I bought all those stocks?"

Taxes, limited partnerships, and real estate investments, as well as antiques and jewels, are also covered in this part of the book. Which do you think is worth more, a one-carat diamond or a one-carat emerald?

High Flyers

Part 5 covers the options that Joe used to make his small fortune. It also explains convertible issues and commodities. Strong hearts and strong stomachs are required for this section. Investors who are not willing to take great risks in order to

"make a killing in the market" are wasting their time by reading this section. On the other hand, if you have a gambling spirit, here is where the action is.

CONCLUSION

There is an old proverb that the longest journey begins with a single step. So it is with investments. The first step was an overview of the wide range of opportunities available to investors. Among them are stocks, bonds, options, commodities, limited partnerships, and real assets.

There is another saying. You have to learn how to walk before you can run. The next step in our journey is to become familiar with stocks and bonds, the most popular forms of investment. You will learn what it means to be a stockholder and how stock values are determined. These are things that you should know *before* you invest. You may recall that Joe did not know anything about the stock market, yet he had the Midas touch. You may not be so lucky, so sit back and read about the market before you commit your funds.

IMPORTANT CONCEPTS

Agency orders
American Depository Receipts (ADRs)
Asked (or offered price)
Auction market
Bid (price)
Bid/ask spread
Blue chip
Blue List
Broker
Call options
Certificates of deposit
Commodities
Commodities Futures Trading Commission (CFTC)
Computer Assisted Execution System (CAES)
Continuous market
Dealer
Equity options
Federal Reserve
Financial futures
Firm quote
Inside market
Intermarket Trading System (ITS)

Internalized order
Investment
Limited partnership
Locked in
Margin
Market makers
Market price
National Association of Securities Dealers (NASD)
National Association of Securities Dealers Automatic Quotation System (NASDAQ)
NASDAQ National Market System (NASDAQ/NMS)
Negotiated market
Nonequity options
Notes
Offered (or ask price)
Over-the-counter (OTC) market
Pink sheets
Preferred stock
Put options
Real assets
Savings account

Securities
Securities and Exchange Commission
  (SEC)
Securities Investor Protection Corpo-
  ration (SIPC)

Small Order Execution System (SOES)
Stock exchange
Time deposits
Transaction accounts
Yellow sheets

QUESTIONS AND EXERCISES

1. List five types of real assets that are suitable for investment purposes. De-
    scribe the benefits and drawbacks of investing in these assets, noting how
    much risk is involved in each.

2. Name the different types of marketable securities issued by corporations.
    Indicate which represent ownership and which represent debt.

3. Describe the similarities and differences between mutual funds and money
    market funds.

4. True or False. Puts are options to sell and calls are options to buy stocks, and
    futures are contracts to buy or sell commodities. Explain what this statement
    refers to.

5. What are the main differences between stock exchanges and the over-the-
    counter market?

6. How do stockbrokers differ from dealers?

7. What is meant by a "firm quote"?

8. Cite the attributes of a continuous market. Explain why your local real estate
    market is or is not a continuous market.

9. Stock A is quoted $25 bid and $26½ asked. Stock B is quoted at $60–$69.
    Which of these stocks is more actively traded? Why?

10. Explain the meaning of the term "liquidity." If liquidity were your main
    concern, would you invest in real estate? Why or why not?

11. How does the Securities Investor Protection Corporation (SIPC) protect
    investors?

12. What are the four desirable features of nonmarketable, deposit-type securi-
    ties?

13. Are stock prices regulated? Is the stock market regulated? Explain each.

14. Describe the basic features of U.S. savings bonds.

15. If you had $10,000 to invest for a month, what would you do with the funds?

16. Use *The Wall Street Journal* to look up a quote on the common stock of a
    corporation. Be sure you understand every part of the quote. Headings at the
    top of the columns should help. If you cannot understand any part of the
    quote, ask the professor for an explanation in class.

EQUITY SECURITIES

S tocks are the most popular type of investment medium for several reasons. One reason that was mentioned in Chapter 1 is that they are marketable. Another reason is that there is a lot of information available about stocks. Stock market information is presented nightly on television as a major news item. Stock prices are quoted on the radio and appear daily in many newspapers. All of this information is presented because millions of individuals are shareholders and their wealth depends, in part, on what their stocks are doing. What does it mean to be a shareholder? And how are stock prices determined?

COMMON STOCK

Business Corporations

A **corporation** is a legal entity created under the laws of a state or nation and is granted certain rights and privileges. There are different types of corporations. They include municipal corporations such as cities or townships that carry out governmental functions; eleemosynary corporations with charitable functions and purposes; professional corporations used by individuals such as doctors and lawyers; and other types of corporations. In this chapter we are concerned with **public business corporations** that are formed by private individuals for the purpose of transacting business in the broadest sense of the term, and where one purpose of the organization is to make a profit. The public business corporation is uniquely suited to accumulate assets and grow because it has an unlimited life

FIGURE 2-1   Corporate pyramid of organization.

span. This allows it to make long-range plans, recruit and develop management talent, and to acquire assets for long-term growth.

Another advantage of a corporation is that it has rights, privileges, and liabilities that are distinct from those of its owners, who are called **stockholders.** This means that the stockholders are not liable for the wrongful acts of the corporation they own — they have **limited liability** — their loss is limited in most cases to their investment; but they hope to profit from its lawful gains in the form of dividends and higher stock prices. The shares of stock provide **liquidity,** because they can be easily sold for cash.

One disadvantage of public corporations is that they are required to make periodic **public disclosures** of their business and financial condition. These disclosures are used by stockholders, analysts, and their competition to monitor the behavior of the corporations. In addition, large corporations are taxed at higher rates than individuals. However, corporations make investment and business decisions to minimize the amount of taxes they must pay. Finally, there may be conflicts between the owner–stockholders and managers of the corporations.

Figure 2-1 shows the corporate pyramid of an organization. The stockholders form the broad base at the bottom of the pyramid. American Telephone and Telegraph has 2.7 million stockholders, General Motors has 1.7 million, and IBM has 0.8 million. Obviously the stockholders cannot get together to make day-to-day decisions about how to run these companies, so they elect directors to represent them. Similarly, the directors elect officers who run the firms.

The basic idea behind this form of organization is that the officers are supposed to run their organizations for the benefit of the stockholders. Some corporate officers do, but some don't. The extreme case of those that don't is presented in Box 2-1. Management guru Peter Drucker, quoting an old proverb, said that "if you don't have gravediggers you need vultures."[1] He went on to say that for the

---

[1] Edward Reingold, "Facing the 'Totally New and Dynamic'," *Time,* January 22, 1990, 6. For further discussion of conflicts between owners and managers see Michael C. Jensen, "Eclipse of the Public Corporation," *Harvard Business Review,* September–October 1989, 61–74.

BOX 2-1

THE EXECUTIVE LIFE[2]

A few corporate executives live lavish and outlandish lives, perhaps to the detriment of their shareholders. The following examples illustrate this extreme. Most corporate officers do not behave like this.

When WPP Group P.L.C. acquired J. Walter Thompson Company, it discovered that its new acquisition's dining room had been transported from an excavated Colonial New England house and reconstructed in the firm's New York office on Lexington Avenue. Of course, uniformed butlers provided water to the firm's executives in cut-glass crystal decanters on silver trays. One executive had a butler deliver a single peeled orange to him every day, at an estimated cost of $300 per orange.

Kohlberg Kravis Roberts & Company acquired RJR Nabisco. Following the acquisition, the company discovered that the acquired firm's former chairman, Ross Johnson, traveled with G. Shepard, but in separate private planes. KKR discovered that G. Shepard was Johnson's dog, and traveled in a separate plane because of his alleged tendency to bite people.

William A. Schryer, chairman and chief executive of Merrill Lynch — the country's largest investment firm, sometimes takes a helicopter from his Manhattan office to his home in Princeton, New Jersey. He says it's strictly business when he has late meetings in New York and early meetings in Princeton. He also took the corporate plane to London to officially open the new headquarters there, two months after it opened and at the same time as the Wimbledon tennis tournament, which he, several directors, and some clients attended. Following the 1987 stock market crash, Merrill Lynch flew its 16 board members and their spouses on the Concorde to Paris, where they stayed at the Ritz Hotel and attended dinners at a private hunting club. Two days after their arrival they held a dinner with secret clients at one of the most exclusive clubs in France. Schryer said it sounds expensive, but compared to what? Merrill Lynch is an international firm and must show its flag. During this period, the firm's earnings declined sharply due to poor cost control. Not the least of their problems stemmed from just before the '87 crash when they moved from the Empire State Building to the World Financial Center, with a 25-year lease for 3.9 million square feet, more than doubling their previous floor space. They can't use all that space and expect to lose more than $100 million on that deal.

---

[2] Based on Deirde Fanning, "The Executive Life," *The New York Times,* February 4, 1990, Section 3, 29; and Kurt Eichenwald, "Changing the Culture of Spending at Merrill Lynch," *The New York Times,* February 4, 1990, Section 3, 12.

> Shearson Lehman Hutton, another beleaguered securities firm, spent $25 million on a Colorado ski lodge. Peter Cohen, Shearson's former chief executive, was an avid skier. Guests at the lodge included former President Gerald Ford and Leonard Firestone, heir to the tire fortune.
>
> Similarly, Time-Warner, Inc., owned a house in Acapulco overlooking the harbor. It had a pool, tennis courts, a screening room, and full-time staff.
>
> Was all of this for the good of the stockholders?

past 30 years, the management of large corporations have not been accountable to their stockholders, and we need vultures. The vultures are corporate raiders who have come to clean up by buying firms that they perceive as being undervalued because they are being run poorly, and either running them better or selling parts of them using the *"chop shop"* theory. This theory holds that the individual parts are worth more than the whole. This is a partial explanation for the large number of hostile takeovers and mergers in recent years. The stockholders, whether they be ordinary citizens or corporate raiders, have power only if they are willing and able to exercise it. Lets examine the process further.

Ownership

Common stock represents ownership in a corporation. But what does ownership mean? Can a stockholder of American Airlines walk into the cockpit of one of their jets and suggest that the plane fly to Hawaii instead of Cincinnati? Can a stockholder of United Artists tell the firm how to direct its films? The answer to both questions is that stockholders do not have the right to tell a company how to conduct its business.

Owning a stock is not the same as owning a car or a house. You can do what you want with your car or house, but as a stockholder–owner, your rights are limited. As shown in Figure 2-2, stockholders are entitled to *vote*. They can vote on important issues such as mergers, and they can vote to elect directors. The directors, in turn, elect the officers that run the company; they establish general operating policies; and they vote on dividend payments. As we shall see later in this chapter, cash dividend payments have a major impact on stock prices.

Common stock is the riskiest type of corporate security. The common stockholders are called the **residual claimants** because they are entitled to what remains of earnings and assets after all prior claims have been satisfied. As residual claimants, common stockholders may receive cash dividends if the corporation is profitable, or they may lose their investment if it goes bankrupt. Nevertheless, common stock offers the greatest opportunity for rewards. The rewards to stockholders consist of cash dividends and capital appreciation.

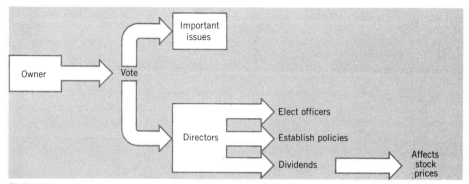

FIGURE 2-2 Common stock ownership.

A stock certificate is one proof of ownership. Figure 2-3 is an example of a typical stock certificate. The front of the certificate shows the name of the issuing company, the name of the owner of the shares, the number of shares represented by the certificate, the name of the registrar, and the par value. It also shows that the stock is fully paid for and nonassessable. On the back of the certificate is a form that must be completed when the holder of the stock decides to transfer ownership of the shares.

Some investors who buy and sell stocks frequently prefer not to have their stocks registered in their names, partially because it may take a month or longer to have a stock certificate registered in the name of the owner. In addition, when a stock is sold, a properly endorsed (signed) certificate must be delivered to the seller's stockbroker. As a result, the shares are commonly registered in **street name** and are held by the brokerage firm for the customer's account. Street name means that the stock is registered in the name of a brokerage firm or some other nominee so the stock certificate can be easily transferred from one owner to another.

Par Value

All stocks are issued with a par value, no-par value, or some nominal value. The **par value,** or nominal value, of a stock is frequently found on the front of the stock certificate or in the corporate charter. One purpose of the par value is to determine the proportionate share of ownership that each share represents. The total par value represents the amount of capital subscribed by the stockholders. Suppose that a company has a total par value of $1 million for all the common stock and that each share has a par value of $25. Each share will represent 1/40,000 ownership in the company.

If the shares are sold to the original stockholders for a consideration equal to or greater than the par value, the stock certificates are designated "fully paid and nonassessable." Excess funds over the par value are put in a capital surplus account. If additional shares are sold by the company for a consideration of less

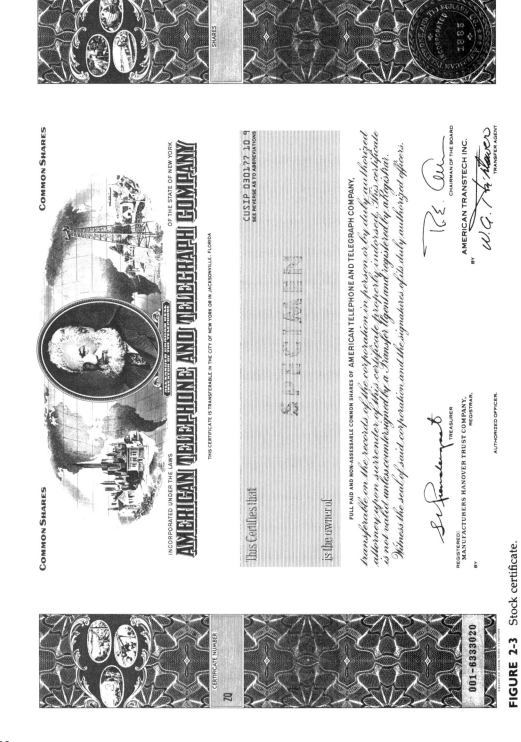

FIGURE 2-3 Stock certificate.

TABLE 2-1   Par Value, Book Value, and Market Value of Selected Stocks[a]

Name of Company	Par Value	Approximate Book Value	Price Range
American Express	$0.60	$13	$39–$26
Gillette	$1.00	$1	$49–$33
Maytag	$1.25	$9	$27–$19
McDonald's	None	$10	$33–$23

[a] Values are for 1989.

than the par value, owners of those shares may be liable for an assessment of the difference in the event of insolvency.[3]

Taxes are another factor affecting par value. Some states charge excise taxes and franchise fees based on the par value of the stock. Such laws encourage the issuance of stock with low par values.

Finally, investors should be cautioned about confusing par value with book value or market price, at which stock trades. Par value is strictly a legal concept. **Book value** is an accounting concept used by security analysts and others. It is determined by dividing the number of common shares outstanding into the stockholders' equity less the value of any preferred stock. Thus, par value, book value, and market price are unrelated. By way of illustration, compare stocks listed in Table 2-1 with regard to par values, book values, and range of market prices. The companies listed exhibit a wide range of par values that have no relationship to the book values or market values of their stocks.

Voting Rights

As previously noted, stockholders have the right to elect the Board of Directors and vote on other important issues. Generally, stockholders are given the opportunity to vote once a year at the corporation's annual meeting, which is usually held in the city of the corporate headquarters. Because many stockholders are unable or unwilling to attend, corporations send their stockholders a **proxy** statement along with the notification of the annual meeting. It is a power of attorney that assigns the owner's right to vote on particular issues to another person or persons. Stockholders' apathy in attending annual meetings or even signing proxies is widespread. As a result, managers may act in their own interests rather than strictly in the interests of the stockholders.

Classified Stocks

In some cases there are class A and class B common stocks, or **dual-class** stocks. Generally, one **classified stock** has voting rights and the other has limited or no voting rights. An unusual example is Resorts International (listed on the Ameri-

---

[3] Model Business Corporation Act Ann. (1960), sec. 17 (1966 Supp.).

can Stock Exchange), whose class B common stock has full voting rights and whose class A common stock has 1/100 vote. However, class B shares are convertible into class A shares. In the more typical situation, class A stock has voting rights and class B stock does not. Dual-class stocks are commonly found in firms where the founding families or entrepreneurs value control more highly than outsiders do. The dual class enables them to retain control by retaining the voting rights in the class of stock that they hold (e.g., Class A stock), and obtain equity financing with nonvoting stock (e.g., Class B stock) when needed.[4]

Ordinary and Cumulative Voting

Typically, stockholders are entitled to cast one vote per share for each vacancy on the Board of Directors. This is known as **ordinary** or **straight voting.** Under this method, a group of investors controlling the majority of the votes could elect all the directors, and minority owners would be excluded from representation on the Board of Directors. An alternative method, **cumulative voting,** gives increased weight to minority owners. With this method, stockholders are entitled to a total number of votes that is determined by the number of shares owned multiplied by the number of vacancies on the board. Stockholders can cast all their votes for one candidate or distribute them as they see fit.

A simple illustration will help to clarify the difference between ordinary and cumulative voting. Assume that a company has 1000 shares outstanding and that there are five directors to be elected. Under ordinary voting, a minority stockholder with 200 shares can cast only 200 votes for each vacancy, while the majority stockholders have 800 votes for each vacancy on the board and can elect all five directors. Thus, a group holding more than 50 percent of the voting stock and voting by the ordinary method can select the entire Board of Directors. However, under cumulative voting, the minority stockholder is entitled to cast a total of 1000 votes ($200 \times 5 = 1000$), and the majority group has a total of 4000 votes ($800 \times 5 = 4000$). The minority stockholder can cast all of his 1000 votes for one directorship vacancy and obtain at least one seat on the board. There is no way that the majority stockholders can combine their votes to capture all of the vacancies.

Dividends

One of the major reasons investors buy common stocks is to receive the cash dividends that many, but not all, companies pay. During the 1980–1989 period, the **average dividend yield** (cash dividend/price) of 500 common stocks used in the Standard & Poor's stock index ranged from a low of 3.08 percent to a high of 5.81 percent. The average for the period was 4.30 percent.

You may be thinking that 5 percent does not seem very high, considering that stocks are risky and you can earn that much or more on risk-free insured deposits

---

[4] For a discussion of dual stocks, see Daniel R. Fischel, *Organized Exchanges and the Regulation of Dual Class Common Stock,* University of Chicago and Lexecon Inc., March 1986.

in banks. However, cash dividends are only part of the return that stockholders expect to earn. They also expect their shares to increase in value. The total expected return includes both cash dividends and higher stock prices.

Dividend Policy

Dividends can be paid in three basic forms — cash, stock, and property, or some combination of the three. The most common dividend is cash, which gives stockholders a monetary return on their investment. However, the Board of Directors of the company decides whether to pay a dividend of any kind. The directors must decide whether the funds available for dividend payments can be used more effectively by retaining them or by paying them out to stockholders. Retaining funds may enable the company to grow at a faster rate, and the value of the stock could appreciate. Paying cash dividends enables the stockholders to share in the profits of the company. An alternative to paying cash dividends is giving stockholders additional shares of stock or property. More will be said about these kinds of dividends shortly.

The needs of the stockholders are one of the important criteria affecting dividend policy. If the stockholders consist largely of those who bought the stock for income, the Board of Directors will favor large cash dividends. If the stockholder group consists mainly of investors who want price appreciation instead of ordinary income, the directors will probably decide to retain most of the earnings.

The directors must also take the needs of the company into account. If the company is losing money, they may decide to reduce the regular dividends as a way of conserving cash. On the other hand, if the company is doing exceptionally well and can spare the funds, the directors may decide to increase the dividend or declare an extra dividend for that year.

Cash dividends normally account for 40 to 60 percent of after-tax profits. The money can be distributed in several ways. Most companies pay dividends on a quarterly basis. Typically, a certain amount, such as $0.50 per share, is paid each quarter. When the earnings of the company become sufficiently high over a sustained period of time, the Board of Directors may decide to increase the regular dividend or to pay an extra dividend. Alternatively, the policy may be to pay a certain percentage (e.g., 40 percent) of available earnings as dividends. This dividend policy is not desirable for investors who want a steady stream of income. Finally, there is the residual dividend policy: Dividend payments consist of whatever earnings remain after the company has taken care of all investment needs.

Timing of Dividend Payments

Investors should know four dates in the process of dividend payment: date declared, date of record, ex-dividend date, and date payable. The **date declared** is the date on which the Board of Directors of the company declares that it is going to pay a dividend in the future. At the same time they announce the **date of record.** Only those stockholders who are recorded on the transfer books on the date of record are entitled to receive the dividend. It takes about four business days from

the time one buys a stock for one's name to be recorded on the company's transfer books, so a date must be established to let buyers know whether they are entitled to receive the dividend. That date is known as the **ex-dividend date.** On the New York Stock Exchange it is usually the fourth business day preceding the record date. Investors who buy a stock after the ex-dividend date are not entitled to receive the dividend because their names cannot be recorded on the company's transfer books by the record date. Such a stock is said to have gone ex-dividend. In some cases, an investor can make a cash transaction for the stock and circumvent the four-day rule. The **date payable** is the date when the dividend will be paid.

Stock Dividends and Splits

From an investor's point of view there is little difference between **stock dividends** and **stock splits.** They are analogous to owning a portion of a pie and cutting it into more slices. The overall size of your share of the pie does not change but you have more slices. Instead of owning 1/10 of the pie, you now own 2/20 of it. Stock prices appreciate because investors foresee higher earnings and dividends, not because the shares have been split.

Stock dividends are usually expressed as a percentage—2 percent, 5 percent, 10 percent, and so on. Most stock dividends are for less than 25 percent. A stockholder who owns 100 shares when a 5-percent stock dividend is declared will receive an additional five shares. Keep in mind that the stockholder still owns the same proportion of the company. When a company pays a stock dividend, it makes an accounting entry to decrease the retained earnings and increase the capital stock by a like amount. In accounting terms, the company capitalizes the retained earnings. For example, assume that the ABC Company has a total equity of $500,000, consisting of 400,000 shares of $1 par value stock outstanding, and retained earnings of $100,000. If the ABC Company declares a 5-percent stock dividend, the shares outstanding will increase by 20,000 to 420,000 and the retained earnings will decline by $20,000 to $80,000. The important point is that the total equity ($500,000) has not changed.

Stock splits are usually expressed as 2 for 1, 3 for 1, or other combinations. A 2 for 1 split means that the stockholder will have two shares for every one share currently held. Most of the stock splits are 2 for 1 to $2\frac{1}{2}$ for 1. When fractional shares occur, companies usually buy or sell them for the convenience of the stockholder. The difference between the stock dividend and the stock split is a matter of accounting entries. When a company pays a stock dividend, it capitalizes retained earnings, as described in the previous example. When the stock is split, the dollar amount of the capital stock remains the same, but the number of shares is increased and the par value is reduced. For example, if the ABC Company had declared a 2 for 1 stock split instead of a stock dividend, the capital stock would have increased to 800,000 shares, and the par value would have declined to $0.50 per share.

Figure 2-4 illustrates the effects of a 100-percent stock dividend or a 2 for 1 stock split on the price of a share of stock. In either case, the number of shares

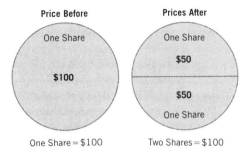

FIGURE 2-4 The price effects on one share of stock at 100-percent stock dividend or a 2-for-1 stock split.

doubles. The figure shows that the stockholder is no better off financially after the number of shares has doubled because the price has been halved. The shareholders gets more shares, but they represent the same amount of wealth.

If the shareholder is no better off, then why do companies split their shares? One answer is that the price of most stocks is between $10 to $50 per share. This is the so-called popular trading range. Some stockholders believe that there might be more trading activity for a stock that sells at $100 per share if the price of the stock were $50 per share. One way to reduce the price is to have a 2 for 1 split.

A psychological benefit of a stock split is that some investors prefer to buy 100 shares of stock rather than an odd lot (fewer than 100 shares), and it is less costly to buy 100 shares of a low-price stock than it is to buy 100 shares of a high-price stock. It "sounds" better to say you own 100 shares of ABC at $50 a share than 50 shares of ABC at $100 a share, although the value is the same.

Finally, stock dividends and stock splits do increase the number of shares that can be bought and sold. This may be important for large traders, such as financial institutions, that restrict their trading activity to stocks with a large "floating supply," or the number of shares normally traded.

In summary, stock dividends and stock splits per se do not increase shareholder wealth. Many investors believe they are better off with stock dividends or splits because they are frequently accompanied by an increase in cash dividends. In that case, it is the increased cash dividends rather than the increased number of shares that increased their wealth.

Property Dividends

Property dividends consist of assets of the corporation. The most common use of property dividends today is distribution of securities owned by the company. In 1962, stockholders of E.I. du Pont de Nemours and Company were given shares of General Motors as a result of antitrust litigation. Some companies use this method to divest themselves of subsidiaries. This type of property dividend is called a *spinoff.* Other types of property dividends include securities and merchandise. During World War I, some companies distributed Liberty Bonds as property dividends. Other companies have given liquor and cigarettes. Merchandise dividends are rarely used today, although some companies do send their stockholders coupons to promote their products.

Dividends: A Determinant of Value

Cash dividends are the principal financial return that investors receive from stocks until shares are sold. It is not surprising, therefore, that stock prices are determined, in part, by current and expected cash dividends. In this section we demonstrate one method of determining the intrinsic value of common stock. **Intrinsic value** is the theoretical value. It is the value that is justified by the facts that analysis reveals. In Part 3 you will learn more about analysis of companies. For the moment, let us say that the analysis includes an evaluation of the financial condition and earning prospects of a company, as well as other factors. To some extent, intrinsic value depends on the views of analysts and investors, each of whom may perceive the value of the same company differently. This is one reason why the market price of a security may differ from its intrinsic value.

The reason for determining the intrinsic value is to find **undervalued stocks** —those whose intrinsic value is greater than their market value. This is how T. Boone Pickens, Jr., made millions of dollars for himself and investors in Mesa Limited Partnership. Mesa explores, develops, and produces oil and gas. When oil prices soared in the 1970s, Pickens realized that it was cheaper and less risky to buy oil companies with proven reserves than it was to explore for new oil and gas. He became known as a corporate raider for his acquisition activities of buying "undervalued" oil companies. Maybe you can do the same!

Present Value

Many methods are used to determine the value of an asset. Virtually all of the modern methods incorporate the use of **present value,** which is the value today of a future payment or series of payments. Present value may be seen in terms of the cliché that a bird in the hand is worth two in the bush. You are better off holding cash today than the promise of receiving the same amount of cash in the future because that promise may never be fulfilled.

Another way to understand this concept is to ask yourself how much money you would pay today for $1 that you will receive a year from now. Would you be willing to pay $1.10, $1.00, or $0.90? Economists believe that having $1 today is better than having the promise of $1 at some time in the future because the promise of future payments is worth less than an immediate payment. Also, you can do something else with the money during the waiting period.

If you would only be willing to pay about $0.90 today for the promise of a $1 payment one year from now, then you have discounted the future payment by 10 percent [$1.00 ÷ (1 + 0.10) = $0.9091]. The discount rate is the interest rate used in the discounting process and is sometimes called the **capitalization rate.** The present value of a future payment can be expressed in an equation as

$$PV = \frac{FV_n}{(1 + k)^n} \tag{2-1}$$

where

PV = present value of a future payment
FV_n = dollar amount of the future payment to be received in period n
k = discount or capitalization rate
n = number of periods (years)

This equation was used to generate the present values of $1 that appear in Table 2-2. In the previous example, $1 was discounted at 10 percent for one year. The present value can be found by referring to the 10-percent column and the one-year row. The answer is 0.9091 for each $1 being considered. If $100 were to be paid in one year, the present value discounted at 10 percent would be $90.91 ($100 × 0.9091 = $90.91).

As the table shows, the amount of present value is determined by the size of the discount rate and the number of periods (years) involved. For example, $1 discounted for 5 years is worth $0.7835 at a 5-percent rate and $0.4972 at a 15-percent rate. The present value decreases as the number of discounting periods increases. Thus, $1 discounted for five years at 5 percent is worth $0.7835, and when discounted for 25 years, it is worth $0.2953. Armed with this background on present value, we will discuss one method of determining stock prices.

Dividend Valuation Model

One widely used method of determining the price of a stock is to capitalize (take the present value of) future cash dividends. The current price of the stock, which is represented by P_0, is the present value of cash dividends that are expected to be paid in the future. To illustrate this method, assume that Spruill Company pays a $2 dividend annually and that it will continue to pay that amount in the future. Assume further that investors expect to earn a 10-percent rate of return on their investment in Spruill. They decided on 10 percent by examining the returns on

TABLE 2-2 Present Value of $1

Year	Discount Rate			
	1%	5%	10%	15%
1	0.9901	0.9524	**0.9091**	0.8696
2	0.9803	0.9070	0.8264	0.7561
3	0.9706	0.8638	0.7513	0.6575
4	0.9610	0.8227	0.6830	0.5718
5	0.9515	**0.7835**	0.6209	**0.4972**
10	0.9053	0.6139	0.3855	0.2472
20	0.8195	0.3769	0.1486	0.0611
25	0.7798	**0.2953**	0.0923	0.0304

For detailed tables see Appendix A at the back of the book.

alternative investments (bank deposits, Treasury securities, and other stocks and bonds), taking into account the riskiness of the company and considering other factors. The price of Spruill is $20 per share and can be determined as follows:

$$P_0 = \frac{D_1}{k}$$ (2-2)

where

$P_0 =$ current price (at time 0)
$D_1 =$ cash dividend in time period 1
$k =$ appropriate discount rate determined by investors, their required (expected) rate of return

$$P_0 = \frac{\$2}{0.10} = \$20$$

This method of determining stock prices applies only if the cash dividends remain unchanged in the future. This condition is met by preferred stocks, which will be discussed shortly, and common stocks whose cash dividends are never going to change.

Since most companies change their cash dividends from time to time, we can modify Equation 2-2 to take the growth rate of cash dividends into account. Let us assume that cash dividends are expected to increase 5 percent annually. Every year cash dividends are 5 percent larger than they were in the previous year. In this case, the value of the stock is $40 per share, and can be determined by using Equation 2-3.[5]

$$P_0 = \frac{D_1}{(k - g)}$$ (2-3)

where

$P_0 =$ current price (at time 0)
$D_1 =$ cash dividend in time period 1
$k =$ rate of return required by investors
$g =$ growth rate of cash dividends

$$P_0 = \frac{\$2}{(0.10 - 0.05)} = \$40$$

Let us consider another example. Suppose the growth rate of cash dividends is 8 percent. Now the stock is worth $100 per share.

$$P_0 = \frac{\$2}{(0.10 - 0.08)} = \$100$$

Keep in mind that all three parts of the equation (cash dividends, its growth rate, and the required rate of return) affect stock prices. If any one of these

[5] The development of this equation is presented in the Appendix at the end of the chapter.

changes, stock prices will change. For example, suppose that interest rates on alternative investments increase and now investors want a 12-percent return on their investment in Spruill Company. If nothing else changes in the equation ($D_1 = \$2, g = 0.08$), the effect of the increased required rate of return will be lower stock prices ($50).

$$P_0 = \frac{\$2}{(0.12 - 0.08)} = \$50$$

The previous examples assumed that cash dividends would grow at a constant rate. This assumption does not hold true for many firms. Relatively new companies may grow at rapid rates for several years and then at a slower pace. The intrinsic value of firms whose growth rate varies over time is explained in Chapter 13.

At this point, it is sufficient to remember that the value of stocks, as well as that of other assets, depends on the present value of future cash flows. In the dividend valuation model, expected cash dividends are the cash flows that we consider. In this regard we are concerned with

- The *amount* of the dividends
- The *timing* of the dividends (i.e., when they are expected to be paid)
- The *riskiness* of the dividends

Keep the amount, timing, and riskiness of cash flows in mind as we learn more about the valuation of securities.

Preemptive Rights

Stockholders have a common law right to maintain their proportionate share of ownership when a company raises new capital by selling stock. Not all states recognize this **preemptive right,** and some have waived it in corporate charters. The preemptive right of stockholders does not usually apply if the company is selling **treasury stock** — outstanding stock the company has acquired — or if new stock is being issued to purchase property such as another company.

Stockholders are generally given one or more rights for each share held. Rights have value and can be bought and sold. They can be traded from the date the offering is announced until they expire, which is usually two or three weeks after the date of record. Between the announcement date and the date of record, the stock is traded with the rights attached or **cum rights.** After the date of record, the stock sells without the rights, or **ex-rights,** and the rights are traded by themselves.

The following example illustrates the theoretical value of a right. Assume that the stock is selling for $40 per share, and the stockholders are offered new shares at $35 per share. In addition, 10 rights are required to buy one new share at the offering price of $35. The theoretical value of a single right is $0.45 and can be

determined by using the following equation:

$$V_1 = \frac{P_0 - S}{N + 1} = \frac{\$40 - \$35}{11} = \$0.45 \tag{2-4}$$

where

$V_1 =$ theoretical value of one right when the stock
is cum rights
$P_0 =$ market price of stock
$S =$ subscription price of one share
$N =$ number of rights required to buy one share

Finally, the rights are given to the stockholders on a document called a **warrant**. This warrant should not be confused with warrants that are long-term options to buy stocks. Long-term purchase warrants are discussed in Chapter 20.

PREFERRED STOCK

Preferred stock is a hybrid type of security. It has some of the characteristics of both corporate bonds and common stock. Like bonds, preferred stocks have a stated rate of return on the face value, but they do not have the collateral security that is generally associated with bonds. Like common stock, they represent ownership in a corporation, but preferred stockholders generally do not benefit from increased earnings or participate in management to the same extent as do the owners of common stock.

Preference as to Dividends and Assets

The term *preferred* means that the owners of preferred stock have a preference over the owners of common stock as to (1) dividends and (2) assets in the event the company is liquidated. The characteristics of preferred stock are quite different from those of common stock, as the following paragraphs show.

Par Value

Most preferred stocks have a par value of $100. Some preferred stocks have a par value of $50 or some other amount, and some even have no-par value. Par values are important because the dividends are frequently expressed as a percentage of the par value. For example, Ohio Edison has an 8.20 percent preferred stock outstanding. The dividend of this stock is 8.20 percent of the $100 par value of the stock, or $8.20 per year. Preferred stocks with no-par value express dividends in dollar amounts, such as $8.

Par value may also affect the priority of preferred stockholders if a company is liquidated. In such cases, preferred stocks with high par values rank ahead of those with lower par values.

Dividends

If cash dividends are declared by a Board of Directors, preferred stockholders have to be paid before common stockholders. If a Board of Directors decides not to pay cash dividends when the dividend on preferred stock is due, the stock is said to be in **arrears.** Many preferred stocks have a cumulative clause, which means that the unpaid dividends accumulate for future payment. Such stocks are called **cumulative preferreds.** The dividends that are in arrears must be paid before any cash dividends can be paid to common stockholders. If the arrearages become too large, preferred stockholders may lose the dividends, or the company may negotiate with them to reduce the amount.

Investors should be very cautious about investing in a noncumulative preferred stock. Holders of noncumulative preferred stock have no claim on earnings if dividends are not earned. Even if dividends are earned and not declared, owners of noncumulative preferred stocks are in a weak legal position. The courts have stated that they have no claim on foregone dividends that have been used for necessary improvements.[6]

Some preferred stocks have a participating clause, which means that the preferred stockholders share in the earnings of the company in addition to their stated dividends. Some **participating preferred** stocks share equally with the common stockholders after the usual dividends have been paid on the preferreds.

Finally, corporate investors can deduct 80 percent of the dividends they receive on certain preferred stock from their taxable incomes. The effect of this tax advantage is that new issues of preferred stock are sold mainly to corporate investors.

Assets

In the event of a company's liquidation, holders of preferred stock with an asset preference provision have priority over common stockholders in asset distribution. The preference must clearly state the priority accorded to various par values and dividend arrearages. In the absence of an asset preference clause, preferred stockholders may be no better off than common stockholders. Before any assets can be distributed to the owners of the company, fixed-claim creditors must be paid. Finally, the asset preference does not apply to mergers or consolidations unless the merger agreement states that it does.

Voting

Preferred stockholders have the same voting rights as common stockholders unless they are expressly denied that right in the corporate articles and stock certificates. In some cases, preferred stockholders can vote only under special circumstances. For example, if the dividends reach a specified level of arrearages, preferred stockholders can elect a certain number of directors.

---

[6] *Wabash Railroad v. Barclay,* 280 U.S. 197 (1930).

Redemption Provisions

Many preferred stocks issued in recent years have **call provisions** similar to those of corporate bonds, which are discussed in Chapter 3. The company has the right to call or purchase outstanding preferred shares and may call the stock because it wants to retire the issue. Because stockholders may be inconvenienced by having their shares called, they receive a premium above the par value. Call premiums are sometimes quite high. General Motors $5 preferred, callable at $120 ($20 premium) is one example of high-call premiums. Thus, if the management of General Motors wants to retire the $5 preferred stock issue, it has to pay $120 per share to the stockholder.

Preferred stocks are frequently called to meet sinking fund provisions. The term **sinking fund** refers to the periodic retirement of part of the stock issue through payments made by the corporation. The sinking fund provision ordinarily requires the obligatory redemption of a certain number of preferred shares for a dollar amount based on the net income after preferred dividends. By way of illustration, Philadelphia Electric Power Company has a sinking fund provision of 25,000 shares per year for its 15.25 percent preferred stock. The stock is callable at 110 through April 1995. If the market price of the stock is less than the call price, the shares will be purchased in the market for the sinking fund. If the market price is higher than the call price, the stock will be called for the sinking fund.

Conversion is another method of retiring preferred stocks, but in this case the decision is made by the stockholder rather than the company. The **conversion privilege** gives the preferred stockholder the right to convert preferred stock into common stock at a predetermined price or ratio. For example, each share of Armco $4.50 cumulative convertible preferred is convertible into 1 share of common stock at $51.80 – $50.00 per share, depending on when it is converted.

In summary, the preferred stockholders have a preference over common stockholders as to cash dividends and the assets of the firm if it is dissolved. If cash dividends are not declared or are in arrears, preferred stockholders are in a weaker investment position than bondholders because they are owners rather than creditors of the company.

From an individual investor's point of view, the best type of preferred stock to own is one that is cumulative, participating, and convertible, in a company that is growing. One advantage preferred stocks may have over common stock of the same company is higher dividends. In the example previously cited, Armco pays a $0.40 cash dividend while the preferred receives $4.50 per share.

INVESTMENT COMPANIES AND MUTUAL FUNDS

Types of Investment Companies

Investment company shares are a special type of equity security. Investment companies are corporations or trusts that sell their own securities to investors, and invest the proceeds in stocks, bonds, and other types of securities. They are

regulated by the Securities and Exchange Commission in accordance with the Investment Company Act of 1940 (1940 Act), which is discussed in Chapter 5. The 1940 Act divides investment companies into three categories: management companies, unit investment trusts, and face-amount certificates. Management companies are further divided into **open-end** and **closed-end companies.**

Mutual Funds

Open-end investment companies are called **mutual funds.** They are open-end because the mutual funds can issue (sell) new shares to investors and redeem (buy back) shares whenever the holder wants to sell their shares back to the company at the current **net asset value (NAV).** NAV is market value of the fund's equity (assets − liabilities = equity) divided by the number of shares outstanding. Basically, it is the market value per share of the mutual fund's portfolio, which is determined by the value of the securities it holds. Mutual funds are the dominant form of investment companies. They account for over three-fourths of the more than 2000 investment companies registered with the Securities and Exchange Commission.

Closed-End Investment Companies

Closed-end investment companies differ from mutual funds in several important respects. Nevertheless most investors still refer to them as mutual funds, although that is not technically correct. Closed-end investment companies issue a fixed number of shares that holders may sell in the stock market like any other stock. Closed-end investment companies do not redeem their shares. They are traded on the NYSE and OTC markets. For example, Adams Express Company is traded on the New York, Boston, Midwest, and Pacific Stock Exchanges. Some sell below their NAV (a discount) and others sell above it (a premium). To a large extent, the discounts or premiums reflect investor's attitudes about the earning prospects for the fund. In other words, the price represents the expected returns discounted by the investor's required rate of return.

Unit Investment Trusts

These are closed-end portfolios of securities that are generally sold to investors by brokers. Units represent an undivided interest in the portfolio. Unit holders receive a proportionate share of the income generated from the trust as it is earned or liquidated.

Face-Amount Certificate Companies

The 1940 Act provides for Face-Amount Certificate Companies, although there are only a few in existence. A face-amount certificate is an unsecured financial obligation that makes payments to the holder on or before its maturity.

Load and No-Load Funds

In the past, mutual funds could be classified as load or no-load. **Load fund** companies have a sales charge, or load, that is paid when the shares are purchased. In the brokerage business, the sales charge is also referred to as the **12b-1 fee,** after the 1980 SEC ruling permitting them to charge such a fee. The sales

MUTUAL FUND QUOTATIONS

Friday, February 2, 1990

Price ranges for investment companies, as quoted by the National Association of Securities Dealers. NAV stands for net asset value per share; the offering includes net asset value plus maximum sales charge, if any.

	NAV	Offer Price	NAV Chg.
AAL Mutual:			
CaGr p	10.67	11.20	+ .06
Inco p	9.50	9.97	− .02
MuBd p	9.83	10.32	− .01
AARP Invst:			
CaGr	28.30	NL	+ .32
GiniM	14.97	NL	− .02
GenBd	14.86	NL	− .02
GthInc	24.05	NL	+ .04
TxFBd	16.38	NL	+ .01
TxFSh	15.19	NL	.....
ABT Funds:			
Emrg p		unavail	
GthIn p		unavail	
SecIn p		unavail	
UtilIn p		unavail	
AdsnCa p	16.83	17.35	+ .10
ADTEK	9.21	9.21	+ .04
AIM Funds:			
Chart p	6.18	6.54	+ .06
Const p	7.56	8.00	+ .10
CvYld p	9.64	10.12	+ .07
HiYld p	6.56	6.89	.....
LimM p	9.75	9.92	− .01
Sumit	7.30	.....	+ .06
Weing p	10.95	11.59	+ .09
A M A Funds:			
ClaGt p	8.67	NL	+ .03
GlbGt p	21.80	NL	+ .08
GlbIn p	19.43	NL	− .01
GlST p	9.81	NL	.....
GrPl p	20.36	NL	+ .09
USGv p	8.52	NL	.....
AMEV Funds:			
AstAl p	11.26	11.79	+ .06
Capitl	14.48	15.20	+ .17
CaAp p	14.02	14.68	+ .17
Fidcur p	23.81	24.93	+ .31
Grwth	19.04	19.99	+ .26
HiYld p	7.63	7.99	− .01
TF MN	9.63	10.08	+ .01
TF Nat	9.83	10.29	.....
US Gvt	9.57	10.02	− .02
AcornF	40.67	40.67	+ .40
Afuture	10.02	NL	+ .14
AAF TF p	10.22	10.70	.....
Advest Advant:			
Govt p	8.31	8.31	.....
Gwth p	12.92	12.92	+ .09
HY Bd p	7.99	7.99	− .02
Inco p	10.33	10.33	+ .04
Spcl p	10.98	10.98	+ .15
AlgrSCp t	13.63	13.63	+ .22
AlgerG t	12.91	12.91	+ .16
Alliance Cap:			
Alian p	5.54	5.86	+ .07
Balan p	11.16	11.81	− .03
Canad p	6.56	6.94	+ .05
Conv p	9.00	9.52	+ .03
Count p	16.61	17.58	+ .22
Govt p	8.20	8.68	− .02
GrInc p	2.48	2.62	+ .01
HiYld p	5.73	6.06	.....
Intl p	17.73	18.76	+ .17
ICalT p	12.14	12.65	.....
InsMu	9.41	9.80	.....
MonIn p	11.52	12.19	− .02
Mortg p	8.63	9.13	− .01
MuCA	9.57	9.97	− .01
MuNY	8.94	9.31	− .01
NtlMu	9.54	9.94	.....
Quasr p	19.47	20.60	+ .25
ST Mlt p	9.77	10.07	.....
Survy p	10.42	11.03	+ .16
Tech p	19.47	20.60	+ .30
AlpnCA	9.92	10.31	.....
AlpnNat	9.77	10.15	.....
Altura Funds:			
Grwth	12.16	12.16	+ .08
Inco f	9.96	9.96	− .01
Amer Capital:			
Cmstk	14.27	15.60	+ .08
CpBd p	6.49	6.81	− .01
Entrp p	10.81	11.47	+ .10
Exch	75.93	.....	+ .71
FdMg p	12.60	13.23	− .01
FdAm p	10.40	11.03	+ .08
GvSc p	9.97	10.47	− .03
Harbr p	13.64	14.47	+ .05
HiYld p	6.30	6.61	.....
Citibank IRA-CIT:			
Balan f	2.10	NL	.....
Equit f	2.30	NL	+ .01
Incom f	1.91	NL	.....
ShtTr f	1.63	NL	.....
Clipper	40.18	40.18	+ .21
Colonial Funds:			
AGold p	23.46	25.16	− .07
CalTE	6.95	7.30	.....
CpCsh p	44.60	45.51	+ .02
CCsII p	42.60	43.47	− .01
DvsdIn	7.10	7.61	+ .01
Fund p	19.42	20.83	+ .06
GvSec p	10.83	11.61	− .04
Gwth p	11.59	12.43	+ .13
HiYld p	6.08	6.38	− .01
Incom p	6.32	6.64	.....
IncPls	8.79	9.43	.....
IntEq p	19.34	20.30	+ .13
MATx	7.08	7.43	.....
MI TE	6.52	6.85	.....
MN TE	6.82	7.16	.....
NY TE	6.60	6.93	.....
OhTE	6 75	7.09	.....
SmlIn p	12.66	13.29	+ .07
TXIns p	7.58	7.96	.....
TxEx p	12.91	13.55	.....
US Gv p	7.01	7.36	− .01
US Id p	16.15	16.96	+ .10
Colonial VIP:			
AggG t	11.29	11.29	+ .14
DvRet t	11.04	11.04	+ .06
FdSec t	9.85	9.85	− .01
HiInc t	8.85	8.85	.....
HYMu t	9.82	9.82	− .01
Co DTE	9.89	10.29	− .01
Columbia Funds:			
Fixed	12.49	NL	− .02
Grth	22.35	22.35	+ .18
Muni	11.50	NL	.....
Specl	38.70	NL	+ .54
Common Sense:			
Govt	10.85	11.64	− .04
Grwth	12.07	13.19	+ .09
GrInc	12.18	13.31	+ .09
MunB	12.29	12.90	.....
CmwlthBal		unavail	
Compass Capital:			
EqInc	9.89	10.36	+ .05
FxdIn	9.87	10.34	− .01
Grwth	10.15	10.63	+ .07
ShInt	9.97	10.44	.....
Composite Group:			
BdStk p	10.19	10.61	+ .04
Gwth p	10.62	11.06	+ .09
InFd p	8.24	8.58	.....
NW50 p	19.47	20.39	+ .25
TxEx p	7.07	7.36	.....
USGv p	9.91	10.32	− .01
ConcCnv	9.59	10.26	+ .04
Conn Mutual:			
Govt	10.40	10.89	− .01
Grwth	12.41	13.24	+ .09
TotRet	12.29	13.11	+ .04
CnstE p	9.90	10.37	+ .06
Copley	13.72	NL	+ .01
Counsellors Fd:			
CapAp	10.64	NL	+ .12
EGth	12.51	NL	+ .16
FixInc	9.47	NL	− .03
IntEqu	12.43	NL	+ .09
IntGvt	10.16	NL	− .02
NYMu	9.58	NL	− .01
CtryCa r	15.96	16.45	+ .11
Cowen t	10.83	11.38	.....
CownOp p	10.37	10.90	+ .17
CmbldG	9.92	9.92	+ .03
DR Funds:			
Bal	9.71	9.71	+ .03
Equity	10.92	10.92	+ .05
EurEq	9.60	NL	+ .04
Dean Witter:			
AmVl t	13.96	13.96	+ .12
CalTF t	11.87	11.87	+ .01
Convt t	8.86	8.86	+ .06
DevGr t	9.81	9.81	+ .18
DvGth t	22.33	22.33	+ .08
GPlus t	8.99	8.99	− .03
HiYld	8.17	8.65	+ .01
Intmd t	9.67	9.67	− .01
Fidelity Invest:			
AgTF r	11.41	11.41	.....
A Mgr	10.62	NL	+ .02
Balanc	10.98	11.20	+ .01
BluCh	13.09	13.36	+ .13
CA TF	11.13	NL	.....
CA In	9.55	NL	.....
Canad r	14.17	14.46	+ .08
CapAp r	16.11	16.44	+ .16
CngS	108.30	108.30	+ .89
ConnT	10.58	NL	.....
Contra	16.23	NL	+ .24
CnvSc	11.27	NL	+ .06
DisEq	12.74	13.13	+ .11
Eq Inc	25.43	25.95	+ .11
EqIdx	12.65	NL	+ .09
Europ r	17.23	17.58	+ .07
Exch	75.43	75.43	+ .52
Fidel	17.15	17.15	+ .14
FlexB	6.74	NL	− .01
Fredm	14.55	NL	+ .12
GloBd r	11.06	NL	− .01
GNMA	10.19	NL	− .02
GovtSc	9.42	NL	− .01
GroInc	16.42	16.76	+ .11
GroCo	17.89	18.44	+ .27
HiInc	6.94	NL	.....
HiYld	12.25	NL	+ .01
InsMu	10.92	NL	.....
IntBd	9.92	NL	− .02
IntGr r	13.77	13.91	+ .07
LtdMn	9.23	NL	− .01
MagIn	56.56	58.31	+ .34
MI TF	10.97	NL	.....
MA TF	11.05	NL	.....
MN TF	10.40	NL	.....
MtgSc	10.05	NL	− .01
MunBd	8.05	NL	.....
Oh TF	10.64	NL	.....
NJ HY	10.41	NL	.....
NY HY	11.66	NL	.....
NY Ins	10.77	NL	− .01
OTC	18.99	19.58	+ .19
Ovrse	28.14	29.01	+ .24
PcBas r	15.42	15.73	+ .05
Pa TF	9.79	NL	− .01
Puritn	13.15	13.42	+ .02
RealEs	9.39	9.58	− .01
ShtBd	9.25	NL	.....
ShtTGv	9.87	NL	− .01
Sht TF	9.45	NL	.....
SprtG	10.31	NL	− .02
Sptcahy	9.93	NL	.....
SpcSit	18.61	19.39	− .02
TX TF	10.26	NL	.....
Trend	41.12	NL	+ .54
UtilInc	12.02	12.27	+ .03
Value	26.82	NL	+ .45
Fidl Inv Instit:			
CTAR r	8.45	NL	.....
EqP G	14.51	NL	+ .26
EqP I	11.28	NL	+ .05
IP LTD	10.16	NL	− .02
IP SG	9.41	NL	.....
TE Ltd	10.56	NL	− .01
QualD	11.26	NL	+ .01
Fidelity Selects:			
SlAir r	10.61	10.83	+ .06
SlAGl r	18.48	18.86	− .08
SlBio r	14.12	14.41	+ .96
SlBrd r	12.83	13.09	+ .19
SlBrk r	8.14	8.31	+ .06
SlChe r	22.68	23.14	+ .18
SlCmp r	11.36	11.59	+ .05
SlDef r	11.68	11.92	+ .02
SlElec r	8.11	8.28	+ .01
SlEUt r	11.07	11.30	+ .01
SlEng r	16.89	17.23	+ .16
SlEnS r	11.45	11.68	+ .19
SlEnv r	10.84	11.06	+ .13
SlFnS r	28.96	29.55	+ .24
SlFd r	21.91	22.36	+ .16
SlHlth r	45.73	46.66	+ .57
SlInd r	12.93	13.19	+ .07
SlLesr r	26.39	26.93	+ .42
SlMD r	10.77	10.99	+ .26
SlMetl r	16.03	16.36	+ .22
SlPap r	11.43	11.66	+ .05
SlPrp r	13.91	14.19	+ .10
Pacif p	12.58	13.21	+ .08
Wldw p	13.40	14.07	+ .07
GW Sierra Tr:			
CalBd	9.89	9.89	− .01
GvSec	9.90	9.90	− .01
GrInc	9.59	9.59	+ .06
Galaxy Funds:			
Bond	9.95	9.95	− .02
Equity	10.54	10.54	+ .05
Gen Elec Inv:			
ElfDiv	11.47	11.47	+ .04
ElfGl	12.49	12.49	+ .05
ElfnIn	10.86	NL	− .02
ElfnTr	29.24	NL	+ .26
ElfnTx	11.00	NL	− .01
S&S	33.23	NL	+ .23
S&S Lg	11.03	NL	− .01
GenSec	11.42	11.42	+ .06
Gintel Group:			
CaAp p	13.41	13.41	+ .15
Erisa p	31.94	31.94	+ .28
GintFd	73.78	73.78	+ .79
Gradison Funds:			
EstGr p	17.46	NL	+ .03
GvIn p	12.77	13.03	− .03
OpGr p	13.88	NL	+ .13
Grnspg	13.14	NL	+ .05
GwWsh p	12.57	13.23	+ .03
Grth Ind	7.37	7.37	+ .07
Guardian Funds:			
Bond	11.53	NL	.....
ParkA	20.57	21.54	+ .15
Stock	20.34	NL	+ .13
HTInsE p	10.45	10.94	+ .03
HanColo	9.50	9.98	.....
Harbor Funds:			
Grwth	12.19	NL	+ .24
Intl	16.97	NL	+ .05
US Eq	11.52	NL	+ .11
Value	12.52	NL	+ .05
Hartwell Fds:			
EGth	14.37	14.81	+ .34
Gwth	18.14	18.70	+ .28
HrvstG p	8.82	9.36	+ .07
HeartG p	9.09	9.52	− .02
HeartId p	13.24	13.86	+ .10
Helmsman Fds:			
DscEq	10.40	10.40	+ .06
GrEq	10.55	10.55	+ .10
Inco	9.50	9.50	− .02
IncEq	10.75	10.75	+ .04
Heritge p	11.52	12.00	+ .09
HrtgCv p	9.01	9.39	+ .05
HiMark		unavail	
Home Group:			
GvSec	9.33	9.80	.....
GroInc	11.05	11.60	+ .05
HY Bd	8.19	8.60	+ .01
NatTF p	6.96	7.31	.....
Hor Man	17.87	17.87	+ .06
Hummer	15.84	NL	+ .12
IAI Funds:			
Apollo	11.84	11.84	+ .10
Bond	9.81	9.81	− .04
IntFd	11.72	11.72	+ .09
Region	18.19	18.19	+ .12
Resve	10.16	10.16	− .01
Stock	15.06	15.06	+ .08
IDS Group:			
Bond p	4.48	4.71	.....
Cal p	4.84	5.10	− .01
Discv p	7.67	8.07	+ .11
Equit p	9.05	9.53	+ .04
Extrl p	3.73	3.93	− .01
FedIn p	4.97	5.23	.....
GlobBd	5.28	5.55	+ .01
Gwth p	20.06	21.11	+ .23
HiYld p	4.47	4.71	.....
Insr p	4.92	5.18	.....
Intl p	9.31	9.81	+ .14
MgdR p	8.93	9.40	+ .08
Minn p	4.93	5.19	− .01
Mutl p	11.57	12.18	+ .01
NY p	4.77	5.02	− .01
US Gvt	8.30	8.69	− .01
UtilFd	9.83	10.29	+ .04
LindDiv	22.74	NL	+ .08
Lindner	18.70	NL	+ .04
Loomis Sayles:			
Capit	16.60	NL	+ .21
Mut	21.21	NL	+ .06
Lord Abbett:			
Affiltd	9.91	10.68	+ .05
BdDeb	8.56	9.23	+ .02
Dev Gt	7.05	7.60	+ .05
FdVl p	11.61	12.52	+ .08
GlEq p	10.68	11.51	+ .06
GlInc p	9.00	9.45	− .02
GvSc p	2.83	2.97	− .01
TaxFr	10.89	11.43	.....
TFCa p	10.26	10.77	− .01
TxNY	10.83	11.37	.....
TFTX	9.42	9.89	.....
ValAp	9.64	10.39	+ .07
Lutheran Bro:			
BroHi	7.93	8.35	.....
Fund	16.00	16.84	+ .14
Incom	8.46	8.91	− .02
Muni	8.15	8.58	.....
MFS:			
MIT	12.79	13.79	+ .06
FinDv	10.80	11.64	+ .09
GrtStk	8.64	9.32	+ .16
CapDv	10.30	11.11	+ .07
Specl	8.50	8.92	+ .08
Sectr p	12.67	13.30	+ .15
EmGt	15.62	16.84	+ .36
TotRet	11.07	11.62	+ .04
GvGu p	9.18	9.64	− .02
GvPl p	7.49	7.86	− .03
IntBnd	11.52	12.09	− .03
FinBd	13.00	14.02	− .02
GovP p	9.36	9.72	− .03
HiIBd	4.84	5.22	− .01
HiInII	7.34	7.71	+ .01
MuBd	10.20	10.71	− .01
TFCA p	5.16	5.42	.....
MMA p	10.58	11.11	− .01
MMD p	10.81	11.35	+ .01
MNC p	11.21	11.77	+ .01
MSC p	11.32	11.88	.....
MuTN p	9.81	10.30	.....
MuVA p	10.98	11.53	.....
MWV p	10.73	11.27	.....
MuHY	9.45	9.92	.....
MFS Lifetime:			
CapG t	11.44	11.44	+ .10
Globl t	13.39	13.39	+ .12
Sectr t	10.08	10.08	+ .11
Emg t	7.54	7.54	+ .17
DivPl t	9.05	9.05	+ .01
GvPl t	7.42	7.42	− .04
HiInc t	5.53	5.53	.....
IntInc t	9.25	9.25	− .02
MuBd t	8.32	8.32	.....
MIM Funds:			
BdInc	9.14	NL	+ .03
SCO Inc	10.20	NL	+ .08
SCO Gr	9.40	NL	+ .10
StkAp	8.22	NL	+ .05
MIMLIC Funds:			
AstAll	11.18	11.77	+ .03
Invl	11.79	12.41	+ .11
MtgSc	10.05	10.58	− .01
MSB Fd p	17.21	NL	+ .16
Mackenzie Grp:			
AmFd	12.75	13.93	+ .15
Canad	10.50	11.05	+ .04
FixInc	9.92	10.41	− .09
GvtSc p	7.57	7.95	− .04
NA TR	6.54	6.88	+ .02
MainStay Funds:			
CaAp t	10.78	10.78	+ .12
Conv t	8.35	8.35	+ .02
CrpBd t	7.01	7.01	+ .01
Globl t	10.17	10.17	+ .06
Gold t	11.11	11.11	− .01
GovPl t	8.73	8.73	− .03
North Am Sec Tr:			
AgAA p	6.33	6.65	+ .03
CnAA p	8.71	9.14	+ .01
Gwth p	9.84	10.33	+ .06
MdAA p	7.43	7.80	+ .02
USGvt p	9.56	10.04	− .01
Nuveen Funds:			
CA Spc	9.72	10.20	.....
CA Ins	9.44	9.91	+ .01
InsNat	9.47	9.94	.....
MunBd	8.77	9.21	+ .01
NYITF	9.20	9.66	+ .01
OhTF	9.41	9.88	+ .01
TF MA	8.76	9.20	+ .01
TFNY	9.39	9.86	.....
Oberws		unavail	
OlyEqIn	12.76	12.76	+ .06
OldDom		unavail	
Olympus Funds:			
Equty t	9.65	10.08	+ .08
PrmIn t	7.42	7.75	+ .04
TE CA	7.48	7.81	.....
TE NY	7.71	8.05	.....
TEHY r	7.72	8.06	.....
USGvt t	9.05	9.45	− .01
Oppenheimer Fd:			
AsetA p	10.39	10.91	+ .03
BlueC p	15.38	16.15	+ .10
CA TE	9.72	10.20	.....
Direct	21.08	23.04	+ .15
EqInc	8.98	9.81	+ .06
GNM p	13.27	13.93	− .01
Global	30.29	33.10	+ .29
Gold	14.80	16.17	+ .07
Hi Yld	13.94	14.95	.....
NYTx p	11.84	12.43	+ .01
90-10	12.42	13.46	+ .01
OTCF p	20.03	21.03	+ .23
Oppen	8.90	9.73	+ .06
Prem	19.47	21.28	+ .16
Rgcy	12.47	13.63	+ .11
Specl	18.32	20.02	+ .12
StrInc	4.94	5.19	.....
Target	17.26	18.12	+ .13
TxFr p	9.30	9.76	.....
Time	15.57	17.02	+ .11
TotRt p	6.35	6.67	+ .06
USGv p	9.33	9.80	− .01
Ostrand	7.33	7.45	− .02
OTC Sc p	15.08	15.79	+ .10
OvIndCA	10.16	10.64	− .01
PNC Ca p	10.23	10.71	+ .08
PNC M p	9.78	10.24	− .02
Pacific Horizon:			
AgGr p	16.80	17.59	+ .35
CATF p	13.63	14.27	+ .01
HYBd	10.82	11.33	− .02
Pacific Inv:			
LowDu	9.91	NL	− .01
ShortT	9.98	NL	− .01
TotRet	9.88	NL	− .02
Paine Webber:			
AstAll t	9.80	9.80	.....
Atlas p	15.13	15.84	+ .09
CalTx	10.80	11.28	+ .01
ClGIn p	15.59	16.32	+ .06
ClHY p	9.95	10.36	.....
CGth p	14.06	14.72	+ .13
CWld p	10.10	10.58	+ .05
GNMA	9.32	9.73	− .01
HiYld	6.93	7.24	.....
InvGr	9.61	10.04	− .01
MstE r	12.56	12.56	+ .08
MstGl t	10.35	10.35	+ .01
MstGt t	13.14	13.14	+ .16
MstIn p	8.69	8.69	− .01
TaxEx	11.06	11.55	.....
Paragon Pt:			
IntBd	9.76	10.20	− .02
LA TF	9.99	10.44	.....
ST Gv	9.91	10.36	.....
ValEq	9.36	9.78	+ .04
ValGr	9.47	9.90	+ .06
Parkstone Fds:			
Bond	9.91	10.38	− .02
Equity	11.37	11.91	+ .04
HiEq	11.73	12.28	+ .03
IntGvt	9.83	10.29	− .01
LtdMt	9.81	10.27	− .01
MuBd	10.01	10.48	.....

	NAV	Offer Price
RNC Group:		
CvSc p	8.86	9.30
Rgcy p	13.94	14.64
Wstw p	10.61	11.14
Rainbw	4.90	NL
ReaGr	13.71	14.39
RchTng	13.67	NL
Rightime Group:		
BlueC p	25.74	27.02
RT fp	31.40	NL
GvSc p	13.88	14.57
Grth p	23.40	24.57
Rochester Fds:		
CnvG p	8.82	9.12
Grth p	6.11	6.32
Muni p	16.19	16.86
Tax p	8.11	8.36
Rodney Square:		
BnUS p	8.08	8.46
Gwth p	11.83	12.55
IntlEq p	12.63	13.40
Royce Funds:		
Inco t	7.19	7.19
Valu t	8.13	8.13
TotRt t	4.49	4.49
Rushmore Group:		
AGas	11.55	NL
Nova	9.45	NL
SMP Id	13.74	NL
OTC Id	11.08	NL
USGLg	9.65	NL
US Gov	9.62	NL
TxFLg	10.08	NL
TxFIn	10.21	NL
SBSF Cv	10.28	10.28
SBSF Gr	15.51	15.51
SEI Funds:		
Bond p	9.80	NL
LtVBd p	9.80	NL
ShtGv p	9.64	NL
IntGv p	9.46	NL
EqInc p	11.75	NL
EqIdx p	12.08	NL
PAMu p	9.94	NL
Valu p	10.67	NL
CapA p	11.68	NL
SFT Group:		
AstAll	9.42	10.30
Envir p	12.51	13.17
Equit p	11.38	11.98
OddLt	20.44	NL
US Gv p	6.64	6.99
SP IFG Fds:		
DEAF f	11.83	NL
IntMu f	10.10	10.10
TIF f	11.22	NL
Safeco Secur:		
CalTF	11.08	NL
Equit	9.75	NL
Grwth	15.24	NL
Inco	15.28	NL
Munic	12.75	NL
USGov	9.19	NL
SalmFi t	9.85	9.85
SalemG p	14.88	14.88
Schield p	10.84	11.29
Schrodr	7.51	7.51
Schrod fp	19.15	19.15
Scudder Funds:		
CalTx	10.29	NL
CapGt	18.11	NL
Devel	21.01	NL
EqtyIn	11.95	NL
Globl	19.17	NL
GNMA	14.32	NL
Gold	12.44	12.44
GrwIn	13.38	NL
Incom	12.71	NL
IntlBd	11.97	NL
Intl Fd	37.93	NL
MMB	8.37	NL
MA Tx	12.28	NL
NYTax	10.66	NL
OHTax	11.98	NL
ST Bond	11.64	NL
TxFHi	11.17	NL
TxFr90	10.05	NL
TxFr93	10.58	NL
TxFr96	10.80	NL
Zr1995	11.25	NL
Zr2000	11.87	NL

FIGURE 2-5 Listing of mutual funds. *Source: The Wall Street Journal*, February 5, 1990, C-20, reprinted by permission, © 1990, Dow Jones & Co., Inc., all rights reserved.

charges range from 4 to $8\frac{1}{2}$ percent or more of the initial purchase. The sales charge is added to the NAV to determine the offering price — the price that investors pay to buy new shares. The sales charge covers the cost of distribution and advertising. Most of it goes to the selling brokerage firm as an inducement to sell mutual fund shares. The fund's sales charge is substantially higher than the 2 or 3 percent charged on stocks.

No-load fund companies do not charge a commission when the shares are bought directly from the fund by mail or phone. However, some no-loads charge commission when investors redeem their shares. Moreover, some mutual funds are charging smaller front-end load and combining them with "back-end" redemption fees. Thus, the distinction between load and no-load is blurred.

Mutual Funds

Figure 2-5 is a partial listing of the mutual funds that appear in *The Wall Street Journal*. Those with N.L. in the "offer price" column are no-load funds. The offer price is the same as the NAV. Most of the Fidelity funds, for example, are no-load. Fidelity and other fund managers have a **family** or **group** of mutual funds to meet the varying investment needs of their investors. For example, they have bond funds, growth funds, overseas funds, and so on.

TABLE 2-3 Total Net Assets of Equity, Bond, and Income Funds by Fund Characteristics, 1988 Year-end (millions of dollars)

Total Net Assets	Dollars $472,296.6	Percent 100.0%
Investment Objective		
Aggressive growth	29,452.3	6.2
Growth	50,547.2	10.7
Growth and income	70,865.3	15.0
Precious metals	3,171.9	0.7
International	6,831.8	1.4
Global equity	11,151.1	2.4
Income-equity	17,509.5	3.7
Option/income	5,286.3	1.1
Flexible portfolio	3,485.7	0.7
Balanced	9,492.9	2.0
Income — mixed	8,768.7	1.9
Income — bond	10,693.3	2.3
U.S. government income	82,688.1	17.5
Ginnie Mae	28,712.0	6.1
Global bond	3,024.3	0.6
Corporate bond	10,463.9	2.2
High-yield bond	33,425.2	7.1
Long-term municipal bond	54,316.3	11.5
State municipal bond, long-term	32,410.8	6.9

Source: Investment Company Institute, *Mutual Fund Fact Book,* 1989.

The investment advisors who manage the portfolios of securities also receive compensation. Their fee is based on the dollar value of the assets under their supervision, and averages about one-half of 1 percent annually. Thus, their income goes up when the funds appreciate in value or when more fund shares are sold.

Investment Objectives

Mutual funds may also be classified by their investment objectives. There are three broad groups of funds: (1) equity, bond, and income funds, (2) money market funds, and (3) short-term municipal bond funds.

Table 2-3 shows the assets and distribution of the **equity, bond, and income funds** by specific investment objective. What these investment objectives mean is explained in Figure 2-6. Total assets for all of these funds amounted to $472.3 billion in 1988. Most of the assets are invested in funds with growth and income as investment objectives.

Aggressive Growth Funds seek maximum capital gains as their investment objective. Current income is not a significant factor. Some may invest in stocks that are somewhat out of the mainstream such as those in fledgling companies, new industries, companies fallen on hard times, or industries temporarily out of favor. They may also use specialized investment techniques such as option writing. The risks are obvious, but the potential for reward should also be greater.

Growth Funds invest in the common stock of more settled companies but, again, the primary aim is to produce an increase in the value of their investments through capital gains rather than a steady flow of dividends.

Growth and Income Funds invest mainly in the common stock of companies with a longer track record — companies that have both the expectation of a higher share value and a solid record of paying dividends.

Precious Metals Funds invest in the stocks of gold mining companies and other companies in the precious metals business.

International Funds invest in the stocks of companies located outside the U.S.

Global Equity Funds invest in the stocks of both U.S. companies and foreign companies.

Income-equity Funds invest primarily in stocks of companies with good dividend-paying records.

Option/Income Funds seek a high current return by investing primarily in dividend-paying common stocks on which call options are traded on national securities exchanges. Current return generally consists of dividends, premiums from writing call options, net short-term gains from sales of portfolio securities on exercises of options or otherwise, and any profits from closing purchase transactions.

Flexible Portfolio Funds invest in common stocks, bonds, money market

FIGURE 2-6 Types of mutual funds. *Source:* Investment Company Institute, Mutual Fund Fact Book, 1989.

FIGURE 2-6 *(continued)*

securities, and other types of debt securities. The portfolio may hold up to 100 percent of any one of these types of securities, or any combination thereof, and may easily change depending upon market conditions.

Balanced Funds generally have a three-part investment objective: 1) to conserve the investors' principal; 2) to pay current income; and 3) to increase both principal and income. They aim to achieve this by owning a mixture of bonds, preferred stocks, and common stocks.

Income-mixed Funds seek a high level of current income for their shareholders. This may be achieved by investing in the common stock of companies that have good dividend-paying records. Often corporate and government bonds are also part of the portfolio.

Income-bond Funds invest in a combination of government and corporate bonds for the generation of income.

U.S. Government Income Funds invest in a variety of government securities. These include U.S. Treasury bonds, federally guaranteed mortgage-backed securities, and other government issues.

GNMA or Ginnie Mae Funds (Government National Mortgage Association) invest in government-backed mortgage securities. To qualify for this category, the majority of the portfolio must always be invested in mortgage-backed securities.

Global Bond Funds invest in bonds issued by companies or countries worldwide, including the U.S.

Corporate Bond Funds, like income funds, seek a high level of income. They do so by buying bonds of corporations for the majority of the fund's portfolio. The rest of the portfolio may

be in U.S. Treasury and other government entities' bonds.

High-yield Bond Funds are corporate bond funds that predominantly invest in bonds rated below investment grade. In return for a generally higher yield, investors bear a greater degree of risk than for more highly rated bonds.

Long-term Municipal Bond Funds invest in bonds issued by local governments—such as cities and states—which use the money to build schools, highways, libraries, and the like. These funds predominantly invest at all times in municipal bonds that are exempt from federal income tax. Because the federal government does not tax the income earned on most of these securities, the fund can pass the tax-free income through to shareholders. For some taxpayers, portions of income earned on these securities may be subject to the federal alternative minimum tax.

Short-term Municipal Bond Funds invest in municipal securities with relatively short maturities. They are also known as tax-exempt money market funds. For some taxpayers, portions of income earned on these securities may be subject to the federal alternative minimum tax.

Long-term State Municipal Bond Funds predominantly invest at all times in municipal bonds, which are exempt from federal income tax as well as exempt from state taxes for residents of the state specified by the fund name. For some taxpayers, portions of income earned on these securities may be subject to the federal alternative minimum tax.

Short-term State Municipal Bond Funds invest in municipal securities with relatively short maturities. Because they contain the issues of only

FIGURE 2-6   *(continued)*

one state, they are exempt from state taxes for residents of the state specified by the fund name. For some taxpayers, portions of income earned on these securities may be subject to the federal alternative minimum tax.

Money Market Mutual Funds invest in the short-term securities sold in the money market. (Large companies, banks, and other institutions invest their surplus cash in the money market for short periods of time.) In the entire investment spectrum, these are generally the safest, most stable securities available. They include Treasury Bills, certificates of deposit of large banks, and commercial paper (the short-term IOUs of large U.S. corporations).

Money market mutual funds had total assets of $272.3 billion at the end of 1988. Their objectives, income, and safety, are obtained by investing in short-term securities such as Treasury bills, CDs, and commercial paper. Some invest in foreign short-term securities. Although money market funds invest in short-term securities, there are differences in risk and return. Those that invest exclusively in short-term Treasury issues will have lower risk and returns than those that invest heavily in short-term foreign securities. Money market funds at securities firms are covered by SIPC insurance. Other money market funds may not be insured. There are more than 400 money market funds from which investors can choose one or more that matches their need. There are no sales charges on money market funds.

Because of their importance, they deserve special attention. In addition to providing yields that are tied to market rates of interest, they are used by many investors as an interest-bearing checking account because they allow checks to be written against their holdings. Most funds require a minimum initial investment that ranges from $250 to $2500 or more, and require a $500 minimum on the amounts that can be withdrawn by check.

Short-term municipal bond funds are basically money market funds that invest in municipal securities. The advantage of these investments is that income from such securities is exempt from federal income tax, except the alternative minimum tax, and in some cases from state taxes. At the end of 1988, $65.7 billion was invested in these funds.

Figure 2-7 illustrates the dramatic growth of mutual funds' assets during the 1980s. The growth in money market funds reflects the public's demand for alternatives to traditional savings and transaction accounts offered by banks and thrifts. The growth of stock, bond, and income funds reflects a major change in the way investors invest in the securities markets. Today more investors are investing indirectly, through mutual funds and other financial institutions, than in previous years. For example, investors who want to invest in a sector of the economy and do not know which companies will succeed or fail, may invest in a **sector fund** that specializes in a particular industry such as health sciences,

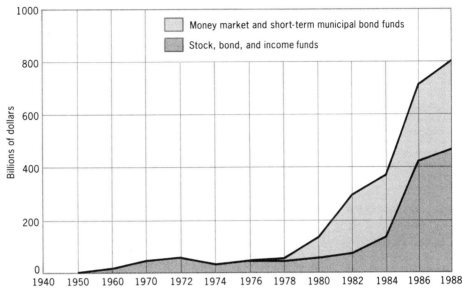

FIGURE 2-7 Assets of mutual funds. *Source:* Investment Company Institute, Mutual Fund Fact Book, 1989.

leisure, insurance, or chemicals. Such funds manage a portfolio of firms that invests heavily in the desired sector.

Benefits for Investors

Investment companies have certain advantages that are lacking in other types of investments. For those investors who do not have the time, knowledge, or desire to analyze and manage securities they offer a professionally managed portfolio, which gives many people a certain sense of security. Moreover, investment company shares can be bought by investors with either small or large sums to invest. Some of the features in the following discussion are also beneficial to investors.

Diversification

One advantage of owning investment company shares is **diversification**—the spreading of risk over a variety of companies, industries, securities, or other forms of investments whose returns are affected differently by changing economic and financial market conditions. One share of an investment company represents ownership of 25 to 100 or more companies that are held in the investment company's portfolio.

Unfortunately, holding so many different companies can also be a disadvantage. By holding so many different companies, the investment company may perform "like the whole stock market." In other words, the diversification may be excessive.

Reinvestment Plans

Most investment companies have provisions for automatic **reinvestment** of dividends and capital gains. Generally, the dividends from investment income are reinvested at the offering price, which may include a sales charge. Many investment companies give their stockholders the option of taking their net realized capital gains in the form of a stock dividend of investment company shares or of receiving cash.

Withdrawal Plans

Some investors want a steady stream of income on a monthly or quarterly basis, and some investment companies offer such programs. Most **withdrawal plans** require an initial investment of $10,000 or more. Income dividends are reinvested or held as cash, and capital gains distributions are accepted as shares. Assume that an investor wants to receive $75 per month. If that amount exceeds income dividends, some shares are redeemed at net asset value to make up the difference in the withdrawal payment. If the fund does well, the investor may never have to dip into capital to pay the withdrawal payment. The higher the amount of withdrawal payments in relation to the principal amount, the greater the risk of depletion of the principal.

Conversion Privilege

Some investment companies belong to a family of funds and permit their shareholders to switch from one fund to another within the family for a small transaction charge. For example, Massachusetts Investors Trust, Massachusetts Investors Growth Stock Fund, Massachusetts Capital Development Fund, and Massachusetts Financial Development Fund are all members of one family of mutual funds. Shareholders can exchange shares in any one of the funds for the shares of any other fund in that family. This privilege is an advantage for those approaching retirement age who have common stock funds and want to switch to funds that emphasize preservation of capital and income.

Retirement Plans

Various types of retirement plans can be funded with mutual fund shares. This means that federal income tax laws permit retirement funds to be invested in mutual fund shares as well as other assets. These families of funds provide flexibility for individuals to adjust their holdings to funds that match their changing needs as they approach retirement.

CONCLUSION

This chapter examines some of the important features of three types of equity securities: common stock, preferred stock, and shares in investment companies. All equity securities represent ownership in a corporation. As owners, common

stockholders generally have the right to vote and share in the profits of the company in the form of dividends. They also benefit from appreciation in the value of their investment. However, should the company be dissolved, the common stockholder is the last person to receive any distribution of assets. Dividends on common stock are paid in cash, stock, or property. The firm's Board of Directors decides on the amount and form of the dividend, and in some cases decides to declare no dividend at all. Stock dividends and stock splits are ways of increasing the number of shares outstanding, but they do not increase the total equity of the company.

The amount of the dividend a common stock pays is an important determinant of the stock's *intrinsic value* — the theoretical value justified by analysis of the stock. There are a number of methods of determining intrinsic value. Most of them use the concept of *present value* — what one would be willing to pay today to receive a given amount of money in the future.

Preferred stockholders have a preference over common stockholders as to assets and dividends. Unfortunately, most preferred stocks have characteristics that make them relatively unattractive to many individual investors. For example, they pay a fixed rate of return that is taxable; many do not have voting privileges; and many are not convertible into some other class of security. Certain features of some preferred stocks are desirable, however. As with common stocks, they may pay no dividends if the Board of Directors so decides, but if the stock has a cumulative clause, the dividends go into arrears and must be paid before any future dividends can be paid to common stockholders. A participating preferred stock gives the stockholder the right to share in dividends with the common stockholders. Moreover, some preferred stocks are convertible to common stocks.

Investment company shares are common shares in a company that specializes in pooling the funds of investors and offering them professional management and diversification of their investments. There are several types of investment companies, but mutual funds are the most common. These may be load or no-load funds. The former require a payment of commission upon share purchase, but the latter do not. Both make about the same return on investment, so the investor does better to choose a no-load fund. Different funds have different investment objectives: They may invest for capital appreciation, for production of income, or for a balance between the two. There are also funds that invest in highly specialized areas. Some funds offer reinvestment and withdrawal plans and conversion privileges so as to meet the needs of their investors more fully.

IMPORTANT CONCEPTS

American Depository Receipts (ADRs)	Classified stock
Arrears	Closed-end investment company
Assets	Common stock
Book value	Conversion privilege
Call provision	Corporation
Chop shop	Cum-rights

Cumulative preferred
Cumulative voting
Dated declared
Date of record
Diversification
Dividend
Dividend valuation model
Dividend yield
Dual-class stock
Ex-dividend date
Ex-rights
Face-Amount Certificate Companies
Family or group of mutual funds
Intrinsic value
Investment company
Limited liability
Load fund
Money market funds
Municipal securities
Mutual fund
Net asset value (NAV)
No-load fund

Ordinary voting
Ownership
Par value
Preemptive rights
Preferred stock
Present value
Property dividend
Reinvestment plans
Residual claimant
Sector funds
Short-term municipal bond funds
Sinking fund
Split (stock)
Stock dividend
Stockholders
Street name
Treasury stock
Undervalued stock
Unit Investment Trust
Withdrawal plans
12b-1 fee

QUESTIONS AND EXERCISES

1. Suppose that you bought 100 shares of Losemore at $60 per share yesterday, and today it is selling for $30 per share. If the basic factors that influenced your decision to buy the stock have not changed (except for the price), would you buy more today? Explain your answer.

2. What rights are stockholders entitled to?

3. Which of the following is better for stockholders: a 2-for-1 split, or a 100 percent stock dividend?

4. Should stock be purchased before or after it goes ex-dividend? Explain.

5. Subscribemore House runs an annual sweepstake that gives the grand-prize winner a choice: a check for $1 million or $50,000 per year for 20 years. If taxes are not a consideration, which would you choose? Why?

6. In valuing a stock, should one discount the future value of dividends 5 years? 10 years? 20 years? Perpetually? Comment on your choice.

7. What is the idea behind the dividend valuation model?

8. How is the discount rate used in the dividend valuation model chosen?

9. Are preferred stocks a suitable investment for investors seeking capital appreciation? Why or why not?

10. How is book value related to the market value of a stock? To the par value?
11. Why do the managements of some firms fear cumulative voting?
12. What does it mean when a preferred stock is in "arrears"?
13. Cite four benefits of owning investment company shares.
14. Distinguish between load and no-load funds.
15. Define the term "net asset value," and indicate which type of securities are routinely traded in terms of their net asset value.

APPENDIX 2A:
DIVIDEND VALUATION MODEL

The price of most common stocks can be calculated by capitalizing (discounting) all the future cash dividends. Stated otherwise, the value of a share of stock is

$$P_0 = \frac{D_1}{(1+k)^1} + \frac{D_2}{(1+k)^2} + \cdots + \frac{D_\infty}{(1+k)^\infty} \qquad (2A\text{-}1)$$

$$P_0 = \sum_{t=1}^{\infty} \frac{D_t}{(1+k)^t}$$

where

$P_0 =$ the price at time 0
$D_1, D_2, D_t =$ the dividends per share expected in periods 1, 2, and t
$k =$ the appropriate discount rate determined by investors

Sigma (Σ) means summation and ∞ stands for infinity.

If the dividends are expected to grow at some constant rate (g), then D_t can be expressed as

$$D_t = D_0(1 + g)^t \qquad (2A\text{-}2)$$

where $D_0 =$ the dollar amount of the dividend in time 0.
Time 0 can be thought of as the current period.

Equation 2A-1 can be rewritten as

$$P_0 = \sum_{t=1}^{\infty} \frac{D_0(1+g)^t}{(1+k)^t} \qquad (2A\text{-}3)$$

or as

$$P_0 = D_0 \left[\frac{(1+g)}{(1+k)} + \frac{(1+g)^2}{(1+k)^2} + \cdots + \frac{(1+g)^n}{(1+k)^n} \right] \qquad (2A\text{-}4)$$

Multiply both sides of Equation 2A-4 by $\dfrac{(1+k)}{(1+g)}$

$$\left[\frac{(1+k)}{(1+g)}\right]P_0 = D_0\left[1 + \frac{(1+g)}{(1+k)} + \frac{(1+g)^2}{(1+k)^2} + \cdots \frac{(1+g)^{n-1}}{(1+k)^{n-1}}\right] \quad \text{(2A-5)}$$

Subtract Equation 2A-4 from Equation 2A-5

$$\left[\frac{(1+k)}{(1+g)} - 1\right]P_0 = D_0\left[1 - \frac{(1+g)^n}{(1+k)^n}\right]$$

$$\left[\frac{(1+k)-(1+g)}{(1+g)}\right]P_0 = D_0\left[1 - \frac{(1+g)^n}{(1+k)^n}\right]$$

Assume $k > g$, as n approaches infinity, $\left[\dfrac{1-(1+g)^n}{(1+k^n)}\right]$ approaches 1, which leaves

$$\left[\frac{(1+k)-(1+g)}{(1+g)}\right]P_0 = D_0$$

Which simplifies to

$$(k-g)P_0 = D_0(1+g) = 1; D_1 = D_0(1+g)$$

$$\therefore P_0 = \frac{D_1}{k-g}$$

CHAPTER 3

DEBT SECURITIES

CORPORATE BONDS
Basic Features
Types of Security
Quality Ratings
Bond Retirement Features
Special Types of Bonds
STATE AND LOCAL GOVERNMENT BONDS
Tax Exemption
Industrial Development Bonds or
   Private Activity Bonds
General Obligation Bonds
Revenue Bonds
	U.S. GOVERNMENT AND FEDERAL AGENCY SECURITIES
	Marketable Treasury Securities
	Nonmarketable Securities
	Government-Sponsored Agencies and
	   Federal Agencies
	CONCLUSION
	IMPORTANT CONCEPTS
	QUESTIONS AND EXERCISES

I t used to be that investors thought of bonds as safe securities. They bought bonds for income and held them until maturity. Now investors know better. Bond prices are just as volatile as stock prices, and some bond issuers default on their payments. Therefore, buying a bond because you want a "safe" investment might not be a good idea. On the other hand, if you want to speculate, consider bonds along with other investment opportunities.

Debt securities, such as bonds, generally arise because organizations borrow funds to finance their operations. Business concerns borrow to finance plant and equipment, and federal, state, and local governments borrow to finance roads, schools, bridges, and so on. In recent years, however, business concerns have also borrowed heavily to finance the purchase of their own stocks, the stocks of other firms, and to pay cash dividends. Borrowing for such purposes is called *restructuring,* because it restructures the relationship between debt and equity in the firms involved.[1]

This chapter examines the different types of *marketable* debt securities. The discussion is limited to those securities that are generally bought by individual investors, rather than those bought by banks or governments. Debt securities are

---

[1] For additional information on restructuring, see William D. Samson and Benton E. Gup, "The Hidden Side of Corporate Restructuring," *Tax Analysts/Tax Notes,* November 13, 1989, 877–888. Also, *The Journal of Applied Corporate Finance,* Spring 1988 issue, is devoted to corporate restructuring.

divided into three categories: (1) corporate bonds, (2) securities of state and local governments, and (3) federal government and agency securities.

CORPORATE BONDS

Basic Features

A **bond** is a credit instrument that promises to pay both principal and interest on a loan on predetermined dates. The details of the loan agreement appear in a deed of trust or **indenture.** The indenture is issued to a trustee, typically a commercial bank, who ensures that the issuing corporation complies with the terms of the agreement. One of the most important terms of the agreement is the unconditional promise to pay the principal amount of the loan on some maturity date and to make periodic interest payments if they are required. Some bonds do not require interest payments. The principal amount, or as it is commonly called, **par value** or **face amount**, can range from $50 to $10,000 or more. However, $1000 is the most common par value. Most bonds mature 15 years or more after they are issued, but some bonds are redeemed before they mature. The indenture also specifies when interest payments will be made. Bonds usually pay interest semi-annually, such as on June 30 and December 31. Some bonds pay interest by means of coupons that are attached to the bond. When interest is due, bondholders detach the dated coupons and present them to the issuer's paying agent or deposit them in their own banks for collection. The indenture may also contain clauses that restrict certain actions by the company (called **restrictive covenants**). For example, bondholders may restrict the amount of additional debt the company can incur.

Coupon and Registered Bonds

Both the principal and interest of **bearer** or **coupon bonds** are payable to the bearer of the security and coupon. Coupons are usually payable semiannually. In contrast, other bonds are **registered** as to principal and, in some cases, interest. These bonds are payable to the person whose name appears on the face of the bond and is recorded on the books of the issuing corporation. The principal advantage of a registered bond lies in the safety it offers: It cannot be sold or cashed in unless it is properly endorsed. The disadvantage is that some coupon bonds are more marketable and command a higher price than registered bonds.

Accrued Interest

When investors purchase bonds, they must pay the current price plus **accrued interest,** the interest earned since the last interest payment or the date of issue, whichever is later. For example, if the last coupon payment was June 1 and the investor purchased bonds for delivery on July 15, the accrued interest would be

calculated for 1 month and 14 days. The investor will regain the amount of interest paid to the seller of the bond when the next coupon is cashed.

Yield

Most investors are concerned with the yield of a bond. Two types of yields must be considered: (1) **current yield** and (2) **yield to maturity.** A third type, yield to call, will be discussed shortly. Current yield is the dollar amount of the coupon divided by the market price of the bond. For example, an 8-percent bond with 15 years to maturity pays $80 interest a year on each $1000 par value. If the bond is selling at par, the current yield is 8 percent ($80 ÷ $1000 = 8%). If the bond is selling below par (at a **discount**) or above par (at a premium), current yield is still calculated in the same manner. Thus, if the bond is selling at $950, the current yield is 8.42 percent.

$$\text{Current yield} = \frac{C}{P_0} \qquad (3\text{-}1)$$

where

$$C = \text{annual income (\$) from bond}$$
$$P_0 = \text{current market price of bond}$$

$$\text{Current yield} = \frac{\$80}{\$950} = 8.42\%$$

If the bond is held to maturity, the market price of the bond will advance to the $1000 par value. When the bond matures, the bondholder will receive $1000 and the $50 difference between the purchase price and the par value. In this case, the yield to maturity will be greater than the current yield, and it can be approximated by Equation 3-2:

$$\text{Yield to maturity} = \frac{C + [(F - P_0)/n]}{(F + P_0)/2} \qquad (3\text{-}2)$$

where

$$C = \text{annual income (\$) from bond}$$
$$F = \text{face value of obligation payable at maturity}$$
$$P_0 = \text{current market price of bond}$$
$$n = \text{number of years to maturity}$$

Substituting in the equation we get

$$\text{Yield to maturity} = \frac{\$80 + [(\$1,000 - \$950)/15]}{(\$1,000 + \$950)/2} = 8.55\%$$

Yield to maturity (YTM) is the average percentage yield earned annually from the purchase date to the maturity date and includes both capital gains and losses. The precise yield to maturity of a bond can be found by solving the following

equation for r, or by using bond value tables that are derived from the equation:

$$P_0 = \frac{C/m}{(1 + r/m)} + \frac{C/m}{(1 + r/m)^2} + \frac{C/m}{(1 + r/m)^3} + \cdots + \frac{F}{(1 + r/m)^{mn}}$$

$$= \sum_{t=1}^{n} \frac{C/m}{(1 + r/m)^{mn}} + \frac{F}{(1 + r/m)^{mn}} \qquad (3\text{-}3)$$

where

P_0 = current market price of bond
C = annual income ($) from bond
r = yield to maturity (%)
m = number of payments per year, generally twice per year
n = number of years to maturity
F = face value of obligation payable at maturity ($)

Accordingly, the precise yield to maturity of the bond in the example is

$$P_0 = \frac{\$80/2}{(1 + 0.086/2)} + \frac{\$80/2}{(1 + 0.086/2)^2} + \frac{\$80/2}{(1 + 0.086/2)^3} + \cdots$$

$$+ \frac{\$80/2}{(1 + 0.086/2)^{30}} + \frac{\$1000}{(1 + 0.086/2)^{30}} = \$950$$

$$YTM = 0.086 \text{ or } 8.6\%$$

Price

From Equation 3-3 we can see that the market price of a bond is the present value of all of the cash flows — interest and principal — and that the yield to maturity r is the rate of return required by bond investors. If we know what return investors want, say 10 percent, we can take the present value of (discount) the interest and principal payments to determine the price.

TABLE 3-1   Present Value of $1 at 10%

Year	Present Value	Present Value of an Annuity
1	0.9091	0.9091
2	0.8264	1.7355
3	0.7513	2.4868
4	0.6830	3.1699
5	0.6209	3.7908
10	0.3855	6.1446
20	0.1486	8.5136
25	0.0923	9.0770

Tables showing both present values and present values of annuities are in Appendixes A and B at the back of the book.

Before calculating the price of a bond, a quick review of present value is in order. The basic idea is how much you would be willing to pay today for $1 that you will receive one or more years from now. Stated otherwise, it is the amount needed today to have $1 at some time in the future given a fixed rate of interest. As shown in Table 3-1, the present value of $1 received at the end of one year is $0.9091. The present value of $1 received at the end of five years is $0.6209. Now let's apply this technique to bond prices. If a bond with five years to maturity pays $70 interest at the end of each of the next five years, the price of the bond, or the present value of the interest and principal amounts discounted at 10 percent, is as follows:

Year	Present Value Interest Factor for 10%	Present Value	
1	2	$3 = 2 \times \$70$	
1	0.9091	$63.64	
2	0.8264	57.85	
3	0.7513	52.59	
4	0.6830	47.81	
5	0.6209	43.46	
Sum	3.7908	$265.35	Present value of interest payments
5	$0.6209 \times \$1,000 = \$621.09$		Present value of principal
Sum		$886.44	Present value of the bond

If the bond had 25 years to maturity, we could determine its price in the same manner. However, there is an easier way to do it. Because bond interest payments are the same dollar amount every year, they can be thought of as an **annuity**—a regular periodic payment. The advantage of this concept is that it reduces the calculations needed to determine the price of a bond. The present value of an annuity, shown in Table 3-1, is merely the sum of the present value interest factors. Thus, the present value of an annuity for two years is $0.9091 + 0.8264 = 1.7355$. Similarly, the present value of an annuity for three years is $0.9091 + 0.8264 + 0.7513 = 2.4868$. For five years the present value of the annuity is 3.7908. This amount can be multiplied by the $70 to give the present value of the interest payments, $265.35. In other words, using the present value of an annuity interest factor table, it is necessary only to multiply one interest factor times the dollar amount of interest payments instead of doing it multiple times using the present value table.

Since the principal amount is paid only once, at maturity, we take the present value of that amount for year 5, $621.00, and add it to the present value of the interest payments to arrive at the price of the bond, $886.30.

In this simplified example we assumed that interest was paid only once a year. If interest were paid twice a year, we would use the formula shown in Equation 3-3. The coupon C and interest rate r would be divided by the number of pay-

ments (2), and the number of periods to maturity would be doubled. Thus, the present value of the annuity for the interest payments for 10 years, with interest paid twice a year, is determined by dividing the $70 interest payment by 2, and by using the present value of an annuity interest factor for 20 years (12.4622) because the number of years was doubled:

$$\$70/2 \times 12.4622 = \$436.17$$

The present value of the principal amount to be paid in year 10 is determined by using the principal amount ($1000), and the present value interest factor for 20 years (0.3769):

$$\$1,000 \times 0.3769 = \$376.90$$

The present value of the bond ($813.07) is the sum of the two figures we just calculated:

$$\$436.17 + \$376.90 = \$813.07$$

The present value of any bond can be determined in the same manner using both the present value interest factor table and the present value of an annuity interest factor table. These tables are in Appendixes A and B at the back of the book. Bond prices may also be determined by using bond value tables, which do the work for you.

Bond Value Table

Bond value tables are a useful aid in determining the yield to maturity or, given the yield, the market price of bonds. Table 3-2 is an example of one page from a bond value table. The coupon rate of the bond—8 percent—and the years and months to maturity are given in the table heading. Yields to maturity are shown in bold type in the far left column. The body of the table gives the market prices of the bonds expressed as a percentage of par value. Thus, 84.63 is equivalent to $846.30 for a $1000 par value bond. To illustrate the use of the table, consider the bond that was used in the previous example. It had an 8-percent coupon, 15 years to maturity, and the market price of the bond was $950. Find the column marked 15-0, which stands for 15 years and no months. Look down that column until you find 95.00, which stands for the bond's price—$950. The yield to maturity—8.60 percent—can be read from the left-hand column.

An alternative way to use the table is to find the market price of a bond for any given yield. What is the market price of an 8-percent coupon bond with 15 years maturity if the yield is 10 percent? The answer can be determined by finding 10 percent in the yield column on the left-hand side of the table and reading across the line to the column for 15-0 years to maturity. The answer is 84.63, or $846.30 per $1000 par-value bond.

Calculators

Some hand-held calculators are programmed to calculate yields to maturity and bond prices. Such calculators eliminate the need for bond value tables and the cumbersome calculations of prices and yields using present value concepts.

TABLE 3-2   Bond Value Table

Yield	14–6	15–0	15–6	16–0	16–6	17–0	17–6	18–0
				Years and Months				**8%**
4.00	143.69	144.79	145.88	146.94	147.98	149.00	150.00	150.98
4.20	140.96	141.97	142.97	143.95	144.91	145.84	146.76	147.66
4.40	138.29	139.23	140.14	141.04	141.92	142.78	143.62	144.44
4.60	135.69	136.55	137.39	138.21	139.01	139.80	140.56	141.31
4.80	133.15	133.94	134.71	135.46	136.19	136.90	137.60	138.28
5.00	130.68	131.40	132.09	132.77	133.44	134.09	134.72	135.33
5.20	128.27	128.92	129.55	130.16	130.76	131.35	131.92	132.47
5.40	125.91	126.50	127.07	127.62	128.16	128.69	129.20	129.70
5.60	123.62	124.14	124.65	125.15	125.63	126.10	126.55	127.00
5.80	121.38	121.84	122.30	122.74	123.16	123.58	123.98	124.38
6.00	119.19	119.60	120.00	120.39	120.77	121.13	121.49	121.83
6.10	118.11	118.50	118.87	119.24	119.59	119.93	120.26	120.59
6.20	117.05	117.41	117.76	118.10	118.43	118.75	119.06	119.36
6.30	116.01	116.34	116.67	116.98	117.29	117.58	117.87	118.15
6.40	114.97	115.28	115.58	115.88	116.16	116.43	116.70	116.96
6.50	113.95	114.24	114.51	114.78	115.05	115.30	115.54	115.78
6.60	112.94	113.20	113.46	113.71	113.95	114.18	114.40	114.62
6.70	111.94	112.18	112.42	112.64	112.86	113.07	113.28	113.48
6.80	110.95	111.17	111.39	111.59	111.79	111.99	112.17	112.35
6.90	109.98	110.18	110.37	110.56	110.74	110.91	111.08	111.24
7.00	109.02	109.20	109.37	109.53	109.70	109.85	110.00	110.15
7.10	108.07	108.22	108.38	108.52	108.67	108.80	108.94	109.07
7.20	107.13	107.27	107.40	107.53	107.65	107.77	107.89	108.00
7.30	106.20	106.32	106.43	106.54	106.65	106.75	106.85	106.95
7.40	105.28	105.38	105.48	105.57	105.66	105.75	105.83	105.92
7.50	104.37	104.46	104.54	104.61	104.69	104.76	104.83	104.90
7.60	103.48	103.54	103.61	103.67	103.73	103.78	103.84	103.89
7.70	102.59	102.64	102.69	102.73	102.78	102.82	102.86	102.90
7.80	101.72	101.75	101.78	101.81	101.84	101.87	101.89	101.92
7.90	100.85	100.87	100.88	100.90	100.91	100.93	100.94	100.95
8.00	100.00	100.00	100.00	100.00	100.00	100.00	100.00	100.00
8.10	99.16	99.14	99.13	99.11	99.10	99.09	99.07	99.06
8.20	98.32	98.29	98.26	98.24	98.21	98.18	98.16	98.14
8.30	97.50	97.45	97.41	97.37	97.33	97.29	97.26	97.22
8.40	96.68	96.62	96.57	96.51	96.46	96.41	96.37	96.32
8.50	95.88	95.81	95.74	95.67	95.61	95.55	95.49	95.43
8.60	95.08	95.00	94.91	94.84	94.76	94.69	94.62	94.56
8.70	94.29	94.20	94.10	94.01	93.93	93.85	93.77	93.69
8.80	93.52	93.41	93.30	93.20	93.10	93.01	92.92	92.84
8.90	92.75	92.63	92.51	92.40	92.29	92.19	92.09	92.00
9.00	91.99	91.86	91.73	91.61	91.49	91.38	91.27	91.17
9.10	91.24	91.09	90.96	90.82	90.70	90.57	90.46	90.35
9.20	90.50	90.34	90.19	90.05	89.91	89.78	89.66	89.54
9.30	89.76	89.60	89.44	89.29	89.14	89.00	88.87	88.74

TABLE 3-2   (continued)

| Yield | Years and Months | | | | | | | 8% |
	14-6	15-0	15-6	16-0	16-6	17-0	17-6	18-0
9.40	89.04	88.86	88.69	88.53	88.38	88.23	88.09	87.96
9.50	88.32	88.13	87.96	87.79	87.62	87.47	87.32	87.18
9.60	87.61	87.42	87.23	87.05	86.88	86.72	86.56	86.42
9.70	86.91	86.71	86.51	86.32	86.15	85.98	85.81	85.66
9.80	86.22	86.01	85.80	85.61	85.42	85.24	85.08	84.91
9.90	85.54	85.31	85.10	84.90	84.70	84.52	84.35	84.18
10.00	84.86	84.63	84.41	84.20	84.00	83.81	83.63	83.45
10.20	83.53	83.28	83.05	82.82	82.61	82.41	82.21	82.03
10.40	82.23	81.97	81.72	81.48	81.25	81.04	80.84	80.64
10.60	80.96	80.68	80.42	80.17	79.93	79.91	79.50	79.29
10.80	79.72	79.43	79.15	78.89	78.64	78.41	78.19	77.98
11.00	78.50	78.20	77.91	77.64	77.39	77.14	76.91	76.70
11.20	77.31	77.00	76.71	76.43	76.16	75.91	75.67	75.45
11.40	76.15	75.83	75.52	75.24	74.96	74.70	74.46	74.23
11.60	75.02	74.68	74.37	74.07	73.79	73.53	73.28	73.04
11.80	73.90	73.56	73.24	72.94	72.65	72.38	72.13	71.89
12.00	72.82	72.47	72.14	71.83	71.54	71.26	71.00	70.76

Source: Reproduced from Pub. #83, *Expanded Bond Value Tables*, p. 879. Copyright © 1970 by Financial Publishing Company, Boston, Mass.

Prices and Yields

There is a very important lesson about the relationship between current yields in the securities markets and the market price of outstanding bonds: *Market yields and market prices of outstanding bonds are inversely related!*

This means that when market rates of interest (commonly referred to as **yields**) increase, the market price of outstanding bonds declines. For example, suppose that yields are 8 percent. In the bond value table shown in Table 3-2, the market price of an 8-percent coupon bond with 15-0 years to maturity is 100.00, or $1000. If yields increase to, say, 12 percent, the market price of the bond will decline to 72.47, or $724.70.

Conversely, when yields fall, the price of outstanding bonds increases. Suppose that market yields fell to 4 percent. The market price of the 8-percent coupon bond with 15-0 years to maturity would increase to 144.79, or $1447.90.

Yields and bond prices change daily, and some of the changes are quite large. Consider the wide swings in long-term bond yields that are depicted in Figure 3-1. The figure covers a time span of more than 50 years. The only period of relatively stable yields for U.S. government bonds was during the 1940s and early 1950s when the Treasury "pegged" interest rates at 2½ percent to help finance World War II. Since then, yields increased irregularly, reaching a peak in the early 1980s and then declining sharply. It follows that bond prices went in the opposite direction.

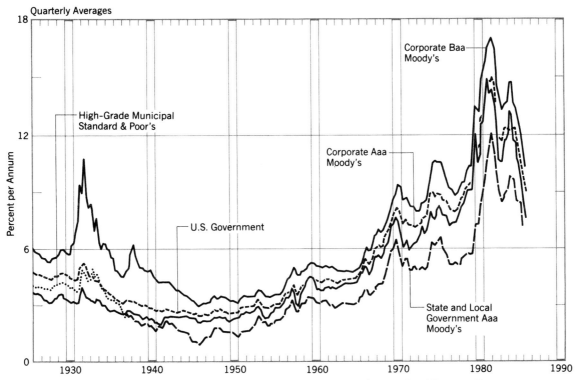

FIGURE 3-1 Long-term bond yields. *Source:* Board of Governors of the Federal Reserve System.

Bond Quotations

Changes in bond prices are reported daily in *The Wall Street Journal* and elsewhere. Figure 3-2 shows a partial listing of bonds listed on the New York Stock Exchange from *The Journal*. At the heads of the columns are the current yield, the volume expressed in $1000 units, and bond prices expressed as a percentage of par. That is, a 90 stands for $900. The listing also shows the high price for the day, the low price, and the closing price. The net change is the difference in the closing price from the previous trading session.

To illustrate how to read bond quotations, consider the last American Telephone & Telegraph (ATT) bond, ATT $8\frac{5}{8}$ 26. This bond has an $8\frac{5}{8}$ percent coupon and matures in 2026. The current yield on the bond is 9.3 percent. The next column gives the volume of bonds traded in thousands of dollars. In this case $76,000 in bonds traded. The last two columns show the closing price of the day along with the change from the previous closing price. The bond closed at $92\frac{3}{8}$, or $923.75.

Notice that the ATT bonds have different coupon rates, reflecting the fact that they were issued at different times and they paid the prevailing rate at the time of issuance.

NEW YORK EXCHANGE BONDS

Quotations as of 4 p.m. Eastern Time
Friday, February 2, 1990

Volume $42,100,000

	Domestic Fri.	Domestic Thu.	All Issues Fri.	All Issues Thu.
Issues traded	562	594	567	597
Advances	211	249	214	249
Declines	230	217	231	220
Unchanged	121	128	122	128
New highs	7	5	7	5
New lows	18	25	18	25

SALES SINCE JANUARY 1
(000 omitted)

1990	1989	1988
$1,172,568	$718,859	$782,061

Dow Jones Bond Averages

–1989– High	–1989– Low	–1990– High	–1990– Low		–1990– Close	–1990– Chg.	–1990– %Yld	–1989– Close	–1989– Chg.
94.15	87.35	93.04	90.82	20 Bonds	91.02	–0.10	9.64	89.37	–0.12
95.26	86.95	94.48	92.09	10 Utilities	92.09	–0.21	9.58	89.49	+0.06
93.26	87.60	91.60	89.56	10 Industrials	89.96	+0.02	9.70	89.25	–0.30

CORPORATION BONDS
Volume, $41,830,000

Bonds	Cur Yld	Vol	Close	Net Chg.
AL Lb 7¾14	cv	5	106	+ 1½
AbbtL 9.2s99	9.2	10	100⅜	...
Advst 9s08	cv	13	81¾	– ⅝
AlaP 7¾s02	8.8	20	88⅛	– 1⅞
AlaP 8⅞s03	9.3	10	95	– 1
AlaP 9¾s04	9.7	1	100½	– 1⅛
AlaP 10⅞05	10.6	3	103	...
AlaP 10½05	10.1	17	103⅞	...
AlaP 8¾07	9.4	6	93⅛	– 1
AlaP 12⅝10	11.9	2	106⅜	...
viAlgl 10.4s02f	...	5	19½	...
AlldC zr96	...	2	57⅞	...
AlldC zr98	...	15	47	...
AlldC zr2000	...	43	37⅜	– ⅛
AldC dc6s90	6.2	2	96 9/16	...
AlldC zr95	...	10	60¼	– ¼
AlldC zr97	...	5	49⅝	+ ¼
AlldC zr99	...	25	42½	...
AlldC zr07	...	15	20¾	– ½
AlldC zr09	...	100	16	– ⅞
Alcoa 6s92	6.5	25	92⅞	...
AMAX 14½94	12.6	95	115½	– ⅛
AmBas 14⅞98	17.7	160	84	+ ⅛
AForP 5s30	9.8	10	51¼	+ 1
ABrnd 8⅝90	8.7	51	98 31/32	...
ABrnd 9⅛16	9.9	60	91¾	– ¼
viACM 6¾91f	cv	10	29	...
AmGnFn 9⅜92	9.4	5	100	+ ¾
AmGnFn zr90s	...	52	93	+ ½
AmMed 9½01	cv	20	58	– 2
AmMed 8¼08	cv	4	51½	– ½
ATT 5½97	6.7	4	82½	+ ½
ATT 6s00	7.5	8	80⅛	+ ½
ATT 5⅛01	7.0	60	72¾	– 1⅝
ATT 8¾00	8.9	334	98	+ ⅛
ATT 7s01	8.2	30	85½	– ⅜
ATT 8.80s05	9.2	79	95⅜	– 1⅝
ATT 8⅝s07	9.1	86	94⅞	+ ½
ATT 8⅝26	9.3	76	92⅜	+ ⅜
Ames 7½14	cv	141	56	...
Amoco 6s98	7.0	35	85¼	– ⅛
AmocoCda 7⅜13	6.3	62	116½	– ½
Anhr 8s96	8.5	8	94⅛	– 3⅝
Anhr 6s92	6.4	15	94	...
ArizP 7.45s02	8.9	55	83¾	– ⅜
ArizP 10⅝00	10.5	35	100¾	+ ¾
AshO 11.1s04	10.9	3	102	– ⅛
AshO 6¾14	cv	40	95	+ ½
Atchn 4s95r	5.4	2	73¾	...
Athlne 15⅝91	15.2	20	103	+ 2½
ARich 7.7s00	8.7	2	88¾	– 2½
ARch 10⅜95	9.8	15	105⅞	+ ⅛
ARch 10⅞05	9.6	20	113⅛	+ ⅛
Avnet 8s13	cv	15	91	+ ½
Avnet 6s12	cv	20	86¼	+ ¼
BRE 9½08	cv	16	98	– ¼
Utilicp 6⅝11	cv	16	91¼	+ ¼
Vestrn 9s11	cv	10	14¾	– ½
WarC 10⅞95	10.8	197	101	– 2⅞
Coastl 8.48s91	8.6	5	98½	+ ⅜
Coastl 11⅛98	10.8	10	102¾	+ 1¾
ColuG 9s94	9.1	2	99⅛	– 1⅜
ColuG 9⅛95	9.2	4	99⅝	– ⅜
ColuG 8¼96	8.7	10	94⅝	– 1⅜
Cmdis 9.65s02	10.1	12	95¼	– ¾
CmwE 8¾05	9.5	40	92½	– ⅝
CmwE 8⅛07J	9.5	5	85⅞	+ ⅞
Compq 6½13	cv	71	129	+ 1⅜
Consec 12¾97	15.1	59	84¼	+ ¼
ConEd 9⅜00	9.4	12	100⅛	...
ConEd 7¾03	8.8	2	88	+ ⅞
ConEd 9⅛04	9.2	10	99	+ ¼
CnNG 9s95	9.0	5	100	...
CnNG 9¼95	9.2	9	100⅛	– ⅛
CnPw 8⅛01	9.4	10	86¾	– 1¾
CnPw 9s06	9.5	30	94⅜	...
CnPw 8⅝07	9.6	13	90¼	– ½
viCtlInf 9s06f	cv	20	5¾	– ⅝
CtlOil 7½99	8.3	2	90¼	– 1⅜
CtlDat 12¾91	12.5	5	102	+ 1¼
CtlDat 8½11	cv	50	86	– ¼
CoopCo 10⅝05	cv	5	67¼	...
Copwld 9.92s08	cv	31	104	+ 1
CrayRs 6⅛11	cv	6	79	– ¾
CritAc 12.3s13	12.0	1	102⅛	...
CritAc 12.35s14	12.0	20	103	...
CritAc 13.10s14	12.7	2	103⅛	...
CritAc 11¼15	11.1	1	101½	– 1
Dana 8⅞08	10.1	4	88	– 2
DataDes 8½08	cv	25	70	...
Datpnt 8⅞06	cv	7	28	...
Deere 8s02	8.4	1	94¾	– ¾
DetEd 9.15s00	9.5	2	96⅛	– 1⅞
DetEd 8.15s00	9.2	20	88½	+ ⅝
DetEd 9⅞04	9.9	74	100	...
Dow 8.92000	9.0	20	99⅜	+ ⅞
Dow 7.4s02	8.5	45	87⅛	– 2⅜
Dow 7⅞07	9.1	20	87	– ¼
duPnt dc6s01	7.7	411	77⅝	+ ⅛
duPnt 8½16	9.2	124	92¼	– ⅝
DukeP 7⅜01	8.5	20	86¾	+ ⅛
DukeP 9¾04	9.7	14	101	+ ⅜
DukeP 8⅜06	9.0	2	93¼	...
DukeP 8⅛07	9.0	8	90½	+ ⅝
DukeP 10⅛09	9.6	4	105	+ 1¼
DuqL 8¾00	9.4	5	93⅛	– 1⅛
DuqL 9s06	9.7	6	92½	– 1¾
DuqL 8⅜07	9.7	2	86½	– 2½
DuqL 10⅛09	10.1	40	100⅜	– ⅜
ECL 9s89f	...	1	94	– 1
EKod 8⅝16	9.8	288	87⅞	– ½
EnvSys 6¾11	cv	26	57	– ½
Equitc 10s04	cv	27	30	...
Exxon 6s97	7.1	125	84⅛	...
Fairfd 13¼92	21.7	6	61	...
Famly 4¾90	4.8	14	98¼	+ 1 29/32
FedN zr19s	...	200	7⅞	– ⅛
Fldcst 6s12	cv	33	65	...
TxAir 10¼09	cv	10	101	– 2
TxAir 4¾97	cv	1	32	– 2½
TxAr n 8½10	cv	2	119½	+ 1½
TxAr 6½96	cv	35	90½	+ 1
TxA ¼05	cv	5	113¼	– ¾
TxA 8⅞01	9.1	5	92⅛	+ ⅛
TCa M 8¾13	cv	16	114	+ 4
Tm ia 9½98	10.4	8	91¾	– ⅛
Tu 12¼94	11.5	80	104½	– ½
Ur Dev 12⅞95	21.3	150	60½	– 6½
Ur Dev 12⅝05	26.9	519	47	+ 2⅜
Vi Dyn 9s16	9.7	5	92⅝	+ 1⅝
W Dyn 9.95s18	10.1	10	99	– ¼
W=I 5.3s92	5.5	2	97	+ ¾
W=I 7½96	8.0	30	94¼	+ ⅞
W=I 8½04	8.9	40	95⅜	– ⅛
WHme 15½95f	...	30	12	– 1⅜
WHme 12¾98f	...	50	12½	– ½
WInst 7¼12	cv	40	109½	+ ½
WMills 8¾95	8.9	4	100¼	...
WA 8s93M	8.3	10	96⅞	– ⅛
WA 7¾94	8.1	25	95⅛	
GrowGp 12½94	13.9	5	90	...
GrowGp 8½06	cv	1	78	...
Grumn 9¼09	cv	14	80½	– ½
Hall 8.7s91	11.3	65	77	...
HalwdGp 13½09	...	3	79⅛	– ⅜
Hercul 8s10	cv	21	94	+ ½
HmeDep 6¾14	cv	52	124½	+ 2½
HomFSD 6½11	cv	24	86	...
HmGrp 14⅞99	16.6	81	89½	– ¼
HudFd 14s08	cv	1	108	...
Humn 8½09	cv	57	110	– ½
viHuntIR 9⅞04f	...	2	6¾	...
IBM Cr 8s90	8.0	180	99¾	– 1/16
ICN 12⅞98	18.2	45	70¾	+ 1¼
IllBel 8s04	8.8	5	91	– 1½
IllPw 10⅛16	10.2	1	99½	...
IllPw 9⅜16	9.9	6	94¾	+ ¾
Inco 6.85s93	7.6	5	90	– 1¾
IndBel 8⅛11	9.0	19	90¼	– 1¾
IndBel 8s14	9.1	10	88⅜	+ ⅜
ItgRs 13⅛95f	...	100	3⅛	– ⅜
ItgRs 10¾96f	...	25	3	– ½
ItgRs 10s90f	...	55	21	+ 1
ItgRs 12¼98f	...	100	2¾	– 1⅛
IBM 9⅜04	9.3	135	100⅝	– ⅛
IBM 7⅞04	cv	238	96⅛	– ⅛
IBM 10¼95	9.9	155	103⅞	– ⅛
IBM 9s98	9.0	35	100⅜	– ⅝
IPap dc5⅛12	...	15	57⅜	– 1⅝
IntRec 9s10	cv	71	59½	+ ½
Intnr 11½94	11.0	20	104½	– 2½
Jamswy 8s05	cv	115	69	...
viJoneL 6¾94f	...	10	17½	+ ½
KerrGl 13s96	13.4	45	97	– 1½
KerrMc 7¼12	cv	98	116	+ 2
KogerP 9¼03	cv	20	87½	+ ⅛
viLTV 5s88mf	...	121	13¼	– ⅛
viLTV 9¼97f	...	15	24	– 3
viLTV 11s07f	...	1	13¾	– ¼
viLTV 14s04f	...	50	25½	+ 1⅜
viLTV 11½97f	...	12	12½	+ ½
viLTV 10⅜99f	...	13	18⅜	– ⅛
viLTV 15s00f	...	55	19	...
Leget 6½06	cv	2	95	+ 1
Litton 11½95	11.1	47	103⅜	– ⅜
Litton flt00	...	1	95¼	...
Litton 12⅝05	11.7	2	108	– 1¼
LoewCp zr04	...	150	38½	+ 1¼
viLomF 7s11f	cv	10	18	...
LglsLt 12⅝92	12.4	30	102	...
LglsLt 11.7s93	11.3	10	104	– ½
LglsLt 11¼14	11.1	15	103½	...
Loral 10¾97	10.7	1	100¼	– 1
NConv 9s08	cv	10	67½	– ½
NtEdu 6½11	cv	315	38	– 1¼
NEnt 4¾96	cv	12	30	+ 5
NtGyp zr04	...	199	43⅜	– ⅝
NMed 12¾99A	12.4	40	102¾	...
NMEd 12s00	11.9	4	101⅛	– ⅛
NMed 12½00	12.3	8	102	...
NMed zr04	...	35	39¼	+ 1¼
NRUt 13½10	12.8	3	105¾	– ⅞
NRUt 14¾11	13.8	7	107¼	...
NRUt 9⅜95	9.3	5	101	+ ½
Navstr 9s04	9.9	8	91	+ 1¾
NavFin 11.95s95	11.9	70	100⅜	– ⅛
NJBTl 7¼11	8.8	24	82¾	...
NJBTl 7¾13	9.3	5	83⅛	– 1⅞
NJBTl 8¼16	9.0	3	91¼	+ 1⅞
NJBTl 8s16	9.0	9	89	+ 2
NoAPh 4s92	cv	2	87⅛	+ ⅞
NwnBl 7⅞11	9.2	5	85¾	– 1¼
NwnBl 10s14	9.7	6	102⅞	+ ¼
NwnBl 9½16	9.6	20	99	+ ⅛
Norton 7¾12	cv	79	108	...
Oakwd 6½12	cv	10	58	– ½
OccP dc9.65s94	9.9	198	97⅜	...
OcciP d8.95s94	9.4	107	95⅛	...
OcciP 10s91	10.0	120	100¼	...
OcciP 10½93	10.4	130	100⅝	– ⅜
OcciP 10⅞96	10.7	50	102	+ ⅜
OcciP 11¾11	11.5	187	102½	– ½
OcciP 10½93	10.1	2	103⅝	+ 1⅛
OcciP 11⅛19	11.1	5	100½	– ¼
OcciP 9⅝99	10.2	37	94⅜	+ ⅛
OcciP 10⅛09	10.6	30	95⅜	– ⅛
OcciP 10⅛01	10.5	9	96⅝	– ⅜
OhBIT 7½11	8.8	50	85½	+ ¾
OhEd 9½08	9.7	20	98¼	...
OhEd 15½10	13.5	24	115	+ 4⅜
OriCap 12½97	12.3	10	101¼	...
Oryx 7½14	cv	13	124	+ 4¾
OutbM 7¾96	8.6	1	90	– 2
OxyOG 6⅝99	8.5	3	78¼	– 1¾
PPG 9s95	9.0	10	100¼	+ ½
PGE 4½96JJ	5.6	1	80½	+ 1¾
PGE 4½96KK	5.8	1	77¾	+ 1⅜
PGE 8⅞s02	9.2	18	96⅞	...
PGE 7½s04	9.0	10	83	– 1¼
PGE 9⅛s06	9.5	20	96¼	– 1
PGE 9⅝s06	9.6	23	100¼	+ ⅛
PGE 9⅜11	9.6	6	97½	+ 1
PcLumb 12s96	15.7	10	76½	+ ½
PacTT 3⅝91	3.9	40	93½	...
PacTT 8¾06	9.3	5	94¼	– ⅛
PacTT 7¼08	8.7	7	83	

Bonds	Cur Yld	Vol	Close	
RJR Nb 13½01	14.3	845	94⅛	+
RJR Nb 15s01	19.9	618	75½	+
RJR Nb 13.7s07	...	9102	68⅜	+
RJR Nb zr09	...	2829	74⅝	+
RJR 7⅜01	9.9	21	74¾	+
RalsP 9½16	10.1	172	93⅝	+
RalsP 9s96	9.1	84	99	–
RalsP 9⅜16	10.1	9	93¼	–
RapA72 7s94	13.5	8	52	+
RapA 10¾03	21.7	95	49½	–
RapA 12s99	21.1	8	57	+
RayJm 7½06	cv	10	101½	–
RelGp 11s96	13.6	30	81	
RelGp 9⅞99	12.3	2	80	+
RepNY 9s01	9.3	5	97	
viRepStl 12⅛03f	...	54	16	
Revl 10⅞10	13.9	25	78½	+
Revln 11¾95	12.9	79	90⅞	+
ReyTb 7⅞94	8.9	8	88¾	
Rohr 7s12	cv	50	73½	–
Rorer 7¾13	cv	2	153	+
Rowan 13¾96	13.2	30	104	–
Ryder 13⅜94	12.4	2	108	+
Ryder 9⅜98	9.6	49	98	+
StLSaF 5s06f	...	3	60	
SallM zr14	...	15	10¼	
Salmnln 8s96	8.7	5	92¼	–
SanD 8¾07	9.3	10	94	+
SFeSP na16s03	...	176	109½	–
Savin 14s00f	...	4	74	–
Scot 8⅞2000	9.1	5	97	–
Seagrm zr06	...	16	35	
Sears 13¼92	12.0	3	110	
SvceCp 6½11	cv	20	81	
ShrLehm 10¾96	10.7	34	100¾	–
ShrLR 10¾03	10.8	22	99½	–
SoestB 6½99	cv	70	75½	
SoCG 8.85s95	8.9	20	99⅛	
SoCG 7⅝97	8.3	10	91⅞	+
SoNG 7.7s91	7.8	7	98⅝	–
viSomk 13¼94f	...	10	2½	–
viSomk 8½98f	cv	87	2	
viSomk 10⅞89fm	...	3	19	+
viSomk 11491f	...	5	19¼	+
SwEng 8½10	cv	10	104½	
StdOil 8⅜07	9.1	40	92½	+
StoneCn 13⅝95	13.3	123	102¼	+
StoneCn 11½99	12.0	61	95½	+
StrTch 13½96	...	215	99½	+
Sunsh 9s94	11.1	28	81	–
Sunsh 9½94	11.2	9	84½	+
Sunsh 9½95	...	5	84⅞	+
Sunsh 8⅞08	cv	6	85	–
TJX 7¼10	cv	6	88	
Teledy 10s04A	10.2	20	98½	+
Teledy 10s04C	10.2	183	98	+
TencoCr 9s95	9.3	5	97¼	–
TennGas dc6s11	9.4	70	63⅞	–
TennGas 10¼16	10.0	10	102⅝	–
TVA 7s97	7.8	10	89⅞	
TV 7.35s98A	8.2	10	90⅛	–
TV 7¾s98C	8.3	5	93⅛	+
TV 7¾98Cr	8.5	5	91⅛	
Tesor dc12¾01	16.6	10	77	
Texco 13⅝94	12.8	7	106½	
Texco 9s96	9.1	15	98⅝	–
Texco 5¾97	7.0	19	81⅞	+
Texco 7¾01	8.9	10	87⅜	–
Texco 8⅞05	9.5	39	93⅝	–
Texco 8½06	9.3	2	91	+
TxInd 9s08	cv	10	89½	–
Thermo 5¾12	cv	17	106	+
Thortc 6½12	cv	6	17	
Thortc 8⅝04	34.5	21	25	+
Tidwtr 7s10	cv	11	71½	+
Time 8¾17	10.4	4	83¾	–
viTodSh 14s96f	...	105	93¾	–
TolEd 7½02	9.2	25	81¼	
TolEd 9.65s06	9.8	10	98	+
Trvlr 8.32s15	cv	7	96¼	

EXPLANATORY NOTES
(For New York and American Bonds)
Yield is current yield.
cv-Convertible bond. cf-Certificates. dc-Deep discount. ec-European currency units. f-Dealt in flat. il-Italian lire. kd-Danish kroner. m-Matured bonds, negotiability impaired by maturity. na-No accrual. r-Registered. rp-Reduced principal. st-Stamped. t-Floating rate. wd-When distributed. ww-With warrants. x-Ex interest. xw-Without warrants. zr-Zero coupon.
vi-In bankruptcy or receivership or being reorganized under the Bankruptcy Act, or securities assumed by such companies.

FIGURE 3-2 Corporate bond quotations. *Source: The Wall Street Journal,* February 5, 1990, C-16, reprinted by permission, © 1990, Dow Jones & Co., Inc., all rights reserved.

A careful examination of the listing reveals that some bonds have a "zr" instead of a coupon rate. AlldC (Allied Chemical) is one example. These are zero-coupon bonds. Other bonds have "cv" in the current yield column. These are convertible bonds. Furthermore, some bonds are selling at low prices **(deep discounts)** and some have high current yields. One reason why bonds sell at deep discounts is because they were issued when yields were lower than they are at the present time. As market rates increased, the prices of the low-yielding bonds

declined. However, as they approach maturity, their prices will converge on their par values.

Other deep-discount bonds may be zero-coupon bonds, bonds that are issued at a discount and pay no current interest. More will be said about them shortly.

Some bonds also sell above their par values, or at a **premium.** Some of these bonds were issued when yields were higher than they are at the present time, and their prices increased when yields fell. Others are convertible bonds and are trading on their stock values. We will cover convertibles later in this chapter and again in Chapter 20.

Types of Security

Corporate bonds can be classified on the basis of the security behind the bonds. **Security** refers to collateral or liens against certain assets of the borrower. However, many bonds are unsecured.

Mortgage Bonds

Bonds that are secured by liens on real estate are known as mortgage bonds. Those secured by a first mortgage on real estate are called **first mortgage bonds.** Similarly, second mortgage bonds are secured by a second mortgage. Because most lenders dislike the idea of holding third, fourth, or fifth mortgages, bonds backed by such collateral are called **general mortgage bonds** or consolidated mortgage bonds. **Closed-end mortgage bonds** have a provision prohibiting other bond issues from using the same property as collateral. Bonds without that restriction are called **open-end mortgage bonds.**

Collateral Trust Bonds

Collateral trust bonds are secured by stocks and bonds owned by the issuing corporation. The collateral is deposited with a trustee, such as a bank, for the benefit of the bondholders. Frequently, corporations use their own bonds as collateral. When collateral trust bonds are secured by mortgage bonds, they have the same priority, or lien, as the mortgage bonds. In such cases, the collateral behind the bonds is usually worth considerably more than the par value of the bonds.

Equipment Obligations

Equipment obligations are a method of financing employed mainly by railroads for acquiring rolling stock, such as railroad cars and locomotives. The obligation is secured by rolling stock and the general credit of the issuing corporation. However, the general credit has little to do with the investment position of such obligations, which is stronger than other types of corporate securities.

The most widely used form of equipment obligations is a lease arrangement called the **Philadelphia plan.** Under this plan, the borrower makes a down payment or advance rental of about 25 percent of the cost of the equipment. Then

the lease payments are made to a trustee for the benefit of certificate holders. Certificates that have been sold to investors in order to pay a manufacturer for equipment are known as **equipment trust certificates.** This type of lease generally runs about 15 years. However, the earnings generated by the rolling stock are usually sufficient to pay off the obligation at a faster rate than the depreciation of the equipment. In addition, the certificates are frequently paid off in serial form, which means they mature at different dates. More will be said about serial bonds later.

Debentures

These bonds are backed by the general credit of the issuing corporation without a specific lien against any particular asset. For the most part, **debentures** are used by industrial companies and public utilities that have high credit ratings. They are the weakest form of bond, but a debenture from a strong corporation may be a better investment than a first mortgage bond from a weak corporation. Care should be taken when comparing the quality of a bond with the security behind it.

Quality Ratings

The fact that the creditworthiness of various companies is different and that their bonds can be backed by security that ranges from first mortgages to their goodwill affects the quality of the bonds they sell. Determining that quality would be a difficult task for most investors. Fortunately, Standard & Poor's and Moody's Investor Service provide **quality rating** services and assign letter ratings to indicate the quality (creditworthiness) of bonds.

As a general matter, bond ratings are based on the following considerations. The first is the financial ability and willingness of the company to meet its financial obligations in accordance with the terms of the bond. The second consideration concerns the nature of the bond itself — what type of bond is it, what type of security is behind it, and so on. Finally, the protection afforded the bondholder in the event the company goes bankrupt is taken into account.

Although bond ratings are assigned at a time a bond is issued, they can change from time to time if conditions within the firm change substantially.

Some corporate bonds are not assigned bond ratings; however, the absence of ratings may or may not reflect the quality of the bond. For example, Standard & Poor's does not publish bond ratings on bond issues that are privately placed with an institutional investor such as an insurance company. In addition, some bond issues are so small (i.e., less than $600,000) and the cost of obtaining a rating so great (in excess of $2500) that it may not be practical to give a rating. Therefore, some high-quality bonds issued by small corporations are not rated. In any case, quality ratings are meant to be investment guides, not absolutes.

The following listing of Moody's and Standard & Poor's quality ratings shows that they range from investment-grade securities to those that are in default. **Investment-grade securities** are eligible for bank investments and meet the minimum standards as legal investments for trust companies, insurance companies, and other fiduciaries in various states. **Junk bonds** are those with below-

investment-grade quality ratings and are speculative in nature. Many junk bonds have been issued in connection with corporate restructuring and takeovers in recent years. Some have defaulted.

Moody's/Standard & Poor's

Investment Grade

Aaa/AAA	This is the highest rating that is given a bond. Bonds with such ratings are referred to as *gilt-edge;* they carry the smallest degree of investment risk, and both principal and interest are protected by substantial margins.
Aa/AA	These are high-grade obligations, and they differ very little from the highest quality bonds. Nevertheless, as risk increases, investors expect a higher return. For example, the yields on seasoned corporate bonds (October 17, 1988) were

Aaa	8.85%
Aa	9.14
A	9.41
Baa	9.75

A/A	Bonds with this rating are regarded as upper-medium-grade bonds. The issuers are financially strong, but they are more susceptible to adverse changes in economic activity than issuers of bonds with higher ratings.
Baa/BBB	These are medium-grade bonds. Under normal circumstances, there is adequate financial coverage, but under adverse economic conditions, there may be a weakened capacity to meet financial obligations. This is the lowest quality investment-grade bond rating.

Junk Bonds

Ba/BB	These bonds have more default risk than those described above, especially under adverse business, financial, and economic conditions. This is the least risky of the speculative-grade bonds. Bonds subordinated to senior debt with a BBB rating are assigned a BB rating.
B/B	These bonds have greater vulnerability to default, but currently have the capacity to meet interest and principal obligations. This rating is also used for subordinated debt to senior obligations with a BB rating.
Caa/CCC	These bonds have an identifiable vulnerability to default, and are dependent on favorable business, financial, and economic conditions to meet their financial obligations. This rating is also used for debt subordinated to senior obligations with a B rating.
Ca/CC	This rating usually applies to debt subordinated to senior obligations with a CCC rating.
C/C	This rating is used when the debt is subordinated to senior debt with a CC rating. It also applies to situations where a bankruptcy petition has been filed, but the debt service payments continue.
D/D	This rating is used when debt service payments are in default. It is also used if a bankruptcy petition has been filed and the debt service payments are in jeopardy.

Plus (+) or minus (−) are used with the above ratings to show relative standing within major rating categories.

BOX 3-1

THE PROBLEM WITH QUALITY RATINGS

One problem with quality ratings is that by the time investors use them, the ratings may be out of date. A related problem is that the quality ratings themselves may not reflect current developments. Consider the case of Continental Illinois Bank & Trust Company, a major U.S. bank with financial problems that were widely recognized by the investment community. One security analyst from Stifel, Nicholaus & Company recommended in February 1984 that conservative investors should sell Continental's stock. Not everyone agreed with that opinion. Over the next few months, however, Continental's financial plight became worse, and by May it was so bad that federal agencies had to support the failing institution. Meanwhile, both Moody's and Standard & Poor's were slow to react to current developments and continued to rate Continental's bonds as A quality—having favorable investment attributes.

How useful are quality ratings if they do not reflect current developments?

Source: Based on Richard Gibson and Wendy L. Wall, "Bank Analysts Try to Balance Their Ratings," *The Wall Street Journal,* May 29, 1984, p. 33.

Bond Retirement Features

Bonds can be retired by five principal methods: (1) being paid off in a lump sum at maturity, (2) being converted, (3) being called, (4) being retired serially, or (5) being retired because of sinking fund commitments. Conversion is one method in which the bondholder, rather than the issuing corporation, decides to retire the bonds. Funds used to pay off bonds at maturity are frequently obtained by selling new bonds to replace the old ones. The new bonds are commonly called **refunding bonds.**

Convertible Bonds

Conversion provisions offer an opportunity for bondholders to share in the growth of the corporation by converting their bonds into common stock at a specified price. For example, a $1000 par value bond may be convertible into common stock at $50 per share. Thus, at $50 per share the bond's worth is equivalent to 20 shares of stock ($1000 ÷ $50 = 20). If the market value of the stock appreciates above $50 per share, the market value of the bond is increased. By way of illustration, assume that the market value of the stock is $60 per share. In this case, the bond is worth $1200 ($60 × 20 = $1200). However, if the market value of the stock falls below $50 per share, the market value of the bond will not

decline below its true value as a bond. Thus, investors can benefit from increases in the value of the company's stock and also have some protection from declines in the value because they hold a bond that is a fixed obligation of the company. **Convertible bonds** are discussed in greater detail in Chapter 20.

Callable Bonds

Corporations frequently reserve the right to call in their bond issues in whole or in part. Corporations have used the call privilege for the following reasons:

1. To avoid high interest rates over long periods of time through calling the issues. However, in the short run, **callable bonds** usually have higher interest rates than noncallable bonds.
2. To eliminate issues with unfavorable provisions in the indenture.
3. To refund and refinance—refunding of high-interest coupon bonds with low-interest coupon bonds when interest rates decline.
4. To force convertible bondholders to convert when it is in the company's interest to do so.
5. To contribute to sinking funds.

Many bonds have a **call-protection clause** that prohibits the company from calling the bond for 5 years, 10 years, or longer. Such clauses typically require the company to pay a premium above the par value of the bond if it is called. The size of the premium depends on when the bond is called. For example, if the bond is called in the sixth year, the premium might be 1.75 percent of the principal amount. Bonds called in later years will have progressively smaller premiums. Some investors calculate the approximate **yield to call** for callable bonds selling above par value. This may be computed by the following equation, which is similar to Equation 3-2, yield to maturity:

$$\text{Yield to call} = \frac{C + [F_c - P_0]/n}{(F_c + P_0)/2} \tag{3-4}$$

where

C = annual income ($) from bond
F_c = dollar amount payable to bondholder when bond is called
P_0 = current market price of bond
n = number of years to the first call date

By the way of illustration, the approximate yield to call for an 8 percent bond, selling at $950 and callable in three years at $1120, is

$$\text{Yield to call} = \frac{\$80 + (\$1120 - \$950)/3}{(\$1120 + \$950)/2} = 13.2\%$$

Note that the yield to call is higher than the yield to maturity on this 15-year bond (the YTM is 8.55 percent) because a call premium ($120) is being paid to bondholders, and the first call date is in three years instead of 15 years.

Serial Bonds

In a **serial bond** issue, the bonds mature at different dates instead of at the same time. Thus, purchasers are offered a variety of maturities to meet their needs. Serial bonds are more common in real estate and equipment financing than in industrial financing because the rental income from real estate is considered more stable than earnings from industrial concerns.

Serial maturities are also advantageous when the collateral depreciates from use. In the case of equipment trust certificates, the bonds are retired at a faster rate than the equipment depreciates.

Sinking Funds

A **sinking fund** provides for periodic retirement of a certain portion of a bond issue through payments made by the corporation. Ordinarily, the payment is made to the trustee of the issue, who either purchases the bonds in the market or calls them. As long as the bonds may be bought in the open market at or below the call price, the company will do so. However, should the market price be above the call price, it is obviously advantageous to retire them by call. In this case, the serial numbers of the bonds that are to be called are drawn by lot.

Under some circumstances, a sinking fund is necessary for the protection of a bond — for example, when the collateral consists of a wasting asset such as a coal mine. Bonds backed by mining properties frequently have a sinking fund based on the tonnage mined.

Special Types of Bonds

Income (or Adjustment) Bonds

Several types of hybrid bonds have been developed mainly from railroad reorganizations. The hybrid securities were exchanged for other types of claims held by investors. When such reorganizations take place, bondholders are asked to take hybrid bonds in order to give the railroad a chance to improve its earnings. **Income** (or **adjustment**) **bonds** are an example of a hybrid security. These bonds promise to pay interest only if it is earned by the corporation. That is, the payment of interest is secured through a charge on the corporation's income, but it is not secured by any assets. One advantage from the corporation's point of view is that if there are no earnings, the company is not harassed to pay interest. From the investor's point of view, the promise of some income is better than receiving no income at all.

The net income, from which interest on the income bonds is paid, is determined before the payment of dividends on common stock and after depreciation has been deducted. The interest on some income bonds is payable before preferred stock dividends and, on others, after such dividends. In addition, it is common practice to make the interest cumulative, especially after a few years. In corporations that are financially weak but have hopes of better times, the interest may be deferred from one to three years, but rarely longer.

Guaranteed Bonds

Guaranteed bonds arise from mergers, consolidations, and financing subsidiaries. Basically, one corporation guarantees the obligations of another corporation. The guarantee applies to the interest, the principal, or both. What the bond guarantees to pay is usually stated on the face or back side of the bond, in which case the bond is referred to as *stamped* or *endorsed.* Bonds that are guaranteed by two or more corporations are called *joint bonds.* The value of the guarantees is as strong as the combined strengths of the corporations involved when proper consideration is given to their intentions to pay off the obligation.

Guaranteed bonds are not the same as **assumed bonds,** which are the obligations issued by one company that has been taken over or "assumed" by another company.

Participating Bonds

A **participating bond** not only bears a fixed rate of interest, like an ordinary bond, but also has a profit-sharing feature. In other words, the bondholder is entitled to participate along with the stockholders in the earnings of the corporation to the extent described in the contract. Bonds of this type are not very common in the United States, but are used more frequently in Europe. They are usually issued by financially weak corporations that need an inducement to attract investors.

Bonds with Warrants

Some bonds are issued with **warrants** that give the holder the right to purchase common stock, or some other form of security, at a specified price. Usually, the price stated on the warrant is higher than the market price on the stock at the time the bond is sold. Most warrants are nondetachable, which means that they may be separated from the bonds only when the bondholder exercises the right of purchase.

Zero-Coupon Bonds

Zero-coupon bonds are bonds that are issued at a deep discount, and the interest is entirely in the appreciation of the bond as it matures. That is, the bondholder receives only the face value of the bond when it matures; there are *no* periodic interest payments. For example, GMAC sold a 10-year bond that will yield 14.25 percent to maturity. The bonds were issued at $252.50. Such bonds help hold GMAC's interest payments down, for a while. These bonds may not be suitable for individual investors because the "gain" is taxed as ordinary income.

The price of zero-coupon bonds is determined by discounting the present value of the face amount of the bond ($1000) by the investor's required rate of return. Because there are no intervening interest payments, only one calculation is necessary to determine the price. In the previous example, the present value interest factor for 14.25 percent for 10 years is 0.2639. Thus, the price of the bond is $1000 × 0.2639 = $263.90. The slight difference between this price and the

one shown above ($252.50) may be due to the fact that the maturity is not exactly 10 years in the future.

Zero-coupon bonds are considered by the Internal Revenue Service as **original issue discount** (OID) securities when they are issued at a price less than the face amount. The OID is the difference between the initial offering price and the face amount. The OID is considered a form of taxable interest, and as it accrues over time, the bondholders must report it as such even though they received no payments from the issuer. Keep this in mind when you are dealing in OIDs!

Indexed Bonds

During the late 1970s and early 1980s, when there were high levels of inflation, some companies and state and local governments issued bonds whose interest payments or principal amounts were indexed so that the bondholder's returns can vary. Most of the bonds issued then were redeemed, but a few are still outstanding. For example, Sunshine Mines issued bonds that are indexed to silver. Each $1000 of face value of Sunshine Mines 8.50 percent, 1995 is worth $1000 at maturity or the market price of 50 ounces of silver, whichever is greater.

STATE AND LOCAL GOVERNMENT BONDS

Thousands of state and local governing bodies in the United States have sold bonds. These bodies include states, cities, counties, park districts, sewer districts, and other special districts and authorities. They sell bonds to help finance roads, sewers, parks, and other capital improvement projects. Such bonds are commonly called **municipal bonds.** Although they have some of the same features as corporate bonds, municipal bonds differ in several respects.

Tax Exemption

The most important difference between municipal bonds and other securities is that the interest earned on certain municipal bonds is exempt from federal income taxes, and in some cases from state income taxes. The federal exemption became law with the enactment of the Federal Income Tax Amendment of 1913. The theory behind the law is that exemption permits state and local governments to finance capital improvement projects at reduced borrowing costs. Thus, the interest rate paid on **tax-exempt** bonds is lower than the interest rate paid on taxable issues of the same quality. For example, in October 1989, the average interest rate on Aaa municipal bonds (Moody's) was 6.90 percent, and the average interest rate on Aaa-rated corporate bonds was 8.85 percent.

The alternatives to borrowing in order to finance capital expenditures are to increase taxes, charge the users of the projects and services, or use some combination of the two. Few taxpayers want to pay higher taxes, and those in high tax brackets are seeking ways to reduce their tax burdens. Thus, municipal bonds benefit both the users of the capital improvements and investors.

TABLE 3-3 Taxable and Tax-Equivalent Yields[a]

	Taxable Income, Single Individual with No Dependents		
Tax-Exempt Yield	Not over $18,850 (15%)	$18,850 to $44,950 (28%)	$44,950 to $93,130 (33%)
5%	5.88%	6.94%	7.46%
8	9.41	11.11	11.94
11	12.94	15.28	16.42
14	16.47	19.44	20.90

[a] Based on 1989 tax tables.

An investor's federal income tax bracket determines the extent to which tax-exempt interest income is beneficial. Table 3-3 gives the approximate yield that taxable securities must earn in various income tax brackets to produce after-tax yields equal to those on tax-exempt bonds. For example, for investors in the $44,950 and over tax bracket, an 8-percent tax-exempt yield is equivalent to an 11.94-percent taxable yield. Investors in high-income tax brackets benefit more than those in lower brackets. The **tax-equivalent yield** for any tax bracket may be determined by the following equation:

$$\text{Tax-equivalent yield} = \frac{\text{tax-exempt yield}}{1 - \text{tax bracket \%}} = \frac{0.08}{1 - 0.33} = 11.94\% \quad (3\text{-}5)$$

State taxes vary from zero in Alaska to as high as 25 percent of the federal tax liability in Vermont. Some states, such as New York and California, do not tax income from municipal bonds issued within those states, but they do tax income from bonds issued in other states. This provides an additional tax incentive to invest in local bonds where that exemption exists.

Industrial Development Bonds or Private Activity Bonds

Some state and local governments issued **industrial revenue bonds (IDBs) or private activity bonds** to fund capital improvements that were used primarily by business concerns. Typically, such bonds originate when a community wants to attract business concerns by leasing buildings to them at low cost. The business, in turn, pays off the bonds from their revenues. Firestone Tire & Rubber Company, Delta Airlines, and International Paper Company are among the leading firms that lease or guarantee IDBs. Because such bonds are backed by business concerns, and their ability to pay the interest on the debt, they are riskier than bonds backed by state and local government. Consequently, IDBs have a higher interest rate than direct obligations of the municipalities.

Private activity bonds were a way for corporations to acquire the use of assets

at lower cost than they could do on their own. In essence, they were tax-exempt corporate bonds.

This changed with the Tax Reform Act of 1986, which removed the tax exemption on certain private activity bonds. The logic is that tax exemption applies only if the proceeds from the bond issue are used exclusively for traditional governmental purposes. Now interest earned on private activity bonds is not tax-exempt from federal income tax unless 95 percent or more of the net proceeds of the bond issue are related to governmental use.

An alternative test is that an issue is a private activity bond if (1) more than 10 percent of the proceeds are used for private business purposes, or (2) if more than 10 percent of the debt service comes from the use of privately used property. This discussion of tests to determine whether an issue is a private activity bond is not complete. Check with your broker, accountant, or tax attorney if you are in doubt about the tax exemption of particular bonds.

General Obligation Bonds

Most municipal bonds are backed by the full faith, credit, and taxing power of the issuer. Such bonds are called **general obligation bonds (GOs)**. Because they are backed by taxing power, and not by the pledge of specific assets, investors should take into consideration the size of the resources being taxed and the dollar amount of the bonds currently being supported by these resources. Taxes are usually based on the assessed value of real estate. In addition, some municipalities have income taxes and sales tax receipts as a source of revenue. Information of this type is available from *Moody's Municipal & Government Manual,* and from annual census data.

Revenue Bonds

The term **revenue bond** applies to municipal bonds that are payable from some specified source of revenue other than the general taxing power of the issuer. The term does not include special assessment bonds that are payable solely from assessed benefits, nor does it include warrants or other debt securities that are issued in anticipation of collecting certain taxes.

The bondholders have a claim against the revenue of specific projects, such as hospitals, wharves, mass commuting facilities, sewage facilities, and other exempt facilities. Because there is a claim against the revenues, the indenture of the bond may prohibit the issuance of additional revenue bonds against those same revenues.

U.S. GOVERNMENT AND FEDERAL AGENCY SECURITIES

The federal government, like state and local governments, must borrow funds to conduct its operations. The difference between receipts and outlays is financed by the U.S. Treasury and by government agencies. The Treasury raises money

through the sale of marketable and nonmarketable debt securities. The marketable securities include **Treasury bills,** notes, and bonds; nonmarketable securities are mainly savings bonds and other special issues.

Marketable Treasury Securities

Treasury Bills

These securities provide investors with a safe return for a short period of time. Although Treasury bills may have a maturity of one year, they are generally issued with a maturity of 13 to 26 weeks. Bills have denominations of $10,000 or more, which precludes many small investors from buying them. Nevertheless, there is still a lot of investor interest in bills.

Treasury bills differ from other types of Treasury securities because they are sold at a **discount.** This means that investors pay less than the full face value for the security when they buy it, and they receive the face value when it matures. To illustrate how this process works, and the returns on buying and selling Treasury bills, we will use the following symbols:

$$A = \text{days to maturity or number of days held}$$
$$B = \text{discount basis (in percent)}$$
$$C = \text{full discount per \$100 maturity value}$$
$$P = \text{dollar price when purchased}$$
$$S = \text{dollar price when sold}$$
$$Y = \text{annualized bond equivalent return}$$

The computation of the discount is based on the actual number of days, usually 360 days per year. The equation for the discount is

$$C = \frac{A}{360} \times B \tag{3-6}$$

$$P = \$100 - C$$

By way of illustration, find the discount price for a Treasury bill due in 90 days on a 12-percent basis.

$$C = \frac{A}{360} \times B$$

$$= \frac{90}{360} \times 12\%$$

$$= 3\%, 3\% \text{ of } \$100 = \$3$$

$$P = \$100 - C$$

$$= \$100 - \$3$$

$$= \$97 \text{ (the dollar price for the 12\% discount basis)}$$

Treasury bills are traded on a 360-day year, while most bonds are traded on a 365-day year. The following equation is used to put Treasury bills on a **bond-equivalent basis** (365-day year):

$$Y = \frac{C}{P} \times \frac{365}{A} \times 100 \tag{3-7}$$

If we use the same data as in the previous example, the bond equivalent yield is 12.54 percent. This conversion permits us to compare the returns on bills to those on bonds:

$$Y = \frac{\$3}{\$97} \times \frac{365}{90} \times 100$$

$$= 12.54\%$$

Finally, some investors **ride the yield curve.** As discount bills mature, their price increases until it reaches face value at maturity. Investors need not hold the bills for their entire life. For example, suppose that the 90-day bill was held for only 30 days and then sold at an 11.50-percent basis. The return for holding the bill for 30 days was 13.55 percent and was determined by the following equation:

$$Y = \frac{S - P}{P} \times \frac{365}{D} \times 100 \tag{3-8}$$

The equation for computing S, the selling price, is Equation 3-9, the same one used to determine P, the purchase price. In this problem, D, the number of days held is 30:

$$A = 90 - 30 = 60$$

$$B = 11.50\%$$

$$C = \frac{60}{360} \times 11.50\% = 0.01916 = \$1.92$$

$$S = \$100 - C = \$100 - \$1.92 = \$98.08 \tag{3-9}$$

Using this information and Equation 3-6, the solution is

$$Y = \frac{\$98.08 - \$97.00}{\$97.00} \times \frac{365}{30} \times 100 = 13.55\%$$

The previous examples are important for two reasons. First, they illustrate how the bond-equivalent yield can differ from the yield on a discount basis. In other words, the yield on Treasury bills is slightly higher than stated when compared to bonds. Second, it was shown that the return can be changed by riding the yield curve. It is not necessary, or even desirable, to hold securities until they mature if you can get a better price by selling them.

Coupon Issues

Treasury bonds, notes, and certificates are issued to the public on a coupon basis. The major difference between the different types of issues is their maturity. Treasury bonds may be issued with any maturity, but most have an original maturity in excess of 10 years. Notes have an original maturity of one to ten years. Certificates have a maturity of one year or less; however, there are no certificates outstanding at this time.

Some brokers and the Treasury strip the coupon interest payments from the principal amount that is due at maturity and sell each separately. This is called **coupon stripping.** Once separated, each coupon and the principal amount are essentially **zero-coupon bonds.** For example, a $1 million face (par) amount 10-percent bond due 15 years from now can be stripped into 30 semiannual zero-coupon bonds, each with a face amount of $50,000, and one 15-year zero-coupon with a face amount of $1 million. The price of each coupon, which is equivalent to a zero-coupon bond, is determined by discounting the present value of the dollar amount of the coupon ($50,000) by the investor's required rate of return. If the required rate of return for a coupon maturing in five years is 10 percent, the price of that coupon is

Coupon	$50,000
Present value @10% for 5 years	$\times 0.621$
Price	$= \$31,050$

Treasury coupon strip issues are called STRIPS (Separate Trading of Registered Interest and Principal of Securities) while brokers have other names including TIGRs (Treasury Investment Growth Receipts, Merrill Lynch), and CATs (Certificate of Accrual on Treasury Securities, Salomon Brothers) to name a few.

Government-Guaranteed Securities

The Government National Mortgage Association (GNMA) and the Federal Home Loan Mortgage Corporation (called the Mortgage Corporation) guarantee in varying degrees mortgage certificates that consist of a large number of mortgages bundled together. The interest and principal payments for **government-guaranteed securities** are collected by a mortgage broker or a bank and are then passed through to the investors. Generally, these **pass-through mortgage certificates** are held by institutional investors because of their large denominations of several million dollars or more. However, some stockbrokerage firms and banks break down the certificates so that small investors can participate too.

Nonmarketable Securities

The Treasury also sells nonmarketable securities, which include U.S. savings bonds (Series EE and HH), certificates, notes (foreign series), and other types of special-purpose securities. Some of the special-purpose securities are used in connection with transactions with foreign governments. Series EE and HH bonds have special tax features that are explained in Chapter 16.

Government-Sponsored Agencies and Federal Agencies

Government agencies or agencies sponsored by the federal government issue securities to obtain a portion of the funds necessary for their operations and to provide credit or stability to some essential sectors of the economy, such as housing and agriculture. These securities are not direct obligations of the Treasury but are backed or guaranteed in one way or another by the federal government. These agencies issue a variety of bonds, notes, and debentures. They usually carry higher interest rates than Treasury securities because investors consider them to

TABLE 3-4   Issuers of Government-Related Securities

Agency	Function
Ordinary Debt Issues	
Farm Credit System	A nationwide system of banks and associations that provides some of the credit needs of farmers, ranchers, and other agricultural businesses.
Federal Home Loan Bank Board	Federal Home Loan banks provide credit for non-bank mortgage lending institutions such as savings and loan associations.
Federal National Mortgage Association (FNMA)	The primary function of FNMA is to buy and sell mortgages to lessen cyclical disruptions in the housing market.
Inter-American Development Bank	An international lending organization whose aim is to further economic and social development of member countries.
Maritime Administration	Sells debt obligations to finance ships and fisheries.
Student Loan Marketing Association	Sells debt obligations to further student loans.
World Bank	The International Bank for Reconstruction and Development is known as the World Bank. It promotes the economic development of member countries.
Mortgage-Backed Issues	
Federal Home Loan Mortgage Corporation	Sells mortgage-backed securities to raise funds for savings and loan associations and other qualified financial institutions.
Government National Mortgage Association (GNMA)	GNMA buys and sells government-backed (e.g., FHA/VA) mortgages.
Tax-Exempt Instruments	
Department of Housing and Urban Development Project Notes	Sells notes that are obligations of public housing agencies.
Federal Financing Bank	The Federal Financing Bank is part of the Treasury and sells securities for various government agencies that are not listed in this table.

be more risky. Moreover, the agencies are not limited on the interest rates they can pay on bonds. Brief descriptions of selected agencies' functions are given in Table 3-4.

Government Securities Quotations

Quotations of governmental securities differ from quotations of corporate bonds. One difference between the quotations for corporate bonds and federal obligations is that corporate bonds are traded in fractions of $\frac{1}{8}$ of a point (0.1250 per $100), while federal securities other than Treasury bills are normally traded in fractions of $\frac{1}{32}$ (0.03125 per $100). Therefore, a price of, say, 99.19 means $99\frac{19}{32}$.

Sometimes transactions are made in fractions of $\frac{1}{64}$, (0.015625 per $100), in which case a quote of 99.5 + means $99\frac{11}{64}$.

$$\frac{5}{32} = \frac{10}{64} + \frac{1}{64} = \frac{11}{64}$$

In contrast, a quote of 99.5 − means $99\frac{9}{64}$.

$$\frac{5}{32} = \frac{10}{64} - \frac{1}{64} = \frac{9}{64}$$

A price of $99\frac{9}{64}$ translates into $991.40625.

Figure 3-3 shows a listing of Treasury bonds, notes, and bills. The first bid price shown is 98.21, or 98 and $\frac{21}{32}$ ($986.5625), for every $1000 of par value. The first asked price is 99.07, which is $992.1875. This means that dealers are willing to buy these securities at 98.21 and sell them at 99.07 percent of par value. Treasury bills have a minimum denomination of $5000. However, the minimum order size from the Treasury for Treasury bills is $10,000. Two-year Treasury notes have a minimum denomination of $5000; and longer term notes and bonds have a minimum denomination of $1000.

The yield shown for government securities is the yield to maturity, which is the average yield over the life of the security. The current yield is used for corporate bond quotations.

Figure 3-3 also shows prices for stripped Treasuries and Treasury bills. Recall that stripped Treasuries are like zero-coupon bonds where the investor receives only the dollar amount of the coupon or the principal at some time in the future.

Notice that for Treasury bills, the bid and asked price are listed in terms of yields. This is because Treasury bills are sold at a discount. As you know, this means that the Treasury sells these securities to investors for less than the face value and redeems them at face value. The difference between the two values is the yield. In the case of Treasury bills, the bid and asked price is the percentage discount from face value. For example, bills maturing February 8 have a bid price of 7.31. Therefore, a seller of a $10,000 Treasury bill would receive $9269.00 (100% − 7.31% = 92.69% × $10,000 = $9,269).

This method of calculating the bid and asked price for Treasury bills results in the bid being higher than the ask, which may confuse some readers. Just

TREASURY BONDS, NOTES & BILLS

Monday, February 5, 1990

Representative Over-the-Counter quotations based on transactions of $1 million or more as of 4 p.m. Eastern time.

Decimals in bid-and-asked and bid changes represent 32nds; 101.01 means 101 1/32. Treasury bill quotes in hundredths. a-Plus 1/64. b-Yield to call date. d-Minus 1/64. k-Nonresident aliens exempt from withholding taxes. n-Treasury notes. p-Treasury note; nonresident aliens exempt from withholding taxes.

Stripped Treasuries -- a-Stripped interest. b-Treasury bond; stripped principal. c-Treasury note; stripped principal.

Source: Bloomberg Financial Markets

GOVT. BONDS & NOTES

Rate	Maturity	Bid	Asked	Bid Chg.	Yld.
3.50	Feb 90	98.21	99.07	...	....
6.50	Feb 90p	99.29	100.00	...	6.31
7.12	Feb 90p	99.29	100.00	...	6.91
11.00	Feb 90p	100.01	100.04	...	5.59
7.25	Mar 90p	99.25	99.28	...	7.92
7.37	Mar 90p	99.25	99.28	...	8.03
10.50	Apr 90n	100.11	100.14	− .01	7.87
7.62	Apr 90p	99.27	99.30	...	7.74
7.87	May 90p	99.28	99.31	...	7.85
8.25	May 90	99.30	100.04	− .01	7.63
8.12	May 90p	99.30	100.01	...	7.90
11.37	May 90p	100.25	100.28	− .01	7.87
7.25	Jun 90p	99.18	99.22	...	8.00
8.00	Jun 90p	99.27	99.31	...	8.02
10.75	Jul 90n	101.01	101.05	...	7.97
8.37	Jul 90p	100.00	100.04	− .01	8.10
7.87	Aug 90p	99.25	99.29	...	8.05
9.87	Aug 90p	100.26	100,30	+ .01	8.01
10.75	Aug 90n	101.08	101.12	...	8.01
8.62	Aug 90p	100.05	100.09	...	8.08
6.75	Sep 90p	99.01	99.05	+ .01	8.10
8.50	Sep 90p	100.03	100.07	...	8.12
11.50	Oct 90n	102.02	102.06	− .01	8.12
8.25	Oct 90p	99.30	100.02	...	8.13
8.00	Nov 90p	99.24	99.28	...	8.14
9.62	Nov 90n	100.30	101.02	...	8.14
13.00	Nov 90n	103.14	103.18	− .01	8.10
8.87	Nov 90p	100.13	100.17	− .01	[illegible]
6.62	Dec 90p	98.18	[illegible]	[illegible]	[illegible]
9.12	Dec 90p	[illegible]	[illegible]	[illegible]	[illegible]
11.75	Jan 91n	[illegible]	[illegible]	[illegible]	8.38
9.00	Jan [illegible]	[illegible]	[illegible]	...	8.40
[illegible]	[illegible]	[illegible]	98.25	...	8.42
[illegible]	[illegible]	100.21	100.25	− .01	8.41
[illegible]	[illegible] 92p	103.00	103.04	...	8.42
[illegible]	Nov 92p	98.10	98.13	− .01	8.40
8.37	Nov 92p	99.25	99.30	...	8.39
10.50	Nov 92n	104.29	105.01	− .01	8.42
9.12	Dec 92p	101.21	101.25	...	8.41
8.75	Jan 93p	100.23	100.27	− .01	8.42
4.00	Feb 88-93	91.00	92.02	...	6.95
6.75	Feb 93	95.17	95.29	+ .02	8.31
7.87	Feb 93	98.25	98.29	...	8.29
8.25	Feb 93p	99.16	99.20	...	8.39
10.87	Feb 93n	106.09	106.13	− .01	8.43
9.62	Mar 93p	103.02	103.06	− .01	8.44
7.37	Apr 93p	96.31	97.03	...	8.43
7.62	May 93p	97.18	97.22	− .02	8.44
10.12	May 93n	104.18	104.22	− .01	8.45
8.12	Jun 93p	99.00	99.04	...	8.42
7.25	Jul 93p	96.13	96.17	− .01	8.43
7.50	Aug 88-93	96.29	97.07	− .01	8.43
8.62	Aug 93	100.12	100.22	− .01	8.39
8.75	Aug 93p	100.25	100.29	− .01	8.45
11.87	Aug 93n	110.01	110.07	− .02	8.46
8.25	Sep 93p	99.09	99.13	− .01	8.44
7.12	Oct 93p	95.24	95.28	− .01	8.44
8.62	Nov 93	100.12	100.22	...	8.40
11.75	Nov 93n	110.05	110.09	...	8.50
9.00	Nov 93p	101.19	101.23	− .01	8.45
7.62	Dec 93p	97.12	97.15	− .01	8.40
7.00	Jan 94p	95.03	95.07	− .01	8.45
9.00	Feb 94	101.24	101.30	− .01	8.42
8.87	Feb 94p	101.08	101.12	− .02	8.46
7.00	Apr 94p	94.27	94.31	...	8.45
4.12	May 89-94	89.06	90.08	− .03	6.79
13.12	May 94p	116.05	116.11	− .02	8.47
9.50	May 94p	103.15	103.19	− .02	8.47
8.00	Jul 94p	98.07	98.11	− .03	8.45
8.62	Aug 94p	100.14	100.18	− .01	8.47
8.75	Aug 94	100.25	101.05	− .03	8.44
12.62	Aug 94p	114.31	115.06	− .03	8.51
9.50	Oct 94p	103.21	103.25	− .03	8.50
10.12	Nov 94	106.00	106.06	− .03	8.51
11.62	Nov 94p	111.26	111.30	− .03	8.52
8.25	Nov 94p	99.02	99.06	− .01	8.45
8.62	Jan 95p	100.15	100.19	− .01	8.47
3.00	Feb 95	89.18	90.20	− .02	5.14
10.50	Feb 95	107.25	107.31	− .03	8.52
11.25	Feb 95p	110.27	111.01	− .02	8.51
7.75	Feb 95p	97.06	97.09	− .02	8.41
8.37	Apr 95p	99.15	99.19	− .02	8.47
10.37	May 95	107.18	107.24	− .02	8.51
11.25	May 95p	111.06	111.12	− .04	8.52
12.62	May 95	116.30	117.04	− .04	8.52
8.87	Jul 95p	101.16	101.20	− .03	8.49
10.50	Aug 95p	108.12	108.18	− .02	8.52
8.62	Oct 95p	100.13	100.17	− .02	8.50
9.50	Nov 95p	104.07	104.11	− .03	8.53
11.50	Nov 95	113.06	113.12	+ .01	8.51
9.25	Jan 96p	103.06	103.10	− .03	8.53
8.87	Feb 96p	101.16	101.20	− .03	8.52
9.37	Apr 96p	103.27	103.31	− .02	8.53
7.37	May 96p	94.12	94.16	− .02	8.52
7.87	Jul 96p	96.24	96.28	− .02	8.51
8.00	Oct 96p	97.12	97.16	− .02	8.49
7.25	Nov 96p	93.11	93.15	− .02	8.54
8.00	Ja 97p	97.16	97.19	− .03	8.46
8.50	May 97p	99.24	99.28	− .04	8.52
8.62	Aug 97p	100.10	100.14	− .03	8.54
8.87	Nov 97p	101.22	101.26	− .04	8.55
8.12	Feb 98p	97.15	97.19	− .05	8.54
9.00	May 98p	102.12	102.16	− .05	8.57
9.25	Aug 98p	103.31	104.03	− .05	8.56
7.00	May 93-98	89.22	90.08	− .04	[illegible]
3.50	Nov 98	89.07	90.09	[illegible]	[illegible]
8.87	Nov 98p	101.23	[illegible]	[illegible]	[illegible]
8.87	Feb 99p	[illegible]	[illegible]	[illegible]	[illegible]
8.50	May [illegible]	[illegible]	[illegible]	[illegible]	8.59
9.12	[illegible]	[illegible]	[illegible]	− .06	8.56
[illegible]	[illegible]	88.24	88.28	− .06	8.56
[illegible]	[illegible] 17k	101.23	101.27	− .09	8.57
[illegible]	Aug 17k	103.01	103.05	− .08	8.57
9.12	May 18k	105.30	106.02	− .10	8.55
9.00	Nov 18k	104.24	104.28	− .09	8.54
8.87	Feb 19k	103.15	103.19	− .12	8.54
8.12	Aug 19k	95.19	95.23	− .08	8.52

STRIPPED TREASURIES

Rate	Maturity	Bid	Asked	Bid Chg.	Yld.
.00	Feb 90a	99.22	99.23	...	7.41
.00	May 90a	97.27	97.28	+ .01	8.02
.00	Aug 90a	95.27	95.29	...	8.13
.00	Nov 90a	93.30	94.01	...	8.15
.00	Feb 91	91.31	92.02	− .01	8.24
.00	May 91a	90.03	90.07	− .01	8.27
.00	Aug 91	88.07	88.12	+ .01	8.27
.00	Nov 91a	86.15	86.20	+ .01	8.28
8.12	Jan 92p	99.18	99.21	...	8.32
.00	Feb 92a	84.15	84.21	+ .01	8.40
.00	May 92a	82.23	82.29	...	8.43
.00	Aug 92a	80.30	81.06	...	8.43
.00	Nov 92a	79.10	79.18	...	8.42
.00	Feb 93a	77.20	77.29	− .03	8.43
.00	May 93a	76.01	76.10	− .01	8.44
.00	Aug 93a	74.14	74.23	− .01	8.44
.00	Nov 93a	72.31	73.09	− .02	8.42
.00	Feb 94a	71.11	71.21	− .02	8.46
.00	May 94a	69.26	70.05	− .01	8.47
.00	Aug 94a	68.12	68.24	− .01	8.46
.00	Nov 94a	67.00	67.12	...	8.45
.00	Feb 95a	65.12	65.24	− .03	8.52
.00	May 95a	64.00	64.12	− .01	8.53
.00	Aug 95a	62.20	63.01	− .02	8.53
.00	Nov 95a	61.11	61.24	− .03	8.53
.00	Feb 96a	59.29	60.10	− .03	8.57
.00	May 96a	58.19	59.00	− .03	8.59
.00	Aug 96a	57.11	57.25	− .03	8.59
.00	Nov 96a	56.06	56.20	− .03	8.58
.00	Feb 97a	54.28	55.10	− .02	8.61
.00	May 97a	53.22	54.04	− .02	8.62
.00	Aug 97a	52.16	52.31	− .03	8.63
.00	Nov 97a	51.13	51.28	− .03	8.63
.00	Feb 98a	50.07	50.22	− .02	8.65
.00	May 98a	49.05	49.20	− .03	8.65
.00	Aug 98a	48.04	48.19	− .02	8.65
.00	Nov 98a	47.05	47.20	− .02	8.64
.00	Feb 99a	46.04	46.20	− .04	8.64
.00	May 99a	45.05	45.21	− .04	8.64
.00	Aug 99a	44.05	44.20	− .05	8.65
.00	Nov 99a	43.07	43.23	− .05	8.65
.00	Feb 00a	42.13	42.29	+ .02	8.62
.00	May 00a	41.13	41.29	− .01	8.65
.00	Aug 00a	40.17	41.00	− .01	8.65
.00	Nov 00a	39.22	40.05	− .01	8.65
.00	Feb 01a	38.22	39.06	− .03	8.68
.00	May 01a	37.28	38.12	− .04	8.68
.00	Aug 01a	37.02	37.18	− .02	8.68
.00	Nov 01a	36.09	36.25	− .03	8.68
.00	Feb 02a	35.17	36.01	− .01	8.67
.00	May 02a	34.26	35.09	− .01	8.67
.00	Aug 02a	34.02	34.17	− .01	8.67
.00	Nov 02a	33.11	33.26	− .01	8.67
.00	Feb 03a	32.21	33.05	− .02	8.66
.00	May 03a	31.31	32.15	− .02	8.66
.00	Aug 03a	31.09	31.25	− .02	8.66
.00	Nov 03a	30.20	31.04	− .04	8.66
.00	Feb 04a	29.30	30.13	− .03	8.67
.00	May 04a	29.10	29.25	− .03	8.67
.00	Aug 04a	28.21	29.05	− .04	8.67
.00	Nov 04a	28.02	28.17	− .05	8.67
.00	Feb 05a	27.15	27.30	− .03	8.67
.00	May 05a	26.28	27.12	− .04	8.67
.00	Aug 05a	26.10	26.25	− .03	8.67
.00	Nov 05a	25.27	26.10	− .03	8.65
.00	Feb 06a	25.06	25.21	− .05	8.67
.00	May 06a	24.21	25.04	− .05	8.67
.00	Aug 06a	24.04	24.19	− .03	8.67
.00	Nov 06a	23.20	24.03	− .04	8.67
.00	Feb 07a	23.04	23.18	− .02	8.67
.00	May 07a	22.20	23.03	− .03	8.67
.00	Aug 07a	22.06	22.20	− .04	8.66
.00	Nov 07a	21.23	22.05	− .03	8.66
.00	Feb 08a	21.08	21.22	− .03	8.66
.00	May 08a	20.26	21.08	[illegible]	[illegible]
.00	Aug 08a	20.11	[illegible]	[illegible]	[illegible]
.00	Nov 08a	[illegible]	[illegible]	[illegible]	[illegible]
.00	Feb 09a	[illegible]	[illegible]	[illegible]	[illegible]
.00	May [illegible]	[illegible]	[illegible]	[illegible]	[illegible]
[illegible]	[illegible]	[illegible]	[illegible]	[illegible]	8.65
[illegible]	[illegible]	[illegible]	12.26	− .01	8.38
[illegible]	[illegible]	12.05	12.12	− .01	8.36
[illegible]	Nov 15b	11.31	12.06	− .01	8.34
.00	Feb 16b	11.30	12.04	+ .01	8.27
.00	May 16b	11.26	12.01	+ .03	8.23
.00	Nov 16b	11.11	11.17	+ .01	8.23
.00	May 17b	10.29	11.04	+ .01	8.22
.00	Aug 17b	10.24	10.30	+ .02	8.20
.00	May 18b	10.09	10.15	+ .01	8.14
.00	Nov 18b	10.00	10.07	...	8.09
.00	Feb 19b	9.30	10.04	...	8.05
.00	Aug 19b	9.20	9.26	− .01	8.02
.00	Nov 94c	66.31	67.06	− .01	8.51
.00	Feb 95c	65.17	65.24	− .01	8.52
.00	May 95c	64.06	64.13	...	8.52
.00	Aug 95c	62.27	63.02	+ .01	8.52
.00	Nov 95c	61.18	61.25	...	8.52
.00	Feb 96c	60.10	60.18	− .01	8.50
.00	May 96c	59.02	59.10	...	8.51
.00	Nov 96c	56.21	56.29	− .01	8.50
.00	May 97c	54.11	54.19	...	8.50
.00	Aug 97c	53.06	54.01	− .01	8.35
.00	Nov 97c	52.03	52.31	− .01	8.35
.00	Feb 98c	50.31	51.27	− .01	8.36
.00	May 98c	49.31	50.27	+ .01	8.35
.00	Aug 98c	48.29	49.25	...	8.35
.00	Nov 98c	47.29	48.26	...	8.35
.00	May 99c	46.01	46.16	...	8.43
.00	Aug 99c	45.02	45.11	− .01	8.48
.00	Nov 99c	44.04	44.13	− .01	8.48

TREASURY BILLS

Rate	Maturity	Bid	Asked	Bid Chg.	Yld.
.00	Feb 08 '90	7.31	7.19	...	7.29
.00	Feb 15 '90	7.50	7.38	+ .21	7.49
.00	Feb 22 '90	7.36	7.25	...	7.37
.00	Mar 01 '90	6.71	6.63	+ .05	6.75
.00	Mar 08 '90	7.52	7.47	− .05	7.62
.00	Mar 15 '90	7.54	7.50	− .10	7.66
.00	Mar 22 '90	7.55	7.50	− .10	7.67
.00	Mar 29 '90	7.54	7.50	− .04	7.69
.00	Apr 05 '90	7.72	7.69	− .03	7.89
.00	Apr 12 '90	7.80	7.75	− .01	7.97
.00	Apr 19 '90	7.91	7.88	+ .03	8.11
.00	Apr 26 '90	7.80	7.78	− .01	8.03
.00	May 03 '90	7.82	7.78	+ .01	8.04
.00	May 10 '90	7.83	7.78	+ .02	8.05
.00	May 17 '90	7.77	7.72	− .03	8.00
.00	May 24 '90	7.75	7.72	− .09	8.01
.00	May 31 '90	7.73	7.69	...	7.99
.00	Jun 07 '90	7.70	7.66	− .01	7.97
.00	Jun 14 '90	7.73	7.69	+ .02	8.01
.00	Jun 21 '90	7.72	7.69	+ .03	8.03
.00	Jun 28 '90	7.71	7.66	+ .04	8.00
.00	Jul 05 '90	7.78	7.75	...	8.12
.00	Jul 12 '90	7.77	7.72	+ .02	8.10
.00	Jul 19 '90	7.76	7.72	+ .02	8.11
.00	Jul 26 '90	7.76	7.72	+ .02	8.12
.00	Aug 02 '90	7.77	7.75	+ .02	8.17
.00	Aug 30 '90	7.76	7.69	...	8.11
.00	Sep 27 '90	7.68	7.63	...	8.06
.00	Oct 25 '90	7.70	7.66	...	8.12
.00	Nov 23 '90	7.71	7.66	+ .01	8.15
.00	Dec 20 '90	7.64	7.59	+ .01	8.11
.00	Jan 17 '91	7.59	7.56	+ .01	8.11

FIGURE 3-3 Listing of Treasury issues. *Source: The Wall Street Journal,* February 6, 1990, C-18, reprinted by permission, © 1990, Dow Jones & Co., Inc., all rights reserved.

remember that large discounts mean low prices. Therefore, a large discount appearing in the bid column means that the buyers are willing to pay a relatively low price for that security.

CONCLUSION

Bonds are one form of long-term debt. Most bonds have the same basic characteristics. They contain a promise to pay the principal amount of the debt on some predetermined date in the future and to pay interest on specified dates throughout the life of the bond. They typically have an original maturity date of 15 years or longer. Other characteristics, such as security behind the bonds, retirement features, sources of revenue to pay the interest and principal, and taxation of interest, vary for different types of bonds. Bonds are issued by business concerns, state and local governments, and the federal government and federally sponsored agencies.

Bonds issued by business concerns are generally secured by specific assets or the general earning power of the issuing corporation. The debt is repaid from corporate earnings or refunding. Corporate bonds can be retired before maturity if they are callable. In addition, some corporate bonds have a conversion provision that enables bondholders to convert their bonds into common stock at a specific price.

Bonds issued by state and local governments are generally not backed by specific collateral. Funds to repay the debt come from the taxing power of the issuing governments or from revenues generated by specific projects. Interest earned from state and local government bonds is exempted from federal income taxes, which makes these bonds attractive investments for persons in high-income tax brackets.

The U.S. Treasury issues bills, notes, and certificates of indebtedness as well as bonds. Debt securities issued by the Treasury are backed by faith in the U.S. government. Debt securities issued by government-sponsored agencies are backed by the issuing agencies, in some instances by collateral, and to a limited degree by the Treasury.

IMPORTANT CONCEPTS

Accrued interest

Adjustment bond

Annuity

Assumed bonds

Bearer bond

Bond

Bond-equivalent basis

Bond value tables

Callable bonds

Call protection

Closed-end mortgage bonds

Convertible bonds

Coupon bonds

Coupon stripping

Creditworthiness

Current yield

Debenture	Par value
Deep discount	Pass-through mortgage certificates
Discount	Philadelphia plan
Equipment trust certificates	Premium
Face amount	Private authority bonds
First mortgage bonds	Quality ratings
General mortgage bonds	Registered bonds
General obligation bonds (GOs)	Restructuring
Government-guaranteed securities	Revenue bonds
Guaranteed bonds	Ride the yield curve
Income bonds	Serial bonds
Indenture	Sinking fund bonds
Indexed bonds	Tax-equivalent yield
Industrial development bonds (IDBs)	Tax-exempt bonds
Investment-grade bonds	Treasury bills
Junk bonds	Warrants (attached to bonds)
Mortgage bonds	Yield (market)
Municipal bonds	Yield to call
Open-end mortgage bonds	Yield to maturity
Original issue discount (OID)	Zero-coupon bonds
Participating bonds	

QUESTIONS AND EXERCISES

1. What is a bond?
2. Assume that a $1000 bond with an 8 percent coupon is maturing in 16 years and is selling at $916.10. What is the yield to maturity of that bond?
3. What is the current yield on the bond in question 2?
4. List the ways corporate bonds differ from municipal bonds.
5. Why do some companies sell bonds with warrants attached?
6. Is a "call" feature desirable from the investor's viewpoint? Why or why not?
7. Determine the tax equivalent yield on the following bonds for an investor in the 33 percent income tax bracket.
   a. U.S. government 6.5 percent note.
   b. General Motors 7s05.
   c. New York 5s99.
8. There is a section in *The Wall Street Journal* bond pages called "Yield Comparisons." Examine it to compare the dollar cost of issuing a $50 million bond issue with a AAA rating versus an A rating, when the bond issue will have a 15-year maturity. (Hint: 1 percent added cost on $50 million is $.5 million.)
9. Why would investors buy zero coupon bonds if they receive no current income until the bond matures?

10. Profitwise has announced a new bond issue: $1000 par value bonds that are convertible into common stock at $80 per share. The common stock is currently traded at $60. Investment analysts consider Profitwise to be a growth company. Will investors find such bonds attractive? Why?

11. Use *The Wall Street Journal* to compare the yields on Treasury bills, Treasury notes, and long-term U.S. bonds. Which is the most risky? Why?

12. Why do investors buy bonds at substantial premiums (e.g., price is $1375) when they know the bond will be worth $1000 when it matures?

13. Would an investor prefer a first mortgage bond or a debenture?

14. What is the price of a 45-day Treasury bill on a 10 percent discount basis?

15. What is the bond equivalent basis of the security in question 14?

CHAPTER 4

RISKS AND RETURNS

MEASURING RISKS AND RETURNS	**RETURNS**
Holding Period Returns	**CONCLUSION**
Proxy for Total Risk	**IMPORTANT CONCEPTS**
SOURCES OF RISK	**QUESTIONS AND EXERCISES**
Market Risk	**APPENDIX 4A: MEASURING**
Business Risk	**RISK—THE STANDARD**
Purchasing Power Risk	**DEVIATION**
Liquidity Risk	

C *aveat emptor*—let the buyer beware—is an appropriate motto for investors because investing in marketable securities abounds with risks. On the other hand, investing in marketable securities offers some exceptional opportunities for profit. This chapter is about the risks and rewards associated with investing in stocks and bonds. First, the concept of risks and returns is explained, and a method of quantifying them is presented. Next, the major sources of risk are considered. Finally, the rate of return on stocks, bonds, and portfolios is discussed.

MEASURING RISKS AND RETURNS

Picture Johnny Carson talking to a guest on the *Tonight Show* and saying "the stock market is risky." Someone in the back of the audience yells "How risky is it?" Johnny looks up, smiles, and says "All right dragon breath; it is so risky that stockbrokers give tranquilizers to their customers before they tell them how their stocks are doing. It is so risky that they put bars on the windows in the offices of stockbrokerage firms so the customers can't jump. It is so risky that gamblers prefer junkets to the New York Stock Exchange instead of to Las Vegas." Risk can be viewed in that context, but we are going to examine it in a more scientific fashion.

In general, the word *risk* refers to the possibility of loss. However, in finance the word has a precise meaning. Risk is the deviation from an expected return on a

security or some other asset. If you expected a return of 20 percent and actually received 16 percent, the difference between the two reflects risk.

In order to quantify risk and explain how it is measured, certain terms must be clearly defined. Let us begin with **total risk,** which is the sum of all risks connected with an investment. Total risk is divided into two parts: (1) **systematic risk** and (2) **unsystematic risk.** Systematic risk is due to some factor that affects the returns on all securities in the same manner. For example, if there was an unexpected announcement that the government was going to nationalize all major firms, stock prices would drop sharply. There is no way to eliminate such a risk, and it is useful to know the extent to which the returns of an asset are affected by such common factors. The degree of systematic risk can be measured by **beta,** which is discussed later in this chapter.

Unsystematic risk, or **residual risk,** as it is sometimes called, is what remains

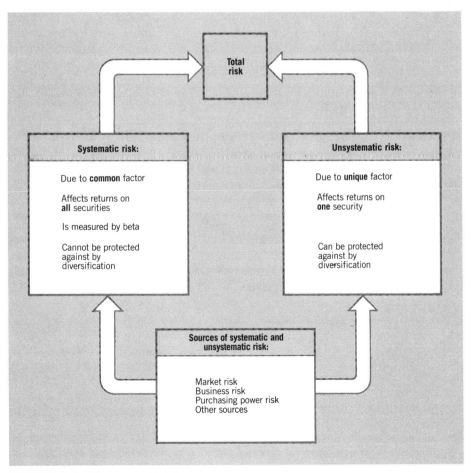

FIGURE 4-1 Elements of total risk.

after systematic risk has been subtracted from total risk. Unsystematic risk is due to unique events that affect the returns of only one security. For example, the Ford Motor Company produced the Edsel and discovered that the demand for that car was substantially less than they had expected. Consequently, the earnings and price of Ford stock were adversely affected, but the earnings and stock prices of other companies were not affected. One can protect against the unique risk of one company by owning shares in a number of different companies — diversifying one's holdings. More will be said about diversification in later chapters.

Figure 4-1 summarizes the concept of total risk of a security. Collectively, systematic risk plus unsystematic risk equals total risk. The major characteristics of systematic and unsystematic risk are listed. Below them are three sources of systematic and unsystematic risk. These sources are discussed in detail in this chapter. Do not be confused because the sources of risk have the word *risk* in their title. It is common usage to speak of fluctuations in stock prices as **market risk.** Similarly, business failures and inflation have commonly been categorized as **business risk** and **purchasing power risk.**

Before we can measure risk, we must have a clear idea of what returns are. Once again, in general usage, returns can be thought of as what investors get back from their investment. To measure these returns, however, requires a more analytical approach.

Holding Period Returns

The return on a security may be measured by the **holding period return (HPR),** which is the total return (income + price at the end of the period) divided by the price at the beginning of the holding period. The length of the holding period is arbitrary. It may be one day, one month, or one year, but all returns should be expressed on an annual basis. Thus, a six-month holding period return is multiplied by 2 to put it on an annual basis. The HPR can be calculated as follows:

$$\text{Stock HPR} = \frac{(D_1 + P_1)}{P_0} \tag{4-1}$$

$$\text{Bond HPR} = \frac{(I_1 + P_1)}{P_0}$$

where

D_1 = expected cash dividends over the holding period (i.e., one year)
I_1 = expected interest payments received over the holding period (i.e., one year)
P_1 = expected price at the end of the holding period
P_0 = expected price at the beginning of the holding period

An HPR of greater than one means that investors expect a return (income + price change) greater than their original investment (P_0). Conversely, an HPR of less than one means that the return is less than the original investment. An HPR of

one means no change in value. By way of illustration, assume that a stock is currently selling at $50 per share. Analysts believe that it will increase to $65 within one year. The stock is paying a $2.50 cash dividend per share, which is not expected to change. The HPR is 1.35. This means that investors expect to receive their original investment plus an additional 35 percent return.

$$\text{Stock HPR} = \frac{(\$2.50 + \$65)}{\$50} = 1.35$$

In reality, things may not come out the way we expect them to. They may be better or worse. Unfortunately, the stock declined to $40 per share instead of increasing in value. In this case, the HPR is 0.85, indicating a loss in value. Investors are receiving 85 percent of their original investment.

$$\text{Stock HPR} = \frac{(\$2.50 + \$40)}{\$50} = 0.85$$

It is also possible for the stock to decline and the dividend to remain the same or increase so that the investors break even. Suppose the price declines to $47.50 and the cash dividend remains $2.50 per share. The HPR is 1.00. The investors' return is equal to their investment.

$$\text{Stock HPR} = \frac{(\$2.50 + \$47.50)}{\$50} = 1.00$$

Now that we understand what is meant by return, we can turn to a measure of risk—or deviation from the return.

Proxy for Total Risk

The word *proxy* means substitute. In this context the **standard deviation** (σ or sigma) is one proxy for total risk, which refers to changes in returns caused by all factors combined. It is a statistical tool that allows us to quantify and compare the riskiness of various assets. Throughout this text, the standard deviation is used as a proxy for risk because it is easily understood and can be used in further statistical calculations. The standard deviation is a measure of dispersion from an average or expected value. The way in which we use it is to measure the degree to which actual HPRs may deviate from the HPR that investors expect to earn. One standard deviation means that the chances are 34 in 100 (i.e., 34%) that the actual HPR will be between the numerical value of the standard deviation and the expected HPR. The following example will illustrate the concept, which is explained in greater detail in Appendix 4A. Consider the two distributions of HPRs shown in Figure 4-2. Both Company A and Company B have an expected HPR of 1.20—the owners expect to earn 20 percent more than their original investment. The standard deviation for Company A is 0.01, which means that the chances are 34 in 100 that the actual HPR will fall between 1.19 and 1.20 (1.20 + 0.01 = 1.19). There is also a 34 percent chance that it may fall as high as 1.21 (1.20 +

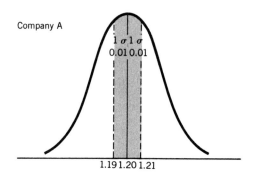

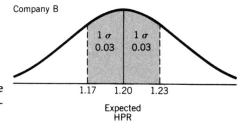

FIGURE 4-2 Two distributions with the same means and different standard deviations.

0.01). In other words, the chances are 68 in 100 (34 + 34 = 68) that the actual HPR will fall between 1.19 and 1.21.

Now examine Company B. It has the same expected HPR (1.20), but the standard deviation is 0.03, much larger than that of Company A. For Company B, the chances are 68 in 100 that the actual HPR will fall between 1.17 and 1.23. Therefore Company B is riskier than Company A because it has the same mean and a larger standard deviation — investors in Company B may lose more or make more than those in Company A.

SOURCES OF RISK
Market Risk

As mentioned previously, risk refers to the possibility of loss or harm. Fluctuations in stock prices can cause losses or gains. This point is demonstrated by the wide swings in stock prices shown in Figure 4-3. This figure shows the declines and subsequent recoveries of stock prices over a long period of time. Figure 4-4 is more dramatic. It shows the decline in the Dow Jones Average that began in August 1987 and ended in the stock market crash of October 1987. The crash affected stock markets and investors throughout the world. Stock markets as a whole are unstable because the values of individual securities are affected by millions of individual investors and financial institutions, each with their own

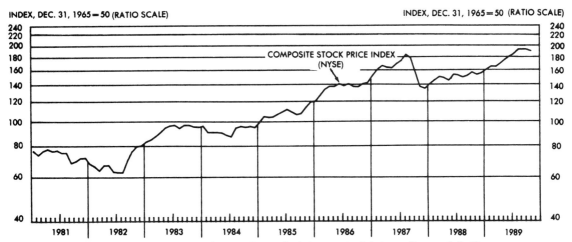

FIGURE 4-3   Common stock prices. *Source:* Council of Economic Advisers, *Economic Indicators.*

expectations and needs. However, these are not the only factors that affect stock prices. More will be said shortly about the major factors affecting values.

Beta

To some extent, stocks are like boats riding the tide. When the tide comes in, boats rise; when the tide goes out, boats fall. However, the size of the tide varies at different places and times. South Korea may have a 40-foot tide and New York may have a 5-foot tide. The fact that all stocks in the same market are affected by a common factor, in the same way boats are affected by tides, is what we call **systematic risk.** Systematic risk is measured by **beta.** Beta measures the extent to which the returns (HPRs) on a stock vary with respect to the returns on the stock market.[1]

Unlike the boat–tide analogy, some stocks are more volatile than others, and the degree of volatility may change over time. Therefore beta values can and do change.

The benchmark is the beta for the stock market index that is being used, and it is equal to 1. Suppose one investment advisory service uses the NYSE Composite Index—a broad measure that includes all stocks traded on the NYSE—

[1] In statistical terms, beta can be defined as the slope (b) of a linear relationship between the expected excess returns over a risk-free rate of individual stocks and the expected excess returns of a portfolio of stocks, or by the relationships shown in the following equation:

$$(ER_{it} - R_{ft}) = b_i(ER_{mt} - R_{ft})$$

where

ER_{it} = the expected return on security i in period t
R_{ft} = the riskless rate in period t
ER_{mt} = the expected return on the portfolio in period t
b_i or beta = the systematic risk measure of stock i relative to the portfolio

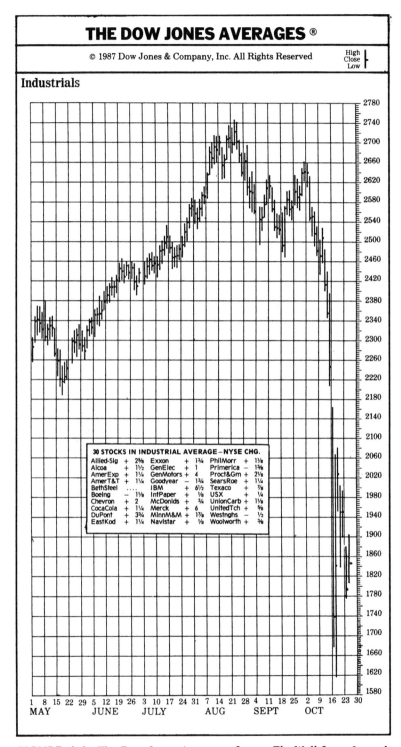

THE DOW JONES AVERAGES ®

High
Close
Low

Industrials

30 STOCKS IN INDUSTRIAL AVERAGE – NYSE CHG.

Allied-Sig	+ 2⅝	Exxon	+ 1¾	PhilMorr	+ 1⅛
Alcoa	+ 1½	GenElec	+ 1	Primerica	− 1⅜
AmerExp	+ 1¼	GenMotors	+ 4	Proct&Gm	+ 2⅛
AmerT&T	+ 1¼	Goodyear	− 1¾	SearsRoe	+ 1¼
BethSteel	....	IBM	+ 6½	Texaco	+ ⅞
Boeing	− 1⅛	IntPaper	+ ⅛	USX	+ ¼
Chevron	+ 2	McDonlds	+ ¾	UnionCarb	+ 1⅛
CocaCola	+ 1¼	Merck	+ 6	UnitedTch	+ ⅝
DuPont	+ 3¾	MinnM&M	+ 1⅞	Westnghs	− ½
EastKod	+ 1¼	Navistar	+ ⅛	Woolworth	+ ⅜

MAY JUNE JULY AUG SEPT OCT

1 8 15 22 29 5 12 19 26 3 10 17 24 31 7 14 21 28 4 11 18 25 2 9 16 23 30

FIGURE 4-4 The Dow Jones Averages. *Source: The Wall Street Journal,* October 27, 1987, reprinted by permission, © 1987, Dow Jones & Co., Inc., all rights reserved.

TABLE 4-1   Betas for Selected Companies

Company	Beta
Iowa–Illinois Gas and Electric	0.60
La-Z-Boy Chair	0.75
WD-40 Company	0.90
Campbell's Soup	1.00
Carnival Cruise "A"	1.25
Ashton-Tate	1.45
Biogen Inc.	1.65
Integrated Devices	1.75

Source: Value Line, New York: Arnold Bernhard & Co., Inc.,
Reprinted by permission; copyright 1990.

to measure beta and another investment advisory service uses the NASDAQ-100 index of OTC stocks. The result is that betas for individual stocks calculated by these two services using different benchmarks may not be the same.

Betas for selected companies are shown in Table 4-1. Keep in mind that the beta for the market index is 1. The betas range from 0.60 to 1.75. The wide range of betas shown in the table supports the old adage that there is a marked difference between the behavior of the stock market and the market for individual stocks. In summary, beta is a measure of systematic risk.

Interest Rate Risk

The previous section pointed out systematic risk in the stock market. Now let us examine the risk of price changes in the bond market, or the so-called **interest rate risk.** We know from the previous chapter that the market prices of outstanding bonds fluctuate when market interest rates change. When market interest rates rise, the market prices of outstanding bonds decline so that the **yield to maturity** of those bonds will equal the current level of interest rates for a similar risk security. As noted in Chapter 3, yield to maturity is the average percentage yield earned annually from the purchase date to the maturity date and includes both capital gains and losses. This concept will now be examined in graphic form.

Figure 4-5 demonstrates the inverse relationship between bond prices and market interest rates (yields) and shows how the maturity of a bond affects the price–interest rate relationship. The bond prices shown in the figure were taken from a bond value table, such as the one described in Chapter 3 (See Table 3-2) on pages 63–64. Let us begin with a 7-percent bond with 25 years to maturity. If market interest rates are 7 percent, the market price of the bond will be $1000.

Suppose that the market rate of interest increases to 9 percent. We know that the market price of the bond will decline, but the extent of the decline depends on the maturity of the bond. If the bond matures in 25 years, the price will decline to $802. If it matures in 15 years, the price will decline to $837. Notice that as the bond approaches maturity, the price approaches the par value. If the bond only had one year to maturity, the price would be $981.

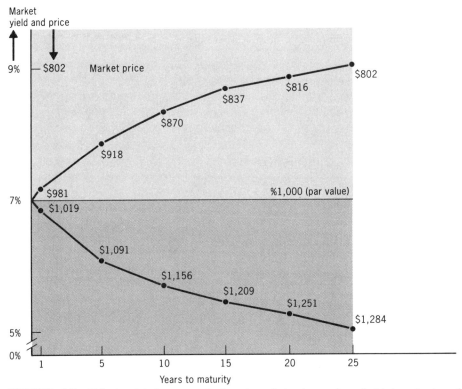

FIGURE 4-5   Relationship between the bond market price and market interest rates of 9% to 5% (1000 25-year, 7% bond). Prices shown are taken from bond value tables.

Conversely, suppose that market interest rates fell from 7 to 5 percent. In this case, the market price of a bond with 25 years to maturity would have increased to $1284! At this point you may want to know why anyone would pay $1284 for a bond that is only going to be worth $1000 when it matures. The investor would have a capital loss of $284. The answer is that the investors who bought that bond received a 5-percent yield to maturity. It did not make any difference to them whether the bond cost $500, $1000, or $1284 as long as they received a 5-percent yield to maturity.

To continue with the example, if market interest rates are 5 percent, the market price of the 7-percent bond will gradually decrease as the bond matures until it reaches par value at maturity.

As shown in Figure 4-6, wide swings in market rates of interest have been commonplace in recent years. In addition, the figure shows that short-term rates are more volatile than long-term rates. Nevertheless, short-term securities are a safer place to "park" funds on a temporary basis than long-term debt securities. The reason is that if interest rates rise, those who hold short-term securities need not take a loss if they are willing to hold the securities until they mature in, say, 60

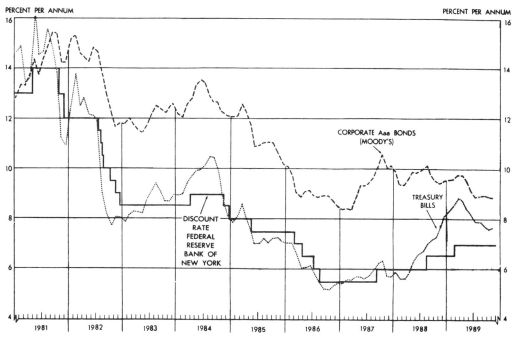

FIGURE 4-6 Interest rates and bond yields. *Source:* Council of Economic Advisors, *Economic Indicators.*

days. However, investors who hold long-term bonds may not be willing to wait 20 years or until rates fall. Therefore, they may have to sell the bonds at a loss to regain their funds at the higher prevailing rates.

Duration

Duration refers to bond's (or stock's) price sensitivity to yield changes. The concept of duration originated in 1938 when Frederick R. Macauley wanted an alternative to the term to maturity for measuring a bond's life.[2] Because it is cumbersome to calculate by hand, not much was done with it until computers and calculators could determine durations quickly. Today, duration has received considerable attention from both academics and practitioners as a means of reducing interest rate risk.

Duration is the weighted average term to maturity of the present value of all

---

[2] Frederick R. Macauley, *The Movements of Interest Rate, Bond Yields and Stock Prices in the United States Since 1856,* New York: National Bureau of Economic Research, 1938. For a modern discussion of duration see Gerald O. Bierwag, *Duration Analysis: Managing Interest Rate Risk,* Cambridge, Mass.: Ballinger Publishing Company, 1987. For stock durations see Martin L. Leibowitz, Eric H. Sorensen, Robert D. Arnott, and H. Nicholas Hanson, "A Total Differential Approach to Equity Duration," *Financial Analysts Journal,* September/October 1989, 30–37.

cash flows received from bonds or stocks. We will focus on the duration of bonds, which can be approximated by using the following equation:[3]

$$D = n - \frac{C[n - (1 + r)PVAIF_{r,n}]}{P_0 \times r} \tag{4-2}$$

where

D = duration in years
C = annual income (\$) from the bond
n = number of years to maturity
r = required rate of return, yield to maturity
P_0 = current market price of the bond
$PVAIF_{r,n}$ = present value of an annuity interest factor at a certain rate r for n years

The PVAIF table can be found in Appendix B at the back of the book.

To illustrate the use of Equation 4-2, assume that a bond has a market price of \$1000, the coupon rate of interest is 12 percent (pays \$120/year), and the term to maturity is five years. The current market yield (required rate of return) is 12 percent. The duration is 4.0 years.

$$D = 5 - \frac{120[5 - (1.12)3.6048]}{1000 \times 0.12} = 4.037$$

Those investors who do not wish to compute durations may use a bond duration table. For example, the duration of a 12-percent bond with five years (and no months; i.e., 5–0) to maturity and a current market yield of 12 percent can be found in Table 4-2. Read down the 5–0 years and months column to the 12.00 yield row. The answer from the table is 3.90, which is more accurate than the 4.0 years approximation derived from using the equation. Nevertheless, if a duration table is not available, the equation gives a ballpark answer.

One additional step is necessary to determine the modified duration that we will use in calculating price changes in bonds.[4]

$$MD = D/(1 + r/2) \tag{4-3}$$

where

MD = modified duration
D = duration
r = required rate of return

The percentage change in bond prices that will occur as a result of changes in market yields can be approximated by Equation 4-4.[5]

[3] John Caks, William R. Lane, Robert W. Greenleaf, and Reginald G. Joules, "A Simple Formula for Duration," *Journal of Financial Research,* 8, Fall 1985, 245–249.

[4] There are several ways to modify duration. The method used here is from *Duration Tables for Bond and Mortgage Portfolio Management,* No. 561, Boston: Financial Publishing Co., 1980.

[5] Bond prices and duration do not change at the same rates, giving rise to "convexity." For solutions to the convexity problem, see "Intro to Convexity," *Financial Futures Professional,* Chicago Board of Trade, July 1989, and "Understanding Negative Convexity," *Financial Futures Professional,* Chicago Board of Trade, September 1989.

TABLE 4-2   Bond Duration at 12% Interest

Yield	Years and Months											
	1-0	1-6	2-0	2-6	3-0	3-6	4-0	4-6	5-0	5-6	6-0	6-6
4.00	.97	1.42	1.85	2.26	2.65	3.03	3.39	3.74	4.08	4.40	4.72	5.03
4.20	.97	1.42	1.85	2.26	2.65	3.02	3.39	3.73	4.07	4.40	4.71	5.02
4.40	.97	1.42	1.85	2.26	2.65	3.02	3.38	3.73	4.07	4.39	4.71	5.01
4.60	.97	1.42	1.85	2.26	2.65	3.02	3.38	3.73	4.06	4.39	4.70	5.01
4.80	.97	1.42	1.85	2.25	2.64	3.02	3.38	3.72	4.06	4.38	4.69	5.00
5.00	.97	1.42	1.85	2.25	2.64	3.02	3.38	3.72	4.05	4.38	4.69	4.99
5.20	.97	1.42	1.85	2.25	2.64	3.02	3.37	3.72	4.05	4.37	4.68	4.98
5.40	.97	1.42	1.85	2.25	2.64	3.01	3.37	3.71	4.05	4.37	4.67	4.97
5.60	.97	1.42	1.85	2.25	2.64	3.01	3.37	3.71	4.04	4.36	4.67	4.97
5.80	.97	1.42	1.85	2.25	2.64	3.01	3.37	3.71	4.04	4.35	4.66	4.96
6.00	.97	1.42	1.85	2.25	2.64	3.01	3.36	3.71	4.03	4.35	4.65	4.95
6.20	.97	1.42	1.85	2.25	2.64	3.01	3.36	3.70	4.03	4.34	4.65	4.94
6.40	.97	1.42	1.85	2.25	2.64	3.01	3.36	3.70	4.02	4.34	4.64	4.93
6.60	.97	1.42	1.84	2.25	2.64	3.00	3.36	3.70	4.02	4.33	4.63	4.92
6.80	.97	1.42	1.84	2.25	2.63	3.00	3.35	3.69	4.02	4.33	4.63	4.92
7.00	.97	1.42	1.84	2.25	2.63	3.00	3.35	3.69	4.01	4.32	4.62	4.91
7.20	.97	1.42	1.84	2.25	2.63	3.00	3.35	3.69	4.01	4.32	4.61	4.90
7.40	.97	1.42	1.84	2.25	2.63	3.00	3.35	3.68	4.00	4.31	4.61	4.89
7.60	.97	1.42	1.84	2.25	2.63	3.00	3.35	3.68	4.00	4.31	4.60	4.88
7.80	.97	1.42	1.84	2.25	2.63	2.99	3.34	3.68	3.99	4.30	4.59	4.87
8.00	.97	1.42	1.84	2.25	2.63	2.99	3.34	3.67	3.99	4.29	4.59	4.87
8.20	.97	1.42	1.84	2.24	2.63	2.99	3.34	3.67	3.99	4.29	4.58	4.86
8.40	.97	1.42	1.84	2.24	2.63	2.99	3.34	3.67	3.98	4.28	4.57	4.85
8.60	.97	1.42	1.84	2.24	2.62	2.99	3.33	3.66	3.98	4.28	4.56	4.84
8.80	.97	1.42	1.84	2.24	2.62	2.99	3.33	3.66	3.97	4.27	4.56	4.83
9.00	.97	1.42	1.84	2.24	2.62	2.98	3.33	3.66	3.97	4.27	4.55	4.82
9.20	.97	1.42	1.84	2.24	2.62	2.98	3.33	3.65	3.96	4.26	4.54	4.81
9.40	.97	1.42	1.84	2.24	2.62	2.98	3.32	3.65	3.96	4.25	4.54	4.81
9.60	.97	1.42	1.84	2.24	2.62	2.98	3.32	3.65	3.96	4.25	4.53	4.80
9.80	.97	1.42	1.84	2.24	2.62	2.98	3.32	3.64	3.95	4.24	4.52	4.79
10.00	.97	1.42	1.84	2.24	2.62	2.98	3.32	3.64	3.95	4.24	4.52	4.78
10.20	.97	1.42	1.84	2.24	2.62	2.97	3.31	3.64	3.94	4.23	4.51	4.77
10.40	.97	1.42	1.84	2.24	2.61	2.97	3.31	3.63	3.94	4.23	4.50	4.76
10.60	.97	1.42	1.84	2.24	2.61	2.97	3.31	3.63	3.93	4.22	4.49	4.75
10.80	.97	1.42	1.84	2.24	2.61	2.97	3.31	3.63	3.93	4.21	4.49	4.74
11.00	.97	1.42	1.84	2.24	2.61	2.97	3.30	3.62	3.92	4.21	4.48	4.74
11.20	.97	1.42	1.84	2.24	2.61	2.97	3.30	3.62	3.92	4.20	4.47	4.73
11.40	.97	1.42	1.84	2.23	2.61	2.96	3.30	3.62	3.91	4.20	4.47	4.72
11.60	.97	1.42	1.84	2.23	2.61	2.96	3.30	3.61	3.91	4.19	4.46	4.71
11.80	.97	1.42	1.84	2.23	2.61	2.96	3.29	3.61	3.91	4.19	4.45	4.70
12.00	.97	1.42	1.84	2.23	2.61	2.96	3.29	3.60	3.90	4.18	4.44	4.69
12.20	.97	1.42	1.84	2.23	2.61	2.96	3.29	3.60	3.90	4.17	4.44	4.68
12.40	.97	1.42	1.84	2.23	2.60	2.96	3.29	3.60	3.89	4.17	4.43	4.67
12.60	.97	1.42	1.84	2.23	2.60	2.95	3.28	3.59	3.89	4.16	4.42	4.67

TABLE 4-2 (Continued)

	Years and Months											
Yield	1-0	1-6	2-0	2-6	3-0	3-6	4-0	4-6	5-0	5-6	6-0	6-6
12.80	.97	1.42	1.84	2.23	2.60	2.95	3.28	3.59	3.88	4.16	4.41	4.66
13.00	.97	1.42	1.83	2.23	2.60	2.95	3.28	3.59	3.88	4.15	4.41	4.65
13.20	.97	1.42	1.83	2.23	2.60	2.95	3.28	3.58	3.87	4.14	4.40	4.64
13.40	.97	1.42	1.83	2.23	2.60	2.95	3.27	3.58	3.87	4.14	4.39	4.63
13.60	.97	1.42	1.83	2.23	2.60	2.94	3.27	3.58	3.86	4.13	4.38	4.62
13.80	.97	1.42	1.83	2.23	2.60	2.94	3.27	3.57	3.86	4.13	4.38	4.61
14.00	.97	1.42	1.83	2.23	2.60	2.94	3.27	3.57	3.85	4.12	4.37	4.60
14.20	.97	1.42	1.83	2.23	2.59	2.94	3.26	3.57	3.85	4.12	4.36	4.59
14.40	.97	1.42	1.83	2.22	2.59	2.94	3.26	3.56	3.85	4.11	4.36	4.58
14.60	.97	1.42	1.83	2.22	2.59	2.94	3.26	3.56	3.84	4.10	4.35	4.58
14.80	.97	1.42	1.83	2.22	2.59	2.93	3.26	3.56	3.84	4.10	4.34	4.57
15.00	.97	1.41	1.83	2.22	2.59	2.93	3.25	3.55	3.83	4.09	4.33	4.56

Source: *Duration Tables for Bond and Mortgage Portfolio Management,* No. 561, Boston: Financial Publishing Co., 1980, 218.

$$\text{Percentage change in bond prices} = -MD \times \Delta i \qquad (4\text{-}4)$$

where

$$MD = \text{modified duration (equation 4-3)}$$
$$\Delta i = \text{change in yield in percentage points}$$

Here is how to use these equations to reduce risk and improve investment performance. Suppose that interest rate forecasts suggest that long-term interest rates are going to decline (the prices of long-term bonds are going to increase). The current yield is 8 percent and it is expected to decline to 7.20 percent. Investors wanting to profit from the price increase will buy long-term bonds. They have a choice of one of the following bonds:

- 12 percent coupon, 20 years to maturity, price $802.10, or
- 6 percent coupon, 20 years to maturity, price $1359.90

Which one should they buy, assuming that investors are interested only in price volatility, and that they do not intend to hold the bonds for a long period of time? The answer is the 6 percent coupon bond because it has the greater price volatility. To determine price volatility we use equations 4-2, 4-3, and 4-4. The 6 percent bond has a duration of 11.2 years and a modified duration of 10.78. The price of this bond will increase 8.6 percent whereas the price of the 12 percent coupon bond will increase only 7.6 percent.

$$D = 20 - \frac{60[20 - (1.08)9.8181]}{802.10 \times 0.08} = 11.2 \text{ years}$$

$$MD = 11.2/(1.04) \qquad\qquad = 10.78 \text{ years}$$

$$\text{Price change} = -10.78 \times -0.80 \qquad = +8.6\%$$

For the 12 percent coupon bond, the figures are

$$D = 20 - \frac{120[20 - (1.08)9.8181]}{1395.90 \times 0.08} = 9.9 \text{ years}$$

$$MD = 9.9/(1.04) \qquad\qquad = 9.52 \text{ years}$$

$$\text{Price change} = -9.52 \times -0.80 \qquad = +7.6\%$$

The actual price changes based on bond value tables are 8.9 and 7.7 percent, respectively. Thus, these equations are only approximations, and they work best when the yield changes are less than 100 **basis points** (1 percentage point = 100 basis points).

The relationship between duration and maturity can be seen in Figure 4-7. A careful examination of the figure reveals the following:

- Except for zero-coupon bonds, duration is always less than the term to maturity. The duration of a zero-coupon bond is equal to its maturity.
- Longer terms to maturity mean higher durations.
- Duration is inversely related to the coupons; i.e., bonds with high coupons have shorter durations than those with low coupons.

We know that the longer the duration, the greater the price volatility of a bond. Thus, investors wanting high price volatility should seek bonds with long terms to maturity and low (no) coupons. Those wanting low volatility should do the opposite.

Factors Affecting Market Values

Market values of securities are influenced by many factors, including (1) **structural changes in the market,** (2) **business activity,** (3) **inflation,** and (4) **investor psychology.**

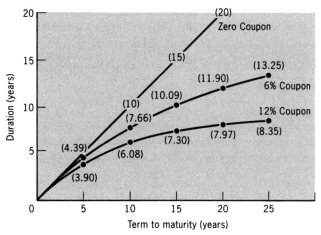

FIGURE 4-7 Duration and term to maturity for selected coupons.

Structural Changes in the Market

The structure of the stock market has changed dramatically in recent years. Originally, individual investors dominated trading activity and were the primary buyers of stocks. Beginning in the 1960s, institutional investors, such as mutual funds and pension funds, began to account for an increasing volume of trading activity. Today the biggest buyers of stocks are the corporations themselves. Mergers, share buyback programs, leveraged buyouts, and other forms of corporate restructuring absorbed $470 billion of stock between 1984 and 1989, almost one sixth of the total market value.[6]

Along the line of corporate restructuring, Michael Jensen wrote an article entitled "The Eclipse of The Public Corporation," which appeared in the *Harvard Business Review*.[7] He observed that publicly held corporations are being replaced by new organizations that have a corporate form but no public stockholders. Their owners are large institutions and entrepreneurs who hire managers to run the corporations on their behalf. They use public and private debt to acquire these organizations. The most obvious manifestation of this trend is the large volume of junk bonds that have been issued to finance leveraged buyouts and other forms of corporate restructuring.

The combination of institutional and corporate trading activity, as well as the increased use of derivative securities (options and futures contracts), has contributed to increased volatility of stock and bond prices during the post–World War II period. Nevertheless, stock prices are less volatile than they were in the 1930s when institutional trading and corporate restructuring were not factors in the market.[8] Stock prices always have been and probably always will be volatile. To paraphrase President Truman, investors who can't stand the "heat" of volatility should stay out of the market.

Globalization, or internationalization, which refers to the increased linkages among financial markets throughout the world, is another important change. The over-the-counter markets and organized exchanges are organizing communication links among international markets that allow trading to go on around the clock because of time differences around the world. For example, the GLOBEX commodity trading system links the Chicago Mercantile Exchange to European and Asian locations, and permits 24-hour trading of options and futures. The NASD is linked to the London and Singapore stock markets. The American, Boston, and Midwest stock exchanges are linked to Canadian stock exchanges.

---

[6] U.S. House of Representatives, *Corporate Finance Trends: 1989.* A Report prepared by the Congressional Research Service for the Subcommittee on Telecommunications and Finance of the Committee on Energy and Commerce, 101st Congress, 1st Session, October 1989, Committee Print 101-N, 7.

[7] Michael C. Jensen, "Eclipse of the Public Corporation," *Harvard Business Review*, September–October 1989, 61–74.

[8] Peter Fortune, "An Assessment of Financial Market Volatility: Bills, Bonds, and Stocks," *New England Economic Review*, Federal Reserve Bank of Boston, November/December 1989, 13–28, and Charles P. Jones and Jack W. Wilson, "Is Stock Price Volatility Increasing?" *Financial Analysts Journal*, November/December 1989, 20–26.

Linkages between other U.S. exchanges and foreign markets are being planned.[9]

The globalization trend is heightened by the television and print media, which keep us abreast of what is happening in financial markets around the world. By way of illustration, recent articles featured in *The Wall Street Journal*[10] and *The New York Times*[11] were "Wall Street is Placing Bets Tokyo's Market Will Fall," and "A Boom on Vienna's Bourse."

Globalization complicates the supervision and regulation of the securities markets by regulatory authorities in the countries involved. Rules that apply in the United States may not apply overseas and vice versa. For example, Westpac Banking Corporations (Australia) wanted to underwrite (sell) new stock issues in the United States.[12] Westpac argued that it was not a U.S. bank as defined in the Investment Company Act. Under our rules, domestic U.S. banks are not permitted to underwrite stocks. The Securities and Exchange Commission did not allow the foreign banks to underwrite stocks on that basis. However, the issue was not settled. Despite the difficulties of regulation and supervision, there has been dramatic growth in the issuance of Eurobonds and Euroequities. **Eurobonds** are debt securities issued multinationally through international syndicates of banks or securities firms in a currency other than that of the country in which the bond is issued. For example, bonds denominated in Japanese yen may be issued in France. Foreign bonds issued in the United States are called **Yankee securities.** **Euroequities** are common and preferred stocks distributed to investors in one or more markets outside the issuer's domestic market by a syndicate of international banks or securities firms.

Business Activity

The stock market is a barometer of business activity; it is one component of the Commerce Departments' Index of Leading Economic Indicators. To understand why this is so, consider the dividend valuation model that was presented in Chapter 2.

$$P_0 = \frac{D_1}{(k - g)}$$

---

[9] U.S. House of Representatives, *Globalization of Securities.* Hearing before the Subcommittee on Telecommunications and Finance of the Committee on Energy and Commerce, 100th Congress, 1st Session, August 5, 1987, Serial No. 100-72, and U.S. Securities and Exchange Commission, *Internationalization of the Securities Markets,* Report of the Staff of the U.S. Securities and Exchange Commission to the Senate Committee on Banking, Housing and Urban Affairs and the House Committee on Energy and Commerce, July 27, 1987.

[10] John R. Dorfman, "Wall Street is Placing Bets Tokyo's Market Will Fall," *The Wall Street Journal,* January 24, 1990, C1.

[11] Johnathan Fuerbringer, "A Boom on Vienna's Bourse," *The New York Times,* February 4, 1990, Section 3, 15.

[12] U.S. House of Representatives, Hearing, August 5, 1987, 118.

where

P_0 = price of the stock today
D_1 = dollar amount of cash dividend in period 1
g = growth rate of cash dividends
k = capitalization rate — the rate of return required by equity investors

When investors believe that business activity is doing well and firms are expected to increase their earnings and cash dividends, stock prices go up. Suppose that a firm currently pays a $1 dividend, that no change is expected in the dividend, and investors require a 10-percent rate of return. The stock is then worth $10 per share.

$$P_0 = \frac{\$1.00}{(0.10 - 0.00)} = \$10$$

Because business activity is increasing, the firm's management decides to increase and maintain the growth rate of cash dividends to 5 percent — an increase of $0.05 from the current cash dividend. Now the stock is worth $21 per share.

$$P_0 = \frac{\$1.05}{(0.10 - 0.05)} = \$21$$

Conversely, an expected slowdown in economic activity can result in lower earnings and reduced dividends for some companies. In either case, the dividend valuation model helps us understand the impact of expected business activities on stock prices and why stock prices reflect expected business activity.

Inflation

Many economists believe that inflation is a monetary phenomenon. A shortage of goods and strong demand can push prices up, but *sustained* price increases cannot continue without increases in the money supply. Inflation affects security prices adversely for several reasons. First, stock prices reflect the earning power of corporations. During periods of rising prices, after-tax profit figures reported by business concerns tend to be overstated for two reasons: (1) they include inventory profits and (2) depreciation is insufficient because it is based on original cost, not replacement cost. In addition, inflation contributes to the greater use of short-term debt, higher borrowing costs, and reduced liquidity, all of which increase the riskiness of companies. Inflation also leaves fewer funds available for dividends. It should also be noted that some companies benefit handsomely by borrowing during periods of inflation if their revenues outpace their rising costs.

Second, inflation affects the capitalization rate that investors use to discount corporate dividends or earnings to determine stock price. The capitalization rate reflects investors' attitudes toward risk and the return they can receive on alternative forms of investment. Because inflation and high levels of interest rates go hand in hand, the capitalization rate, which is in the denominator of the equation, will be high. For some of the reasons stated previously, dividends, which are in

BOX 4-1

HOW MUCH FINANCIAL RISK ARE YOU WILLING TO TAKE?

One of the most important concepts in finance is the trade-off between risk and expected returns. The extent to which you are willing to trade off risk against expected financial returns depends on your current and future income and expenses as well as your attitudes about risk. Let us explore your attitudes about risk. Answer each of the following questions by selecting a number between 1 and 5: 1 means definitely yes, 3 means maybe, and 5 means definitely not.

	Yes		Maybe		No
1. If you purchased a stock yesterday at $30 per share and today it is selling at $10 per share, would you be worried about the stock?	1	2	3	4	5
2. If you thought the stock was a good buy at $30 would you buy more stock at $10 per share?	1	2	3	4	5
3. Suppose you call your broker and she does not know what was happening, but she has heard rumors that the stock might go lower. Would you sell your stock?	1	2	3	4	5
4. You receive a telephone call from a Canadian broker telling you that silver prices are going to rise over the next six months and there is very little downside risk. He has given you detailed data to prove his point. Now he wants you to invest in silver futures contracts. Will you invest?	1	2	3	4	5
5. Your best friend knows the president of a large firm. Your friend has some "inside" information about a forthcoming acquisition by that firm. Will you buy stock in it?	1	2	3	4	5
Total	. . . .

Now add up all of the points from each of these questions. If your score is *less* than 15, you are willing to take large risks in hopes of making big gains. If your score is *more* than 15, you are averse to large risks. Of course, this exercise is not definitive, but it does provide some information about your attitudes toward risk.

the numerator of the equation, may grow at a slower pace than inflation. The result is lower equity security prices.[13]

For example, assume that a company currently pays a $1 dividend that is expected to grow at a rate of 5 percent, while investors require a 10-percent rate of return. The stock is then worth $21.

$$P_0 = \frac{\$1.05}{(0.10 - 0.05)} = \$21$$

If, as a result of inflation, investors require a 12-percent rate of return and the dividends still grow at 5 percent, the price of the stock will fall to $15.

$$P_0 = \frac{\$1.05}{(0.12 - 0.05)} = \$15$$

Finally, inflation creates "illusions" for some investors. They are led to believe that the relatively high returns they are receiving are "beating" inflation. For example, suppose an investor in the 40-percent income tax bracket is receiving a 15-percent return on a money market fund and the annual rate of inflation is 10 percent. The investor is losing 1 percent in real terms.

15%	Return on money market fund
− 6%	40-percent tax bracket
9%	Net to investor
−10%	Inflation
=− 1%	Loss

Investor Psychology

It is generally recognized that investor psychology plays a significant role in the price swings that take place in the stock market. The collective views of investors are reflected by the changing groups of stocks that are in fashion at any given time and by investors' reactions to domestic and international events. In some ways the stock market is analogous to women's fashions. One year purple is in vogue, and next year some other color ascends to the leading spot. Similarly, investors may consider computer and airline stocks to have the greatest profit potential one year, and oil and gold stocks to have the greatest potential the following years. Thus, the stock market is always changing as investors continuously search for new and profitable investments.

John Maynard Keynes summed up this aspect of investor psychology in the following statement:

> Professional investment may be likened to those newspaper competitions in which the competitors have to pick out the six prettiest faces from 100 photographs, the prize being awarded to the competitor whose choice most

---

[13] The same argument can be developed for bonds by using Equations 3-3 in Chapter 3. In this case, the current market rates of interest reflect investor-required rates of return.

nearly corresponds to the average preferences of the competitors as a whole. So, each competitor has to pick not those which he, himself thinks likeliest to catch the fancy of the other competitors, all of whom are looking at the problem from the same point of view. It is not a case of picking those who, to the best of one's judgement, are really the prettiest, or those which average opinion generally thinks the prettiest; we have reached the third degree where we devote our intelligence to anticipating what average opinion expects the average opinion to be. And there are some, I believe, who are practicing the fourth, fifth and higher degrees.[14]

The reactions of investors to news events are equally important. For example, when the President is going to make a speech in which major changes in economic policies are expected to be announced, investors may withhold buying because they are waiting for new information about the state of the economy, or they may sell early in anticipation of bad news.

Business Risk

The previous section examined market risk and some of the factors that influence it. This section examines business risk. In the narrow sense of the term, business risk refers to the possibility that a firm will fail. In a broader context, business risk includes a firm's being in distress, endangered, or otherwise limited in the scope of its activities. The discussion of business risk is divided into two parts: (1) failure and (2) government actions.

Failure

A firm's failing — bankruptcy or going out of business because of losses — is a terrible thing for stockholders and creditors because they may lose most or all of their investments. However, from society's point of view, the loss of some firms may be desirable. For example, the failure of some inefficient and uneconomical airlines paved the way for new firms to enter the market. Fortunately, failure is a relatively rare occurrence. In 1987, a recession year, only 107 of every 10,000 business concerns failed. Most of the firms that failed had liabilities of less than $100,000, and the largest number were engaged in retail trade.[15] Although relatively few firms fail, many more merge or sell out at distressed rates, which can also result in losses to stockholders.

Government Actions

Government policies and regulations affect business risk. The government grants monopolies to some business concerns and attempts to break up other concerns because they are monopolies. Public utilities, such as gas and electric companies,

---

[14] John Maynard Keynes, *The General Theory of Employment, Interest and Money,* New York: Harcourt Brace & World, 1936, 156.

[15] Data on active corporations and failures are summarized in U.S. Department of Commerce, *Statistical Abstract of the United States* (revised annually).

are given exclusive geographic areas. The usual line of reasoning used to justify such "natural" monopolies is that it is not economically feasible to have competing companies providing the same basic service because of the high fixed costs of operation. The result is a local monopoly.

Although local monopolies are tolerated, big monopolies are considered to be undesirable. The Antitrust Division of the U.S. Department of Justice filed suit against the world's biggest corporation—American Telephone & Telegraph Company. The company was accused of conspiring to monopolize local and long-distance telephone service, telecommunications services, and the manufacture of telecommunications equipment. The final outcome was the breakup of the Bell system. Antitrust suits have also been filed against General Motors, the Du Pont Company, IBM, and other large companies.

The judicial system decides the outcomes of antitrust suits. Once a case is decided, it can be reversed by a higher court. For example, a federal appeals court in Denver reversed a trial court decision that found IBM had violated certain provisions of the Sherman Anti-Trust Act, and the company did not have to pay $259.5 million in damages to Telex Corporation. Thus, the risk of antitrust actions involves both the executive branch of the government and the judicial system as well as the timing of the eventual settlement of litigation.

The government also regulates the rates charged by electric companies, the drugs that pharmaceutical companies can market, certain exports and imports, and so on. Every industry in the United States is influenced by government policies and regulations. In some cases the government shields companies from competition, and in other cases it encourages competition. An example of government action increasing competition occurred when the airlines were deregulated. The deregulation stimulated the growth of small "feeder" airlines.

Foreign governments can also intervene in business affairs. Companies with overseas operations are subject to the policies of foreign governments. In some cases, company assets have been nationalized by foreign governments. Anaconda Company, one of the world's largest producers of copper, had its interests in Chile nationalized. The company received $67 million in cash as a partial settlement and $188 in promissory notes. Aramco (Arabian-American Oil Company)—previously owned by Exxon Corporation, Texaco, Standard Oil Company of California, and Mobile Oil Corporation—was taken over by Saudi Arabia. Other countries, seeing the successes of the Arabs, may follow a similar pattern with their natural resources in an attempt to control their development without foreign ownership.

Purchasing Power Risk

Purchasing power risk applies largely to investments with fixed returns such as bonds, preferred stocks, and savings accounts. The risk is that the rate of inflation will erode the purchasing power of the fixed payments. Assume that a 20-year bond pays $100 interest each year and that the rate of inflation is 7 percent. For each year the bond is held, the purchasing power of the $100 interest payment is

worth 7 percent less than the previous year. By the end of the fifth year, the $100 will have a purchasing power of only $71.30. By the end of the tenth year, the purchasing power will have declined to $50.83. When the bond matures at the end of 20 years, the purchasing power of the $100 interest payment and the $1000 principal will be $25.84 and $258.40, respectively.

The previous illustration points out one of the major risks of holding securities with a fixed return. The purchasing power risk is compounded by the fact that during inflationary periods market interest rates generally rise and the market price of outstanding fixed payment securities, such as bonds, declines. Thus, investors have a loss in purchasing power and an unrealized loss in capital value, which would be realized if the security were sold before maturity.

Liquidity Risk

Liquidity risk is the risk that investors may not be able to convert their investments into cash without a significant loss in value. Liquidity risk differs from the other sources of risk because it does not affect any of the variables in the dividend valuation model. Nevertheless, it is a real risk faced by investors. During the stock market crash on October 19, 1987 ("**Black Monday**"), some investors found they were unable to sell their securities when over-the-counter market makers did not answer their telephones to take orders because they were overwhelmed. In addition, the relative spreads—the difference between the bid and asked prices—were much larger in the OTC market than on the New York Stock Exchange, indicating less liquidity in the OTC market than on the NYSE.[16]

Liquidity risk is not limited to securities. Investors in real estate, limited partnerships, art, and other investments face it too. Markets for many investments are "thin"—meaning very few market makers, or no market makers at times.

RETURNS

Many investors have dreamed of buying stocks and having the price quadruple in a few days' time or less. As mentioned in Chapter 1, Robert Scheller became an instant millionaire in 20 minutes with Genentech. Most investors can only savor such successes and hope that they, too, will find the mother lode.

What should the average investor expect to earn on securities? To answer that question, this section examines the realities of returns on common stocks and bonds.

The **total return** on a security includes both income and changes in price. In the case of stocks, the dividend income tends to be relatively stable whereas there are wide changes in the prices of stocks, which have the major impact on stock returns. In any given year the total return on the Standard & Poor's Composite Index, representing 500 common stocks with the largest market values in the

---

[16] Alison Leigh Cowan, "Crisis Pushes Nasdaq's Limits," *The New York Times,* October 30, 1987, Y27, Y34.

United States, may be up 53 percent (1954) or down 43 percent (1931), due primarily to changes in stock prices.

Figure 4-8 shows the returns and standard deviations for stocks and bonds. The geometric mean annual return is the rate of return compounded annually from 1926 to 1987, a 62-year period. The arithmetic mean return is the simple average of the series. The standard deviation measures the extent to which observations deviate from the arithmetic mean of the series. The figure shows that small-company stocks provided the highest returns (17.7 percent) and carried the most risk, as measured by the standard deviation (35.9 percent). This means that some made as much as 53.6 percent ($17.7 + 35.9 = 53.6$) or more, while others lost 18.2 percent or more ($17.7 - 35.9 = -18.2$). The average return on common stocks (S&P 500) is 12 percent, and the risk is less (21.1 percent).

The average returns on bonds are lower, about 5 percent, and are related to their maturities and the quality of the issuer. Long-term corporate bonds are riskier than government bonds of the same maturity and returned about 0.6 percent more. Similarly, longer- and intermediate-term government bonds yielded more than short-term Treasury bills.

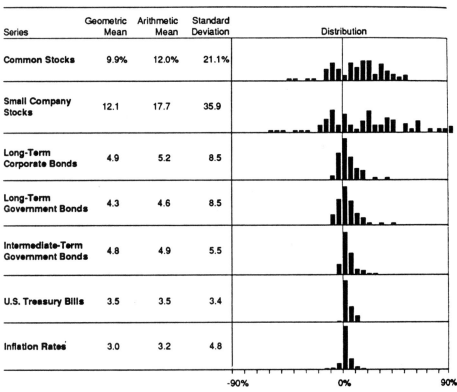

Series	Geometric Mean	Arithmetic Mean	Standard Deviation	Distribution
Common Stocks	9.9%	12.0%	21.1%	
Small Company Stocks	12.1	17.7	35.9	
Long-Term Corporate Bonds	4.9	5.2	8.5	
Long-Term Government Bonds	4.3	4.6	8.5	
Intermediate-Term Government Bonds	4.8	4.9	5.5	
U.S. Treasury Bills	3.5	3.5	3.4	
Inflation Rates	3.0	3.2	4.8	

-90%   0%   90%

FIGURE 4-8 Summary statistics of annual returns, 1926–1987. *Source:* Roger G. Ibbotson and Rex A. Sinquefield, *Stocks, Bonds, Bills, and Inflation: Historical Returns,* Homewood, Ill: Richard D. Irwin, Inc., 1989.

The average rate of inflation during the period covered was 3.2 percent. Subtracting the inflation rate from the returns gives us the returns adjusted for inflation, or the **real returns.** Thus, the real return of common stocks is about 9 percent, and the real return of Treasury bills is about 0.5 percent.

Collectively, Figure 4-8 illustrates the relationship between risk and return. The higher the risk, the higher the expected returns. Those who invested in small-company stocks earned the highest returns on average over the 62-year period, but they also had the highest risks. Investing in Treasury bills was the least risky and least rewarding investment strategy. If the past provides any useful information about the future, this pattern is likely to continue.

CONCLUSION

Investing in marketable securities is risky because there is a possibility of loss. Fluctuations in prices, inflation, and government policies contribute to the risk. However, the risk is not the same for every company. The stocks of steel companies are affected more by changes in business conditions than are the stocks of cigarette companies. Similarly, government policies may have a greater impact on the drug industry than on toy manufacturers. Even different types of securities have different degrees of risk. U.S. government bonds are considered safe, but they, too, are affected by rising interest rates. Nonmarketable securities, such as certificates of deposit, are affected by purchasing power risk. Every type of investment, including gold, real estate, artwork, and antiques, is subject to one kind of risk or another. There is no perfectly safe investment medium.

Common stocks are a relatively risky form of investment. However, they also offer potentially substantial rewards. Studies cited in this chapter found that common stocks provided higher returns than other forms of investment for which data were available. The returns were realized over long periods of time and not from trading on a day-to-day basis. Moreover, the returns varied widely from year to year. Commissions and income taxes can reduce short-term trading profits significantly.

Bonds are generally considered safer investments than common stocks. Nevertheless, the market price of bonds can fluctuate, and there may be some loss of purchasing power because of inflation. One of the major advantages of investing in bonds is that the current yield on bonds is generally higher than the current yield on common stocks. In November 1989, for example, yields on Aaa-rated corporate bonds were 8.89 percent, while dividend yields on common stock were 3.39 percent. Thus, some investors who were uncertain about the future direction of the stock market took temporary refuge in debt securities.

IMPORTANT CONCEPTS

Beta

Black Monday

Business risk

Eurobond

Euroequity

Globalization

Holding period returns (HPR)   Standard deviation
Interest rate risk   Systematic risk
Liquidity risk   Total return
Market risk   Total risk
Purchasing power risk   Unsystematic risk
Real return   Yankee securities
Residual risk   Yield to maturity

QUESTIONS AND EXERCISES

1. What does it mean when a stock has a beta of 1.5?
2. Alfaco pays a quarterly cash dividend of $0.75. The price of its stock is currently $66 per share, and it is expected to increase to $81 per share a year from now. What is the expected holding period return (HPR) on the stock for the next year? Interpret this.
3. Using data from the *Federal Reserve Bulletin, The Wall Street Journal,* or other sources, how do the holding period returns for the Standard and Poor's 500 Stock Index compare to the holding period return for AAA-rated corporate bonds?
4. Examine publications such as *Business Week* and *U.S. News* to determine the outlook for interest rates six months from now. What will the 90-day Treasury bill rate be then? Give an exact number, such as 10 percent. Given that rate, what will happen to stock prices?
5. Compare the volatility of Treasury bills to the volatility of AAA-rated bonds. Which is the more volatile?
6. To what extent will a labor strike at a major airline affect the betas of its stock?
7. Use Figure 4-5 to explain interest rate risk.
8. Explain how inflation affects stock prices.
9. Government policies and regulations affect business risk. Cite three industries in your area that are heavily regulated and three that are not regulated.
10. What is liquidity risk?
11. A broker calls you and tells you that hundreds of investors who have taken her advice have earned at least 30 percent annual return on their stock market investments year after year. She wants you to be one of her customers. Based on this information, would you deal with her? Explain.
12. What is the difference between systematic and unsystematic risk?
13. Define the term business risk. What is the ultimate business risk?
14. How does investor psychology affect the stock market?
15. What groups of stocks are the current stock market leaders (e.g., computers, oil, chemicals, airlines, etc.)? Do you think they will be the leaders next month?

APPENDIX 4A:
MEASURING RISK—THE STANDARD DEVIATION

In this chapter and elsewhere in the text, the standard deviation is used as a proxy for measuring the total risk of a security. This appendix explains how to calculate the standard deviation and explains what it means.

EXPECTED VALUE

Risk is measured by the deviation from an **expected value.** The following example will illustrate the use of the standard deviation to measure risk. Assume that a securities analyst was asked to estimate the holding period returns for Company X. After careful consideration of all the available facts, the analyst concluded that the HPRs for the company would range from 1.10 to 1.70.

In order to obtain greater accuracy, the analyst assigned the probabilities shown in Table 4A-1 to various HPRs. The analyst believed that the chances were 7 in 100 that the HPR for Company X would be 1.10. The chances were 15 in 100 that the HPR would be 1.30. In a similar way, the analyst estimated the likelihood (probability) of each of the HPRs' occurring. The probabilities are generally expressed as percentages and must total 100 percent, or unity (1.00).

The weighted average, or expected HPR, is obtained by multiplying the HPR by its respective probability.[17] The expected HPR for Company X is 1.40. The expected return is the most likely return that an investor can expect. In this case, an investor can expect a return of the original investment plus 40 percent (1.40).

Although the investor expects a 1.40 HPR, the chances are that he or she will not get exactly that amount. The actual return can deviate from the expected return for a variety of reasons. One reason is that the stock price did not increase as much as anticipated. The difference between the expected HPR and other possible returns can be measured by the standard deviation (σ), which acts as a proxy for risk.

STANDARD DEVIATION

The standard deviation can be calculated as shown in Table 4A-2. The expected HPR (1.40) is subtracted from each of the possible outcomes. These differences

---

[17] The following equation gives the expected HPR:

$$E_r = \sum_{i=1}^{n'} P_i r_i$$

where

E_r = expected return
P_i = probability associated with return i
r_i = possible return i
n' = number of observations from which $\sum_{i=1}^{n'} P_i = 1$

TABLE 4A-1   Calculating Expected Returns for Company X

(1) Holding Period Returns	(2) Probability	(3) (1) × (2)
1.00	0.00	0.000
1.10	0.07	0.077
1.20	0.10	0.120
1.30	0.15	0.195
1.40	0.36	0.504
1.50	0.15	0.225
1.60	0.10	0.160
1.70	0.07	Expected 0.119
	1.00	return = 1.400

are squared (multiplied by themselves) to eliminate the negative (−) numbers. Next, the squared differences are multiplied by their respective probability. Recall that all the outcomes do not have an equal chance (probability) of occurring. The last step—adding the weighted values in column 4 of Table 4A-2—provides a weighted average of the squared deviations (0.0236). This weighted average is called variance, which is a measure of dispersion.[18] The standard deviation is the square root of the variance.

In this example, the standard deviation is approximately 0.15. One standard deviation from the expected return indicates that the HPR could range from 1.25 to 1.55 (1.40 ± 0.15).

The chances that the actual HPR will lie within one standard deviation from the expected HPR are 68 in 100. The chances that the actual return will lie within two standard deviations from the expected HPR are 95 in 100.

Numbers, tables, and statistics are confusing to some people, so let us look at the same information in graphic form. Figure 4A-1 shows a normal probability function or curve. The area under the curve represents 100 percent of all possible HPRs for Company X. The expected HPR of 1.40 is in the middle. We know that one standard deviation represents 34 percent of the area under that curve. In this

---

[18] The following equations give the variance and the standard deviation:

$$V = \sum_{i=1}^{n'} P_i(r_i - E_r)^2$$

where

V = variance
P = probability of event i occurring
r = possible returns
E_r = expected returns
$\sigma = \sqrt{V}$

TABLE 4A-2   Calculating the Standard Deviation for Company X

(1) Difference: HPR − Expected HPR	(2) Difference Squared: $(1)^2$	(3) Probability	(4) Weighted Value: $(2) \times (3)$
$1.10 - 1.40 = -0.30$	0.09	0.07	0.0063
$1.20 - 1.40 = -0.20$	0.04	0.10	0.0040
$1.30 - 1.40 = -0.10$	0.01	0.15	0.0015
$1.40 - 1.40 = \ \ \ 0.00$	0.00	0.36	0.0000
$1.50 - 1.40 = +0.10$	0.01	0.15	0.0015
$1.60 - 1.40 = +0.20$	0.04	0.10	0.0040
$1.70 - 1.40 = +0.30$	0.09	0.07	0.0063
		1.00	0.0236

$$\text{Variance} = 0.0236$$
$$\text{Standard deviation} = \sqrt{\text{Variance}} = 0.1536$$

case, one standard deviation is 0.15, and if we *subtract* that from 1.40, we get 1.25. In other words, 1.25 is one standard deviation less than the expected HPR. This means that the chances are 34 in 100 (34 percent) that the actual HPR will be between 1.25 and 1.40.

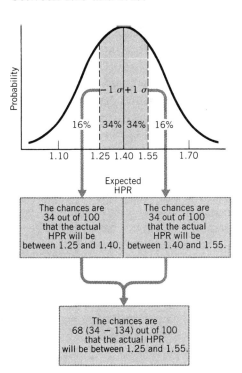

FIGURE 4A-1   Probability function for Company X.

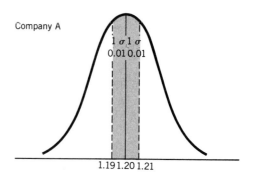

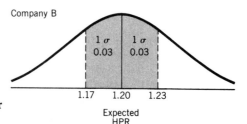

FIGURE 4A-2 Standard deviations for Companies A and B.

Now we do the same thing by *adding* one standard deviation to the expected HPR to get 1.55 (1.40 + 0.15 = 1.55). Once again, the chances are 34 in 100 that the actual return will fall between 1.40 and 1.55.

When we consider one standard deviation on either side of the expected HPR, we can say that the chances are 68 in 100 that the actual return will fall between 1.25 and 1.55. Does that mean that the actual return will fall between those two numbers? No. But it does mean that there is a 68 percent chance that it will happen.

Information about standard deviations can be used to compare the relative risk of different securities. Consider the two distributions shown in Figure 4A-2. Both Company A and Company B have the same expected HPR of 1.20. However, Company A has a standard deviation of 0.01 while Company B has a standard deviation of 0.03. Therefore, Company B has a greater degree of risk than Company A.

PART TWO

THE SECURITIES BUSINESS

Mechanics of Investing
Examines How the Securities Markets Function

The next four chapters focus on the major participants in the securities business and the rules under which they operate. A thorough understanding of how to buy and sell securities and the rules of the game are essential before investing. Otherwise, investing would be like playing poker and not knowing the difference between a flush and a straight.

Chapter 5 looks at the role of investment bankers, the firms that bring the buyers and sellers of new security issues together. Different types of stockbrokerage firms are also examined, as are the principal laws affecting the buying and selling of securities.

Chapter 6 explains what you should know when you deal with a stockbroker. How to select a stockbroker, buying securities on margin, and investment advice are a few of the topics covered. Chapter 7 describes the operations of the New York Stock Exchange and demonstrates the mechanics of trading securities. Here you will learn about different types of orders, such as short sales, that you can use to your advantage. Finally, Chapter 8 explains how to interpret various stock and bond market indicators, such as the Dow Jones Averages.

HOW THE SECURITIES BUSINESS WORKS

I n the broadest sense of the term, the securities business includes those organizations that raise funds by selling securities such as stocks and bonds, the investors who buy those securities, and the firms that bring the two groups together. This chapter focuses mainly on the firms that bring the buyers and sellers of funds together and the regulations that govern them.

AN OVERVIEW OF THE SECURITIES MARKETS

The securities markets, depicted in Figure 5-1, are divided into the **primary market** and the **secondary market.** A primary market is analogous to a new car dealer and the secondary market to a used-car dealer. The new- and used-car markets are closely interrelated, and the same dealer generally handles both types of cars. Many people buy new cars, hold onto them for a few years, and then sell them or trade them in for a new car. The existence of a used-car market encourages people to buy new cars because they know that they can get rid of them if

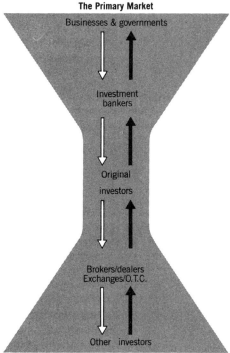

The Primary Market

FIGURE 5-1   The securities market.

they wish to do so. Some individuals would be reluctant to buy new cars if they had to keep them until they fell apart.

A similar situation exists in the securities markets. Business concerns and governments sell securities to investors through **investment bankers** (the new securities dealers), or underwriters, as they are sometimes called. Most investment bankers are part of stockbrokerage and securities firms that deal in the secondary market (existing securities). The leading investment banking firms include the largest stockbrokerage firms in the United States, such as Merrill Lynch, Pierce, Fenner & Smith; Salomon Brothers, Inc.; and the First Boston Corporation.

The significance of the secondary market is that it permits short-term investors to provide long-term capital to business and government. Short-term investors are willing to buy long-term stocks and bonds because the securities can be sold on short notice. Philadelphia Electric Company originally sold 500,000 shares of preferred stock to investors. Some investors may want to hold the shares for years, while others may want to sell them within days because they need the funds for other purposes. In either case, Philadelphia Electric and other companies would find it difficult and costly to sell long-term debt securities if investors had to hold debt securities until they matured and equity securities forever.

The secondary market also provides **marketability** and **liquidity** for invest-

ments. Marketability means that investors can sell their securities. Liquidity means that investors can sell their securities on short notice with little or no loss from current values. Without the existence of marketability and liquidity, investors would require higher returns because of the increased risk of holding securities and the inconvenience of not being able to sell them. More will be said about the secondary market shortly.

THE ROLE OF INVESTMENT BANKERS

Investment bankers play an important role in our economy. They bring organizations that need capital together with those that have funds to invest. In this way they help to allocate financial resources where they are needed, and, by assisting companies to raise capital, they are helping the economy grow. The principal functions of investment bankers, assisting borrowers and underwriting securities, are explained next.

Assisting Borrowers

Business concerns that need long-term financing sometimes seek advice from investment bankers, who are in constant contact with the securities markets and know how and when to sell different types of security issues. For example, assume that a corporation wants to issue additional bonds. The investment banker may advise the corporation that first mortgage bonds with five-year call protection would be better received by the market than debentures with seven-year protection.

Timing

Timing is also important. If the bond calendar (the dollar volume of new issues being offered) is heavy for, say, June, the investment banker may suggest another month when the supply of new bond issues is more conducive to the sale of the corporation's bonds. Also, the demand for bonds must be considered. For example, individual investors may be less willing to invest in bonds just before income tax payment dates than at other times.

Timing is equally important for stocks. Investors are more receptive to new issues when the stock market is soaring and stock values are appreciating than when stock prices are plunging to untested depths.

Pricing

Investment bankers also give advice on **pricing new issues** (the price or interest rate at which they are sold to investors). Suppose that a stock has an intrinsic value of $40 per share. In order to make the new issue attractive to investors, the investment banker suggests selling it to them at $36 per share. By pricing the stock so that it is **undervalued** (it is worth more than the current market price), inves-

tors will want to buy the new stock because they believe that the price will increase as soon as it is issued. On the other hand, if the investment banker priced the stock too low, it would alienate the issuer. Therefore, the stock must be priced to be fair to both the seller and the buyer. Correct pricing creates a demand for the stock, which reduces the investment banker's risk and ensures that the company will receive the capital it needs. The risk is reduced because investors' strong demand for the stock will ensure that the entire issue will be sold, and the investment banker will not have to hold the new shares longer than necessary.

By suggesting the type of security to issue, the timing, and the pricing, investment bankers help organizations obtain long-term funds at the lowest possible cost. They also provide similar services for organizations that sell short-term securities such as commercial paper.

Underwriting Securities

Investment bankers **underwrite** securities by buying a new issue from a corporation and selling the securities to investors. The investment banker makes money by buying the securities at one price and selling them to investors at a higher price. Their fees range from less than 1 percent to more than 10 percent, depending on the size of the issue, their efforts, and the degree of risk involved. In general, it costs relatively more to underwrite a small issue than a large one. The reason is that one must do about the same amount of work for each. For example, registration statements have to be filed with the **Securities and Exchange Commission (SEC).**

Prospectus

Before large issues of a new security can be sold to investors through the mail or the channels of interstate commerce, the **Securities Act of 1933** requires that the issuing company must register with the Securities and Exchange Commission and provide prospective investors with a **prospectus.** Some of the basic information that a prospectus must contain is:

1. Price to public, commissions and discounts to underwriters, and proceeds to issuer
2. Names of underwriters and amounts underwritten
3. Use of proceeds to registrant
4. Sales other than for cash
5. Capital structure
6. Financial statements
7. Organizational form of registrant (e.g., corporation) and name of state or jurisdiction in which organized
8. List of controlling interests of the registrant
9. Description of business

10. Description of property
11. History of organization if less than five years old
12. Pending legal proceedings
13. Description of the type of security being registered and provisions pertinent to investors
14. List of directors and executive officers and their remuneration
15. Information about options to purchase securities from the registrant or its subsidiaries
16. Principal holders of the type of securities being issued.
17. Interests of management and others in certain transactions

Many companies issue a preliminary prospectus to investors so that they may become acquainted with most of the details of the security offering. A preliminary prospectus is also known as a *red herring;* it is incomplete and contains some statements on the front page printed in red ink (see Figure 5-2).

Underwriting

There are four common ways that new securities can be distributed, but underwriting is the most common. When this method is used, one or more investment banks guarantee the success of the new issue by buying all the securities from the issuer and reselling them to the public. The group of firms that buys the securities is known as a *syndicate,* and the originating investment banker is the *syndicate manager.* Each firm agrees to buy a stipulated amount of the new issue. The syndicate's profit is the difference between the price it paid the issuer and the price at which it sells the securities to the public. If the price of the security declines during the offering period, the underwriter may lose money.

Best Efforts

The second method protects investment bankers from such losses. They agree to use their **best efforts** to sell the securities, but they do not guarantee success by buying the entire issue. This method shifts the risk from the investment banker to the issuing company.

Stand-By Underwriting

The third method, a compromise between the other two methods, is called **stand-by underwriting.** It is most widely used when an established corporation wants to sell additional securities to existing security holders, and the underwriter agrees to buy the unsold portion of the issue. For example, the underwriter may subscribe to whatever rights are not exercised in a rights offering to security holders. The underwriter will exercise the rights, buy the new securities, then sell them to the public.

PROSPECTUS

SUBJECT TO COMPLETION, DATED AUGUST 23, 1989

$1,000,000,000

Motorola, Inc.

Liquid Yield Option™ Notes due 2009
(Zero Coupon-Subordinated)

The Issue Price of each Liquid Yield Option™ Note ("LYON"™) will be $306.56 (30.656% of principal amount at maturity) and there will be no periodic payments of interest. The LYONs will mature on September   , 2009. The Issue Price of each LYON represents a yield to maturity of 6.00% per annum (computed on a semi-annual bond equivalent basis) calculated from September   , 1989. The LYONs will be subordinated to all existing and future Senior Indebtedness of the Company. As of July 1, 1989, the Company had approximately $1,625 million of consolidated indebtedness outstanding (excluding accrued interest thereon), which would have constituted either Senior Indebtedness or indebtedness of subsidiaries of Motorola, Inc. to which the LYONs are effectively subordinated. See "Capitalization" and "Description of LYONs-Subordination of LYONs."

Each LYON will be convertible at the option of the Holder at any time on or prior to maturity, unless previously redeemed or otherwise purchased, into common stock, par value $3 per share, of the Company (the "Common Stock") at the Conversion Rate of   shares per LYON. The Conversion Rate will not be adjusted for accrued Original Issue Discount but will be subject to adjustment upon the occurrence of certain events affecting the Common Stock. Upon conversion, the Holder will not receive any cash payment representing accrued Original Issue Discount; such accrued Original Issue Discount will be deemed paid by the Common Stock received on conversion. See "Description of LYONs-Conversion Rights." On August 22, 1989, the last reported sale price of the Common Stock on the New York Stock Exchange Composite Tape was $56⅛ per share.

LYONs will be purchased by the Company at the option of Holders on September   , 1994, September   , 1999 and September   , 2004 at Purchase Prices equal to the Issue Price plus accrued Original Issue Discount to such dates. The Company, at its option, may elect to pay any of such Purchase Prices in cash, shares of Common Stock or Ten-Year Subordinated Extension Notes of the Company. See "Description of LYONs-Purchase of LYONs at the Option of the Holder." In addition, 35 business days after the occurrence of any Change in Control of the Company occurring on or prior to September   , 1994, each LYON will be purchased at the option of the Holder by the Company for a Change in Control Purchase Price, in cash, equal to the Issue Price plus accrued Original Issue Discount to the date set for such purchase. The Change in Control purchase feature of the LYONs may in certain circumstances have an anti-takeover effect. See "Description of LYONs-Change in Control Permits Purchase of LYONs at the Option of the Holder."

Prior to September   , 1991, the LYONs are not redeemable unless the closing sale price of the Common Stock equals or exceeds $ per share (as adjusted upon the occurrence of certain events) for at least 20 trading days within 30 consecutive trading days ending not more than five trading days prior to notice of redemption. Subject to the foregoing, the LYONs are redeemable at the option of the Company at Redemption Prices equal to the Issue Price plus accrued Original Issue Discount to the date of redemption. See "Description of LYONs-Redemption of LYONs at the Option of the Company."

For a discussion of certain Federal income tax consequences to Holders of LYONs, see "Certain Tax Aspects."

Application will be made to list the LYONs on the New York Stock Exchange.

THESE SECURITIES HAVE NOT BEEN APPROVED OR DISAPPROVED BY THE SECURITIES AND EXCHANGE COMMISSION NOR HAS THE COMMISSION PASSED UPON THE ACCURACY OR ADEQUACY OF THIS PROSPECTUS. ANY REPRESENTATION TO THE CONTRARY IS A CRIMINAL OFFENSE.

	Principal Amount at Maturity	Price to Public	Underwriting Discount	Proceeds to Company(1)
Per LYON	100%	30.656%	%	%
Total (2)	$1,000,000,000	$306,560,000	$	$

(1) Before deducting expenses payable by the Company estimated at $

(2) The Company has granted the Underwriter an option, exercisable within 30 days after the date of this Prospectus, to purchase up to an additional $150,000,000 aggregate principal amount at maturity of LYONs on the same terms and subject to the same conditions as set forth above to cover over-allotments, if any. If the option is exercised in full, the total Principal Amount at Maturity, Price to Public, Underwriting Discount and Proceeds to Company will be $1,150,000,000, $352,544,000, $, and $, respectively. See "Underwriting."

The LYONs are offered by the Underwriter, subject to prior sale, when, as and if delivered to and accepted by the Underwriter, and subject to certain other conditions. The Underwriter reserves the right to withdraw, cancel or modify such offer and to reject orders in whole or in part. It is expected that delivery of the LYONs will be made in New York, New York on or about September   , 1989.

™ Trademark of Merrill Lynch & Co., Inc.

Merrill Lynch Capital Markets

The date of this Prospectus is September   , 1989.

FIGURE 5-2 Prospectus offered for Motorola.

Privately Placed

Finally, some companies sell their securities directly to financial institutions, such as insurance companies. In 1989, 36 percent of the corporate bond offerings were handled in this manner. Investment bankers who arrange such deals are paid a fee for their services.

Existing securities are also handled by investment bankers. The term **secondary distribution** refers to the sale of extremely large blocks of existing securities. For example, suppose a stockholder wanted to sell 2 million shares of McDonald's Corporation. If the stock were sold in the ordinary way, the price might be driven down owing to the large number of shares being offered. In a secondary distribution, the entire block is offered at a reduced price in order to induce investors to buy the stock.

CORPORATE SECURITIES OFFERINGS

Issuers

The data presented in Table 5-1 reveals that $376.2 billion of new corporate stocks and bonds were issued in 1989. Stocks accounted for about 15 percent of the total and bonds for the remainder. Real estate and finance companies were the largest issuers of both stocks and bonds. Manufacturing concerns were the next largest issuers.

Institutional Trading

Financial institutions, such as mutual funds, account for well over half of the trading volume of the New York Stock Exchange. The growth of block transactions is evidence of the trading activity, since these institutions buy and sell in large volume. A **block transaction** is a transaction involving 10,000 shares or more. In 1965 there were 2171 block transactions accounting for 3.1 percent of

TABLE 5-1 New Corporate Securities Offerings, 1989 ($ Billions)

Industry Group	Stocks	Bonds
Manufacturing	$9.3	$76.3
Commercial and miscellaneous	7.4	49.3
Transportation	1.9	10.0
Public utilities	3.1	17.1
Communications	1.9	8.5
Real estate and financial	34.0	157.4
	$57.6 +	$318.6 = $376.2

Source: Federal Reserve Bulletin, November 1990

the NYSE's reported volume. In 1988 there were 768,419 block transactions accounting for 54.5 percent of the reported volume.

Financial institutions make extensive use of program trading to facilitate the rapid execution of orders and to take advantage of differences between the prices of securities in stock and futures markets. There are four types of program trading.[1] The first type involves the New York Stock Exchange automated stock routing system, called SuperDot, that links institutions via computers to the appropriate individuals on the floor of the exchange to trade their stocks. Super-Dot is the acronym for Super Designated Order Turnaround, which is discussed further in Chapter 7. The NYSE defines *program trading* as "the simultaneous placement of buy or sell orders of at least 15 different stocks valued at more than $1 million."

The second type of program trading is called **portfolio insurance** or **dynamic asset allocation** and involves the use of stocks and stock index futures. Stock index futures are futures contracts on a stock index such as the Standard and Poor's 500 Stock Index (S&P 500). The futures contracts *obligate* their owners to buy or sell a commodity at a predetermined price on a specific date. The commodity — the S&P 500 futures contract — is a portfolio of stocks represented by the price index. Investors and speculators trade the futures contracts instead of dealing in the underlying stock issues. Some institutions sell stock index futures when the stock market declines instead of selling the underlying stocks. In other words, they hedge the decline in stocks by selling the futures contracts. They do this because it is faster and cheaper to sell futures contracts for 5000 shares than it is to sell 5000 shares. Managers who tried this strategy during the market decline in October 1987 found it wanting. It didn't work; therefore this technique is no longer widely used.

The third type is known as **tactical asset allocation.** It involves stocks, bonds, and cash equivalents. Portfolios of stocks are bought when they are "undervalued" according to some predetermined valuation formula and sold when they are overvalued. It also uses stock futures and bonds to augment the portfolios. The stocks are commonly traded on the NYSE SuperDot system.

The final type of program trading is called **index arbitrage.** It attempts to take advantage of the differences between the price of stock index futures and the price of the securities represented by them. Computers monitor the price of the stocks underlying the indexes. When the stock values exceed the value of the index, computers automatically sell stocks represented by the index and buy futures contracts or options. When the stock values are less than the index, computers automatically buy stocks and sell futures contracts or options. The simultaneous purchase and sale of essentially the same commodity — the futures contracts or options on the stocks and the underlying stocks — at different prices is called **arbitrage.** Since the value of the underlying stocks may be $50 million or more, such trades are normally done by financial institutions, such as pension

[1] "The Realities of Program Trading," *Market Perspectives,* Chicago Mercantile Exchange, January/February 1990.

funds, which control such wealth. The arbitrage can be done at a very low cost because the pension funds pay no taxes on the trades and their commission cost is as low as $0.30 per $1000 of transaction. In contrast, individuals pay taxes on trades and their commission may be 1 percent or more.

In program trading, computers are used to facilitate transactions by reducing the length of time necessary to make decisions and to execute orders. Program trading could exist without computers, but it would be cumbersome and time-consuming to execute orders.

Black Monday

Portfolio insurance is supposed to protect institutions from sharp declines in stock prices. However, on Black Monday—the day the market crashed in 1987—portfolio insurance exacerbated the 508-point decline in the Dow Jones Industrial Average. When institutions sold futures contracts, the prices of the futures contracts were driven below the values of the underlying stocks. The program-trading computers, sensing the gap in prices, instructed fund managers to sell stocks and buy futures.

Since stocks were declining faster, the institutions sold more futures contracts to protect their portfolios, but the sales drove the prices of the futures contracts lower due to the selling pressure. Once again the program-trading computers picked up the disparity between the prices of the contracts and the prices of the underlying securities, and instructed fund managers to sell stocks and buy futures contracts. Thus arbitrageurs doing program trading and institutions using portfolio insurance contributed significantly to the crash on Black Monday.

THE STOCKBROKERAGE INDUSTRY

There are more than 6000 brokers and dealers doing business in the United States. Not all of these firms deal in corporate securities. Some deal only in government issues, bonds, real estate ventures, or other specialized investments.

Brokers and dealers can be classified by their membership on various stock exchanges and by the types of services they offer.

Membership on Stock Exchanges

Member Firms

Some brokers and dealers are members of a stock exchange such as the New York Stock Exchange. As such, they are able to buy and sell securities on that exchange. The NYSE, the nation's largest stock exchange, has limited membership; as of 1988 there were 555 member firms, of which only 363 do business with the public. The remainder deal with other brokers and institutions.

In order for a firm to be a member of the NYSE it must meet the rules of the

exchange and acquire a seat.[2] Membership, commonly called a **seat,** can be traded with the approval of the Board of Directors of the exchange. The price of a seat ranged from a low of $17,000 in 1942 to a high of $1,150,000 in 1987. The price was $820,000 in 1988.

Once the firm is a member (a **member firm**), it must meet certain financial requirements and standards. For example, each member doing business with the public is required to have a fidelity bond to protect its clients against fraudulent trading practices and other problems that may arise. In addition, each member doing business with the public is required to have a minimum amount of net capital (assets less liabilities) to further protect its customers. Not all member firms deal with the public; some deal with other brokers, dealers, and financial institutions.

Nonmember Firms

Nonmember firms are those that are not members of a stock exchange, and they deal mainly in over-the-counter securities. To handle their trading activity on a particular stock exchange, they engage the services of a **correspondent firm.** Correspondent firms are members of the principal stock exchanges and, for a fee, they provide services for nonmember firms, including execution of orders, research, safekeeping of securities, and so forth. Correspondent firms are commonly large firms that do retail business as well.

Services Provided

Full Service, Full Commission

The largest firms are members of the principal stock exchanges, with branch offices throughout the country and often around the world. Merrill Lynch, Pierce, Fenner & Smith is perhaps the largest brokerage firm in the United States. It has more than 400 offices and more than 11,000 account executives (salespersons). E. F. Hutton, Prudential-Bache, and Paine Webber are some of the other large firms.

Merrill Lynch, and some of the other large firms, have diversified into financial services, offering residential brokerage, mortgage banking, and insurance. Nevertheless, they are known mostly for their **retail** securities business — dealing mainly with individual investors. They also engage in **wholesale** activities — dealing with financial institutions. Salomon Brothers and First Boston are examples of wholesale brokers. As full-service firms, they offer their clients a variety of services such as research on selected securities, new stock issues, investment advice, and trading on foreign exchanges. They frequently charge higher commissions than discount brokers to cover the costs of offering full service.

---

[2] For additional information on the requirements for membership, see Rule 325 in the New York Stock Exchange's *Constitution and Rules, April 30, 1987.* Chicago: Commerce Clearing House, 1987.

TABLE 5-2 Typical Discount Commission Schedule for Stocks and Warrants Traded in the United States[a]

Dollar Range per Transaction	Commission Rates
$0–$2,500	$19 + 1.6% of principal amount
$2501–$6000	$44 + 0.6
$6001–$22,000	$62 + 0.3
$22,001–$50,000	$84 + 0.2
$50,001–$500,000	$134 + 0.1
$500,001 or more	$234 + 0.08

[a] The minimum commission per stock transaction is $34.00. The maximum is $49.00 for the first 100 shares, plus $0.45 per share thereafter. This schedule applies to stocks selling for $1 or more.

Discount Brokers

Discount brokers, such as Charles Schwab, StockCross, and Quick & Reilly, execute orders but do not provide the wide range of costly services offered by full-service, full-commission firms. Commission rates for different types of securities (stocks, bonds, mutual funds, options) and minimum charges vary widely among firms. The cost at a discount broker may be higher than the cost at a full-service, full-commission firm on some transactions. An example of a commission schedule for a discount broker is listed in Table 5-2. A comparison of full versus discount commission is shown in Table 5-3.

Some discount brokers provide more services than others and may charge commensurately higher commissions, but they are still lower than those charged by full-service firms. For example, Charles Schwab offers mutual funds, a computer service to make cash transfers from your checking or savings account into you account at Schwab, and other investment-related services, some of which have fees. A comparison of Schwab's commissions with those of other discount brokers reveals that they are lower on some transactions and higher on others.[3]

	StockCross	Schwab	Quick & Reilly
100 shares @ $35	$34	$ 49	$ 38
500 shares @ $35	68	121	130

Between the large-size firms and the discount brokers, there are thousands of small- and medium-size firms that compete for retail and wholesale business.

[3] *The Wall Street Journal,* January 26, 1990, C2.

TABLE 5-3   Comparison of Typical Commission Costs

Shares per Order	Price per Share	Full Commission	Discount Commission
100	$60	$ 98.00	$ 49.00
500	15	181.00	96.50
3000	25	879.25	209.00

Some of these firms have their own research departments, underwrite securities, and provide other services. Investors must decide what level of service they want, which firms can deliver the service desired, and how much they are willing to pay for it.

REGULATION OF THE SECURITIES INDUSTRY

During World War I, millions of Americans made their first investment by buying government bonds to support the war effort. This experience set the stage for other investors to put their savings into stocks and bonds in the years to come. In the late 1920s, investment in securities had become rampant. In August 1929, the *Ladies' Home Journal* published an article entitled "Everybody Ought to Be Rich." The article explained that an investment of $15 a week in good common stocks would grow to $80,000 in 20 years. Stocks could be bought on **margin** (credit), which made them more attractive, since investors would only have to put down one quarter or less of the value of the stock. It was truly the golden age of the stock market — at least until stock prices began to decline in September 1929. Between September 3 and November 13, stock prices dropped drastically from their spectacular highs. The price of American Telephone & Telegraph stock went from $304 to $197 a share, and General Electric went from $396 to $168. Thousands of people were ruined financially by the Great Crash.

The fraudulent activities and other excesses that developed during this period led to the passage of legislation to protect investors. The principal laws affecting investors are reviewed in the following sections.

Securities Act of 1933

The purpose of the **Securities Act of 1933** is to provide for full and fair disclosure of the character of new securities sold in interstate commerce and to prevent fraud in their sale. The Act covers (1) registration of securities with the Securities and Exchange Commission, (2) unlawful representation, (3) requirements for prospectuses, and (4) penalties and liabilities for false registration statements and false statements in communications and prospectuses. The penalties include fines and imprisonment.

Investors should recognize that registration of securities does *not* mean that the Securities and Exchange Commission endorses the investment merits of the secu-

---

BOX 5-1

ILLEGAL PRACTICES OF PROMOTERS, UNDER-WRITERS, AND BROKER–DEALERS

Government regulations prohibit promoters, underwriters, and broker–dealers from certain illegal practices that are used in the new issue market. Some of these practices are

1. Stimulating the preoffer publicity to condition the market for an offering.

2. Holding back a portion of an offering to increase its scarcity value and sell the shares at a higher price in the after-issue market.

3. Manipulating the price or volume of transactions to stimulate interest in the stock.

4. Requiring investors who want to buy new issues to agree to buy additional shares at higher prices in the after-market, purchase shares of other promotional offerings, or not sell their shares.

5. Violating the customer suitability (e.g., selling speculative stocks to investors who need preservation of capital), funds segregation (mixing investors' funds with those of others in an improper fashion), escrow, net capital (the minimum amount of capital a firm must have to satisfy regulations), and other requirements.

Source: Based on the written statement of John Shad and John Fedders, Securities and Exchange Commission Hearings on Fraud and Abuse in the "Hot Issues" and "Penny Stock" Markets, to the Subcommittee on Securities of the Senate Committee on Banking, Housing and Urban Affairs, 98th Congress, 1st Session, December 15, 1983.

---

rity. It does mean that the company has provided the information called for by the Act.

Certain types of securities are exempted from registration. They include government securities, commercial paper, and other short-term securities that mature in nine months or less, certain securities issued by banks and common carriers, and security offerings of less than $500,000.

The Act requires that investors be given a prospectus telling them some facts they need to know about the company in order to make informed investment decisions. The contents of a prospectus were discussed previously in this chapter.

Securities Exchange Act of 1934

The 1933 Act is concerned primarily with the initial distribution of securities, and the **1934 Exchange Act** deals with trading outstanding securities. The Exchange Act regulates the securities exchanges and OTC markets operating in interstate

commerce. It also restricts the amount of credit (margin) used in the nation's securities markets and provides remedies for fraud and manipulation of these markets. The principal sections of the Exchange Act are presented here.

Securities and Exchange Commission

The Exchange Act created the Securities and Exchange Commission, which consists of five members appointed by the President for a five-year term. The commission and its staff are responsible for enforcing federal securities laws.

The SEC has several divisions that carry out its many activities. The Market Regulation Division is responsible for securities markets, broker–dealers, and the **National Association of Securities Dealers.** The Investment Management Regulation Division oversees investment companies and advisors, and the Corporate Regulation Division supervises public utility holding companies, bankruptcies, and reorganizations. Financial reports are handled by the Division of Corporation Finance, and enforcement is handled by the Division of Enforcement.

Exchanges

Securities exchanges operating in interstate commerce and through the mails were also brought under the purview of the Exchange Act. As of 1989, 9 securities exchanges were registered with the commission:

American Stock Exchange

Boston Stock Exchange

Chicago Board Options Exchange

Cincinnati Stock Exchange

Midwest Stock Exchange

New York Stock Exchange

Pacific Stock Exchange

Philadelphia Stock Exchange

Spokane Stock Exchange

Margin Requirements

The Exchange Act gave the Board of Governors of the Federal Reserve System the right to limit the amount of credit that may be extended on securities as collateral by prescribing a maximum loan value. The Federal Reserve System manages the nation's money supply and also supervises the regulation of margin credit. The margin requirements are expressed as a percentage of the market value of the collateral at the time the credit is extended. Effective January 3, 1974, brokers and dealers (Regulation T), banks (Regulation U), and other lenders (Regulation G) could grant a 50-percent margin on stocks, convertible bonds, and short sales. Thus, an investor buying $10,000 worth of marginable stock (e.g., 100 shares

selling at $100 per share) would have to deposit only $5000. The remainder would be lent by a broker or bank.

Securities listed on registered stock exchanges and certain OTC stocks, as determined by the Federal Reserve, are eligible for margin.

Registration

Securities traded on registered stock exchanges, as well as many of those traded in the over-the-counter market, must be registered with the Securities and Exchange Commission. To register a security, a company must provide the SEC with the following information:

1. Organization, financial structure, and nature of business
2. Terms, position, rights, and privileges of the different classes of securities that are outstanding
3. The terms on which the securities are to be offered to investors, including offerings during the preceding three years
4. A list of directors, officers, underwriters, and stock owners holding 10 percent or more of any equity issues; their remuneration; and their interest in the security
5. Remuneration to key officers
6. Bonus and profit-sharing arrangements
7. Management and service contracts
8. Options
9. Balance sheets and income statements for not more than the three preceding fiscal years, certified by independent public accountants if required by the commission

In addition to this information, the company must file periodic reports with the Securities and Exchange Commission. The annual report form (Form 10-K) updates the information covered in the original filing. It is the centerpiece for corporate disclosures, encompassing both new offerings and continuous reporting requirements. Semiannual financial reports (Form 9-K) and reports concerning matters of important and immediate interest to stockholders must also be filed (Form 8-K).

Manipulation

The Exchange Act prohibits any person from manipulating the prices of securities in any form. The following **manipulation** techniques are specifically prohibited by the law.

1. Making wash sales (a buy and sell order given at the same time) to create the appearance of active trading.
2. Creating the false appearance of active trading to induce buying and selling by others.

3. Pegging, fixing, or otherwise stabilizing prices except as used by underwriters during an initial offering of securities.
4. Making false or misleading statements about securities.

Insider Trading

Officers, directors, and others owning 10 percent or more of the controlling stock must advise the SEC of their transactions in the securities. The purpose of this is to prevent insiders from taking advantage of information that is not available to other investors. Insider transactions appear in *The Wall Street Journal* and elsewhere when they are released by the SEC.

Insider trading refers to the trading of securities in breach of a fiduciary duty, or relationship of trust or confidence, while in possession of material nonpublic information about the issuer or the market in which the securities are traded. Federal securities laws prohibit such trading by officers, directors, and others in a position of trust or confidence with the issuer or its shareholders. This extends to others who get material nonpublic investment "tips" from such persons. In the case of *SEC* v. *Kerheve,* the SEC alleged that two foreign nationals, who resided in Cairo, Egypt, and who knew of a major oil find in Egypt, unlawfully traded the securities of Texas International Company. The defendants paid over $50,000 plus penalties. In the case of *SEC* v. *Wang and Lee,* the SEC alleged that an analyst in an investment firm provided information about proposed mergers to a foreign national investor who traded those securities and made at least $19 million in illegal profits.[4] The analyst was fined $200,000 and sentenced to a three-year prison term to be followed by three years of probation. About $12 million was recovered from the foreign investor.

Investment Swindles

Investment swindles are widespread because many investors are gullible and greedy. Fraudulent investments amount to more than $10 billion annually. The frauds include investments in securities, commodities, and other so-called investment opportunities. One type of investment fraud is called "the infallible investor." All that it requires is a telephone and a list of prospective investors taken from a telephone book or some other source. Joe, a fraudster posing as a broker, calls Ms. Jones and tells her not to invest with someone she does not know. To demonstrate the quality of his firm's research, Joe tells Jones about a stock (or commodity) that is expected to make a significant increase in value and it does.

A second phone call is made. This time Joe tells Jones about a stock that is going to decline in value, but Joe does not solicit business from Jones yet. Joe explains that his firm's research can help Jones make sound investment decisions. To borrow an analogy from fishing, Joe is setting the hook before reeling in the big fish. Within a few days the price of the stock declines as predicted.

When Joe calls the third time, Jones is a true believer in the firm's research and

[4] U.S. Securities and Exchange Commission, *Fifty-Fourth Annual Report, 1988,* 10–11.

is eager to make a large investment in Joe's recommendations. And Joe makes the big catch when Jones invests thousands of dollars.

What Ms. Jones did not know is that Joe had a calling list of 200 people. In the first call he told 100 that the stock would appreciate in value and the other 100 that it would go down in value. When it came time for the second call, he called only those who had received the correct forecast. Of these, he told half that the stock would go up and the other half that it would go down. Jones was in the group that got correct forecasts on both calls. She was ripe for Joe's picking. However, Jones could have avoided getting "taken" by asking the following questions:

1. Where did you get my name?
2. What risks are involved in the proposed investment?
3. Can you send me a written explanation of the investment so I can consider it at my leisure?
4. Would you mind explaining your investment proposal to a third party, such as my attorney, accountant, or banker?
5. Can you give me the names of your firm's principals and officers?
6. Can you provide references?
7. Do you have any documents such as a prospectus or risk disclosure statement that you can provide?
8. Are the investments you are offering traded on a regulated exchange?
9. What government or industry regulatory supervision is your firm subject to?
10. How long has your company been in business?
11. What has your track record been?
12. When and where can I meet with you or another representative of your firm?
13. Where, exactly, will my money be? And what type of regular accounting statements do you provide?
14. How much of my money would go for commissions, management fees, and the like?
15. How can I sell the investments when I decide I want my money?
16. If disputes should arise, how can they be resolved?

If you do not get satisfactory answers to each of these questions, don't invest! These questions were developed by the **National Futures Association,** a Congressionally authorized self-regulatory organization of the futures industry.[5]

The Maloney Act

The Maloney Act (Section 15A of the Securities Exchange Act of 1934) provided for the establishment of national securities associations to supervise the over-the-

---

[5] The questions and example of the infallible forecaster are based on *Investment Swindles: How They Work and How to Avoid Them,* National Futures Association, 200 West Madison St., Suite 1600, Chicago, Ill. 60606.

counter markets. This Act set out the legal basis for the formation of the National Association of Securities Dealers (NASD) in 1939.

According to the certificate of incorporation of the NASD, the principal purpose of the organization is:

> To promote through cooperative effort the investment banking securities business, to standardize its principles and practices, to promote therein high standards of commercial honor, and to encourage and promote among members observance of Federal and State Securities laws.[6]

To accomplish these and other goals, the NASD developed (1) the **Rules of Fair Practice,** (2) the **Code of Procedure,** (3) the **Uniform Practice Code,** and (4) other rules and regulations. The Rules of Fair Practice are the standards that members of the NASD are required to use in conducting their business. These rules cover recommendations made to customers, charges for services, guidelines for selling mutual funds, and provisions for the supervision of registered representatives.

The Code of Procedure prescribes methods for handling trade practice complaints. Persons having a complaint are required to make their grievance known in writing on a form supplied by the Board of Governors of the NASD. The complaint may be heard by the District Business Conduct Committee. The committee investigates the allegations made in the complaint to determine if any rules have been violated and then makes its recommendations, in writing, to all interested parties. The Board of Governors of the NASD can review and overrule the committee's decisions.

The Uniform Practice Code concerns all over-the-counter transactions in securities between members of the NASD that are compared, cleared, or settled through the facilities of the National Clearing Corporation (except for certain exempted securities). The code defines and establishes procedures for the delivery of securities, procedures for transactions in securities that are ex-dividend or ex-rights, and other procedures that are associated with transferring and clearing securities.

With the exception of the **National Association of Securities Dealers Automated Quotations** (NASDAQ, pronounced *naz-dak*), the activities of the NASD are unknown to most investors. NASDAQ provides current quotations and other pertinent information on about 5000 over-the-counter securities.

As described more fully in the by-laws, the purposes of the NASD are as follows:

- To promote the investment banking and securities business
- To standardize its principles and practices
- To promote high standards of commercial honor and to promote among members observance of federal and state securities laws

---

[6] National Association of Securities Dealers, *Reprint of The Manual,* September 1987, Chicago: Commerce Clearing House, 1989, paragraph 1003.

- To provide a medium through which the membership may consult with governmental and other agencies
- To cooperate with governmental and other agencies in the solution of problems affecting the securities business and investors
- To adopt and enforce rules of fair practice in the securities business
- To promote just and equitable principles of trade for the protection of investors
- To promote self-discipline among members
- To investigate and adjust grievances between the public and members

Investment Company Act of 1940 and Investment Adviser Act of 1940

Two acts passed in 1940 gave the SEC regulatory authority over investment companies and investment advisors. The **Investment Company Act of 1940** provides a regulatory framework within which investment companies must operate. All investment companies with 100 or more stockholders are required by the Investment Company Act of 1940 to register with the Securities and Exchange Commission. This legislation was designed to ensure that investors have detailed information about the financial condition of investment companies and their operating policies. Some of its key features are

1. **Diversification.** Investment companies must invest at least 75 percent of their assets in cash and securities. No more than 5 percent of the assets can be invested in any one company, nor can investment companies hold more than 10 percent of any company's controlling stock.
2. **Management.** Management must be approved by the stockholders.
3. **Tax Exemption.** Investment companies are exempt from federal income tax providing they distribute 97 percent of their income to their stockholders.
4. **Reports.** Investment companies are required to report all financial activities to the SEC twice a year.
5. **Shares.** Before buying shares of an open-end investment company, investors must be given a prospectus containing sufficient information to make an intelligent appraisal. Each share must represent a proportionate share of ownership and no security may have a prior claim. Finally, the shares may be redeemed at net asset value.
6. **Categories.** The Act divides investment companies into three categories:
   a. Management companies — these are subdivided into **open-end** (mutual funds) **companies** and **closed-end companies.**
   b. Unit investment trusts — in these trusts, each investor holds a certificate that represents a group or unit of securities. For example, a unit may consist of 25 shares of stock of 10 different companies. Unit trusts are managed by a trustee acting on behalf of the investors, who are the beneficial owners of the trust property.
   c. Face-amount certificate companies — these companies get their invest-

ment fund by selling face-amount certificates, which are unsecured obligations to pay either a stated sum to the holder on a specified date if he makes all payments required by the contract or a cash surrender value prior to maturity.

Some of the important provisions of this act were summarized in the 1973 Annual Report of the SEC, as follows:

(1) Prohibits changes in the nature of an investment company's business or its investment policies without shareholder approval; (2) protects against management self-dealing, embezzlement or abuse of trust; (3) provides specific controls to eliminate or mitigate inequitable capital structures; (4) requires that an investment company disclose its financial condition and investment policies; (5) provides that management contracts be submitted to shareholders for approval, and that provision be made for the safekeeping of assets; and (6) sets controls to protect against unfair transactions between an investment company and affiliates.[7]

The Investment Adviser Act of 1940 requires that persons engaged for compensation in the business of advising others on the buying and selling of securities must register with the SEC. Banks, brokers, accountants, and others whose investment advice is incidental to the performance of their business do not have to register with the SEC. The Act also prohibits fraudulent, deceptive, or manipulative practices. In 1970, the requirements of this Act were extended to include advisors to registered investment companies.

Securities Investor Protection Act of 1970

The **Securities Investor Protection Act of 1970** created the **Securities Investor Protection Corporation (SIPC),** a nonprofit membership corporation, to provide financial protection for customers of failing brokers and dealers who are members of the SIPC. Each customer's claims are covered up to a maximum of $500,000, except claims for cash are limited to $100,000. The SIPC does *not* protect investors from losses arising from fluctuations in securities prices, and commodity accounts are not covered by the SIPC.

All stockbrokers and dealers are registered under the Securities Exchange Act of 1934, and virtually all members of national securities exchanges belong to the SIPC. At the end of 1988, 12,022 firms were members of the SIPC.

The SIPC, with government assistance, is accumulating a fund to pay claims arising from members' failures. Members contribute an assessment on the revenues from their securities business to the fund, and as assessments grow, government assistance will diminish.

Since the inception of the fund at the end of 1981, 197 broker–dealers have had consumer protection proceedings initiated against them under the provisions

[7] *39th Annual Report of the Securities and Exchange Commission,* Washington, D.C.: U.S. Government Printing Office, 1973, 97.

of the 1970 Act.[8] A total of $941 million has been advanced to customers of those failed firms.

Commodities Futures Trading Commission

Federal Regulatory Agency for Futures Trading

The Commodity Futures Trading Commission (CFTC) was created by Congress in 1974 to regulate and oversee the trading of commodity futures contracts on U.S. Futures exchanges. **Futures contracts** are commitments to buy or sell commodities at a specified time and price in the future. Futures contracts on agricultural commodities have been traded in the United States for more than 100 years and have been under federal regulation since 1920. Today, futures contracts are traded on a broader array of commodities, including Treasury bills and industrial materials. And Congress has expanded the definition of commodities beyond agricultural products to include all other goods, articles (except onions), services, rights, and interests in which there is *dealing* in futures contracts. Futures contracts may be traded only on exchanges licensed by the CFTC.

There are some contracts similar to futures for which licensed exchanges do not exist. Two examples are forward contracts and leverage contracts. In **forward contracts** the buyer and seller agree on the price and delivery of a specified quantity and quality of goods at a specified date in the future. **Leverage contracts** call for the delivery of a commodity with the total cost of the commodity spread out over a period of time. A leverage contract usually involves a small down payment and a big "balloon" payment at a later date. Such contracts are subject to CFTC regulation. The CFTC, however, does not regulate cash commodity transactions.

CFTC's Duties

The CFTC approves all of the rules and practices on U.S. commodities exchanges. Before a commodity may be traded on an exchange, it must be shown that the contract will serve come economic purpose and that trading in it will not be contrary to the public interest. In addition, the contract must not distort the normal market flow for that particular commodity. Companies and individuals who handle funds for customers dealing in futures contracts, or offering advice about futures contracts, must be approved by the CFTC. The CFTC also regulates some of the activities of those firms to safeguard customer's funds.

CONCLUSION

From a broad perspective, the securities industry is composed of firms and governments that require funds, investors who provide them with funds, and investment bankers and stockbrokerage firms that bring them together. Investment

---

[8] *Annual Report* 1988, Washington, D.C.: Securities Investor Protection Corporation, 1989.

bankers typically buy new securities from business and government, and in turn sell them to investors. Investment banking firms are generally associated with stockbrokerage firms, which help them distribute the new issues to investors and act as brokers and dealers in the secondary securities market. The investors include both individuals and institutions, such as pension plans. In recent years, institutional trading has become increasingly important.

In an effort to ensure that the securities markets would function properly, and as a result of widespread manipulation and other unsavory practices, Congress passed legislation in the 1930s that established the Securities and Exchange Commission. One function of the SEC is to supervise the workings of the stock exchanges and securities markets. In recent years there has been additional legislation regulating the securities markets. In 1970, the Securities Investor Protection Corporation (SIPC) was created to protect customers of brokers and dealers that failed. The Securities Acts Amendments of 1975 broadened the powers of the SEC to create a regulating scheme for municipal securities professionals, transfer agents, and clearing agencies.

Finally, Congress created the Commodities Futures Trading Commission to regulate futures trading, which now includes commodities such as Treasury bonds and foreign exchange.

IMPORTANT CONCEPTS

Arbitrage
Best efforts underwriting
Black Monday
Block transaction
Closed-end investment companies
Commodities Futures Trading Commission (CFTC)
Correspondent firm
Discount broker
Dynamic asset allocation
Insider trading
Investment Adviser Act of 1940
Investment banker
Investment Company Act of 1940
Liquidity
Maloney Act
Manipulation techniques
Margin
Marketability
Member firm
National Association of Securities Dealers (NASD)

National Association of Securities Dealers Automated Quotations (NASDAQ)
Nonmember firm
Open-end investment companies
Portfolio insurance
Primary market
Privately placed
Program trading
Prospectus
Registration of securities
Retail (brokerage business)
Rules of Fair Practice
Seat on the NYSE
Secondary distribution
Secondary market
Securities Act of 1933
Securities Exchange Act of 1934
Securities Exchange Commission (SEC)
Securities Investor Protection Act of 1970

Stand-by underwriting
Stock index futures
Tactical asset allocation
Undervalued

Underwrite
Uniform Practice Code
Wholesale (brokerage business)

QUESTIONS AND EXERCISES

1. Where is the secondary securities market located? New York City?
2. How do underwriters of securities benefit the economy?
3. What information is found in a prospectus?
4. Are "red herrings" the same thing as lox (smoked salmon)? Explain.
5. Distinguish between "best efforts" and "standby" underwriting.
6. Explain what is meant by "program" trading.
7. Explain the term "member firm."
8. Use the telephone book to obtain a listing of brokers in your area. Call the firms and obtain information necessary to classify them by size, membership, and geographic area that they serve.
9. Can you buy or sell stocks listed on the New York Stock Exchange from a nonmember firm? Explain.
10. Do all brokers charge the same commission and offer the same services?
11. What is the intent of the Securities Acts of 1933 and 1934?
12. What are the principal federal agencies involved in regulating securities trading?
13. Suppose you had a complaint about your broker, who you believe misrepresented certain securities. What legal remedies do you have?
14. What does SIPC do?
15. Your broker has a new stock issue and you want to buy some shares. He said he will sell you some if you also invest in another stock he is recommending. What should you do? Explain.

CHAPTER 6

SERVICES OF STOCKBROKERAGE FIRMS

S tockbrokerage firms provide services to investors who want to buy and sell securities and related investments. As noted in Chapter 5, there are more than 6000 brokers and dealers in the United States. Of that total, about 555 are members of the New York Stock Exchange. Firms that are members of the NYSE handle most stock transactions executed in this country. Because these firms dominate stock trading, the rules presented in this chapter are those of the NYSE.

STOCKBROKERS

How to Select a Stockbroker

Selecting a **stockbroker** is like selecting a doctor or a lawyer. There is no simple way to select the "right" doctor, lawyer, or stockbroker for you. However, here are some suggestions that you may find helpful.

Services Required

First, decide what brokerage services you need. A listing of stockbrokerage firm services is covered later in this chapter. If you decide that you want someone only to execute the orders to buy and sell securities, then a discount broker may satisfy

your needs. If you want to invest in a local company that you know, perhaps a small firm would be the answer. However, if you are a novice investor and require a lot of information of one sort or another, then a larger firm should be considered.

Some investors have specialized investment needs. For example, they may want **tax-sheltered investments**—those that provide tax benefits that defer or reduce income tax payments. As a general rule, larger stockbrokerage firms have greater access to such investments than small firms. Many of the tax deals are public, but some are **private placements**—sold to a few select individuals.

This first step in selecting a stockbroker is analogous to selecting a doctor. If you just want a routine checkup, a general practitioner will suffice. However, if you have a toothache or need eyeglasses, you go to doctors that specialize in those areas. Once you have decided whether you want a general practitioner or a specialist, you still have to select the right one for you.

Reputation

One way of selecting a doctor or stockbroker is by reputation. Reputation takes years to build but can be destroyed in a day by bad service, errors, and so on. Two aspects of reputation should be considered. The first deals with the reputation of the firm. Most stockbrokers or, to be precise, **registered representatives,** work for stockbrokerage firms. Actually, the term *stockbrokerage firms,* although widely used, is outdated. Many firms now offer such a wide variety of services that the term *securities firm* or even *financial supermarket* may be more appropriate. In any case, these firms develop a reputation for service, research, underwriting, and other activities.

Several factors affect the reputation of a stockbrokerage firm. One is membership on the principal stock exchanges. Being a member firm of the New York Stock Exchange, for example, carries with it a certain degree of prestige. In addition, member firms have to follow certain rules concerning their conduct and financial strength that are designed to enhance public confidence in those firms.

Size is another factor that affects reputation. Merrill Lynch is the biggest stockbrokerage firm in the world, and it is known worldwide. And everyone knows that when E. F. Hutton speaks, everyone listens. These and other large firms offer virtually any service you may wish. On the other hand, there are some excellent small firms too, but because of their size, they may not have the international, national, regional, or even local reputation of the big firms. Nevertheless, if you can find them, they may satisfy all of your investment needs.

The second aspect of reputation is the reputation of the individual who handles your account—your stockbroker. First, you must recognize that individual stockbrokers reflect the policies and practices of the firms they represent. This is why selecting a firm is so important. The firm provides the stockbroker with research information and various services to sell to you. Therefore, you probably should not select a firm that specializes in municipal bonds for banks if you are interested in speculating in commodities or Canadian gold mining stocks, even if the stockbroker is your sister-in-law.

Next, you should know that individual stockbrokers, like stockbrokerage firms, specialize. Some stockbrokers deal primarily in commodities, while others focus on options or a wide range of securities. If you are interested in options, seek out a firm and a broker within that firm that do what you want.

Finally, you should ask your friends or other acquaintances whom they use and whether they are satisfied. Keep in mind, however, that sometimes this information can be misleading because their needs may differ from yours. Equally important, many investors do not know what to expect from a stockbroker.

What to Expect from a Stockbroker

There are many misconceptions about what a stockbroker is and what one does. Stockbrokers are hired by stockbrokerage firms to buy and sell securities and other services. The firm expects stockbrokers to generate enough commission income to cover the costs of operation it assigns to them. For stockbrokers, the operative words, are *buy, sell,* and *commission.*

"Well," says Gloria Campbell, who is a novice investor, "I don't know what to buy and I want my stockbroker to give me advice."

A stockbroker is not an investment advisor. Nevertheless, a stockbroker can refer to research provided by the firm and tell Campbell, "My firm recommends the following stocks that have potential for long-term growth and provide a reasonable income from dividends, too." The stockbroker should *not* say, "Gloria, this is the stock for you! It has virtually no risk, and I have that good old feeling that this one is going to be a real winner. It is selling for $36 now and I see it going to at least $68 within the next three months! Should I put your order in for 200 or 400 shares?"

Campbell replies that her stockbroker did tell her what to buy and the stocks did increase in value. "Why not stick with a winner? My stockbroker seems to know the score, and I'm making money."

There are several problems with what Campbell said. First, the stockbroker cannot "tell" someone what to buy or sell. The actual decision is up to the investor. Second, during the period when Gloria bought the stocks, perhaps the entire stock market was enjoying a bull market (rising stock prices), and it may have been hard to find any stock that was going down. Finally, the stockbroker is not an investment analyst. Analyzing stocks is a full-time job, and that is why stockbrokerage firms spend millions of dollars annually on their research departments. Research takes time, and more will be said about analyzing securities in Part 3.

"O.K., I get the point," says Campbell, "but my stockbroker does do a good job of watching out for my stocks and managing all of them for me."

Unfortunately, the stockbroker is not a portfolio manager either. By way of illustration, assume that a stockbroker has 200 customers and each of them owns shares in 10 different companies. The customers could have a total of 2000 different companies. Realistically, some of the customers will own shares in the same companies, so let's say that there are only 1000 different companies. Keeping informed requires a *minimum* of three hours' research on each company

---

BOX 6-1

RED FLAGS

Not all of the risk to investors in the stock market is confined to stocks. There may be some risk in dealing with certain stockbrokers, particularly in the hot market for newly issued stock. Certain telltale signs should serve as red flags to warn investors. These red flags are

1. Extremely low priced "penny" stocks
2. Unsolicited, high-pressure telephone sales
3. Tie-in agreements, under which investors are pressured to buy additional shares at a later date, or shares of a different firm
4. Brokers who do not provide price quotations
5. Securities with extremely wide spreads between the bid and asked price
6. Brokers who resist sales orders
7. Brokers who promote extraordinary profits

Source: Based on the written statement of John Shad and John Fedders. Securities and Exchange Commission Hearings on Fraud and Abuse in the "Hot Issues" and "Penny Stock" Markets, to the Subcommittee on Securities of the Senate Committee on Banking, Housing and Urban Affairs, 98th Congress, 1st Session, December 15, 1983.

---

during a year. Thus, the total time spent on research would be 3000 hours a year. This exceeds the normal work year of 2000 hours (50 weeks $\times$ 40 hours per week = 2000) by 50 percent! Stockbrokers who are supposed to be generating commissions cannot spend that much time on research. It follows that they cannot be expected to manage their customers' portfolios. Yet, some stockbrokerage firms and investment advisors do offer this service for a fee.

In summary, the stockbroker is a salesperson whose income depends on commissions. The stockbroker is not a securities analyst, investment advisor, or portfolio manager. However, because stockbrokers are involved with securities on a day-to-day basis, they may have some useful insights about the market and particular stocks. Therefore, their advice, along with all of the other information that is available, should be weighed before making an investment decision. The decision is up to the investor, and no one else should make it or take the responsibility for it. Do not be like Sadie Badmouth who says, "I have a lousy stockbroker. My stockbroker told me to buy two different stocks, and they both went down."

OPENING AN ACCOUNT

Let us assume that you have found a stockbrokerage firm and a stockbroker that are suitable to you. Now it is necessary to open an account so that you can do

business with the firm. Rule 405 of the New York Stock Exchange states that every member organization is required to use due diligence to learn the essential facts about every customer and every order accepted by that organization. The basic facts required to open an account include information about the applicant's occupation and background. In some cases, additional credit information is required, and special instructions for handling securities are given.

The "know-your-customer" rule allows the firm some discretion in making decisions on individual accounts based on the known facts of a customer's financial circumstances. It permits the exercise of normal, prudent, business judgment in an industry where sizable financial transactions frequently are made on credit. A customer in moderate financial circumstances, for example, who normally makes small trades might be asked for advance payment on a transaction involving a substantial sum of money. Some customers also have been known to "forget" having placed an order when a stock drops dramatically soon after purchase. While customers are legally responsible for their debts, and legal action is a likely outcome if the amount involved is significant, the know-your-customer rule offers member firms some protection against customers who are unwilling or unable to pay for their purchases, and some opportunity to avoid losses before they are incurred.

Types of Accounts

The two basic accounts for buying and selling stocks, bonds, and convertible bonds are the **cash account** and the **margin account.** The cash management-type account, combining all customer assets into a master account, is also an increasingly popular vehicle for securities customers. It includes checking and savings privileges, and is part of the growing trend toward financial supermarkets that was mentioned earlier. Special accounts are needed to deal in options or commodities.

Cash Account

With a cash account the customer pays in full for the purchase of securities on or before the **settlement date.** No credit is extended. The settlement date for most stock transactions is five business days after the date of the transaction. Business days do not include Saturdays, Sundays, holidays, or other days when stockbrokerage firms and banks are not open for business. The settlement date for stocks bought on a Monday of a normal business week would be Monday of the following week. Similarly, when securities are sold, they must be delivered to the brokerage firm on or before the settlement date. A brokerage firm will normally not make payment on the funds realized from a sale prior to the end of the five-day settlement period, but sometimes special arrangements can be made for expedited payment.

Margin Account

Customers who may want to buy some of their securities on margin, or credit extended by the brokerage firm, will open a margin account. The margin account

then can be used to buy stocks or bonds on margin, with the firm financing part of the cost. Fully paid cash transactions can also be handled in a margin account. The current minimum **equity** required to open a margin account and trade on margin is $2000, although some firms may require a larger opening balance.

When a margin account is opened, the customer signs an agreement promising to observe the regulations of the Federal Reserve Board, the New York Stock Exchange, and the firm. The agreement gives the brokerage firm the authority to use the customer's securities in the margin account as collateral for its own loans. Firms use these borrowed funds to pay for stocks that customers buy on margin and for other purposes. The agreement also allows the firm to "borrow" securities in the margin account to make loans to other customers who are making short sales. This concept is discussed further in the section on short sales later in this chapter.

The initial margin requirement can be satisfied by depositing cash or securities that have a loan value equal to the amount required. A 50-percent margin requirement means that the customer must deposit 50 percent of the value of the stocks purchased and the stockbrokerage firm will extend credit on the remaining 50 percent. By using securities the customer owns as collateral, the total value of the transaction can be borrowed. Assume that a customer buys $10,000 worth of stock. If the margin requirement is 50 percent, the initial margin requirement is $5000, or $10,000 in collateral securities. The stockbrokerage firm lends the customer 50 percent of the value of the collateral securities, or $5000, plus the remaining $5000. If the margin requirement were 80 percent, the initial margin requirement would be $8000, or $40,000 in collateral securities. In this case the stockbroker would lend 20 percent of the value of the collateral securities, or $8000, plus the remaining $2000.

The customer is charged interest on the borrowed funds. The interest rate is based on the borrowing costs of the stockbrokerage firm. Stockbrokerage firms charge interest on funds due them, and member firms may pay interest on the **credit balance** (amount the firm owes the customer).

The interest is charged as long as there are borrowed funds. Some customers who buy stocks on margin have large **debit balances** (funds owed) for years. They are under no pressure from the stockbrokerage firms to pay off their accounts. In fact, customers who use margin accounts provide stockbrokerage firms with two sources of income: (1) income from commissions when they trade and (2) interest income from the charges on their margin accounts.

Because stock prices can decline, minimum margin requirements have been established by the Federal Reserve Board. The minimum maintenance margin must be at least equal to

1. 25 percent of the market value of all securities long in the account (the term *long* means stocks that are held in the account)
2. $2.50 per share or 100 percent of the market value, in cash, whichever amount is greater, for each stock short in the account selling at less than $5 per share (the term *short* refers to stocks that have been sold short)

3. $5 per share or 30 percent of the market value, in cash, whichever is greater, for each stock short in the account selling at $5 or above

4. 5 percent of the principal amount of 30 percent of the market value in cash, whichever is greater, of each bond "short" in the account.

Moreover, every margin account must have a minimum **equity** of $2000, except that cash need not be deposited in excess of the cost of any security purchased. Many individual firms require a higher minimum equity.

If the value of the securities in the margin account declines sufficiently, the customer will be sent a **margin call.** This notice states the amount of additional cash or securities that the customer must deposit to meet the minimum margin requirement. A customer cannot meet a margin call by selling securities already in the margin account, but must deliver additional securities or cash.

If the customer does not satisfy the margin call, the stockbrokerage firm can sell the securities the customer has in his or her account in order to meet the call. Moreover, the member firm has the authority to sell a customer's securities for the firm's protection *without* sending margin calls to that customer. This procedure is called a **sellout.** However, as a general practice, member firms notify customers before selling their securities to meet margin requirements.

Calculating Margins

Investors with margin accounts should know how to compute margins and how the margins in their accounts stand in order to use margins to their advantage. This section explains how to calculate margins for stocks. The margin requirements for government bonds (U.S. and tax-exempt), options, and marginable corporate debt securities are different than those presented here. If the market value of a stock held in an account appreciates, the investor may be able to buy additional stock without putting up any more money, or the investor may want to borrow money from the account. Margin calculations require the use of several new terms.

Basic Definitions

When a customer buys a security on margin, the amount owed to the stockbrokerage firm is called the *debit balance*. The debit balance also reflects interest charges on the margin accounts and cash withdrawals by the customer.

The *credit balance* is the amount of money the stockbrokerage firms owes the customer. Credit balances arise when securities are sold, dividends or interest are paid on securities that are held (long) in the account, and cash is deposited.

The equity in an account is defined as the market value of the collateral securities less the debit balance

$$\text{Equity} = \text{market value of collateral } (V) - \text{debit balance } (D) \qquad (6\text{-}1)$$

As previously noted, margin accounts must maintain a minimum equity of $2000 or more.

Margin

The margin for a stock that is held (long) in the account can be calculated in the following manner:

$$\text{Margin} = \frac{\text{market value of collateral } (V) - \text{debit balance } (D)}{\text{value of collateral } (V)} \qquad (6\text{-}2)$$

To illustrate the use of the equation, assume that a customer bought 100 shares of Astro-Growth Company at $40 per share, and the initial margin requirement is 50 percent. The customer deposits $2000 and borrows the remaining $2000 from the stockbrokerage firm. For simplicity, commissions and taxes are excluded from the calculations. The margin in the example is 50 percent.

$$\text{Margin} = \frac{\$4000(V) - \$2000(D)}{\$4000(V)} = 50\%$$

What happens to the margin if the price of Astro-Growth goes up to $60 per share? The debit balance remains unchanged, but the value of the collateral has increased to $6000. Thus, the margin has increased to 66.6 percent.

$$\text{Margin} = \frac{\$6000(V) - \$2000(D)}{\$6000(V)} = 66.6\%$$

At this point, the customer can withdraw part of the unrealized paper profit of $2000, or additional securities can be bought without putting up any more cash.

Because the initial margin requirement is 50 percent, the customer can withdraw 50 percent of the paper profit in cash. The result is that the debit balance will increase to $3000 and the margin will be 50 percent.

$$\text{Margin} = \frac{\$6000(V) - \$3000(D)}{\$6000(V)} = 50\%$$

The amount that can be withdrawn depends on the initial margin requirement. If the initial margin requirement had been 70 percent, only 30 percent of the profit can have been withdrawn. The amount that can be withdrawn is known as the **excess**.

Buying Power

Instead of withdrawing cash, the investor could use the paper profit to buy additional securities. The dollar amount of securities that can be bought is known as buying power. The buying power can be determined by multiplying the excess by 100 percent divided by the initial margin requirement. If the profit is $2000 and the initial margin requirement is 50%, the buying power will be $2000.

$$\text{Excess} = \$2000 \times 50\% \text{ margin} = \$1000 \qquad (6\text{-}3)$$

$$\text{Buying power} = \$1000 \text{ (excess)} \times 100\% \div 50\% \text{ (margin)}$$

$$= \$2000$$

If the initial margin requirement had been 70 percent, the excess would have been $600 ($2000 × 30% = $600) and the buying power would have been $857.14 ($600 × 100 ÷ 70% = $857.14).

Minimum Margin Requirements

When the margin in the account is below the initial margin requirements of the Federal Reserve, the account is said to be a **restricted account.** For example, assume that the price per share of Astro-Growth declined from $40 to $32. The margin in the account would be 33.33 percent, well below the initial margin requirement of 50 percent.

$$\text{Margin} = \frac{\$3000(V) - \$2000(D)}{\$3000(V)} = 33.3\%$$

Because the account is restricted, the customer cannot withdraw cash unless additional securities are deposited. However, as long as the margin is above 30 percent, the customer can sell a security and buy another security of the same dollar value and on the same day without putting up additional collateral or cash. The advantage of "dollar for dollar—same-day substitution" is to permit customers to change the securities they hold if it is to their advantage to do so.

The minimum margin permitted by the New York Stock Exchange is 25 percent. The value of the collateral that will result in a 25-percent margin can be determined by multiplying the debit balance (D) by 4/3, or 1.3333. Thus, in the Astro-Growth example, where the debit balance (D) was $2000, the minimum value of the collateral can be substituted into the margin equation to show that the margin would be 25 percent.

$$\text{Minimum value of collateral} = \text{debit balance} \times 1.3333$$

$$\$2666.60 = \$2000 \times 1.3333$$

$$\text{Margin} = \frac{\$2666.60(V) - \$2000(D)}{\$2666.60} = 25\%$$

If the margin in an account is below 25 percent, the account in **undermargined.** Before the margin falls that low, a customer would be sent a margin call to deposit additional cash or securities. If the customer does not comply with the margin call, or if securities purchased are not paid for, the stockbrokerage firm can sell out the customer's securities.

Leverage

As used here, the term **leverage** refers to the magnifying effect the use of borrowed funds in a margin account can have on profits, losses, and the return on investments. Profits or losses are represented by the difference between the equity in the account and the customer's original investment outlay. For example, assume that 100 shares of Astro-Growth were purchased at $40 per share and the

initial margin requirement was 50 percent. Thus, the customer's original investment outlay was $2000. If the price of the stock remained unchanged, there would be no profit (or loss), which is the difference between the purchase price and selling price.

$$\text{Equity } (V - D) \quad - \text{ original investment} = \text{profit} \quad (6\text{-}4)$$
$$[\$4000(V) - \$2000(D) = \$2000]$$
$$\$2000 \quad - \quad \$2000 \quad = \$0$$

However, if the price of the stock increased by 50 percent, to $60 per share, the profit would increase from $0 to $2000, which represents a 100-percent return on the original investment.

$$\text{Equity } (V - D) \quad - \text{ original investment} = \text{profit}$$
$$[\$6000(V) \qquad\qquad - \$2000(D) \qquad = \$4000]$$
$$\$4000 \qquad\qquad - \$2000 \qquad = \$2000$$

$$\text{Return on investment} = \text{profit/original investment}$$
$$= \$2000/\$2000$$
$$= 100\%$$

If the stock had been paid for in full instead of using margin, the return on investment would have been only 50 percent.

The degree of leverage is related to the proportion of borrowed funds. If the margin requirements are low, the proportion of borrowed funds will be relatively large, and so will the leverage. To illustrate the difference, assume that the initial margin requirement had been 40 percent instead of 50 percent. The original cash outlay would have been $1600. The price increase from $40 to $60 per share would still result in a $2000 profit, but the return on the original investment would increase to 125 percent because less original investment was required ($1600).

$$\text{Equity } (V - D) \quad - \text{ original investment} = \text{profit}$$
$$[\$4000(V) - \$2400(D) = \$1600]$$
$$\$1600 \quad - \quad \$1600 \quad = \$0$$
$$[\$6000(V) - \$2400(D) = \$3600]$$
$$\$3600 \quad - \quad \$1600 \quad = \$2000$$

$$\text{Return on investment} = \text{profit/original investment}$$
$$= \$2000/\$1600$$
$$= 125\%$$

However, leverage is like a double-edged sword because it magnifies losses as well as profits. Investors should give serious consideration to that fact before opening a margin account.

Statements of Accounts

Customers are kept abreast of the debits, credits, and balances in their accounts through **confirmations** and **monthly statements.**

Confirmations

When securities are bought or sold, the transaction is reported to the customer on a confirmation. Figure 6-1 shows a typical customer confirmation. In general, confirmations contain the following information:

1. Trade and settlement dates
2. Number of securities bought or sold
3. Description of security
4. Price
5. Dollar amount of transaction
6. Amount of commission
7. Other fees or taxes
8. Net amount due to customer or broker
9. Other relevant information concerning transaction
10. Name of customer and account number

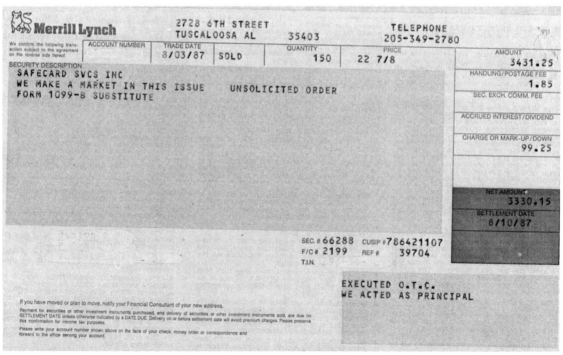

FIGURE 6-1   Example of a confirmation.

Customers should examine confirmations to determine whether any errors have been made. The errors could result from a misunderstanding between the customer and the broker or from clerical mistakes. For example, the customer may give the stockbroker an order to buy 100 *Telephone.* To the customer, the name *Telephone* may signify Bell South Corporation. However, to the stockbroker *Telephone* means American Telephone & Telegraph Company. Thus, the stockbroker would buy 100 American Telephone & Telegraph when the customer wanted 100 Bell South Corporation. Moreover, sometimes the use of nicknames or symbols for stocks can result in misunderstandings and errors between the time an order is given and the time it is executed and delivered to the customer. Finally, because stockbrokerage firms handle so many orders, some clerical errors are bound to occur in which transactions are assigned to the wrong accounts or the wrong number of shares are purchased, sold, or recorded on the confirmation. If the customer does not catch an error on the confirmation, the monthly statement offers another chance.

Monthly Statements

The purpose of the monthly statement is to let customers know the financial status of their account. Figure 6-2 shows a typical monthly statement. These statements list the number of securities bought, sold, or held in the account; describe each transaction; and tell the amounts that have been credited or charged to the account. All dividends, interest payments or charges, and any other pertinent information appear on the monthly statements.

REGISTRATION OF STOCK CERTIFICATES

Individuals who trade on margin generally leave their stock certificates with the stockbrokerage firm. This firm may put the stock in **street name,** which means that the stock certificate is registered in the name of the stockbrokerage firm rather than in the name of the customer (owner). These registration records are kept in the books of the **transfer agent,** usually a commercial bank that keeps track of who owns what amount of stock of a certain company. When stocks are bought or sold, the seller's name is removed from the books of the transfer agent and is replaced by the buyer's name. In order to transfer stock, the seller must deliver a stock certificate to the stockbrokerage firm. The stockbrokerage firm then handles the paperwork involved in the transfer. However, the stock certificate must be in **good delivery.** That is, it must be a certificate that can be legally transferred from one owner to another.

Customers may encounter a number of problems when they decide to transfer securities to other owners or when they register securities. Some of these problems are discussed in the following sections.

Individual Names

A stock certificate can be registered in any name. Customers can instruct their brokers to register stock in the name of George Washington, Moon Mulligan, E. T.

Merrill Lynch
Pierce Fenner & Smith Inc.
Member, Securities Investor Protection Corporation (SIPC)

Statement of Security Account

ACCOUNT #	F/C # 2199	PAGE # 1	SS OR ID	TELEPHONE # 205-349-2780

OFFICE SERVING YOUR ACCOUNT 2728 6TH STREET TUSCALOOSA AL 35403	FINANCIAL CONSULTANT

PERIOD STARTING AUG 29 1987	PERIOD ENDING SEP 25 1987	TYPE CASH	BUYING POWER

***** ACCOUNT PORTFOLIO *****

OPENING BALANCE $10.60CR	CLOSING BALANCE $65.60CR	MARKET VALUE $8917	TOTAL FUND SHARE $19,154.10	TOTAL EVALUATION $28,136.70

***** DIVIDEND, INTEREST AND/OR CHARGE INFORMATION *****

DESCRIPTION	MONTHLY	YEAR TO DATE
DIVIDENDS (REPORTABLE)	$55.00CR	$174.90CR
GROSS PROCEEDS (REPORTABLE)	$.00	$10,000.00CR

***** MONTHLY AND YEAR TO DATE FUND SUMMARY *****

FUND NAME a $1.000 PER SHARE	OPENING BALANCE	CLOSING BALANCE	DIVIDEND/INTEREST MONTHLY	DIVIDEND/INTEREST YEARLY
ML READY ASSET TRUST	$19,067.68	$19,154.10	$86.42	$771.44

***** DAILY ACTIVITY REVIEW *****

DATE	TRANSACTION	DESCRIPTION	PRICE	AMOUNT
08 28	OPENING BALANCE			$10.60CR
09 10	*DIVIDEND	50 INTL BUSINESS MACH		$55.00CR
09 25	CLOSING BALANCE			$65.60CR

YOUR INVESTMENTS		CURRENT PRICE	MARKET VALUE	CURR. YIELD	EST. INCOME
33	**AMERICAN TEL & TEL	33.875	$1117	3.54	$40
50	**INTL BUSINESS MACH	156.000	$7800	2.82	$220
TOTAL MARKET VALUE OF PRICED INVESTMENTS			$8917		$260

FIGURE 6-2 Typical monthly statement.

Being, or Flash Gordon, and this registration will pose no problem until the securities are to be sold. At that time, the certificate has to be in good delivery. In order to transfer stock, the seller must sign the form that appears on the back side of the stock certificate, and that signature must correspond *exactly* to the name that appears on the face of the certificate. If the name on the face of the certificate is *Flash L. Gordon,* the signature on the back of the certificate must read *Flash L. Gordon,* not *F. L. Gordon* or *Flash Gordon.*

Names should be registered so that there can be no confusion as to ownership of the stock. Shares registered in the name of *Mrs. Flash L. Gordon* could belong to Flash's past, current, or future wife. If the stock is registered in the name of *Alice Mergletroid Gordon,* the confusion is eliminated.

On some occasions the registered owner cannot sign the certificate. The owner may be incapacitated or out of the country. To take care of such a contingency, owners can give assignment or power-of-substitution to some other person. These are legal and notarized documents permitting some individual to sign the certificate on the owner's behalf.

The situation becomes complicated when the registered owner is dead and the securities have become part of the deceased's estate. Obviously, the deceased cannot sign the certificate. However, the certificate would then be in good delivery if it has a power-of-substitution executed by the executors or trustees under certain types of trust, or by other persons who have been authorized to sign for the deceased. Sometimes court documents are also required to complete the transaction.

Joint Tenants

Stock certificates can be registered in the names of two or more individuals. In the case of **joint tenants,** both registered owners have to sign the certificate for the stock to be in good delivery. There are several types of joint accounts.

Husband and Wife

A husband and wife may wish to register a stock in both their names. Generally, the certificate has both names followed by the phrase, *joint tenants with rights of survivorship and not as tenants in common.* Sometimes the phrase is abbreviated as **JT TEN.** This legal phrase means that if one spouse dies, the stock will pass to the other because they are not tenants in common. A tenant is one who holds or possesses title and the word *common* means that other persons share in the power to use the property. An alternate form of the phrase is *tenants by the entireties,* which has the same meaning for a husband and a wife.

Such joint accounts are sometimes desirable and convenient, but they are not a substitute for a will. Many disputes arise because of the uncertain legal effects of joint ownership. For example, Mrs. Jones and her son owned property jointly with rights of survivorship. The jointly held property was sold, and the proceeds from the sale were deposited in a bank account that was in the names of Mrs. Jones and her sister. When Mrs. Jones died, there was extensive litigation to determine the claim of Mrs. Jones's son to his share of the bank account.

Business Partners

Business partners may wish to buy stock jointly, but they want to be sure that their individual shares of the property go to their respective estates in the event of death. This can be accomplished by registering the stock in both names followed by the phrase, *joint tenants with rights of survivorship as tenants in common.* As tenants in common, they jointly share in the ownership of the property, and each is entitled to his or her share upon the death of the other. Thus, one partner would not be entitled to all the securities upon the death of the other partner. Instead, the shares would be divided equally between the surviving partner and the estate of the deceased partner.

Accounts for Minors

Stocks bought for minors can be registered to (*Joe Blow*) *as Custodian for* (*Sam Blow*) *under the* (*Ohio*) *Uniform Gifts to Minors Act.* In this case, the stock belongs irrevocably to the minor with an adult acting as the custodian. Alternatively, a trust can be established for the minor and the stock registered to (*Joe Blow*) *as Trustee for the minor* (*Sam Blow*). The trust agreement should explain in detail the limitations of the trustee's powers and the trustee's obligations to the minor. Stocks should *not* be registered in the name of a minor. Few stockbrokerage firms will open accounts for minors because a minor can void a contract without going through legal recourse. Without an account, a minor would have great difficulty in selling securities.

INVESTOR SERVICES

Stockbrokerage firms provide investors with a broad spectrum of financial services. This section presents the types of services that the major firms offer to their customers.

Research

Timely information about various industries and companies is an essential ingredient for successful investing. Research reports on recommendations can be purchased from firms specializing in gathering this information, such as Standard & Poor's, Moody's, and Value Line. In addition, many stockbrokerage firms have their own research departments in which analysts study particular industries or firms. Some analysts have the coveted title CFA behind their names, which stands for **chartered financial analyst.** This professional designation is awarded by the Institute of Chartered Financial Analysts to those who have years of study and experience and have completed difficult examinations. The CFA suggests that the holder is qualified to analyze and make recommendations on securities. An increasing number of security analysts hold a CFA.

The major function of research departments is to give stockbrokers information and recommendations for their customers. Most stockbrokers are deluged with recommendations to buy this, sell that, switch from one stock to another, and hold on to something else. Recommendations to buy or sell a particular stock can have an important impact on stock prices. Therefore, large stockbrokerage firms have to be very careful about what they recommend. Research departments generate so many recommendations partially because stockbrokers serve customers with many different needs, thus necessitating the covering of thousands of securities. Examples of these varying needs can be seen in the customers who are active traders and require the latest information affecting the prices of their securities, the longer term investors who want in-depth studies of industries and companies, and investors who just want general information about investment opportunities.

Finally, customers should be aware of the disclaimer appearing on many research reports and recommendations. Basically, the disclaimer states that the report is based on information believed to be reliable and that opinions stated in the report are subject to change. It also states that the firm making the report may own shares of the security being recommended. In essence, the disclaimer informs customers that recommendations published last week may not be valid this week because of changing circumstances. Thus, investors should not base investment decisions on recommendations and reports that have not been thoroughly reviewed, and keep the disclaimer and the date when the information was assembled in mind.

Other Services

Listed below are some of the other services stockbrokerage firms may offer their customers. Although this list is not complete, it includes the most important services offered. Some of these services are provided at no extra charge other than the usual commissions and taxes when a security is bought or sold.

1. Full brokerage services in securities, options, and commodities
2. Extension of credit on margin accounts
3. Underwriting and private placement of securities
4. Opportunities in tax-sheltered investments such as oil and gas, cattle, equipment leasing, and real estate
5. Financial advice and consultation
6. Custodian service for securities
7. Transfer of ownership of securities
8. Current and past quotations of security prices for tax and estate purposes
9. Cash management services including money market funds, checking accounts, and credit cards

CONCLUSION

One way to select a stockbroker is to "let your fingers do the walking" through the yellow pages. However, this is not the method recommended here. A better method is to determine your investment needs and then find a firm and a broker that match your needs. You can use the yellow pages to discover which firms are available in your area. Many firms that are not located throughout the United States have toll-free telephone numbers, so do not eliminate firms that are located in remote places. Once you have contacted the stockbrokerage firm of your choice, be sure that you understand what the stockbroker is expected to do for you. If you want someone to hold your hand every time your stock goes down $\frac{1}{8}$ point, you should (1) not invest in risky securities and/or (2) talk to a psychologist instead of a stockbroker.

Stockbrokerage firms offer a number of different types of accounts and services to their customers. The cash account operates on a cash basis, while a margin account involves the customer's borrowing part of the money being invested from the firm. The Board of Governors of the Federal Reserve System establishes the initial and minimum margin requirements — the percentage of the total investment the customer must purchase with cash or secure with collateral. The New York Stock Exchange and the stockbrokerage firm may make additional requirements on margin accounts. Margin accounts magnify the profits, losses, and returns on investments that a customer would get with a cash account.

The investor also needs to check each security transaction carefully to ensure that no error has occurred. For this purpose stockbrokerage firms issue confirmations of single transactions and monthly statements of all transactions for that month.

Investors may register their stocks in the name of the stockbrokerage firm in order to facilitate transfer. If the stock is registered in an individual's name, that individual must sign the stock certificate with the exact name under which it is registered before the stock can be transferred to another owner. Occasionally it is necessary to assign a power-of-substitution so that another person can sign the stock certificate on behalf of the owner.

Stocks may also be registered in the names of more than one person. Husbands and wives can register their stock as *joint tenants with rights of survivorship not as tenants in common* so that one will receive all the stock when the other dies. Partners can register stock as *joint tenants with rights of survivorship as tenants in common* so that the estate of a deceased partner receives that partner's share of the stock. Stocks should not be registered to minors. An adult can act as custodian for a minor's stock, or a trust can be established for the minor.

The services that a stockbrokerage firm offers may also include giving customers research reports and recommendations on investment opportunities. The customer will probably consider this information but should make sure it is up-to-date before acting on it. It is wise to make independent investigations as well. A stockbrokerage firm may also offer brokerage service for options, commodities, and tax-sheltered investments; underwriting and private placement of

securities; custodian services and transfer of ownership for securities; and evaluation of securities for tax and estate purposes.

IMPORTANT CONCEPTS

Buying power	Margin call
Cash account	Minimum margin requirement
Chartered Financial Analyst (CFA)	Monthly statement
Confirmation	Private placement
Credit balance	Registered representative
Debit balance	Restricted account
Equity	Sellout
Excess	Settlement date
Good delivery	Stockbroker
Initial margin requirement	Street name
Joint tenants	Tax-sheltered investment
Leverage	Transfer agent
Margin account	Undermargined

QUESTIONS AND EXERCISES

1. Should investors rely on stockbrokers to manage their investment portfolios? Why or why not?
2. Suppose you had $80,000 to invest in the stock market. How can you find a stockbroker that will provide the services you want? What services do you want?
3. Call several stockbrokers and ask them to send you information about particular stocks. Compare their reports and service and explain the differences between them.
4. Why does the New York Stock Exchange have the "know your customer" rule?
5. Explain how stocks can be purchased without putting up any cash.
6. Compute the initial margin requirement if an investor purchased $70,000 worth of stock and the margin requirement is (a) 50 percent, (b) 70 percent, and (c) 100 percent.
7. If stock is bought on margin and the stock appreciates in value, does the debit value have to be paid off?
8. Assume that the value of collateral securities has increased from $20,000 to $25,000 and the debit balance is $16,000. If the initial margin requirement is 50 percent, how much in additional securities can be purchased at this time?
9. An investor has an excess of $7,000 and the initial margin requirement is 30 percent. What is the buying power?

10. If stock were purchased at $80 per share and the initial margin requirement was 40 percent, what is the minimum price to which the stock could decline before it would be sold by the broker?

11. List five items that are found on a customer confirmation when a security is bought or sold.

12. What are the advantages of having a stock in street name?

13. If you and a friend decide to buy stock together, how should the stock be registered?

14. Is it advisable for minors to buy stock and register it in their own name? Explain.

15. "Chartered Financial Analyst" is a professional designation. Who might want such a designation and why?

CHAPTER 7

THE NEW YORK STOCK EXCHANGE

T he New York Stock Exchange (NYSE) is the largest stock exchange in the United States. It is a marketplace for the securities of major corporations. The securities of these corporations are held by more than 47 million individual investors and thousands of institutions. This chapter examines the history of the exchange, its organization, and some of the trading rules that affect you as an investor. The chances are that some stocks you will buy will be listed on the New York Stock Exchange. Therefore, it may be helpful to know something about how it operates and its rules before you play the market. After all, you would not play chess or Monopoly before you knew the rules, would you?

DEVELOPMENT AND ORGANIZATION

Brief History

Wall Street's name is derived from a wall built by the early Dutch settlers to protect their settlement from Indian attack and to keep their cattle from wandering into what today is New York's lower Manhattan financial district. Very early in its history the area developed into a political and financial center. It was on Wall Street, in 1768, that the New York State Chamber of Commerce pressed for the fight against the Stamp Act and the tax on tea. It was on Wall Street, in 1789, that George Washington took the oath of office to become the first President of the

United States, and it was on Wall Street, in 1791, that the Bill of Rights was adopted.

It was also on Wall Street that the 1789–1790 Congress voted to issue $80 million in stock to help pay for the costs of the Revolutionary War. The market for government stock was not organized. Trading took place in coffee houses, offices, and elsewhere. On May 17, 1792, a group of 24 persons who traded stock decided to do something about a permanent place to buy and sell securities at established hours. These traders agreed to meet daily at regular hours under an old buttonwood tree to conduct their business. This so-called Buttonwood Tree Agreement marked the first regular meeting of what is now known as the **New York Stock Exchange.** In addition to government stock and shares in insurance companies, shares in the First Bank of the United States, the Bank of New York, and other banks were also traded. In 1793, trading was moved inside to the Tontine Coffee House.

After the War of 1812, demand for funds from U.S. industry increased. New York State issued bonds to pay for the Erie Canal. New York Gas Light Company was the first public utility to be traded on the exchange. The railroads issued securities to finance their westward expansion.

As the list of securities being traded grew, it became apparent that a more formal organization was required of the exchange. On March 8, 1817, the first formal constitution of the New York Stock and Exchange Board, as it was called at that time, was enacted. This constitution was the forerunner of the Constitution and Rules that are now in force. The Exchange moved many times until it finally settled in its present site at 20 Broad Street in New York City.

Organization

The New York Stock Exchange is organized as a not-for-profit corporation under New York State law. The NYSE exists to provide a meeting place where members can transact their business of buying and selling securities and other related activities.

Government

The government of the New York Stock Exchange is vested in a Board of Directors consisting of 24 persons elected by the members of the exchange, including a chairman, executive vice president, and president. Twelve of the directors represent the public, and they are not permitted to be affiliated in any way with brokers or dealers in securities. In order to make the board representative of the diverse membership it serves, the remaining 12 directors represent different factions of the securities business. At least two of the latter group must be members whose firms engage in business involving direct contact with securities customers and who spend a substantial part of their time on the trading floor of the NYSE.

The Board of Directors is the chief policymaking body of the New York Stock Exchange. However, the actual management and administration of the affairs of the exchange is the responsibility of the chairman of the Board of Directors.

Subject to the approval of the board, the chairman appoints the treasurer, secretary, and other officers who run the exchange on a day-to-day basis. The chairman also has the power to appoint all other employees of the exchange and to fix their duties, responsibilities, and conditions of employment.

Membership

There are 1366 full memberships or seats on the NYSE, and the number of seats has been fixed at that level since 1953. Full members have physical access to the trading floor of the New York Stock Exchange (see Figure 7-1), and distributive rights in the net assets of the exchange. There are additional members who have physical or electronic access to the trading floor on an annual basis.

Only those individuals who hold memberships, or alternates who have been approved by the Board of Directors, can trade on the floor of the exchange. Thus, the XYZ stockbrokerage firm of Los Angeles, which is *not* a member firm, must use a **correspondent firm** to transact its business on the floor of the NYSE.

Six classes of members transact business on the floor of the New York Stock Exchange: (1) **commission brokers,** (2) **floor brokers,** (3) **registered competitive market makers (RCMM),** (4) **competitive traders,** (5) **specialists,** and (6) **odd lot brokers and dealers.**

FIGURE 7-1   NYSE Trading Floor.

Commission Brokers

Commission brokers are employed by member firms to execute their customers' orders on the NYSE. These firms are generally engaged in commission business and frequently have several commission brokers handling their orders. Sometimes the volume of business is so large that the firm's commission brokers cannot handle all of the orders. Therefore, they may use a floor broker to handle some of the excess volume.

Floor Brokers

These brokers execute orders for other members of the exchange, such as the commission broker. Floor brokers used to be known as $2 brokers because they received a $2 commission for every 100 shares they handled.

Registered Competitive Market Makers

RCMMs trade for their own accounts and their firms' accounts. They may be called on by an exchange official to make a bid or offer on a specific security to reduce the price spread or to add to the depth of the market. They may also be asked to assist a commission broker or floor broker in executing a customer's orders that might otherwise go unexecuted.

Competitive Traders

Members of the exchange who buy and sell for their own accounts, hoping to profit from their trading skills, are known as competitive traders.

Specialists

A specialist is a member of the exchange who specializes in dealing in one or more stocks. The specialist for a particular stock works at the post, a designated place of the trading floor, where that stock is traded. The specialist's principal function is to maintain a **fair and orderly market** in the stocks to which he or she is assigned. The term *fair* means free from manipulation and deceptive practices. *Orderly* refers to a continuous market that is evidenced by frequent trading without unreasonable price variations between sales without appropriate volume. An example of a market that is not orderly would be a 100-share trade at $20 per share and the next trade of 100 shares at $25 per share.

In order to maintain a fair and orderly market, specialists act as **agents** (acting on behalf of others) or **principals** (acting on their own behalf).

Agent.   A specialist may handle *limit orders* for other members of the exchange. Limit orders are orders to buy or sell stock at a particular price, such as $40 per share. Suppose that a commission broker received an order to buy 300 shares of stock at $40 per share and the stock is currently selling for $47 per share. It does not make sense for the commission broker to stay at that post until the stock price declines to $40 per share; it may never get there. Therefore, the commission

broker will give the order to the specialist to enter in his or her book. The book contains limit orders to buy the stock below the current market price and to sell the stock above the current market price. When the market price moves up or down, the specialist executes the orders in the book at the limit price or better. In this case, the specialist will attempt to buy the stock for the commission broker at or below $40 per share if the market price of the stock declines. The specialist receives a commission for acting as an agent for other exchange members.

Principal. Specialists also buy and sell for their own accounts in order to ensure a continuous market. Let us say that a stock has just traded at $30 per share. The highest price that anyone will pay for 100 shares of the stock is 29\frac{1}{4}$ (the best bid). The lowest price at which anyone is willing to sell the stock is 30\frac{1}{2}$ (the best offer). Accordingly, the market for stock is 29\frac{1}{4}$ bid — 30\frac{1}{2}$ offered. The specialist may bid $30, thereby narrowing the spread between the bid and asked price to $\frac{1}{2}$ point. By reducing the spread between the bid and asked price and bidding the stock price up, the specialist adds to the continuity of the market. If need be, the specialist will raise the price further to ensure continuous trading. Similarly, specialists will sell from their own accounts to maintain a continuous, fair, and orderly market.

There may appear to be some conflict of interest between the specialist's role as an agent and as a broker. However, the exchange has strict rules governing the conduct of the specialist's operations. Basically, specialists are prohibited from trading for their own accounts while holding orders from others at the same price. In other words, the public comes first. To ensure that specialists deal fairly, the exchange maintains constant surveillance over them.

Odd Lot Brokers and Dealers

These are members of the New York Stock Exchange who buy and sell odd lots. A typical unit of trading or **round lot** is 100 shares, and any number less than that is called an **odd lot.** Specialists may also act as odd lot brokers and dealers.

Technology

The development of the computer and the movement toward a **national market system** where all market participants will be linked together are having an impact on the NYSE.

Designated Order Turnaround System

The **SuperDot System** is one link in the development of computerized trading. It enables members to transmit orders on listed stocks directly from their offices to the proper trading post on the floor of the exchange where it is given to a specialist for execution.

The SuperDot technology has been expanded to include the **Opening Automated Reporting Service (OARS),** which facilitates the processing of orders received on the floor of the exchange prior to the opening of the market.

Other advances on the floor of the exchange include the **Limit Order System,** which electronically files orders that are to be executed when they reach a specific price; the **Electronic Display Book System,** which is used by specialists; and the **Automated Bond Systems (ABS),** which provides current quotes and trades on all nonconvertible bonds listed on the exchange.

Intermarket Trading System (ITS)

The ITS is one of the key building blocks of the national market system. It is an electronic communication network that links the trading floors of the American, Boston, Cincinnati, Midwest, New York, Pacific, and Philadelphia Stock Exchanges and the National Association of Securities Dealers (NASD). It enables brokers, specialists, and market makers to deal on the various exchanges when it is to their advantage to do so. Information about the prices and volume of securities being offered or sought is available on the nationwide consolidated tape. The technology exists to permit an investor to enter orders on his or her personal computer to buy and sell securities anywhere in the world. At the present time there are several experiments being conducted with "home banking," and buying and selling securities is the next step. Slowly but surely, the securities industry will evolve to make this a reality.

Listing

As noted previously, the New York Stock Exchange was organized so that members of the exchange could trade in stocks of listed companies. In order for a company to be listed on the NYSE it has to meet certain qualifications and follow the rules of the exchange. First, the company must meet financial standards such as

1. Demonstrated earning power under competitive conditions of $2.5 million before federal income taxes for the most recent year and $2 million pretax for each of the preceding two years, *or* an aggregate for the last three fiscal years of $6.5 million *together with* a minimum in the most recent fiscal year of $4.5 million. (All three years must be profitable.)
2. Net tangible assets of $18 million, but greater emphasis will be placed on the aggregate market value of the common stock.
3. A total of $18 million in market value of publicly held common stock. The dollar amount varies depending on the stock market activity.
4. A total of 1.1 million common shares publicly held.
5. 2000 holders of 100 shares or more, *or* 2200 total stockholders *together with* an average monthly trading volume (for the most recent six months) of 100,000 shares.

In addition to these requirements, the exchange must determine whether there is a sufficient degree of national interest in the company and whether its prospects for growth and stability are favorable. Finally, the company has to agree to

provide all stockholders with timely financial reports, notices of meetings, proxies, and other relevant information. As a matter of practice, the exchange does not list nonvoting common stocks.

At the end of 1988 2234 stock issues of 1681 companies were listed on the New York Stock Exchange. Some companies have both common and preferred shares listed on the exchange. In addition, 3106 bond issues were listed. The listed companies are the leading commercial enterprises in the United States.

Companies find it to their advantage to be listed on a national stock exchange, and *listing* on the New York Stock Exchange carries with it an element of prestige. Listing on the Big Board gives an aura of success to a company. It shows that the company has arrived! This position gives companies certain leverage when borrowing funds and making mergers and also has some advertising value. Because of mergers, bankruptcy, and other reasons, some companies are "delisted."

EXECUTING ORDERS ON THE EXCHANGE

The complex process of trading on the New York Stock Exchange is best explained by examining the various types of orders that are used to buy and sell securities. When a customer gives a stockbroker an order to buy or sell a stock, the stockbroker writes the order on an order form that gives all of the details of the transaction. Let us say an order is entered to buy 100 International Business Machines (IBM) at the current market price. The order is transmitted from the stockbroker's office to the firm's commission broker on the floor of the NYSE (see Figure 7-2). The commission broker takes the order and goes to the post where that particular stock is traded. At that post are assembled commission brokers from other firms who also have orders to buy and sell IBM stock. The broker with the order to buy stock asks, "How's IBM?" which means the broker wants a current quote on the stock. Someone in the crowd around the post, such as the specialist in IBM, will quote the stock at say "$125 – $126" (meaning $125 bid — $126 asked). The broker knows the stock can be bought at the asked price — $126, but the broker's job is to get the best price available. Since there is a one-point spread between the bid and asked price, the broker may offer to buy 100 shares at 125\frac{1}{2}$, thinking that $\frac{1}{2}$ is the lowest spread that would be acceptable to sellers. If the broker is correct another broker in the crowd will shout "sold 100 at 125\frac{1}{2}$." Thus, the two brokers have agreed on a price, and the transaction is complete. The commission broker will now report back to the firm that its customer bought stock at 125\frac{1}{2}$ per share. Similarly, the seller will be notified that the stock was sold at 125\frac{1}{2}$ per share.

When the transaction takes place, an employee of the exchange records the name of the stock, the number of shares, the price, and the names of the firms involved in the trade. The name of the stock is recorded as a symbol. The symbol for IBM is IBM. Symbols have from one to three letters. For example, General Electric Company is GE and Occidental Petroleum Corporation is OXY. The information on the name, number of shares, and the price at which they were

FIGURE 7-2   NYSE Trading Floor and Post.

traded is fed into the market data system computer. The information is then transmitted and displayed on ticker and display units located throughout the United States, Canada, and Western Europe. The process described here was for an order to buy a **round lot** of stock at the current market price. That is only one of the various types of orders investors use.

Kinds of Orders

Orders to deal in stocks can be classified according to the size of the order, type of transaction, price limits, time limits, and other special features.

Size of Order

The size of the order refers to the number of shares being traded. As previously noted, 100 shares is the normal unit of trading and is known as a round lot. In the case of some preferred stocks and inactive stocks, the round lot can consist of ten

shares. An **odd lot** is anything less than the normal unit of trading. Thus, 1 to 99 shares is an odd lot for the normal unit of trading, and 1 to 9 shares is an odd lot for stocks whose unit of trading is 10 shares. Some brokers charge a fee, called an **odd lot differential,** for dealing in odd lots. The amount varies from firm to firm.

In addition to round lots and odd lots, there are also block transactions. A **block** is a transaction of 10,000 shares or more, or a quantity of stock with a market value of $200,000 or more, whichever is less. **Blocks of stock** are normally traded by institutions. In 1988, block transactions accounted for 54.5 percent of all the reported volume on the exchange.

Types of Transactions

An order is always either to buy stock or to sell stock. Orders to sell have to be marked long or short. The term *long* means that the seller owns the stock to be sold. The term *short* means that the seller may not own the stock to be sold.

Short Sale

A **short sale** is defined as the sale of a (borrowed) security at a high price in anticipation of buying that security back at a lower price (and replacing the borrowed security). The usual transaction, familiar to most investors, is (1) buying stock at a low price such as $30 per share, and then (2) selling it at a higher price such as $40 per share. The profit is the difference between the price at which the stock was bought and sold. In a short sale, the process is reversed because investors believe the price of the stock is going to decline. First, the stock is sold (1) at the higher price. If the stock declines, it is then purchased at the lower price (2). Again, the profit is the difference between the purchase and sale price. Both transactions are illustrated in the following example:

	Normal Transaction			Short Sale	
Step 2	Sell high	$40 per share	Step 1	Sell high (Borrowed stock)	$40 per share
Step 1	Buy low	$30 per share	Step 2	Buy low (Cover short; replace borrowed stock)	$30 per share
	Profit	$10 per share		Profit	$10 per share

When a short sale occurs, a stockbrokerage firm lends the seller stock to deliver to the buyer. The seller's account is credited with the sale, but the funds cannot be withdrawn if that is the only transaction in the account. At some time in the future, the short seller has to buy stock to replace the borrowed stock, along with any dividends that may have been paid during the period. This is known as **covering the short** position.

Short sales can be used in a variety of ways. Speculators sell short when they think the price of a stock is going to decline. Short sales can also be used to lock in

the profits of stocks that are owned and to transfer taxes from one calendar year to another. For example, assume that an investor bought a stock that increased in value but does not want to take the capital gains this tax year. The investor can sell **short against the box.** The *box* refers to the fact that the investor is holding the stock in a safety deposit box or elsewhere. Early in the next calendar year, the investor can deliver his own stock to close out the short position. In this way, the profit in the stock was locked in and the taxes were deferred from one year to another. If the stock price went up or down during the period the investor was short, the long position and short position in the stock exactly offset each other, providing insulation from price changes.

Price of Order

Orders must specify if a security is to be bought or sold at the market price or at a limited price. **Market orders**—orders at the market price—are filled at the best available price at that time. The New York Stock Exchange has rules dealing with the auction process. Basically, a transaction goes to the highest bid or lowest offer. Nevertheless, problems can arise when a number of bids are made at the same price. In such a case, Rule 72 holds that the bid made first has priority, then come bids of equal or greater size than the amount of shares offered. In other words, the priorities are time and size. A few examples will help to clarify the way the rule works.

Assume that all bids and offers are at the same prices and that the bidder or offerer marked with an asterisk(*) has a clearly established time priority. The letters *A, B, C,* and so on represent various brokers. The following example demonstrates time priority:

Bids	Offers
A – 100* shares	*D* – 200
B – 100	
C – 100	

A had the time priority, so *A* gets 100 shares. *B* came before *C*, so *B* gets 100 shares. *C* gets nothing because there was **stock ahead** in the priority system. *C* can try again in the next auction for the stock.

Both time and size priorities are illustrated in the following example:

Bids	Offers
A – 100* shares	*F* – 1000 shares
B – 200	
C – 400	
D – 300	
E – 500	

A has time priority and gets 100 shares. The remaining 900 shares are allocated on the basis of size priority. Thus, *E* gets 500, and *C* receives 400. *B* and *D* get no stock in this auction because of stock ahead.

This final example shows what happens when offers (or bids) are made simultaneously.

Bids	Offers	
E – 600 shares	*A* – 400 shares	
	B – 400	Offered simultaneously
	C – 400	
	D – 200	

A, *B*, and *C* are on parity and have a precedence as to amount over *D*. Thus, *D* is out of the auction because of stock ahead. *A*, *B*, and *C* can match for 400 shares — that is, they flip coins to see which one will get 400 shares. The two losers can then flip to see which one will get the remaining 200 shares. Alternatively, the brokers can agree to split the lot amount themselves unless any member of the crowd objects. For example, *A*, *B*, and *C* may agree to take 200 shares each.

As these examples show, orders for several hundred shares can be filled at different prices and times. Moreover, some limit orders may not be filled even if the stock trades at the limit price.

Limits, or limited orders, are orders to buy or sell stock at a specific price. A limit order to buy stock is placed *below* the current market price, and a limit order to sell stock is placed *above* the current market price. For example,

$45 sell limit

$40 current market price

$35 buy limit

In this example, if the current market price of a stock is $40 per share, an investor may want to wait days or weeks until the stock declines to $35 per share before buying. In this case, the investor can enter a buy limit order at $35. The limit orders are entered on the **specialist's book** or the Electronic Display Book System. If and when the stock declines to $35, the specialist will try to execute the order in the auction market. Sell limit orders are handled in the same manner.

Time Limits

Orders that are not filled by the end of each trading day are canceled unless some other time limit is specified. Orders that are entered for just one day are called **day orders.** Limit orders for longer periods of time are called open orders. Open orders, or **good until canceled** orders, can remain on a specialist's book for six months, or until they are renewed or canceled by the customer. Frequently, customers forget that they have open orders and are surprised to find they have bought or sold stock. To help customers recall their obligations, many stockbrokerage firms send them periodic notices, reminding them of their open orders.

Stop Orders

Stop orders are used to protect a profit or to minimize a loss. They are placed on opposite sides of the market from limit orders. For example, a sell limit is placed above the market price, whereas a sell stop is placed below the market price. And a buy limit is below the market price, whereas a buy stop is above the market price. Thus,

To illustrate the use of stop orders, assume that an investor bought a stock at $25 per share for which the current market price is $40 per share. If the stock continues to advance in price, the investor will not want to sell. Thus, he does not want to put a sell limit order at, say, $45 per share. However, if the stock goes down, he wants to lock in most of the profit, so he puts a sell stop order at $35 per share. If the stock declines to $35, the stop order becomes a market order at that time. The stop price can be thought of as a trigger that activates a market order.

Another use of the stock order is to protect a profit from a short sale. Let us say that a speculator sold stock short at $60, and the current market price is $40. The speculator can put a buy stop order at, say, $45 to protect her profit. If the stock continues to decline, the price of the stop order can be lowered to enlarge the profit.

The stop order can also be used to minimize losses. If an investor thinks a stock bought today might decline in value, the loss can be minimized by using a sell stop order. In the case of a short sale, speculators can protect themselves against losses if stock prices rise by placing a buy stop order above the price at which the stock was sold short. If a stock was sold short at $40 per share, a buy stop order could be placed at, say, $43. If the stock price increased instead of declining, the loss would be limited to $3 per share.

The stop order can also have a limit price. For example, an order could be entered to buy 100 shares of XYZ at $55 stop limit $58. This means that the customer is willing to buy the stock at about $55 per share but not more than $58 per share. Limits can be used on sell stop orders.

Stop orders should not be confused with **stopping stock.** Stopping stock means that a member of the exchange guarantees to buy or sell a stock at a specified price. Such stops occur periodically when a member of the exchange has a market order and thinks a better price can be gotten for the customer.

Finally, there is a word of caution about stop orders. Before placing a stop order on a stock, investors should examine charts showing that stock's price move-

ments. If the stock typically experiences wide price swings, the investor should take this into account. If the stop order is placed too close to the current market price, it could be executed at the wrong time from the investor's point of view. There is no exact method to determine how close the stop price should be to the market price. Each stop price must be determined individually, according to the investor's needs and the type of stock being considered.

Special Odd-Lot Orders

Rule 124 of the exchange describes special odd-lot orders, which are *not* applicable to round-lot transactions. Three examples of such orders are

1. **Buy on offer.** The order is filled at the round-lot price prevailing at the time the odd-lot broker receives the order, plus any odd-lot differential.
2. **Sell on Bid.** An order to sell on bid marked "long" shall be filled at the round-lot bid price prevailing at the time the odd-lot broker receives the order minus any differential. Short sales shall not be accepted.
3. **With or Without Sale.** A limited order to buy or sell ("long") marked "With or Without Sale" shall be filled on an effective round-lot transaction, or an effective bid or offer, whichever occurs first after the odd-lot broker receives the order, plus or minus any differential. Short sales shall not be accepted.

Special Round-Lot Orders

Rule 13 of the exchange defines special orders that are applicable to round lots. Three examples of such orders are

1. **Fill-or-kill order.** These market or limited orders are to be executed in their entirety as soon as they are represented in the trading crowd. If the orders are not executed, they are canceled.
2. **All-or-none order.** This order is similar to the fill-or-kill order, but it is *not* canceled if it is not executed as soon as it is represented in the trading crowd.
3. **At the opening or at the opening only order.** Market or limited orders can be entered to be executed at the opening of the stock or not at all. If the order is not filled in whole or in part, it is canceled.

This review of the trading practices on the New York Stock Exchange provides some idea of the way orders are executed. If investors understand the various types of orders and know how to use them properly, they can increase their profits by buying and selling at the right times and prices.

CONCLUSION

The New York Stock Exchange is the leading exchange in the United States. Historically, it developed out of the need for a specific place to buy and sell securities. Today, because of computers and improved communication systems, it

is no longer necessary to have one or several "places" to buy and sell securities. Transactions can be handled by computers and people located virtually anywhere. Along this line, the exchange is developing its technology and linking up with the other exchanges.

Although the New York Stock Exchange is our leading exchange, it has been losing market share of trades in stocks listed on that exchange.[1] An increasing number of trades in listed stocks are being executed in the over-the-counter market and on other stock exchanges, including those in foreign countries. In 1989 the NYSE handled only 69.23 percent of the trades in its listed stocks.

The NYSE is governed by a Board of Directors, the chairman of the board, and officers appointed by the chairman. Only members of the exchange or their alternates can trade on the floor of the exchange, and a stockbrokerage firm must have at least one member on its staff before it can be considered a member firm.

There are six classes of members that trade securities on the floor of the exchange: commission brokers, floor brokers, registered competitive market makers, competitive traders, specialists, and odd lot brokers and dealers. Each class has its own specific functions, although there is some overlap in what they are permitted to do in some cases.

A company whose stock is listed on the New York Stock Exchange is in a prestigious position because the public knows the exchange demands that it meet certain financial requirements for size and stability before its stock is accepted for listing. Nevertheless, some listed companies do go broke. Investors find it to their advantage to buy listed stocks, too. Information about the price of these stocks is available daily, and margin credit on them can be obtained easily.

The actual process of trading on the New York Stock Exchange is complex, and is governed by the rules and regulations of the exchange. These practices are emulated by other stock exchanges in the United States and elsewhere. Securities are bought and sold through the execution of a wide variety of orders. In order to trade effectively on the exchange, an investor must understand these various options so that stocks can be bought and sold at the most advantageous times.

IMPORTANT CONCEPTS

Agent	Competitive trader
All-or-none order	Consolidated tape
Automated Bond System (ABS)	Correspondent firm
Block of stock	Covering the short
Buy on close	Day order
Buy on offer	Designated Order Turnaround
Cash trade	(SuperDot) System
Commission broker	Electronic Display Book System

[1] Craig Torres and William Power, "Big Board is Losing Some of its Influence Over Stock Trading", *The Wall Street Journal*, April 17, 1990, A1, A10.

Fair and orderly market
Fill-or-kill order
Floor broker
Good until canceled
Intermarket Trading System (ITS)
Limit order
Listing
Market order
National Association of Securities
   Dealers (NASD)
National market system
New York Stock Exchange
Odd lot
Odd-lot differential

Opening Automated Reporting Sys-
   tem (OARS)
Opening only order
Principal
Registered competitive market maker
   (RCMM)
Round lot
Sell "long"
Short against the box
Short sale
Specialist
Specialist's book
Stock ahead
Stopping stock

QUESTIONS AND EXERCISES

1. What is the significance of the Buttonwood Tree Agreement?
2. What is the primary function of the New York Stock Exchange?
3. Who can buy and sell securities on the floor of the New York Stock Exchange?
4. What are the six classes of membership that are permitted to conduct business on the floor of the New York Stock Exchange?
5. Describe the role of commission brokers.
6. What is the primary function of the specialist?
7. As an agent, what type(s) of orders are found in the specialist's book?
8. What are the major companies in your area? Determine if they meet the minimum requirements to be listed on the New York Stock Exchange.
9. Explain how a short sale works.
10. Explain how the New York Stock Exchange is moving toward a national market system.
11. Last week you gave your broker an order to buy 100 shares of Telephone at $30 per share. You read in the newspaper that Telephone traded at that price, but your order was not executed. What could have caused your order to remain unfilled?
12. Compare the purpose of limit and stop orders.
13. Is stopping a stock the same as a stop order?
14. Is the auction method of trading used on the New York Stock Exchange outdated?
15. Which is riskier, selling stock short or buying stock?

CHAPTER 8

AVERAGES AND INDEXES

"What's the market doing?" is probably the most common question stockbrokers are asked. The answer is usually something like, "The Dow is up two points but utilities are weak," or "The Standard & Poor's 500 is unchanged, but all of your stocks are off at least three points." Stock market indicators such as the Dow Jones Averages and Standard & Poor's Indexes provide important clues about the performance of the stock market. They are reported daily in many newspapers and on television and radio. Newscasters generally report changes in the averages with considerable solemnity. It is considered good when they are up and bad when they are down. There is even a degree of mysticism associated with the averages. Some investors claim that they use the averages to predict accurately the future course of stock market activity. Others make profound statements like "The Dow will break 3000 on December 13 at 1:35 P.M." Such statements are intended to persuade listeners that the speaker is a sophisticated investor indeed. Thus, the averages have assumed a degree of importance beyond being a mere statistical indicator of stock market prices. The purpose of this chapter is to acquaint investors with the major stock and bond market indicators, the data they represent, and the way some of them are determined. In Chapters 19 and 21 you will discover how to speculate on some of these indicators with options and futures contracts.

STOCK MARKET INDICATORS

Dow Jones Stock Averages

The Dow Jones Averages are the best known and most widely quoted of the stock market indicators. Charles Henry Dow — co-founder of Dow Jones, which pub-

lishes *The Wall Street Journal* — began publishing his stock average of 11 "representative stocks," including nine industrials and two railroads, on July 3, 1884, in the *Customer's Afternoon Letter*. Ultimately, the *Afternoon Letter* became part of *The Wall Street Journal*, which began publication in 1889.

Currently, the Dow Jones Averages are presented in chart and statistical form daily in *The Wall Street Journal*. The chart shows the **Dow Jones Industrial Average (DJIA).**

Figure 8-1 depicts the DJIA for a six-month period, which is sufficient time to observe substantial changes in stock market activity. The patterns of ups and downs shown in the chart have particular meaning to **technical analysts** — investors who interpret charts and other data to obtain clues about the future direction of stock market prices. Technical analysis is discussed in Chapter 14.

The vertical lines shown in the chart indicate the high and low average for a day, and the horizontal bar represents the closing average. Also shown are charts for the Transportation and Utility Averages. Notice the differences and similarities in the movements of the three averages — they rise and fall at different times and rates. This suggests that factors, such as interest rates, the cost of fuel, or balance of payments, for example, affect each of these groups differently. Thus, while the industrials are rising, the utilities may be falling. There is an important lesson to be learned here: No single stock market indicator explains all of the diverse trends occurring in the market.

Statistical data about the three averages also appear daily in many local newspapers. The statistics show hourly averages at five-minute intervals, percentage changes, and volume of shares sold for each of the averages. The data in the shares-sold column reveal that the bulk of trading activity takes place with the industrial stocks.

Dow Jones Industrial Average

The first DJIA was published in 1896 and it included 12 industrials. General Electric is the only one of the original industrial stocks still listed in the average. In 1916 the number was increased to 20, and in 1928 it was expanded to its current level of 30 industrial stocks. The companies used to compute the DJIA are among the largest in the nation. The four largest companies in the average, in terms of market value, are Exxon, IBM, General Electric, and AT&T. The 30 DJIA stocks may represent 20 to 25 percent of the market value of all companies traded on the New York Stock Exchange. Because of their dominant size, and because many stocks tend to move together, general stock market trends can be inferred from the Dow averages.

One of the criticisms leveled against the usage of the DJIA as a representative indicator of stocks listed on the New York Stock Exchange is that it is derived from a small group of **blue-chip** stocks. The term *blue chip* means that the company is well established and has a reputation for quality goods, service, and financial strength. An average composed largely of such stocks does not represent the large number of medium and relatively small companies that are traded on the exchange. The companies used to compute this average are listed in Figure 8-1. As a

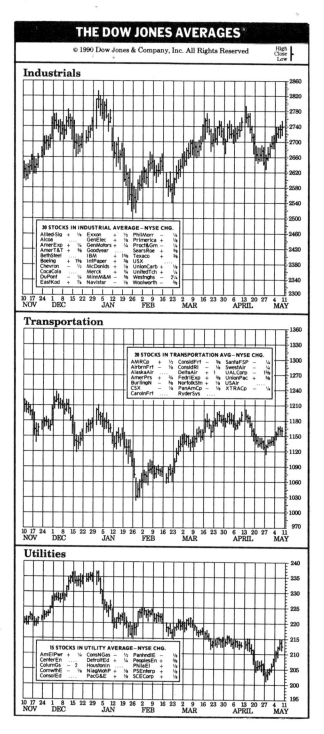

FIGURE 8-1 The Dow Jones averages. *Source: The Wall Street Journal,* May 11, 1990, reprinted by permission, © 1990, Dow Jones & Co., Inc., all rights reserved.

result of mergers, bankruptcies, and other factors, the companies used in the averages change from time to time.

Computing the Industrial Average

The DJIA can be thought of as a portfolio of stocks that originally consisted of one share for each of the 30 different companies. Over the years, some of the companies have split stock and paid stock dividends. The following illustration of a three-stock average shows how the average is calculated and how splits are taken into account. Assume that three stocks—A, B, and C—are selling at $5, $15, and $10 per share, respectively. The average price is determined by summing the value of the shares ($30) and dividing by the number of shares (3):

$$
\begin{array}{rl}
A = & \$\ 5 \\
B = & 15 \\
+C = & 10 \\
\hline
\text{Total} = & \$30
\end{array}
$$

$$
\text{Average} = \frac{\text{total}}{\text{number of shares}} = \frac{\$30}{3} = \$10
$$

In this example the divisor is 3. The divisor changes when stocks are split or substitutions are made in the list of stocks.

Let us say that stock B is split, with each $15 share being exchanged for three $5 shares. On the day the stock is split, the closing price from the previous day is totaled again. However, this time the split stock is added in at its reduced value.

$$
\begin{array}{rl}
A = & \$\ 5 \\
B = & 5 \\
+C = & 10 \\
\hline
\text{Total} = & \$20
\end{array}
$$

The new sum ($20) is divided by the previous day's average ($20/$10 = 2), and the resulting number (2) becomes the new divisor that is used to compute the current day's average.

Suppose that on the day the stock split occurred, the stock market went up, and stock A closed up 1 point at $6, the split stock (B) closed up 2 points at $7, and stock C closed up 3 points at $13. The average is computed by dividing the new total value ($26) by the new divisor (2) to obtain $13.

$$
\begin{array}{rl}
A = & \$\ 6 \\
B = & 7 \\
+C = & 13 \\
\hline
\text{Total} = & \$26
\end{array}
$$

$$
\text{Average} = \frac{\text{total}}{\text{divisor}} = \frac{\$26}{2} = \$13
$$

If the divisor had *not* been changed to reflect the split stock, the average would have been $8.67 ($26/3 = $8.67), which is clearly inaccurate. Thus, the divisors

are changed every time a stock split or stock dividend in excess of 10 percent occurs. It must be noted that as a result of the split, the divisor used to compute the DJIA is never equal to the number of shares in the list. The divisors used to calculate the Dow Averages appear daily in *The Wall Street Journal* beneath the statistical data on the averages. In Figure 8-1, the divisor for the DJIA is 0.555. Thus, a DJIA of, say, 2000, means that if no splits, stock dividends, or substitutions had ever occurred, the average price of the 30 industrial stocks would have been $2000 per share. During this century, the DJIA has ranged in value from a low 52.96 in 1900 to a high of 2810.15 in 1989.

The method used to calculate the Dow Averages has been criticized on several grounds. One criticism is that its calculation gives equal weight to equal dollar price changes. For example, assume that the average is based on two stocks, X selling for $20 per share and Y selling for $200 per share. The average price of these two stocks is $110:

$$\text{Average} = \frac{\$20 + \$200}{2} = \$110$$

If stock X increases $10 in value to $30, and stock Y increases by $10 to $210, the average will be $120:

$$\text{Average} = \frac{\$30 + \$210}{2} = \$120$$

The $10 increase in both stocks was given the same weight in the average, thus increasing it by $10. However, the $10 increase represents a 50 percent increase in stock X, a 5 percent increase in stock Y, and a 9.1 percent increase in the average. This method of calculating averages is called an **unweighted arithmetic mean,** and it differs from some of the other methods used to calculate the averages that will be discussed shortly. The disadvantage of the unweighted arithmetic mean is that extremely high or low values distort the average.

Another problem with the Dow Averages is that the divisor is not adjusted for stock dividends of less than 10 percent. This policy creates a statistical bias against growth stocks that tend to split and declare stock dividends more frequently than nongrowth stocks. Because the divisor is not reduced, the averages are somewhat lower than they would be otherwise.

The Transportation Average

The Dow Transportation Average originally consisted of 20 railroad stocks and was referred to as the Rail Average. In January 1970, the composition of this average was changed to include airlines, freight forwarders, companies engaged in mixed modes of transportation, and railroads. The companies used to calculate this average are shown in Figure 8-1.

The transportation average is calculated in the same manner as the DJIA. However, the divisor for the transportation average is not changed if a stock split or dividend causes a change of less than 2 points.

The Public Utility Average

The utility average consists of 15 utility stocks and is computed in the same manner as the industrial and transportation averages. The companies used in this average are shown in Figure 8-1.

The 65-Stock Average

The 65-stock average is a composite of the industrial, transportation, and utility averages. It is computed like the other averages. The divisor is changed whenever necessary to adjust for splits or other variations.

The Dow Averages have significance beyond their function as indicators of stock market prices. First, they are the oldest stock market average. Second, *The Wall Street Journal* is the most widely read daily financial publication, and it is owned by Dow Jones and Company. Needless to say, *The Wall Street Journal* gives more space to the Dow Averages than other averages and indexes. Third, a lot of stock market lore and mystique is associated with the Dow Averages. Some of this is explained in Chapter 14, where **charting** is discussed. Finally, the companies that make up the industrial average are among the largest companies in the world. To paraphrase an old saying—what affects General Motors affects the rest of the market.

Standard & Poor's Stock Price Indexes

In 1923, Standard & Poor's Corporation published a stock price index that was based on 233 stocks and included 26 subgroup indexes. In 1957, the coverage was expanded to include 500 stocks broken down into 95 subgroups. However, the four main groups are those familiar to most investors: industrials, rails, utilities, and the 500-stock composite—commonly called the Standard & Poor's 500 Stock Index, or the S&P 500. The composite index included 425 industrials, 15 railroads, and 60 public utilities until 1976, when the composition was changed to 400 industrials, 20 transportation, 40 public utilities, and 40 financial. In 1988 Standard & Poor's adopted a flexible structure within the S&P 500 Index. There is no longer a fixed number of industrial, utility, financial, and transportation companies. Standard & Poor's continues to calculate the broad sector indexes, but they are now called the S&P Industrial Index and the S&P Utility Index; they are *not* referred to as the S&P 400 Industrials, the S&P 40 Utilities, etc. The result of these changes is an index that is more representative of the stock market, including some over-the-counter stocks that are included in the financial group. In addition, Standard & Poor's publishes indexes that cover capital goods companies, consumer goods, high-grade common stocks, and low-priced common stocks. As new industries evolve in the economy, they are added to the published indexes. Pollution control and offshore drilling are examples of recent additions to the indexes. Financial data on all of the industry groups are published in Standard and Poor's *Analyst's Handbook* and *Security Price Index Record*. Data on the indexes are published in the Daily News section of *S&P's Corporation Records*, *Outlook*, and *Current Statistics*.

Standard & Poor's uses the **base-weighted aggregative** method to calculate its indexes. The indexes are expressed in relative numbers, with the average value for the base period (1941–1943) equal to 10. The following example illustrates how the index is calculated. Assume that in the base period the average market value for the 400 industrial stocks was $30 billion. The index for that period was arbitrarily assigned a value of 10 and was calculated in the following manner.[1]

$$\text{Index} = \frac{\text{current market value of group}}{\text{market value of group in base period}} \times 10$$
$$\text{1941–1943}$$
$$= \frac{\$30}{\$30} \times 10 = 10$$

where

$$\text{Market value} = \text{average market price of shares} \times \text{number of}$$
$$\text{shares outstanding}$$

Suppose that the market value of the 400 industrial stocks increased to $120 billion. The index would have to quadruple to reflect the increased value. As shown in the following example, the index was 40:

$$\text{Index} = \frac{\$120}{\$30} \times 10 = 40$$

Figure 8-2 reflects the approximate numbers for the Standard & Poor's Price Indexes from 1931 to 1986. This index ranged from about 5 in 1931 to over 350 in 1989. The figure shows that the overall trend of the stock market was upward, but it was punctuated by periodical wide swings. The most notable decline in the index occurred during the Great Crash in 1929 and the Depression in the 1930s.

New York Stock Exchange Indexes

In 1966 the New York Stock Exchange established the **NYSE Common Stock Index,** or **Composite Index** as it is called now, which covers all of the stocks listed on the exchange — stocks from more than 1500 companies. This index provides

---

[1] In symbolic terms the index can be expressed as

$$\text{Index} = \frac{\Sigma P_1 Q_1}{\Sigma P_0 Q_0} \times \text{BI}$$

where

P_1 = the current market price
P_0 = the market price in the base period
Q_1 = the number of shares currently outstanding
Q_0 = the number outstanding in the base period
BI = base index number such as 10 or 100
Σ is the Greek letter sigma and indicates summation. In this case, sigma indicates the summation of all the market values of the companies composing the group.

STANDARD & POOR'S PRICE INDEX
QUARTERLY AVERAGES

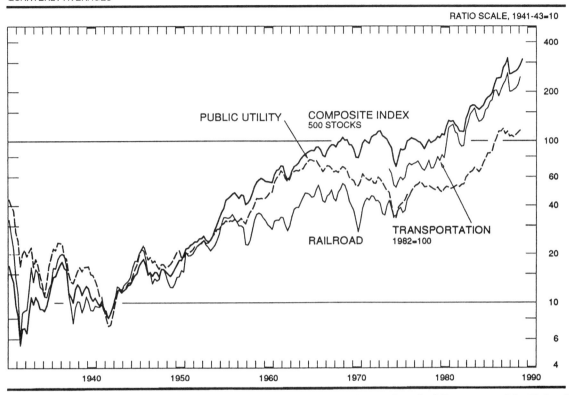

FIGURE 8-2 Standard & Poor's price index, quarterly averages. *Source:* Board of Governors of the Federal Reserve System.

the most comprehensive measure of market activity on the exchange. In addition to the common stock index, there are four subgroup indexes: industrial, transportation, utility, and finance.

The New York Stock Exchange indexes are computed by the same method Standard & Poor's uses to calculate its indexes. However, the NYSE uses December 31, 1965, as the base, and the index for the base is 50.

American Stock Exchange Market Value Index

In September 1973, the American Stock Exchange (AMEX) introduced the **market value index** to replace the price change index in use at that time. The market value index covers all of the common shares listed on the AMEX as well as warrants and American depository receipts (ADRs).

The method of calculating this index differs from the methods described for the other averages. The AMEX selected August 31, 1973, as the base period and set the index number arbitrarily at 100. In 1983 the index number was changed to

50. The index is calculated by dividing the total market value of all of the securities covered in the index on that day by the total market value of all of the securities covered in the previous period and multiplying this number by the index for the previous period.

$$\text{Current index} = \frac{\text{total current market value}}{\text{total market value in previous period}} \times \begin{array}{l}\text{index in}\\\text{previous}\\\text{period}\end{array}$$

The AMEX Market Value Index gives the relative change in the value of the securities covered. If the value of the securities increased 5 percent, the index would increase by a like amount.

NASDAQ

NASDAQ is an acronym for the National Association of Securities Dealers Automated Quotations. NASDAQ indexes cover more than 4000 over-the-counter companies. There are seven NASDAQ indexes:

Composite

Industrials

Banks

Insurance

Other finance

Transportation

Utilities

The NASDAQ indexes are calculated in a manner similar to the Standard & Poor's indexes and New York Stock Exchange indexes, with a few minor differences. The initial base period for NASDAQ indexes is February 5, 1971, and the index number for the base period is 100.

Global Stock Market Indicators

One of the outcomes of Black Monday (October 19, 1987), when the DJIA plunged 508 points (23 percent), was that investors learned that international financial markets were linked together when large declines also occurred on the Tokyo exchange and elsewhere (see Figure 8-3). Subsequently radio, television, and print media have increased their reporting of selected foreign stock market indicators, including the Nikkei index of stocks in Tokyo and the *Financial Times* 100 index of stocks in London. Today investors want to know what happened on the Tokyo and London stock exchanges before they begin trading on the New York Stock Exchange. The Tokyo exchange closed at 1 A.M. New York time, and the London exchange opened at 4 A.M. The New York Stock Exchange opens at 9 A.M.

Although the Tokyo and London stock exchanges get the most media expo-

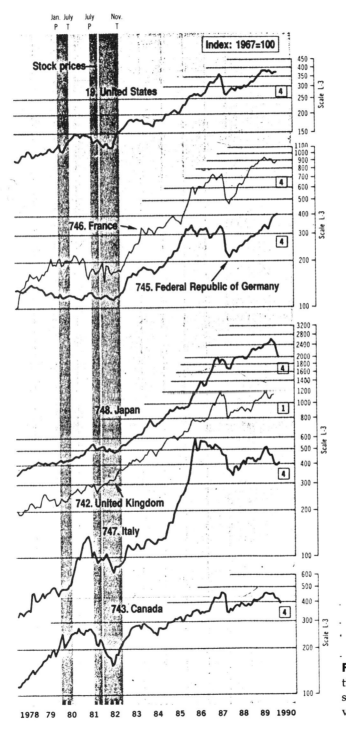

FIGURE 8-3 International comparisons of stock prices. *Source:* Survey of Current Business.

sure, they are not the only exchanges in those countries. As shown in Table 8-1, there are eight stock exchanges in Japan and 13 in the United Kingdom.

While most investors are aware of stock exchanges in Tokyo and London, they may not be aware of smaller and emerging markets. These markets include the other exchanges listed in Table 8-1, and those in Austria, Denmark, Finland, Hong Kong, Italy, New Zealand, Norway, Singapore, South Africa, South Korea, Sweden, Taiwan, and Thailand. Selected foreign stock market indicators are reported in *The Wall Street Journal*, but are not widely reported in the United States. This listing of markets is not complete, and new exchanges are opening to handle the growing volume of international financial transactions.

The question of which stock market indicator the average investor should use is a difficult one to answer because it depends on what the investor wants to know about the market. The stock market indicators discussed here are generally recognized as being the most popular. However, other indicators are available to investors. Moody's Industrial Average, Moody's Railroad Stock Average, the *New York Times* Index, *Barron's* 50 Stock Average, and Value Line averages are examples of other stock market indicators. The major stock market indicators are reported daily in *The Wall Street Journal* and in some other news periodicals. Although the major stock market indicators are calculated in different ways and have different bases, they all indicate similar patterns of stock market activity (see Figure 8-4). Those investors who want information about a particular group of stocks should choose their indicator carefully.

BOND MARKET INDICATORS

Indicators of bond market activity receive less public attention than the stock market indicators because most bonds are held and traded by financial institutions, such as commercial banks, insurance companies, and pension funds. Nevertheless, many individuals invest in corporate, municipal, and U.S. government

TABLE 8-1   Number of Stock
Exchanges in Selected Countries as of 1988

Country	Number of Exchanges
Australia	6
Belgium	4
Canada	5
France	7
Japan	8
Switzerland	7
United Kingdom	13

Source: Based on information presented Norman Berryessa and Eric Kirzner, *Global Investing: The Templeton Way,* Homewood, Ill.: Dow Jones-Irwin, 1988, 85–103.

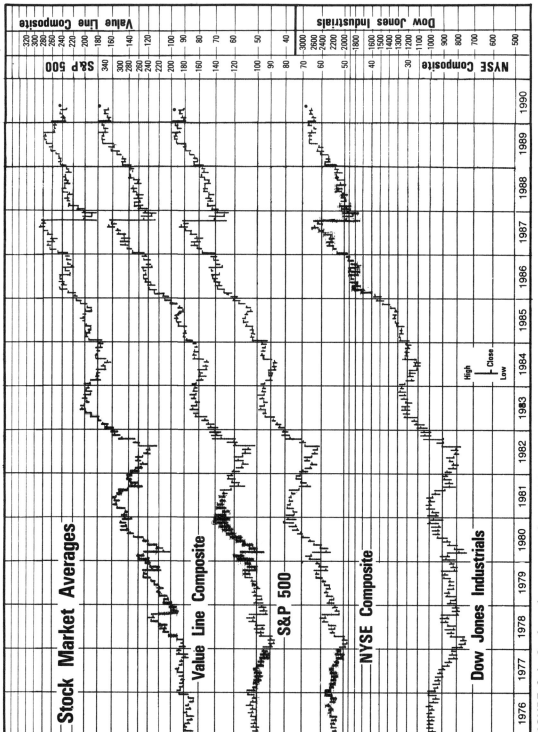

FIGURE 8-4 Stock market averages. *Source:* Value Line Investment Survey.

obligations. Investing in corporate and government obligations becomes particularly attractive when the yields on those securities exceed the yields that can be paid by commercial banks and other financial institutions.

In addition, some investors find it profitable to "play" the bond market. Recall that when market interest rates decline, the market price of outstanding bonds advances. Conversely, a rise in market interest rates is accompanied by declining bond prices. Thus, bond investors should keep a close watch on the level of interest rates and try to anticipate what they will be in the future. The remainder of this chapter deals with selected bond market indicators and the way some of these indicators can be used as forecasting tools.

Moody's Bond Yields

Moody's Investors Service publishes average **bond yields** on various types of bonds in their manuals. Those bonds listed are newly issued domestic, corporate, industrial, municipal, and so on. Current data on some of the averages published by Moody's appear in the *Federal Reserve Bulletin* and *Federal Reserve Chart Book* (annual).

Figure 8-5 shows long-term yields on various types of debt securities. The corporate, state, and local (municipal) bonds are rated Aaa or Baa. As noted in Chapter 3, the quality rating of bonds is indicated by symbols. Bonds with Aaa ratings are prime quality or **gilt-edge securities.** Bonds with Baa ratings are upper- to medium-grade securities. Although not shown, bonds with Caa (or Ca, C) ratings have a poor investment standing.

Figure 8-5 shows that interest rates have moved erratically in recent years. The wide swings in the levels of interest rates provided investors with the opportunity to profit from trading in bonds. The figure also shows that lower quality bonds yield more than bonds with high-quality ratings. The average yields on the Baa seasoned corporate bonds are higher than the average yields on the Aaa seasoned corporate bonds. The difference, or **spread,** between yields reflects the additional compensation investors require to hold relatively risky securities. This requirement also causes a substantial spread between U.S. government bonds, which are considered to have no risk of default, and corporate bonds. The relative low yields on the state and local bonds reflect their tax-exempt status as well as their Aaa rating.

Credit Markets

The Wall Street Journal devotes a daily column to **credit markets** — the market for bonds and other debt instruments — highlighting the previous day's trading activity. It covers factors such as Federal Reserve policies and Treasury financing that affect the credit markets. A careful reading of this column reveals that many of the factors affecting bonds also affect stocks. For example, suppose that the Treasury announces its intention to sell a very large amount, say $60 billion, of Treasury notes. In order to sell a large volume of any inventory, the price is reduced to make the goods attractive to prospective buyers. Likewise, reducing the prices of Treasury notes means higher yields to investors. Higher Treasury

LONG-TERM BOND YIELDS

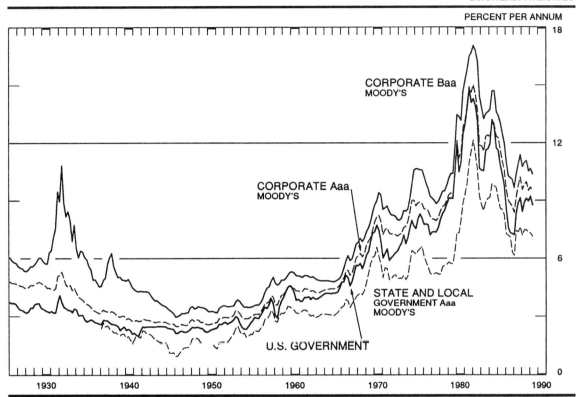

FIGURE 8-5 Long-term bond yields, quarterly averages. *Source:* Board of Governors of the Federal Reserve System.

yields—interest rates—however, signal lower stock prices. Both stock and bond prices are inversely related to market rates of interest. Accordingly informed stock market investors must be aware of activities in the credit markets.

The Wall Street Journal also contains myriad data on corporate, government, and municipal bonds, mortgage-backed securities, and selected foreign bonds. The data are useful to sophisticated investors but may overwhelm novices who do not know GICs from CMOs.[2] However, data and graphs of yield curves are relatively easy to understand.

Yield Curves

Investor's attitudes about the current and future course of market interest rates are reflected to some extent in the maturity of the debt securities that they buy. If

[2] Guaranteed investment contracts and collateralized mortgage obligations.

bond investors believe that interest rates are going to rise significantly, they will tend to avoid buying long-term bonds because the price of bonds will decline. Those investors who hold long-term bonds may sell them in anticipation of the price decline. On the other side of the market, borrowers who sell bonds to raise capital may try to sell as many bond offerings as they can before the general rise in interest rates. Such actions will cause the market rates on long-term bonds to rise.

If the investors who sold or avoided long-term bonds invested in short-term securities, their demand would force the price of those securities up and the interest rates down. Because of their short term to maturity (e.g., 1 year), the prices of such securities change by smaller dollar amounts than the prices of long-term bonds (e.g., 15 years). In other words, short-term securities have less market risk than long-term securities.

In review, if investors believe that interest rates are going to rise significantly, the long-term rates may rise and the short-term rates may fall. This can be shown graphically in what is called a **yield curve,** which shows the relationship between interest rates and the maturity of debt securities. In the case just described, the yield curve will be sloped upward, as shown in Figure 8-6.

If investors expect interest rates to decline significantly, long-term bonds become attractive investments for two reasons. First, they will provide the investor with a relatively high return as long as the bond is held. Second, if interest rates do decline, the bond will increase in value. Borrowers who anticipate a decline in interest rates will withhold new issues from the market to take advantage of lower rates in the future.

If those who are investing in long-term holdings have obtained their funds by selling their short-term holdings, the short-term interest rates will rise. Then, the yield curve will be sloped downward (see Figure 8-7).

A yield curve normally has some positive slope because long-term securities are considered riskier than short-term securities. Thus, lenders want a premium to hold the riskier long-term securities. Figure 8-8 shows a representative normal yield curve of Treasury securities. The configuration of this yield curve suggests that investors did not expect significant changes in the levels of interest rates in the immediate future.

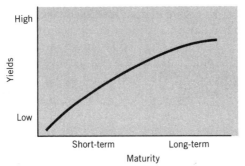

FIGURE 8-6 Upward-sloping yield curve.

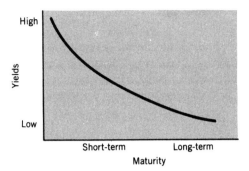

FIGURE 8-7 Downward-sloping yield curve.

In review, yield curves are one indicator of investor's attitudes about the future course of interest rates. Upward-sloping yield curves with more than the normal slope suggest that they believe long-term interest rates will rise. Conversely, downward-sloping yield curves suggest a fall in long-term interest rates. Yield curves for Treasury securities, municipals, and corporates can be obtained daily from *The Wall Street Journal.*

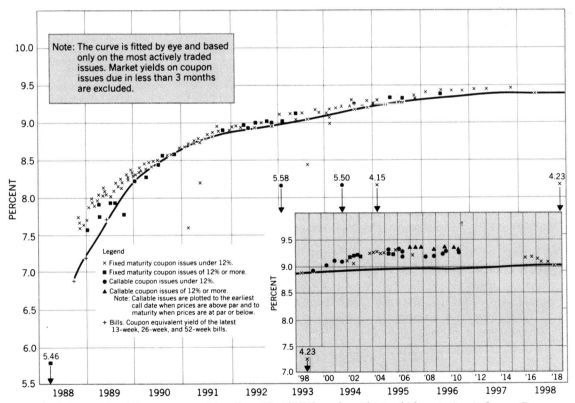

FIGURE 8-8 Yields of Treasury securities, June 30, 1987 (based on closing bid quotations). *Source: Treasury Bulletin.*

CONCLUSION

A number of stock and bond market averages and indexes are available to indicate to the investor "how the market is doing." The Dow Jones Averages are the oldest and most significant of these indicators. They show separate averages for industrials, transportation, and utilities as well as a composite average — all measuring trading activity on the New York Stock Exchange. Standard & Poor's stock price indexes and the New York Stock Exchange indexes also measure activity on the exchange. Although the calculations for each of the indicators differ, they all give about the same information with respect to aggregate stock price movements. Investors who want specific information about particular groups of stocks on the New York Stock Exchange should select the particular indicator that suits their needs. The American Stock Exchange Market Value Index and NASDAQ give information about stock prices on the American Stock Exchange and on the over-the-counter market.

Bond market indicators consist largely of average yields for different qualities and types of bonds. Some investors use newsletters and current periodicals to keep themselves informed about the bond market and future developments. Others use yield curves to provide some limited insight about the future course of interest rates and bond prices.

IMPORTANT CONCEPTS

American Stock Exchange Market
   Value Index
Base-weighted aggregative method
Blue chip
Bond yield
Charting
Credit Market
Dow Jones Bond Average
Dow Jones Industrial Average (DJIA)

Dow Jones Transportation Average
Gilt-edge security
New York Stock Exchange Composite
   Index
Spread between yields
Standard & Poor's 500 Stock Index
Technical analyst
Unweighted arithmetic mean
Yield curves

QUESTIONS AND EXERCISES

1. What is a "blue chip" stock?
2. What does it mean when the Dow Jones Industrial Average changes by 10 points?
3. Suppose that four companies listed in the Dow Jones Industrial Average pay 5 percent stock dividends. How does that affect the Dow Jones Industrial Average?
4. Why are the Dow Jones Averages so popular?
5. What is the base number for the Standard and Poor's 500 Stock Index?

6. What is the base number for the New York Stock Exchange Index?

7. What stock market index measures the performance of the over-the-counter stocks?

8. Examine the major stock indexes for the past five years. Why do they perform differently?

9. Which stock market index is best? Explain.

10. How do the market yields on Baa-rated bonds compare to those on Aaa-rated bonds?

11. What is a yield curve?

12. What are the implications of an upward-sloping yield curve?

13. If long-term interest rates are expected to decline, would you buy or sell long-term bonds?

14. Read the Bond Markets section of *The Wall Street Journal*. What is the yield on new Aaa-rated bonds? What happened to prices of last week's new bond issues?

15. Predict what the Dow Jones Industrial Average will be one month from today. Follow up and see what the average really is in one month.

PART THREE

ANALYZING SECURITIES

Analysis of Investment Opportunities
How To Analyze Investment Opportunities

his part of the book deals with analyzing securities in order to determine
their values and when to buy and sell them. The method suggested here
consists of evaluating information derived from a variety of sources,
which are described in Chapter 9. The analysis begins with understanding the
economic environment (Chapter 10), and then the focus narrows to industries
(Chapter 11) and companies (Chapters 12 and 13). This process is called a **fundamental analysis.** It is analogous to pouring sand through a funnel containing
several filters of different sizes (**see** funnel below). The coarse grains of sand, or

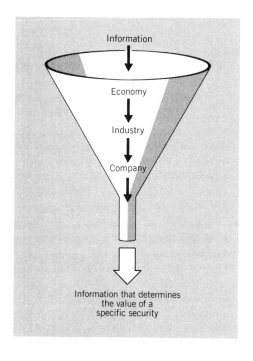

Information

Economy

Industry

Company

Information that determines
the value of a
specific security

information, are filtered to obtain relevant facts about the economy. Finer grains of sand are filtered for particular industries. The finest grains concern specific companies. The residue that falls out at the bottom is the information that is used to determine the intrinsic value of a firm's securities. An alternative approach, called **technical analysis,** is explained in Chapter 14. This approach uses charts of stock price movements and volume to determine which securities should be bought and sold and the timing of those transactions.

SOURCES OF INFORMATION

W hat do the Central Intelligence Agency (CIA), British intelligence (MI-5), and Russian intelligence (KGB) have in common with investing in stocks? The answer is that they obtain large volumes of seemingly unrelated data and try to sift through it to obtain useful information that can be used by their respective governments. Investors do much the same thing. They obtain bits and pieces of data from which they glean information and then make investment decisions.

According to W. Lee Hoskins, president of the Federal Reserve Bank of Cleveland, "We live in an age where information is critical. Households and businesses invest considerable amounts of time and other resources monitoring economic and business developments. These market participants incorporate their expectations of the future into their decisions. Expectations, based on accumulated information, are used to help resources find their highest financial rate of return."[1]

By way of illustration, there is a story about a man who lived near a large manufacturing company. Once a week, a truck stopped at his house to pick up trash. The man always chatted with the driver of the truck and asked him how things were going. One day the driver said that the manufacturing company down the street was keeping him very busy, since the company had more trash than his truck could handle. The man rationalized that the manufacturing company must be doing a large volume of business because it had such a large output of trash. Based on this information, he bought a substantial number of shares of the manufacturing company's stock at a reasonable price. Sometime later, the

---

[1] W. Lee Hoskins, "A Monetary Policy for the 1990s," *Economic Review,* Federal Reserve Bank of Cleveland, May 1, 1990.

driver of the truck revealed that he was not very busy. The volume of trash from the manufacturing company had diminished. The man interpreted this information to mean that business had tapered off, and he sold his stock at the highest price for that year. The point of this story, which is supposed to be true, is that information about stocks can come from virtually any source. It is up to the person receiving the information to use it or disregard it.

One of the problems today, however, is that there can be too much information, or it may not be obvious what information is important for investment purposes. For example, you may have read interesting articles or seen television broadcasts but not realized the investment implications of them. By way of illustration, there are numerous articles and broadcasts concerning the **European Economic Community** (EEC), which consists of Belgium, Denmark, France, Germany, Greece, Ireland, Italy, Luxembourg, the Netherlands, Portugal, Spain, and the United Kingdom. What are the investment implications of the EEC's creating a single integrated market? In 1988, 23 percent of our U.S. merchandise exports were to the European Community.[2] Will the EEC erect trade barriers that will harm U.S. exporters, or will it welcome our imports? How can you benefit from the EEC?

At this point you have to make an intellectual jump from thinking about political and economic changes in the EEC to asking what industries and companies will benefit or be harmed? Consider, for example, the communications industry — broadly defined. Increased trade between nations requires greater communication. Two companies that may benefit from such increased communication are Reuters Holdings PLC and L.M. Ericsson Telephone. American Depository Receipts (ADRs) of both these foreign companies are traded over the counter. Reuters (United Kingdom) is the world's leading electronic publisher and provides real-time and historical financial and business information. Ericsson (Sweden) is an international leader in telecommunications, including mobile and wired communications for private and public networks.

This example illustrates the general pattern of how to organize information. We start from broad concepts, such as the EEC. Next we narrow the scope to selected industries, and then focus on particular companies. Organization of information is the cornerstone of successful investment.

ORGANIZING INFORMATION

There is no shortage of information about which stocks to buy and sell. In fact, there is so much information available that it is a difficult task to pick out what is

---

[2] Norman S. Fieleke, ''Europe in 1992,'' *New England Economic Review,* Federal Reserve Bank of Boston, May/June 1989, 13–26.

useful. What is useful, of course, depends on the objectives of the reader. However, it is helpful to think of the information in terms of its relationship to the investment process. One useful way to organize information is to categorize it in the manner shown in the following list:

1. Information about the state of the economy and the economic outlook
2. Information about particular industries
3. Information about specific companies
4. General information about the stock market

This ordering of subjects reflects the approach used in later chapters to analyze securities. In general terms, the analysis of securities begins by examining major trends in economic activity because the level of stock market prices is significantly affected by business activities and inflation. For example, if projections indicate a downturn in economic activity, there is a strong likelihood that the stock market will precede the course of the economy. Some industries are more affected by changes in business activity than others. The housing industry, for example, is considered cyclical; that is, the number of houses being started and built corresponds directly to the ups and downs of the economy. Other industries, such as drugs, are not affected as much by the level of economic activity. Knowing what the economy is going to do in the future provides important insights about what stocks to buy and sell today. For example, you may decide that based on projections of an ageing population, you think that the drug industry may have some investment potential.

The next step in analyzing securities is to examine particular industries such as drugs. As previously noted, some industries are affected more by changes in economic activity than others. In addition, each industry has unique characteristics investors should know about before they invest in that industry. For example, changes in technology and marketing have had a substantial effect on the computer and drug industries.

The third step in security analysis is to obtain information about specific companies. By combining information obtained about the economy and industry with information about specific companies, the investor will be able to determine whether the securities of that company are worth investing in.

The final step is timing — determining the proper time to buy or sell securities. Assume that an investor has decided to invest in General Motors. However, information about the stock market indicates that the stock should not be bought at this time because the market is declining sharply, and all reports suggest that stock prices will decline further. Thus, the decision to buy stock is modified by the condition of the market.

In review, investors frequently find that they have access to more information than they can use. By organizing information in the manner described, they can make better use of information, thus saving time in analyzing securities.

SOURCES OF INFORMATION

Periodicals

Articles about companies and industries are published in hundreds of periodicals. Fortunately, from the investigator's point of view, *The Predicast F&S Index*[3] tells where to find articles about companies, industries, and products in more than 750 financial publications. Such information includes mergers, products, sales, profits, and other factors that influence earnings. Each entry in the index contains a brief description of the article and the source from which the entry was taken. The index is arranged in two sections. Section 1 uses the **Standard Industrial Classification (SIC)** code to classify groups of related products. SIC codes are a method developed by the U.S. government to classify business concerns on the basis of the products they produce. For example, *chemical products (not elsewhere classified)* have a SIC code of 283. *Drugs and pharmaceuticals* (SIC code 2830) is a subgroup of chemical products. Thus, someone wanting specific information about drug consumption could find that subject listed under the appropriate SIC code . Section 1 contains an alphabetical guide to SIC codes. Section 2 contains an alphabetical listing by company name. The *F&S Index* is published weekly and cumulatively monthly, quarterly, semiannually, and annually. The *F&S Index,* as well as the other sources mentioned here, are available at many public libraries.

Business Periodicals Index is another reference source that can save you a lot of time when you are researching articles. This index covers articles about companies and industries published by major business periodicals.

Several magazines and newspapers generally recognized as being especially useful to investors are *Forbes, Fortune, BusinessWeek, The Wall Street Journal, Barron's, The New York Times,* and *USA Today.*

Forbes specializes in timely articles and commentaries on many companies, industries, and personalities. Particular issues contain special annual reports that rank mutual funds by stock market performance and list the largest corporations by revenue, profitability, growth, and stock market performance.

Fortune examines particular companies and industries in depth. In addition, it lists the 500 largest U.S. industrial corporations, the 50 largest banks, and the 50 largest merchandising, transportation, life insurance, and utility companies in various issues. Moreover, it contains articles about the economy and investing.

BusinessWeek covers a wide variety of business-related topics as well as articles about specific companies and industries. It is an excellent source of information.

The Wall Street Journal is published by Dow Jones & Company each Monday through Friday. It deals primarily with current investment and financial information. Later in this chapter, various part of *The Wall Street Journal* are used to illustrate how to read a financial page. Students and investors will benefit substantially from reading the *Journal* because of its timely articles on subjects related to investing.[4]

---

[3] The *F&S Index* is published by Predicasts, 1100 Cedar Avenue, Cleveland, Ohio 44106.

[4] Special student subscription rates are available for Dow Jones publications. Contact the Educational Service Bureau, Dow Jones & Company, P.O. Box 300, Princeton, N.J. 08540.

Barron's, also published by Dow Jones, is a weekly financial newspaper. It is a rich source of statistical information about the stock market. In addition to quotations on stocks, bonds, and options, *Barron's* publishes data on stock price movements, Dow Jones hourly averages, foreign stock indexes, and a variety of other economic and financial indicators.

The New York Times is a daily newspaper with excellent coverage of business and financial news. The Sunday edition contains a large section devoted to business activity.

USA Today, a national daily newspaper, contains a section earmarked for business activity and the securities market. It is up-to-date and easy to read.

In addition to the periodicals mentioned, other popular, financially oriented publications include the *Commercial and Financial Chronicle, Money,* and *Changing Times.* All of the periodicals mentioned have national coverage. Some concentrate on particular geographic areas, such as *Financial Trend: The Newsweekly of Southwestern Industry and Investments* and *Northwest Stock Guide.*

Financial Services

Many companies provide investors with written and computerized financial data, recommendations to buy and sell securities, charts, and other information for a fee. Three popular financial service organizations are *Standard & Poor's Corporation, Moody's Investor Services,* and the *Value Line Investment Survey.*[5]

Standard & Poor's Corporation

Standard & Poor's offers many financial services. To examine each of these services in depth is beyond the scope of this text, but some of the publications most helpful in analyzing securities are listed in the following discussion.

Standard & Poor's Corporation Records provides continuously updated financial information on 6000 or more companies. The six loose-leaf volumes contain a detailed description of each company's background, financial structure, and securities. For keeping abreast of the latest information there is the daily Monday through Friday publication, *Daily News Section.*

Industry Surveys cover more than 50 leading industries. The economics and investment qualities of the industries are examined in detail. In addition, a monthly Trends and Projections section forecasts industry trends.

Stock Reports are concise descriptions of a company's activities, an analysis of its financial results backed by statistical data, and an opinion of the investment merits of the stock. Stock reports are published for stocks listed on the New York Stock Exchange, American Stock Exchange, and for selected over-the-counter stocks. Figure 9-1 is a stock report for Johnson & Johnson, which is listed on the New York Stock Exchange. When using such a report, the investor should make

---

[5] Investors who want specific information should write to:
  Standard & Poor's Corporation, 25 Broadway, New York, N.Y. 10014
  Moody's Investor Services, 99 Church Street, New York, N.Y. 10007
  The Value Line Investment Survey, 711 Third Avenue, New York, N.Y. 10017

Johnson & Johnson

1268

NYSE Symbol JNJ Options on CBOE (Jan-Apr-Jul-Oct) In S&P 500

Price	Range	P–E Ratio	Dividend	Yield	S&P Ranking	Beta
Nov 13'89	1989					
56	56⅝–41½	18	1.16	2.1%	A	0.91

Summary

This well-known health care firm has one of the broadest product lines in the industry, offering consumer products, ethical and over-the-counter pharmaceuticals, and various other medical and dental items. Above-average growth prospects for major markets coupled with new product contributions should support good sales and earnings growth in the years ahead.

Current Outlook

Earnings for 1990 are estimated at $3.75 a share, up from the $3.25 likely for 1989.

An increase in the $0.29 quarterly dividend is likely in early 1990.

Sales for 1990 should post show further progress. Despite persisting softness in U.S. health and beauty aid markets and intensified competition in the sanitary protection line, volume should be lifted by continued strong gains in pharmaceutical sales and further growth in professional lines. New products, including Hismanal antihistamine, Eprex anti-anemia treatment and Acuvue disposable contact lenses, will be an added plus. Margins should be well maintained on the better volume and cost efficiencies.

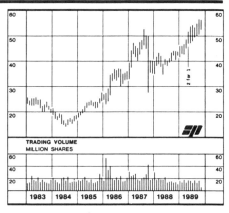

Net Sales (Million $)

Quarter:	1989	1988	1987	1986
Mar.	2,445	2,311	1,981	1,743
Jun.	2,390	2,290	2,010	1,732
Sep.	2,451	2,199	1,993	1,782
Dec.	---	2,200	2,028	1,746
	---	9,000	8,012	7,003

Sales for the nine months ended September 30, 1989 rose 7.1%, year to year, reflecting higher sales in all three major business segments. Net income advanced 11%, to $2.64 a share from $2.31, as adjusted for the May, 1989 2-for-1 split.

Common Share Earnings ($)

Quarter:	1989	1988	1987	1986
Mar.	0.95	0.81	0.68	d0.375
Jun.	0.89	0.79	0.65	0.520
Sep.	0.80	0.71	0.61	0.510
Dec.	E0.61	0.56	0.48	0.280
	E3.25	2.86	2.42	0.930

Important Developments

Oct. '89— The company's over-the-counter pharmaceuticals (OTC) joint venture with Merck announced plans to acquire the U.S. OTC drug business of ICI Americas, Inc. for $450 million. That business includes the Mylanta line of antacid products and the Mylicon line of anti-gas products. JNJ also recently announced a joint agreement with Abbott Laboratories and Chiron Corp. for the development of diagnostic tests. Management noted that four recent product introductions recorded substantial sales growth during the third quarter. These include Acuvue, the world's first disposable contact lens; Hismanal, a once-a-day, less-sedating antihistamine; Eprex, an anti-anemia agent used by dialysis patients; and Prepulsid, a gastro-intestinal prokinetic.

Next earnings report expected in mid-February.

Per Share Data ($)

Yr. End Dec. 31	1988	1987	1986	¹1985	1984	1983	1982	1981	1980	1979
Tangible Bk. Val.	8.69	8.32	7.03	9.17	8.02	7.91	7.40	6.76	6.12	5.41
Earnings²	2.86	2.42	0.93	1.38	1.29	1.40	1.26	1.09	0.96
Dividends	0.96	0.80½	0.68¾	0.63¾	0.58¾	0.53¾	0.48½	0.42⅝	0.37⅛	0.33⅜
Payout Ratio	33%	33%	72%	38%	42%	42%	35%	34%	34%	35%
Prices—High	44⅛	52¾	37⅛	27⅝	21½	25¾	25⅝	19¾	17	13½
Low	34⅝	27½	23⅝	17⅝	14	19½	16¼	14⅛	11	10⅞
P/E Ratio—	15–12	22–11	40–26	16–10	16–10	20–15	18–12	16–11	16–10	14–11

Data as orig. reptd. Adj. for stk. div(s). of 100% in May 1989, 200% May 1981. 1. Reflects merger or acquisition. 2. Bef. spec. item(s) of -0.14 in 1982. d-Deficit. E-Estimated.

November 21, 1989

Standard & Poor's Corp.
25 Broadway, NY, NY 10004

FIGURE 9-1 Standard & Poor's stock report. *Source:* Standard & Poor's Corporation, reprinted by permission.

Income Data (Million $)

Year Ended Dec. 31	Revs.	Oper. Inc.	% Oper. Inc. of Revs.	Cap. Exp.	Depr.	Int. Exp.	Net Bef. Taxes	Eff. Tax Rate	¹Net Inc.	% Net Inc. of Revs.
1988	9,000	1,795	19.9	664	391	135	1,396	30.2%	974	10.8
1987	8,012	1,565	19.5	515	356	140	1,193	30.2%	833	10.4
1986	7,003	1,259	18.0	446	275	87	391	15.7%	330	4.7
²1985	6,421	1,090	17.0	366	251	75	899	31.8%	³614	9.6
1984	6,124	972	15.9	366	226	86	755	31.9%	515	8.4
1983	5,973	953	16.0	401	210	88	724	32.5%	489	8.2
1982	5,761	874	15.2	470	176	74	787	33.5%	523	9.1
1981	5,399	869	16.1	389	152	61	784	40.3%	³468	8.7
1980	4,837	755	15.6	364	139	³37	675	40.7%	401	8.3
1979	4,212	685	16.3	273	121	22	592	40.5%	352	8.4

Balance Sheet Data (Million $)

Dec. 31	Cash	Curr. Assets	Curr. Liab.	Ratio	Total Assets	Ret. On Assets	Long Term Debt	Common Equity	Total Inv. Capital	% LT Debt of Cap.	Ret. On Equity
1988	660	3,503	1,868	1.9	7,119	14.5%	1,166	3,503	4,669	25.0	28.3%
1987	741	3,272	1,763	1.9	6,546	13.4%	733	3,485	4,238	17.3	26.5%
1986	953	3,202	2,293	1.4	5,877	6.2%	242	2,824	3,096	7.8	11.0%
1985	736	2,897	1,172	2.5	5,095	12.7%	185	3,351	3,698	5.0	19.5%
1984	443	2,514	1,042	2.4	4,541	11.7%	225	2,932	3,291	6.8	17.7%
1983	427	2,457	924	2.7	4,462	11.2%	196	3,027	3,268	6.0	16.7%
1982	366	2,253	900	2.5	4,210	13.0%	142	2,800	2,987	4.8	19.5%
1981	427	2,202	881	2.5	3,820	13.0%	92	2,528	2,661	3.4	19.4%
1980	359	1,971	774	2.5	3,343	12.8%	70	2,269	2,372	3.0	18.7%
1979	311	1,718	629	2.7	2,874	13.3%	70	1,987	2,085	3.3	18.9%

Data as orig. reptd. 1. Bef. spec. item(s) in 1982. 2. Reflects merger or acquisition. 3. Reflects acctg. change.

Business Summary

This company is one of the world's leading manufacturers of health care products. Sales and operating profits were divided as follows in 1988:

	Sales	Profits
Consumer	41%	26%
Pharmaceutical	26%	49%
Professional	33%	25%

Foreign operations accounted for about 49% of sales and 61% of operating profits in 1988.

Consumer products encompass baby toiletries, first aid products, and nonprescription drugs. Some of the better known products include Johnson's baby powder, shampoo, oil and lotion; Tylenol analgesic; Stayfree, Carefree, and Sure & Natural feminine hygiene products; Band-Aid adhesive bandages, and Reach toothbrushes.

Pharmaceuticals consist of prescription drugs, contraceptives, therapeutics and veterinary products. Some items are Ortho-Novum oral contraceptives, Haldol tranquilizer, Tolectin antiarthritic, Nizoral and Miconazole antifungals, Eprex anti-anemia agent, Imodium antidiarrheal, Retin-A for acne, and Hismanal antihistamine. Professional items include ligatures and sutures, mechanical wound closure products, diagnostic products, dental products, medical equipment and devices, surgical dressings, surgical apparel and accessories, surgical instruments, intraocular lenses and hyaluronic acid.

Dividend Data

Dividends have been paid since 1905.

Amt. of Divd. $	Date Decl.	Ex-divd. Date	Stock of Record	Payment Date
0.50	Jan. 9	Feb. 14	Feb. 21	Mar. 7'89
2-for-1	Feb. 13	---	Apr. 26	May 10'89
0.29	Feb. 13	May 22	May 26	Jun. 6'89
0.29	Jul. 24	Aug. 16	Aug. 22	Sep. 5'89
0.29	Oct. 23	Nov. 15	Nov. 21	Dec. 5'89

Next dividend meeting: early Jan.'90.

Capitalization

Long Term Debt: $1,069,000,000.

Common Stock: 333,134,851 shs. ($1 par).
The Robert Wood Johnson Foundation owns about 8.4%.

Institutions hold some 62%.

Shareholders of record: 54,500.

Office—One Johnson & Johnson Plaza, New Brunswick, N.J. 08933. Tel—(201) 524-0400. Chrmn & CEO—R. E. Larsen. Secy—J. T. Woodward III. Treas—A. J. Markey. Investor Contact—Jo Ann H. Heisen (201) 524-3376. Dirs—J. E. Burke, R. E. Campbell, D. R. Clare, J. G. Cooney, C. C. Garvin, Jr., P. M. Hawley, J. J. Heldrich, C. H. Johnson, A. D. Jordan, R. S. Larsen, R. Q. Marston, J. S. Mayo, T. S. Murphy, P. J. Rizzo, R. B. Smith, R. N. Wilson. Transfer Agent & Registrar—Morgan Shareholder Services Trust Co., NYC. Incorporated in New Jersey in 1887. Empl—81,300.

Information has been obtained from sources believed to be reliable, but its accuracy and completeness are not guaranteed.   H.B. Safflas

FIGURE 9-1 *(continued)*

sure that it is relatively current. The date of publication is at the bottom of the front page. The recent market price, dividend, and yield are presented at the top of the report. The next item is the summary of the information presented in the sections on prospects, recent developments, fundamental position, and other parts of the report. The summary is Standard & Poor's opinion of the investment merit of the stock in capsule form. Companies such as Standard & Poor's do *not* make strong recommendations such as "this stock is great and is going to double within the next year so it should be bought now." They use phrases like "the stock is suitable for accounts seeking income and long-term appreciation," or "the stock is speculative." Thus, the prudent investor should take all of the information in the report and other sources into account when analyzing a security.

Beneath the summary is a chart showing the price of the stock over a period of four or more years. This chart permits comparisons between the company's market performance and that of other companies in the same industry and the stock market as a whole, which is represented by the Standard & Poor's average.

The remainder of the report is self-explanatory. However, one additional feature should be noted: the address of each company is printed on the bottom of the second page of the report. Investors seeking annual reports and other information can contact the company at that address.

Stock Guides are a pocket-sized monthly summary of investment data on more than 5000 common and preferred stocks. Figure 9-2 shows two pages from a stock guide. There are 44 columns of data for each company. The publication lists the name of the company, the market where it is traded, quality ranking, principal business, and pertinent financial data. Its convenient size and the large volume of data it contains make it a useful tool for investors. Standard & Poor's has a similar service for bonds.

Trendline consists of charts instead of numerical data. The information, such as stock prices and volume of trading, is of particular concern to investors who are interested in "technical analysis," which is explained in Chapter 14. There it will be shown why investors may be better off buying a stock at a higher price than at a low price!

Moody's Investor Services

Moody's, like Standard & Poor's, offers a variety of financial services. However, Moody's is more widely known for its annual reference manuals. The following list provides a brief description of some of its services:

Moody's Industrial Manual and *Moody's OTC Industrial Manual* provide comprehensive financial data on a large number of domestic industrial companies and a limited number of Canadian and other foreign companies. Companies are classified alphabetically and also by industry and product.

Moody's Bank and Finance Manual contains extensive data on banks, investment companies, insurance companies, and real estate investment trusts.

Moody's Public Utility Manual provides financial data on the major electric and gas utility companies.

116 JAY-KAN — Standard & Poor's Corporation

¶S&P 500 •Options Index	Ticker Symbol	Name of Issue (Call Price of Pfd. Stocks)	Market	Com. Rank. & Pfd. Rating	Par Val.	Inst. Hold Cos	Inst. Hold Shs. (000)	Principal Business	Price Range 1971-88 High	1971-88 Low	1989 High	1989 Low	1990 High	1990 Low	Feb. Sales in 100s	February, 1990 Last Sale Or Bid High	Low	Last	%Div Yield	P-E Ratio
1	JAYJ	Jay Jacobs	OTC	NR	1¢	19	860	Apparel strs/whsle apparel	15½	4	9⅝	6	6¾	5⅝	1213	6⅛	5¾	5⅞B	...	10
2	JBBB	JB's Restaurants	OTC	B−	10¢	42	3629	Family type restaurants	15¾	1	7¾	5¾	6¾	5⅞	4192	6¾	6	6 3/16B	...	14
3	JEAN	Jean Philippe Fragrances	OTC	NR	.001	1	17	Mkts imported fragrances	1 7/16	¾	1 5/16	⅞	1 1/16	9/16	1941	⅞	9/16	⅝B	...	10
4	JEFG	Jefferies Group	OTC	B	1¢	29	2253	Equity securities broker	22¼	7¾	15¼	10¾	12¾	11¼	1233	12	11¼	12B	1.7	21
5	JBNK	Jefferson Bankshares	OTC	A−	2.5	24	1189	Commercial bkg,Virginia	39½	6½	26½	19½	24½	21¾	1157	23¼	21¾	22¼B	4.5	9
¶6	JP	Jefferson-Pilot	NY,B,C,M,P,Ph	B+	1¼	204	20771	Insurance hldg co, life	42½	6	45½	29¾	44¼	37¼	7272	41¼	37⅝	40¼	3.4	11
7•[1]	JERR	Jerrico Inc[53]	OTC	A−	No	..	...	Restaurant shoppes	26⅜	5/16	25½	14⅛	23½	20¼	363	21½	20¼	19½B	...	15
8	JGRP	Jesup Group	OTC	NR	1¢	10	359	Mfrs cast acrylic sheet	57½	10	14¼	5½	10	6¼	426	8¼	6¼	7B	...	d
9	JET	Jetronic Indus	AS	C	10¢	6	212	Mfr electr eq:furniture strs	10	11/16	3⅞	1½	3	1⅝	293	2½	1⅝	1¾B	...	d
10	JEM	Jewelmasters Cl'A'	AS	NR	1¢	5	139	Mfr,sell jewelry thru dept str	16½	2	5½	1⅝	2¼	2	132	2¼	2	2B	5.0	d
11	JHM	JHM Mtge Sec Pfd L.P.	NY	NR	No	1	2	Mtge broker/investment co	10¼	9½	9¾	5¼	6⅞	5⅝	1516	6¼	5⅝	5⅞	19.7	..
12•[1]	JLUB	Jiffy Lube Int'l[54]	OTC	NR	.025	..	...	Franchises auto lube centers	25¼	4⅞	8½	1⅜	3	1¾	12452	2¾	2¼	2⅝B	...	d
13	JLGI	JLG Indus	OTC	B−	20¢	25	1335	Mobile aerial lifts:cranes	22¼	3¾	23	14⅞	17	15½	1230	17	15½	16¾B	1.2	8
14	JMBRS	JMB Realty Tr SBI	OTC	LIQ	No	7	257	Real estate investment trust	19	3⅞	12½	7½	9	7¼	95	8¼	7¼	7½B	...	23
15	JALC	John Adams Life	OTC	C	No	7	309	Hldg co: life insurance	18⅛	1¼	1⅝	1⅛	1⅝	1⅛	16	1½	1¼	1¼B	...	d
16	JHS	John Hancock Inc Sec[59]	NY,B,M	NR	No	13	45	Closed end invest:debt	22⅛	10	16⅛	14⅛	15¾	14⅞	742	15⅝	14⅞	15¼	9.6	..
17	JHI	John Hancock Inv Tr[59]	NY,B,M	NR	No	14	38	Closed-end investment co	27⅝	13⅛	22¼	19¼	21⅞	19⅞	489	21⅛	19⅞	20⅝	†9.8	..
¶18•[2]	JCI	Johnson Controls	NY,B,M,P,Ph	A−	16⅔¢	205	20305	Mfr bldg controls:auto prod	40	1 11/16	46¾	27⅞	32¼	27⅛	10118	30¼	27⅛	28¼	4.2	12
19	JHSN	Johnson Electronics	OTC	C	25¢	6	447	Mfr FM/SCA radio receiv'g eq	21	1/16	2¾	1⅜	1¾	1 7/16	1039	1¾	1 7/16	1¾B	...	d
¶20•[3]	JNJ	Johnson & Johnson	NY,B,C,M,P,Ph,To	A	1	907	207608	Health care products	52¾	9½	59½	41½	60¾	51⅛	115105	56⅝	52	53⅝	2.2	17
21	JNU	J&J,Americus(Unit)	AS,M	NR	No	2	1595	Unit Trust,Johnson & Johnson	50½	34¾	54	42⅝	58	53	47	58	53	54½B	2.1	..
22	JNS	Score	AS,M	NR	No	14	885	Capital appreciation	21⅛	3¾	14¾	4½	15¾	9¼	4029	11⅞	9¾	10¼	...	..
23	JNP	Prime	AS,M	NR	No	24	1348	Divd income pay'g component	38⅝	26	46¾	37⅛	46½	43¼	1520	46½	43¾	45½	2.5	..
24	JPC	Johnson Products	AS,M	C	50¢	6	280	Personal grooming aids	37⅜	1⅜	3¾	1⅝	3⅜	3	204	3¼	3	3B	...	33
25	JWAIA	Johnson Worldwide'A'	OTC	NR	5¢	56	2973	Recreational prod/inking	22½	8	27½	20¼	24	20¼	2253	24	20¼	22¼B	...	14
26	JII	Johnston Indus	NY,M	B	10¢	22	1829	Mfrs ind'l/apparel textiles	18¾	9/16	14⅝	10⅛	10⅞	9	1101	10	9	9⅛	5.5	10
27	JOIN	Jones Intercable	OTC	B	1¢	31	2225	Cable television systems	16¾	⅛	20⅞	12½	16¼	10½	2019	13¼	10½	10⅞B	...	d
28	JOINA	Class A (1/10 vtg)	OTC	NR	1¢	50	5012		16⅝	2⅞	20⅞	11⅛	16⅛	10⅜	9069	14⅛	10⅜	10⅞B	...	d
29	JTV	Jones Intercable Inv Cl'A'[61]	AS,M	NR	No	11	369	Acquire,operate CATV system	17½	10⅛	15⅝	12¾	14	10⅝	3354	13¾	10⅝	10¾	13.0	d
30	JMED	Jones Medical Indus	OTC	NR	4¢	5	160	Mfr brand/generic drug prod	6⅞	2⅝	10⅞	4⅝	11¾	9	3329	11⅝	9	10 3/16B	0.8	23
31	JPS	Jones Plumbing Sys	AS	C	20¢	1	5	Mfg/dstr plumbing repair prod	13¼	1 1/16	4¼	2	2⅞	2½	27	2⅝	2½	2½	...	8
32	JOR	Jorgensen (E.M.)Co.[65]	NY,B,M,P	B	1	36	2155	Nationwide metals supplier	33⅜	3⅞	32¼	27⅜	41⅛	29½	7884	41⅛	40⅛	41	2.4	16
33	JOSL	Joslyn Corp	OTC	B	1¼	40	1733	Tel & elec transm eqp	37	4⅜	30¾	27	29¾	28¼	417	29¼	28¼	28¼B	5.7	11
¶34•[4]	JOS	Jostens Inc	NY,B,M,Ph	A+	33⅓¢	201	22179	School class rings,yearbook	25	⅞	30⅜	18⅛	29⅛	22½	7377	27⅛	24⅛	25¾	2.8	18
35	JOL	Joule Inc	AS	NR	1¢	13	408	Office/engineering temp help	13	2¼	3⅛	1½	2¼	1¾	69	2¼	1⅞	2B	...	67
36	JPI	J.P. Industries	NY,B,M	B+	10¢	46	3970	Plumb'g prod/transp'n parts	24⅞	5	18¼	12⅛	15	10⅝	6669	15	10⅝	13⅝	...	10
37	JJS	Jumping-Jacks Shoes	AS	D	1¢	7	163	Mfr/dstr children's shoes	7⅞	15/16	3⅛	1	1¾	1⅜	128	1½	1⅜	¼B	...	d
38	JUNO	Juno Lighting	OTC	B+	1¢	62	5958	Mfrs recessed/track light'g	25¾	3¼	20¼	13	19¾	17⅛	4504	19⅝	18¾	19½B	1.0	14
39	JSTN	Justin Indus	OTC	B	2½	29	2849	Bldg mtl:leather gds,towers	13⅞	1	16⅞	9⅜	17¾	13⅞	10180	17¾	13⅞	16½B	2.4	20
40•[5]	JWP	JWP, Inc	NY,M,Ph	B	10¢	117	8538	Specialty maint:dstr water	22	9/16	31½	16⅛	35	29	18358	32¾	29	31⅛	...	16
41	KHLR	Kahler Corp	OTC	B−	10¢	16	362	Lodg'g,formal wr,text care	23	3⅞	21	14	15¾	14	217	15	14	14¾B	...	d
42	KAMNA	Kaman Corp Cl'A'[69]	OTC	A	10¢	74	8612	Bearings,music,aerosp,av svs	21⅜	⅝	14⅞	7⅝	9½	7½	10418	8⅛	7¾	8⅛B	5.4	17
43	MKCO	Kamenstein (M.)Inc	OTC	B−	1¢	5	238	Mfrs wood household prod	9⅞	1¼	5¼	2¾	5¾	3⅞	365	5½	4¼	4¾B	...	7
44	KPP	Kaneb Pipeline Ptnrs L.P.[71]	NY	NR	No	3	107	O&G pipeline/transportation	....	....	22⅛	19⅛	22⅛	18¾	896	20¼	18¾	18¾	11.7	..

Uniform Footnote Explanations-See Page 1. Other: [1]P:Cycle 1. [2]Ph:Cycle 1. [3]CBOE:Cycle 1. [4]NY:Cycle 3. [5]ASE:Cycle 1. [51]Excl 9,000 jr com shrs. [52]®$1.96,'88. [53]Investor grp(98%)plan mgr. [54]100% non-taxable,'89. [55]Pfd units. [56]80%(Fully-diluted)owned by Pennzoil. [57]Liq divd. [58]Liq divd: 100% non-taxable,'89. [59]Shrs Ben Int. [60]®$2.42,'89. [61]L.P.units. [62]15 Wk Dec'86. [63]Fiscal Jun'88 & prior. [64]Yr Jun'88 d▲1.47. [65]Kelso & Co offer,$41.50 to Mar 19. [66]Fiscal Sep'87 & prior. [67]®$1.30,'88. [68]Sub pfd in M$. [69]Non-vtg. [70]®$1.31,'88. [71]Sr pref units. [72]Incl 4.65M Sr pref.units & 6M pref units.

Common and Convertible Preferred Stocks — **JAY-KAN 117**

Splits ♦ Index	Cash Divs. Ea. Yr. Since	Dividends Latest Payment Period $	Date	Ex. Div.	Total $ So Far 1990	Ind. Rate	Paid 1989	Financial Position Mil-$ Cash& Equiv.	Curr. Assets	Curr. Liab.	Balance Sheet Date	Capitalization Lg Trm Debt Mil-$	Shs. 000 Pfd.	Com.	Earnings $ Per Shr. Years End	1985	1986	1987	1988	1989	Last 12 Mos.	Interim Earnings Period	$ per Shr. 1988	1989	Index
1	....	None Since Public			...	Nil	....	8.41	28.6	10.5	11-30-89	.....	...	5801	Fb	0.42	0.69	0.42	0.50	....	0.58	9 Mo Nov	0.29	0.37	1
2♦	....	0.04	2-28-86	2-10	...	Nil	....	8.52	13.2	8.68	9-25-89	20.6	...	[61]4956	Sp	0.60	d0.67	d0.19	0.08	0.48	0.47	12 Wk Dec	0.05	0.05	2
3	....	None Since Public			...	Nil	....	1.52	4.01	0.74	9-30-89	.....	...	7499	Dc	...	0.01	0.09	0.07	....	0.06	9 Mo Sep	0.04	0.03	3
4	1988	Q0.05	3-15-90	2-9	0.05	0.20	0.20	Book Value $12.75			12-31-88	p40.1	...	p6081	Dc	0.96	1.70	0.79	[52]2.17	P0.58	0.58				4
5♦	1935	Q0.25	1-31-90	12-29	0.25	1.00	1.00	Book Value $19.43			3-31-89	p7.11	...	p6945	Dc	■2.03	▲1.99	▲2.18	▲2.44	P2.44	2.44				5
6♦	1913	Q0.34	3-2-90	2-5	0.34	1.36	1.34	Equity per shr $33.76			12-31-88	.....	...	p37601	Dc	2.92	3.02	3.72	2.59	P3.65	3.65				6
7♦	1976	0.04	9-11-89	8-21	...	Nil	0.12	17.3	61.9	51.8	6-28-89	106	...	19587	Je	1.06	1.29	1.19	△0.91	1.30	1.30				7
8♦	....	None Since Public			...	Nil	....	8.65	88.3	88.1	12-31-89	152	...	3049	Sp	1.75	1.15	d10.05	d0.80	d7.57	d8.50	3 Mo Dec	d2.03	d2.96	8
9♦	....	None paid			...	Nil	....	0.81	24.1	14.5	10-31-89	7.11	...	2457	Ja	0.62	0.41	d2.17	△d0.18	....	d0.22	9 Mo Oct	*0.06	*0.02	9
10	1989	0.10	7-26-89	6-26	...	0.10	0.10	1.10	36.4	19.2	10-28-89	7.50	...	±1953	Ja	±0.72	±0.71	±0.22	△±0.34	....	d0.07	9 Mo Oct	△±d0.46	±d0.87	10
11	1989	0.29	2-8-90	1-25	0.29	1.16	[54]0.92	Net Asset Val $8.49			6-30-89	84.6	...	[55]5000	Dc	...	...	...	§8.48	....	....				11
12♦	....	None Since Public			...	Nil	....	6.80	47.9	91.5	12-31-89	125	...	15752	Mr	*0.11	□0.30	0.44	d5.31	....	d9.33	9 Mo Dec	d2.74	■d6.76	12
13	1987	Q0.05	4-2-90	3-9	0.10	0.20	0.16¼	2.13	65.4	27.4	10-31-89	11.0	...	3510	Jl	*0.28	*0.20	0.60	1.53	2.16	2.10	6 Mo Jan△	1.00	0.94	13
14	....	[57]0.35	1-31-90	1-8	[57]0.35	Nil	[58]3.45	Equity per shr $10.54			11-30-89	.....	...	1423	Au	2.45	1.84	1.27	0.79	2.66	0.33	3 Mo Nov	2.50	0.17	14
15	....	None Since Public			...	Nil	....	Book Value $3.82			12-31-88	p0.52	...	2843	Dc	△1.31	△Nil	△d0.89	d0.28	....	d0.12	9 Mo Sep	d0.19	d0.03	15
16	1973	Q0.36¾	12-29-89	12-12	...	1.47	1.47	Net Asset Val $15.42			2-23-90	.....	...	9464	Dc	§16.22	§16.90	§15.30	§15.24	....	....				16
17	1971	†0.51	12-29-89	12-12	...	1.99	†1.99	Net Asset Val $20.59			2-23-90	.....	...	6953	Dc	§21.85	§22.85	§20.57	§20.46	....	....				17
18♦	1901	Q0.30	3-31-90	3-5	0.60	1.20	1.16	27.0	1101	838	9-30-89	p445	...	39400	Sp	2.40	2.36	2.20	2.83	[60]2.55	2.38	3 Mo Dec	0.84	0.67	18
19	....	0.01¼	2-5-73	2-6	...	Nil	....	0.18	2.15	1.72	9-30-89	4.49	...	1621	Dc	0.21	0.04	d0.21	d0.88	....	d0.90	9 Mo Sep	d0.41	d0.43	19
20♦	1905	Q0.29	3-6-90	2-13	0.29	1.16	1.12	596	3754	1837	10-01-89	★1324	...	333033	Dc	1.68	0.92	2.41	2.86	P3.25	3.25				20
21♦	1987	Q0.284	3-15-90	2-13	0.284	1.135	1.09½	Net Asset Val $42.56			12-31-88	.....	...	3477	Dc	...	...	§39.19	§42.56	....	....	Expires 6-30-92			21
22♦	....	None Since Public			...	Nil	....	....	....	....	....	.....	...	...	Dc	...	...	....	....	....	....				22
23♦	1987	Q0.284	3-15-90	2-13	0.284	1.135	1.09½	Termination claim $59				.....	...	...	Dc	...	...	....	....	....	....				23
24	....	0.09	5-20-80	4-30	...	Nil	....	1.61	14.2	8.89	11-30-89	.....	...	3988	Au	d1.13	d0.50	*0.17	d0.94	*0.31	0.09	3 Mo Nov	*0.29	0.07	24
25	....	None Since Public			...	Nil	....	11.5	94.8	29.0	9-29-89	14.7	...	±7829	Sp	...	...	1.21	1.80	1.71	1.63	3 Mo Dec	0.14	0.06	25
26♦	1988	0.50	9-14-89	8-11	...	0.50	0.50	6.15	37.8	14.3	12-31-89	13.1	...	5042	Je	1.51	2.00	1.73	1.89	1.54	0.90	6 Mo Dec	0.81	0.17	26
27♦	....	5%Stk	5-7-85	4-1	...	Nil	....	Book Value Neg			5-31-89	324	...	±12420	My	±0.24	±0.48	±0.46	±□2.35	d1.96	d2.26	6 Mo Nov	d0.87	□d1.17	27
28♦	....	5%Stk	5-7-85	4-1	...	Nil	....	....	....	....	....	.....	...	8166	My	±0.24	±0.48	±0.46	±□2.35	±d1.96	d2.26	6 Mo Nov	±d0.87	□d1.17	28
29	1987	Q0.35	5-15-90	2-23	0.75	1.40	1.60	Equity per shr Neg			9-30-89	45.6	...	±8323	Dc	...	±[62]d0.05	d1.12	d1.37	....	d1.42	9 Mo Sep	d1.04	d1.09	29
30♦	1989	0.02	1-5-90	12-22	0.02	0.08	0.074	1.77	5.48	3.54	9-30-89	5.40	...	3455	Dc	0.17	0.23	0.25	0.35	P0.46	0.46				30
31	....	0.04	10-10-86	9-8	...	Nil	....	0.23	16.1	8.59	9-30-89	7.71	...	5759	Dc	0.42	d0.88	[63]d1.37	p[64]0.40	....	0.32	9 Mo Sep	0.33	0.25	31
32	1952	Q0.25	2-9-90	1-25	0.25	1.00	1.00	0.12	162	80.5	9-30-89	14.5	...	6327	Dc	1.48	d2.35	0.78	1.42	P2.65	2.65				32
33	1936	Q0.40	3-13-90	2-26	0.80	1.60	1.59	15.3	101	43.2	9-30-89	.....	...	4730	Dc	2.37	2.25	■d1.06	2.68	P2.61	2.61				33
34♦	1960	Q0.18	3-1-90	2-9	0.18	0.72	0.66	4.84	278	155	12-31-89	56.2	...	39933	Je	0.88	0.95	▲1.22	△2.42	1.39	1.44	6 Mo Dec	0.34	0.39	34
35♦	....	None Since Public			...	Nil	....	0.10	11.2	6.01	12-31-89	.....	...	3700	Sp	0.21	0.45	0.48	△d0.11	d0.07	0.03	3 Mo Dec	d0.07	0.03	35
36♦	....	None Since Public			...	Nil	....	1.76	220	57.5	9-30-89	191	...	10800	Dc	0.87	1.08	[66]1.32	[67]1.35	P1.31	1.31				36
37	....	None Since Public			...	Nil	....	File Bankruptcy Chapt 11				.....	...	2675	Ap	0.39	0.45	d0.11	d0.85	d0.15	d0.40	6 Mo Oct	d0.30	d0.55	37
38♦	1987	Q0.05	1-15-90	12-11	0.05	0.20	0.18	19.3	41.2	6.39	2-28-89	6.76	...	9170	Nv	0.69	0.81	1.07	△1.21	P1.39	1.39				38
39♦	1984	Q0.10	1-9-90	12-21	0.10	0.40	0.267	3.34	137	38.9	12-31-89	56.2	...	8548	Dc	1.71	0.57	0.09	0.89	0.84	0.84				39
40♦	....	5%Stk	12-5-73	11-9	...	Nil	....	37.9	659	432	9-30-89	286	[68]6	21340	Dc	0.37	0.80	1.20	1.48	P1.90	1.90				40
41♦	....	0.142	10-31-84	10-10	...	Nil	....	0.03	6.62	10.6	10-01-89	68.8	★142	1561	Dc	d1.73	*△0.10	0.04	0.15	....	d0.86	9 Mo Sep	0.50	△d0.51	41
42♦	1972	Q0.11	4-16-90	3-27	0.22	0.44	0.44	5.44	319	117	9-30-89	136	...	±18004	Dc	±1.11	±1.16	±1.37	±[70]1.42	P±0.48	0.48				42
43	....	None Since Public			...	Nil	....	0.24	12.9	5.23	9-30-89	0.49	...	2296	Dc	d0.10	0.04	0.02	0.52	....	0.65	9 Mo Sep	0.21	0.34	43
44	1990	0.538	2-14-90	1-8	0.538	2.20	....	3.98	9.24	2.40	p6-30-89	p16.7	...	[72]±13810	Dc	...	...	...	p1.33	....	....	6 Mo Jun	n/a	p0.60	44

♦Stock Splits & Divs By Line Reference Index [2]3-for-2,'85. [5]3-for-2,'86:4-for-3,'89. [6]3-for-2,'86. [7]4-for-3,'86. [8]1-for-5 REVERSE,'89. [9]10%,'85,'86. [12]2-for-1,'87. [18]2-for-1,'86. [20]2-for-1,'89. [21]2-for-1,'89. [22]2-for-1,'89. [23]F2-for-1,'89. [26]3-for-2,'89. [27]Adj to 5%,'85. [28]Adj to 5%,'85. [30]10%,'89. [34]2-for-1,'86. [35]3-for-2,'87. [36]2-for-1,'86. [38]2-for-1,'85,'87. [39]3-for-2,'90. [40]2-for-1,'86:3-for-2,'89. [41]3-for-1,'86. [42]3-for-2,'85:8-for-5,'87.

FIGURE 9-2 Standard & Poor's stock guide. *Source:* Standard & Poor's Corporation, reprinted by permission.

Moody's Transportation Manual gives information about companies involved in all forms of transportation. The manual also contains maps.

Moody's Municipal & Government Manual contains data on debt obligations of various government institutions in the United States, Canada, and the British Commonwealth as well as some data on international organizations.

In addition to the manuals, Moody's also publishes *Moody's Handbook of Widely Held Common Stocks* (issued four times a year), *Dividend Record, Bond Record, Bond Survey,* and other timely information about stocks and bonds. There is considerable overlap between the information published by Moody's and Standard & Poor's.

The Value Line

A number of organizations provide financial services similar to those offered by Value Line, but space does not permit an examination of them all. Value Line's services should be considered representative.

The *Value Line Investment Survey* is a weekly publication consisting of three parts. Part I is a summary and index of the 1500 or more stocks covered by this service. The index is in alphabetical order and lists statistical data for each company. In addition, performance and safety rankings are shown. Each company is ranked on a scale of one to five, with one the highest score and five the lowest score. This score is based on how the company is expected to perform in the stock market over the next 12 months and the degree of safety of the investment. Part I also lists stocks that are expected to appreciate within the next 12 months and over the next few years.

Part II, "Selection & Opinion," reviews the business outlook, discusses the stock market and investment strategy, and recommends specific stocks for purchase.

Part III contains one-page summaries of the business and financial activities of each company (see Figure 9-5). The information presented in the summaries is similar to that discussed in Standard & Poor's Stock Reports (see Figure 9-3). However, this service has features that are not available elsewhere. As previously mentioned, Value Line ranks companies according to performance and safety. In Part III each company is ranked according to price stability and growth persistence on a scale of 100 to 5, with 100 the highest score and 5 the lowest. These four rankings (performance, safety, stability, and growth) simplify the mass of information into a manageable amount for making decisions.

Value Line also forecasts earnings, prices, and other key data. It is one of the few sources that publishes figures on beta, the systematic risk factor discussed in Chapter 4.

Dow Jones Information Services

In this age of the computer, it is possible to get up-to-date information on your home or office computer. Dow Jones provides news from *The Wall Street Journal, Barron's,* and the *Dow Jones "Broad Tape"* as recent as 90 seconds and as far back as

JOHNSON & JOHNSON NYSE-JNJ

RECENT PRICE	55	
P/E RATIO	15.4	(Trailing: 16.9 / Median: 14.0)
RELATIVE P/E RATIO	1.24	
DIV'D YLD	2.1%	
VALUE LINE	225	

TIMELINESS 2 (Relative Price Performance Next 12 Mos.) Above Average

SAFETY 1 Highest (Scale: 1 Highest to 5 Lowest)

BETA 1.05 (1.00 = Market)

1992-94 PROJECTIONS

	Price	Gain	Ann'l Total Return
High	95	(+75%)	16%
Low	80	(+45%)	12%

Insider Decisions

	M	J	J	A	S	O	N	D	J
to Buy	0	0	0	0	0	0	0	0	0
Options	0	1	0	0	0	4	0	3	3
to Sell	0	2	3	1	0	1	0	0	0

Institutional Decisions

	2Q'89	3Q'89	4Q'89
to Buy	157	162	178
to Sell	226	167	165
Hld'g(000)	194072	200424	192780

Percent shares traded: 6.0 / 4.0 / 2.0

High/Low prices: 13.4/10.8, 16.9/11.0, 19.7/14.1, 25.6/16.3, 25.8/19.5, 21.4/14.0, 27.6/17.6, 37.1/22.9, 52.7/27.5, 44.1/34.6, 59.5/41.5, 60.8/51.1

Target Price Range 1992 | 1993 | 1994 | 1995

2-for-1 split ↓
3-for-2 split ↓
12.0 x "Cash Flow" p sh
Relative Price Strength

Options: CBOE

	1974	1975	1976	1977	1978	1979	1980	1981	1982	1983	1984	1985	1986	1987	1988	1989	1990	1991	© VALUE LINE, INC.	92-94E
Sales per sh A	5.59	6.39	7.22	8.30	9.74	11.47	13.05	14.43	15.23	15.61	16.75	17.56	20.26	23.28	27.02	29.15	31.55			44.60
"Cash Flow" per sh	.64	.73	.81	.95	1.12	1.29	1.45	1.66	1.85	1.98	2.03	2.36	1.75	3.45	4.10	4.60	5.10			7.20
Earnings per sh B	.47	.53	.59	.71	.83	.96	1.08	1.26	1.40	1.44	1.38	1.68	.93	2.42	2.86	3.25	3.70			5.50
Div'ds Decl'd per sh C	.12	.14	.18	.23	.28	.33	.37	.43	.49	.54	.59	.64	.69	.81	.96	1.12	1.25			1.65
Cap'l Spending per sh	.45	.39	.34	.49	.64	.74	.98	1.04	1.24	1.05	1.00	1.00	1.29	1.50	1.99	2.25	2.50			2.75
Book Value per sh F	2.88	3.31	3.73	4.21	4.74	5.41	6.12	6.76	7.40	7.91	8.02	9.16	8.17	10.13	10.52	12.65	15.00			23.90
Common Shs Outst'g E	346.70	348.21	349.51	351.03	359.12	367.27	370.83	374.12	378.25	382.66	365.69	365.70	345.70	344.19	333.07	333.00	333.00			325.00
Avg Ann'l P/E Ratio	35.0	28.0	24.5	16.6	15.4	12.5	12.3	13.6	14.6	15.8	12.5	13.3	34.6	17.9	14.2	15.4	Bold figures are Value Line estimates			16.0
Relative P/E Ratio	4.90	3.73	3.14	2.17	2.10	1.81	1.63	1.65	1.61	1.61	1.16	1.08	2.35	1.20	1.17	1.16				1.35
Avg Ann'l Div'd Yield	.7%	1.0%	1.2%	2.0%	2.2%	2.8%	2.8%	2.5%	2.4%	2.4%	3.4%	2.9%	2.2%	1.9%	2.4%	2.3%				1.9%

CAPITAL STRUCTURE as of 10/1/89

Total Debt $1584 mill. Due in 5 Yrs $1217 mill.
LT Debt $1202 mill. LT Interest $106 mill.
incl. $100 mill. capitalized leases.
(Long term interest earned: 14.0x; total interest coverage: 11.0x)

(23% of Cap'l)
Leases, Uncapitalized Annual rentals $75 mill.

Pension Liability $19 mill. in '88 vs. None in '87
Pfd Stock None

Common Stock 333,085,439 shs. (77% of Cap'l) as of 10/27/89

	1980	1981	1982	1983	1984	1985	1986	1987	1988	1989	1990		92-94E
Sales ($mill) A	4837.4	5399.0	5760.9	5972.9	6124.5	6421.3	7002.9	8012.0	9000.0	9757.0	10500		14500
Operating Margin	15.6%	16.1%	15.2%	16.0%	15.9%	17.0%	18.0%	19.5%	19.9%	21.0%	21.0%		21.5%
Depreciation ($mill) D	138.7	152.4	176.2	209.8	226.3	250.5	275.2	356.0	391.0	440	470		525
Net Profit ($mill)	400.7	467.6	523.4	547.0	514.5	613.7	329.5	833.0	974.0	1082.0	1230		1800
Income Tax Rate	40.7%	40.3%	33.5%	33.4%	31.9%	31.8%	15.7%	30.2%	30.7%	31.0%	31.0%		31.0%
Net Profit Margin	8.3%	8.7%	9.1%	9.2%	8.4%	9.6%	4.7%	10.4%	10.8%	11.1%	11.7%		12.5%
Working Cap'l ($mill)	1197.5	1321.0	1352.9	1533.3	1471.3	1724.2	908.9	1509.0	1635.0	1900	2100		2550
Long-Term Debt ($mill)	70.1	91.7	142.2	195.6	224.8	185.3	241.9	733.0	1166.0	1100	1050		1500
Net Worth ($mill)	2269.1	2527.9	2799.5	3026.5	2932.0	3350.9	2824.2	3485.0	3503.0	4200	5000		7750
% Earned Total Cap'l	17.3%	18.1%	18.1%	17.3%	16.7%	17.6%	11.1%	20.6%	22.0%	21.5%	21.0%		20.5%
% Earned Net Worth	17.7%	18.5%	18.7%	18.1%	17.5%	18.3%	11.7%	23.9%	27.8%	25.5%	24.5%		23.5%
% Retained to Comm Eq	11.6%	12.2%	12.2%	11.3%	10.0%	11.4%	3.0%	15.9%	18.5%	17.0%	16.0%		16.5%
% All Div'ds to Net Prof	34%	34%	35%	37%	43%	38%	74%	33%	34%	34%	34%		30%

CURRENT POSITION ($MILL)

	1987	1988	10/1/89
Cash Assets	741	660	596
Receivables	953	1135	1333
Inventory (LIFO)	1165	1273	1343
Other	413	435	482
Current Assets	3272	3503	3754
Accts Payable	568	651	503
Debt Due	356	522	382
Other	839	695	952
Current Liab.	1763	1868	1837

ANNUAL RATES

of change (per sh)	Past 10 Yrs.	Past 5 Yrs.	Est'd '86-'88 to '92-'94
Sales	11.0%	9.5%	11.5%
"Cash Flow"	12.5%	11.0%	15.0%
Earnings	11.5%	8.5%	17.5%
Dividends	13.5%	11.0%	12.5%
Book Value	8.5%	5.5%	16.5%

QUARTERLY SALES ($ mill.) A

Calendar	Mar.Per	Jun.Per	Sep.Per	Dec.Per	Full Year
1986	1743	1732	1782	1746	7003
1987	1981	2010	1993	2028	8012
1988	2311	2290	2199	2200	9000
1989	2445	2390	2451	2471	9757
1990	2650	2650	2600	2600	10500

EARNINGS PER SHARE A B

Calendar	Mar.Per	Jun.Per	Sep.Per	Dec.Per	Full Year
1986	d.37	.52	.51	.27	.93
1987	.68	.65	.61	.48	2.42
1988	.81	.79	.71	.55	2.86
1989	.95	.89	.80	.61	3.25
1990	1.05	1.00	.90	.75	3.70

QUARTERLY DIVIDENDS PAID C■

Calendar	Mar.31	Jun.30	Sep.30	Dec.31	Full Year
1986	.163	.175	.175	.175	.69
1987	.175	.21	.21	.21	.81
1988	.21	.25	.25	.25	.96
1989	.25	.29	.29	.29	1.12
1990	.29				

BUSINESS: Johnson & Johnson is a leading manufacturer of health care products. Its segments are: Consumer (toiletries, first aid products, hygienic and baby care); professional (medical equipment, surgical products and apparel, and dental products); and pharmaceutical (contraceptives, therapeutics and veterinary). Brands include Tylenol, Band-Aid, Stayfree, Modess, and Reach. International business, 44% of sales (61% of operating profits); R&D, 7.5%. '88 depreciation rate: 9.9%. Has 81,300 employees, 54,500 stockholders. R.W. Johnson Foundation owns 8.6% of stock, directors 1.6%. Chairman & Chief Executive Officer: Ralph S. Larsen. Incorporated: New Jersey. Address: 501 George Street, New Brunswick, New Jersey 08903. Telephone: 201-524-0400.

Sales in Johnson & Johnson's Consumer segment are staging a rebound, especially internationally. Soaring inflation rates in Brazil are spurring demand for the company's well-known brand name products, and a new line of Stayfree sanitary pads is helping the company regain share in the female protection market. Moreover, the cash cow Tylenol is benefiting from an early flu season and an extension of the product line. These factors will help lift first-quarter earnings more than 10% to $1.05 a share, we think.

But the pharmaceutical business will likely be the biggest contributor to growth in the future. The potential for the company's licensed anti-anemia drug Eprex is vast; AIDS patients and cancer victims are just two of the many groups of people that will benefit from it. Unfortunately, J&J is still embroiled in a dispute with Amgen, the licensor, and it hasn't received FDA approval for many applications. Still, Eprex will probably be a big product for the company in the years ahead. J&J's joint venture with Merck to commercialize Merck's prescription drugs is gaining momentum, and it is also likely that a number of potentially big drugs will be approved late this year or early in 1991. The contraceptive operations are one of the few of the company's lines that aren't growing. The AIDS epidemic has led to a significant increase in the use of condoms for birth control at the expense of oral contraceptives. Then too, demographic shifts are expected to continue decreasing the percentage of women of child-bearing age. J&J remains committed to research and development in all of its businesses though, so we think new products will pick up the slack of this lagging operation.

This stock is a good choice for year ahead performance. We look for share net to rise 12%-14% in 1990, and solid growth is likely on tap thereafter. This high-quality stock has well-defined, if a little below average, prospects out to the 1992-94 horizon.

Stuart J. Benway   March 23, 1990

Restated Sales (and Pretax Margins) by Business Line

	1987	1988	1989	1990
Consumer	3396 (8.2%)	3692 (8.8%)	3915 (8.5%)	4200 (8.5%)
Professional	2621 (12.0%)	2970 (11.4%)	3190 (12.5%)	3400 (13.0%)
Pharmaceutical	1993 (30.1%)	2338 (31.4%)	2652 (32.0%)	2900 (32.0%)
Company Total	8012 (14.9%)	9000 (15.5%)	9757 (16.0%)	10500 (17.0%)

(A) Year ends on Sunday nearest to the end of December. (B) Primary shares. Excludes extraordinary charge: '82, 27¢. Includes nonrecurring charges: '83, 31¢; '86, $2.20.

Next earnings report due late April. (C) Next dividend meeting about April 27. Goes ex about May 25. Dividend payment dates: March 8, June 6, Sept. 6, Dec. 6. ■ Dividend reinvestment plan available. (D) Accelerated depreciation in U.S. (E) In millions, adjusted for stock splits. (F) Includes intangibles in '88: $609 million, $1.83/sh.

Company's Financial Strength	A++
Stock's Price Stability	90
Price Growth Persistence	65
Earnings Predictability	50

Factual material is obtained from sources believed to be reliable, but the publisher is not responsible for any errors or omissions contained herein.

FIGURE 9-3 The Value Line Investment Survey. *Source:* Value Line Investment Survey.

90 days. In addition, information about current stock quotes and the Dow Jones Averages is available for a fee. In addition to Dow Jones, other companies sell stock market data for home computers.

Newsletters

The term *newsletter* is used here to refer to the many reports, surveys, bulletins, and similar publications that provide investment advice for a fee. Some reports tell you how to stay continuously invested for maximum potential capital gains, how to interpret recent monetary trends, or how to protect your life savings. Others pinpoint industries and companies to watch and some to avoid.

Such newsletters usually discuss the outlook for the economy and the stock market, then recommend selected securities for your consideration. Because the publishers of the newsletters are in the business of selling advice, they may recommend several hundred securities over the period of a year. They are bound to be correct at least part of the time because of the large number of securities they recommend. Standard & Poor's and Value Line also publish newsletters.

Some large commercial banks publish periodic newsletters free of charge. Bank newsletters are generally concerned with the economic outlook, monetary policy, and other topics of national importance, such as the balance of payments. Topics that have appeared in recent bank newsletters are "Economic Growth in the Next Decade," "Economic Forecasting—How Good a Track Record?," and "Good Times for Stocks." Particular industries are discussed in bank newsletters, but these publications do not make investment recommendations.

Chart Services

Graphs, or charts, that depict the prices of securities on a daily or monthly basis are available from a variety of firms. Figure 9-4 is one example of a graph. Such charts permit investors to make visual comparisons of trends in stock prices. A picture is worth a thousand words. The charts are also used by technical analysts, who interpret price patterns that appear in the charts, to predict stock price movements. More will be said about technical analysis in Chapter 14.

Electronic Data Bases

Electronic data bases are available from Standard & Poor's, Value Line, and other sources for a fee. Standard & Poor's *Stockpak,* for example, is a computerized version of the *Stock Guide* shown in Figure 9-2.[6] It permits investors with access to personal computers to use the data base of about 5000 companies. Investors can use their own criteria to select stocks from the data base. By way of illustration,

---

[6] For information on Stockpak call 212-208-8581.

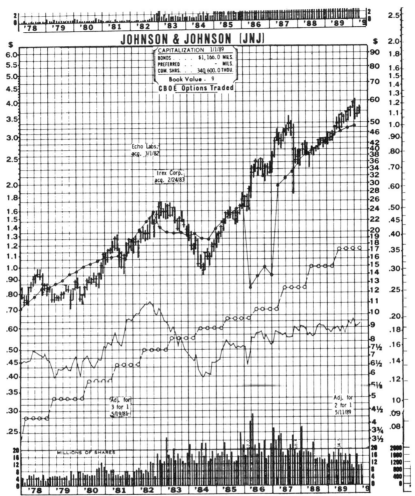

FIGURE 9-4 The SRC Blue Book. *Source:* Securities Research Company, a division of Babson-United Investment Advisors, Inc., Wellesley Hills, Mass.

stocks with yields in excess of 15 percent and five-year growth rates of earnings in excess of 12 percent may be used as the criteria for selecting stocks. Stockpak also has graphic capabilities. Value Line's VALUE SCREEN/Plus permits users to create stock portfolios and do limited statistical analysis on about 1600 companies in the data base, which is updated monthly.[7] One advantage of computerized data base services is that they allow users to sort through a monumental amount of statistical data about stocks in a matter of seconds. VALUE SCREEN users can use the following variables to select the securities they desire.

---

[7] For information on Value Screen call 800-654-0508.

Ratings and Estimates

Timeliness rank	Price stability index
Safety rank	Beta
Financial strength rating	Current earnings per share (EPS)
Industry code	Current dividend
Industry rank	Technical rank

Market Data

Recent price	Price/book value
52-Week high price	13-Week % price change
52-Week low price	26-Week % price change
Current P/E ratio	Market value ($ millions)
Current yield (%)	Options listing

Historical Measures

Sales ($ millions)	Last quarter EPS % change
% Return/new worth	12-Month EPS % change
% Retained/common equity	5-Year EPS growth
Book value per share	5-Year dividend growth
Debt as % of capital	5-Year book value growth

Growth Projections

Estimated % change EPS 1st quarter	Projected EPS growth
Estimated % change EPS 2nd quarter	Projected dividend growth
Estimated % change EPS fiscal year	Projected book value growth
Projected 3–5 year % appreciation	Projected 3–5 year average return

---

Other on-line computerized data services, such as QuoTrek, Dow Jones News/Retrieval, and Warner provide real-time price information about stocks, bonds, options, and commodities. Investors can even enter their orders by computer, or just by using their touch-tone telephones. For example, Charles Schwab's *Telebroker Service* permits customers to get real-time quotes, review account information, and trade securities. Dow Jones *JournalPhone* (1-900-JOURNAL) provides current stock quotes, stock market information, and news including sports and weather for fee ($0.85/first minute, $0.75/additional minutes).

Government Sources

The U.S. government and related agencies are good sources of statistical data on the economy and various industries.

Current Economic Data

Several publications are generally recognized as the primary sources of current and past economic data. The monthly publications in the following list present

data in chart and tabular form:

Survey of Current Business, U.S. Department of Commerce

Economic Indicators, U.S. Council of Economic Advisers

Federal Reserve Bulletin, Board of Governors of the Federal Reserve System

More will be said about these and other government publications in Chapters 10 and 11, which focus on analyzing the economy and industries.

Additional statistical data and timely articles about business activity are published by the 12 Federal Reserve Banks.

The Federal Reserve Bank of St. Louis is particularly helpful because it publishes *U.S. Financial Data,* a weekly that analyzes current interest rate and money market conditions, and *National Economic Trends,* a monthly that comments on the national business situation, using both charts and tables. For additional information about these and other Federal Reserve publications, write to specific Federal Reserve Banks.[8]

Industry Data

The Census Bureau, which is part of the U.S Department of Commerce, Social and Economic Statistics Administration, conducts periodic censuses of various industries. The economic censuses cover

Retail trade

Wholesale trade

Selected service industries

Construction industries

Manufacturers

Mineral industries

Transportation

The major items collected in the economic censuses include financial data (total sales, capital expenditures, etc.) and other information (number of employees,

---

[8] The addresses of these banks are

Federal Reserve Bank of Boston, 30 Pearl Street, Boston, Mass. 02106

Federal Reserve Bank of New York, 33 Liberty Street, New York, NY. 10045

Federal Reserve Bank of Philadelphia, 925 Chestnut Street, Philadelphia, Pa. 19101

Federal Reserve Bank of Cleveland, East 6th Street and Superior Avenue, Cleveland, Ohio 44101

Federal Reserve Bank of Richmond, 9th and Franklin Streets, Richmond, Va. 23213

Federal Reserve Bank of Atlanta, 104 Marietta Street, Atlanta, Ga. 30303

Federal Reserve Bank of Chicago, 230 South LaSalle Street, Chicago, Ill. 60690

Federal Reserve Bank of St. Louis, P.O. Box 442, St. Louis, Mo. 63166

Federal Reserve Bank of Minneapolis, 73 South 5th Street, Minneapolis, Minn. 55480

Federal Reserve Bank of Kansas City, Federal Reserve Station, Kansas City, Mo. 64198

Federal Reserve Bank of Dallas, Station K, Dallas, Tex. 75222

Federal Reserve Bank of San Francisco, P.O. Box 7702, San Francisco, Calif. 94120

number of establishments, etc.) that make them useful tools for securities analysts.

The U.S. Department of Commerce also publishes the *U.S. Industrial Outlook* annually. The publication provides an analysis and outlook on major industries and gives a good overview of each industry and some of the problems it faces.

Company Data

All companies whose stocks are widely held by investors must file periodic reports with the Securities and Exchange Commission (SEC). When companies issue new securities they must file a registration statement (Forms S-1 and 10) that gives detailed information about the securities to be issued, the company, and its financial position. Investors buying the new securities are given a prospectus, which gives them some of the information found in the registration statement. A **red herring** is a preliminary prospectus issued before the final terms of the issue have been settled. Once securities are issued, companies must file an annual report **(Form 10-K)** with the SEC. The annual report contains detailed financial data about the company, as well as information about its operations. Additional information about an annual report (10-K) appears in Chapter 12, where it is discussed as a tool for analyzing companies. The 10-K is one of the most comprehensive and reliable sources of company data available.

Companies must also file an interim report (Form 8-K) if some significant event occurs such as a merger, sale of a substantial portion of the assets, or defaulting on securities. Copies of these reports can be obtained from the SEC. Many libraries maintain 10-Ks on file or on microfiche, and companies may provide them free of charge to their shareholders.

Information on more than 11,000 publicly held corporations that file financial reports with the SEC is available on personal computers. The data are provided by Disclosure, and are available at many public and university libraries at a nominal charge, or can be purchased by individual investors.[9] The Disclosure Database is available on disks for use with personal computers. It can be used to obtain reports, financial ratios, and other information necessary for security analysis.

Stockbrokerage Firms

All of the leading stockbrokerage firms have research departments that publish investment information. Most of the information is used inside the firm by its registered representatives or stockbrokers. For example, assume that an investor calls her stockbroker and states that she is interested in buying a stock that will provide income and some growth. The stockbroker may respond to the client's request by using a reference book or computerized information supplied by the firm. This reference book may contain lists of stocks recommended for growth, income, or some combination of the two. In addition, it may be classified by industry with specific comments about the companies in each group. Thus, the

---

[9] Disclosure, 5161 River Rd., Bethesda, Md. 20816.

stockbroker can tell the client that the firm, which has spent millions of dollars on research, recommends XYZ Corporation for her consideration. Most stockbrokerage firms have reference books similar to the one mentioned here.

Some investors want to know what stocks they can buy in the morning and sell by afternoon to make a quick profit. Many stockbrokerage firms can give their "traders" current information that can help them make their decisions.

Finally, some of the information published by stockbrokerage firms is for public consumption. The public information may range from a comment about a stock to an in-depth analysis of the economy, industries, and companies. Other information may concern taxes, options, commodities, and similar topics of interest to investors. Figure 9-5 is one example of a Merrill Lynch research report and opinion (all QRQs). It contains recommendations on the suitability of the stock for different investment objectives, a review of company developments, and other information. More detailed reports are available on many companies.

Trade Publications

Trade magazines contain financial data and articles about various industries. For example, *Iron Age* publishes "Steel Financial Analysis" and "Nonferrous Industry Financial Analysis" on a periodic basis. Financial data about the petroleum and chemical industry can be found in *National Petroleum News* and *Chemical Week.* A complete listing of all of the trade associations and their publications would fill a book. Investors should be aware that such publications exist and that they are an important source of information.

Sources of Information About Foreign Securities

Obtaining information about foreign countries and foreign companies is becoming easier as global trading of securities spreads. *The Wall Street Journal, Business-Week, Forbes,* and other publications mentioned previously have regular sections devoted to international finance, providing information ranging from political analysis to stock prices and foreign exchange rates. *The Economist* and *Euromoney* are especially useful in analyzing trends in foreign markets.

General economic information about other countries can be obtained from the International Monetary Fund (IMF), the Organization for Economic Cooperation and Development (OECD), and the United Nations (UN).[10] For example, each year the IMF publishes the *World Economic Report, International Capital Markets, Developments and Prospects,* and other reports. The OECD publishes data as well as economic surveys. The UN publishes a monthly statistical bulletin.

Moody's International Manual provides specific information about a large number of foreign companies whose securities are publicly traded. Keep in mind that foreign companies have different accounting practices than ours, and are not subject to the same rules of financial disclosure. This means that even if you are

[10] International Monetary Fund, 700 19th St. N.W., Washington, D.C. 20431; OECD, Publications and Information Centre, 1750 Pennsylvania Ave. N.W., Washington, D.C., 20006; United Nations, Sales Section, New York, N.Y., 10017.

able to get information about foreign companies, you may not be able to interpret what it means. Fortunately, Moody's, Standard & Poor's, Value Line, and other investment advisory services interpret such information about selected foreign securities.

THE COST OF INFORMATION

As mentioned at the beginning of this chapter, many of these sources of information are available at public libraries and from stockbrokerage firms. Nevertheless, some investors prefer the convenience of having their own copies of publications or information available to them on their own computers. The cost of information can range from a few dollars to hundreds of dollars per year. Before spending several hundred dollars for investment information, ask yourself if it is worth the

```
***************     QRQ FCR AE      ***************
           MERRILL LYNCH RESEARCH 05/17/90   15:52
           JOHNSON&JOHNSON   (JNJ     )
INVESTMENT OPINION              ANALYST:   OLWELL
 I.T.   3 NEUTRAL
 L.T.   2 ABOVE AVG.            EXCH/OPT       NYSE/CBOE
 INC.   7 SAME/HIGHER           CURR PRICE        60 7/8
 SUIT   INVEST. GRADE           PRICE RANGE           NA
 CHAR   GROWTH                  P/E CUR/NXT    16.2/14.0

 EPS                            INDIC DIV / DIST
  ACT DC89       3.25            CURR      1.160 / 1.9%
  EST DC90       3.75            NEXT      1.340 / 2.2%
  EST DC91       4.35            EST 5YR GR      15.000%
  EST 5YR GR        15.000%
  INTR 03MR      1.11 V      .95  BKVAL  DC89       12.10
  EST  03JE      1.02 V      .89  MKT VAL(MIL)   20277.46

JNJ IS A DIVERSIFIED HEALTHCARE COMPANY - CONSUMER
PRODUCTS, HOSPITAL SUPPLY PRODUCTS, AND
PHARMACEUTICALS. HOSPITAL SUPPLY GROUP IS BEING
HURT BY SLOWDOWN IN HEALTHCARE ACTIVITY.
INTERNATIONAL CONSUMER SALES ARE CURRENTLY BEING
IMPACTED BY DOLLAR. BELIEVE COMPANY WILL ONLY BE
AN AVERAGE PERFORMER OVER INTERMEDIATE TERM.

RSCH COMMENT DRA 4/27/90            IND CODE  145300
```

FIGURE 9-5 QRQ report. *Source:* Merrill Lynch, Pierce, Fenner & Smith, reprinted by permission.

YOUR KEY TO QRQ

9999 QR O OPN 010981-1010	Date and time QRQ was requested
	Company name
	Closing price on day previous to date shown
12 TYPICAL MFG PX 45	Indicated annual dividend based on recently declared
DIV 2.25	dividends
SYMBOL TYP	Stock symbol
INTR T APREC NEUTRAL /3/	This is our recommendation based on our opinion of
	prospects for intermediate-term appreciation (up
L.T. APREC OK TO BUY /2/	to one year). Recommendations include "Buy,"
	"OK to Buy," "Neutral," "OK to Sell," and "Sell."
INCOME QFLD HIGH YIELD /7/	This is our recommendation based on our opinion of
	prospects for long-term appreciation (one to three
EARNS 9 MOS SP80 3.95 VS 3.75	years). Recommendations are as above.
EARNS EST DC 80 5.25 VS 5.00	"Qualified high yield" means yield is about 5% or
	more, dividend considered secure. "Qualified low
EARNS EST DC 81 5.50	yield" means yield is below 5%, dividend consid-
	ered secure. "Unqualified" indicates either no
SUITABILITY—INV GRADE	cash dividend or dividend considered insecure.
INVEST CHAR—DEFENSIVE	Most recent interim reported earnings compared to
	same period a year earlier.
RSCH COMMENT 15 1/2/81	Our full-year earnings estimate compared to last
	comparable period reported.
OPT CB—	The next year's earnings estimate.
DOE/	Suitability classifications describe the strength of the
	company and the quality of the security. Invest-
FAVORABLE EARNS COMPARISON AIDED	ment Grade is the highest classification, followed
BY CONTINUED GROWTH IN DEMAND,	by Good Quality, Speculative, and High Risk.
HIGHER PRICES AND EFFECTIVE COST	Investment Characteristic describe the nature of the
CONTROLS. ESTIMATE HIGHER EARN-	business in which company is engaged. Char-
INGS IN 1981. LABOR NEGOTIATIONS	acteristics include Growth, Defensive, and
IN PROGRESS. SUCCESSFUL $50 MYN	Cyclical.
DEBT OFFERING MADE IN SEP. WE	Indicates additional Merrill Lynch Research material is
THINK SHRS REPRESENT EXCELLENT	available on company.
VALUE FOR QUALITY CONSCIOUS IN-	Indicates options in this stock are traded on the
VESTORS SEEKING INCOME AND LT	Chicago Board Options Exchange.
APREC.	Research Analyst responsible for this opinion
	Text

FIGURE 9-5   *(continued)*

cost. For example, $500 sounds like a lot of money, but it takes only a 5-point increase in 100 shares of stock to pay for the service. If the service offers advice and you act on that advice to increase profits or reduce losses, it is worth the cost if the hoped-for results are achieved.

CONCLUSION

Investors find no shortage of information about the securities market. Rather, the problem lies in organizing the available information in a useful manner. The approach suggested here is to first consider general information about the state of

the economy, next information about particular industries, then information about specific companies, and finally information about the securities market and the timing of a purchase or sale.

Periodicals are one useful source of information. The *F&S Index* and the *Business Periodicals Index* cover articles on business and finance. Both can be useful in finding articles about a particular topic of general interest, an industry, or a company.

In addition to periodicals, a number of financial services research and publish a large amount of financial information. Standard & Poor's, Moody's, and the Value Line are examples of such organizations. Newsletters also contribute to the flow of information about events affecting the securities market. Current stock market data are available on home computers for a fee.

The U.S. government publishes a large amount of statistical data on the economy as a whole and particular industries within it. The annual economic census volumes cover retail and wholesale trade, manufacturing, service industries, and so on. The Federal Reserve Banks, particularly the St. Louis bank, publish analyses of interest rate and money market trends as well as general information on the economy. Every company whose stock is widely held must file an annual report with the Securities and Exchange Commission. This information is also available to investors, for a fee.

Stockbrokerage firms are another source of information. The research departments of many large firms develop in-depth studies and make recommendations to their customers on the basis of these studies. Trade publications and publications dealing with financial and operating ratios of various companies are also available. Some investment information services are even computerized, and other sources deal specifically with investment companies.

In deciding how to get the information needed for informed investment decisions, you should consider the cost of information. Most of the sources mentioned here are available in public libraries, but if an investor uses information successfully to make a profit on the securities market, the decision to spend some money for readily available, accurate information may be a wise one.

Daily newspapers contain the most current financial news. *The Wall Street Journal* is an excellent source of information about financial matters in general and the securities market in particular. Aside from the many articles about world news and its effect on business activities, *The Wall Street Journal* also prints stock, bond, and government securities quotations. From these quotations the investor can tell at a glance what the prices, dividends, or yields of these securities are. Other daily newspapers also print quotations from the securities market.

Investors, as one can easily see, are more likely to be smothered by information than to lack it. With a little effort, they can collect and organize in a useful manner all the information needed to make informed decisions.

IMPORTANT CONCEPTS

Business Periodicals Index   Form 10-K
F&S Index   Moody's Investor Services

Red herring   Value Line Investment Survey
Standard & Poor's Corporation
Standard Industrial Classification
   code (SIC)

QUESTIONS AND EXERCISES

1. Articles about various companies appear in many periodicals. If you wanted information about a specific company, where would you begin your search?

2. There is a wide range in the quality of reporting of daily stock market activity. Compare the information from *The Wall Street Journal, Barron's, The New York Times,* and your local newspaper.

3. Some investors use charts to obtain information about stocks. What sources provide charts of price and volume?

4. The U.S. government is an excellent source of statistical data and information about various industries. Examine a recent issue of the *Survey of Current Business* and find the following information: (a) What happened to the prices of oil and lumber in the last six months? (b) What is the dollar value of residential construction and domestic automobile production?

5. Suppose that you are asked to analyze a bank stock. The bank has a ratio of loans to deposits of 70 percent. Use the *Federal Reserve Bulletin* to compare this ratio to that of other large banks.

6. The outlook for interest rates is important for investors. Draw the recent trend of 3-month Treasury bills and AAA-rated corporate bonds. Data can be obtained from various government publications or other sources. What can you learn from this chart about the future course of interest rates?

7. Many stockbrokerage firms publish reports about the economic outlook. Call several firms and obtain such reports. Then compare them. What do you think housing starts will be next year? Give both the number of units and the dollar amount of construction.

8. Is an investment service that costs $800 per year expensive? Explain.

9. Examine Figure 9-4. List five stocks whose earnings have increased significantly in recent years. What other information, if any, would you want to know about these companies before buying their stock?

10. Based on the information presented about Johnson & Johnson in this chapter, is it a good buy? (Assume the data are current.)

11. Which one of the sources concerning Johnson & Johnson did you find the most useful? Why?

12. What major news events of the past week have had an impact on stock prices? Why?

13. What are the major sources that you should use to analyze the outlook for the airline industry?

14. Assume that you want to buy a growth-oriented mutual fund. What sources of information would you use?

15. How much time (hours) do you think it takes to analyze a stock before you would consider investing in it? Keep in mind, there is a chance that you may lose all of your money. Estimate the cost of your analysis.

ANALYZING THE ECONOMY

T he process of security analysis begins by gathering information about the economy. This gives us the "big picture" of coming events and important clues about which industries should be good investment opportunities. Equally important, it provides information about which industries to avoid.

STOCK PRICES AND ECONOMIC ACTIVITY

According to the U.S. Department of Commerce, stock prices are a **leading economic indicator.** This means that they usually reach peaks and troughs before business cycles change direction. Since World War II, declines in stock prices have led business cycle peaks by about 10 months on average, and advances in stock prices have led business cycle troughs by five months on average.[1]

These averages are subject to wide variations, and sometimes the stock market anticipates changes in business activity that do not materialize. The market break in 1987 is one example.

Figures 10-1 and 10-2 illustrate the relationship between the Standard & Poor's Industrials, business cycles (shaded areas represent recessions), and two industry groups. Figure 10-1 shows that the hotel and motel industry outperformed the S&P Industrial index, while Figure 10-2 shows that machine tools generally underperformed the index. The effects of the recession on these indus-

---

[1] Data on stock prices and business cycles can be found in *Survey of Current Business,* published monthly by the U.S. Department of Commerce.

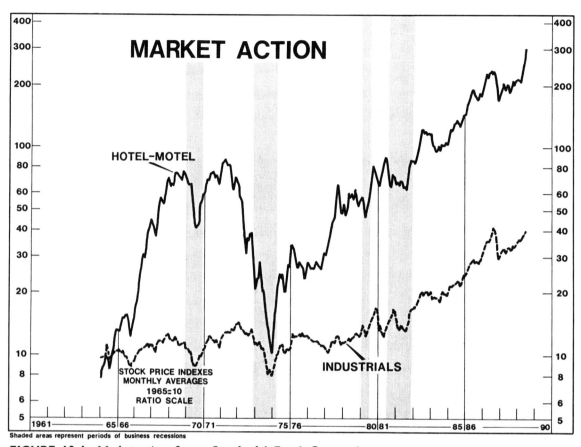

FIGURE 10-1   Market action. *Source:* Standard & Poor's Corporation.

trial groups and the Industrial index also differed. Thus, not all stocks or groups of stocks behave the same as an index that represents their collective behavior.

The Dividend Valuation Model

The relationship between stock prices and economic activity can be explained in terms of the **dividend valuation model** that was presented in Chapter 2. According to the model, the market value of stocks is found by discounting future dividends. For a constant growth rate stock, the equation is

$$P_0 = \frac{D_1}{k - g} \qquad (10\text{-}1)$$

where

P_0 = market value at time 0
D_1 = dollar amount of the dividend in time period 1
k = discount rate; the rate of return required by equity investors
g = growth rate of dividends

FIGURE 10-2 Market action. *Source:* Standard & Poor's Corporation.

Stock prices are tied to the level of economic activity through expected dividends (D_1) and the discount rate (k). When the economy is growing, corporate earnings and dividends increase. However, if the economic outlook is bleak, corporate earnings may decline and some corporations may curtail dividend payments. Thus, a growing economy and growing corporate earnings and dividends go together.

Interest Rates

The discount rate used in the dividend valuation model (k) is the rate of return that equity investors expect to earn on their stocks. This rate is influenced by the rates of return that investors can earn on alternative investments such as bank deposits, money market funds, and Treasury bills. Figure 10-3 shows the relationship between stock prices and short-term interest rates such as those on Treasury bills. A close examination reveals that they tend to be inversely related. This means that when market rates of interest go up, stock prices tend to go down. Conversely, when market rates of interest decline, stock prices tend to increase.

INTEREST RATES AND BOND YIELDS

In March, short-term interest rates fell and long-term rates rose.

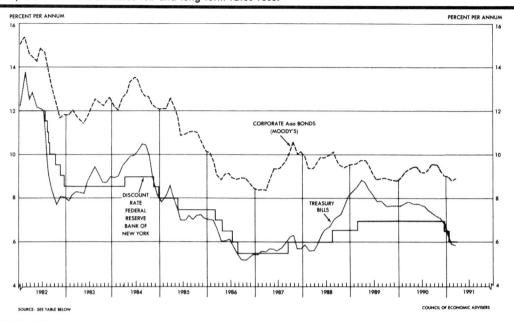

COMMON STOCK PRICES AND YIELDS

Stock prices rose in March.

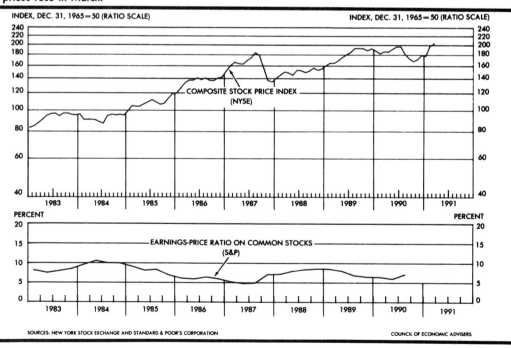

FIGURE 10-3 Common stock prices and yields. *Source:* Department of Commerce.

The stock market index and interest rates shown in Figure 10-3 do not move in precisely the opposite direction because the prices of some stocks are less sensitive to changes in market rates of interest than others. Nevertheless, it often holds that when interest rates fall, stock prices rise.

In order to explain this phenomenon, let us assume that cash dividends paid by corporations are fixed in the short run. This is a realistic assumption because corporations do not change their dividends on a day-to-day basis. But investors can change their expectations that often. If they believe interest rates are going to rise, they will want higher returns on their stocks. The result is that stock prices will fall. A simple numerical example will clarify this point. If the cash dividend is $1 and the required rate of return is 10 percent, the market price of the stock is $10 per share:

$$P_0 = \frac{D_1}{k - g}$$

$$= \frac{\$1}{0.10} \quad (g = 0 \text{ because the dividend is not going to change})$$

$$= \$10$$

If investors expect interest rates to increase, and require, say, a 15-percent return, the price per share will decline to $6.67.

$$P = \frac{\$1}{0.15}$$

$$= \$6.67$$

The reverse, of course, is also true. Declining market rates of interest are usually associated with higher stock prices. This pattern does not always appear when examining broad stock market indexes, for two principal reasons. The first reason is that some companies may increase dividends at the same time interest rates are rising, thereby offsetting higher discount rates and lower stock prices. Similarly, some companies may cut dividends at the same time interest rates are falling, thereby offsetting lower discount rates and higher stock prices. The second reason is that interest rates are only one of the factors that influence stock prices. Nevertheless, it generally holds that when market rates of interest increase, stock prices decline. Although this example concerns stocks, the same process applies to the prices of bonds that are outstanding.

TRENDS

Economic Data

The U.S. government, which is the chief source of economic data, publishes thousands of economic series and other statistics continuously. Many series that are important for investors are published in the **Federal Reserve Bulletin, Sur-**

vey of Current Business, and Economic Indicators. This short list of sources is not exhaustive, but much of the current data are contained in these four publications. There is some duplication of series in these publications, particularly for national income data.

The Federal Reserve Bulletin, which is published monthly, is a particularly good source of data on interest rates, money stock, flow of funds, and other financial data. It also contains articles about current economic and financial developments. *Survey of Current Business* is best known for the detailed coverage of the national income and product accounts it provides. The *Survey*, a monthly publication, has more than 350 statistical series covering many phases of general business, commodity prices, construction, real estate, domestic and foreign trade, employment and income, and finance. The *Survey* also has an in-depth review of the current business situation and other pertinent articles. The monthly issue is supplemented weekly with the latest economic data available. *Economic Indicators*, published monthly, covers many of the major economic series in chart and table form. Each chart is accompanied by a brief explanation of the most recent developments. Collectively, these sources provide investors with most of the data about the economy that they will require.

Gross National Product

Perhaps the most widely used measure of overall economic activity is the **gross national product (GNP).** The GNP is the market value of goods and services produced by the nation's economy within a specified period of time. Typically, data are estimated for a calendar or fiscal year or a quarter of a year and expressed at an annual rate. The quarterly data are multiplied by four so they can be compared to annual data. The GNP is the most comprehensive single measure of economic activity.

Figure 10-4 shows the growth in the GNP, which is $5.6 trillion. It is mind boggling to think in such quantities, but that is the size of it. To some extent, the growth in GNP is overstated because it is expressed in **current (nominal** or today's) **dollars,** and it includes the inflation that has occurred. To solve this problem, the GNP is also measured in **constant (1982) dollars.** The difference between the GNP in current dollars and in 1982 dollars represents inflation. The growth in 1982 dollars is sometimes referred to as *real growth* because the current dollar GNP has been deflated to remove the effects of inflation.

Investors should know the GNP and its major components because nominal and real GNP data are key elements of economic forecasts. Recall that stock prices reflect what is happening in the economy. Thus, if the economic outlook is for sustained real growth, stock prices should benefit. On the other hand, if the forecast calls for large increases in the nominal GNP and high rates of inflation, stock prices will decline as investors increase their capitalization rates and hope that their dividend payments will not be cut.

The components of the GNP give important clues about spending patterns in the economy as a whole. By way of illustration, let us examine the major compo-

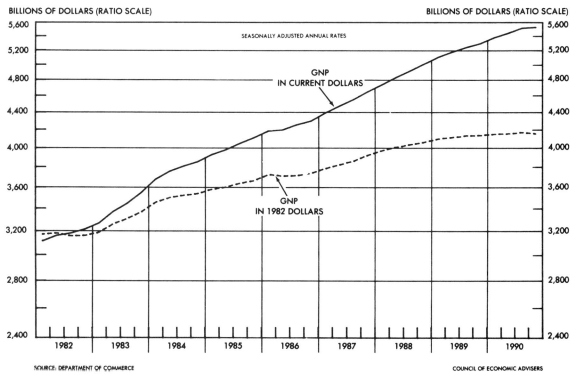

BILLIONS OF DOLLARS (RATIO SCALE)   BILLIONS OF DOLLARS (RATIO SCALE)

SEASONALLY ADJUSTED ANNUAL RATES

GNP
IN CURRENT DOLLARS

GNP
IN 1982 DOLLARS

1982   1983   1984   1985   1986   1987   1988   1989   1990

SOURCE: DEPARTMENT OF COMMERCE   COUNCIL OF ECONOMIC ADVISERS

FIGURE 10-4   Gross national product. *Source:* Department of Commerce, Council of Economic Advisers.

nents of the GNP:

Personal consumption expenditure

Gross private domestic investment

Net exports

Government purchases

These components are listed in Table 10-1.

Personal Consumption Expenditures.   The personal consumption series reflects the market value of goods and services purchased by individuals and nonprofit institutions or acquired by them as income in kind. The three major parts of personal consumption expenditures are **durable goods,** nondurable goods, and services. *Durable goods* include items that have a life expectancy of three years or more. Automobiles, household appliances, and mobile homes are examples of durable goods. Durable goods are the most volatile part of consumer expenditures because these purchases can be postponed if consumers think they may be laid off or may need the money elsewhere. *Nondurable goods* are items that usually last for less than three years. They include food, gas, and clothing. Nondurables are purchased as they are needed and are generally less volatile than durable goods. Finally, *services* are intangible commodities such as transportation, medical care,

TABLE 10-1   Gross National Product and Income (billions of current dollars except as noted)

Account	1986	1987	1988
Gross National Product			
1. Total	**4,231.6**	**4,524.3**	**4,880.6**
By Source			
2. Personal consumption expenditures	2,797.4	3,010.8	3,235.1
3. Durable goods	406.0	421.0	455.2
4. Nondurable goods	942.0	998.1	1,052.3
5. Services	1,449.5	1,591.7	1,727.6
6. Gross private domestic investment	659.4	699.9	750.3
7. Fixed investment	652.5	670.6	719.6
8. Nonresidential	435.2	444.3	487.2
9. Structures	139.0	133.8	140.3
10. Producers' durable equipment	296.2	310.5	346.8
11. Residential structures	217.3	226.4	232.4
12. Change in business inventories	6.9	29.3	30.6
13. Nonfarm	8.6	30.5	34.2
14. Net exports of goods and services	−97.4	−112.6	−73.7
15. Exports	396.5	448.6	547.7
16. Imports	493.8	561.2	621.3
17. Government purchases of goods and services ..	872.2	926.1	968.9
18. Federal	366.5	381.6	381.3
19. State and local	505.7	544.5	587.6
By Major Type of Product			
20. Final sales, total	4,224.8	4,495.0	4,850.0
21. Goods	1,686.7	1,785.2	1,931.9
22. Durable	724.2	777.6	863.6
23. Nondurable	962.5	1,007.6	1,068.3
24. Services	2,119.3	2,304.5	2,499.2
25. Structures	425.6	434.6	449.5
26. Change in business inventories	6.9	29.3	30.6
27. Durable goods	1.2	22.0	25.0
28. Nondurable goods	5.6	7.2	5.6
29. **Total GNP in 1982 dollars**	**3,717.9**	**3,853.7**	**4,024.4**
National Income			
30. Total	**3,412.6**	**3,665.4**	**3,972.6**
31. Compensation of employees	2,511.4	2,690.0	2,907.6
32. Wages and salaries	2,094.8	2,249.4	2,429.0
33. Government and government enterprises .	393.7	419.2	446.5
34. Other	1,701.1	1,830.1	1,982.5
35. Supplement to wages and salaries	416.6	440.7	478.6
36. Employer contributions for social insurance	217.3	227.8	249.7
37. Other labor income	199.3	212.8	228.9
38. Proprietors' income[a]	282.0	311.6	327.8
39. Business and professional[a]	247.2	270.0	288.0

TABLE 10-1 *(Continued)*

Account	1986	1987	1988
40. Farm[a]	34.7	41.6	39.8
41. Rental income of persons[b]	11.6	13.4	15.7
42. Corporate profits[a]	282.1	298.7	328.6
43. Profits before tax[c]	221.6	266.7	306.8
44. Inventory valuation adjustment	6.7	−18.9	−25.0
45. Capital consumption adjustment	53.8	50.9	46.8
46. Net interest	325.5	351.7	392.9

Source: Federal Reserve B.

[a] With inventory valuation and capital consumption adjustments.
[b] With capital consumption adjustment.
[c] For after–tax profits, dividends, and the like, see table 1.48.

and entertainment. The data in Table 10-1 show the dollar amounts spent on these three types of consumer expenditures. The bulk of the funds are spent on nondurable goods and services. Durable goods, particularly automobiles, have been affected in recent years by higher gasoline prices and the trend toward smaller cars. Investors should be particularly aware of trends in these areas and their implications for long-term investments; for example, in recent years consumers have become more service-oriented.

Gross Private Domestic Investment. Gross private domestic investment (GPDI) is composed of fixed investment and changes in business inventories. *Fixed investment* is the change in private capital that results from business concerns, nonprofit organizations, and individuals investing in equipment and structures. It includes business equipment, factories, stores, schools, hospitals, homes, and other fixed items. The function of fixed investment is to provide the capacity to produce goods and services for future consumption. For the moment, let us focus on one part of fixed investment, *producers' durable equipment* (Line 10, Table 10-1). This category includes electrical machinery, trucks, buses, trailers, and other business equipment. A perusal of the data for producers' durable equipment shows the swings that occur from year to year. Similarly, the data for residential structures (Line 11, Table 10-1) show frequent and considerable changes.

What do these fluctuations mean for investors? The answer is that the various components of GPDI are cyclical. When there is a housing boom, companies involved in residential construction, lumber, plumbing, appliances, and furnishings have the opportunity to make a substantial profit. However, if the outlook calls for lower housing starts, companies engaged in housing-related activities should be viewed with caution. The same holds true for producers' durable goods. Companies that make machine tools benefit from business expansion and have reduced rates of growth during recessions.

Changes in **business inventories** represent the monetary value of changes in

TABLE 10-2 Cross-Classification of Cyclical Indicators by Economic Process and Cyclical Timing

Cyclical Timing \ Economic Process	I. Employment and Unemployment (15 series)	II. Production and Income (10 series)	III. Consumption, Trade, Orders, and Deliveries (13 series)	IV. Fixed Capital Investment (19 series)	V. Inventories and Inventory Investment (9 series)	VI. Prices, Costs, and Profits (18 series)	VIII. Money and Credit (28 series)
A. Timing at Business Cycle Peaks							
Leading indicators (61 series)	Marginal employment adjustments (3 series) Job vacancies (2 series) Comprehensive employment (1 series) Comprehensive unemployment (3 series)	Capacity utilization (2 series)	Orders and deliveries (6 series) Consumption and trade (2 series)	Formation of business enterprises (2 series) Business investment commitments (5 series) Residential construction (3 series)	Inventory investment (4 series) Inventories on hand and on order (1 series)	Stock prices (1 series) Sensitive commodity prices (2 series) Profits and profit margins (7 series) Cash flows (2 series)	Money (5 series) Credit flows (5 series) Credit difficulties (2 series) Bank reserves (2 series) Interest rates (1 series)
Roughly coincident indicators (24 series)	Comprehensive employment (1 series)	Comprehensive output and income (4 series) Industrial production (4 series)	Consumption and trade (4 series)	Business investment commitments (1 series) Business investment expenditures (6 series)			Velocity of money (2 series) Interest rates (2 series)
Lagging indicators (19 series)	Comprehensive unemployment (2 series)			Business investment expenditures (1 series)	Inventories on hand and on order (4 series)	Unit labor costs and labor share (4 series)	Interest rates (4 series) Outstanding debt (4 series)
Timing unclassified (8 series)	Comprehensive employment (3 series)		Consumption and trade (1 series)	Business investment commitments (1 series)		Sensitivity commodity prices (1 series) Profits and profit margins (1 series)	Interest rates (1 series)

B. Timing at Business Cycle Troughs

Leading indicators (47 series)	Marginal employment adjustments (1 series)	Industrial production (1 series)	Orders and deliveries (5 series) Consumption and trade (4 series)	Formation of business enterprises (2 series) Business investment commitments (4 series) Residential construction (3 series)	Inventory investment (4 series)	Stock prices (1 series) Sensitivity commodity prices (3 series) Profits and profit margins (6 series) Cash flows (2 series)	Money (4 series) Credit flows (5 series) Credit difficulties (2 series)
Roughly coincident indicators (23 series)	Marginal employment adjustments (2 series) Comprehensive employment (4 series)	Comprehensive output and income (4 series) Industrial production (3 series) Capacity utilization (2 series)	Consumption and trade (3 series)	Business investment commitments (1 series)		Profits and profit margins (2 series)	Money (1 series) Velocity of money (1 series)
Lagging indicators (41 series)	Job vacancies (2 series) Comprehensive employment (1 series) Comprehensive unemployment (5 series)		Orders and deliveries (1 series)	Business investment commitments (2 series) Business investment expenditures (7 series)	Inventories on hand and on order (5 series)	Unit labor costs and labor share (4 series)	Velocity of money (1 series) Bank reserves (1 series) Interest rates (8 series) Outstanding debt (4 series) Bank reserves (1 series)
Timing unclassified (1 series)							

Source: Survey of Current Business, January 1990.

227

physical inventories held by business concerns. Inventories include raw materials and goods in various stages of completion as well as finished goods.

Net Exports.   Exports include both goods and services. The goods consist of commodities, produced goods, raw materials, and so on. Services include items such as ocean and air fares paid to U.S. carriers, insurance, and profits earned by U.S. business concerns operating abroad. The import items include goods as well as military expenditures by U.S. service personnel abroad and earnings of foreigners on their investments in the United States.

Government Purchases.   Government expenditures reflect the role of governments in our economy. The largest single expenditure item in this category is for national defense. However, the role of state and local governments is becoming increasingly important.

In summary, the GNP and its component parts give a broad perspective of the economy and its various sectors. Economic forecasts make extensive use of the terms covered here. Investors should be familiar with the meaning of these terms and use the information to determine the future direction of the stock market and particular industries.

Business Indicators

Economic forecasts are usually cast in terms of the GNP and its components, but the current state of the economy is usually measured by business indicators. Many of the business indicators are published in *The Survey of Current Business.* The part of the *Survey* devoted to cyclical indicators it is particularly useful. It is designed to help analyze current economic conditions and prospects. In this portion of the *Survey,* economic time series are classified into three cyclical timing categories: (1) **leading,** (2) **roughly coincident,** and (3) **lagging indicators** (see Table 10-2). The *leading indicators* are economic time series that usually reach peaks and troughs before general economic activity. Stock prices are one of the leading economic indicators. These series provide information about the future direction of economic activity. The index composed of 12 leading indicators is particularly sensitive to changes in business activity. *Roughly coincident indicators* are economic series that reach peaks and troughs at about the same time as general economic activity. These series are used to confirm the dates when the peaks and troughs occurred. The index of wholesale prices and the unemployment rate are examples of coincident indicators. *Lagging indicators* are those that reach peaks and troughs after general economic activity. For example, consumer installment debt tends to lag behind peaks and troughs. The relationships between the cyclical indicators and various economic processes are shown in Table 10-2. The large number of economic series shown in the table is enough to confuse most investors. Fortunately, indicators such as these are usually reported in the financial press and are interpreted for the readers. Nevertheless, the point here is that cyclical indicators provide important clues about the state of the economy.

Anticipations and intentions data are also published in the *Survey*. As the name implies, economic series in this part of the *Survey* provide information about the future plans of businesses and consumers regarding their economic activity. Such intentions cover expenditures for new plant and equipment, inventories, and buying and income expectations. The results of these series are also reported in the financial press.

The remainder of the *Survey* is packed full of other economic series that are designed to provide insights into the state of the economy, but the average investor need not be concerned with them because they are highly technical.

Selected Indicators

Four other economic indicators deserve special mention: the **index of 12 leading indicators,** the **index of industrial production,** the **unemployment rate,** and the **consumer price index.** The *index of 12 leading indicators* combines 12 economic series into one manageable number. Historically, the index leads peaks by 11 months and troughs by 2 months. This index is closely watched by analysts and has received widespread public attention because it is easy to understand.

The *index of industrial production* is a coincident indicator that gives detailed information about production (final and intermediate products) and materials for a variety of industries. The index has a base year of 1977, which was set equal to 100. Therefore, an index of 140 means that industrial production is 40 percent higher than it was in 1977. Figure 10-5 shows the total index and the index for manufacturing.

A large part of the volatility of durables is attributable to automobiles. The indexes are useful because data are published on several hundred individual industries and are relatively current.

Investors interested in analyzing international economic performance can find some data and charts in the *Survey of Current Business.* Figure 10-6 shows indexes of industrial production in the United States and other countries.

The *unemployment rate* for all civilian workers is actually a summary number for various groups of employment. Indexes are also published for men, women, whites, blacks, and for various industries, such as construction and manufacturing. Similarly, the *consumer price index* is a summary number. The consumer price

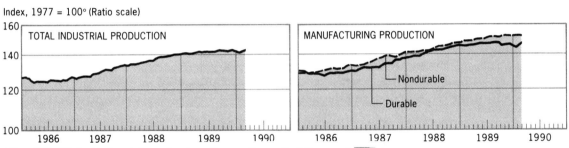

FIGURE 10-5 Industrial production. *Source:* Council of Economic Advisers.

International Comparisons: Industrial Production

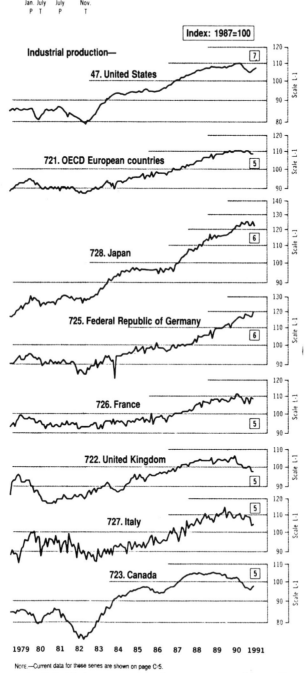

NOTE.—Current data for these series are shown on page C-5.

FIGURE 10-6   International comparisons. *Source:* Department of Commerce, *Survey of Current Business.*

index represents the average costs for city wage earners and clerical workers. Price indexes are published for various components of housing (rent, fuel, and so on), health, recreation, food, apparel, and transportation.

The unemployment rate and consumer price index are important to economists, politicians, and individuals. News concerning these two indicators is widely disseminated by the news media. One does not have to be an economist to know that rising rates of unemployment and prices are bad, or that falling rates of unemployment and lower prices are signs that things are getting better. Investors can use a general knowledge of these indicators in assessing securities.

Monetary Indicators

One of the major functions of the **Federal Reserve System** is to affect the flow of bank credit and money in order to influence decisions to lend, spend, and save money throughout the economy. There is considerable agreement among economists that changes in the monetary policies of the Federal Reserve have an important influence on spending and security prices. However, there is less agreement on how the monetary transmission process works. Several views of the transmission process are synthesized in Figure 10-7. In general, a change in monetary policy leads to changes in the relative prices of real assets and securities as well as changes in wealth. These factors, in turn, affect spending.

The Federal Reserve carries out monetary policy by influencing the amount of

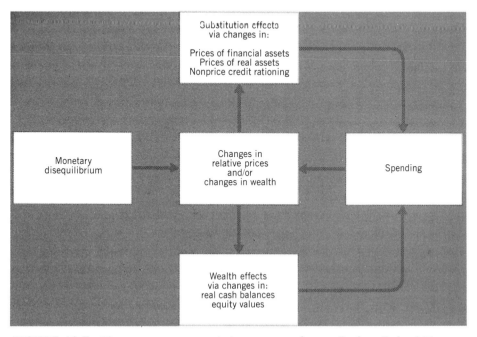

FIGURE 10-7 The monetary transmission process. *Source: Review,* Federal Reserve Board of St. Louis, November 1974.

credit that financial institutions can make available to borrowers and its cost. The cost of credit is interest. The relationship between interest rates and stock prices was explained earlier in this chapter. All that needs to be said about them now is that Federal Reserve policies are very important in influencing the level of interest rates. This is why many sophisticated investors are "Fed watchers." By examining data published by the Federal Reserve, they hope to determine the course of interest rates, economic activity, and, of course, stock prices.

The Federal Reserve Bank of St. Louis is one of the best sources of information about the current posture of monetary policy. The bank publishes *U.S. Financial Data* weekly and *Monetary Trends* monthly. Both publications contain an analysis of monetary developments, charts, and data on monetary indicators and interest rates.

Demographic Factors

During the 1900–1990 period, the population of the United States increased from 76 million to about 250 million. As our population grew, changes occurred in the geographic location and composition of our population that have important implications for investments. One trend concerns the aging of our population. This trend is revealed in the following statistics, which show that the younger population peaked in 1980 and has since declined, and that the older population is increasing in size. Data on population, projections, and immigration are readily available in the *Statistical Abstract of the United States,* which is the source of the figures presented here.

	Percentage of Population	
Year	Age 18–24	Age 65 or more
1960	8.9%	9.2%
1980	13.3	11.3
1987	11.2	12.2
2010 (projection)	9.6	13.9

As the population ages, the types of goods and services required will change accordingly. For example, young adults have different tastes and needs when it comes to entertainment, travel, housing, and medical care than senior citizens. Thus, companies that provide medical care to senior citizens will benefit because that population is growing, while firms that cater to teenage tastes, that make candy, for example, may suffer.

Population growth depends on the birth rate and immigration. Both of these factors have changed dramatically. The birth rate per 1000 women declined from 118.0 in 1960 to 65.4 in 1986. Lower birth rates have investment implications for

Housing	Size and type required
Transportation	Size and type required
Clothing/toys	Lower demand for products aimed at children
Entertainment	More funds for adult entertainment

BOX 10-1

WHAT DO BLUE JEANS AND BEER HAVE IN COMMON?

As people get older, their tastes and waistlines change. The baby boom generation is aging, and as a result, their preferences for certain products are changing. That means business concerns may gain new customers or lose old ones. Manufacturers of jeans and brewers of beer — which both depend heavily on 18- to 25-year-olds for sales — have to adapt. Producers of these products are scrambling to introduce new products that will appeal to the baby boomers. Some jeans manufacturers are diversifying into other types of sportswear, and the brewers are introducing lower calorie beers to appeal to weight-conscious customers.

The baby boomers are in the family formation stage, when they will be buying homes, condominiums, furniture, and cars. This opens up new markets for firms that can satisfy their needs. Along this line, make a list of five products or services that you intend to buy within the next year. Also determine who manufactures those products. If your peers have similar wants, then perhaps some of these companies might be worthwhile investments.

Product	Manufacturer
1. _____	_____
2. _____	_____
3. _____	_____
4. _____	_____
5. _____	_____

With respect to immigration, the United States is receiving fewer Europeans and more Asians and Hispanics. Sixty-two percent of the immigrants in 1987 settled in four states: California, New York, Florida, and Texas. This influx of population affects housing, food distribution, utilities, and so on. This listing is not complete, but illustrates how this information about population growth might be used in making investment decisions.

Regional Differences

Although this chapter is about the economy, there are significant differences in economic activity among the various geographic regions of the United States. In the 1980s depressed energy prices, real estate prices, and farm prices had a devastating effect on the economy in the Southwest, while the economy in the Southeast prospered. These conditions are temporary and may be reversed in the future as economic activity changes.

One reason for regional differences in economic activity involves the migration of the population. For example, between 1990 and 2000, the population of the Midwest is expected to decline 0.3 percent, while that of the West is expected to increase 13.7 percent. You can use this type of information in the following way: Many investment opportunities are local or regional in nature. Banks, utility companies, and medical facilities are examples. By way of illustration, banks in San Diego, California, may benefit from an inward migration by making loans to home buyers, who will also finance appliances, cars, and new businesses. In contrast, banks in Des Moines, Iowa, may lose customers who move west, and lending opportunities along with them.

CONCLUSION

There is a close relationship between selected aspects of economic activity and stock prices. In general, stock prices decline during recessions and increase as business activity expands. However, stock prices are closely related to the level of interest rates, which can change significantly over short periods of time. Since interest rates and stock prices are inversely related, when interest rates rise, stock prices decline. The investor, however, is usually more interested in identifying economic trends that affect particular industries and companies. To make an informed assessment, investors need to understand and consider the relevant indicators of economic activity.

The gross national product and its components give important clues about the future course of stock and bond prices. Information about economic activity is widely disseminated through various government publications, periodicals, and the news media.

In addition, trends in population affect the growth of the economy and various sections of it. All of these factors, if applicable, should constitute part of the analysis of a security. The next step is to narrow the focus from the big picture of the entire economy to a more restrictive view of a particular industry.

IMPORTANT CONCEPTS

Business Condition Digest
Business inventories
Coincident economic indicator
Constant (real) dollars
Consumer price index
Current (nominal) dollars
Demographic factors
Dividend valuation model
Durable goods
Economic Indicators
Federal Reserve Bulletin
Federal Reserve System

Government purchases
Gross national product (GNP)
Gross private domestic investment
Index of industrial production
Index of 12 leading economic indica-
    tors
Lagging economic indicators
Leading economic indicators
Net exports
Personal consumption expenditures
Unemployment rate

QUESTIONS AND EXERCISES

1. If market rates of interest are expected to increase, what should happen to stock prices? Why?

2. If market rates of interest are expected to increase, what should happen to the price of 90-day Treasury bills? Why?

3. What was the gross national product in current and real dollars in the last quarter for which data are available?

4. Compare consumer spending on durables and on services in the past few years. What does this information suggest to you about the future?

5. Describe what is happening in the nation's balance of payments account. What are the implications of this for the stock market?

6. List five leading economic indicators.

7. What is meant by a "coincident" economic indicator?

8. What is the current level of unemployment for men, women, and teenagers?

9. Describe the relationship between monetary policy and stock prices.

10. Are stock prices a leading, lagging, or coincident indicator?

11. An aging population, such as ours, is good for some industries. Name three industries that are helped by this demographic trend.

12. Extrapolate the current trend in the cost of oil and predict what impact this will have on the airline industry.

13. How will a reduction in the birth rate affect housing and automobile sales?

14. Some analysts say the temperature of the world is rising over a period of many years. What groups of stock will be affected by this trend?

15. AIDS is a national problem. What industries may benefit from this disease?

ANALYZING INDUSTRIES

C hapter 10 examined general economic trends and pointed out how they affected the securities markets. Now the focus narrows to particular industries. It is important to know some basic facts about industry analysis because the behavior of individual firms can depend on the organization and characteristics of its industry.

GENERAL CHARACTERISTICS

The term **industry** is widely used, generally understood, and very hard to define. One definition is that an industry consists of firms selling identical products. Another is that it is a distinctive group of productive enterprises. Yet another is that it is a specific branch of manufacture and trade, such as the steel industry. Again, an industry can be defined as a group of sellers of similar products who supply a common group of buyers. All of these definitions are useful until one tries to assign firms to particular industries. For example, General Electric Company produces jet engines, toasters, electrical generators, light bulbs, ovens, and thousands of other products. GE also owns NBC (broadcasting) and RCA (electronics). Ford Motor Company produces steel, glass, and of course, automobiles. The government has developed a system of classification to solve some of the problems associated with defining an industry — the **Standard Industrial Classification.**

Standard Industrial Classification

The Standard Industrial Classification (SIC) system promotes the comparability of statistics describing various aspects of the economy. In this system, establishments are classified by the primary type of activity in which they engage. An establishment is defined in the *Standard Industrial Classification Manual* as an economic unit where business is conducted or where services or industrial operations are performed. Examples of establishments are banks, hotels, mines, and ranches. A business enterprise may consist of one or more establishments. Nevertheless, business enterprises can be classified by their SIC codes, which group establishments into eleven major divisions.

Division A: Agriculture, forestry, and fishing	01–09
Division B: Mining	10–14
Division C: Construction	15–17
Division D: Manufacturing	20–39
Division E: Transportation, communications, electric, gas, and sanitary services	40–49
Division F: Wholesale trade	50–51
Division G: Retail trade	52–59
Division H: Finance, insurance, and real estate	60–67
Division I: Services	70–89
Division J: Public administration	91–97
Division K: Nonclassifiable establishments	99

Each division is composed of a number of major industry groups, which are assigned a two-digit SIC code. Food and kindred products (SIC 20), paper and allied products (SIC 26), and primary metal industries (SIC 33) are examples of the major groups and two-digit codes that are a part of Division D—Manufacturing. As shown in Table 11-1, the major groups are further subdivided into three-, four-, and five-digit SIC codes. In this example, the major industry group is food and kindred products (SIC 20), which includes establishments that manufacture and process food and beverages. The three-digit code (201) designates a specific industry—in this case, meat products. Entire companies are

TABLE II-I SIC Classifications

SIC code	Designation	Name
20	Major industry group	Food and kindred products
201	Industry group	Meat products
2011	Industry	Meat packing plants
20111	Product	Fresh meat

TABLE 11-2   Food, Beverages, and Tobacco Product Shipments, 1987–1989 (in millions of dollars)

SIC Code	Industry	1987	1988[a]	1989[a]
201	Meat products	69,401	74,616	78,813
2011	Meat packing plants	40,658	43,508	44,710
2013	Sausage and other prepared meats	14,385	14,789	15,214
2015	Poultry slaughtering and processing	14,358	16,319	18,889
202	Dairy products	39,364	39,685	42,613
2021	Creamery butter	1,610	1,547	1,522
2022	Cheese, natural and processed	10,733	11,105	12,608
2023	Dry, condensed, and evaporated products	5,814	5,727	6,061
2024	Ice cream and frozen desserts	4,189	4,091	4,229
2026	Fluid milk	17,018	17,215	18,193
203	Preserved fruits and vegetables	34,626	36,896	40,442
2032	Canned specialties	4,459	4,750	5,121
2033	Canned fruits and vegetables	12,219	12,760	14,332
2034	Dried fruits, vegetables, and soups	2,050	2,064	2,561
2035	Pickles, sauces, and salad dressings	4,488	4,974	5,413
2037	Frozen fruits and vegetables	6,234	6,905	7,151
2038	Frozen specialties, nec[c]	5,176	5,443	5,866
204	Grain mill products	33,624	35,714	39,043
2041	Flour and other grain mill products	4,778	5,399	6,100
2043	Cereal breakfast foods	5,081	5,554	6,416
2044	Rice milling	1,257	1,290	1,316
2045	Prepared flour mixes and doughs	2,712	2,750	2,860
2046	Wet corn milling	4,434	4,570	5,030
2047	Dog, cat, and other pet food	4,701	5,171	5,791
2048	Prepared animal feed	10,661	10,980	11,530
205	Bakery products	20,733	22,813	25,284
2051	Bread, cake, and related products	13,486	15,042	16,854
2052	Cookies and crackers	5,874	6,356	6,950
2053	Frozen bakery products, except bread	1,373	1,415	1,480
206	Sugar and confections	19,015	19,426	20,420
2061	Raw cane sugar	1,232		
2062	Cane sugar refining	2,438	5,458	5,844
2063	Beet sugar	1,832		
2064	Candy and other confectionery products	7,312	7,692	8,138
2066	Chocolate and cocoa products	3,274	3,366	3,480
2067	Chewing gum	869	890	918
2068	Salted and roasted nuts and seeds	2,058	2,020	2,040
207	Fats and oils	15,700	16,707	17,183
2074	Cottonseed oil mills	435	448	470
2075	Soybean oil mills	7,799	8,267	8,598
2076	Vegetable oil mills, nec	492	530	540
2077	Animal and marine fats and oils	2,111	2,132	2,175
2079	Shortening and cooking oils	4,863	5,330	5,400

TABLE 11-2 *(Continued)*

SIC Code	Industry	1987	1988[a]	1989[a]
208	Beverages	45,010	47,482	50,040
2082	Malt beverages	13,505	14,059	14,719
2083	Malt	530	541	555
2084	Wine, brandy, and brandy spirits	3,123	3,204	3,300
2085	Distilled and blended liquors	3,145	3,220	3,317
2086	Soft drinks and carbonated water	19,807	21,352	22,783
2087	Flavoring extracts and syrups, nec	4,900	5,106	5,366
209	Miscellaneous foods	28,267	30,215	32,064
2091/92	Processed fishery products	5,945	6,123	6,290
2095	Roasted coffee	5,467	5,740	5,999
2096	Potato chips and similar products	4,988	5,415	5,820
2097	Manufactured ice	281	300	315
2098	Macaroni and spaghetti	988	1,037	1,110
2099	Food preparations, nec	10,598	11,600	12,530
20	Total food products	305,740	323,554	345,903
2111	Cigarettes	16,741	18,544	19,612
2121	Cigars	204	200	197
2131	Chewing and smoking tobacco	1,039	1,057	1,066
2141	Tobacco stemming and redrying	2,159	2,313	2,346
21	Total tobacco products	20,143	22,114	23,221
	Grand total food and tobacco products[b]	325,883	345,668	369,124

Source: U.S. Department of Commerce: *U.S. Industrial Outlook 1990.*

[a] Estimated.

[b] Detail may not equal total due to rounding.

[c] nec, not elsewhere classified.

usually classified by a three-digit code. The four-digit code (2011) indicates the next level, which is meat packing plants— establishments primarily engaged in slaughtering. Specific products, such as fresh meat, are assigned five-digit codes.

Each major industry group includes a wide variety of industries. Table 11-2 shows the industries that fall under the food and kindred products group (SIC 20). This table was taken from the *U.S. Industrial Outlook,* which is published annually by the U.S. Department of Commerce. The *Outlook* discusses major groups and industries and makes projections. For example, the value of shipments for meat packing plants (SIC 2011) was estimated to be about $44.7 billion in 1989. This industry includes Oscar Mayer's (owned by Philip Morris), Swift Independent Packaging Company, and other firms.

SIC codes are widely used and provide a uniform method for describing industries and companies. In some cases, companies that engage in a variety of activities are assigned several different SIC codes. Ford Motor Company, for

example, is assigned SIC codes 3711–3713 and 3715. All of these codes are part of major group 37—Transportation equipment.

Economic Structure

Another way to classify industries is according to their economic structure, which is based on the number of firms in the industry, the nature of the product, the degree of price control, and other factors. Economic structures may be divided into four groups: (1) **pure competition, (2) imperfect or monopolistic competition, (3) oligopoly,** and (4) **monopoly.** Table 11-3 highlights some of the key elements of each of these categories.

Pure Competition

Pure competition prevails when a large number of firms are producing an identical product. There are so many producers that no single firm can affect the price of the product. Thus, the profitability of the firm depends largely on the supply and demand for that product. Wheat farming is one example of pure competition. Wheat is a homogeneous product, and the number of wheat-producing farmers is so large that no single producer can affect the market price. Nevertheless, if the growing conditions are favorable, all the wheat farmers can produce a large crop. If the demand for the wheat does not increase correspondingly, the price of the wheat will fall because of the increased supply. Thus, increased output by all of the firms in this industry can result in lower prices for the product. What happens if the growing conditions are unfavorable and the demand for wheat increases? In this case wheat prices will rise, and the firms may benefit from lower output. The key features of pure competition are that the firms have no control over price and no way to differentiate their products.

Imperfect Competition

Product differentiation is one of the principal differences between imperfect competition and pure competition. The term *product differentiation* means that there is a real or imagined difference between products. Beer is such a product.

TABLE 11-3 Characteristics of Various Economic Structures

Structure	Number of Firms	Differentiation of Products	Degree of Control over Price by Firms
Pure competition	Many	Identical (e.g., wheat)	None
Imperfect competition	Many	Real or imagined differences (e.g., beer)	Some
Oligopoly	Few	Identical or slight differences (e.g., steel)	Some
Monopoly	One	One product (e.g., public utility)	Considerable

There are a large number of beer producers, and each firm spends considerable amounts of money on advertising trying to convince buyers that its brand is better than that of its competition. Some claim that light beers are better than dark beers. Others claim that the particular water used to make their beer gives it a special quality that cannot be duplicated elsewhere. This differentiation among the various beer products allows the producers to develop brand loyalty in their customers and to have some control over the price of their products. Those who are convinced that Coors beer is better than Olympia or Budweiser will pay a premium price to get what they want. However, if the premium becomes too large, they may switch to some other beer that costs less.

Oligopoly

Oligopoly is derived from Greek roots meaning *few sellers.* The steel industry is one example of an oligopoly because a few large firms — U.S.X. (formerly U.S. Steel), Bethlehem, Armco, and Inland — dominate the production of steel in the United States, and steel products — bar, wire, and sheet — are virtually identical from one producer to another. Because only a few firms produce the same products, each producer is keenly aware of the pricing policies of the others. Frequently, one firm is regarded as a leader, and the others follow the prices set by that firm. Some nonprice competition also exists. That can take the form of engineering services provided with the product, or rapid delivery of an order.

Many oligopolies are capital-intensive, which means that large capital outlays are required to produce products like steel, automobiles, and jet engines. The high entry costs, size, and complexity of producing such products tend to restrict the entry of new firms into that market. That is not the case in imperfect competition where the cost of entering the industry is typically lower. For example, for the cost of a Coleman camp stove, one can open a hamburger stand and try to compete with McDonald's fast food chain.

Monopoly

Monopoly consists of a single firm selling a product that does not have any close substitutes. A local public utility, such as an electric company, is a monopoly. Because of the high costs of producing and delivering electricity to users, electric utilities are granted franchises to be the sole producer of electricity in a given area. Consumers may use their own generators for their electrical needs, but they cannot sell this electricity to other consumers. Thus, consumers are at the mercy of the one firm. If they do not like the service or the cost, they are at a disadvantage because there are no other firms to turn to for the product. Their only recourse is to complain to whatever government agency granted the charter and sets the rates for the electricity.

Utility companies cannot charge whatever rates they desire. Typically, utilities seeking higher rates are required to present their requests to a government agency; then public hearings are held on the request. In general, utilities are permitted to charge rates that are sufficiently high to give them a reasonable rate

of return on their investments so they can attract future capital for expansion. However, consumers have been disputing what should be considered a reasonable rate of return.

Another example of a monopoly is the only bank in a small, isolated town. Those who need to borrow funds and do not have access to other banks will be forced to pay the local bank's rates. The local banker could charge higher rates than banks located elsewhere because the customers are unwilling or unable to go elsewhere for funds. Similarly, the local banker could pay lower interest rates on deposits than would be available elsewhere.

In review, the economic structure of industry ranges from pure competition to monopoly. Most industries fall in between these two extremes. They exhibit some of the characteristics of imperfect competition and some of the characteristics of oligopoly. Most industries deal in products that have substitutes. If the price of one product becomes excessively high, some consumers will switch to lower cost products. In some industries, the producers are quite price conscious. With gasoline, for example, the difference in quality between most major brands is negligible, and if one firm starts cutting prices to attract customers, other firms typically follow and drive the price of gasoline down. At some point it becomes unprofitable for all concerned (except consumers), and the price will rise. Such gas wars are generally local in nature, but they do demonstrate some of the features of imperfect competition and oligopoly.

These same traits are observable on a larger scale. In the 1960s, Detroit automotive manufacturers failed to recognize the demand for smaller and more efficient cars, and foreign manufacturers captured a large share of the automobile market. It was not until the mid-1970s that the Detroit automotive manufacturers seemed to realize the trend was toward smaller cars and began to produce them en masse. More will be said about autos shortly.

Supply and Demand

Investors should analyze factors that affect the long-run supply and demand for the output of an industry. For example, the demand for petroleum products is expected to increase in the future. However, the industry faces a major supply problem. Most of the world's proven oil reserves are held by foreign powers that can raise prices and withhold supplies of crude oil. In addition, it is widely recognized that most of the world's oil supply will be depleted in a few decades.

In contrast, the baby food industry has problems with demand. If there is a trend toward reduced population growth, there will be fewer babies in the future, and less baby food will be required. Similarly, there will be less demand for other baby products: toys, furniture, diapers, and so on.

The process of analyzing industry output in terms of supply and demand brings some important issues into sharp focus and provides greater understanding of the industry outlook.

Industry Life Cycle

Industries evolve through stages of development called the **industry life cycle.** The life cycle is analogous to the development of a human. The rate of growth is rapid in the early stages of development and tapers off as adulthood approaches. After a relatively long period of maturity, some stagnation and decay sets in.

The industry life cycle is the same as a product life cycle, but we are applying the concept to a firm or an industry. As noted earlier in this chapter, there may be little or no difference between a product, a firm, and an industry. Figure 11-1 illustrates a typical industry (product) life cycle that is divided into four phases: **pioneering, expansion, stabilization,** and **decline.**

Pioneering Phase

In this discussion we assume that a firm has one major product line that will carry it to great heights or force it to slide into oblivion. Many newly formed companies do have a single thrust, but there are also many established companies that can afford to broaden their product lines and speculate on new ventures. The conse-

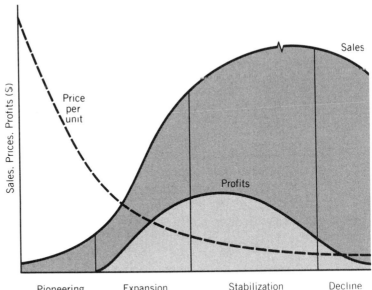

	Pioneering	Expansion	Stabilization	Decline
No. of firms	Few	Increasing	Decreasing	Few
Profits	Loss	Increasing	High	Declining—Loss
Risk	High	High	Decreasing	Low

FIGURE 11-1 Industry life-cycle.

quences of failure for them may not be as severe as for the new company. Keeping this factor in mind, we can focus on a single-product company in the early phases of the life cycle.

The personal computer industry is a product of space age technology. The principal innovator was Apple Computer, Inc., founded in 1977 by two engineers from Atari, Inc., and Hewlett-Packard Co. The Apple I was introduced in 1978. The price for a 16k Apple I without disk drives or a monitor was about $1800. (By 1986, the price of a 64k Apple with drive and monitor was less than $1000). The product was an instant success and Apple II was introduced the following year. From 1977 to 1979, Apple's net income went from zero to $5.1 million; and by 1990 it exceeded $474 million!

Expansion Phase

The expansion phase of the life cycle is characterized by increasing competition, declining prices, and rising industry profits. It is a period of spectacular successes and spectacular failures. Only the fittest firms survive.

Apple's success attracted more then 150 competitors, including Tandy (Radio Shack), IBM, Hewlett-Packard, Digital Equipment, and others. The failures began. The increased production and sales of personal computers drove prices down. In 18 months (December 1981 to June 1983) the price of personal computers fell by 75 percent.[1] The combination of lower prices and poor management decisions contributed to the failure of Osborne Computer Corporation, Archieves, Inc., and Victor Technologies, Inc., to name a few. According to the cover story in *BusinessWeek*, the battle for supremacy in the personal computer market was over; there were few survivors, and IBM was declared the winner.[2] But the personal computer industry is still in the expansion phase of its life cycle and only time will tell who the winner will be.

Although *costs* are not depicted in Figure 11-1, they must be mentioned in connection with profits. Cost is important to pricing, and pricing affects profits. One reason for IBM's success is that it mass-produced personal computers in automated factories. A personal computer was made every 45 seconds. IBM's low-cost production gave it a competitive advantage over high-cost producers. Recall that profit is the difference between revenue and cost. So when IBM cut prices, the revenue per unit fell. Since IBM's costs per unit were falling too, it maintained its profit. However, the profits of higher cost producers were squeezed because their revenue per unit fell more than their cost per unit. In some cases revenue was less than cost, and the firms went out of business.

The expansion phase of the life cycle is exciting because, to paraphrase Charles Darwin, only the fittest firms survive. Poorly managed or unlucky firms may drop out of the race for survival. However, some poorly managed companies survive in spite of themselves. One reason for this is that the demand for their products or services may be so great that even if they do a poor job they survive. They are in

[1] Bro Uttal, "Sudden Shake-up in Home Computers," *Fortune,* July 11, 1983, 105–106.

[2] "Personal Computers: And the Winner is IBM," *BusinessWeek,* October 3, 1983, 76–95.

the right place at the right time. Poor-quality management also increases the possibility of a takeover — being acquired by another firm. Managers of another firm may believe they can do a better job than the existing management and bid for the company's stock.

Well-managed firms may be attractive takeover targets for other firms seeking to enhance their growth by buying growth firms instead of expanding internally. The fastest way to enter a new market is to buy a firm that already has a substantial presence in that market. For example, North Carolina National Bank (NCNB) bought a large bank in Dallas, Texas, and instantly became a large competitor in that market area.

In summary, both poorly managed and well-managed companies may be takeover targets. The takeover may be friendly or hostile. In friendly takeovers the managers willingly sell the company. In hostile takeovers the managers frequently employ a variety of tactics to prevent the acquisitions and to save their jobs. Such tactics are not necessarily for the benefit of the stockholders. **Golden parachutes** are one example. With a golden parachute, managers are paid large sums of money if their firm is acquired and they are fired.

During the 1980s, acquiring companies paid the stockholders of the acquired firms premiums of 42 percent, on average, over the market price of the stock at the time the takeover was announced.[3] The stockholders of the acquiring firms, on the other hand, generally do not make out as well as the sellers. Most studies of mergers suggest that the acquiring firms frequently pay too much for the acquired firms.

Stabilization Phase

During the stabilization phase of the life cycle, total sales continue to increase, albeit at a slower rate, while prices decline to a low level and industry profits fall. Finally, the number of firms in the industry continues to diminish. Consider the automobile industry. During the expansion phase of the life cycle there were about 1500 automobile companies.[4] Today there are only a small handful of producers, and the prices of mass-produced cars are relatively low.

The fact that there is such a wide variety of automobile models today tells us something about the firms that survived the stabilization phase. Each of the firms has three essential ingredients:

1. Sufficient *capital* to finance expansion and continued operations despite falling prices.

2. Sufficient *technology* to provide a continuous stream of new products.

3. Sufficient *scale* or size so that products can be mass-produced at the lowest possible cost.

[3] U.S. Department of Commerce, *Statistical Abstract of the United States, 1989,* Table 872: Also, for a general discussion of premiums for acquired and acquiring firms, see Benton E. Gup, *Bank Mergers: Current Issues and Perspectives,* Norwell, Mass: Kluwer Academic Publishers, 1989.

[4] Donald L. Kemmerer and C. Clyde Jones, *American Economic History,* New York: McGraw-Hill Book Company, 1959, 325.

At the top of the sales curve shown in Figure 11-1 is a break in the line. This break suggests that the length of the stabilization phase may be longer for some firms and industries than others. For electric utilities, for example, it may go on for many years. In high-technology industries, however, it may last for a year or less.

Declining Phase

The final phase of the life cycle is akin to old age in human beings. The firm or industry is over the hill and on the way out. However, there is one significant difference between humans and firms or industries. Once humans have matured, it is unlikely that they can be rejuvenated, but rejuvenation is possible with industries. For example, higher energy costs have contributed to the rejuvenation of the coal industry.

Rejuvenation

Consider the case of ceiling fans. They were a common means of cooling homes until central air conditioning became popular. Subsequently, the ceiling fan industry declined (Figure 11-2). However, the fickle finger of fate was at work. When energy prices soared in the late 1970s and early 1980s, people sought ways to reduce the costs of cooling their homes. Once again they turned to ceiling fans, and the rejuvenated industry grew again.

Using the Life Cycle

Figure 11-2 shows where selected industries are located on the life cycle. To some extent, their placement on the life cycle was a matter of judgment. In addition, the characteristics of the life cycle shown in Figure 11-1 are useful guides in placing industries and firms. With a little practice, it is easy to determine where a firm or industry should be placed on the life cycle.

The placement of an industry in the life cycle provides a lot of information

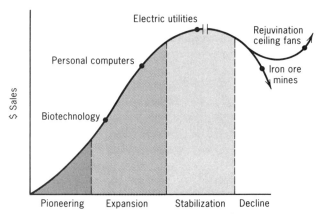

FIGURE 11-2   Selected industries on a life cycle curve.

useful to prospective investors. For example, the genetic research industry is in the pioneering phase of the life cycle. From this we know that there are only a few firms to select from if we wish to invest. We also know that the risk of investing in such firms is *very* high. Offsetting this fact is the knowledge that there may be some tremendous gains to be had by investing. Are you willing to take the risk?

The personal computer industry is in the expansion phase. This tells us that there will be continued rapid growth, but there are substantial risks involved, too. Which firms will survive to enter the stabilization phase?

Electric utilities are in the stabilization phase. Hence, they will continue to grow, but at a slower pace than industries in the earlier phases. Moreover, they tend to be profitable and are reasonably safe investments. However, some mining operations may not be safe investments for the long run. Some of the iron mines in the Mesabi range are running out of good-quality iron ore. That is the nature of mining; quality ore is removed, and all that remains is a hole in the ground.

In the next chapter we will see how the life cycle can be used effectively to provide information about specific firms.

Finally, it must be recognized that the life cycle is presented here to provide a general framework that can be applied to some industries and firms. Not all industries develop in the manner described here. Technological developments like the Polaroid camera, birth control pill, and jet engine did not lead to a large number of firms. High capital costs, patents, and technical knowledge helped to keep other firms out of those industries. Thus, the life cycle is an imperfect tool, but so are most of the other tools at our disposal.

ROLE OF GOVERNMENT, SOCIAL TRENDS, AND TECHNOLOGY

Industries operate in a system that is bounded by laws, society, and other factors. This section examines some aspects of the role of government and the way social trends and technology affect selected industries.

Government Involvement

Virtually every industry is subject to varying degrees of government regulation. The extent of the regulation can affect the limits of growth and profitability of an industry. The following examples illustrate selected aspects of government control in particular industries.

Public Utilities

The term **public utility** generally refers to businesses that serve a public interest. Traditionally, such firms include those that supply water, natural gas, electricity, telephone and telegraph services, and radio and television. These firms usually have high capital requirements. For example, it is very costly to build the electric generators and all of the transmission wires, transformers, and other equipment

needed to supply and deliver electricity to customers. It is argued that having several firms supply the same service would be inefficient. For this and other reasons, public utilities are owned or regulated by governments. In essence, they are given a franchise that makes them a monopoly — the only firm that is permitted to provide that service in a given area. Although the utility is a legal monopoly, it cannot charge unreasonable prices for its services. Utility rates are set high enough to provide the firm with a reasonable rate of return. The fact that the rate structure is regulated does not guarantee the utility a profit. Increasing costs, poor management, and shifting demands can undermine profits.

Regulated Industries

Certain industries that, according to the U.S. Constitution, are "clothed with a public interest" are subject to public regulation. In 1887, the Interstate Commerce Commission was created to regulate railroads. Later, its jurisdiction was extended to include common and contract motor carriers. Other federal regulatory agencies, such as the Federal Maritime Board, Civil Aeronautics Board, Federal Power Commission, Federal Communications Commission, and the Federal Reserve Board, were established to regulate various industries. The principal **regulated industries** are as follows:

Transportation:
Railroads

Local and highway passenger carriers

Water carriers

Airlines and air cargo carriers

Natural gas pipelines

Financial industries:
Banks and nonbank financial institutions

Insurance carriers

Securities and commodities brokers and dealers

Utilities:
Gas, electric, water, sewer, etc.

Telephone and telegraph

Radio and television broadcasting

The regulatory agencies set the rules that these industries must live by, and, in turn, the agencies affect the profits of individual companies. For example, the Federal Aviation Administration (FAA) sets certain standards for aircraft safety. These standards include how often aircraft should be inspected, crew qualifications, and certain types of equipment that must be installed before aircraft can fly into major airports. Complying with the regulations is costly and time-consuming, but presumably increases the safety of flying. However, some aircraft operators believe that many of the FAA regulations are excessive and add to costs but

not to safety. Similar arguments can be made in connection with most regulatory agencies and regulated industries.

Antitrust Regulation

A number of laws attempt to curb anticompetitive practices. The principal **antitrust laws** are the Sherman Antitrust Act (1890), the Clayton Anti-Trust Act (1914), the Robinson-Patman Act (1936), and the Celler-Kefauver Act (1950). The Sherman Act was designed to protect trade and commerce against unlawful restraint and monopoly. The Clayton Act supplemented the Sherman Act. One of the key provisions of the Clayton Act is Section 7, which forbids any corporation to acquire the stock of any other corporation where the effect of the acquisition might be to substantially lessen competition or result in a restraint of trade. The Robinson-Patman Act made certain types of price discrimination illegal. Finally, the Celler-Kefauver Act strengthened Section 7 of the Clayton Act.

Enforcement of the antitrust laws is entrusted to the Antitrust Division of the Department of Justice and the Federal Trade Commission. Given the manpower limitations of these agencies and the cost and effort required to prosecute an antitrust case, the enforcement of the laws has been directed primarily at key cases that are expected to have a major impact on other companies. Many of the antitrust cases concern large, well-known companies, such as DuPont Company, Radio Corporation of America (RCA), and American Telephone & Telegraph, which was broken up into smaller units. Individuals or companies can also seek remedies under the antitrust laws. *Telex v. IBM* is one example of litigation by a firm that believed it was injured by anticompetitive practices.

Antitrust considerations are also taken into account by various federal agencies in performing their functions. For example, the Board of Governors of the Federal Reserve System considers antitrust implications when reviewing applications for bank mergers and bank holding company acquisitions.

Government as Buyer

The U.S. government is the largest single buyer of goods and services in this nation's economy. In 1989 the government spent $403 billion on goods and services. Of that amount $302 billion was spent on national defense. Some industries and firms produce defense products largely for the government. Fighter aircraft, guided missiles, bombs, and similar products have a limited domestic market. Thus, firms that produce such products compete vigorously to obtain defense contracts worth millions of dollars. Although defense contracts are worth millions of dollars, the firms that receive them are not especially profitable because the government views such firms as though they were a utility and permits them to earn only a reasonable rate of return. Furthermore, because of competition to get the contracts, the firms bid as low as possible, which means slim profit margins. In addition, the cost of producing complex military items has frequently exceeded producers' estimates, thereby reducing their profits further.

BOX 11-1

REGULATION OF BANKS

Many industries are regulated, banks among them. Banks are creatures of law. They can do only what the laws and regulations permit them to do. Rarely do the laws and regulations work to the competitive advantage of banks or other regulated industries. For example, although banks are heavily regulated, their competitors do not have to comply with the same rules. They compete with Sears, General Electric, Merrill Lynch, General Motors Acceptance Corporation, and many other firms offering financial services. The principal bank regulators are:

The Comptroller of the Currency	Regulates National banks
The Federal Reserve	Regulates banks that are members of the Federal Reserve System
State bank regulators	Regulate nonmember state-chartered banks
Federal Deposit Insurance Corporation	Insures deposits

A bank that wants to acquire a bank in another state may have to deal with all of the agencies listed above as well as the Department of Justice. If Sears or GE wants to do business in other states, they do not have to deal with these agencies. Regulations tend to stifle competition.

Social Trends

Consumers and government are becoming increasingly aware of the social responsibility of business concerns. The term **social responsibility** is used here in a very broad context. The automobile industry has been particularly affected by this growing awareness. In recent years automobile manufacturers have been required by government to strengthen bumpers, provide seat belts, and improve fuel economy and the quality of their antipollution systems. These changes were brought about because citizens' groups pressured Congress to make the automobile industry improve its products.

The drug industry is also being forced to change its ways by the Food and Drug Administration and by consumers. The Food and Drug Administration is accelerating its program to remove from sale drugs that are found to be ineffective and to restrict the labeling claims on proprietary drugs and other items. For example, Carter's Little Liver Pills were found to contain no liver, and the manufacturer was required to change the name of the product. A manufacturer of denture cream claimed that people who used their product could eat apples, corn, and similar items. However, tests revealed that some users' teeth got stuck and re-

mained in the items they were eating. The manufacturer changed the advertisement. Consumers are also getting into the act. More consumers are asking for drugs by their *generic* names then ever before. The generic name is the common chemical name as opposed to the trademark name. Generally, drug companies charge more for a product sold under the trade name than the same product sold under the generic name.

Biodegradable and *recycling* are now commonplace words in our language. These words became widely used when people became concerned about the effect of industrial outputs on the environment. Today industry spends billions of dollars annually on pollution and environmentally related equipment. Such equipment is generally used to meet government standards on waste, water, and air. Other environmental issues include the disposal of hazardous materials, such as radioactive waste, or the disposal of bulk waste products. In some cases, industries have turned waste materials into profitable products. For example, tree bark was once considered a bulky waste product for the lumber industry and a major source of pollution. Some lumber firms now use tree bark in mulch and soil conditioners. Recycling of paper and metal products is an additional example of using waste products constructively.

These social trends present growth opportunities for some lines of business and mark a decline in growth for others. For example, Waste Management and Browning Ferris are the leading firms in the waste-disposal business. The more garbage and trash we create, the more these firms grow. Likewise, the trend toward increased health care has brought about a reduction in the rate of growth of domestic cigarette consumption. This same trend affects the volume of meat, poultry, and fish we consume. This trend has been to the detriment of the meat producers and processors and to the benefit of poultry and fish producers. The point is that social trends have an impact on business concerns and the earnings and stock prices of those firms.

Technology

Technology refers to the application of science to industrial and commercial objectives. The computer, avionics, and aerospace industries are examples of high-technology industries that push the frontiers of industrial development forward. One distinguishing feature of these industries is the rapidity of change as new products emerge. In the time span of a few years, jets replaced propeller-driven airliners on many routes. Fast computers replace slow computers. Satellites replaced underwater cables for transcontinental communications. Pocket calculators replaced desk calculators and slide rules. Typically, the price of such products declines sharply after the prototypes have been developed and large-scale production is under way. Producing products that can become obsolete overnight because of rapid change is a hazardous business. Nevertheless, companies such as Xerox, IBM, and Polaroid have developed new technologies and created new areas for growth. However, the list of companies that have attempted to produce similar products and failed is much longer.

Another feature of high technology is that it costs a lot of money for research and development. Typically, the major leaders in new technology are business concerns that can afford the capital outlays. IBM, American Telephone & Telegraph, General Electric, and Texas Instruments are examples of large firms that are leaders in new technology. Most small firms cannot afford to do research or absorb the cost of new products that fail. However, many technological innovations spawned in the laboratories of large firms may be produced in whole or part by small firms. For example, the production of a nuclear submarine requires thousands of component parts from hundreds of different manufacturing firms. Even though a large firm may be the primary contractor for the submarine, many other firms help to produce it and benefit from its development.

GROWTH

Growth is another word, like *industry,* that is difficult to define. Growth is frequently expressed in terms of increases in earnings, assets, sales, or some measure of output. An industry spokesperson may point to a chart that shows a sharply rising curve and announce proudly that sales increased at a 6-percent rate over the past two years, which was a marked improvement over the previous two-year period. A 6-percent increase sounds good until one compares it to the nation's economy, which has been growing at a 9-percent rate. This example illustrates that growth is both an absolute and a relative concept. The industry did grow at a 6-percent rate; however, it was growing at a slower pace than other industries.

What is a growth industry? Is it one that grows 4, 8, or 12 percent? Is there a special rate above which an industry automatically qualifies as a growth industry? The answer to these questions is that *a growth industry is one that consistently grows faster than other industries.* Moreover, the growth rate of a growth industry may vary over a period of time for a variety of reasons, including changes in economic activity. As noted in Chapter 10, many industries are considered cyclical because their production or sales increase and decrease with general business activity. The

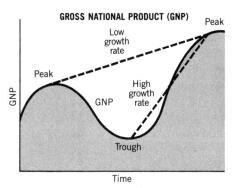

FIGURE 11-3 Measuring growth.

growth rates of such industries may depend on when the measurements are made during the business cycle. For example, Figure 11-3 shows hypothetical peaks and troughs of a cycle. If the growth rate is measured from peak to peak it will be lower than if it is measured from the trough to the next peak. Both growth rates are correct, but someone wanting to show a high growth rate will use one, and someone wanting to show a low growth rate will use the other.

Economic Growth

The actual growth rate of the economy as measured by the **gross national product (GNP)** varies from year to year. Figure 11-4 presents two growth triangles that can be used to measure the compounded annual growth rate of the GNP in current (nominal) dollars and in real dollars. Real GNP is what the GNP would have been had there been no inflation in the economy. In this case the GNP is measured in 1982 dollars. The triangles are used in the following manner. Assume that you are interested in determining some of the growth rates between the second quarter of 1987 and the fourth quarter of 1989. Using the top panel of Figure 11-4, find the 2-87 column under *initial quarter.* Read down that column to the *terminal quarter* 4-9, and the answer is that the growth rate was 7.3 percent annually. The growth rate expressed in real terms (lower panel) was 3.6 percent. Again, the difference between the nominal and real growth rates represents information.

Since the growth rate of the economy changes continuously, it is not surprising that the growth rates of industries vary from year to year and over longer periods of time. Keep in mind that the economy is only one of the many factors discussed in this chapter that affect industry growth. Changes in technology, laws, natural disasters, and other factors also affect industry growth. The precise impact of such events cannot be predicted accurately. Nevertheless, investors can take advantage of available information and techniques to make an educated guess about the future. Some information about the future is better than none.

Motor Vehicle Sales

Assume that an investor is considering investing in the automotive industry and wants to know about its future growth. One simple technique is to rely on published forecasts. For example, the *U.S. Industrial Outlook 1990,* has estimated automotive sales by market segment, source, and market share for 1988–1994 (see Table 11-4). The figures show the role of imports in the domestic automotive market. The data in these tables are accompanied by text explaining the trends. A partial explanation of the trends in this industry is that

The improved outlook for sales of North-American built passenger cars during this period is attributed to new product offerings and new vehicle manufacturers. The forecast masks a shift in nameplate mix, with Japanese auto producers making and selling more in the United States, while the Big Three make and sell less. This trend, combined with growing North

GROSS NATIONAL PRODUCT IN CURRENT DOLLARS
(Compounded Annual Rates of Change)

TERMINAL QUARTER	2-85	3-85	4-85	1-86	2-86	3-86	4-86	1-87	2-87	3-87	4-87	1-88	2-88	3-88	4-88	1-89	2-89	3-89	4-89	BILLIONS OF DOLLARS ANNUAL RATES
3-85	7.0																			4,047.0
4-85	6.6	6.2																		4,107.9
1-86	6.8	6.7	7.3																	4,181.3
2-86	5.4	4.9	4.3	1.3																4,194.7
3-86	5.5	5.1	4.7	3.5	5.7															4,253.3
4-86	5.3	4.9	4.6	3.7	5.0	4.2														4,297.3
1-87	5.8	5.6	5.4	5.0	6.2	6.5	8.8													4,388.8
2-87	6.1	5.9	5.9	5.6	6.7	7.0	8.5	8.2												4,475.9
3-87	6.3	6.2	6.2	6.1	7.0	7.4	8.4	8.3	8.4											4,566.6
4-87	6.6	6.5	6.6	6.5	7.4	7.7	8.6	8.5	8.7	9.0										4,665.8
1-88	6.6	6.5	6.6	6.5	7.2	7.5	8.2	8.0	7.9	7.7	6.5									4,739.8
2-88	6.7	6.7	6.8	6.7	7.4	7.6	8.2	8.1	8.1	8.0	7.5	8.6								4,838.5
3-88	6.8	6.8	6.8	6.8	7.4	7.6	8.1	8.0	8.0	7.9	7.5	8.1	7.5							4,926.9
4-88	6.8	6.9	6.9	6.9	7.4	7.6	8.1	7.9	7.9	7.8	7.5	7.9	7.5	7.5						5,017.3
1-89	6.9	6.9	7.0	6.9	7.5	7.6	8.0	7.9	7.9	7.8	7.6	7.9	7.6	7.7	7.9					5,113.1
2-89	6.9	6.9	7.0	6.9	7.4	7.6	7.9	7.8	7.9	7.6	7.5	7.7	7.5	7.5	7.9	7.1				5,201.7
3-89	6.9	6.9	6.9	6.9	7.3	7.5	7.8	7.7	7.6	7.5	7.3	7.5	7.3	7.2	7.5	6.7	6.2			5,281.0
4-89	6.8	6.7	6.8	6.7	7.1	7.3	7.5	7.4	7.3	7.2	7.0	7.1	6.8	6.7	6.7	6.0	5.4	4.6		5,342.2
1-90	6.8	6.8	6.8	6.8	7.2	7.3	7.5	7.4	7.3	7.1	7.1	7.1	6.9	6.8	6.7	6.4	6.2	6.2	7.8	5,441.2E
	2-85	3-85	4-85	1-86	2-86	3-86	4-86	1-87	2-87	3-87	4-87	1-88	2-88	3-88	4-88	1-89	2-89	3-89	4-89	
										INITIAL QUARTER										

E— ESTIMATED

FIGURE II-4 Growth rate of GNP. *Source:* Prepared by Federal Reserve Bank of St. Louis, April 27, 1990.

PREPARED BY FEDERAL RESERVE BANK OF ST. LOUIS
APRIL 27, 1990

GROSS NATIONAL PRODUCT IN 1982 DOLLARS
(Compounded Annual Rates of Change)

TERMINAL QUARTER	2-85	3-85	4-85	1-86	2-86	3-86	4-86	1-87	2-87	3-87	4-87	1-88	2-88	3-88	4-88	1-89	2-89	3-89	4-89	BILLIONS OF DOLLARS ANNUAL RATES
3-85	4.1																			3,635.8
4-85	3.5	3.0																		3,662.4
1-86	4.5	4.7	6.6																	3,721.1
2-86	2.9	2.5	2.3	-1.8																3,704.6
3-86	2.5	2.1	1.8	-0.5	0.8															3,712.4
4-86	2.5	2.1	1.9	0.4	1.6	2.3														3,733.6
1-87	2.9	2.7	2.6	1.7	2.8	3.8	5.4													3,783.0
2-87	3.1	2.9	2.9	2.2	3.2	4.0	4.9	4.4												3,823.5
3-87	3.3	3.2	3.2	2.7	3.6	4.3	5.0	4.8	5.3											3,872.8
4-87	3.6	3.7	3.7	3.3	4.1	4.8	5.4	5.4	5.9	6.6										3,935.6
1-88	3.6	3.6	3.6	3.4	4.1	5.1	4.9	4.8	5.3	5.3	4.0									3,974.8
2-88	3.7	3.7	3.7	3.4	4.0	4.5	4.6	4.6	4.8	4.9	3.9	3.7								4,010.7
3-88	3.6	3.6	3.6	3.3	3.8	4.2	4.4	4.4	4.2	4.0	3.6	3.4	3.2							4,042.7
4-88	3.6	3.5	3.6	3.3	3.8	4.1	4.3	4.3	4.2	4.0	3.5	3.2	2.9	2.7						4,069.4
1-89	3.6	3.5	3.6	3.3	3.8	4.1	4.3	4.2	4.2	3.8	3.5	3.3	3.2	3.1	2.5					4,106.8
2-89	3.5	3.5	3.5	3.3	3.7	4.0	4.0	4.0	4.0	3.8	3.3	3.1	3.0	3.0	2.8	3.0				4,132.5
3-89	3.5	3.4	3.4	3.1	3.6	3.9	3.9	3.8	3.6	3.4	3.0	2.8	2.7	2.6	2.2	2.0	1.1			4,162.9
4-89	3.3	3.3	3.3	3.1	3.5	3.7	3.8	3.6	3.4	3.3	2.9	2.7	2.6	2.5	2.2	2.0	1.6			4,174.1
1-90	3.3	3.2	3.0	3.0	3.4	3.6	3.7	3.5	3.4	3.3	3.3	2.9	2.7	2.6	2.5	2.5	2.0	1.6	2.1	4,195.8E
	2-85	3-85	4-85	1-86	2-86	3-86	4-86	1-87	2-87	3-87	4-87	1-88	2-88	3-88	4-88	1-89	2-89	3-89	4-89	

INITIAL QUARTER

E— ESTIMATED

PREPARED BY FEDERAL RESERVE BANK OF ST. LOUIS
APRIL 27, 1990

FIGURE II-4 (Continued)

TABLE 11-4   U.S. Automobile Sales, 1988–1994 (in thousands of dollars)

Vehicle Category and Source	1988	1989[a]	1990[a]	1991[a]	1992[a]	1993[a]	1994[a]
Total	$10,540	$9,975	$9,890	$10,020	$10,200	$10,335	$10,445
Small	2,663	2,325	2,160	2,270	2,330	2,345	2,380
North American	960	860	815	920	950	1,040	1,100
Captives[b]	388	390	325	360	360	350	355
Imports from Japan	922	825	780	735	720	650	600
Imports from Europe	50	25	30	20	20	20	25
Other imports	343	225	210	235	280	285	300
Compact	3,594	3,520	3,495	3,380	3,463	3,565	3,615
North American	2,799	2,795	2,740	2,650	2,720	2,855	2,935
Imports from Japan	716	625	650	600	625	600	575
Imports from Europe	79	70	60	65	60	60	55
Other imports	0	30	45	65	60	50	50
Intermediate	2,362	2,260	2,410	2,525	2,600	2,620	2,610
North American	2,169	2,000	2,135	2,195	2,215	2,225	2,245
Imports from Japan	74	140	175	250	300	325	300
Imports from Europe	119	120	100	80	85	70	65
Large/luxury	1,921	1,870	1,825	1,845	1,805	1,805	1,840
North American	1,556	1,510	1,400	1,385	1,360	1,355	1,345
Imports from Japan	111	140	235	270	270	275	300
Imports from Europe	254	220	190	190	175	175	195

American overcapacity, will lead to some plant closures and accompanying regional unemployment problems during the early and mid-1990s. Much of the anticipated decline in employment will likely be addressed by attrition, but layoffs and worker transfers cannot be ruled out.[5]

Industry Growth

If you were to guess what are the most and least profitable industries in the United States, the odds are that you would not select beverages and tobacco as being number one or metals being last, but, as shown in Table 11-5, you would be wrong. A brief examination of the tobacco industry reveals why tobacco is a profitable industry. Although there is a growing awareness of the health hazards of smoking and decreased domestic consumption of tobacco products, as well as increased taxes, and increased government intervention in the tobacco industry, the industry has prospered. Why? One reason is increased foreign demand, especially from the Far East. American cigarette brands are favored over other brands. As new overseas markets open up due to easing import barriers, the

[5] U.S. Department of Commerce, *U.S. Industrial Outlook 1990.* 38-3.

TABLE II-4 (Continued)

				Sales and Market Share			
Source	1988	1989[a]	1990[a]	1991[a]	1992[a]	1993[a]	1994[a]
Sales	$10,540	$9,975	$9,890	$10,020	$10,200	$10,335	$10,445
North American	7,484	7,165	7,090	7,150	7,245	7,475	7,625
Imports	3,056	2,810	2,800	2,870	2,955	2,860	2,820
Japanese-made	2,076	1,935	2,000	2,045	2,095	2,025	1,960
Japanese nameplates	1,823	1,730	1,840	1,855	1,915	1,850	1,775
Captives[b]	253	205	160	190	180	175	185
Non-Japanese, except Korean	980	875	800	825	860	835	860
European	502	435	380	355	340	325	340
Other imports	343	255	255	300	340	335	350
Other captives	135	185	165	170	180	175	170
South Korean[c]	419	320	290	290	315	325	320
Market share							
North American	71.0%	71.8%	71.7%	71.4%	71.0%	72.3%	73.0%
Imports	29.0	28.3	28.3	28.6	29.0	27.6	27.0
Japanese-made	19.7	19.4	20.2	20.4	20.6	19.6	18.8
Japanese nameplates	17.3	17.3	18.6	18.5	18.8	17.9	17.0
Captives[b]	2.4	2.1	1.6	1.9	1.8	1.7	1.8
Non-Japanese, except Korean	9.4	8.9	8.1	8.2	8.4	8.0	8.3
European	4.8	4.4	3.8	3.5	3.3	3.1	3.3
Other imports	3.3	2.6	2.6	3.0	3.3	3.2	3.4
Other captives[b]	1.3	1.9	1.7	1.7	1.8	1.7	1.6
South Korean[c]	4.0	3.2	2.9	2.9	3.1	3.1	3.1

Source: U.S. Department of Commerce, *U.S. Industrial Outlook 1990.*

Notes: Totals may not add up due to rounding. This forecast assumes that the Japanese Voluntary Export Restraints ended March 31, 1990; real gas prices increase no more than 1 percent per year, and the value of the yen ranges between 130 and 145 to the dollar.

[a] Forecast.

[b] Foreign-made, but sold under domestic nameplates.

[c] Not included in the totals.

demand for American tobacco products will increase further. As shown at the bottom of Table 11-2, total tobacco product shipments (SIC code 21) increased sharply in recent years. The largest demand is for cigarettes (SIC code 2111). The strong growth in sales and profitability in this industry paid off for investors.

Total returns to tobacco stock investors (dividend yield and price appreciation) were 48.7 percent in 1986 and 19.2 percent in 1987.[6] In the metals industry, total returns to investors were − 9.5 percent in 1986, and 50.5 percent in 1987. These widely divergent figures suggest the tenuous relationship between short-term performance of stocks and industry growth. Industry growth is only one of many factors affecting stock prices.

[6] U.S. Department of Commerce, *Statistical Abstract of the United States, 1989,* Table 887.

TABLE 11-5 Industry Profitability and Growth, 1983–1987

Industry	Return on equity[a]		Sales[b]		Earnings per share	
	5-year rank	5-year average	5-year rank	5-year average	5-year rank	5-year average
All-industry medians	(x)	**12.8**	(x)	**6.8**	(x)	**5.3**
Beverage and tobacco	1	20.5	11	8.2	1	12.9
Communications media	2	19.1	5	11.5	2	12.9
Financial services	3	18.7	1	17.1	8	9.5
Industrial, office services	4	18.1	4	11.8	3	12.2
Health	5	17.5	8	10.8	7	10.0
Electrical equipment	6	16.3	23	5.6	12	7.5
Food processors	7	16.3	18	6.3	11	8.0
Retailing	8	16.1	3	13.6	5	11.8
Food distributors	9	16.1	10	9.4	10	8.2
Electric utilities	10	14.4	21	5.8	16	5.3
Banks and thrifts	11	14.4	6	11.4	6	11.1
Telecommunications	12	13.8	22	5.8	19	2.8
Aerospace and defense	13	13.6	17	6.5	13	6.1
Consumer products	14	13.4	12	7.7	14	5.8
Natural gas	15	12.9	26	3.8	24	−.5
Apparel, shoes, and textiles	16	12.8	15	7.0	26	−3.6
Insurance	17	12.6	2	14.4	4	12.0
Packaging	18	11.6	13	7.7	9	8.8
Computers and electronics	19	11.3	7	11.2	20	1.1
Conglomerates	20	11.1	27	3.8	22	.3
Paper	21	10.9	19	6.1	15	5.7
Chemicals	22	10.6	28	2.1	27	−7.3
Automotive	23	10.5	14	7.5	17	3.5
Leisure and recreation	24	10.4	20	6.0	21	1.0
Construction	25	10.3	24	4.9	23	−.1
Surface transportation	26	9.3	16	6.8	25	−3.1
Air transport	27	7.3	9	10.8	18	2.8
Oil	28	6.8	31	−5.6	28	(NS)
Heavy equipment	29	5.6	30	−.2	28	(NS)
Coal	30	4.5	25	4.0	28	(NS)
Metals	31	[c]	29	.1	28	(NS)

Source: U.S. Department of Commerce: *Statistical Abstract of the United States, 1990,* No. 894.

Notes: **In percent, except ranks. For fiscal years ending in the 12-month period ending September 30.** Included in the Forbes Universe of 1000 companies is every firm with revenue of over $475 million in 1987. Represents industry medians; calculated by listing companies in rank order and selecting the midpoint. Where there is an even number of companies, an arithmetic average of the two middle companies is substituted.

NS, not significant, X, not applicable.

[a] Represents net income divided by common shareholders' equity. Common shareholders' equity is total shareholders' equity including the stated value of all preferred stock at the beginning of each year minus the involuntary liquidating value of nonconvertible preferred shares.

[b] Net sales plus other operating revenue.

[c] Deficit.

CONCLUSION

No standard procedure can be used to analyze industries because each industry has unique features that must be taken into account. Some of the factors that investors should consider are definition of the industry, its economic structure, supply and demand, industrial life cycle, role of government, and projections of industry trends.

The U.S. government's Standard Industrial Classification (SIC) code numbers can help investors to define the particular industries they are interested in. Economic data about industries are usually published according to these classifications and can be a valuable source of information to investors.

The economic structure of an industry varies with the number of firms in the industry, the nature of the product, the degree of competition, the extent of government regulation, and so on. Economic structure can be divided into four classes: pure competition, imperfect competition, oligopoly, and monopoly. Investors should be aware of the economic structure of any industry they are considering investing in because this structure will affect the way the industry will perform in relation to overall economic conditions and the pressures of the marketplace.

Two other factors should have a bearing on an investor's long-range plans. A look into the future can often help investors determine what the supply and demand for an industry's product will be. These conditions will affect sales and production in the industry. In addition, many industries, like human beings, go through a life cycle with several stages of predictable growth. If an investor knows whether an industry is in the pioneering, expansion, or stabilization stage, predictions of performance become easier. Changes caused by life-cycle stages can also affect short-term profits for the investor who is trading in the securities market.

The ever-increasing and constantly changing involvement of government in industry is another factor that must be considered. Government control, regulation, and antitrust actions affect most industries to some degree. The government as a buyer of industrial products can also have a considerable effect, particularly on industries that manufacture products for national defense.

In recent years, rising consumer consciousness has heightened expectations of social reponsibility on the part of industries. This responsibility affects some industries more than others, but it is a rare factory nowadays that is not deeply involved in controlling pollution created by its manufacturing processes.

Variations in rates of technological change also have an effect on industries. Some constantly seem to find this year's product becoming obsolete before the end of January, while others have considerable stability in their technological processes. These conditions affect competition and performance in the entire industry.

Finally, the investor should have some awareness of the rate of growth of the particular industry being considered. The concept of rate of growth is complex, and an industry's growth rate should be considered in the context of the rate of growth of the overall economy as measured by an indicator such as GNP.

The analysis of an industry can be cursory or in-depth, depending on the needs of the investor. In most cases, investors use industry analyses supplied by stock-brokerage firms or investment advisory services rather than attempting to interpret the primary sources themselves.

IMPORTANT CONCEPTS

Antitrust laws
Declining phase (life cycle)
Expansion phase (life cycle)
Gross national product (GNP)
Growth
Imperfect competition
Industry
Industry life cycle
Monopoly
Oligopoly

Pioneering phase (life cycle)
Public utility
Pure competition
Regulated industries
Social responsibility
Stabilization phase (life cycle)
Standard Industrial Classification
   (SIC) code
Technology
U.S. Industrial Outlook

QUESTIONS AND EXERCISES

1. True or False. A two-digit SIC code can be used to determine specific products such as iron bars. Explain.
2. Give two examples of firms that are monopolies. What do they monopolize?
3. The soap industry is one example of imperfect competition. How many brands of soap can you list?
4. Supply and demand play an important role in assessing the outlook for an industry. What are some of the supply and demand factors that affect the demand for nuclear power?
5. Cite two industries that are currently in the pioneering phase of the life cycle.
6. Name an industry that is in the declining phase of the life cycle. What can be done to rejuvenate it?
7. Name an industry that is not heavily regulated. Explain why it is not.
8. Visit a local business and determine all of the government agencies that it must report to, or that monitor its activities.
9. If the local electric company is a monopoly, can it raise prices at will?
10. Antitrust laws are designed to make the economic system competitive. Do you think that breaking up large companies would be beneficial or harmful? Explain.
11. The Food and Drug Administration requires extensive testing of new drugs and more truthful labeling of certain products. Is this good or bad for the stock market? Explain.

12. Draw a diagram showing the relationship between housing starts (on the X axis) and interest rates (on the Y axis). If interest rates are expected to increase, predict what will happen to housing starts.

13. Keeping Figure 11-3 in mind, what is the appropriate length of time to use when measuring the growth rate of a company's dividends?

14. What is meant by a growth industry?

15. Deregulation has occurred in the airline industry. What has been the impact on competition?

ANALYZING COMPANIES

This is the first of two chapters dealing with analyzing companies. In this chapter we examine two of the four broad categories of factors affecting the behavior of companies, which, as shown in Figure 12-1, are government/law, funding costs, competition, and management factors. The role of government/law was explained in the previous chapter. Funding costs refer to the cost of borrowing funds and selling stock. These costs are determined by market conditions at the time the funds are raised and by the risk characteristics of the issuing firms. The risk characteristics of the issuer are influenced by other factors, including the two shown in the chart—competition and management decisions—which are the two topics examined in this chapter. Competition includes the products and markets in which firms operate. Management includes decisions to expand, diversify, and merge, to mention a few. How well managers deal with all of these factors is reflected in their firms' financial statements, which show their assets (what they own/control), liabilities (what they owe), how much money they earn, and so on. A description of a financial statement is presented in this chapter, and an in-depth analysis of them appears in the next chapter.

PRODUCTS AND MARKETS

Investors can obtain valuable insights into the potential of individual companies by examining the quality of products and services they produce. The basic premise presented here is that successful companies are those that do an excellent job

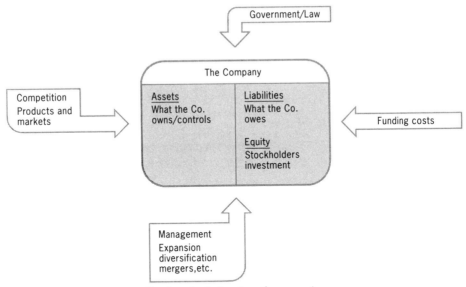

FIGURE 12-1   Factors affecting the behavior of companies.

of selling their products or services. Moreover, astute investors may be able to perceive some of the differences between the quality of products and use this information in assessing the value of a stock.

Consumer Goods and Services

Differences between the quality of products and services are easier to observe in companies that produce consumer goods than in companies that produce an item such as basic chemicals or metals. Therefore, let us start with a company that has a relatively narrow product line that is readily recognized by most investors. McDonald's Corporation is one of the leading fast food merchandisers. According to the U.S. Department of Commerce, there are about 87,000 eating and drinking establishments in the United States. McDonald's accounts for more than 10,700 of that total.[1] Their drive-in self-service restaurants with the famous golden arches are recognized by millions for popularly priced hamburgers, french fries, and similar products served in an informal atmosphere. The service and quality of products are maintained at a uniform standard throughout the United States. Thus, a hamburger bought in California should taste the same as one bought in Illinois or Florida. The company is very careful about selecting sites for its outlets, and it advertises heavily.

The investors who recognized that this company was doing something better than other fast-food companies and took advantage of that insight could have

[1] Based on information from the Value Line Investment Survey, March 30, 1990; published by Arnold Bernhard & Co., Inc., New York, and from the U.S. Department of Commerce.

profited handsomely by buying the stock before the general public caught on to McDonald's.

Many consumer-oriented companies have broader product lines than McDonald's. For example, Gillette Company offers a wide variety of products used in personal care, but they are known mainly for their shaving products. Similarly, Revlon is best known for its cosmetic line.

Brand Names

Some companies have been so successful in marketing particular products that the brand names of those products, for example, Coke, Kleenex, and Jell-O, have become household words. The expression "Let's go have a Coke" usually means, "Let's go get a soft drink." In this instance, Coca-Cola produced a product so widely known that there is tremendous brand loyalty, which means sales for the company and profits for its stockholders. Similarly, Kleenex is commonly used to refer to facial tissue, and Jell-O refers to gelatin-type desserts. Do you know who manufactures Kleenex and Jell-O?[2] Coke, Kleenex, and Jell-O are outstanding products, but they are only some of the many products produced by their manufacturers. Some companies produce hundreds of consumer products. Obviously, some products will be more successful than others. The weaker product lines are dropped, and new products are introduced to stir consumers' imaginations and tap their purses. Products, like industries, can have life cycles. A product can be in strong demand for a few years, and then fade away into obscurity. Such fads are evident in the garment industry, where clothing fashions change from year to year.

Number of Products

The number of products a company sells and the stability of the demand for these products is important. For example, Bristol-Myers Company produces hundreds of ethical and proprietary products. **Ethical products** are dispensed by prescription only, and **proprietary products** are sold over the counter. Benoxane and Cefadyl are examples of ethical products. Benoxane is an anticancer agent that is used against Hodgkin's disease and other cancers of the lymphatic system, and Cefadyl is a broad-spectrum injectable antibiotic. Although there is a demand for such products, it is the medical profession, not the public, that determines the quantity of an ethical product sold. In addition, there are few competitive products because most firms cannot afford the research and development costs of a product with a limited market. The demand for products such as these increases only in proportion to the diseases they are designed to cure. Moreover, the product has the potential to become outdated by a competitor's newer and better product.

Bristol-Myers' proprietary products include Clairol (hair coloring); Final Net (hair spray); Windex, Drano, and Vanish (household products); Poly-Vi-Sol (vitamins); Enfamil (baby formula); Vitalis (hair dressing); and Ban (deodorant). In

---

[2] Kleenex is manufactured by Kimberly-Clark Corporation and Jell-O by Philip Morris.

some cases the company offers several similar products to obtain a larger market share. For example, both Excedrin and Bufferin are Bristol-Myers' products.

The size of Bristol-Myers and the number of products it produces work both for and against the company. On the one hand, it has a large number of products that span the markets for such items as hair products, household products, and specialized medicines. Accordingly, sales should increase as the market for such products grows. On the other hand, the introduction of a new product may have little impact on the sales and earnings of the company. Nevertheless, many companies that produce consumer goods find it continuously necessary to introduce new products and retire old products that have become unprofitable. This pattern is the consequence of the **life cycle** of products.

Product Life Cycle

In Chapter 11 we used the industry/product life cycle in connection with analyzing industries. Now we will use it to give us some insights about the behavior of individual companies. By way of illustration, let us consider the life cycle of McDonald's Corporation. McDonald's licenses and operates the leading fast-food chain. As shown in Figure 12-2, it is in the stabilization phase of the life cycle. This position on the life cycle tells us that McDonald's is a survivor. Many fast-food chains have come and gone, but McDonald's has grown and prospered. Its position also tells us that McDonald's will continue to grow, but at a slower pace than before. One reason is that there is increased competition. When McDonald's was in the early portion of the expansion phase of the life cycle in the 1950s, there were relatively few fast-food chains. Today, however, one has a choice of Wendy's, Burger King, Pizza Hut, Taco Bell, and the list goes on. Other factors affect the growth of McDonald's, too. For example, there is increasing consumer preference for "healthier" and "lighter" foods such as salads and pasta dishes. There is the trend toward home delivery of hot, prepared food. Finally, as the population matures and incomes rise, there is increasing demand for "upscale" food service—better service and quality at a higher price.

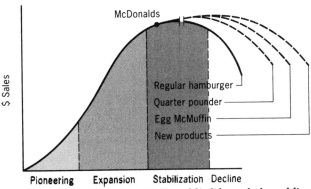

FIGURE 12-2   Extending McDonald's life cycle by adding new products.

As McDonald's revenues increased over the years, the company shared an increasing portion of its income with the shareholders. McDonald's paid its first cash dividend of $0.01 per share in 1976 (adjusted for stock splits). Since then, cash dividends have increased each year. In 1989 the cash dividend per share was $0.30. The dividend payout ratio — the percent of net income per share paid as cash dividends — was 15 percent. This means that the company retained 85 percent of its net income to foster future growth.

Since there are more than 10,700 McDonald's outlets and competition is increasing, how will McDonald's grow? Figure 12-2 provides a partial answer to that question. Part of the growth will come from the addition of new products. When the growth rate of regular hamburgers slowed, McDonald's added the Quarter Pounder. When its growth slowed they introduced the Egg McMuffin. Then came McNuggets (chicken), light salads to appeal to weight- and health-conscious patrons, and so on. The same concept applies to other companies as well. When the sales on one product line begin to falter, they introduce additional products. The addition of new products permits them to extend the duration of their life cycles.

Diversification and new products increase the costs of operating the business, which tends to retard profits. In addition, one can speculate that such diversification is a signal that the firm's growth rate is going to slow down. Its major source of growth has tapered off, and it is looking for new avenues of growth. Is that what happened to Xerox, Polaroid, and IBM?

Diversification generally works best for companies if they expand into areas or acquire firms in markets that they know. By way of illustration, Coca-Cola Company has expanded its product line to include Diet Coke, Sprite, and 17 other soft drinks, which are doing quite well. It was not as successful with its acquisition of Columbia Pictures Enterprises, or ventures into coffee, tea, wine, bottled water, and pasta businesses. Likewise, Exxon, the oil company, ventured into office machines and was a flop. Winnebago, the recreational vehicle company, ventured into advertising via satellites and it flopped too. The lesson to be learned here is that diversification into ventures unrelated to the core business is more risky than expanding the core business.

Some companies venture into other areas when their domestic core businesses are shrinking. For example, USX (formerly U.S. Steel) bought Marathon Oil, and Philip Morris (tobacco) bought Kraft Foods (Maxwell House, Jell-O, Birds Eye, Oscar Mayer, etc.).

Our discussion of the product life cycle has focused on the "typical" shape of the life cycle shown in the left panel of Figure 12-3. There are other shapes, including the "fad," that deserve our consideration. The term *fad* usually applies to fashions or trends that are relatively short-lived. The same concept applies to products. Some products enjoy very rapid growth. Then the original product is typically emulated by other products, and it fades or disappears altogether. Fads include Batman, Cabbage Patch dolls, C.B. radios, E.T., hoola-hoops, pet rocks, and others. Investors should consider whether the investments they are consid-

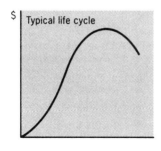 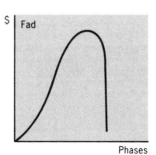

FIGURE 12-3   Life cycles.

ering are in fad products, which are short-lived, or ones that have longer term potential.

Derived Demand

The demand for one product frequently creates demand for other products. For example, the demand for computers created a demand for computer programs. Similarly, the demand for digital watches and calculators created a demand for the semiconductors that make them work. Therefore, companies like National Semiconductor and Texas Instruments, which produce semiconductors, benefited from the demand for digital watches and calculators. There are many other examples of **derived demand.** Think of the variety of materials used in producing an automobile. If the demand for automobiles changes, it affects the demand for steel, plastics, textiles, tires, and electronics.

Elasticity of Demand

The term **elasticity of demand** refers to the effect that price changes have on the quantity of goods demanded. If the quantity of goods demanded changes by a larger percentage than the price, the demand for the product is said to be elastic. For example, if the price of color televisions decreases 10 percent and the demand increases 20 percent, the demand for color televisions is said to be elastic. In contrast, if the price for table salt declines 10 percent and the demand does not change, it is considered inelastic. The general concept of elasticity is important in evaluating the impact of price changes on the demand for products.

The **elasticity of demand** helps to explain the large increases in the sales of personal computers when the prices were reduced. It also explains why consumers began to buy smaller and more economical cars when the price of gasoline increased to record levels.

To a large extent, elasticity of demand is influenced by substitution of other products. If the price of one brand of toothpaste doubled and the prices of other brands remained the same, some consumers would switch to the lower cost products. When the price of meat increases, some consumers switch to lower cost poultry, or they reduce the amount of meat they consume.

Some products have strong brand loyalty, which affects their elasticity of demand. Crest toothpaste is one such product. If the price of Crest were to increase $0.10 or $0.20 per tube, most loyal users would continue to buy it rather than switch to another product. This inelasticity of Crest gives its manufacturer, Proctor & Gamble, a competitive advantage over other toothpaste manufacturers.

Geographic Markets

The size and location of markets are relatively easy to determine and can be classified as local, regional, national, and international.

Local Markets

Public utilities are an example of firms that serve local markets, although some utilities serve larger regions. To a large extent, the growth rate of local utilities is influenced by the growth rates of the areas they serve. For example, during the 1970–1980 period, the population in Houston, Texas, increased 29 percent, while that in the New York City area declined about 10 percent. Assuming that Houston continues to grow more rapidly than New York City, one would expect investors to view utilities serving Houston with greater favor than those serving New York City. Keep in mind that population is only one of the factors affecting utilities. Other factors include the consumer–industrial–commercial mix, sources of power (coal, gas, nuclear), age of equipment, and rate structure.

Local market conditions do not go unnoticed by investors. If the stock market is efficient, then local market conditions will be reflected in the stock prices. In other words, savvy investors know that Houston is growing faster than New York City, so Houston utilities may be "fully priced" — they are not undervalued.

Regional Markets

Some firms serve particular regions of the country, especially when they are relatively small and growing. Ryan's Family Steak House, for example, is a rapidly growing family-style steak house–type restaurant chain with about 70 outlets located primarily in the Southeast. As it grows, it is entering Ohio and Indiana, and it can be expected to enter other bordering states as well. Ryan's is in the growth phase of the life cycle.

Shoney's Incorporated is a larger full-service restaurant with over 680 outlets located primarily in the Southeast. Shoney's is more mature than Ryan's, and has expanded as far west as Oklahoma. It has diversified by adding specialized restaurant chains and motels, Captain D's (seafood), Lee's Famous Recipe (chicken), and Shoney's Inns. Referring back to the life cycle, we can observe how Shoney's strategy differs from that of McDonald's. McDonald's began as a specialized fast-food producer of hamburgers and is expanding into other food lines. Shoney's began as a full-service restaurant and is expanding into other product areas by opening specialized restaurants and by expanding its geographic market.

To some extent, the success of both Ryan's and Shoney's is due to economic growth and prosperity in the Southeast. Without that growth, consumers would have had less disposable income and may have chosen lower cost alternatives to eating out.

National Markets

Most major firms conduct their business on a national or international scale. Automobile manufacturers, computer manufacturers, and oil companies are examples. Such firms are affected more by national economic conditions than by local or regional conditions. Nevertheless, regional conditions are still important. For example, take the case of a major carpet manufacturer. One of the most important markets for carpeting is provided by new housing starts. In recent years there have been wide swings in new housing starts and changes in the composition of housing. In 1978 housing starts were 2.0 million units per year. The total declined to 1.0 million units in both 1981 and 1982, rebounded to 1.8 million units in 1986, then declined to 1.3 million in 1989. During the 1978–1989 period, the average purchase price of a new single-family home increased from about $63,000 to about $150,000. As prices increased, some consumers switched to lower cost alternatives, such as multifamily dwellings and mobile homes. Therefore, carpet manufacturers' sales depended both on the level of housing starts and the composition of housing. Moreover, there were regional differences. There were fewer housing starts in the New England states than in the South. Manufacturers could offset their reduced sales in the New England states with increased sales in the South.

International Markets

The United States is both a major exporter and importer of goods. We sell agricultural products, military hardware, machinery, computers, and many other products overseas. On the other side of the international balance sheet, we import oil, steel, radios, shoes, and a myriad of other products. Firms that buy and sell in international markets face a variety of problems that do not confront domestic firms. For example, these firms must deal with different ways of doing business in foreign countries, fluctuating exchange rates (two or more currencies), different tax structures, unstable governments, and problems of divided allegiance.

On balance, the problems overseas are extremely difficult for most investors to analyze. Therefore, one should proceed cautiously and conservatively in assessing the contributions of overseas divisions of international companies. For example, Anaconda (now owned by Atlantic Richfield Oil) has reserves of copper ore in Chile and the United States, while Phelps Dodge has reserves of copper ore, primarily in the United States. If one were to assign dollar values to each ton of copper ore in reserve, the domestic reserves would be valued at a higher rate than those overseas.

Market Share

Regional geographic markets should not be confused with **market share.** As used here, the term *market share* refers to the percentage of sales (or some similar number) accounted for by a particular firm. In the case of a local utility company that has a monopoly, one firm accounts for all the sales in the area—a 100-percent share of the market. Similarly, if there are five commercial banks in a metropolitan area, one bank may account for 40 percent of the deposits and the other banks the remainder. The first bank's market share would be 40 percent. There is a strong relationship between market share and profitability.

Competitive Advantage

Michael Porter wrote a book entitled *Competitive Advantage: Creating and Sustaining Superior Performance.*[3] According to Porter, the success or failure of a firm depends on lowering costs or offering unique benefits to buyers that justify a premium price. *High capital investments* in plant and equipment provide a competitive advantage to some firms. Few firms can afford to duplicate the capital investments of public utility companies. *Government regulations* also give utilities and other firms a competitive advantage by keeping other firms out of their markets or regulating the rates they charge. Sometimes such regulations are a disadvantage. The banking industry is saddled with regulations, such as limitations on branch banking, that were designed to protect it from competition. These same regulations inhibit banks from competing effectively with other firms that provide financial services, such as Sears, General Electric, and Merrill Lynch, which are not subject to the same restrictive regulations.

Like capital investments in plant and equipment, large amounts of money and time spent on research and development are not easily duplicated. At major drug companies, it takes years to develop new drugs, test them, and have them approved by the Food and Drug Administration.

Firms also gain a competitive advantage by being *innovators.* The first firm to develop a new product may be able to dominate the market. One way to do this is to protect the new product with *patents* that prohibit competitors from producing exactly the same product. Xerox, for example, dominates the market for copy machines.

Reputation and *name recognition* also provide a competitive advantage. The names "Cadillac" and "Rolls Royce," for example, are associated with quality.

Financial strength can be a competitive advantage. A firm must be able to raise funds at favorable rates in order to expand, produce, and sell products and services. More will be said about financial strength.

Finally, firms must be able to sustain their competitive advantages over time in order to benefit. Having a temporary advantage may not be sufficient to add much value to a firm's earning power or share price.

---

[3] Published by The Free Press, New York, 1985.

MANAGEMENT

Some companies succeed because of their management. Other companies succeed in spite of their management. In either case, management has something to do with profits which, in turn, influence share prices.

Analyzing Management

Every student of management has studied the Sears, Roebuck–Montgomery Ward case. After World War II, the management of Montgomery Ward believed that the country was in for a depression of major proportions. Accordingly, it invested heavily in liquid assets that were considered safe and did not expand the number of its retail sales outlets. In contrast, the management of Sears foresaw the postwar boom, and it expanded the number of its retail sales outlets dramatically. The net result of these management decisions was that Sears became the world's leading general merchandiser and Montgomery Ward grew at a slower pace.

Given 20–20 hindsight, it is clear that the Sears management made the correct decision. However, investors buying or analyzing securities today cannot afford to wait 40 years or more for history to judge current management decisions.

Most investors do not have the time, money, or knowledge necessary to analyze the top management of a General Motors or even the local utility company. Such an analysis would require in-depth interviews with the top management team and key directors. Obviously, the interviewer would have to know the proper questions to ask. It would also require a thorough search of articles and speeches by management. In short, an investor who owns several hundred shares of General Motors probably would not go to such lengths to learn about the top management team.

Several sources of information provide limited insights about management. One such source is the annual meeting. Companies listed on the New York Stock Exchange notify their stockholders of the time and place of the annual meetings. Some unlisted companies hold their meetings at inconvenient times and places to keep stockholder participation at a minimum. Wherever or whenever the annual meetings are held, they give stockholders the opportunity to question the management's practices and policies.

Stockholders may also receive annual reports, which usually contain very little intrinsic information about management. Typically, such reports show a picture of the top management personnel around a conference table. In addition, there is a letter from the president. When earnings are rising and the outlook is reasonably good, the letters tend to be relatively long and full of glowing reports of the past and promises for the future. If the earnings are depressed, the president's letter tends to be short and full of explanations as to why factors over which the company has no control contributed to lower profits. Many annual reports contain pictures of company products, discussions of market factors, and other useful information. However, the most important part of the annual report is the financial statement, which is discussed at the end of this chapter and more fully in Chapter 13.

Business periodicals are another source of information about management. Magazines such as *Forbes, BusinessWeek,* and *Fortune* contain articles about management personalities, philosophies, and corporate strategies. Some names appear more frequently than others in the financial press, such as those of T. Boone Pickens and Saul Steinberg, entrepreneurs who have used mergers to achieve corporate growth, personal wealth, and individual power. When such empire builders acquire a company, changes will occur. However, it is not easy to predict the direction of change. Some of their ventures have paid off handsomely, and others have failed.

In summary, it seems reasonable that in the long run well-managed companies should be more profitable than similar companies with inferior management. In other words, one can judge management by its deeds instead of its words. In this case, their deeds are the ability to be more profitable than other companies over a period of years.

One place to begin measuring the accomplishments of management is in the Security and Exchange Commission's **Form 10-K.**

Form 10-K

According to the Securities and Exchange Act of 1934, Section 13, companies that are registered with the SEC are required to file an annual report known as Form 10-K. Form 10-K is important because it is the best source of financial information and other information that may not be available elsewhere.

Investors can obtain copies of Form 10-K in several ways. First, some companies use Form 10-K as the basis for their annual reports. Second, companies must provide stockholders with copies of their Form 10-K on request. The number of pages in the report depends on the size of the company and the complexity of its operations. Some reports may contain 30 pages, others 1000 pages. The number of pages is important for several reasons. Companies are generally more willing to supply relatively small reports and somewhat reluctant to supply large ones unless the investor pays for the cost of copying. Finally, the reports are available at the SEC's offices and library. This source is mentioned last because it is generally faster to deal directly with private business concerns than to obtain reports from government agencies.

For those investors who do not wish to go to the time or expense of obtaining Form 10-K or other documents filed with the SEC (e.g., quarterly reports), similar information can be found in a company's annual report and Standard & Poor's and Moody's publications. Form 10-K information is available on personal computers from Disclosure. These sources were discussed in Chapter 9.

FINANCIAL STATEMENTS

The **balance sheet, income statement, cash flow statement,** and **statements of shareholders equity** are the principal financial statements issued by corporations. As previously noted, annual reports and Form 10-Ks are two sources of the

BOX 12-1

MUCH CAN BE LEARNED BY READING THE *ACCOUNTING POLICIES* SECTION IN ANNUAL REPORTS

In December 1987, the Financial Accounting Standards Board ("FASB") adopted Statement of Financial Accounting Standards No. 96, "Accounting for Income Taxes" ("Statement No. 96"). Statement No. 96 originally required all companies to adopt the new rules effective for fiscal years beginning after December 15, 1988. However, due to continued implementation concerns, in December 1989 the FASB delayed the effective date to fiscal years beginning after December 15, 1991.

For regulated companies, Statement No. 96 requires that all deferred tax liabilities be recognized and that a long term deferred asset and a deferred tax liability be recorded to reflect the amount of cumulative tax benefits previously flowed through to ratepayers and the revenue to be recovered through rates when the related taxes become payable in future years. Under Statement No. 96, the effect of changes in corporate income tax rates on deferred income taxes, absent regulation, is recognized as an adjustment to income tax expense. It is not anticipated that any of these changes will have a material impact on net income. However, the accounting for and the impact on net income related to these adjustments will depend on the rate making treatment authorized in future regulatory proceedings.

> *Income Taxes:* Income tax expense is based on reported earnings before income taxes. Deferred income taxes reflect the impact of temporary differences between the amount of assets and liabilities recognized for financial reporting purposes and such amounts recognized for tax purposes. These deferred taxes are measured by applying currently enacted tax laws. In years prior to 1988, deferred taxes were accounted for at the tax rates in effect when the asset or liability was recorded, with no adjustment for subsequent rate changes. Deferred investment tax credits are being amortized as a reduction of income tax expense over the average useful life of the applicable classes of property.

> *Inventories:* Raw materials, finished goods and work in process are stated at the lower of average cost or market.

> *Cash Equivalents:* All highly liquid investments with a maturity of three months or less at date of purchase are considered to be cash equivalents.

> *Translation of Foreign Currency:* Assets and liabilities of foreign subsidiaries are translated at rates of exchange in effect at the close of their fiscal year. Revenues and expenses are translated at the weighted

(continued on next page)

average exchange rates during the year. Translation gains and losses are accumulated as a separate component of shareholders' equity. Foreign currency transaction gains and losses are included in income.

Research and Development: All research and development costs are charged to expense as incurred.

Marketable Securities: Marketable securities, other than equity securities, are valued at cost. Marketable equity securities are valued at the lower of aggregate cost or market value, and changes in market value are reflected in income. Dividend and interest income are accrued as earned. The cost of marketable securities sold is determined by the specific identification method.

Inventories: Inventories are stated at the lower of cost or market, with cost determined under the first-in, first-out method.

Property, Plant, and Equipment: Property, plant and equipment are carried at cost less accumulated depreciation and amortization. Depreciation is computed based on the estimated useful lives using the straight-line method. Leasehold improvements are amortized over the term of the lease using the straight-line method.

Intangible Assets: Intangible assets consist primarily of patents, trademarks, product technology, and acquired license agreements and are stated at cost less accumulated amortization. Amortization of intangibles is computed based on the straight-line method over periods ranging from eight to twelve years.

original financial statements which have not been altered to fit a vendor's data base or investment service. Always use the original source when possible. The aim here is to introduce these financial statements so that the reader will become familiar with them before attempting to analyze them. An analysis of financial statements is presented in Chapter 13.

Balance Sheet

A balance sheet, sometimes called a statement of financial position, represents the financial position of a company on one particular date. It is analogous to taking a snapshot that captures a person at a particular moment in time. Each person is unique, and so are corporations. No two firms are exactly alike. It is the unique features, whatever they may be, that differentiate firms — Coca-Cola is different from Pepsi, although both sell beverages; Ford is different from Chrysler, although both sell cars, and so on. Despite the differences among firms, we can compare their financial statements because they use generally accepted accounting practices. However, because each firm is unique, the comparisons are not precise in the same sense that an engineer must be precise in designing a space-

ship to go to Mars. Recognizing this shortcoming, we will examine Dayton Hudson Corporation in this chapter and the next in order to illustrate the general process of financial analysis. Dayton Hudson is one of the nation's largest retailers. It owns 657 Target, Mervin's, and Dayton Hudson Department Stores in 33 states. These are large-scale retail stores.

Figure 12-4 shows the consolidated statements of financial position (balance sheet) of Dayton Hudson Corporation. The term "consolidated statements" means that the financial statements for the firm's subsidiaries are combined here.

The balance sheets for two fiscal years are shown to demonstrate financial changes that occurred between balance sheet dates. Notice that the **fiscal years,** which are used for accounting purposes, do not coincide with calendar years. Examining data for a period of years may reveal trends and changes that cannot be detected in one year.

This financial statement is called a balance sheet because the two parts of the statement must balance — the **total assets** must equal the **total liabilities** and **shareholders' equity.**

$$\text{Assets} = \text{liabilities} + \text{shareholders' equity} \qquad (12\text{-}1)$$

In brief, the assets represent resources owned or controlled by the company. Liabilities are amounts owed by the company to others for goods they purchased on credit, borrowed funds, and other debts. Shareholders' equity represents the amounts that shareholders can claim after all of the liabilities have been paid. It is what the shareholders "own."

In Chapter 2 you learned that both common and preferred shareholders have an equity interest; i.e., own, the company. But in Dayton Hudson's balance sheet, only the common stock is included in shareholder's equity — total common shareholders' investment (line 27). The *redeemable preferred stock* (line 22) is listed above the *loan to ESOP* (line 23). An **ESOP** is an employee stock ownership plan. Dayton Hudson loaned the ESOP funds to buy the redeemable preferred stock. Dividends on the preferred stock will be used to repay the loan to the corporation. The redeemable preferred is *convertible* into shares of the common stock. According to the Securities and Exchange Commission, redeemable preferreds have characteristics of both debt and equity, and must be distinguished from the permanent equity capital.[4] Thus, it is a hybrid security that we will consider a liability for purposes of our analysis.

From Equation 12-1, we know that total assets equal total liabilities plus equity. It follows that total liabilities equal total assets (line 13) less equity (line 27). Figures are for 1990 and are shown in millions of dollars.

$$\begin{array}{ccc} \text{Total liabilities} = & \text{total assets} & - \text{equity} \qquad (12\text{-}2) \\ \$4931 & = \$6684 & - \$1753 \end{array}$$

Total liabilities in 1989 were $4662 million.

[4] See SEC, Accounting Series Release 268 for details on this subject. Some details about the redeemable preferred stock and the ESOP are printed in the footnotes of Dayton Hudson's 1989 Annual Report.

CONSOLIDATED STATEMENTS OF FINANCIAL POSITION

Dayton Hudson Corporation and Subsidiaries

(Millions of Dollars)		February 3, 1990	January 28, 1989
ASSETS			
Current Assets			
1	Cash and marketable securities	$ 103	$ 53
2	Accounts receivable (net of allowance for doubtful accounts of $37 and $35)	1,138	1,223
3	Merchandise inventories (net of accumulated LIFO provision of $169 and $154)	1,827	1,669
4	Other	39	36
5	**Total Current Assets**	3,107	2,981
	Property and Equipment		
6	Land	545	497
7	Buildings and improvements	2,749	2,566
8	Fixtures and equipment	1,422	1,335
9	Construction-in-progress	157	308
10	Accumulated depreciation	(1,350)	(1,220)
11	**Net Property and Equipment**	3,523	3,486
12	Other	54	56
13	**Total Assets**	$ 6,684	$ 6,523
	LIABILITIES AND COMMON SHAREHOLDERS' INVESTMENT		
	Current Liabilities		
14	Commercial paper	$ 234	$ 148
15	Accounts payable (including outstanding drafts of $276 and $248)	1,166	1,056
16	Accrued liabilities	536	566
17	Income taxes—payable and current deferred	187	138
18	Current portion of long-term debt	72	95
19	**Total Current Liabilities**	2,195	2,003
20	**Long-Term Debt**	2,510	2,383
21	**Deferred Income Taxes and Other**	225	276
22	**Redeemable Preferred Stock**	379	—
23	**Loan to ESOP**	(378)	—
	Common Shareholders' Investment		
24	Common stock	71	78
25	Additional paid-in capital	34	25
26	Retained earnings	1,648	1,758
27	**Total Common Shareholders' Investment**	1,753	1,861
28	**Total Liabilities and Common Shareholders' Investment**	$ 6,684	$ 6,523

FIGURE 12-4 Balance sheets.

Companies borrow funds (liabilities) and sell stock (equity) in order to acquire more assets. As shown in line 13, total assets grew from $6523 million in 1989 to $6684 million in 1990. Most of the growth was financed with increased borrowing.

Assets

Two of the major categories of assets are *current assets* and *property and equipment,* which is also called *fixed assets.* The term "current" generally means that the assets can be converted into cash or used within a short period of time such as a year or less. The principal current assets are cash and marketable securities (line 1), accounts receivable (line 2), and inventories (line 3).

Cash (line 1) is exactly what the name implies. It includes coin and currency as well as money on deposit at banks. It is used to meet the day-to-day transaction needs of the firms. When there is more cash on hand than is required to meet these needs, it is invested in short-term **marketable securities** such as U.S. government securities or commercial paper. These securities earn interest whereas cash is a nonearning asset. Some firms "park" large amounts of funds in marketable securities while they are waiting to make large acquisitions that will be financed by cash.

Accounts receivable (line 2) arise when goods are sold on credit to customers. Payment for those goods may not take place for several days, weeks, or months.

Inventories (line 3) consist of merchandise for sale at Dayton Hudson. The composition of inventories depends on the type of business. In manufacturing firms, it also includes raw materials, goods in the process of being produced, and finished materials.

The function of current assets can be considered in terms of the **working capital cycle.** As Figure 12-5 shows, the sales of inventories lead to an increase in both cash and credit sales. The credit sales increase accounts receivable. When the accounts receivable are collected, cash increases. The cash in turn is used to purchase new inventories and pay operating expenses, such as wages, rent, and insurance.

Although the diagram in Figure 12-5 is simplified, it is useful in illustrating selected financial problems. For example, if credit sales grow rapidly and the collection of accounts receivables is slow, the company will be caught in a financial bind and will be unable to buy new inventories and pay expenses. Second, if sales increase at a slower rate than inventories, an excessive amount of funds will be tied up in inventories and fewer funds will flow back into cash to pay expenses. Finally, if sales increase, what should the company do with its cash receipts? Should it increase inventories or invest in short-term securities. Can you think of other uses of cash?

Property and equipment (lines 6 – 11) or **fixed assets** include land, buildings, and fixtures. In other firms it includes plant and equipment. These fixed assets are used to produce or merchandise the goods and services the firm sells.

Buildings, fixtures, machinery, and equipment wear out over time. Because of the wear, they are valued at their cost less accumulated depreciation.

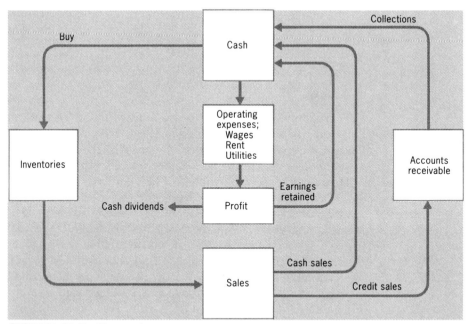

FIGURE 12-5   The working capital cycle.

In summary, total assets consist of current and noncurrent assets. Current assets are considered short-term because they can be converted into cash or used in the business in a relatively short period of time. In contrast, noncurrent assets are not normally sold. They are used in the production or sale of goods and services.

Liabilities

The major categories of liabilities are **current liabilities** and long-term debt. Current liabilities (lines 14–18) are debts that are due within one year. As shown in Figure 12-4, the principal current liabilities are accounts payable and accrued liabilities. **Accounts payable** (line 15) represent amounts that are owed to business creditors. When Dayton Hudson buys suits, for example, it may have 30 days to pay for them. During that period, Dayton Hudson owes the manufacturer for the suits. That same amount is recorded on the books of the manufacturer as an account receivable.

Accrued liabilities (line 16) consist of wages and salaries that are due to employees, interest on borrowed funds, and similar expenses. The accrued expenses item indicates the extent to which such expenses were owed on the date of the balance sheet.

In summary, current liabilities are short-term liabilities. These short-term debts may not be paid off completely at a given time. Many companies roll over their short-term debts; that is, they continuously borrow short-term funds. The

amount of short-term funds borrowed depends on the company's financial needs and the outlook for interest rates.

Long-term liabilities form the second major category of liabilities. Long-term liabilities include all debts and other obligations that do not mature in one year. As noted previously, we are including the redeemable preferred stock (line 22) and the loan to the ESOP (line 23) as long-term liabilities.

Common Shareholders' Investment (Equity)

This portion has two categories of concern to us: contributed capital and retained earnings. Contributed capital includes common stock (line 24) and additional paid-in capital (line 25). This represents the capital stock, valued at par, and the amounts paid in capital in excess of par. **Retained earnings** reflect profits that have been retained by the firm instead of being paid out to shareholders in the form of cash dividends.

Retained earnings belong to the common stockholders. They are not usually retained in the form of cash where they could be distributed to shareholders at a later date. Instead they are invested in various assets and used to repay debts.

Income Statement

The income statement, or **results of operations,** shows how much money a firm earned or lost during its fiscal year. It is a statement of revenues and expenses. The balance sheet is like a snapshot taken on one day, but the income statement is analogous to a movie because it shows what happens over the period of one year. Stated otherwise, it reflects the earnings or losses between two balance sheet dates.

Figure 12-6 shows the income statement for Dayton Hudson. It consists of three broad parts. The first part lists the revenues from sales and other sources of income (line 1). The second part shows the expenses associated with producing those revenues (line 7). The two largest expenses include the cost of the goods that they sell and occupancy expense (rent), and the selling, publicity, and administrative expenses. Depreciation, interest and other expenses are relatively small. The third part of the statement shows the profits, also called **net earnings or net income** (line 10). By definition, profits are the amount that remains after expenses have been deducted from revenues.

The net earnings divided by the number of common shares outstanding gives us *primary earnings per share* (line 11). If the redeemable preferred stock is converted into common stock, there will be more shares outstanding. This condition is reflected in the *fully diluted earnings per share* (line 12).

Common Shareholders' Investment

The disposition of the profits is shown in Figure 12-7. Figure 12-7, line 11 (and Figure 12-4, line 27) shows that total common shareholders' investment on

CONSOLIDATED RESULTS OF OPERATIONS

Dayton Hudson Corporation and Subsidiaries

(Millions of Dollars, Except Per-Share Data)		1989		1988		1987
1	Revenues	$ 13,644	$	12,204	$	10,677
	Costs and Expenses					
2	Cost of retail sales, buying and occupancy	9,890		8,980		7,950
3	Selling, publicity and administrative	2,264		2,038		1,769
4	Depreciation	315		290		231
5	Interest expense, net	267		218		152
6	Taxes other than income taxes	230		206		176
7	Total Costs and Expenses	12,966		11,732		10,278
8	Earnings Before Income Taxes	678		472		399
9	Provision for Income Taxes	268		185		171
10	Net Earnings	$ 410	$	287	$	228
	Earnings Per Share:					
11	Primary	$ 5.37	$	3.45	$	2.41
12	Fully Diluted	$ 5.35	$	3.45	$	2.41
	Average Common Shares Outstanding (Millions):					
13	Primary	76.3		83.3		94.8
14	Fully Diluted	76.6		83.3		94.8

FIGURE 12-6 Consolidated results of operations.

CONSOLIDATED STATEMENTS OF COMMON SHAREHOLDERS' INVESTMENT

Dayton Hudson Corporation and Subsidiaries

	(Millions of Dollars)	Total	Common Stock	Additional Paid-in Capital	Retained Earnings
1	**Balance January 31, 1987**	$ 2,180	$ 97	$ 19	$ 2,064
2	Consolidated net earnings	228			228
3	Dividends declared	(87)			(87)
4	Stock option activity	5	1	4	
5	Stock repurchase	(340)	(12)		(328)
6	**Balance January 30, 1988**	1,986	86	23	1,877
7	Consolidated net earnings	287			287
8	Dividends declared	(85)			(85)
9	Stock option activity	2		2	
10	Stock repurchase	(329)	(8)		(321)
11	**Balance January 28, 1989**	1,861	78	25	1,758
12	Consolidated net earnings	410			410
13	Dividends declared	(87)			(87)
14	Stock option activity	9		9	
15	Stock repurchase	(440)	(7)		(433)
16	**Balance February 3, 1990**	$ 1,753	$ 71	$ 34	$ 1,648

Preferred Stock

Authorized 5,000,000 shares, $.01 par value; 438,353 shares (Series B ESOP Convertible Preferred Stock) outstanding at February 3, 1990; no shares outstanding at January 28, 1989.

Common Stock

Authorized 500,000,000 shares $1 par value; 70,874,232 shares issued and outstanding at February 3, 1990; 77,648,989 shares issued and outstanding at January 28, 1989.

Junior Preferred Stock Rights

In September 1986, a distribution of preferred share purchase rights was declared. Terms of the plan provide for a distribution of one preferred share purchase right on each outstanding share of Dayton Hudson common stock. Each right will entitle shareholders to buy one-hundredth of a share of a new series of junior participating preferred stock at an exercise price of $150, subject to adjustment. The rights will be exercisable only if a person or group acquires ownership of 20% or more of Dayton Hudson common stock or announces a tender offer to acquire 20% or more of the common stock.

These financial statements should be read in conjunction with the Analysis of Operations on pages 17-21 and the information on pages 26-29.

FIGURE 12-7 Consolidated statements of common shareholders' investments.

January 28, 1989, was $1861 million. During the next fiscal year, Dayton Hudson earned $410 million (Figure 12-6, line 10; Figure 12-7, line 12). Of that amount, $87 million was paid out in the form of cash dividends. Dayton Hudson also repurchased $440 million of its own shares, thereby reducing the number of shares outstanding (Figure 12-6, line 13) and helping to increase the earnings per share (Figure 12-6, line 11). The resulting common shareholders' investment at the end of the period is $1753 million (Figure 12-4, line 27; Figure 12-7, line 16).

Cash Flow

The **Statement of Cash Flows** is the final statement that we will consider. Cash flow is a misnomer because it includes the disposition of cash and other funds. For example, depreciation (Figure 12-8, line 2) is a noncash expense. It provides a source of funds through the reduction of federal income taxes that must be paid. Similarly, deferred taxes (Figure 12-8, lines 3 and 4) represent the differences between alternative methods of calculating certain expenses to be depreciated each year. This difference is due to the fact that the firm may use one accounting method for reporting to shareholders and another method for reporting taxes to the Internal Revenue Service. The deferred items reconcile the two methods.

The cash flow statement is divided into three broad categories designating the sources of the cash flow. The first is *cash flow provided by operations* (Figure 12-8, line 10). The amounts shown here represent the ability of Dayton Hudson to generate funds from its normal operations. These funds can be used to repay debts and to expand.

Cash flows from investing activities (Figure 12-8, line 13) reveals the amount of funds spent on investing in property and equipment and the sale of property.

Cash flows from financing activities (Figure 12-8, line 22) summarizes the firm's financial activities — borrowing, stock repurchases, payments of dividends, and so on.

When all of these three categories are summed and added to the cash held by Dayton Hudson at the beginning of the year, we get the cash held at the end of the fiscal year (Figure 12-8, line 25; Figure 12-4, line 1).

Auditor's Statement

At the end of the financial statements, the independent auditor certifies the report. The **auditor's statement,** or certification, should say that the financial statements fairly represent the financial condition of the company, that they are in conformity with generally accepted accounting principles, that the same methods were used in previous years to provide consistency, and that the auditor used such tests of the accounting records as were considered necessary. In other words, the auditor is saying the financial statements do not misrepresent the facts. However, there is a growing concern as to the manner of reporting financial statements and as to whether accountants have their client's or the investors'

CONSOLIDATED STATEMENTS OF CASH FLOWS

Dayton Hudson Corporation and Subsidiaries

(Millions of Dollars)		**1989**	1988	1987
	Operating Activities			
1	Net Earnings	**$ 410**	$ 287	$ 228
	Reconciliation to cash flow:			
2	Depreciation and amortization	**319**	292	232
3	Non-current deferred tax provision	**19**	27	5
4	Current deferred tax provision	**(29)**	(56)	(36)
5	Decrease/(increase) in accounts receivable	**91**	(149)	(21)
6	(Increase) in inventory	**(158)**	(46)	(311)
7	Increase in accounts payable	**110**	1	213
8	Increase/(decrease) in income taxes payable	**33**	35	(18)
9	Other	**(56)**	146	18
10	**Cash Flow Provided by Operations**	**739**	537	310
	Investing Activities			
11	Expenditures for property	**619**	690	787
12	Disposals of property	**(234)**	(18)	(86)
13	**Total from Investing Activities**	**385**	672	701
14	**Net Financing (Sources) Requirements**	**(354)**	135	391
	Financing Activities			
15	Increase/(decrease) in commercial paper	**86**	(205)	353
16	Additions to long-term debt	**242**	691	451
17	Purchase and redemption of debt	**(30)**	(39)	—
18	Principal payments on long-term debt	**(95)**	(17)	(19)
19	Repurchase of common stock	**(440)**	(329)	(340)
20	Dividends paid	**(85)**	(85)	(87)
21	Other	**18**	(3)	(16)
22	**Total from Financing Activities**	**(304)**	13	342
23	**Net Increase/(Decrease) in Cash and Cash Equivalents**	**50**	(122)	(49)
24	Cash and cash equivalents at beginning of year	**53**	175	224
25	**Cash and Cash Equivalents at End of Year**	**$ 103**	$ 53	$ 175

Amounts in these statements are presented on a cash basis and therefore may differ from those shown in other sections of this annual report. For purposes of these statements, all short-term investments purchased with a maturity of three months or less are considered cash equivalents.

Investing and financing activities not reported in the Statements of Cash Flows, because they do not involve cash, include financing activities in 1989 of the issuance of $379 million of ESOP preferred stock in consideration for a $379 million 15-year loan from the ESOP. Non-cash investing and financing activities also include capital lease activity. In 1989, disposition of capital leases on buildings and equipment were $(12) million. In 1988 and 1987, obligations were incurred when leases were entered into for buildings and equipment of $2 million and $8 million, respectively. In addition, non-cash capital expenditures resulting from assumed liabilities and asset reclassifications were $3 million in 1989 and $43 million in 1987.

Interest paid (including interest capitalized) during 1989, 1988 and 1987 was $269 million, $196 million and $141 million, respectively. Income tax payments of $248 million, $179 million and $218 million were made during 1989, 1988 and 1987, respectively.

The net change in commercial paper includes the repayment of $6 million of commercial paper with maturities over 90 days in 1988 and the issuance of $66 million and repayment of $60 million of commercial paper with maturities over 90 days in 1987.

In 1989, the reconciliation of net earnings to cash flow and disposals of property include the sale of Lechmere.

These financial statements should be read in conjunction with the Analysis of Operations on pages 17-21 and the information on pages 26-29.

FIGURE 12-8 Consolidated statements of cash flows.

interests in mind. The following accountants' report, which appeared on the cover of *Forbes* (March 15, 1977), reflects this concern:

To the directors and stockholders:

We have examined the Consolidated Balance Sheet of the company and Consolidated subsidiaries as of December 31, 1976 and 1975. In our opinion, these financial statements present fairly the financial position of the companies, in conformity with generally accepted accounting principles consistently applied.

On the other hand, there is a growing body of opinion that holds that our opinion is not worth a damn.

There is some evidence to support this position. Auditors gave Continental Bank a clean bill of health shortly before it failed. They did so because it was still a "going concern" before the federal regulators stepped in and took charge.

Finally, footnotes attached to financial statements deserve careful attention. Footnotes may concern litigation, acquisitions, leases, details of compensation plans, and other information explaining various aspects of the financial statements.

CONCLUSION

In analyzing a company, investors should examine its products, market, and management. Different industries have different types of products, but the successful company is one that does a good job of selling its products. In a company selling consumer goods, product quality, consumer response to products, and advertising effectiveness will affect sales. Products also have a life cycle similar to that of an industry. This cyclical pattern accounts for the constant introduction of new products and the retiring of old ones that are no longer appealing to consumers.

In order to be successful, a company must be aware of and responsive to consumer demand. The development of a new or existing product can sometimes create a demand for other products — derived demand. The nature of demand changes with the product. A necessity such as salt is in constant demand, and price changes will have little effect on its sales. Such a product is said to have inelastic demand. On the other hand, the sale of home computers will be sharply affected by price. When the percentage of change in sales is greater than the percentage of change in price the demand for the product is said to be elastic. Investors should be aware of changes in consumer demand and their possible effect on a particular company.

A company's market may be local, regional, national, or international. The extent of its market area will have a significant effect on the way it does business and on its potential success. An investor should also be aware of a company's

market share—that portion of its total market that a company's business accounts for. Market share figures are often a good indication of a company's position in relation to its competitors.

Success of products and high market share are usually clear-cut signs of success. It is more difficult for an investor to assess the effectiveness of a company's management. The annual report and the annual stockholders' meeting may offer some clues, but usually the quality of management must be deduced from the company's success in the marketplace and its financial success over the years.

A company's financial statements—balance sheet, income statement, and statement of change in financial position—give the investor an opportunity to see the current and ongoing financial position of the company. More is said about analysis of financial statements in the next chapter.

IMPORTANT CONCEPTS

Accounts payable
Accounts receivable
Accrued expenses
Assets
Auditor's statement
Balance sheet
Beta
Cash flow
Competitive advantage
Current assets
Current liabilities
Deferred taxes
Depreciation
Derived demand
Dividend payout ratio
Earnings per share
Elasticity of demand

Employee stock ownership plan
  (ESOP)
Ethical products
Fixed assets
Form 10-K
Income statement
Intangible assets
Liabilities
Life cycle
Market share
Proprietary products
Ratio of long-term debt to equity
Retained earnings
Stockholders' equity
Systematic risk
Working capital cycle

QUESTIONS AND EXERCISES

1. List three products whose names are household words. What companies make these products?

2. Why do some companies make two or more products that are in direct competition with each other? Give an example of such a company.

3. Select three products that you bought recently. Who made them? Where do the companies that made them fit on the life cycle?

4. What is the meaning of the term "derived demand?" How can this concept be applied in considering the outlook for the sale of personal computers?

5. The term "price elastic demand" means that the demand for a product is responsive to changes in price. Are the following products highly price elastic, moderately price elastic, or inelastic: (a) automobiles, (b) aspirin, (c) salt?

6. Cite five firms in different industries that sell their products or services on a regional basis.

7. Assume that you were asked to analyze a local bank. You can ask any five questions of top management (within reason). What questions will you ask?

8. What is Form 10-K?

9. Explain the difference between a balance sheet and an income statement.

10. If a firm has a large stockholders' equity, does that mean it has a lot of cash being held for stockholders? Explain.

11. Do intangible assets have value? Explain.

12. Why is depreciation important?

13. How do you analyze the quality of management of a company that is located in a foreign country?

14. Why is market share important?

15. One clue about the quality of a company is the quality of service they provide. Rate your local supermarket food chains and discount stores on the basis of quality. How do they compare?

CHAPTER 13

FINANCIAL STATEMENT ANALYSIS AND VALUATION

FINANCIAL ANALYSIS	Capital Asset Pricing Model
Ratios and Indicators	Price/Earnings Ratio
Percentage Statement Analysis	Price/Cash Flow Per Share
Statement of Cash Flows	Book Value
PROBLEMS WITH ACCOUNTING METHODS	Mergers
Inventory Valuation	**CONCLUSION**
DETERMINING VALUES	**IMPORTANT CONCEPTS**
Dividend Valuation Method	**QUESTIONS AND EXERCISES**

The reason for analyzing companies is to determine their intrinsic value. Analysis of financial statements is a basic tool used in making this determination, and this chapter explains techniques for interpreting and analyzing these statements. In addition, the chapter points out some of the difficulties that investors who are not security analysts can have in understanding financial statements. Finally, four methods of determining intrinsic value are presented.

FINANCIAL ANALYSIS

Balance sheets and income statements provide basic financial data about companies. It is up to investors to interpret the raw data and convert it into useful information. The aim of this section is to explain how to use the data to analyze financial trends and the financial condition of the firm.

Financial trends develop over time. The longer the time period we examine, the more likely we are to discover trends. Whenever possible, data should be analyzed over a period of five years or more.

The financial condition of a firm is relative to what other firms in the industry and the economy are doing. For example, suppose that revenues increase 15 percent per year. Is that good or bad? The answer is that it depends on what other firms in the same industry are doing. If their revenues are increasing 10 percent

per year, it is good. If their revenues are increasing 20 percent per year, it is bad. Accordingly, the best way to evaluate the condition of a firm is to compare it with similar firms. This is not easy to do because each firm is unique. Nevertheless, some industry data may be helpful.

Selected measures of industry performance can be found in the *Standard & Poor's Analysts Handbook,* Robert Morris Associate's *Annual Statement Studies,* Dunn & Bradstreet's *Industry Norms & Key Business Ratios,* and the U.S. Department of Commerce's *Statistical Abstract of the United States.* Periodicals, such as *BusinessWeek* and *Fortune,* publish some industry and company data too. The good news is that these sources provide industry data. The bad news is that the data may not apply to the firm you are analyzing. In fact, unless interpreted correctly, the data may be misleading. For example, the industry average for a particular ratio may be 22 percent and the firm you are analyzing has a ratio of 18. Is that good or bad? The word *average* refers to the middle value. By definition, half the companies are below average and half the companies are above average. Thus, being below average does not necessarily indicate a problem. However, it is important to know how far below average the ratio may fall before a problem is indicated.

Another issue in interpreting the data is that your firm may be in the expansion phase of the life cycle and the industry data may be dominated by firms in the stabilization phase. One would not expect the financial characteristics in firms in different phases of the life cycle to be the same. The firm in the expansion phase may be borrowing heavily and not paying any cash dividends. The mature firms may be reducing their debts and paying out most of their earnings in the form of cash dividends. Therefore the data are not strictly comparable.

The key to analyzing financial statements is good judgment. Such judgment is acquired only through experience and by analyzing many financial statements. We will analyze Dayton Hudson's financial condition one step at a time to make it as understandable as possible. For simplicity, we will use the data from the annual report, which is readily available to investors and analysts. The analysis covers two years, and does not make industry comparisons because of some of the reasons cited previously. Our mission is to determine the financial condition of the firm. To do that we use three general approaches: (1) ratio analysis, (2) percentage analysis, and (3) cash flow analysis. The starting points for the analyses are Figures 13-1 and 13-2, which present Dayton Hudson's balance sheet and income statements. Figure 13-3, the statement of common shareholders' investment, is also included for your convenience.

Notice that the income statement (Figure 13-2) covers 1989, 1988, and 1987. These are fiscal years. The end of fiscal year 1988 was January 28, 1989. The end of fiscal year 1989 was February 3, 1990. These are the dates used in the balance sheet (Figure 13-1). To avoid confusion about dates, we will adopt the convention of referring to the fiscal year. Thus, the balance sheet date February 3, 1990, is for fiscal 1989 data, and January 28, 1989, is for fiscal 1988 data.

Because income statements cover a one-year period, and balance sheets cover a one-day period, some analysts use average data from two balance sheets (i.e.,

CONSOLIDATED STATEMENTS OF FINANCIAL POSITION

Dayton Hudson Corporation and Subsidiaries

(Millions of Dollars)	February 3, 1990	January 28, 1989
ASSETS		
Current Assets		
1 Cash and marketable securities	$ 103	$ 53
2 Accounts receivable (net of allowance for doubtful accounts of $37 and $35)	1,138	1,223
3 Merchandise inventories (net of accumulated LIFO provision of $169 and $154)	1,827	1,669
4 Other	39	36
5 **Total Current Assets**	3,107	2,981
Property and Equipment		
6 Land	545	497
7 Buildings and improvements	2,749	2,566
8 Fixtures and equipment	1,422	1,335
9 Construction-in-progress	157	308
10 Accumulated depreciation	(1,350)	(1,220)
11 **Net Property and Equipment**	3,523	3,486
12 Other	54	56
13 **Total Assets**	$ 6,684	$ 6,523
LIABILITIES AND COMMON SHAREHOLDERS' INVESTMENT		
Current Liabilities		
14 Commercial paper	$ 234	$ 148
15 Accounts payable (including outstanding drafts of $276 and $248)	1,166	1,056
16 Accrued liabilities	536	566
17 Income taxes–payable and current deferred	187	138
18 Current portion of long-term debt	72	95
19 **Total Current Liabilities**	2,195	2,003
20 **Long-Term Debt**	2,510	2,383
21 **Deferred Income Taxes and Other**	225	276
22 **Redeemable Preferred Stock**	379	—
23 **Loan to ESOP**	(378)	—
Common Shareholders' Investment		
24 Common stock	71	78
25 Additional paid-in capital	34	25
26 Retained earnings	1,648	1,758
27 **Total Common Shareholders' Investment**	1,753	1,861
28 **Total Liabilities and Common Shareholders' Investment**	$ 6,684	$ 6,523

FIGURE 13-1 Balance sheet.

CONSOLIDATED RESULTS OF OPERATIONS

Dayton Hudson Corporation and Subsidiaries

(Millions of Dollars. Except Per-Share Data)	1989	1988	1987
1 **Revenues**	$ 13,644	$ 12,204	$ 10,677
Costs and Expenses			
2 Cost of retail sales, buying and occupancy	9,890	8,980	7,950
3 Selling, publicity and administrative	2,264	2,038	1,769
4 Depreciation	315	290	231
5 Interest expense, net	267	218	152
6 Taxes other than income taxes	230	206	176
7 **Total Costs and Expenses**	12,966	11,732	10,278
8 **Earnings Before Income Taxes**	678	472	399
9 **Provision for Income Taxes**	268	185	171
10 **Net Earnings**	$ 410	$ 287	$ 228
Earnings Per Share:			
11 Primary	$ 5.37	$ 3.45	$ 2.41
12 Fully Diluted	$ 5.35	$ 3.45	$ 2.41
Average Common Shares Outstanding (Millions):			
13 Primary	76.3	83.3	94.8
14 Fully Diluted	76.6	83.3	94.8

FIGURE 13-2 Consolidated results of operations.

290

CONSOLIDATED STATEMENTS OF COMMON SHAREHOLDERS' INVESTMENT

Dayton Hudson Corporation and Subsidiaries

(Millions of Dollars)	Total	Common Stock	Additional Paid-in Capital	Retained Earnings
1 **Balance January 31, 1987**	$ 2,180	$ 97	$ 19	$ 2,064
2 Consolidated net earnings	228			228
3 Dividends declared	(87)			(87)
4 Stock option activity	5	1	4	
5 Stock repurchase	(340)	(12)		(328)
6 **Balance January 30, 1988**	1,986	86	23	1,877
7 Consolidated net earnings	287			287
8 Dividends declared	(85)			(85)
9 Stock option activity	2		2	
10 Stock repurchase	(329)	(8)		(321)
11 **Balance January 28, 1989**	1,861	78	25	1,758
12 Consolidated net earnings	410			410
13 Dividends declared	(87)			(87)
14 Stock option activity	9		9	
15 Stock repurchase	(440)	(7)		(433)
16 **Balance February 3, 1990**	$ 1,753	$ 71	$ 34	$ 1,648

Preferred Stock
Authorized 5,000,000 shares, $.01 par value; 438,353 shares (Series B ESOP Convertible Preferred Stock) outstanding at February 3, 1990; no shares outstanding at January 28, 1989.

Common Stock
Authorized 500,000,000 shares $1 par value; 70,874,232 shares issued and outstanding at February 3, 1990; 77,648,989 shares issued and outstanding at January 28, 1989.

Junior Preferred Stock Rights
In September 1986, a distribution of preferred share purchase rights was declared. Terms of the plan provide for a distribution of one preferred share purchase right on each outstanding share of Dayton Hudson common stock. Each right will entitle shareholders to buy one-hundredth of a share of a new series of junior participating preferred stock at an exercise price of $150, subject to adjustment. The rights will be exercisable only if a person or group acquires ownership of 20% or more of Dayton Hudson common stock or announces a tender offer to acquire 30% or more of the common stock.

These financial statements should be read in conjunction with the Analysis of Operations on pages 17-21 and the information on pages 26-29.

FIGURE 13-3 Consolidated statements of common shareholders' investment.

1990 and 1989) to put the figures from both statements on a comparable basis. We will *not* adopt that convention here unless the data are reported as an average in the financial statement. For example, the income statement reports the average number of common shares outstanding (Figure 13-2, lines 13, 14).[1] Instead, except for shares outstanding, we will use year-end balance sheet data as it appeared in Dayton Hudson's annual report. As long as we are consistent in our methodology, the interpretation of the data should be about the same. In other words, the method suggested here requires fewer computations and less data, and produces similar results. Both methods are widely used.

Ratios and Indicators

Financial analysis is analogous to a physician giving a physical examination. Physicians poke, probe, and perform a variety of diagnostic tests. They look for symptoms of hidden problems, such as cancer. If a patient is not breathing and is turning blue, there is an obvious problem, and the physician looks for the cause. If everything is normal, the patient is pronounced healthy. We are going to do the same thing in the financial sense. There is no single ratio or indicator that tells us if a firm is doing well or poorly. To make that determination we must consider a variety of ratios and indicators that provide information about the firm's financial health. Then we will consider them collectively to make our decision.

Financial ratios are divided into four broad categories: (1) profitability, (2) liquidity, (3) efficiency, and (4) leverage. Investors interested in the long-run prospects of the firm want to know if it is profitable, so that is why we are starting there. We look at liquidity next because a firm has to be liquid to survive in the short term. If a firm cannot pay bills that are due now, we do not have to consider what the firm will be like three years from now because it will be bankrupt! Next we look at how efficiently the firm is using its resources. Finally, we consider leverage — the relationship between debt and equity. This has become particularly important in recent years as firms have borrowed large sums to acquire other firms, buy back their own stock, and pay dividends.

Profitability

Profits are the ultimate test of management's effectiveness, and the question of profitability is uppermost in the minds of investors. One measure of profit is **net earnings** (Figure 13-2, line 10). This is most usually expressed as **earnings per share** (EPS) (Figure 13-2, lines 11 – 12). Primary *EPS* is determined by dividing net earnings, or **net income,** as it is commonly called, by the average number of shares of common stock that are outstanding (Figure 13-2, line 13). *Fully diluted*

[1] The weighted average used by Dayton Hudson is based on the period of time that the shares are outstanding, and not the average between two balance sheet dates. Most of the shares were repurchased in the third quarter of 1989, for example. Therefore, even if we averaged the two year-end periods for 1988 and 1989, we would not compute the same average as shown in Figure 13-2, line 13. The difference is 2.1 million shares.

EPS takes into account the conversion of convertible securities—in this case redeemable preferred stock. For 1989, the figures for primary EPS, which we will use in our analysis, are:

Fiscal 1989

$$EPS = \text{net income/number of shares outstanding}$$
$$\$5.37 = \$410/76.3 \text{ shares}$$

(13-1)

The numbers are shown in millions of dollars except for per share data. The EPS increased from $2.41 in 1987 to $5.37 in 1989 indicating good growth, which is what stockholders like. However, a word of caution about interpreting these EPS figures is in order. Notice that the average number of shares outstanding (Figure 13-2, line 13) declined from 94.8 million in 1987 to 76.3 million in 1989. Thus, while net income (the numerator in the equation) is increased, the number of shares outstanding (the denominator) decreased sharply. As shown in the Statement of Common Shareholders' Investment (Figure 13-3, lines 5, 10, and 15), Dayton Hudson was a major buyer of its own stock. During the 1987–1989 period, the Board of Directors of Dayton Hudson authorized the repurchase of 27 million shares of stock. Therefore the growth in EPS was not due exclusively to increased profits.

In the previous example, the primary EPS for 1989 was $5.37. The fully diluted EPS was $5.35. The difference between the two in this case is small. When the difference between the two is substantial, you should use fully diluted EPS. When using fully diluted EPS, adjustments also must be made to the liability and equity portions of the balance sheet to reflect the changes that will occur—convertible debt (or preferreds) will decrease and common equity will increase. That is an unnecessary complication here.

In addition to looking at net income and earnings per share, analysts are interested in the return on common shareholders' investment in the firm. This return is called **return on equity (ROE).** It is calculated by dividing net income by common shareholders' investment.

$$ROE = \text{Net income/common shareholders' equity}$$ (13-2)

Analysts are also interested in the productivity of assets for shareholders, bondholders, and other creditors. This measure is called **return on assets (ROA).** It is calculated by dividing net income by total assets.

$$ROA = \text{Net income/total assets}$$ (13-3)

The relationship between these two ratios is presented in the following equation:

$$\text{Return on equity} = \text{Return on assets} \times \text{leverage ratio}$$

$$\text{ROE} = \text{ROA} \times \text{LR}$$

$$\text{NI}/\text{E} = \text{NI}/\text{A} \times \text{A}/\text{E} \tag{13-4}$$

where

NI = net income or net earnings
E = common shareholder's equity
A = total assets

From this equation we can see that the ROE can be increased in three ways. First, a firm can operate more efficiently and increase its ROA. It can earn more income per dollar of assets.

Second, a firm can increase its financial leverage, which can be measured by dividing total assets by equity. Recall that total assets are equal to liabilities plus equity. The larger the leverage ratio (LR), the more assets are being financed by debt instead of equity. An LR of 1 means that every $1 of assets is financed by $1 of equity. A LR of 3 means that $3 of assets are being financed by $1 of equity; the remainder is financed by $2 of debt. The concept of leverage is discussed later in this chapter.

Finally, firms can increase both their ROAs and their financial leverage to improve their ROEs. This was the case for Dayton Hudson. The ROE increased from 15.4 percent in fiscal 1988 to 23.3 percent in fiscal 1989.

$$\text{ROE} = \text{ROA} \times \text{LR}$$

$$\text{NI}/\text{E} = \text{NI}/\text{A} \times \text{A}/\text{E}$$

Fiscal 1989 $410/$1753 = $410/$6684 \times $6684/$1753

$$0.233 = 0.061 \times 3.8$$

Fiscal 1988 $287/$1861 = $287/6523 \times $6523/$1861

$$0.154 = 0.044 \times 3.5$$

Profitability can also be computed in terms of revenues (or net sales, where available). The **profit margin** is computed by dividing net income by revenue (Figure 13-2, lines 1 and 10). The resulting figure is the percentage of profit for each dollar of revenue. The profit margin for Dayton Hudson is 3 percent, up from 2.4 percent in the previous year. The larger the profit margin the better. An increasing profit margin is a good trend.

$$\text{Profit margin} = \text{net income}/\text{revenue}$$

$$0.030 = \$410/\$13,644 \tag{13-5}$$

Although a firm may be profitable in the sense that it has high returns on assets, equity, and revenues, cash dividends are the only returns that shareholders receive until they sell their shares. The cash dividends per share were $1.045 in 1988 and $1.17 in 1989. These figures are commonly shown in the income statement, but Dayton Hudson did not do so.

Using these dividends and the primary EPS, we compute the **dividend payout ratio,** the percentage of earnings paid out as cash dividends.[2]

$$\text{Dividend payout ratio} = \text{cash dividends}/\text{EPS}$$
$$0.2178 = \$1.17/\$5.37$$

(13-6)

The payout ratio of 21.78 percent means that Dayton Hudson shares about one fifth of its net income with its shareholders and retains the remainder for growth. Assuming that no additional borrowing takes place, the estimated future growth rate of the firm is based on the retention of earnings. This estimate is called the **internal growth rate.** It is equal to ROE times the proportion of earnings that are retained — what is left after the dividend is paid. The internal growth rate is 18.2 percent.

$$\text{Internal growth rate} = \text{ROE} \times (1 - \text{dividend payout ratio})$$
$$0.1822 = 0.233 \,(1 - 0.2178)$$

(13-7)

The usefulness of this number in estimating growth depends on the stability of both ROE and the dividend payout ratio and no additional borrowing. At best, the internal growth rate is a rough approximation of expected growth.

Liquidity

The following indicators show a firm's ability to meet its current obligations. Recall that current liabilities are those that are due within one year. Generally, such obligations are paid out of current assets, which consist mostly of assets that can be converted into cash on relatively short notice. The dollar difference between current assets and current liabilities is commonly called **net working capital.** It represents the amount of current assets that are left after current obligations have been accounted for. Using data from the balance sheet (Figure 13-1, lines 5 and 19), the net working capital is $912, compared to $978 the previous year. It is too early in the analysis to say whether the decline in net working capital is good or bad. It must be interpreted in light of the other ratios and indicators.

---

[2] A similar ratio could be computed from the Statement of Shareholders' Investment (Figure 13-3, lines 12 and 13). The results will be different, however, because EPS is based on the average number of shares outstanding. In addition, this statement shows dividends *declared.* The dividends declared in the third quarter of 1989 had *not been paid* by the end of the fiscal year.

$$\text{Net working capital} = \text{current assets} - \text{current liabilities}$$
$$\$912 = \$3107 \qquad - \$2195$$

(13-8)

The **current ratio** is a broad measure of liquidity and is computed by dividing current assets by current liabilities (Figure 13-1, lines 5 and 19). The current assets are 1.42 times ($\times$) the amount of current liabilities, down from 1.49$\times$ the previous year.

$$\text{Current ratio} = \text{current assets}/\text{current liabilities}$$
$$1.42\times = \$3107/\$2195$$

(13-9)

The **acid-test ratio** is computed by adding cash (and marketable securities) to accounts receivable and dividing by current liabilities. It is a narrow measure of liquidity because it does not include inventories, which may not be liquid if they are not what the customers want to buy. The acid-test ratio for fiscal 1989 is 56.5 percent, down from 63.7 percent the previous year.

$$\text{Acid-test ratio} = (\text{cash} + \text{accounts receivable})/$$
$$\text{current liabilities}$$
$$0.565 = (\$103 + \$1138)/\$2195$$

(13-10)

The lower liquidity (net working capital, current ratio, acid-test ratio) can be interpreted in several ways. First, it suggests that the firm is using its assets more efficiently, which contributed to the increased profitability. Second, it raises the question of how much more liquidity can be reduced without increasing the riskiness of the firm's ability to pay its short-term debts. Unfortunately, we cannot answer that question with the information shown. To answer it, we need longer term financial and industry data for comparison.

Efficiency

These ratios measure how efficiently the firm is using its assets and liabilities. Recall the working capital cycle that was discussed in Chapter 12. The cycle showed that inventories are sold giving rise to accounts receivable and cash sales. Thus, the faster inventories are sold and the faster receivables are collected, the more money is available for expenses and profits. The inventories are acquired on credit, giving rise to accounts payable. We get some idea of efficiency by examining the number of day inventories, accounts receivable, and accounts payable on hand. For example, holding 40 days' inventory is less costly, i.e., more efficient, than holding 45 days' inventory, assuming that we can service our customers with that inventory.

Two steps are required to calculate the number of days of inventory that are outstanding. The first step is to calculate **revenue per day.** It is computed by

dividing total revenue (Figure 13-2, line 1) by 360 days. Most financial analysts use 360 days rather than 365 to calculate this and other ratios. It does not make any difference in the interpretation of the results which number of days is used in the calculation as long as you are consistent. The second step needed to calculate **days' inventory outstanding** is to divide inventory (Figure 13-1, line 3) by the revenue per day.

$$\text{Step 1: Revenue per day} = \text{revenue}/360$$

$$\$37.90 = \$13,644/360 \text{ days}$$

$$\text{Step 2: Days' inventory outstanding} = \text{inventory}/$$
$$\text{revenue per day}$$

$$48.2 \text{ days} = \$1827/\$37.90$$

(13-11)

There were 48.2 days' inventory outstanding in 1989 and 49.2 days outstanding in 1988. This indicates that the firm used its inventory more efficiently. It is making more sales on less inventory.

A sale is not complete until the funds are collected. We can evaluate the efficiency of Dayton Hudson's collection policies by examining the **days' receivables outstanding.** This ratio is computed by dividing the accounts receivable (Figure 13-1, line 2) by the revenue per day computed previously. On average there were 30.02 days' receivables outstanding in 1989 and 36.08 days in the previous year. This shows that Dayton Hudson made a significant improvement in its collection policies, which contributed to increased profitability.

$$\text{Days' receivables outstanding} = \text{accounts receivable}/$$
$$\text{revenue per day}$$

$$30.02 \text{ days} = \$11.38/\$37.90$$

(13-12)

Current assets are financed in part with current liabilities. The largest current liability is accounts payable. We can determine the **days' accounts payable outstanding** by dividing accounts payable (Figure 13-1, line 15) by revenue per day. The data reveal that 43.95 days of payables were outstanding in 1989 compared to 31.15 days the previous year. This increase means that Dayton Hudson has slowed its payment of current debts to suppliers, and is using the funds to finance inventories and receivables. Without more information, one can only guess whether the suppliers will continue to finance Dayton Hudson in this manner or if they will demand more rapid payment. If the latter occurs, Dayton Hudson will have to seek longer term, higher cost funds for financing assets to replace the low-cost financing from accounts payable.

$$\text{Days' payables outstanding} = \text{accounts payable}/$$
$$\text{revenue per day}$$

$$43.95 \text{ days} = \$1666/\$37.90$$

(13-13)

Leverage

Financial leverage refers to the relationship of fixed obligations, such as bonds and preferred stock, to stockholders' equity. Companies that have a high proportion of bonds and preferred stocks are said to be highly leveraged. Leverage increases the volatility of earnings per share and the financial risk of the company. Both of these effects are illustrated in the example given in Table 13-1, which shows three companies with different degrees of leverage. These degrees are indicated by the fixed interest expenses payable on the bonds and the earnings per share. Company A has no leverage because it is financed entirely by 100 shares of common stock and has no fixed expenses. Company B has 50 shares of common stock and 50 bonds with moderately high fixed expenses. Company C is highly leveraged and has 10 shares of common stock, 90 bonds, and very high fixed expenses. The interest expenses of $1 per bond must be deducted from earnings before computing earnings per share. If each company earned $100, their respective stockholders would earn $1 per share. However, if the earnings increased to $200, Company A would earn $2 per share, Company B would earn $3 per share, and Company C would earn $11 per share ($200 earnings = $90 interest/10 shares = $11 per share). If total earnings fell to $50, Company C would be unable to meet its interest payments. This example demonstrates that leverage can magnify changes in earnings per share. When total earnings increased 100 percent, Company C's earnings increased 1000 percent. However, when earnings declined 50 percent, the highly leveraged Company C was unable to cover fixed expenses. Thus, leverage is a two-edged sword.

The **leverage ratio** (L/R), which was discussed in connection with equation 13-4, is measured by dividing total assets by common shareholders' equity. The ratio increased from 3.5 in 1988 to 3.8 in 1989, indicating increased use of borrowed funds. We know that part of this increase comes from accounts payable.

TABLE 13-1   Degrees of Leverage for Three Companies

	Company A	Company B	Company C
Number of shares of stock	100	50	10
Number of bonds	None	50	90
Fixed interest expense ($1 per bond)	None	$50	$90
Earnings per share			
Total earnings			
$100	$1	$1	$1
200	2	3	11
50	0.50	0	−4

$$\text{Leverage ratio} = \text{total assets/equity}$$
$$3.8 = \$6684/\$1753 \tag{13-14}$$

The **long-term debt to total capital ratio** reveals that Dayton Hudson increased its long-term debt as well. This ratio increased from 52.7 percent in 1988 to 55.9 percent in 1989. The ratio is computed by dividing long-term debt by total capital. Total capital includes common shareholders' interest and all long-term sources of debt. One way to calculate total capital is to subtract current liabilities from total liabilities and common shareholders' equity (Figure 13-1, lines 19 and 28). For 1989 total capital is equal to $6684 - $2195 = $4489. Long-term debt (Figure 13-1, line 20) is $2510. The resulting ratio is 55.9 percent.

Long-term debt as % of total capital

$$= \text{Long-term debt/total capital}$$
$$0.559 = \$2510/\$4489 \tag{13-15}$$

Being in debt is fine as long as the operating earnings are sufficient to cover the interest expense. The extent of the coverage is measured by the **times interest earned ratio.** Operating earnings are earnings before interest and income taxes (EBIT). EBIT is calculated by adding earnings before income taxes to interest expense (Figure 13-2, lines 8 and 5). In 1989 the EBIT was $678 + $267 = $945. The ratio computes to 3.53 times in 1989, up from 3.17 times the previous year. An increasing ratio is good. It indicates less risk for the firm and its creditors.

$$\text{Times interest earned} = \text{EBIT/interest expense}$$
$$3.53X = \$945/\$267 \tag{13-16}$$

All of the ratios and indicators presented in this section are summarized in Table 13-2. In review, the data reveal that Dayton Hudson's profitability increased due to increased returns on assets and increased financial leverage. The increased returns on assets are attributable to increased efficiencies, particularly in collecting accounts receivable. On the other side of the balance sheet there was a marked slowdown in paying current liabilities. The financial leverage position increased, but interest expense is well covered.

Percentage Statement Analysis

Figures 13-4 and 13-5 are the items on balance sheets and income statements expressed as a percentage of total assets and revenues, respectively. Examining the financial statements on a percentage basis allows comparisons among firms of different sizes, and provides a different perspective than the ratios and indicators.

TABLE 13-2   Summary of Ratios and Indicators (Data are for fiscal 1989, $ millions, except per share data)

Profitability Measures

EPS = net income/number of shares outstanding
$\$5.37 = \$410/76.3$ shares   (13-1)

ROE = net income/common shareholders' equity   (13-2)

ROA = net income/total assets   (13-3)

$ROE = ROA \times LR$

$NI/E = NI/A \times A/E$ (13-4)

$\$410/\$1753 = \$410/\$6684 \times \$6684/\$1753$

$0.233 = 0.061 \times 3.8$

Profit margin = net income/revenue
$0.030 = \$410/\$13644$ (13-5)

Dividend payout ratio = cash dividends/EPS
$0.2178 = \$1.17/\$5.37$ (13-6)

Internal growth rate = ROE $\times$ (1 − dividend payout ratio)

$0.1822 = 0.233 (1 - 0.2178)$ (13-7)

Liquidity Measures

Net working capital = current assets − current liabilities

$\$912 = \$3107 - \$2195$ (13-8)

Current ratio = current assets/current liabilities

$1.42\times = \$3107/\$2195$ (13-9)

Acid-test ratio = (cash + accounts receivable)/current liabilities

$0.565 = (\$103 + \$1138)/\$2195$ (13-10)

Efficiency Measures

Step 1: Revenue per day = revenue/360

$\$37.90 = \$13644/360$ days   (13-11)

Step 2: Days' inventory outstanding = inventory/revenue per day

48.2 days = $\$1827/\$37.90$

Days' receivables outstanding = accounts receivable/revenue per day

30.02 days = $\$11.38/\$37.90$ (13-12)

Days' payables outstanding = accounts payable/revenue per day

43.95 days = $\$1666/\$37.90$ (13-13)

TABLE 13-2 *(continued)*

Leverage Measures

Leverage ratio = total assets/equity

$$3.8\times = \$6684/\$1753 \tag{13-14}$$

Long-term debt as % of total capital

$$= \text{Long-term debt/total capital} \tag{13-15}$$
$$0.559 = \$2510/\$4489$$

Times interest earned = EBIT/interest expense

$$3.53\times = \$945/\$267 \tag{13-16}$$

The balance sheet figures support what we learned previously about declines in receivables and common shareholders' equity and increased current liabilities. It also shows the relative growth of buildings and improvements (Figure 13-4, line 7). The income statement reveals a decline in the cost of retail sales, buying, and occupancy expenses (Figure 13-5, lines 2 and 7) that contributed to increased earnings (line 10) relative to sales.

Statement of Cash Flows

Cash flow is especially important in the analysis of firms that are highly leveraged or that are in the process of restructuring their capital. Cash flow gives an indication of a firm's ability to pay interest and principal on debts. It also provides information about how funds are being obtained and used.

Unfortunately, the term "cash flow" is misleading because it may not accurately reflect the timing or the magnitude of cash inflows or outflows of a firm because of the accrual method of accounting. Under this method, revenues are recorded when they are earned, not when they are received. Expenditures are recorded as soon as they result in liabilities for the benefits received rather than when they occur.

Equally important, there are numerous ways to calculate cash flow.[3] We begin with one method approved by the Financial Accounting Standards Board for presentation in annual reports (Figure 13-6). This so-called "indirect method" is what most companies use in their annual reports. The fact that there are different measures of cash flows for different purposes means that one must understand which measure is being used. Let's examine Figure 13-6 — the Statement of Cash Flows for Dayton Hudson. The statement is divided into three principal parts: cash flow from operations (lines 1–10), from investing activities (lines 11–13), and from financing activities (lines 15–22). When the amount of cash on hand at

[3] Benton E. Gup and Michael T. Duggan, "Cash Flow: The Tip of an Iceberg," *Business Horizons*, September 1988.

Dayton Hudson Corporation and Subsidiaries

(Millions of Dollars)	February 3, 1990	January 28, 1989
ASSETS		
Current Assets		
1 Cash and marketable securities	1%	0%
2 Accounts receivable (net of allowance for doubtful accounts of $37 and $35)	17	19
3 Merchandise inventories (net of accumulated LIFO provision of $169 and $154)	27	26
4 Other	0	0
5 **Total Current Assets**	46	46
Property and Equipment		
6 Land	8	8
7 Buildings and improvements	41	39
8 Fixtures and equipment	21	20
9 Construction-in-progress	2	5
10 Accumulated depreciation		
11 **Net Property and Equipment**	53	53
12 Other		
13 **Total Assets**	100%	100%

LIABILITIES AND COMMON SHAREHOLDERS' INVESTMENT

Current Liabilities

14	Commercial paper	4%	2%
15	Accounts payable (including outstanding drafts of $276 and $248)	17	16
16	Accrued liabilities	8	9
17	Income taxes–payable and current deferred	3	2
18	Current portion of long-term debt	1	1
19	**Total Current Liabilities**	33	31
20	**Long-Term Debt**	38	37
21	**Deferred Income Taxes and Other**	3	4
22	**Redeemable Preferred Stock**	6	—
23	**Loan to ESOP**	6	—
	Common Shareholders' Investment		
24	Common Stock	1	1
25	Additional paid-in capital	0	0
26	Retained earnings	25	27
27	**Total Common Shareholders' Investment**	26	29
28	**Total Liabilities and Common Shareholders' Investment**	100%	100%

Figures may not add to totals due to rounding.

FIGURE 13-4 Consolidated statements of financial position.

303

Dayton Hudson Corporation and Subsidiaries

(Millions of Dollars, Except Per-Share Data)	1989	1988	1987
1 **Revenues**	100%	100%	100%
Costs and Expenses			
2 Cost of retail sales, buying and occupancy	72	74	74
3 Selling, publicity and administrative	17	17	17
4 Depreciation	2	2	2
5 Interest expense, net	2	2	1
6 Taxes other than income taxes	2	2	2
7 **Total Costs and Expenses**	95	96	96
8 **Earnings Before Income Taxes**	5	4	4
9 **Provision for Income Taxes**	2	2	2
10 **Net Earnings**	3	2	2

Figures may not add to totals due to rounding.

FIGURE 13-5 Consolidated results of operations.

the beginning of the year and all of the cash flows during the year are taken into account, the resulting figure is the cash balance shown in the balance sheet. (Figure 13-6, line 25 is the same as Figure 13-1, line 1).

As a starting point, cash flow from operations is the most important feature for investors. It tells how well Dayton Hudson's operations are doing in terms of generating cash. If the firm is not generating adequate cash from operations to meet its financial obligations, it is in trouble. The cash flow from operations is determined by adding to net income (line 1), depreciation, changes in inventory, accounts receivable, accounts payable, and the other items shown.

Depreciation represents a decline in the value of fixed assets, such as buildings and equipment. They wear out over time, and funds may be set aside to replace them. The Internal Revenue Code permits firms to use depreciation as an expense for tax purposes, but it does not require a cash outlay. The deduction of depreciation from revenues reduces income before taxes. When we calculate cash flow per share later in this chapter (Equations 13-24 and 13-25), depreciation is added back to net income to reflect the amount of cash that is available because it is a noncash outlay. In contrast, buying inventories requires cash or credit. Similarly, increasing accounts receivable requires funding.

In general, more cash flow is preferred to less. However, this is not always the

CONSOLIDATED STATEMENTS OF CASH FLOWS

Dayton Hudson Corporation and Subsidiaries

(Millions of Dollars)	1989	1988	1987
Operating Activities			
1 Net Earnings	**$ 410**	$ 287	$ 228
Reconciliation to cash flow:			
2 Depreciation and amortization	**319**	292	232
3 Non-current deferred tax provision	**19**	27	5
4 Current deferred tax provision	**(29)**	(56)	(36)
5 Decrease/(increase) in accounts receivable	**91**	(149)	(21)
6 (Increase) in inventory	**(158)**	(46)	(311)
7 Increase in accounts payable	**110**	1	213
8 Increase/(decrease) in income taxes payable	**33**	35	(18)
9 Other	**(56)**	146	18
10 **Cash Flow Provided by Operations**	**739**	537	310
Investing Activities			
11 Expenditures for property	**619**	690	787
12 Disposals of property	**(234)**	(18)	(86)
13 **Total from Investing Activities**	**385**	672	701
14 **Net Financing (Sources) Requirements**	**(354)**	135	391
Financing Activities			
15 Increase/(decrease) in commercial paper	**86**	(205)	353
16 Additions to long-term debt	**242**	691	451
17 Purchase and redemption of debt	**(30)**	(39)	—
18 Principal payments on long-term debt	**(95)**	(17)	(19)
19 Repurchase of common stock	**(440)**	(329)	(340)
20 Dividends paid	**(85)**	(85)	(87)
21 Other	**18**	(3)	(16)
22 **Total from Financing Activities**	**(304)**	13	342
23 **Net Increase/(Decrease) in Cash and Cash Equivalents**	**50**	(122)	(49)
24 Cash and cash equivalents at beginning of year	**53**	175	224
25 **Cash and Cash Equivalents at End of Year**	**$ 103**	$ 53	$ 175

Amounts in these statements are presented on a cash basis and therefore may differ from those shown in other sections of this annual report. For purposes of these statements, all short-term investments purchased with a maturity of three months or less are considered cash equivalents.

Investing and financing activities not reported in the Statements of Cash Flows, because they do not involve cash, include financing activities in 1989 of the issuance of $379 million of ESOP preferred stock in consideration for a $379 million 15-year loan from the ESOP. Non-cash investing and financing activities also include capital lease activity. In 1989, disposition of capital leases on buildings and equipment were $(12) million. In 1988 and 1987, obligations were incurred when leases were entered into for buildings and equipment of $2 million and $8 million, respectively. In addition, non-cash capital expenditures resulting from assumed liabilities and asset reclassifications were $3 million in 1989 and $43 million in 1987.

Interest paid (including interest capitalized) during 1989, 1988 and 1987 was $269 million, $196 million and $141 million, respectively. Income tax payments of $248 million, $179 million and $218 million were made during 1989, 1988 and 1987, respectively.

The net change in commercial paper includes the repayment of $6 million of commercial paper with maturities over 90 days in 1988 and the issuance of $66 million and repayment of $60 million of commercial paper with maturities over 90 days in 1987.

In 1989, the reconciliation of net earnings to cash flow and disposals of property include the sale of Lechmere.

FIGURE 13-6 Consolidated statements of cash flows.

case. For example, a negative cash flow may be good if a firm is growing rapidly; i.e., acquiring assets. Conversely, a positive cash flow may be bad. This could mean a firm is liquidating too many assets. The point is that cash flows must be interpreted in conjunction with other information to assess a firm's financial condition.

Cash flow from investing activities (Figure 13-6, line 13) concerns the acquisition and disposal of property other than current assets. The footnote at the bottom of the tables explains that Dayton Hudson sold Lechmere retail stores.

Cash flow from financing activities (Figure 13-6, line 22) summarizes the sources and selected uses of external funds raised. The principal source of funds was additions to long-term debt. The principal use of the funds was the repurchase of common stock.

PROBLEMS WITH ACCOUNTING METHODS

An analysis of historical data highlights trends and specific items that give clues about the company's future. However, they may be false clues because of some special problems with accounting data that can lead investors to false conclusions. To some extent this is so because there is considerable latitude in the accounting methods used in preparing financial statements. One consequence of the variation in methods is that it is extremely difficult to compare companies that use different methods of accounting. Moreover, unless one has a good background in finance or accounting, the discrepancies or implications of the financial statements are not readily apparent.

Unfortunately, there is no easy solution to the problem of discovering which methods overstate or understate earnings. Most investors accept the financial statements as they are presented in Form 10-K or elsewhere at face value. Unless one is a trained security analyst or certified public accountant, there is little reason to try to adjust a company's financial statement to compensate for the various methods of accounting. Without experience, one could make adjustments that could be just as misleading as the original figures. The objective here is to make you aware of some accounting methods that may provide misleading information. Cash flow is one example. Inventory policy is another.

Inventory Valuation

Two commonly used methods to value inventories are first in, first out (FIFO) and last in, first out (LIFO). The FIFO method values ending inventory at the cost of more recent purchases. Thus, the cost of older purchases flows through to the income statement as cost of goods sold. In contrast, ending inventory under LIFO is valued at the cost of older purchases because the cost of more recent purchases flows through to the income statement as cost of goods sold. The following example illustrates the difference between the two methods.

	FIFO	LIFO
Sales	$140,000	$140,000
Less: Cost of goods sold[a]	79,000	84,000
Equals: Gross profit	$ 61,000	$ 56,000
Less: Operating expenses	30,000	30,000
Equals: Operating income	$ 31,000	$ 26,000
Less: Taxes (50%)	15,500	13,000
Equals: Net income	$ 15,500	$ 13,000

[a] Beginning inventory   1,000 units @ $10
    Purchase   3,000 units @ $11
    Purchase   5,000 units @ $12
    Purchase   1,000 units @ $13
    Total available for sales 10,000 units
    Less units sold   7,000 units
    Equals ending inventory   3,000 units

    Cost of goods sold:
      FIFO   1,000 @ $10   LIFO   1,000 @ $13
             3,000 @ $11   5,000 @ $12
             3,000 @ $12   1,000 @ $11
             7,000 @ $79,000   7,000 @ $84,000

During periods of rising prices, inventory cost calculated by the FIFO method will produce a higher value than that calculated by the LIFO method. Therefore, the cost of goods sold is lower and the net income is higher with the FIFO method. That is one reason why many firms have switched to the LIFO method.

DETERMINING VALUES

The reason for analyzing a security is to determine its intrinsic value — what it is worth. This determination is based on factors that were covered in previous chapters: long-term trends; the outlook for the economy, the industry, the company; an analysis of a company's financial condition; and the condition of the stock market. Investors may put different weights and interpretations on these factors. Stated otherwise, value, like beauty, is in the eye of the beholder.

We usually think of stock values in terms of **price per share.** We should also think about the market value of the firm, or **market capitalization,** which is the price per share times the number of shares outstanding. When the number of shares outstanding is changing, as in the case of Dayton Hudson, market capitalization gives a different perspective on value than price per share. For example, the average price of Dayton Hudson in 1989 was $53 per share and there were 76 million shares outstanding on average. The market capitalization of Dayton Hudson was $4.028 billion. During the previous year, the price was $38 and there were 83 million shares outstanding, resulting in a market capitalization of $3.154

billion. The average price per share increased 39.5 percent [($53 – $38)/$38 = 0.395], while the market capitalization increased 27.7 percent.

Market capitalization = price per share × common shares outstanding

1989 $4.028 billion = $53/per share × 76 million shares   (13-17)

1988 $3.154 billion = $38/per share × 83 million shares

This section presents four methods of determining intrinsic value per share. The first method, dividend valuation, is based on projections of dividend growth. The other methods are relative measures of value. They argue that value is some multiple of earnings, cash flows, or book value. Each method has good and bad points, which are also discussed. All the methods are widely used, but there is no convincing evidence that any one of them is consistently better than the others.

The best way to value a stock is to use all of these methods to determine the range of intrinsic values. If the values are all about the same, say $30/share, then you can be reasonably certain that your estimates and judgments are correct. If, however, they produce values that range from $1/share to $300/share, you had better check your assumptions and calculations. Something is wrong!

Finally, some investors reject all of these methods and rely on a method called charting. Charting is explained in the next chapter.

Dividend Valuation Method

The **dividend valuation method** was introduced in Chapter 2, and selected parts of it are reviewed here. This method discounts all the future cash dividends of a company by an appropriate discount rate. When this method is used, the intrinsic value of a share of stock can be determined by the following equation:

$$P_0 = \frac{D_1}{k - g}$$ (13-18)

where

P_0 = price of the stock today
D_1 = dollar amount of dividend the company is paying per share in year 1
g = growth rate of dividends
k = capitalization rate; i.e., the rate of return required by equity investors

Let us assume that a company is expected to pay a $2.50 dividend per share next year, D_1, and that amount is expected to grow at an annual rate of 8 percent. Assume further that investors can invest in virtually risk-free government securities that yield about 10 percent. Since investing in this company is substantially riskier than investing in government securities, the investors want a **risk premium,** an amount over the risk-free rate of, say, 5 percentage points. Therefore,

the capitalization rate, or required rate of return, is 15 percent. The intrinsic value of one share of stock of this company is

$$P_0 = \frac{D_1}{k - g}$$

$$= \frac{\$2.50}{0.15 - 0.08} = \$35.71$$

The assumption of a constant growth rate of dividends does not apply to all companies. We know from our examination of the life cycle that firms in the pioneering phase generally pay no cash dividends. As the firms mature in the expansion phase, they begin to pay small dividends at first and then increase them as their financial condition warrants.

In addition to considering dividends over a life cycle, you should also take business cycles into account. For example, when the steel business is good, steel companies frequently increase their cash dividends. In contrast, when the steel business is bad, they frequently reduce their cash dividends. Thus, it should be clear that a valuation model based on the simplifying assumption of dividends growing at a constant rate forever may not produce satisfactory results. However, the value of a firm whose growth rate of dividends varies over time can be determined by the following equation:

$$P_0 = \sum_{t=1}^{n} \frac{D_0(1 + g_x)^t}{(1 + k)^t} + \sum_{t=n+1}^{\infty} \frac{D_n(1 + g_y)^{t-n}}{(1 + k)^t} \qquad (13\text{-}19)$$

where

g_x = growth rate of dividends for n years
g_y = growth rate of dividends for years $n + 1$ and beyond
Sigma (Σ) stands for summation, ∞ for infinity

This equation can be expanded to include any number of growth rates or time periods. The ability to change growth rates allows you to value stock over the life cycle of a firm as the rates of growth change. If the growth rate of dividends is expected to grow at one rate for a period of time and then at a constant rate, the equation for the variable growth rate model is

$$P_0 = \sum_{t=1}^{n} \frac{D_0(1 + g_x)^t}{(1 + k)^t} + \frac{D_{n+1}}{k - g_y} \left[\frac{1}{(1 + k)^n} \right] \qquad (13\text{-}20)$$

To illustrate how to use Equation 13-20, assume that the Planet Company is currently paying a cash dividend of $0.04. Further, Planet will increase its dividends 50 percent per year for five years. Thereafter, it will increase its dividends at a rate of 10 percent per year. Finally, investors require a 15-percent rate of return. Thus, the first step in using the equation is to list the assumptions. This step, and the others required to determine the value, are listed in Figure 13-7. Let us solve the problem step by step.

The second step is to calculate the present value of the dividends for each of the

Step 1   Assumptions:

a. The initial cash dividend (D_0 is 0.04).
b. The growth rate of cash dividends is 50 percent per year for the first five years (g_x) and 10 percent per year thereafter (g_y).
c. The rate of return required by equity investors, the capitalization rate, is 15 percent.

Step 2   Calculate the present value of dividends for the first five years.

Years	Dividends $D_0(1+g_x)^t$ 0 $\$0.040$	$\times$	Capitalization Rate $k=0.15$	$=$	Present Value
1	0.060		0.870		$0.052
2	0.090		0.756		0.068
3	0.135		0.658		0.089
4	0.023		0.572		0.116
5	0.304		0.497		0.151
					$0.476

Step 3   Value at the end of five years for the remaining life of the company.   Dividend in the 6th year is the dividend in the 5th year (0.304) times the growth rate of 10 percent.

$$D_6 = D_5(1+g_y)$$
$$= \$0.304(1+0.10)$$
$$= \$0.334$$

The value at the end of the fifth year P_5 is equal to the dividend in the sixth year D_6 divided by the capitalization rate less the growth rate of dividends.

$$P_5 = \frac{D_6}{k-g_y}$$
$$= \frac{\$0.334}{0.15-0.10}$$
$$= \$3.32$$

Step 4   The present value of stock at the end of year five.

$$P_5 \left[\frac{1}{(1+k)^n} \right]$$
$$= \$6.69 \, (0.497)$$
$$= \$3.32$$

Step 5   The value today P_0 equals the present value of the dividends for the first five years (step 2) plus the present value of the stock at the end of five years (step 4).

$$P_0 = \text{Step } 2 + \text{Step } 4$$
$$= \$0.476 + \$3.32$$
$$= \$3.80$$

FIGURE 13-7   Calculating the intrinsic value of the Planet Companies.

first five years. Recall that the present value of dividends is what dividends received in the future, say, over the next five years, are worth today when discounted by the required rate of return. Thus, the present value is $0.476.

Step three is to determine the value at the end of five years for the remaining life of the company. The value at the *end* of five years is $6.69. This is the value of the security in year six and forever after. During this period, the growth rate of dividends slowed to 10 percent per year.

Step four ascertains the present value of the $6.69, which comes to $3.32. The final step is to add the present value of the stock for the first five years ($0.476) to the present value of the stock for the remaining years ($3.32) to arrive at the present value of the stock today—$3.80 per share.

In summary, the usefulness of this model is highly dependent on the validity of the assumptions used. If the assumptions are wrong, the model will not give a correct estimate of intrinsic value. The dividend method of determining the intrinsic value of a stock is based on two crucial assumptions. One is that the capitalization rate is larger than the growth rate ($k > g$). The second is that the company will pay cash dividends now or at some predictable time and rate in the future. If the company is never going to pay dividends, other methods of valuation are available. One method deserves special mention here. It is called the **bigger fool theory.** According to this theory, an investor buys a stock that is never going to pay any cash dividend because the investor thinks that a bigger fool will buy it at a higher price.

Capital Asset Pricing Model

The effective use of the dividend valuation model depends on the correct estimation of the capitalization rate as well as other factors. The capitalization rate can be thought of as the minimum rate of return that investors require. The required rate of return for any common stock is equal to the risk-free rate of return plus a risk premium:

$$k = R_f + \text{risk premium}$$
$$R_f + b(k_m - R_f)$$

(13-21)

where

$$k = \text{required rate of return}$$
$$R_f = \text{risk-free rate of return}$$
$$b = \text{beta}$$
$$k_m = \text{rate of return on the market}$$

This equation represents the **capital asset pricing model (CAPM),** and it may be used in the manner described below. The ideas behind the CAPM are discussed in terms of the figure presented in Figure 13-8. The vertical axis depicts required rates of return, and the horizontal axis depicts risk as measured by beta. Recall that beta is a measure of systematic risk. A beta of 1 means that a stock has the same degree of systematic risk as the market as a whole, or average risk. In

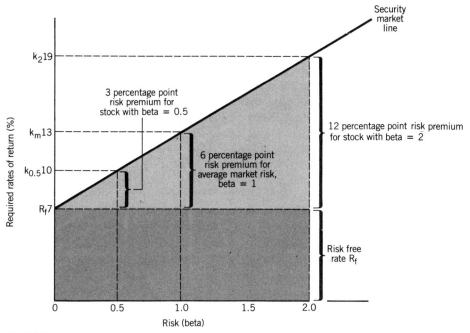

FIGURE 13-8   Security market line (SML).

contrast, a beta of 2 implies a high degree of systematic risk, and a beta of 0.5 implies a low degree of systematic risk.

The **security market line (SML)** represents the relationships between the required rates of return on various assets and risk as measured by beta. The SML is positively sloped, which means that investors require higher rates of return as risk increases.

By definition, common stocks are risky. Therefore, rational investors require a minimum of the risk-free rate of return plus some risk premium. The risk-free rate of return is represented by the rate of return on Treasury bills. In Figure 13-8, the risk-free rate of return is 7 percent.

If investors expect to take an average risk in the stock market, they should expect an average rate of return. The average rate of return shown here is 13 percent. It is determined by finding the average risk on the horizontal axis (beta = 1), then following the dashed line to the 13 percent on the vertical axis. In this case, the risk premium, or the difference between the risk-free rate of return and the market return k_m is 6 percentage points. If a stock has a high degree of systematic risk (beta = 2), the figure shows that the risk premium is 12 percentage points, and the required rate of return k_2 is 19 percent. Similarly, a stock with a small degree of systematic risk (beta = 0.5) has a risk premium of 3 percentage points, and the required rate of return $k_{0.5}$ is 10 percent.

In summary, the required rate of return for any stock can be determined by multiplying the stock's beta by the average market risk premium for that stock (in

this example it is 6 percentage points), and adding that to the risk-free rate of return. For example, if a stock has a beta of 1.5, the required rate of return is

$$k = R_f \quad + b(k_m - R_f),$$
$$k = 0.07 + 1.5(0.13 - 0.07)$$
$$= 0.07 + 1.5(0.06)$$
$$= 0.16, \text{ or } 16\%$$

The CAPM is based on investors' expectations about future returns, which may not be the same as historical returns. When the historical returns of a stock are compared to the historical returns of the market, using a statistical technique called linear regression, the result is a **characteristic line** described by the following equation:

$$k = a + bk_m + e \qquad (13\text{-}22)$$

where

k = return on an individual stock
a = alpha, the intercept on the Y axis
b = beta
k_m = rate of return on the market
e = error term in the regression equation

The characteristic line shown in Figure 13-9 has an **alpha** of 3 percent and a beta of 1.2. The alpha is the expected return on the stock if the return on the market, which is represented by the *Standard & Poor's 500 Stock Index,* is zero. However, if the return on the market is, say, 10 percent, the return on this stock will be 15 percent.

$$k = a \quad + bk_m \qquad + e$$
$$= 3\% \ + 1.2(10\%) + 0$$
$$= 15\%$$

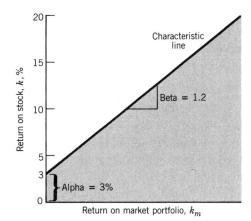

FIGURE 13-9 Characteristic line.

Price/Earnings Ratio

The **price/earnings ratio** is one of the most widely used methods of determining the value of common stock. Perhaps the major reason for its popularity is that it is easy to calculate and convenient to use. The price/earnings ratio (P/E ratio) is determined by dividing the market price of a stock by its earnings per share. If a stock is selling for $60 per share and its earnings are $3, the P/E ratio, or earnings multiplier, is 20. Thus, investors are paying 20 times earnings to buy shares in that company. It is much easier to think about a multiplier of 20 than to think about equations and discounting. The P/E ratio method embodies some of the theoretical considerations of the dividend valuation method, but they are generally not made explicit. Nevertheless, the P/E ratio is related to the dividend valuation model in the following manner:

$$P/E = \frac{D/E}{k - g} \tag{13-23}$$

Ideally, the P/E ratio should use expected dividends D_1 and expected earnings E_1. However, *The Wall Street Journal* and other financial publications use historical data to calculate P/E ratios. Therefore, no time subscript has been attached to the dividends D or the earnings E. It should also be pointed out that Equation 13-23 does not apply when a company pays no cash dividend. Generally speaking, companies with high growth rates tend to have higher P/E ratios than companies growing at a slower pace.

To illustrate how P/E ratios can change, make a list of the current P/E ratios for the stocks listed in Table 13-3. You may use the spaces provided in the table for your listing. Current P/E ratios can be found in *The Wall Street Journal* under *NYSE-Composite Transactions*. P/E ratios of the same stock can change from day to day because of price fluctuations. Moreover, a temporary aberration in quarterly earnings per share may be overlooked by investors. For example, a company may have had a labor strike that affected earnings for one quarter. Once the strike ended, earnings returned to their normal rate of growth. In such a case, investors may have overlooked the temporary decline in earnings, and the reported P/E ratio would appear artificially high. On any particular day, the P/E ratio listed in the newspaper may not accurately reflect investor's expectations. Therefore, P/E ratios should be observed for at least two or three earnings quarters. Alternatively, one can calculate the ratio on the basis of the average quarterly earnings per share for the year.

What do P/E ratios tell us? P/E ratios indicate how investors view the growth potential of particular stocks. Persistently high P/E ratios imply high continued rates of growth, and low ratios imply low rates of growth. The determination of what one considers high or low P/E ratios is largely subjective. Most investors would agree that a company producing a drug that can cure a common cold has more growth potential than one producing metal trash cans. The former may sell at 40 times earnings and the latter at 4 times earnings. But there is no precise way to determine if the drug company should sell at 39, 40, or 41 times earnings or that

TABLE 13-3 Dow Jones Industrial Stocks and Price/Earnings Ratios as of June 1990

Stock	Ratio	Today's Ratio
Allied Signal	10	—
Alcoa	7	—
American Express	50	—
AT&T	17	—
Bethlehem Steel	7	—
Boeing	24	—
Chevron	· · ·	—
Coca-Cola	17	—
DuPont	11	—
Eastman Kodak	25	—
Exxon	20	—
General Electric	15	—
General Motors	10	—
Goodyear	14	—
IBM	17	—
International Paper	7	—
McDonald's	17	—
Merck	21	—
Minnesota Mining	15	—
Navistar	· · ·	—
Philip Morris	13	—
Primamerica	11	—
Proctor & Gamble	21	—
Sears Roebuck	9	—
Texaco	12	—
USX	10	—
Union Carbide	6	—
United Technologies	11	—
Westinghouse	11	—
Woolworth	13	—

P/E ratios for firms with losses shown as · · ·

the trash can company should sell at 3, 4, or 5 times earnings. Thus, investors must use good judgment and common sense in evaluating P/E ratios. As noted previously, it is possible that a stock selling at 5 times earnings could be overvalued and one selling at 41 times earnings could be undervalued. Judge each stock on its own merits.

Along this line, an examination of current and past trends of P/E ratios may yield some useful information. Let us say that an investor is considering the stock of a paper company that is selling for 23 times earnings. The average P/E ratio for stocks in that industry is, say, 14. Moreover, for the past 10 years that paper

company sold at P/E ratios ranging from 12 to 17 annually. In the absence of any other information, the investor would be justified in believing that the stock may be overvalued. Although P/E ratios are easy to calculate and convenient to use, at times they can be difficult to evaluate because they depend in part on the elusive quality called an investor's good judgment.

Price/Cash Flow Per Share

Because a large number of firms are highly leveraged or are restructuring, an increasing number of analysts are using multiples of cash flow in addition to P/E ratios. As previously noted, the term cash flow means different things to different analysts, and it is not always clear what they mean. For example, an article in *Fortune* explained that Akzo, a Netherlands-based company, was selling at six times cash flow.[4] Cash flow was not defined. Merrill Lynch reported that Boeing was expected to have $10.75 cash flow/share in 1991.[5] Cash flow was not defined. In contrast, an article in *Forbes* explained that Perkin-Elmer company should generate "free cash flow," which is net income plus depreciation less capital spending, of $2.50/share.[6] The *Value Line Investment Survey* defines cash flow per share as net profit plus noncash charges less preferred dividends paid, divided by the number of common shares outstanding. Because of differences in the definitions of cash flow, it must be interpreted with caution.

For investors who do not have a background in finance or accounting, we define *cash flow* as cash flow from operations (Figure 13-6, line 10). To obtain *cash flow per share*, divide this cash flow by the average number of common shares outstanding (Figure 13-2, line 13). The 1989 cash flow per share for Dayton Hudson is $9.69. If the price of Dayton Hudson is $53/share, then the stock is selling at 5.47 times cash flow per share. This multiple can be compared to that of other firms in the industry. A low multiple is safer than a high one. What is low or high is, of course, relative to other firms.

Cash flow/share = cash flow from operations/
           number of shares outstanding

$9.69/share = $739/76.3 million
                                    (13-24)

Times cash flow = price per share/cash flow per share

5.47 × = $53/$9.69
                                    (13-25)

The figures used here are based on data given in the financial statements and the average price of the stock to keep the example simple. When possible, use current prices and financial data. In either case, be consistent in your use of the figures.

[4] "A New Improved Chemical Stock at Half-Price," *Fortune*, July 2, 1990, 28.
[5] Merrill Lynch, *Equity Ideas*, "Boeing," May 1, 1990.
[6] Suzanne Loeffelholz, "The Case for Technology," *Forbes*, June 25, 1990, 186–187.

Book Value

The **book value** of a stock share is determined by dividing the number of shares of common stock outstanding into the firm's net worth. If there are preferred shares outstanding, their value is subtracted from the net worth before dividing by the number of common shares. In general, the book value is not an important consideration in determining the market price. The current market price of most business concerns is based primarily on the earnings they will generate in the future. Nevertheless, the book value is an important determinant of value in some cases.

Book value plays a greater role in influencing the value of financial business concerns than industrial concerns. The closest relationship is with mutual funds, which were discussed in Chapter 2. Mutual funds are open-ended investment companies. Their value is the net asset value, which is equivalent to book value. Life insurance companies are another example of the importance of book value. Life insurance policies in force are the basic earnings asset of life insurance companies. Analysts frequently assign definite values to the various types of life insurance in force. For example, every $1000 of face value of ordinary life insurance may be assigned a value of $15, and every $1000 of term insurance may be assigned a value of $5. These amounts are included in various calculations that are used to determine *adjusted book value* and *adjusted earnings.* Thus book value, or some similar value, is widely used by analysts of life insurance companies.

Book values can also be used in determining the value of natural resource companies. Definite values can be assigned to natural resources such as oil, coal, copper, gas, and timber. To a large extent, the value of such companies depends on the value of the natural resources they have access to. Accordingly, analysts may assign so many dollars per barrel of proven oil reserves in the United States and smaller values for proven oil reserves located in politically unstable countries. These values, in turn, can be used to evaluate the intrinsic value of natural resource companies.

Book values are important in the case of failing firms. The financial history of the United States abounds with the names of business concerns that have failed or otherwise gone out of existence. Two examples are Braniff Airlines and W.T. Grant. In such cases the stockholders' immediate concern is what they can salvage from their investment in the company. If the company is liquidated, the stockholder is the residual claimant, which means that the stockholders are entitled to whatever is left after all other claims have been paid. The book value per share will give the stockholder a rough approximation of this value.

Mergers

Evaluating Mergers

Although you may have used all of the techniques described here to determine the value of a firm, someone else may have determined a different value. For example, suppose that you had analyzed Conoco Oil Company in early 1981 and had determined that the value was $50 per share. However, other investors

evaluated Conoco and decided that they were willing to pay a higher price for control of the company. Some of the bids in this merger were

Dome Petroleum	$65 per share
Seagram	$75 per share
DuPont	$98 per share
Mobil	$120 per share

DuPont was successful because it controlled enough shares of Conoco at $98 per share to acquire it. The point is that various investors see the same investment from different points of view and are willing to pay different prices for it. To use a slang expression: different strokes for different folks.

Market Value Exchange Ratio

In recent years there have been many large mergers and many opportunities to profit from them. The value of the terms of proposed mergers to the stockholder of the firm being acquired may be measured by the **market value exchange ratio.** It is the ratio of what stockholders are offered relative to what they have. If the ratio is greater than 1, they have an increase in wealth — they are offered more than they have. If the ratio is less than 1, they will be worse off if they accept the merger terms. As a general rule, acquiring firms pay a premium to the seller to make the deal attractive.

$$\text{Market value exchange ratio} = \frac{\text{market value of benefits offered to sellers}}{\text{market value of benefits offered to buyers}} \quad (13\text{-}26)$$

To illustrate the use of the market value exchange ratio, consider the following situations. The buyer is offering the seller the following terms for each share of common stock:

1. $2 cash + 0.4 shares of common stock valued at $50 per share, or
2. 0.375 shares of common stock valued at $50 per share and 0.25 shares of preferred stock valued at $30 per share

The seller's stock is currently $20 per share. For simplicity, we will ignore the tax effects of the exchange and cash dividends. The ratio focuses on the *immediate* value of the exchange. Using equation 13-26, the seller is better off with the second offer, which gives the largest premium.

$$\text{Offer 1} = \frac{\$2 + 0.4(\$50)}{\$20} = 1.1$$

$$\text{Offer 2} = \frac{0.375(\$50) + 0.25(\$30)}{\$20} = 1.3$$

BOX 13-1

FIGHTING WORDS

Some mergers are considered hostile because one firm wants to take over another firm that does not want to be acquired. To fight so-called **corporate raiders,** some firms have developed "defensive merger tactics" that have given rise to new terms.

Golden Parachutes
Executives of takeover targets may be guaranteed that they will not lose income if they lose their jobs due to a merger or if they are fired. They have employment contracts—called **golden parachutes**—that guarantee them large payments. Such payments can amount to as much as $10 million! The idea behind such payments is twofold. First, golden parachutes are supposed to discourage unfriendly takeovers. Second, they are good deals for the executives who get them. What about the stockholders? They get stuck making the payments if the firm is acquired.

Pac-Man Defense
The **Pac-Man defense** is named after the well-known video game. The basic idea is that the takeover target defends itself by trying to acquire the corporate raider's firm.

Scorched Earth
Sometimes a raider will try to acquire an entire firm to get one or two divisions that it wants. The **scorched earth defense** means the target company sells those divisions to another firm if the target is acquired. This is supposed to make the target unattractive to the raider.

Shark Repellent
A firm can change its by-laws to make it difficult for a raider to acquire it. For example, it may require that 80 percent of the stockholders approve the merger. This is one kind of **shark repellent.**

White Knight
A **white knight** is a friendly firm that agrees to buy the takeover target to prevent it from being acquired by the raider. Sometimes black knights wear white armor. Consider Pullman Inc., which was fighting an unfriendly takeover by J. Ray McDermott & Co. Pullman sold out to Wheelabrator-Frye, a white knight. However, Wheelabrator really didn't want all of Pullman; it wanted only the construction division. So Wheelabrator dismantled Pullman and distributed shares in Pullman's various divisions to the shareholders. Was Wheelabrator really a white knight?

P/E Ratios

P/E ratios are important in assessing the effect mergers have on the combined earnings of the merged firms. By way of illustration, examine the financial data presented in Table 13-4. The table shows that the buyer's stock earns $5 per share (EPS) and has a P/E ratio of 12, which means that the market price of the stock is $60 per share.

Let us see how the combined earnings will be affected if the same seller has a high P/E ratio, the same P/E ratio, or a low P/E ratio relative to the buyer. If the seller's P/E ratio is 16, the total equity of the seller's firm will be $9.6 million. If the seller's P/E is 12, the equity will be worth $7.2 million, and if the P/E is 8, it will be worth $4.8 million.

Now let us assume that the buyer pays the seller the full price of the equity (the market value exchange ratio is 1.0) by exchanging shares of common stock. As shown in Table 13-5, if the seller had a high P/E ratio, the buyer would have to give the seller 160,000 shares of stock. This is determined by dividing the total value of the seller's equity by the market price of the buyer's stock ($9.6 million/ $60 = 160,000). Notice that the combined earnings of both companies ($1,000,000 + $600,000 = $1,600,000) and the increased number of total shares outstanding (200,000 + 160,000 = 360,000) result in lower earnings per share for the buyer. Before the merger the buyer had $5 earnings per share, but after the merger the buyer had $4.44 per share!

If the price of the stock of the merged company is $60 per share, the initial P/E ratio of the combined company will be higher (13.5) than before (12). If the seller had the same P/E ratio as the buyer, the buyer's earnings per share would be the same — $5. If the seller had a low P/E ratio relative to the buyer's, the combined earnings per share would have increased to $5.71, and the initial P/E ratio after the merger will be the same as before (12).

The *initial* effect of the buyer's and seller's price/earnings ratio on earnings per share of the buyer is listed in Table 13-6. If the buyer's P/E ratio is greater than the seller's, the buyer's earnings per share will increase. This was the case when the seller's P/E was 8 and the earnings increased from $5 per share to $5.71 per share.

TABLE 13-4 Selected Financial Data Before Merger

	Buyer	Seller		
		High P/E	Same P/E	Low P/E
Earnings	$1,000,000	$600,000	$600,000	$600,000
Number of shares	200,000	300,000	300,000	300,000
EPS	$5	$2	$2	$2
P/E ratio	12	16	12	8
Market value				
Per share	$60	$32	$24	$16
Total equity	$12 million	$9.6 million	$7.2 million	$4.8 million

TABLE 13-5 Selected Financial Data After Merger

	High P/E (16)	Same P/E (12)	Low P/E (8)
Cost at market value	$9,600,000	$7,200,000	$4,800,000
Addition to buyer's capital shares[a]			
Market value of seller's stock	$\dfrac{\$9,600,000}{\$60} = 160,000$ shares	$\dfrac{\$7,200,000}{\$60} = 120,000$ shares	$\dfrac{\$4,800,000}{\$60} = 80,000$ shares
Buyer's price per share			
Combined earnings	$1,600,000	$1,600,000	$1,600,000
Number of shares after merger	360,000	320,000	280,000
EPS of combined company	$4.44	$5.00	$5.71
Initial P/E ratio of combined company	$\dfrac{\$60}{\$4.44} = 13.5$	$\dfrac{\$60}{\$5.00} = 12.0$	$\dfrac{\$60}{\$5.71} = 10.5$

[a] The market value exchange ratio is 1.0.

$$\frac{\text{Market value offered seller}}{\text{Market value of seller's stock}} = \frac{\$60/\text{share} \times 160,000 \text{ shares}}{\$9,600,000} = \frac{\$9,600,000}{\$9,600,000} = 1.0$$

TABLE 13-5   The Initial Effect of P/E Ratios on
Earnings per Share of the Buyer

Buyer's P/E		Seller's P/E	Earnings per Share of Buyer
Buyer	>	Seller	Increase
Buyer	=	Seller	Same
Buyer	<	Seller	Decrease

If the P/E ratios are the same, there will be no change in the earnings. However, if the buyer's P/E is less than the seller's, the initial earnings will decline. Thus, when the seller had a P/E ratio of 16, the combined earnings fell to $4.44 per share.

The word *initial* was highlighted in the previous paragraph to call it to your attention because the initial earnings are a starting point for the combined companies. The important thing is what the combined companies are going to be in the long run. Figure 13-10 illustrates the point. Without the merger, expected earnings will increase over the years. With the merger, there is an initial dilution in earnings; but over the years the combined earnings potential is greater than the earnings would have been without the merger.

Merger Terms

When there is a merger or a major change in the capital structure of a firm, shareholders are usually asked to consider selling or exchanging the shares they hold for cash or new securities. The offer to buy the stock is called a **tender offer.** A tender offer can be made by the acquiring firm, the firm to be acquired, or anyone else wishing to buy the stock. If shareholders decide to accept the tender

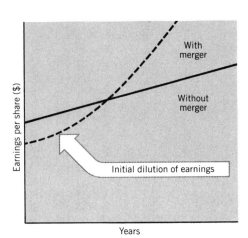

FIGURE 13-10   Expected earnings per share with and without merger.

offer, they must sell — tender — the stock on or before a certain date for the cash price stated. If they decide not to accept the tender offer, they may keep their shares or sell them in the stock market in the usual way.

When debt or equity securities are offered instead of cash, the tender offer is called an **exchange offer.** The tender can also be for some combination of cash and securities. In addition, it can be for all of the shares outstanding, or for a limited number of shares.

CONCLUSION

A number of financial ratios and indicators can help investors determine the financial condition of a company, particularly when the company's figures are compared with those of the industry as a whole. Investors should look at a range of these indicators to get a sense of the company's overall financial state. Most if not all of the financial data and ratios can be obtained in computerized form. But do not be satisfied with that alone. Read the footnotes and the text of the annual reports and Form 10-Ks. Sometimes they reveal more important information than the ratios.

Analysis and interpretation of a company's balance sheets, percentage of income statements, and cash flow can also give useful clues as to its financial condition. However, variations in ways of reporting depreciation, inventory, and income from installment sales make it difficult for an ordinary investor to analyze these statements with complete accuracy.

The goal of analyzing a company's financial condition is to determine the intrinsic value of its stock — what one ought to pay for it. In general, the value of companies is predicted on future earnings. Thus, an investor must attempt to forecast what the company's earnings potential is. An investor can use a dividend valuation method or can estimate future earnings from the price/earnings ratio of the company over a period of time. No method is completely accurate, however. Book value is usually not closely related to the price of a stock, although for financial institutions and life insurance companies, book value may be a close approximation of actual value.

Even if a company has an outstanding financial record of growth, the stock may not appreciate in value because the growth prospects may already be capitalized. Alternately, the company may be a diamond in the rough. If no one recognizes it as such, the stock will not perform well. Therefore, sponsorship of a stock is required if it is to be recognized as a growth stock. The term *sponsorship* means that a stockbrokerage firm or investment advisor makes continuous recommendations to buy a particular stock. In addition, the firm publishes periodic reports in order to keep clients interested in that company, thus pushing a stock into the investment community's notice. Those who are interested in learning more about these subjects should take additional finance, economics, and accounting courses.

IMPORTANT CONCEPTS

Accelerated depreciation	Inventory
Acid – test ratio	LIFO
Alpha	Long-term debt as a percentage of
Average collection period	total capital
Bigger fool theory	Market capitalization
Book value	Market value exchange ratio
Call provision	Net income
Capital asset pricing model (CAPM)	Net working capital
Cash flow	Pac-Man defense
Characteristic line	Payout ratio
Corporate raiders	Percentage of income statement
Cost of long-term debt	Price/earnings (P/E) ratio
Current ratio	Profit margin
Debt coverage	Quick ratio
Dividend valuation method	Rate of return on equity
Earnings per share	Return on assets
Exchange offer	Risk premium
FIFO	Scorched earth
Financial leverage	Security market line (SML)
Financial risk	Shark repellent
Fixed asset turnover	Sponsorship
Golden parachute	Tender offer
Installment contract	White knight

QUESTIONS AND EXERCISES

1. Which financial ratio is the most important?
2. The value of a company can be determined by the dividend valuation method. Which financial ratio provides information about a firm's dividend policy?
3. There is a saying that in order to survive in the long run, you have to survive the short run. Which ratios can be used to determine if a firm can meet its current obligations?
4. Of the liquidity ratios presented in this chapter, which one provides the best measure of liquidity?
5. The inventory turnover ratio measures how many times an inventory is sold each year. What would be the inventory turnover for *Time Magazine* and Zales Jewelry?
6. It is useful to compare the ratios of a company to an industry average. Can the ratios for all companies be above average? Explain.

7. When comparing a firm's ratios to an industry average, is it bad to be below average? Explain.

8. Why are high degrees of financial leverage acceptable in some industries and not in others?

9. If high degrees of financial leverage are considered risky, why do investors buy bank stocks and mutual fund shares, both of which have very high degrees of financial leverage?

10. Is it possible to make a meaningful comparison of the financial statements of Ford to that of a small manufacturing company?

11. If a firm has a negative cash flow, does that mean it is in financial trouble? Is a positive cash flow good? Explain.

12. What assumption is made in the dividend valuation model about the growth rate of dividends? Is it realistic?

13. Explain the basic idea behind the capital asset pricing model.

14. Explain how price/earnings ratios can be used to determine stock values.

15. Are mergers good or bad for: (a) investors, (b) companies that merge, (c) the economy?

CHAPTER 14

TECHNICAL ANALYSIS, FORMULA PLANS, AND INVESTMENT STRATEGIES

CHARTS
Bar Charts
Point and Figure Charts
The Dow Theory
Chart Patterns
TECHNICAL INDICATORS
Interpreting Stock Market Trends
Efficient Markets
FORMULA PLANS
Dollar Cost Averaging
Constant Ratio Plans

Variable Ratio Plans
Other Formula Plans
INVESTMENT STRATEGIES
Small-Company Stocks
Low P/E Stocks
High Dividend Yields
Low Price to Book Value
CONCLUSION
IMPORTANT CONCEPTS
QUESTIONS AND EXERCISES

K nowing *when* to buy and sell securities is just as important as knowing which ones to buy and sell. There are three basic approaches to the problem of timing the purchase and sale of securities. The first is the fundamental approach, which uses an analysis of the economy, industries, and companies to arrive at an intrinsic value for a security. According to this approach, stocks should be purchased when they are undervalued and sold when they are overvalued. This method was discussed in Chapters 10, 11, 12, and 13. The second method is called technical analysis. If focuses on the supply and demand conditions that affect a stock or the stock market. About 40 to 50 technical methods are used to analyze stock market trends, but at the present time charting has the greatest number of disciples. The third method of timing is formula plans. This method advocates buying and selling securities according to a predetermined set of rules.

CHARTS

Chartists believe that the patterns of stock prices depicted on charts give all the information an investor needs to buy or sell a security at the right time. The

investor does not even need to know the name of the company or the type of business it is in. All that is necessary is a proper interpretation of the charts. Two types of charts are used: (1) bar charts and (2) point and figure charts.

Bar Charts

Figure 14-1 shows a typical **bar chart.** This chart depicts price changes and the volume of shares traded on the vertical axis and time on the horizontal axis. The price change is indicated by a vertical bar showing the high price, low price, and closing price for uniform time intervals. These time intervals can be daily, weekly, or monthly. The number of shares traded, or volume, is shown at the bottom of the chart. Some bar chartists contend that price, volume, and time are essential ingredients for the proper interpretation of the patterns that develop. Other chartists depend primarily on price changes.

Point and Figure Charts

Point and figure charts differ from bar charts in three respects. First, only significant price changes are recorded. Thus, a stock is required to fluctuate a certain number of points (1, 2, or 3) before the change is recorded. Second, there is *no* time dimension, such as daily or weekly recordings. However, some point and figure chartists do record the month in which price changes occur. Finally, no volume is recorded. Thus, point and figure charts reflect only price change and the direction of that change.

Construction of a point and figure chart requires three basic steps:

1. Every time the price of a stock increases by, say, one point ($1) mark an X in the appropriate box.

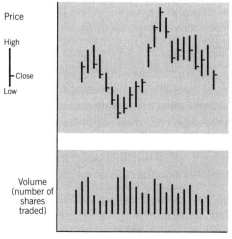

FIGURE 14-1   Typical bar chart.

2. Every time the price of a stock declines by one point mark an *O* in the appropriate box.

3. Every time the direction of price change is reversed, start a new column.

Figure 14-2 shows a typical point and figure chart. According to the chart, the stock increased in price from $20 per share to $23. These increases are recorded by *X*s in the first column on the left side of the chart. Then the price of the stock declined to $17, as noted by the *O*s in the second column. The *6* in the second column means that the price decline occurred during the sixth month (June) of the year. The *6* was substituted for the *O* merely to indicate the approximate date. July (*7*) and August (*8*) are also shown. Some chartists use the first letter of the month (*A* for August) instead of the numerical configuration (*8* for August).

Since similar types of patterns develop in both types of charts, our discussion of charting patterns will cover only bar charts.

The Dow Theory

Chartists rely on the assumption that stock prices do have predictable patterns — an assumption based on the **Dow theory.** This theory was named after Charles H. Dow, editor of *The Wall Street Journal* from 1900 to 1902.[1] Dow wrote a number of articles on stock price movements, but he never really developed a theory. When Dow died in 1902, he was succeeded as editor by William P. Hamilton, who developed what is now referred to as the Dow theory. The original purpose of the Dow theory was to predict changes in business activity, but it became a popular tool for forecasting changes in stock prices. Chartists and other stock market technicians generally recognize the Dow theory as the foundation of technical stock market studies.

In order to measure the trends of the stock market's average prices, Charles Dow developed the forerunner of the Dow Jones Averages in 1897. He used two averages. One was composed of 20 railroad companies, which represented the dominant industry in the securities market at that time. The second average was composed of 12 industrial issues. These two averages provided the basic information used in developing the Dow theory.

Structure of Theory

According to the theory, the averages reflect everything except acts of God. Because stock prices are determined by thousands of investors who possess varying amounts of information about particular stocks, the prices serve as a mirror of their collective views.

There are three basic trends in stock price movements, and these trends are analogous to the movements of the sea. The primary and most important move-

[1] The discussion of the Dow theory and some of the material used in this chapter draw on the work of Robert D. Edwards and John Magee, *Technical Analysis of Stock Trends,* 4th ed. Springfield, Mass.: John Magee, 1958. Many chartists consider the concepts found in this book the cornerstone of their theories.

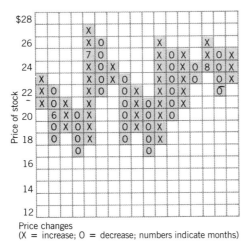

FIGURE 14-2 Typical point and figure chart.

Price changes
(X = increase; O = decrease; numbers indicate months)

ment is analogous to the tide (see Figure 14-3). **Primary movements** are relatively long in duration and may last for a year or more. They are generally known to investors as bull markets and bear markets. In a **bull market** stock prices rise over an extended period of time, and in a **bear market** protracted declines in stock prices occur.

Secondary movements are like the waves and frequently move against the tide. They provide intermediate **corrections** during bull markets and **recoveries** during bear markets. The corrections (or recoveries) can produce stock price declines (or increases) of one third to two thirds the magnitude of the underlying primary trend. If the railroad average increased 30 points, the correction could produce a decline of at least 10 but no more than 20 points. In addition, any price

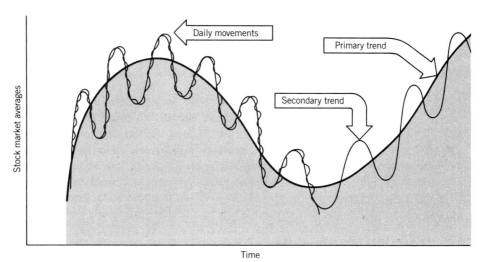

FIGURE 14-3 Dow's three stock market trends.

change that moves in the opposite direction of the underlying primary trend for at least three weeks is considered a secondary trend.

Daily movements are like the ripples in the sea. They have no importance in and of themselves, but collectively the daily movements make up the secondary trends.

Major Trends

A bull market develops in four phases. Phase 1 is called **accumulation.** In this period stock prices are generally considered low. The investing public is disgusted with the stock market because of the previous decline in stock prices, and only those investors who believe that stocks are undervalued and will appreciate in the future begin to accumulate shares.

Phase 2 of the bull market is characterized by steady advances in stock prices and increased trading activity. During this phase, corporate earnings improve, and the general outlook for business activity is encouraging.

During Phase 3, all of the business and financial news is favorable, and the investing public is becoming excited about the stock market. The increases in the averages are spectacular and are reported as major news items. Moreover, everybody is talking about which stocks to buy. It's a wonderful time, and the outlook is terrific.

By this time most of the stocks are fully priced. That is, their market value and theoretical value are about equal. Therefore, in Phase 4 the low-priced stocks with no apparent value become the target for speculators. Such stocks are called **cats and dogs,** and speculation in them is rampant in Phase 4.

Phase 1 of a bear market, **distribution,** actually begins in the last two phases of a bull market. During this phase, investors who bought stocks when they were priced low begin to sell their holdings. As stock prices advance in the later stages of the bull market, these investors liquidate all of their holdings and get out of the market. The investing public notices that the trading volume is still relatively high, but it is diminishing on the rallies. The rallies become less frequent, and the potential for making profits becomes increasingly rare.

During Phase 2 of the bear market, **panic,** stock prices decline sharply. The investing public and speculators frantically sell stocks in order to avoid bigger losses later, but the more they sell, the faster stock prices decline.

Phase 3 is a **secondary recovery** caused by the oversold condition of the market. That is, stock prices declined too fast, and in this phase stock prices will recover about one third of their losses. Nevertheless, selling will still continue because the outlook is bleak.

Phase 4 is the **long slide** during which stock prices decline gradually over an extended period of time. When the prices fall low enough, some investors will begin to accumulate stocks and start the whole process all over again.

Confirmation of Trends

A primary trend is not recognized as such until it has been confirmed by (1) both the industrial and transportation averages, or (2) by **making a line,** then **break-**

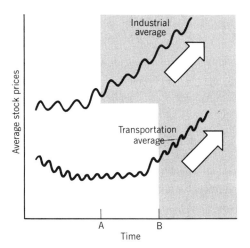

FIGURE 14-4 Bull market confirmation by the averages.

ing out. Figure 14-4 illustrates confirmation by the averages. At point A the industrial average begins a strong advance, and each trough in the secondary movements is higher than the preceding one. However, the bull market is not confirmed until point B, when the transportation average begins a similar advance.

Making a line, the second method of **confirmation,** is illustrated in Figure 14-5. The line is the stock average's fluctuation within a narrow trading range over an extended period of time. The duration can range from several weeks to several months. Confirmation occurs when the average breaks out, or penetrates, the upper level of the line. As a general rule, long and narrow lines contribute to stronger breakouts than short lines.

In either case, a bull market may be under way for a long time before it is confirmed. The confirmation is up to the individual analyst. By using bar charts

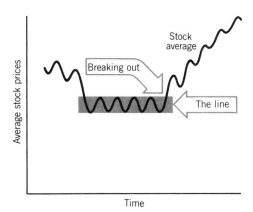

FIGURE 14-5 Bull market confirmation by making a line and breaking out.

instead of point and figure charts and by using different scales on graph paper, two analysts tracking the same averages may get entirely different perspectives.

Volume

The volume of stock transactions is another important indicator of stock price trends. The general rule is that volume should go with the trend. In other words, volume should rise when stock prices increase and diminish when stock prices decline. The rule implies that a large volume indicates determination on the part of investors. If stock prices rise on strong volume, there is a good chance that prices will continue to advance. However, if prices advance on weak volume, there is a good chance that the advance will fade, and prices will decline.

Chart Patterns

The Dow theory provided some of the theoretical background for the development and interpretation of chart patterns. Chartists use these patterns to predict the future direction of stock prices. A number of recognizable patterns are thought to indicate specific future movements.

Reversal

A **reversal pattern** indicates a change in the direction of stock prices. Figure 14-6 shows three types of reversal patterns. All three suggest that stock prices have been advancing and are going to decline. The first pattern is called **head and shoulders.** The shoulders are denoted by S and the head by H. When the stock price drops below the right shoulder, the stock has broken out on the down side. The rounded top is sometimes called an **inverted saucer** or **dome.** The characteristic feature of this pattern is the gradual rounding of the top.

The third pattern is a **triple top.** According to chartists, the triple top means that a stock has tried to penetrate some price level three times and failed. Since what cannot go up must come down, the price of the stock is expected to decline.

The three patterns could be turned upside down and used to indicate reversal patterns for stocks that have declined and are going to advance in the future. Some astute chartists claim to be able to predict not only reversals in prices but also the extent of the price changes that will occur.

Consolidation

After stock prices have changed significantly, the stocks have to pause to consolidate their gains or losses before making another major price change. Figure 14-7 shows some typical consolidation patterns. The triangles are sometimes called **flags** or pennants, depending upon their shape and the interpretation of the pattern. Sometimes triangles appear in a series. When this pattern occurs, the change in stock price is expected to follow the same direction as the slope of the previous triangle.

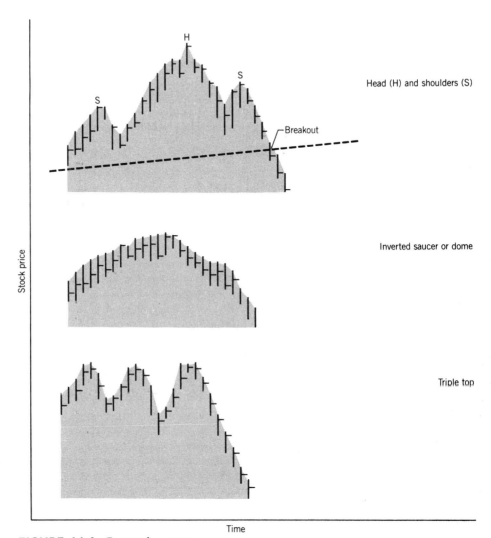

Head (H) and shoulders (S)

Inverted saucer or dome

Triple top

FIGURE 14-6   Reversal patterns.

A line is another consolidated pattern. The base of the line is called the *support level* because the demand for the stock at that price is great enough that the price should not decline below that level. If it did break out on the down side, chartists would sell the stock because they would expect the price to decline further. The top of the line is called the **overhead resistance level.** Whenever the stock reaches this price, a sufficient supply of stock is being offered for sale to keep the stock from advancing any futher. Until this overhanging supply is exhausted or removed by the sellers, the stock will not be able to advance further. Once the supply is removed, the stock can break out and move to higher levels.

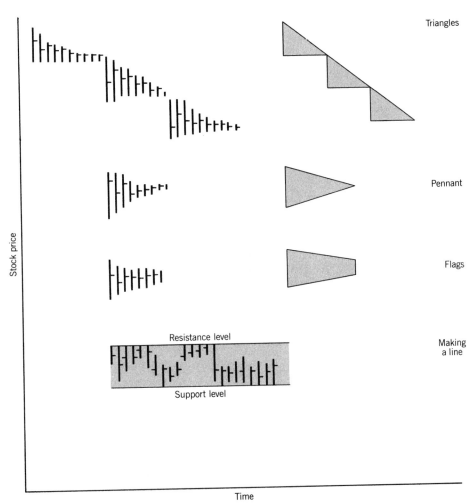

FIGURE 14-7   Consolidation patterns and lines.

Trendlines

A **trendline** indicates the direction in which a stock has been moving. There are upper and lower limits on this movement, but the movement is either up or down rather than horizontal. Figure 14-8 illustrates a trendline. Chartists believe that a trendline will continue in the same direction. When it changes, the reversal patterns discussed earlier are used to predict the turning points.

Patterns as an Investment Aid

Many traders and investors use support and resistance levels to determine when to buy or sell securities. Let us say that Big Steel has an intrinsic value of $45 per share and is currently selling for about $42 per share. Big Steel appears to be a

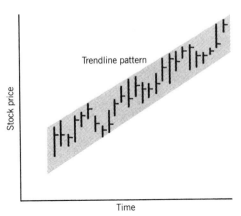

FIGURE 14-8 Trendline patterns.

good investment because it is selling below its theoretical value. However, it may be a better buy at $44 per share than it is at $42 per share! Figure 14-9 shows that Big Steel has been trading in the $40 to $43 price range for the past six months. There appears to be strong support at $40 and strong overhead resistance at $43. The chart suggests that Big Steel will continue to trade within that trading range until it breaks out either on the up or the down side. At this point, investors have the four choices that are presented here. They may also use options that will be explained in Chapter 19.

1. Buy the stock at the current market price, about $42 per share. In this case, the stock is below the theoretical value, but it may not get above $43 per share for a long time because of the overhead resistance.

2. Place a limit order to buy the stock at $40 per share. If and when the stock declines to $40, the limit order will be executed and the stock bought. Using this approach, the investor buys the stock at the lower end of the trading range. When the stock goes to $43 per share, it can be sold at a profit that will

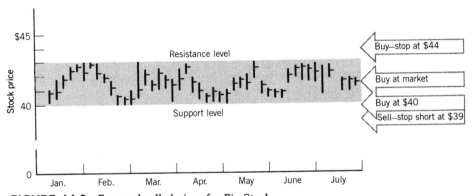

FIGURE 14-9 Buy and sell choices for Big Steel.

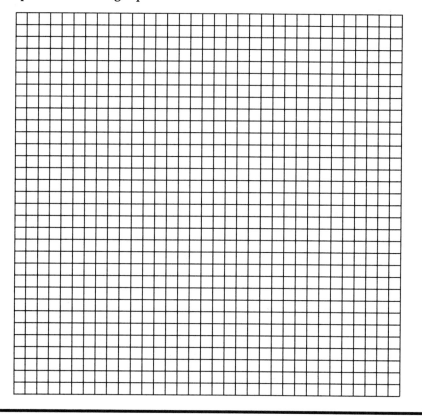

BOX 14-1

MAKE YOUR OWN CHART

Select any stock and plot its price for the last 30 trading days. Do you see any patterns? Do you think that the patterns would be different if you plotted the prices over a longer period?

cover the commission and taxes and leave a small profit. Alternatively, the stock can be held for appreciation in hopes that it will break out of its trading range.

3. Enter a buy-stop order at $44 per share. The buy-stop order will be executed only if the stock price reaches $44. In other words, the stock will not be bought if it stays within its trading range. In this case, the investor has no money tied up in a stock that is moving sideways. If and when the stock does move, it can still be bought below its intrinsic value.

4. Enter a sell-stop short order. The same logic that was used to place orders when buying stock can be applied to a short sale. It would be better to enter a

sell-stop short order at $39 per share than to sell short at $41 per share, because the stock will have to penetrate the strong support level at $40 before it will be a good candidate for a short sale. Clearly, this is a different ball game than the one most fundamental analysts and investors play.

A Picture Is Worth 1000 Words

You do not have to be a chartist to recognize that charts provide valuable information about the direction of stock prices and timing. Figure 14-10 is a page from *The SRC Blue Book of 5-Trend Cycli-Graphs,* one of the many charting services available for a fee. This chart service shows 12 years of monthly prices, volume, dividends, and other information for more than 1100 stocks. We are concerned primarily with price. Four companies are depicted in Figure 14-10. The charts for Wallace Computer Service and Warner-Lambert reveal substantial growth. In contrast, the chart for Wang Laboratories reveals a declining trend, and the one for Washington National suggests no growth. Based on this information alone, most investors seeking price appreciation would consider Wallace Computer Services and Warner Lambert, and reject the other two stocks as possible investments. Speculators, on the other hand may find Wang and Washington National more attractive. Should Wang be "shorted?" Will Washington "break out"? Weekly or daily charts may help to answer such questions.

TECHNICAL INDICATORS

Technical indicators are statistics, such as the **short interest** or the **advance/decline index,** that technical analysts use to interpret stock market trends. Most of the technical indicators make sense when examined individually—that is, the logic behind them appears sound. However, when many technical indicators are examined at the same time, the interpretation of their collective meaning is often contradictory and confusing. One technical analyst issued the following report:

> The breadth of the market remains pretty bearish, but the odd-lot index is still in balance and is more bullish than bearish. While the short interest is not bearish, brokers' loans are at a dangerously high level. Business indices are beginning to turn sharply upward and most psychological indications are generally bullish. The index of 20 low-priced stocks remains in a general uptrend, but the confidence index still is in a long-term downtrend. The Canadian gold price index is still in a downtrend, which normally implies a higher stock market ahead. Professional and public opinion remains cautiously optimistic, which is also an indication of a higher stock market, but on a decline below 800 the Dow Jones Industrial averages would give a definite sell signal.[2]

---

[2] Ken Ward, "The Stock Market Now," an address before the Association of Customers Brokers, New York, April 7, 1964. The quote was one cited by Ward to show confusion among some technical analysts.

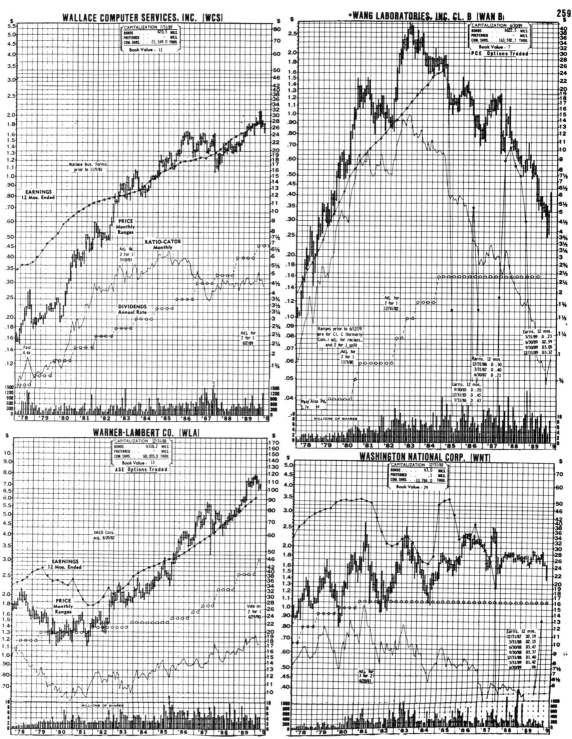

FIGURE 14-10 Charts. *Source:* The SRC Blue Book of 5-Trend Cycli-Graphs.

The author of this technical report presented numerous technical indicators that collectively add up to organized confusion. Some of the major technical indicators are described in the following sections. Each indicator makes sense by itself, but interpreting all of them at the same time may yield the same type of confusion found in the passage quoted.

Interpreting Stock Market Trends

Short Interest Ratio

The logic behind this ratio is that speculators and other investors sell stocks short at high prices in anticipation of buying them back at lower prices. Accordingly, a large volume of short sales implies that the short sellers will cover (buy stock) their short positions at some lower price. In other words, if and when stock prices do rise, short sellers will provide support. They will attempt to maximize profits (or minimize losses) by buying the stock at the lowest possible price, which in turn contributes to rising stock prices. The process of forcing the short sellers to buy as the stock price advances is called **squeezing the shorts.**

The short interest ratio is derived by dividing the reported short interest, or the number of shares sold short on the New York Stock Exchange, by the average volume for about 30 days (e.g., July 15 to August 15). When short sales increase relative to total volume, the indicator rises. A ratio above 150 percent is considered bullish, and a ratio below 100 percent is considered bearish.

The Odd-Lot Ratio

This indicator relates odd-lot sales to purchases. The **odd-lot ratio** is sometimes referred to as a yardstick of uninformed sentiment or an index of contrary opinion because it is believed that odd-lot investors do the right things at the wrong times.

Mutual Funds' Cash Ratio

The **mutual funds' cash ratio,** which relates mutual funds' liquid assets to their total assets, gives some indication of these institutions' short-term ability to invest in the stock market. A high cash ratio is considered bullish because the funds have cash to invest in equities. An increasing cash ratio is bearish because they are withholding funds from the market.

Advance/Decline

The advance/decline is the net difference between the number of New York Stock Exchange stocks rising and the number of stocks falling, added to (or subtracted from) the previous total. This indicator measures the breadth of the market. The more issues that advance (and the fewer that decline), the more bullish the indicator is. For example, a rally that consists of a large number of stocks is considered stronger than one led by a small number of leading stocks.

Barron's Confidence Index

The confidence index is published weekly in *Barron's*. It is the ratio of a group of lower grade bonds to a group of higher grade bonds. A high **Barron's Confidence Index** indicates confidence that the stock market will advance because investors are buying more lower quality bonds in relation to higher quality bonds. Moreover, bond investors are supposed to be sophisticated investors who know what they are doing. Presumably, their insights are better than those of stock investors.

Insider Transactions

The Securities and Exchange Commission (SEC) requires that officers and major stockholders (insiders) of companies that are registered with the SEC report their purchases and sales of their companies' stocks. If the insiders are buying heavily, it is considered a bullish indicator. If the insiders are selling heavily, it is considered a bearish indicator. Stockholders do not like to hear that the president is selling large blocks of stock in the company. Although the president's reason for selling the stock may not be related to the future growth of the company, it is still considered bearish, as investors figure the president, as an insider, must know something bad about the company that they, as outsiders, do not know.

The list of technical indicators is not exhaustive, but it includes those most widely used. Studies have been made to determine the statistical validity of **insider transactions** and other technical indicators, but for the most part the results of the studies give no definitive answers as to whether technical stock market indicators are effective predictors of stock market prices.

Efficient Markets

Most technical analysis is based on the premise that price movements of stock can be used to predict future price movements. However, a growing body of literature claims that this premise, which is basic to technical analysis, is wrong. This literature claims that technical analysis is wrong because the stock market is said to be **efficient** and security prices fully reflect all available information. Thus, the current prices of securities reflect theoretical values because a sufficiently large number of investors are buying and selling securities on the basis of the same information. Price changes are caused by changing basic factors (dividends, earnings, economic outlook, and so on). Speculators who are alert to the price changes will buy or sell securities until they have returned to their theoretical values. When the basic factors that determine the theoretical value change, some investors perceive them at the same time and in the same way so the price change is immediate. Therefore, the current price of a security gives no information about future price movements, and prices are independent of each other. The fact that the price of a security increased today gives no indication as to whether the price will increase, decrease, or remain unchanged tomorrow or next week.

Random Walk

According to this theory, stock prices are said to follow a **random walk** because each price is independently or randomly determined. The random walk hypothesis offers an explanation of stock price movements in an efficient market. Paul Samuelson, a noted economist, explained the efficient market concept by saying:

> If intelligent people are constantly shopping around for good value, selling those stocks they think will turn out to be overvalued and buying those they expect are now undervalued, the result of this action by intelligent investors will be to have existing stock prices already have discounted in them an allowance for their future prospects. Hence, to the passive investor, who does not himself search out for under or overvalued situations, there will be presented a pattern of stock prices that makes one stock about as good or bad as another. To the passive investor, chance alone would be as good a method of selection as anything else.[3]

There is considerable debate over how efficient the efficient markets are. The debate centers around the fact that the random walk hypothesis *does not* say that price changes are unpredictable. It *does* say that price changes are not predictable by using the linear combinations of previous price changes. It is possible that other factors do have some predictive value. Other factors may include information about the economy or the company that are not available to the general investing public. In addition, the random walk hypothesis deals with the ability to predict the actual values of price changes. The hypothesis does not deal with relative price changes, insider information, fraud, or other factors. Therefore, it may be possible to determine from a given number of stocks the ones that are most likely to advance or decline in relation to the rest of that group.

Pro and Con Opinions

As a consequence of these differences of opinions, the debate about efficient markets has taken three forms: (1) the weak form, (2) the semistrong form, and (3) the strong form. The random walk hypothesis is the **weak form.** It asserts that future price changes cannot be predicted on the basis of past prices. This form refutes the basic premise of charting and much of the technical analysis of stock market indicators. The **semistrong form** incorporates a wider range of information. According to this form, the investing public has access to a wide variety of information and fully reflects that information in the price of the security. In essence, the semistrong form suggests that fundamental analysis is futile. Finally, the **strong form** asserts that no amount of information, public or private, is of use because the market anticipates information and fully reflects it in the current

---

[3] This quote appeared in Burton G. Malkiel, *A Random Walk Down Wall Street,* New York: Norton, 1973, 167–168.

price. For all practical purposes, those who believe in the strong form can throw darts at the stock quotation section of the newspaper as a means of selecting stocks.

Efficient Market	Includes
Weak form	Stock prices–random walk
Semistrong form	Publicly available information
Strong form	All information, public and private

If all of what we said about efficient markets is true, then how do we explain the fact that some investors consistently make extraordinary profits? The answer is that the theory tells us that on average, investors will earn an average return, which is historically about 12 percent (see Chapter 4 for details). However, the average return is subject to wide variation. Figure 14-11 will help clarify this point; it shows that the average return on the stock market is 12 percent. Most investors will earn about 12 percent, but some will earn 40 percent or more while others will lose everything. It is the different degrees of risk, as well as the random chance of earning high returns, that attracts many investors and speculators to the stock market.

This debate about the efficient market concept indicates that the jury of academicians and investors has not yet decided beyond the shadow of a doubt on the degree of market efficiency. Nevertheless, a substantial body of evidence leads one to believe that the stock market is reasonably efficient. Therefore, one can question the usefulness of both fundamental and technical analysis. In spite of the fact that these tools are not perfect, they are all that most investors have available to them. Moreover, they do provide useful information about financial management, marketing, and other areas of interest. As long as the tools work, it makes sense to use them. If they do not work, or if other tools are better, it is time to change to methods that bring better results. Modern portfolio theory, one attempt to find a better method for selecting assets for inclusion in a portfolio, is discussed in Chapter 15.

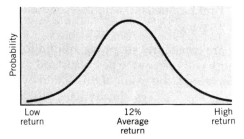

FIGURE 14-11   Stock market returns.

FORMULA PLANS

Formula plans can be used to simplify the investing process and to avoid bad timing when buying and selling securities. Although these plans eliminate some of the problems associated with timing, the investor still must select the security that is to be bought or sold. The most widely used formula plans are discussed in the following sections.

Dollar Cost Averaging

Dollar cost averaging is a systematic way to buy shares at an average cost that is lower than the average price of those securities. Dollar cost averaging works in the following way. Assume that an investor wants to make regular monthly investments of $100. As Table 14-1 shows, the price of the shares ranged from a low of $23 per share in April to a high of $45 per share in November. By investing the same dollar amount regularly, the investor bought more shares when the price was low and fewer shares as the price advanced. In April, 4.345 shares were purchased (stock price $23), and in November, 2.222 shares were purchased (stock price $45). When all the months are accounted for, the average cost per share, $34.713 ($1200/34.569 shares = $34.713), was lower than the average price of the shares, $36.167 (sum of monthly prices/12 = $36.167).

Dollar cost averaging should be used over an extended period of time for the

TABLE 14-1 Dollar Cost Averaging[a]

Month	Price per Share		Number of Shares Purchased
January	$35		2.867
February	31		3.125
March	28		3.571
April	23		4.345
May	28		3.571
June	34		2.941
July	39		2.564
August	43		2.326
September	44		2.272
October	41		2.439
November	45		2.222
December	43		2.326
Average price	$36.167	Total number of shares purchased	34.569
Average cost per share	$34.713		

[a] Regular investment of $100 per month and purchase of fractional shares are assumed.

best results. When this method of investing is used, low stock market prices are better for the investor than high prices because more shares can be purchased for the same dollar amount.

Constant Ratio Plans

Investment portfolios can be divided into two parts: (1) a defensive part, composed of debt securities that are not supposed to fluctuate in price, and (2) an aggressive part, composed of common stocks to provide growth. The size of each part depends on the goals of the investor. If the goal is growth, the portfolio may contain 70 percent aggressive securities and 30 percent defensive securities. If the goal is preservation of capital and income, these percentages may be reversed. These schemes are called **constant ratio plans.**

Let us examine a balanced portfolio with 50 percent aggressive securities and 50 percent defensive securities. If the portfolio begins with $100,000, $50,000 will be invested in stocks and $50,000 in bonds. If the stock prices appreciate to, say, $80,000, the portfolio will be out of balance. Therefore, half of the gain ($15,000) in the common stocks will be sold and the funds reinvested in bonds to restore the 50–50 balance.

Constant ratio plans are simple to use and may produce profits. However, certain guidelines must be established before using such a plan. For example, investors must establish the percentage mix of their portfolios in relation to their investment goals. This is relatively easy to do if investors know what they want. It is more difficult to determine when the ratio should be reestablished. Three criteria can be used to make this determination. Reestablish the ratio

1. When security prices change by a certain percentage (e.g., 5 percent) or by a dollar amount (e.g., $5).
2. When some stock index, such as the Dow Jones Industrials or Standard & Poor's 500 Stock Index change by some predetermined amount.
3. At an established time interval, such as weekly or monthly.

After investors have settled these questions, they still must select the stocks and bonds that are to be bought or sold for their portfolios.

Variable Ratio Plans

The **variable ratio plan** permits the ratio of aggressive and defensive securities to change as security prices fluctuate. The basis of the variable ratio plan is a trend-line that represents a value above which stocks will be sold (and bonds purchased) and below which stocks will be purchased (and bonds sold). The trendline can be determined by using statistical techniques, such as regression analysis, or by any method the investor chooses.

When the trendline is plotted, it should be bound by decision lines that reflect decision rules as to when stocks are to be bought or sold. Figure 14-12 illustrates the variable ratio plan. When the stock is advancing and passes decision line 2, 10

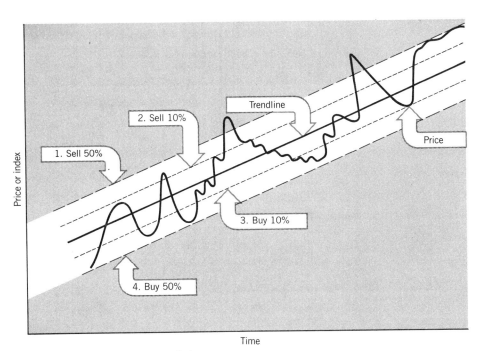

FIGURE 14-12   Variable ratio plan.

percent of the stocks will be sold. Similarly, the decision lines beneath the trendline indicate the proportion of shares to be purchased if stock prices decline. The percentages selected for the decision rules illustrated in Figure 14-12 were arbitrary, and investors may develop decision rules based on their own needs. Moreover, this methodology can apply to a single stock as well as to a portfolio of securities.

The variable ratio plan has several shortcomings. First, the trendline could be miscalculated. In this case, the purchases and sales could be made at the wrong times. To some extent, this problem might be overcome by using charts such as those discussed earlier in this chapter. Conceivably, the trendline and decision rules could be based on chart trendlines and support and resistance levels.

Another problem with the variable ratio plan is that it requires continuous supervision. Decisions have to be made when the securities reach predetermined prices. Because most investors do not have the time to keep track of their stocks each day, they should consider the use of *limit buy and sell orders* and *stop-loss orders*, which were discussed in Chapter 7. Another alternative is using stock options, which are discussed in Chapter 19.

Other Formula Plans

Formula plans can be based on price/earnings ratios, the current dividend yield of the stock, and other statistics. For example, one can develop a set of decision

rules stating that a selected stock should be bought when it is selling at less than 12 times earnings and should be sold when it is selling at more than 16 times earnings. Similarly, a selected stock should be bought when the current dividend yield (cash dividend/market price = current dividend yield) is more than 4 percent and sold when it is less than 2 percent.

Formula plans such as these can produce profits under the right circumstances. The key to success is remembering that the investor still is required to select securities that will appreciate over a period of time. If they continuously decline in value, nothing except a short sale (or the purchase of a put option) will result in profit. In addition, the investor has to adhere to the formula plan. Some investors have a tendency to deviate from their plans. When stock prices are falling dramatically and the formula plan calls for regular periodic investment, some investors want to wait and try to buy more shares at lower prices. On the other hand, who wants to sell stocks when they are increasing in value? Maybe they can be sold for higher prices at a later date. It takes an investor with a strong will to adhere to the decision rules. Those who are not willing to abide by the rules are wasting their time using formula plans.

INVESTMENT STRATEGIES

Although there is no magic "formula plan," there are investment strategies that have produced higher total returns than the stock market as a whole during various time periods. There is no guarantee that they will do so in the future, however. Four investment strategies that have produced excess returns are investing in small-company stocks and investing in stocks with low price/earnings (P/E) ratios, high dividend yields, and low price to book value ratios.

Small-Company Stocks

Over a 62-year period (1926–1987) small-company stocks had an arithmetic average total return of 18 percent, compared to 12 percent for large-company stocks represented by the Standard & Poor's 500 Stock Index.[4] The standard deviations, a measure of dispersion, was 36 percent for the small-company stocks and 21 percent for the large-company stocks. This means that although the small stocks had higher total returns on average, the returns on those stocks were more variable than they were for large-company stocks. Most of the high returns for small-company stocks occurred in the early 1940s and between 1974 and 1983. In

[4] Data are based on Roger G. Ibbotson and Rex A. Sinquefield, *Stocks, Bonds, Bills, and Inflation: Historical Returns (1926–1987)*, Charlottesville, Va.: Institute of Chartered Financial Analysts, 1989; Roger G. Ibbotson and Gary P. Brinson, *Investment Markets, Gaining the Performance Advantage*, New York: McGraw-Hill, 1987. See also John R. Curran, "High-Scoring Strategies with Stocks," *Fortune*, Fall 1985, 25–40; Donald B. Keim, "The CAPM and Equity Return Regularities," *Financial Analysts Journal*, May/June 1986, 19–34. The Keim article reviews the scientific literature of the so-called market anomalies.

other time periods, the returns were lower than for large-company stocks, especially during the 1929–1932 stock market crash. Likewise, small stocks performed worse than large stocks in the 1987 stock market crash. Another interesting aspect of the higher returns on small stocks is that much of the excess returns occurred during the first few days of January. Some observers attribute the **January effect** to investors' selling stocks for tax losses at the end of the year and repurchasing them in the following year. Others attribute it to measurement errors. A January effect has been found in larger stocks as well.

It is not surprising that small-company stocks outperform large-company stocks, at least some of the time. According to the life cycle hypothesis discussed in Chapters 11 and 12, one would expect high returns from firms in the expansion phase of the life cycle. On the other hand, firms in that phase of the life cycle also face high risks, and many do not survive. They may go out of business or be acquired by larger firms. The data on small firms suggest that they do offer high returns, if you are willing to accept the risk that accompanies them.

Low P/E Stocks

The average P/E ratio of the Standard & Poor's 500 Stock Index over the 60-year period (1926–1985) was 14 times earnings (standard deviation was 4). The highest ratio was 23 times earnings in 1933 and the lowest was 6.64 times earnings in 1948. It peaked at 22 times earnings in 1961 and 20 times earnings in 1987 just before stock market declines in both years. In 45 of the 60 years, the ratio was above 10 times earnings. During the 1967–1984 period, stocks with low P/E ratios outperformed others.

The "stock market" tends to do things in excess. Investors pay excessively high P/E ratios for growth stocks with good track records. On the other side of the coin, investors excessively discount firms with slower growth prospects. Thus, low P/E stocks may be poor investments, or they may just be undervalued. That is why we analyze stocks—to determine whether they are overvalued or undervalued. If low P/E stocks are frequently "good investments," then stocks with excessively high P/E ratios should be avoided.

High Dividend Yields

Corporate directors have to make a choice of whether to retain earnings to help finance the growth of their companies or to pay out earnings in the form of cash dividends to shareholders. All other things being equal, firms with high dividend payout ratios grow at a slower pace than firms that retain their earnings. Understanding this will help investors to choose among stocks with various dividend policies and dividend yields. The average dividend yield of the Standard and Poor's Index over the 60-year period was 4.71 percent. Although there are some periods where high-yielding stocks had higher total returns than lower yielding stocks, there was nothing to indicate that buying high-yield stocks per se led to superior returns.

Low Price to Book Value

Market to book value ratios may be an unreliable guide to investment values because accounting values that appear in the financial statements may have little relationship to the economic value of the underlying assets. For example, suppose a firm owns real estate in downtown Los Angeles. The real estate has been fully depreciated and is carried at a nominal value on the firm's books. The current value of the real estate, however, is worth millions of dollars. In this case, the book value of the firm will understate the true value. Alternatively, during periods of high inflation, a firm's depreciation may not provide sufficient funds to replace equipment at higher costs. Here the book value overstates the true value. Despite such problems, stocks with low price to book value ratios had higher total returns over the past decade than those with higher ratios. The average market to book ratio during the 40-year period 1946–1985 was 1.54. The highest ratio was 2.08 in 1967 and the lowest 1.01 in 1974.

So where does this leave us with respect to investment strategies? A review of 60 or more years of stock market performance suggests that these strategies do not provide consistent high returns. However, they should be considered along with other factors affecting investment values when making investment decisions.

CONCLUSION

Investors who have determined what kind of securities fit their investment goals must still decide when to buy and sell these securities if they are to manage their portfolios effectively. Investors use many methods for making these decisions. The fundamental approach based on analysis of the economy, industry, and company was discussed in earlier chapters. Technical analysis, particularly charting, offers another approach to making buy and sell decisions. Formula plans, which set up decision rules for the timing of purchases and sales, offer still another approach.

Technical analysis is based primarily on the Dow theory that there are patterns in stock market fluctuations. According to this theory, market fluctuations have three types of movement: primary—the bull and bear markets all investors are familiar with, which last for a year or longer; secondary—fluctuations of a few weeks' duration, often in opposition to the primary movement; and daily—small fluctuations that taken together form the secondary movements. The theory also holds that the primary movements occur in predictable phases. Trading volume is also considered to be part of the predictable pattern.

Considering this theoretical background, we can easily see why chartists believe that the patterns of past and present stock prices indicate the direction of future prices. Chartists analyze bar charts and point and figure charts to determine future prices and base their buying and selling decisions on these determinations. To the chartist, a specific pattern on the charts indicates the particular direction stock prices will take. The chartist may set up a complex set of buy and sell choices on the basis of these patterns.

In addition to charts, other technical indicators can be used in market analysis. These ratios and indexes may be of value, but studies have not yet proven their effectiveness in predicting price changes. Furthermore, they can be confusing and contradictory when considered together.

In direct opposition to the theory behind technical analysis, we have the efficient market theory, which holds that past and present prices of stock cannot be used to predict future prices. The market is said to reflect perfectly all available information. Thus, the current or past price of a stock gives no indication of its future price. Furthermore, all prices are thought to be independent of each other. This theory gives rise to the random walk hypothesis, which holds that each stock price is independently and randomly determined. Investors who believe in the efficient market theory might choose the securities in their portfolios by random chance — a throw of dice or some similar gamble. Formula plans provide a predetermined method for solving the problem of when to buy or sell stocks.

Finally, we examined four investment strategies that provided superior returns during certain times in the past. However, they should not be relied upon to provide consistently high returns.

IMPORTANT CONCEPTS

Accumulation
Advance/decline index
Bar chart
Barron's Confidence Index
Bear market
Breaking out
Bull market
Cats and dogs
Chartists
Confirmation
Constant ratio plan
Correction
Daily movement (Dow theory)
Distribution
Dollar cost averaging
Dow theory
Efficient markets
Flags
Formula plans
Head and shoulders
Insider trading
Inverted saucer (dome)
January effect

Long slide
Making a line
Mutual funds' cash ratio
Odd-lot ratio
Overhead resistance level
Panic
Point and figure chart
Primary movement (Dow theory)
Random walk
Recoveries
Reversal pattern
Secondary movement (Dow theory)
Secondary recovery
Semistrong form (random walk)
Short interest
Squeezing the shorts
Strong form (random walk)
Technical indicator
Trendline
Triple top
Variable ratio plans
Weak form (random walk)

QUESTIONS AND EXERCISES

1. What basic concept underlies all technical analysis?
2. Does a bar chart or point-and-figure chart give a better basis for making a technical analysis? Explain.
3. Describe the basic features of a bull market.
4. Assume that Zilchco's stock has been making a line between $40 and $42 per share. From a technical point of view, is the stock a better buy at $41 or $43 per share? Explain.
5. There is a rumor that Zilchco may go out of business. Is it a better short at $42 or $39 per share? Explain.
6. Examine the chart of the Dow Jones Industrial Average that appears in *The Wall Street Journal* and explain what patterns, if any, you see developing. How might the pattern you see affect your decision to buy stock today?
7. Why does volume play such an important role in technical analysis?
8. Why is a high short interest ratio bullish?
9. Explain the efficient market hypothesis. Track the daily closing price of any actively traded stock and determine if it follows a random walk.
10. What is the idea behind dollar cost averaging?
11. Will investors earn a higher return by buying small-company stocks or large-company stocks? Explain.
12. What is the January effect?
13. What do you think about an investment strategy that focuses on buying stocks with low P/E ratios?
14. What is the track record of the strategy of buying high-yielding stocks?
15. What is the track record of the strategy of buying stocks with low price-to-book-value ratios?
16. Of the investment strategies discussed, which is best?

PART FOUR

INVESTMENT ADMINISTRATION

Decisions: Which Investments to Choose
Managing Your Investments

The previous parts of this book explained various investment alternatives, how the securities business works, and how to analyze securities. Now it is time to put some of the major pieces of the puzzle together so that you will know how to make investment decisions. Chapter 15 explains the process. Part of this chapter is devoted to modern portfolio theory. Do not let the word "theory" scare you. It is explained in simple terms. Chapter 16 discusses taxes and how to avoid paying them by using tax shelters such as real estate investments and oil wells. Chapter 17 is about real estate. Everyone has to live somewhere, and if you own a house or a condo, you are a real estate investor. Chapter 18 focuses on investing in tangible items such as works of art and gems. Diamonds and gold have become popular investments in recent years. But watch out! Their prices fluctuate just like those of any other commodity. Another caveat is how easily you can be cheated when buying works of art or antiques if you are not very careful.

MAKING INVESTMENT DECISIONS

nvestors frequently ask me to recommend a good stock for them. When I hedge and mumble that there are a lot of good investments they usually reply, "If you had $10,000 to invest, what would you buy?" I answer that question in the following way: "If you walked into a physician's office and said, 'Doc, what is a good medicine to take?' your physician would not want to prescribe anything for you without a thorough examination to determine what is wrong and whether it would respond to medication." This analogy also applies in the recommendation of investments. The needs of the investor must be known before a stock can be recommended. This chapter explains how investors can go about determining what their needs are in order to make prudent investment decisions.

FINANCIAL PLANNING

Financial planning is the *process* of selecting financial products and services that will maximize an individual's wealth while taking their other needs into account. The word *process* is emphasized because planning involves a series of five steps: (1) setting goals, (2) analyzing current and future needs, (3) asset allocation, (4) taking action, and (5) reviewing and revising the plan as necessary. Figure 15-1 illustrates this process. Individual investors should do steps 1–3 *before* dealing in securities. Once actions are taken and reviewed, the arrow points back to step one. Thus, it is a continuous process in which goals are revised as needs and the suitability of investments change.

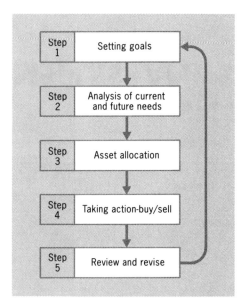

FIGURE 15-1   The process of financial planning.

In this chapter we examine the first three steps of financial planning. Step 4, taking action, consists of buying and selling securities, which was covered in earlier chapters. Unless you take action to buy and sell securities, the first three steps of financial planning are a waste of time. Step 5 is reviewing the success or failure of the portfolio to meet your goals, and then revising goals or investments accordingly.

Setting Financial Goals: The Risk–Return Trade-off

"If you don't know where you are going, it does not make any difference what road you take to get there." This saying can be reworded to apply to investment decisions: If you don't know what your investment objectives are, it does not make any difference what securities you buy.

Many investors make bad investment decisions because they have never bothered to ask, "What are my investment goals?" To answer that question, we assume that the *investment goal is to maximize wealth.* Wealth, or net worth, is the difference between what is owned or controlled (assets) and what is owed (liabilities).

Maximizing wealth must be considered within the context of how much financial risk one is willing to take. **Financial risk** refers to the amount of money that can be lost. The amount of financial risk individuals take depends on their age, their level of income — including the timing of when they get it — the amount of funds to be put at risk, personal preferences, temperament, and other factors. These factors must be considered collectively to make an intelligent judgment about how much risk is suitable. For example, a wealthy octogenarian may enjoy

betting small amounts of money on a state lottery or dealing in commodity contracts. The risk of loss is great in each case, but the dollar amount of the loss to this person is trivial. Conversely, a young adult may require all the money he or she can raise to meet current needs and cannot afford to speculate or make long-term investments. In contrast, another young adult is willing to borrow large sums to invest in a real estate venture.

Many investors believe that they are willing to take financial risks. But are you? Suppose that you bought stock at $70 per share yesterday. Today the stock is worth $35 per share — you have lost half your investment although you did not "realize" the loss for tax purposes. You think that the intrinsic value of the stock is still $70 per share. What would you do today: hold your shares and hope that they increase in value, sell them before they go lower, or buy more? The least risky course of action is to sell the stock now because it may go lower. The most risky course of action is to buy more shares. What would you do?

Investors' temperaments — their willingness to take risks — are important. And every investor should determine how much risk is personally acceptable. Once a wealthy physician told her stockbroker that she wanted to speculate in 10 shares of General Electric (GE). In this investor's mind, investing a small portion of her wealth in one of the largest companies in the United States was speculative, although the generally held perception is that GE is a conservative investment. This difference in views is important because it points out the psychological aspect of risk. The physician would not be happy owning stocks that decline overnight, even though the company had excellent management and stable dividends.

The best investment decision for you depends on the risk–return trade-off you are willing to make. It may not result in the greatest increase in wealth, but at least you will be able to sleep at night and not worry about your investments.

Each person is different. That is why you will not find a magic formula in this book or elsewhere that will explain the proper mix of investments that are suitable for you or anyone else. A substantial amount of judgment is required to determine how much financial risk is acceptable for each individual. What is appropriate for one person may not be suitable for another. Sound judgment is one of the most important tools that investors can use to determine the appropriate level of financial risk.

Figure 15-2 depicts two risk–return attitudes in graphic form. The heavier line represents **risk averters,** who are willing to take on additional risk only if it is accompanied by higher expected returns. Notice that the slope of the line is gradual at first and then becomes almost vertical. The vertical pattern means that some degree of risk is unacceptable, even when the expected returns are very high. For example, would you be willing to bet all of your income for the next five years on the outcome of a horse race if the odds were 20 to 1 against you? If you win, you receive 20 times your income. If you lose, you must give up *all* of your income for the next five years. Most investors would be unwilling to take such a risk.

Nevertheless, there are individuals who enjoy taking big risks for high returns.

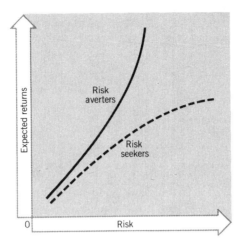

FIGURE 15-2 Risk return attitudes.

These **risk seekers** are represented by the dashed line in Figure 15-2, which shows expected returns increasing with risk. An example of a risk seeker is the person who buys $20,000 worth of state lottery tickets. The chances of losing $20,000 is great, but there is a very small chance of winning $10 million.

Figure 15-3 illustrates the two extremes of investment goals: capital appreciation and preservation of capital. The figure depicts these goals at opposite ends of a teeter-totter. Investors can shift the weight so that capital gains dominate, or they can favor preservation of capital and income. Most investors want some combination of the two—income and capital gains.

Decision Rules

Investors can control the degree of risk they take in deciding between capital gains and preservation of capital by using decision rules. The term **decision rule** means defining investment goals in terms of specific numbers or investment criteria for individual stocks and other securities. Examples of rules covering stocks for a conservative investor are

1. Stock price   Expected growth of 10%/year
2. Dividend yields   Must be 3% or more
3. Quality ratings   Aaa, Aa, A
4. Financial ratios   Low debt to equity, high ROA strong cash flow, low P/E
5. Listing   Must be listed on NYSE or NASDAQ

Such rules are useful because they force investors to think about what they are buying or selling. For example, a 55-year-old widow who is living on a small pension and social security became interested in personal computers and invested a large portion of her wealth in a new software company. One does not have to be a trained investment advisor to realize that she was unwise in investing most of her wealth in an unproven, speculative company. If she had used decision rules

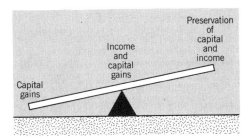

FIGURE 15-3   Investment goals.

about her income in relationship to the quality of the stocks she bought, she probably would not have invested as much in this speculative venture.

Once the investment objective and decision rules have been determined, they reduce the search time and cost of finding appropriate securities. Let's say that the goal is income plus some capital gains. For simplicity, assume that dividend income means a yield of 3 percent or more and that capital gain means expected stock price increases of 10 percent or more per year. The average dividend yield of the Standard & Poor's 500 stocks in 1990 was 3.6 percent. There is no need to consider stocks that yield 2 percent because the decision rule calls for 3 percent or more. Now thousands of securities that do not meet the income/capital gains criteria have been eliminated from consideration.

Decision rules for a speculator may be radically different. The speculator may include certain chart patterns (e.g., breakouts, making a line, etc.) in his rules. Dividends and quality may not be important. He may consider only those stocks whose price is expected to change 20 percent or more. Speculators are interested in price changes, and this decision rule eliminates less volatile stocks.

The important point here is that each investor must develop rules that are suitable for his or her needs. What is good for you may not be good for your father, and vice versa.

Exceptions to the Rules

A few decision rules are useful, but too many rules can be counterproductive. There is no "correct" number of rules. Whatever works best for you with the least number of rules is the best guideline.

Equally important, decision rules for selecting individual stocks do not apply to the management of the entire portfolio. For example, the widow could have invested a small amount in the speculative software company to provide growth in her portfolio. She could have had a few speculative growth stocks along with conservative investments so that the entire portfolio provides the desired stability and income. Obviously, a different set of rules is needed for portfolio management. Examples of such rules are

1. Number of stocks   Hold ten or more firms in unrelated industries
2. Taxes   Hold 20% tax-free securities
3. Liquidity   Hold no less than 30% short-term liquid assets

4. Real estate   No more than 30% of total value of the portfolio

5. Income   A portfolio yield of 5 percent

Analysis of Current and Future Needs

The second step in financial planning is to analyze current and future needs. Figure 15-4 illustrates the types of information you need to know in order to plan for the future. It includes personal data, the dollar amount and timing of expected financial needs, the current financial position, and information about goals and risk.

Because it takes time to accumulate wealth to fund future financial needs, it is important to consider tomorrow's needs today. It takes time to accumulate savings for the down payment on a house. It takes time to accumulate a sufficient amount to pay for children's college education. It takes time to accumulate wealth for retirement. Let us examine some of the factors listed in Figure 15-4 in greater detail.

Personal Data

Date of birth	_____
Marital status	_____
Age of spouse	_____
Number of dependents	_____
Ages of dependents	_____

Financial Needs
(Rank in order, 1, 2, etc.)

	Time Horizon (years)	$ Amount
_____ Buy a home	_____	_____
_____ Buy car, boat, etc.	_____	_____
_____ Retirement income	_____	_____
_____ Increase income	_____	_____
_____ Increase savings	_____	_____
_____ Minimize current taxes	_____	_____
_____ Estate planning	_____	_____
_____ Finance education	_____	_____

FIGURE 15-4 Sample worksheet.

_____ Dependent care   _____   _____

_____ Other   _____   _____

Financial Profile

Assets/liabilities

Cash and short-term investments $ _____

Stocks $ _____

Investment companies $ _____

Fixed-income securities $ _____

Retirement plans $ _____

Real estate $ _____

Other investments $ _____

Personal assets $ _____

Insurance $ _____

Mortgage loans $ _____

Personal loans $ _____

Other debts $ _____

Income

Annual income $ _____

Investment Goals

Mark (x) on the line below to your overall investment objective.

Growth   Balanced   Income

_____   _____   _____

Do you have the time to manage your assets?   ___ Yes   ___ No

Do you have the knowledge to manage your assets?   ___ Yes   ___ No

Do you want to manage your assets?   ___ Yes   ___ No

Risk Profile

Mark (x) on the line below the word that best describes your attitude about financial risk.

Conservative   Moderate   Aggressive   Speculator

_____   _____   _____   _____

Income

The dollar size of one's income and accumulated wealth sets the upper limit on how much can be invested in securities. However, size is not the only factor. Stability of income must also be taken into account. Take the case of two investors—Andrew and Anna. Andrew works for a large department store and receives his salary on a regular, monthly basis. Anna sells encyclopedias. Some months she earns a very high income, and other months are lean. At the end of the year, Anna receives a bonus based on her annual sales. Although both people make the same amount of money annually, their ability to invest differs. Andrew can invest on a regular, monthly basis if he wishes to do so. Because Anna's monthly income is uneven, she will probably invest when she gets her year-end bonus. If Anna invests some of her September income when sales are high, she might have to sell some securities in the following months when sales and income are low.

Permanence of income is another important factor. James has been the senior bookkeeper for a large supply company for the past 35 years. During that time he invested about 10 percent of his annual salary in securities. He is going to retire in four years and will have to live on a small pension because his income will decline sharply. Taking these factors into account, he decided to invest in certificates of deposit at a local bank instead of investing in stocks that could decline in value.

Germaine is 25 years old and has just been promoted to assistant vice-president of a bank. Further promotion and salary increases are assured because her father is chairman of the board and owns the bank. Germaine can afford to invest a substantial portion of her income because she knows that her income will continue to increase. In fact, some day Germaine will inherit the bank. These examples point out that future income needs must be taken into account. Expected changes in income also affect attitudes about risk.

Age

Germaine and James also have different investment needs because of their respective ages. James' primary concern at this stage of his life is preservation of capital in order to have sufficient income on which to live. In contrast, Germaine does not have to worry about preservation of capital or income. She can afford to speculate. There is ample time for her to recover her losses, and she is not dependent on the securities for income.

Dependents

The number of dependents and the degree of dependency must also be considered. The financial needs of dependents vary over time. The amount of money required to finance children of kindergarten age is significantly different from the amount required to finance children in college. In addition, many families provide some degree of support for parents and other relatives. Hospital bills and nursing home fees for the elderly can be very high.

Investors can arrange their investment programs to take into account the cash outlays required by their dependents. Parents can make investments so that when children go to college ample funds will be available. Such investment programs should be started when the children are infants. The amount that is set aside for this or other purposes is a personal decision. It is tempting to say that the children are only three years old and there is plenty of time to invest for them in the future, so let us go ahead and get a new car and fix the television set. The result of such procrastination is that most families do not have an investment program to take care of their dependents. Actually, most families do not even think about investments. Sellers of life insurance say that procrastination is the greatest cost of insurance. Instead of buying insurance when they are young and healthy and the rates are low, people wait until they are old, sick, and the rates are prohibitive. The same problem is relevant to investing in securities.

Financial Factors

Two additional financial factors deserve mention: income tax bracket and life insurance. Federal income taxes that apply to investing are discussed in Chapter 16. It is sufficient to say here that your income tax bracket has an important influence on the type of investments you should make. Those in high income tax brackets favor tax-exempt income.

Life insurance is the second factor. Each investor has to decide how much life insurance is adequate. Let us say that the decision is that $100,000 will be an adequate amount. Then the investor should investigate the various types of policies that are available. In very general terms there are (1) **term**, (2) **whole life**, and (3) **endowments.** Other types of insurance, such as 20 pay life and universal life, are combinations of term and whole life.

Term insurance provides limited protection for a stated period of time, such as five years. The face amount of the policy is payable to a beneficiary on the death of the insured if it occurs within a specified period. As a general rule, term insurance provides only protection. It does not provide any form of savings. However, it does offer protection at the lowest cost.

Whole life insurance, or **ordinary life insurance,** as it is sometimes called, provides permanent protection. The face amount of the policy is paid upon the death of the insured whenever it occurs. Such insurance policies provide protection as well as a savings plan. Because of the savings feature, some insurance companies call whole life insurance an investment. However, the yield on savings (cash value) may be relatively low. This is one reason why some investors buy lower cost term insurance and invest the difference in premiums in higher yielding investments.

Endowments are savings plans that are supplemented with some insurance protection. They are typically used to accumulate funds for retirement or to put children through college. The face amount of the endowment policy is payable upon the death of the insured during a specified period, or it is payable at the end of the period if the insured is living.

The relative costs of these policies differ significantly. At age 20, a man buying a $10,000 insurance policy could pay the following annual premiums:

5-year term	$50
Whole life	$133
20-year endowment	$453

These premiums are rough approximations. Actual premiums can vary widely between companies. Nevertheless, these figures point out the substantial differences in cost that reflect the savings features of the whole life and endowment policies. Before investing in life insurance, compare the costs and returns with other forms of investment such as savings accounts, stocks, bonds, and investment company shares.

Universal life insurance is one of the life insurance industry's hottest products. Universal life is a combination of term insurance with a tax-deferred savings feature whose yield can vary with market rates of interest. Insurance salespeople like the product because of the large commission they receive. Policyholders like it because it provides higher yields than traditional whole life policies. Another benefit to policyholders is that they can vary both the premiums and death benefits within prescribed limits. In addition, some universal policies permit policyholders a choice of investments (e.g., stocks and bonds) for the variable portion of their policies.

Time and Knowledge

A lot of people spend their waking hours earning money but very little time figuring out how to manage their hard-earned wealth. It takes time to analyze securities and to manage a securities portfolio. It is unwise to buy securities and then forget about them. Economic conditions, technology, and consumer tastes change, and stocks that were in favor last year may not be in favor this year. Accordingly, prudent investors review their portfolios periodically.

The process of selecting and reviewing securities requires a certain degree of knowledge on the part of the investor. Because the process takes time as well as knowledge, some investors prefer to turn the task over to professional investment advisors.

Professional investment advisors charge a fee for their advice. A typical fee is ½ of 1 percent of the net asset value of the amount being managed. This fee amounts to $500 for every $100,000 of funds under management. Most investment advisors do not deal with small accounts — $300,000 or less — because they cannot earn enough from such an account to pay for the time required to manage it properly.

Bank trust departments are another alternative. They charge fees similar to those of investment advisors. Moreover, the banks are usually more willing to deal with smaller trust accounts.

Financial planners, individuals and firms selling financial advice, are becoming increasingly popular. Table 15-1 is a partial list of financial planning practi-

TABLE 15-1   Financial Planning Practitioners

Certified Financial Planner (CFP)	Financial planning
Chartered Financial Consultant (Chfc)	Financial planning/insurance
Certified Public Accountant (CPA)	Accounting
Chartered Life Underwriter (CLU)	Insurance
Chartered Property and Casualty Underwriter (CPCU)	Insurance
Doctor of Philosophy (Ph.D.)	Finance/accounting
Registered Health Underwriter (RHU)	Insurance
Juris Doctorate (J.D.)	Law
Master of Laws (LL.M.)	Law/tax
Chartered Financial Analysts (CFA)	Investments
Registered Investment Advisor (RIA)	Investments
Registered Representative (broker)	Investments
Member Appraisal Institute (MAI)	Real estate
Residential Manager (RM)	Real estate
Certified Employee Benefits Specialist (CEBS)	Pensions
Enrolled Agent (EA)	Taxes

tioners who offer financial advice for a fee. An examination of the list reveals a wide range of backgrounds and certifications. Generally these certifications require experience, knowledge, testing, and continuing education in their respective fields. However, only the Certified Financial Planners focus primarily on financial planning. Nevertheless, no single individual is expert in all the areas listed. Even Certified Financial Planners need to cooperate with legal, tax, and other experts to provide comprehensive service.

Those who offer financial planning services may be highly qualified, they may be adequate, or they may be charlatans. Investors can reduce their chances of falling prey to a charlatan by first checking with their state's securities office and asking the following questions:[1]

- Is the planner registered by the state to sell the securities being offered?
- Does the planner have a record of disciplinary actions from the state, SEC, NASD, or other organizations?
- Has the planner been sued by his or her clients?
- Does the planner have the educational/professional qualifications that he or she claims?

Financial planners affiliated with banks, insurance companies, stockbrokerage firms, and other financial organizations may try to sell their own products and services, which may or may not be the best ones for you. Other financial planners

---

[1] For additional information call the North American Securities Administrators Association (202-737-0900). Also see Ellen E. Schultz, "New Breed of Financial Sharks Feeds on Investor Fears," *The Wall Street Journal*, June 15, 1990, C1.

| BOX 15-1 |

WHAT TO EXPECT FOR YOUR MONEY FROM A FINANCIAL PLANNER

How much financial planning will cost depends on the level of income and the level of service required. The following is provided for purposes of illustration, and actual costs may differ.

Level of Income	Service	Cost
$25,000	Basics of financial planning, credit counseling, specific product information. Use of computer software to give "answers" and "programs." One-time advice and not much personal attention.	$50–$300
$25,000–$50,000	Personal financial management, limited investment and tax advice, some estate planning, all to be reviewed annually. Limited service provided by planner.	$300–$1000
$50,000–$250,000	Personal financial management with detailed investment and tax advice, trust and estate and retirement planning, reviewed annually. Some use of software, but more individual attention by a planner.	$1000–$5000
$250,000 or more	Personal financial management with detailed investment and tax advice, risk management, tax shelters, venture capital, retirement and estate planning, with continual review by a team of planners. Lots of personal attention.	$5000 or more

---

offer "comprehensive" financial planning for a fee. They tell you what to do, and you use a broker to execute the orders. As shown in Box 15-1, the size of the fee depends on the amount of service provided. The fees are for managing money and do not include commissions. Alternatively, a *wrap fee* covers the planner's/manager's fee, commissions, and custodial fees. Wrap fees range from 3 percent for accounts of $500,000 or less ($15,000/year maximum) down to 2.5 percent for accounts of $2.5 million or more ($62,500/year minimum).

Investment companies are the final alternative presented here. They provide

continuous management and well-diversified portfolios. However, the securities they deal in are not tailored to meet the investor's exact needs. In this regard, the investment advisor is analogous to a custom-fitted suit, and the investment company is the factory production model. They both manage securities, but presumably the firm with the personal touch does a better job.

In summary, securities require constant supervision, which means time and knowledge on the part of the investor. Investors who are not willing to make such an effort should consider professional management for their funds if they can afford to do so. Those who cannot afford professional management and are not willing to spend time managing their portfolios should not be surprised if the results they obtain are less than they hoped for.

Asset Allocation

Asset allocation refers to the proportion of total assets to be invested in stocks, bonds, real estate, and other investments. Table 15-2 illustrates asset allocation of cash, stocks, and bonds for different types of investors. The term cash as used in the table refers to high-quality, short-term investments such as bank deposits, U.S. Treasury securities, and money market funds. Bonds refer to longer term investments, including corporate and government bonds, mortgage-backed securities, guaranteed investments, and annuities. Stocks refer to equity securities, options, futures contracts, and so on. Thus, the asset allocation shown in the table is a rough approximation of how funds might be allocated. For example, two conservative/income investors, each with 15 percent in cash, might have different investments. One might have half of the cash invested in a tax-exempt money market fund and the other half in CDs. The other may have 95 percent of the cash in U.S. Treasury bills and notes and the remainder in an interest-bearing transaction account.

Asset allocation is *dynamic*. As your needs change, the best asset allocation to satisfy those needs changes too. Equally important, asset allocation also depends on economic and market conditions at the time you are making decisions. For example, investors should allocate a higher proportion of their funds in stocks when the economy is growing vigorously than when it is sliding into a recession.

TABLE 15-2   Assets Allocation

	Cash	Stocks	Bonds
Conservative/ income (%)	15	20	65
Conservative/ growth (%)	10	70	20
Moderate risk (%)	5	55	40
Aggressive/ growth (%)	0	70	30

As economic and market conditions change, the stock and bonds being held must be reevaluated. The process of selecting the "right" combination of securities can be mind-boggling. For example, suppose that an investor wants to hold a portfolio of two stocks and can choose from a selection of three stocks. As shown in the following example, there are three combinations of stocks the investor can hold.[2]

	Stocks		
Combinations	1	2	3
1	x	x	
2		x	x
3	x		x

Now suppose that the portfolio consists of five stocks. If there are only five stocks to choose from, there is only one possible combination. If there are 10 stocks to choose from there are 252 combinations. If there are 100 stocks to choose from there are 75 million combinations!

	Stocks			
	5	10	50	100
Portfolio (5)	1	252	2,118,759	75,287,520

Since there are about 40,000 or more securities from which portfolios can be formed, it is easy to understand why there are so many combinations and why some perform better than others. Because there are so many combinations, investors use their goals and decision rules to reduce the number of choices to a manageable level. Even then, there are a large number of combinations. Fortunately, computer technology and portfolio theory help us with this task.

MODERN PORTFOLIO THEORY

Modern portfolio theory deals with the rules for the intelligent selection of investments under conditions of risk. Although it is a useful aid to the individual investor, most do not possess the knowledge of statistics required to examine the theory in detail. To make the theory understandable to all readers, some technical features of the theory are omitted from the description given here.

Modern portfolio theory recognizes that most investors hold more than one security and are more interested in the performance of their entire portfolio than

[2] The combination C of n stocks taken x at a time can be determined by

$$C_x^n = \frac{n!}{x!\,(n-x)!}$$

that of any one stock or bond. Therefore we must examine what happens to the notions of risk and return in the context of a portfolio. Indeed, some very interesting things happen!

Risk and Return

The concepts of risk and return were introduced in Chapter 4 and are reviewed here.

Expected Return

The expected return of a security is defined as the average **holding period return.** Recall that the holding period return (HPR) can be measured in the following manner:

$$HPR = \frac{D_1 + P_1}{P_0}$$

where

$D_1 =$ expected dividends over the holding period
$P_1 =$ expected price at the end of the holding period
$P_0 =$ current market price, or price at beginning of holding period

The following example illustrates the use of this equation. A stock is currently selling for $60 per share; the annual cash dividend is $2.50 and will remain at that level in the foreseeable future; and the price of the stock is expected to decline to $50 by the end of the holding period. The HPR will be 87.5 percent, as the following computation shows:

$$HPR = \frac{D_1 + P_1}{P_0}$$

$$= \frac{\$2.50 + \$50}{\$60}$$

$$= 87.5\%$$

An HPR of 87.5 percent means the investment declined 12.5 percent. In contrast, an HPR of 120 percent means the investment appreciated 20 percent.

Risk

In general terms, **risk** refers to the possibility of loss. Risk can be measured in statistical terms by the standard deviation (designated by sigma, σ). The standard deviation measures the variability of a set of observations from the average or predicted value of a distribution. For example, if the expected holding period return of a security is 87.5 percent, the likelihood of any deviation from that return is considered to be risk. If the probability distribution for the expected

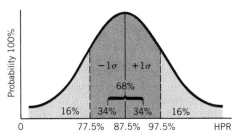

FIGURE 15-5   Probabilities for expected HPRs.

return is normal (symmetric) for that same stock, with a standard deviation of, say, 10 percent, the laws of probability tell us that the chances are 68 in 100 that the future HPR will fall between 77.5 and 97.5 percent. Figure 15-5 illustrates the normal probability distribution of the standard deviation for this example. The figure also shows that the chances are 32 in 100 that the HPR will be less than 77.5 percent or more than 97.5 percent. If the standard deviation were 5 percent instead of 10 percent, the risk associated with the predicted value would be substantially less. A small standard deviation implies less risk than a large one.

Systematic and Unsystematic Risk

Two additional concepts of risk are used in portfolio theory: **systematic** and **unsystematic risk.** Systematic risk can be attributed to a common source, such as changing economic conditions, and affects all stocks in the same manner. Systematic risk is measured by **beta,** a concept that was introduced in Chapter 4. A beta of 1 means that the returns of a stock are just as volatile as the returns of the stock market as a whole. A beta of greater than 1 means that the stock returns fluctuate more than the stock market as a whole, and a beta of less than 1 means that they fluctuate less.

Systematic risk cannot be eliminated by diversification because all stocks are affected in much the same manner. Nevertheless, an investor can increase or decrease the average systematic risk of a portfolio by altering the proportions of stocks held. For example, assume that a portfolio is divided equally among the four stocks—A, B, C, and D—which have the beta values listed:

Stock (1)	Proportion of Portfolio (2)	Beta (3)	(2) × (3) (4)
A	25%	0.9	0.225
B	25	1.6	0.400
C	25	1.0	0.250
D	25	0.7	0.175
			1.050 = Average portfolio beta

In this example, the average portfolio beta is 1.050, which means that the portfolio is slightly more volatile than the stock market as a whole. If the investor wanted a more aggressive portfolio, a greater proportion of the stocks could be shifted into stocks with higher beta values:

Stock (1)	Proportion of Portfolio (2)	Beta (3)	(2) × (3) (4)
A	5%	0.9	0.045
B	80	1.6	1.280
C	10	1.0	0.100
D	5	0.7	0.035
			1.460 = Average portfolio beta

With this change, the average portfolio beta increases to 1.460. Thus, investors can alter the composition of their portfolios to achieve a desired level of systematic risk. The relationship between various levels of systematic risk and expected returns associated with that risk will be discussed shortly.

Unsystematic risk can be attributed to unique events, such as a flood, fire, or labor strike, that can affect an individual company. This risk can be eliminated by diversification because the effect of such events on the price of one company's stock should have no relationship to other companies' stock prices. Collectively, systematic risk plus unsystematic risk equals total risk.

Diversification

Diversification means spreading risk over a variety of companies, industries, securities, or other forms of investments whose returns are not perfectly correlated (i.e., they have different patterns). The key to proper diversification is to invest in securities or companies with holding period returns that are affected differently by changing economic and financial market conditions. For example, automobile companies are affected by different factors than cigarette companies. If there is a recession, consumers may withhold purchases of automobiles, but they probably would not smoke less. Therefore, the earnings of the automobile manufacturers will probably decline, while those of the cigarette manufacturer could increase because consumers are nervous about the recession and they may smoke more. Thus, investing in General Motors Corporation and RJR Nabisco (Winston, Salem, Camel, etc.) would be proper diversification, but investing in General Motors and Ford Motor Company would not, because both companies are in the automotive industry. Similarly, investing in General Motors and Goodyear Tire and Rubber Company would not be a good idea because tire sales are closely related to automobile sales. The sales and earnings are ultimately translated into stock prices and returns. The *principle of diversification* that should be

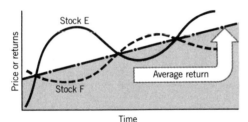

FIGURE 15-4   Effect of diversification.

followed is *to invest in stocks whose variations of holding period returns tend to offset each other.* This principle is shown graphically in Figure 15-6. As the price of Stock E advances, the price of Stock F declines somewhat. When Stock E declines, Stock F advances. The fact that the advances and declines tend to offset each other reduces the risk, and the potential returns, of the portfolio.

A well-diversified portfolio that eliminates diversifiable risk should contain at least 10 different stock issues according to one study and at least 30 different stock issues according to another.[3] The correct answer probably lies between the two numbers.

If the number of stocks is sufficiently large, the returns earned from the portfolio will not differ significantly from those of the stock market as a whole. For example, mutual funds typically invest in stocks of 160 or more companies. Based on this fact alone, one would expect that the average return from the mutual funds would not differ significantly from the average return of the stock market. In fact several studies found the average return of mutual funds did not differ significantly from those of stocks that were selected at random. One reason for their lackluster performance is the large number of companies in their portfolios.

Excessive diversification can have other disadvantages. The transaction costs of buying and selling securities can become too high. The cost of time and information necessary to manage the additional securities also increases, and it becomes virtually impossible for most investors to manage a large number of securities.

Risk Aversion

After we understand the measurement of expected returns and the various kinds of risk involved in investing, we still need some way of assessing how much risk an individual investor is willing to assume in order to get a certain rate of return. Earlier in this chapter we learned that most investors are averse to risk. Thus, most rational investors will take an additional risk only if it gives the promise of

---

[3] J. Evans and S. Archer, "Diversification and the Reduction of Dispersion: An Empirical Analysis," *Journal of Finance,* December 1968, 761–767, and M. Statman, "How Many Stocks Make a Diversified Portfolio?" *Journal of Financial and Quantitative Analysis,* September 1987, 353–363. Statman argues for the larger number.

increased returns. But the question of how much risk for how much return remains.

Risk and Utility Theory

Utility theory provides a means of assessing an investor's willingness to assume a specific amount of risk to get a specific rate of return. The range of possible uses of utility theory is too complex to treat fully here. In essence, the risk–return issue is addressed by constructing a utility schedule for a given investor. This process involves asking a series of questions designed to establish the investor's indifference curves. These curves are drawn along the points at which the investor's aversion to the risk involved and desire to reap the returns expected are exactly equal. Figure 15-7 illustrates a series of such utility curves. An investor can get a particular level of utility or satisfaction from any combination of risk and return shown on the curve. In other words, the investor will get the same satisfaction from the combinations of risk and return at points A, B, and C on utility curve U_3 (see Figure 15-7).

Note that the utility curves are concave, moving upward and to the right. This configuration suggests that the investor's aversion to risk increases as the amount of risk increases. The figure also shows three utility curves, U_1, U_2, and U_3. Curve U_3 gives the greatest amount of satisfaction because it provides the highest expected return (E_3) for any given level of risk (R_1). When investors have a choice, they should select the highest utility curve they can attain.

Portfolio Selection

When the risks associated with individual securities have been taken into account, the investor has the task of selecting those securities that provide the best combination of risk, return, and utility.

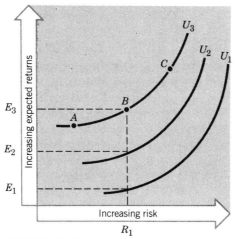

FIGURE 15-7 Utility curves.

Dominance Rules

The securities that provide the best relationship between risk and return are selected on the basis of two **dominance rules:**

1. The security with the *least risk* is preferred to all other securities with the same rate of return.
2. The security with the *highest expected return* is preferred to all other investments with the same degree of risk.

To illustrate the application of these rules, let us examine the expected returns and the risks for seven securities:

Security	Expected Return	Risk (σ)
A	5%	2%
B	8	12
C	4	2
D	8	4
E	6	8
F	7	11
G	10	11

The first rule tells us that Security D dominates Security B because both have the same expected return (8 percent), but Security D is less risky than Security B($\sigma_D = 4$ percent, $\sigma_B = 12$ percent). On the basis of the second rule, Security G dominates Security F. Both securities have the same degree of risk ($\sigma = 11$ percent), but Security G has a higher expected rate of return than Security F (10 percent versus 7 percent). Security A dominates Security C for exactly the same reason. Securities such as C, E, and F are inferior to other securities with higher rates of return and less risk.

Efficient Portfolio

A portfolio that consists of dominant securities is called an **efficient portfolio.** Figure 15-8 shows a plot of the returns and risks for the seven securities in the example. The line *ADG* is called an **efficient frontier.** It is the line drawn through the points that offer the maximum rate of return for each degree of risk in the set of securities under consideration.

Only seven securities were used to illustrate the concepts explained here. In reality, of course, you may be selecting from hundreds or thousands of securities, all of which could lie in the shaded area on Figure 15-8.

Single-Index Model

The large number of securities available for consideration by the investor makes the number of calculations necessary to determine an efficient frontier unman-

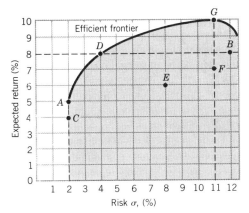

FIGURE 15-8 Selection of an efficient portfolio from seven securities.

ageable. To reduce the number of calculations, William Sharpe developed a **single-index model.**[4] Instead of directly measuring the relationships among hundreds of securities, you can estimate relationships between a selected number of securities and some stock market index, such as the Standard & Poor's 500. The stock market index thus becomes a proxy for the market portfolio of securities. The single-index model contributed significantly to the development of capital market theory, or, as it is frequently called, the capital asset pricing model (CAPM). The capital asset pricing model was introduced in Chapter 13 as a method for estimating the rates of return required by investors. Now we will see other uses for the CAPM.

Capital Market Line

So far only risky securities such as those represented by the efficient frontier (*ADG*) in Figure 15-8 have been considered. Now the scope of assets will be broadened to include risk-free securities as well as risky ones. Constructing a **capital market line** (CML) gives an investor a method for determining efficient combinations of risk-free and risky securities.

Figure 15-9 illustrates the CML. The risk-free security is represented by point R_f, which is located on the vertical axis. Point M represents a market portfolio of risky securities that is recognized by all investors as being the best combination of risk and return. The expected rate of return from the market portfolio (E_M) is the (weighted) average return on all securities in the market. Point L represents a portfolio containing some of the risk-free securities and some securities in the market portfolio. This combination has an expected rate of return (E_L) that is greater than R_f and less than M. Point B extends the CML to include the investment of funds borrowed at the risk-free rate and used to increase the size of the

[4] William F. Sharpe, "A Simplified Model of Portfolio Analysis," *Management Science,* vol. 9, no. 2 (January 1963), 277–293.

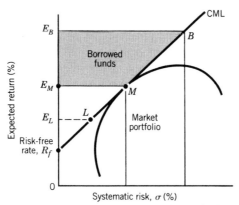

FIGURE 15-9   Capital market line (CML).

market portfolio. Notice that the use of borrowed funds increases not only the size of the portfolio but also the expected return and the risk.

Astute investors recognize that portfolios consisting of various combinations of risk-free and risky securities can be constructed on the CML. For example:

1.   All funds can be invested in the risk-free security R_f that will yield a low rate of return R_f.
2.   All funds can be invested in the market portfolio M that will yield an expected return of E_M, which is higher than the return on the risk-free security.
3.   Some funds can be invested in the risk-free security and the remainder in the market portfolio, which will yield a return of E_L, somewhere between the risk-free return and the rate of return from the market portfolio.
4.   Funds can be borrowed to increase the amount invested in the market portfolio M, which will yield a return of E_B, greater than the return from the market portfolio.

Thus, the CML is an efficient frontier for combinations of both risk-free and risky portfolios of securities.

Note that all the portfolios on the CML contain only systematic risk; that is, they are all efficiently diversified. The diversifiable risk has been removed, and only the nondiversifiable (systematic) or market risk remains.

Utility Theory and the CML

Let us return to the concept of utility theory. Recall that the utility curves for an individual investor give the specific amounts of risk that the investor is willing to assume in order to get specific rates or expected return (see Figure 15-7). It is possible now to integrate the CML with the various utility curves to locate the optimal portfolio for each of the curves. Figure 15-10 illustrates this process.

The optimal portfolio is indicated by the point at which the highest utility curve that the investor can reach is tangent to the CML. The first portfolio is tangent to

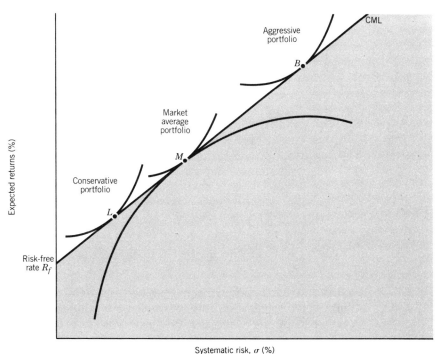

FIGURE 15-10   Use of utility curves and the CML to determine optimal portfolios.

the CML at point L, which represents a portfolio containing risk-free securities and market portfolio securities. This portfolio is labeled "conservative" because of the proportion of funds invested in risk-free securities. The market average portfolio is one in which the funds are invested in the portfolio of market securities M. In this case, the investor is willing to let these investments rise and fall with the security market prices. The aggressive portfolio indicates that the investor wants a higher rate of return and is willing to take on dollar investment in the market portfolio of securities. In other words, the investor wants a higher degree of return and is willing to take on the higher degree of risk that is necessary to obtain it.

Security Market Line

The CML deals with the expected rate of return on portfolios that contain only systematic risk (beta). The relationship between the expected rate of return on individual securities and risk can be described by the **security market line (SML),** which is depicted on Figure 15-11. In this figure, the vertical axis shows the expected rate of return on securities. Note that the SML intersects the vertical axis at the risk-free rate R_f. The horizontal axis indicates systematic risk as measured by beta. The beta for the risk-free security is zero.

The securities (or portfolios) that lie on the SML are in equilibrium with respect

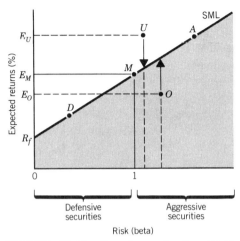

FIGURE 15-11　Security market line (SML) and equilibrium points of stock prices.

to risk and return, which means that there is no tendency to change. For example, point M represents a security (or market portfolio) that has a beta of one. Recall that a beta of one means that the security is as volatile as the stock market as a whole. Accordingly, that security should earn a return that is equal to the average return of the stock market E_M. If the expected return for M is above or below the market return E_M, the security is not in equilibrium.

Points U and O represent securities that are not in equilibrium. Point U indicates that the security is undervalued because its return E_U, relative to its systematic risk, is higher than the market rate. Therefore, increased demand for that security will force the price upward and the return downward until the security finds equilibrium at a point on the SML. Security O is overvalued. In this case, the return on Security O (E_O) is low relative to its systematic risk. Accordingly, investors will sell the security, forcing the price down and the return up until it, too, finds equilibrium on the SML.

Finally, since the horizontal axis indicates market risk, the investor can ascertain something about the volatility of various securities. Securities such as D, which lie to the left of M and have a beta of less than one, are called **defensive securities.** These securities tend to fluctuate less than the stock market as a whole. On the other hand, securities such as A are called **aggressive** because they have a beta that is greater than one and tend to fluctuate more than the market as a whole.

CONCLUSION

Investing is not simply a matter of selecting stocks or bonds. Many factors that affect the individual investors have to be taken into account. Investors should establish investment objectives based on such factors as the need for growth, the degree of risk they wish to assume, and their income. The next step is to develop

some decision rules that implement the objectives. Clearly defined objectives and decision rules make it much easier to choose securities that are suitable to individual needs.

Once the securities are purchased, they must be reviewed periodically because economic and financial conditions change and tax advantages should be considered. Investors must be willing to spend time and become informed if they expect to handle their investments effectively. Alternatively, professionals can be hired to manage investments through an investment advisor, a bank trust department, or an investment company.

Prudent investors not only select securities that are appropriate to their individual needs, but they also diversify the securities in their portfolios. The development of modern portfolio theory has led to a greater understanding of diversification and asset selection under conditions of risk. Because security markets are reasonably efficient—that is, security prices fully reflect all available information—the concepts of CML and SML are reasonable approximations of reality. Thus, through proper diversification, the diversifiable risk of a portfolio can be reduced to virtually zero, thereby leaving only the systematic risk. Moreover, by using utility theory, investors can determine the degree of systematic risk and the commensurate returns that will satisfy their particular needs and give the greatest amount of satisfaction (utility). These theoretical tools give investors an opportunity to use a rational process in portfolio selection that takes into account both market conditions and subjective attitudes toward risk.

IMPORTANT CONCEPTS

Aggressive securities
Asset allocation
Beta
Capital gains (goal)
Capital market line
Decision rules
Defensive securities
Diversification
Dominance rules
Efficient frontier
Efficient portfolio
Endowment
Expected return
Financial planner
Financial risk

Holding period return
Income (goal)
Modern portfolio theory
Ordinary life insurance
Personal financial software
Risk
Risk averters
Security market line
Single-index model
Systematic risk
Term insurance
Unsystematic risk
Utility theory
Whole life insurance

QUESTIONS AND EXERCISES

1. List five or more decision rules that apply in determining securities you might buy.

2. Many investors claim that they want growth stocks and that they are willing to take some risks. Define growth and risk in terms of numbers that can be used as decision rules.

3. Assume that you inherited $100,000 from your Aunt Minnie. Her will stipulated that you must invest *all* of the funds in common stock with the dual objective of growth and income. Construct a common stock portfolio that meets these objectives.

4. Given the current economic outlook, how would you invest your Aunt Minnie's $100,000 if you were not limited to common stocks?

5. Offer three or more examples to show that most individuals are risk averters.

6. Life insurance is an important consideration in one's total financial portfolio. Explain what type of insurance you would recommend for a young married couple who are starting their first jobs after graduation.

7. Explain the concepts of systematic and unsystematic risk.

8. What is diversification?

9. How many securities should an investor have in a portfolio? Explain.

10. How many possible combinations of stocks are there? How do you go about selecting the correct ones for you?

11. Briefly describe the concept of an efficient portfolio.

12. If you were a financial planner, explain what sort of portfolio (including goals, risks, types of securities) you would recommend for: (a) a 3-year-old child who has been left $40,000 in trust; (b) a 35-year-old millionaire who has $950,000 to invest; (c) a 65-year-old widow who has $400,000 in pension benefits, life insurance proceeds, and cash.

13. Suppose the 3-year-old's portfolio is to be 30 percent invested in "defensive" stocks and debt securities to provide him with income when he reaches college age. What is meant by "defensive," and what stocks do you recommend?

14. Continuing with the previous question, what debt securities do you recommend?

15. Suppose the millionaire wants to speculate with half her funds. What are your recommendations?

TAXES AND TAX SHELTERS

T his chapter is about income taxes and investment techniques that can be used to reduce tax payments. The *Tax Reform Act of 1986,* a major revision of the U.S. tax code, had a major impact on investors. Selected highlights of that Act that affect investors are explained here.

INCOME TAXES

If you earn a sufficient amount of money, you must pay federal income tax, *unless* you have enough deductions to eliminate the tax payments. Before examining some methods investors can use to reduce tax payments, let us examine the tax rate schedule.

Tax Rate Schedule

Table 16-1 shows the 1990 tax rate schedule for a single individual with no dependents. By way of illustration, assume that Jean Spruill is a single taxpayer with taxable income of $50,000. Using the figures from Table 16-1, her income tax is $11,619.

Taxable Income	Tax Rate	Tax
$19,450	15%	$ 2,917.50
27,600	28	7,728.00
2,950	33	973.50
$50,000		$11,619.00

Jean is in the 33 percent **marginal tax bracket.** This means that she pays 33 percent on the additional income earned over a certain amount. In this case, she pays 33 percent tax on the additional $2,950 earned over $47,050.

Do not confuse the marginal tax bracket with the average tax bracket. The **average tax bracket** is the total amount of income tax divided by total taxable income. Jean has a marginal tax rate of 33 percent and an average tax rate of 23.24 percent.

$$\frac{\text{Total federal income tax}}{\text{Taxable income}} = \frac{\$11,619}{\$50,000} = 23.24\%$$

Capital Gains and Losses

A **capital asset** is usually defined as personal property that is used for pleasure or investment. A home, car, stocks, and bonds are examples of capital assets. Gains (or losses) from the sale or exchange of such assets are called **capital gains** (or capital losses). In the past, such gains (or losses) were divided into two categories, short-term and long-term, depending on how long they were held. Short-term capital gains were taxed at a higher rate than long-term capital gains. Under the Tax Reform Act of 1986, the tax advantage of long-term capital gains was eliminated and all gains are now taxed at the ordinary income tax rates.

Capital losses can be used to offset capital gains. If capital losses exceed capital gains, up to $3000 per year can be used to offset ordinary income. For example, suppose that an investor had $4000 in capital gains and $6000 in capital losses. The $2000 in capital losses in excess of the capital gains can be used to offset ordinary income on a dollar-for-dollar basis. If the excess capital loss had been, say, $5000, only $3000 in ordinary income could have been offset in one year and the remainder carried over into the following tax year.

TABLE 16-1   1990 Income Tax Schedule for a Single Individual, No Dependents

Taxable Income	Tax Rate
$0–$19,450	15%
$19,450–$47,050	28%
$47,050–$97,620	33%
Over $97,620	Special worksheet required to compute tax

Selling Short

Capital gains or losses can be deferred from one year to the next by selling short against the box. A short sale is the sale of a borrowed stock. The short position is closed out when the borrowed stock is returned to the lender. One can return stock to the lender by buying it on the open market or by delivering stock that one owns. A **short sale against the box** occurs when you sell short and intend to deliver your own stock that is held in a "safety deposit box" or elsewhere.

Capital gains or losses do not have to be reported until the short position is closed out. The following example illustrates the use of short sales to obtain a tax advantage. Assume that in May, 100 shares of Matrix Electric was purchased at $75 per share and by December the stock was selling for $50 per share. Investment analysts believed that the stock price would go lower. The investor who bought the stock in May did not need a capital loss or the $3000 offset that year because of other losses. He also did not want to hold the stock any longer because of the unfavorable outlook. One solution was to sell the stock short against the box and recognize the tax loss next year. Another solution was to buy a put option. A put option can be used to defer a gain or a loss to the next year.

Put Options

A put option is a contract that gives the buyer the right to sell stock to the seller of the option a specified number of shares (e.g., 100 shares) of the underlying common stock at a predetermined price within a given period of time. The buyer pays the seller a premium (say $400) for the contract. For that amount, the buyer has locked in the price at which the stock can be sold. This explanation will make more sense after you have read about puts in Chapter 19.

TAX SHELTERS

Certain types of investments enjoy special tax benefits and are generally referred to as **tax-sheltered investments.** The Tax Reform Act of 1986 reduced the attractiveness of tax-sheltered investments. Under that Act, losses from passive activities can be used only to offset income from such activities, with certain exceptions to the rules. **Passive activities** are those involving the conduct of a business in which the taxpayer does **not** materially contribute on a regular, continuous, and substantial basis. The term passive income generator, or **PIG,** is commonly used to refer to such income generated from passive activities. One of several tests of material participation used by the Internal Revenue Service is whether the taxpayer has participated in the activity for more than 500 hours per tax year. Income from most limited partnerships is passive income. However, income from a *working interest* (a special kind of limited partnership) in oil and gas properties is an exception to the rule. Income from rental property is passive income because the income comes from payments rather than the performance of services. However, special rules apply to real estate rental activity in which the

taxpayer actively participates. Because the tax laws are complex and confusing, no attempt is made here to examine them in detail. You should seek expert advice before making investment decisions that will affect your taxes.

A Word of Caution

Before investing in a tax shelter, consider the following advice.

For the Wealthy

Tax shelters are designed for investors who have substantial wealth. In addition to being wealthy, investors in tax shelters should have sufficient liquidity that they do not have to depend on income from the tax shelter or the ability to sell it. Many tax shelters provide little or no income for many years and are difficult if not impossible to sell.

For Risk Takers

There are risks in any investment, but tax shelters frequently involve high-risk investments. For example, oil and gas drilling programs are risky. The odds of finding a new exploratory well that is profitable are less than 15 in 100. This means that about 85 of every 100 wells that are dug are dry holes — no oil. Even if oil is found, it may not be in sufficient quantity to be profitable. However, some of the wells that "hit" are big winners and very profitable investments. It is because oil and gas drilling programs are risky that the government encourages exploration by giving tax incentives. If you are not willing and able to afford losing your investment, avoid risky tax shelters.

Limited Partnerships

Many investors use limited partnerships as a means of investing in tax-sheltered investments. A limited partnership, as used in this context, is an agreement between an individual or company (called the **general partner**) who has investment expertise and the investors (called **limited partners**) who provide most of the funds and want to earn a profit and obtain tax benefits. Thus, these partnerships are tax conduits through which income and losses are passed through to the limited partners.

General Partner

The general partner organizes and operates the tax-sheltered investment. Fees for organizing the deal and operating the investment on a day-to-day basis are paid by the limited partners before their funds are put to work on the investment project. Thus, the general partner stands to benefit even if the proposed investment is not profitable for the limited partners.

In addition, the general partner may share in the profits from the investment, even if the general partner invested no funds of his or her own. The financial arrangements between the general partner and the limited partner vary widely,

but the general partner rarely loses any money no matter what the outcome of the investment.

Information about the financial arrangements between the general partner and limited partners is explained in the **prospectus.** The Securities and Exchange Commission requires a prospectus to be issued to prospective investors in limited partnerships that are offered to the public (called **public programs**). No such requirement exists for **private programs,** where just a few individuals are involved. In either case, the limited partner should understand the financial arrangements before investing.

Limited Partner

The basic function of the limited partner is to provide capital. The limited partner has no responsibility for managing the investment, and liability is limited to the amount of funds he or she has invested plus his or her share of retained earnings. Generally, limited partners have no obligation to contribute additional capital to the partnership, and therefore have **no economic risk of loss** in partnership liabilities. The concept of **limited liability,** the potential for profit, and the fact that the tax benefits pass directly to the partners make limited partnerships a suitable investment vehicle for qualified investors.

Finally, many limited partnerships are operated on a **blind pool** basis. This means that the general partner has flexibility as to the parcels of real estate, oil wells, or other types of investments that can be made with the partnership's funds. Other limited partnerships may invest in specific projects such as a large commercial office building.

Master Limited Partnership

Master limited partnerships (MLPs) are partnerships whose ownership interest (called units) is traded on stock exchanges or over the counter.[1] The first such partnership was formed in 1981 by Apache Petroleum Company, and it is traded on the New York Stock Exchange. Most MLPs are energy companies. From an investor's point of view, the marketability of MLPs is their major advantage over regular limited partnerships. Special tax rules apply to publicly traded partnerships.

Against this background, let us examine some tax shelters.

OIL AND GAS INVESTMENTS
Tax Benefits

High energy costs and a limited supply of oil and gas have drawn increased attention to oil and gas investments. The dream of participating in a major oil discovery and the hope of obtaining tax advantages are sufficient inducements

[1] J. Markham Collins and Roger P. Bey, "The Master Limited Partnership: An Alternative to the Corporation," *Financial Management*, Winter 1986, 5–14.

for some investors. One tax inducement concerns **intangible drilling costs.** Integrated producers of domestic oil and gas wells can write off 70 percent of such costs in the first year and the remainder on a straight-line basis over five years. If a dry well is drilled, the entire expense is written off the year the hole is completed. Intangible drilling and development costs include the amount paid to drilling contractors plus the cost of certain items used in the process of drilling (except for equipment). Such costs may amount to 50 to 90 percent of the investment in the first year and 100 percent over several years.

Depletion allowance is another tax incentive. If a well is successful, part of the income derived from it is tax-free because oil and gas are wasting assets: they cannot be replaced. The depletion allowance is 15 percent of gross income. Gross income is income before operating expenses and production taxes.

Stock Ownership

Investors can buy limited partnerships in oil and gas investments to obtain tax benefits and income. Other investors not interested in the tax benefits of a partnership might consider investing in stocks of oil exploration companies. Companies such as Apache Petroleum and Mesa Limited Partnerships, which are traded on the New York Stock Exchange, manage drilling programs funded by limited partnerships. Stockholders of these companies do not receive the same tax advantages as working interest owners. However, they do enjoy the liquidity of their investments and the potential for appreciation, which are not available to the working interest owners. Thus investors should carefully weigh all of the advantages and disadvantages of limited partnership investments before committing their funds.

REAL ESTATE

Although Chapter 17 deals with real estate investments, we will examine the tax aspects of real estate here. The tax benefits of owning real estate for investment purposes include the deductions for operating expenses, interest expense, depreciation, and certain tax credits.

At Risk

Deductible losses from real estate tax shelters are limited to the dollar amount the taxpayer is "at risk" in the project. The **at-risk rules** generally refer to the amount of money that an investor can lose in an investment. The amount includes the investor's contributions in terms of cash and assets as well as borrowed amounts for which the investor is personally liable.

Exception to Passive Activity

As mentioned previously, real estate (or equipment) rental is considered a "passive activity." Deductions and credits from passive activities may be used to offset

income from other passive activities. There is an exception to the rule in the case of certain real estate activities. An individual who "actively" as opposed to "materially" participates may apply up to $25,000 of real estate losses and tax credits against nonpassive sources of income. "Active" participation requires 10 percent or more ownership. It also requires less bona fide involvement than "material" participation. The $25,000 maximum allowance is reduced by 50 percent when the taxpayer's adjusted gross income exceeds $100,000. Active participation in rentals is not required to take low-income housing and rehabilitation tax credits.

Operating Expense

Operating expenses include all expenses of operating the investment property except mortgage charges and depreciation. Operating expenses include property taxes, maintenance, insurance, power, and so on.

Interest Expense

Interest expense is a deductible item for both homeowners and investors. Homeowners may deduct mortgage interest expense on their principal residence and a second residence (e.g., vacation home). The deduction does not include interest on that portion of the mortgage that exceeds the lesser of the original purchase price (plus improvements) of the residence or its fair market value. The latter restriction does not apply to mortgage loans outstanding before August 16, 1986, or to mortgage loans where the funds are used for qualified educational and medical expenses.

Interest expense is a major part of mortgage payments, particularly in the early years of the mortgage. For example, the first year's mortgage payment on a 25-year, $60,000 loan at 14 percent is $8667.12. Of that amount, $8382.18 is interest expense, which can be deducted from taxes.

Depreciation

Depreciation is an accounting method that allocates the cost of an asset over a recovery period. Residential rental property has a recovery period of 27.5 years, and nonresidential real property has a recovery period of 3.5 years. The cost is recovered using straight-line depreciation. Basically, the straight-line method means that an equal amount is depreciated each year. For example, on January 1 an investor purchased residential rental property for $150,000. The annual depreciation is $5454.54 ($150,000/27.5).

Suppose the property is sold for $150,000 after three years. The book value of the property, which is the cost less accumulated depreciation, is $133,636.36 ($5454.54 × 3 = $16,363.64). Since the property was sold for more than its book value, the $16,363.64 depreciation will be recaptured as ordinary income. Had the property sold for, say, $170,000, the $16,363.64 depreciation would have been recaptured as ordinary income, and the additional $20,000 above the cost would be taxed as a long-term capital gain. If the property sells for less than $133,636.36, a long-term capital loss is established. Depreciation can provide

important tax advantages in terms of sheltering current income and delaying the payment of taxes.

Tax Shelter

The taxable income from real estate investment is determined by cash flow before taxes, loan amortization (the reduction in the principal amount of the loan, also called equity buildup), and depreciation.

$$TI = CFBT + A - D \qquad \text{(16-1)}$$

where

$$TI = \text{taxable income}$$

$$CFBT = \text{cash flow before taxes}$$

$$A = \text{loan amortization}$$

$$D = \text{depreciation}$$

The cash flow is income received during period less operating expenses and mortgage payments. Since only the interest portion of the mortgage payment is tax-deductible, the amortization is added back into the equation. Recall that depreciation is an accounting method for allocating costs. It is *not* a cash disbursement and does not affect cash income. It does, however, reduce taxable income, thereby allowing the investor to retain cash that is not taxed immediately. Thus, depreciation provides a tax shelter.

By way of illustration, assume that cash flow before taxes is $8000, amortization is $5000, and depreciation is $10,000. Although the cash flow is $8000, only $3000 is taxable.

$$TI = CFBT + A - D$$
$$= \$8000 + \$5000 - \$10,000$$
$$= \$3000$$

As long as depreciation exceeds amortization, some portion of the cash flow before taxes will be tax-sheltered. However, if depreciation is equal to or less than amortization, all of the cash flow is taxable and there is no tax shelter.

Rehabilitation Tax Credits and Low-Income Housing

In an effort to restore some of our older structures, Congress has provided certain tax incentives for qualified properties. The tax incentives are tax credits. For example, on certified residential and nonresidential historic structures, the tax credit is 20 percent of the qualified rehabilitation expenditures. For nonresidential buildings placed in service before 1936 it is 10 percent of the qualified rehabilitation expenditures. Similarly, certain tax credits are available to encourage investment in low-income housing projects. **Tax credits** reduce the amount of taxes to be paid. This should not be confused with **deductions,** such as depreciation and

---

BOX 16-1

WHAT TO DEPRECIATE

Here are three suggestions that may save you a lot of money by taking full advantage of depreciation.

1. When calculating the cost basis for depreciation, be sure to include closing fees, title insurance, attorney's fees, and other expenses.
2. Do not confuse personal property, such as the stove and refrigerator, with real estate. Personal property has a shorter recovery period than real estate and can be depreciated faster.
3. Land cannot be depreciated, but buildings and improvements can be. The percentage of property that can be depreciated to land that cannot be depreciated is called the **improvement ratio.** Frequently, the ratios used by mortgage lenders and tax assessors differ. Investors are better off using the higher ratio because they get more depreciation.

---

interest expense, which are subtracted from gross income and reduce the amount of income that is taxed.

RETIREMENT PLANS

Individual Retirement Accounts

Deductible contributions to individual retirement accounts (IRAs) provide an immediate tax reduction. In addition, all dividends, interest, and profits earned in the IRA accumulate and compound tax-free until the employee retires or withdraws the funds. Funds cannot be withdrawn from an IRA before age $59\frac{1}{2}$ without penalty, except in the case of death or disability. So do not invest in an IRA if you need liquidity before reaching that age. Distributions from IRAs must begin by age $70\frac{1}{2}$.

A point of clarification is in order. The IRA itself is not an investment. It is a retirement plan that can invest in stocks, bonds, mutual funds, certificates of deposits, and so on. Therefore, an individual has tremendous latitude as to the type of investment to make with an IRA.

Figure 16-1 lists the criteria for IRA deductions. The three principal criteria are (1) adjusted gross income (AGI), (2) whether an individual is already covered by a retirement plan, and (3) the individual's filing status. AGI is total income less allowable adjustments to income, including alimony paid, deductions for self-employed health insurance, deductions for certain IRA contributions, and other adjustments. Annual IRA contributions are the lesser of $2000 ($2250 for a spousal IRA) or 100 percent of taxable compensation.

The $2000 contribution to the IRA is a tax deduction. For taxpayers in the

CAN YOU TAKE AN IRA DEDUCTION?

This chart sums up whether you can take a full deduction, a partial deduction, or no deduction as discussed in this chapter.

If Your Modified AGI* is		If You Are Covered by a Retirement Plan at Work and Your Filing Status is			If You Are Not Covered by a Retirement Plan at Work and Your Filing Status is			
At Least	But Less Than	•Single •Head of Household	• Married Filing Jointly (even if your spouse is not covered by a plan at work) • Qualifying Widow(er)	Married Filing Separately**	Married Filing Jointly (and your spouse is covered by a plan at work)	• Single • Head of Household	• Married Filing Jointly or Separately (and your spouse is not covered by a plan at work) • Qualifying Widow(er)	Married Filing Separately (even if your spouse is covered by a plan at work)***
		You Can Take	You Can Take	You Can Take	You Can Take	You Can Take	You Can Take	You Can Take
$-0-	$10,000	Full deduction	Full deduction	Partial deduction	Full deduction	Full Deduction	Full Deduction	Full Deduction
$10,000	$25.000	Full deduction	Full deduction	No deduction	Full deduction			
$25,000	$35,000	Partial deduction	Full deduction	No deduction	Full deduction			
$35,000	$40,000	No deduction	Full deduction	No deduction	Full deduction			
$40,000	$50,000	No deduction	Partial deduction	No deduction	Partial deduction			
$50,000 or over		No deduction	No deduction	No deduction	No deduction			

Maximum deduction. You can deduct IRA contributions up to the amount of your allowable deduction (full or partial), or 100% of your taxable compensation, whichever is less.

$200 floor. The partial deduction has a $200 floor. For example, if your deduction would have been reduced to less than $200 (but not zero), you can deduct IRA contributions up to $200 or 100% of your taxable compensation, whichever is less. If the deduction is completely phased out (reduced to zero), no deduction is allowed.

*Modified AGI (adjusted gross income) is: (1) for Form 1040A—the amount on line 11, or (2) for Form 1040—the amount on line 31, figured without taking into account any IRA deduction or any foreign earned income exclusion and foreign housing exclusion (deduction).
**If you did not live with your spouse at any time during the year, your filing status is considered, for this purpose, as Single (therefore your IRA deduction is determined under the "Single" column).

***You are entitled to the full deduction only if you did not live with your spouse at any time during the year. If you did live with your spouse during the year, you are, for this purpose, treated as though you are covered by a retirement plan at work (therefore, your IRA deduction is determined under the "Married Filing Separately" column in the "If You Are Covered by a Retirement Plan..." section of the chart).

FIGURE 16-1 IRA deductions. *Source:* Department of the Treasury, Internal Revenue Service.

28-percent income tax bracket, this means that Uncle Sam has contributed $560 ($2000 × 28% = $560) in the form of taxes saved to the retirement plan, and the after-tax cost of the contribution is only $1440.

Taxpayers with an AGI of $10,000 or less may take an IRA deduction regardless of whether they have a retirement plan at work or their filing status. Taxpayers who are covered by retirement plans at work are limited in the amount of IRA deductions they may take. Taxpayers in this category filing single returns and with an AGI of $35,000 or less and those filing jointly with an AGI of $50,000 or less are qualified for IRA deductions. Taxpayers with an AGI of $50,000 or more who are covered by other plans cannot deduct IRA contributions.

Taxpayers who are not entitled to make full or partial contributions to an IRA may make *nondeductible* contributions to an IRA. The earnings on such nondeductible contributions are not taxed until they are withdrawn. Special rules apply in figuring taxes on the distributions if both deductible and nondeductible contributions are involved in the IRA. Nondeductible contributions are not taxed, and

deductible contributions are taxed when they are distributed. Therefore investors must keep accurate records of their IRA investments.

Taxpayers who are not covered by retirement plans at work are entitled to full deductions, with a few exceptions. The exceptions are for those filing jointly where one spouse is covered by a retirement plan at work. In this case there is an upper limit to the AGI where IRA deductions are allowed.

Keogh Plans

Keogh plans are retirement plans established by self-employed individuals. Sometimes they are called H.R. 10 plans. In addition, there are **Simplified Employee Pensions** (SEPs), which also cover certain business owners and their employees. These individuals can put the lesser of $30,000 or 15 percent of self-employment income per year in a retirement plan.

Elective Deferrals

Individuals covered by certain kinds of retirement plans can choose to have part of their pay contributed by the employer to a retirement plan rather than receiving it currently as compensation. The amounts are called **elective deferrals** because the individual elects to set aside money into the retirement plan. There is a $9,500 limit for qualified individuals on amounts that can be set aside each year. The tax on the elective deferral is deferred until the money is distributed by the plan. Elective deferrals can be made under cash or other deferred arrangements known as section 401(k) plans, section 501(c)(18) plans, SEPs, and other arrangements. The term "section" refers to sections of the Internal Revenue Code. Check with your employer on how this may apply to you.

Tax-deferred annuities are a popular method of investment and income tax deferral. Tax-deferred annuities are sold by insurance companies. Because you invest in annuities for the long term, you should investigate the quality of the insurer. Such information is available from A. B. Best, an insurance rating service. In the case of fixed-rate deferred annuities, you may also want to determine whether the company is paying the same rates on both old and new policies, or if they pay high rates during the first few years of their policies and then lower the rates.

MUNICIPAL BONDS

As discussed in Chapter 2, state and political subdivisions issue so-called **municipal bonds** to finance qualified government activities such as school districts, waste disposal plants, and so on. The interest income from qualified securities is exempt from federal income tax and, in some states, from state income tax. Not all debt securities issued by state and local subdivisions are tax-free. Check carefully before you invest.

The after-tax equivalent yield for any tax-exempt yield and tax bracket can be

determined by the equation that follows. By way of illustration, assume that the tax-exempt yield is 8 percent and the investor is in the 28-percent marginal tax bracket. The after-tax equivalent yield is 11.11 percent. In other words, investing in the tax-exempt yield of 8 percent is equivalent to investing in a taxable security yielding 11.11 percent.

$$\text{Tax-free yield} = \frac{\text{tax-exempt yield}}{1 - \text{tax bracket}} = \frac{0.08}{1 - 0.28} = 11.11\%$$

Although municipal bonds are issued by state and local governments, they are not risk-free. Some major cities, including New York and Cleveland, have had financial problems in the past. Therefore investors should evaluate the quality of these securities just as thoroughly as any other prospective investment.

Finally, there are some money market funds that provide tax-free income by investing in short-term municipal securities. Likewise, there are tax-free mutual funds for investors with other investment needs.

U.S. GOVERNMENT SERIES EE/HH SAVINGS BONDS

U.S. Government Series EE Bonds have tax-saving features. They are sold at 50 percent of their face value in denominations ranging from $50 to $10,000. Interest accrues through periodic increases in the redemption value. Although they have a maturity of 12 years, the maturity may be extended up to 30 years. The interest rates on newly issued bonds are based on current market rates, and if they are held five years or more, they will earn at least 85 percent of the average yield on Treasury notes with a five-year maturity or 6 percent, whichever is higher. Bond-holders *defer* any federal taxes due on the bonds until they are redeemed. The amount taxed is the difference between the purchase price and the redemption price, plus accrued interest if held beyond the original maturity. In addition, beginning in 1990, the interest from newly purchased Series EE bonds may be *excluded from income* if the redemption proceeds are used to pay qualified education expenses for the bondholder, his or her spouse, or dependents. The term "excluded from income" means that the interest does not have to be reported.

Interest payments on Series HH bonds are paid semiannually by electronic transfer. They have an initial maturity of 10 years and are guaranteed to earn interest for 20 years. The interest payments on these bonds are subject to federal income tax, but not to state or local taxes.

CONCLUSION

Why pay taxes if you do not have to? Perhaps some individuals are altruistic, but most are concerned with their own welfare. In that regard, there are ways to reduce one's tax payments and defer them to some time in the future. In this chapter we examined various "tax shelters," including oil and gas, real estate, and

municipal bonds. One reason why some of these investments are tax-sheltered is to encourage investment. In the case of oil and gas exploration the risk is very high. There is less risk in municipal securities, but it is there. Caveat emptor — let the buyer beware.

Investors may also invest in IRAs, Keogh Plans, or SEPs if they are qualified to do so. These are retirement plans that have wide latitude in their investment alternatives.

IMPORTANT CONCEPTS

At-risk rules	Master Limited Partnership (MLP)
Average tax bracket	Municipal bonds
Blind pool	Operating expenses
Capital gains (losses)	Passive activities
Depletion allowance	Private programs
Depreciation	Prospectus
Elective deferrals	Public programs
General partner	Put option
Individual retirement account (IRA)	Selling short
Intangible drilling costs	Short sale against the box
Interest expense	Simplified Employee Pension (SEP)
Keogh plans	Tax Reform Act of 1986
Limited partner	Tax shelter
Marginal tax bracket	Working interest

QUESTIONS AND EXERCISES

1. How does the marginal tax rate differ from the average tax rate?
2. Jose has a taxable income of $75,000. Using Table 16-1, compute his income tax. What are his marginal and average tax rates?
3. What are the tax implications of having a capital loss?
4. Selling short against the box has an important tax advantage. Explain what it is.
5. Explain the meaning of the term "tax shelter."
6. Are tax shelters suitable investments for anyone who pays taxes? Explain.
7. Limited partnerships are widely used in real estate and oil and gas investments. Explain how they are organized, and who generally benefits the most.
8. What are the tax benefits of oil and gas investments?
9. What are the tax benefits of real estate investments?
10. Explain the meaning of the term "at risk" in connection with income taxes.

11. Explain the meaning of the term "passive activity" in connection with income taxes.

12. Who benefits from using an IRA? Explain.

13. What is a Keogh Plan?

14. Explain the tax advantage of municipal bonds.

15. An investor in the 33 percent tax bracket owns a municipal security that has a tax-exempt yield of 10 percent. What is the equivalent yield of that security?

REAL ESTATE INVESTMENTS

W ill Rogers said something to the effect that they stopped making land a long time ago, but they are still making people. Therefore, the price of land will go up as the increasing population crowds the limited land that is available for development. Will was right! Real estate prices have soared. As shown in Figure 17-1, the average purchase price of a new home increased from $74,400 in 1979 to $162,100 in 1990. Population, inflation, and other factors contributed to the rising prices. But will prices continue to rise in the future? The answer is a resounding yes and no. The price of real estate, like that of any other commodity, can go up or down. The direction depends on location, design, financing, and other factors. We will examine various ways in which investors can participate in real estate investments.

OWNING REAL ESTATE

The word *own* refers to the legal right to the possession of a thing such as real estate. The extent to which an investor "owns" a real estate investment varies from being the sole owner of the investment to being a stockholder in a corporation that owns the investment. Some of the principal methods of owning and investing in real estate are described in the following sections.

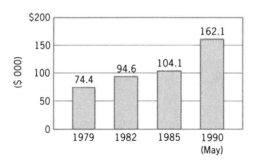

FIGURE 17-1 The average purchase price of a new home financed with a conventional mortgage in the United States. *Source:* Federal Reserve Bulletin.

Methods of Owning Real Estate

Direct Ownership

An individual can own the house that he or she lives in. Most homeowners borrow funds from a financial intermediary to pay for the house and then repay the loan over a period of years. Similarly, an investor could own an apartment building, office building, or shopping center. However, **ownership** of large-scale residential, commercial, and industrial property is frequently beyond the financial means of a single investor. Accordingly, there are various ways in which investors can pool their funds to acquire large properties.

Condominiums

Condominium means joint sovereignty. In real estate, it refers to an apartment complex or office building that is jointly owned by the residents. The owner has legal title to his or her respective apartment or office, and joint interest, along with the other owners, in common areas, such as the roof, parking area, and swimming pool. The owners can buy, sell, rent, and use their units subject to the rules of the condominium. Owners are usually required to make separate monthly payments for common services like trash collection and maintenance.

Cooperatives

In a **cooperative** each owner owns a proportionate share of a nonprofit corporation that holds legal title to that building. The owner of the cooperative leases his or her unit from the cooperative and pays monthly fees for common services. The owner has the right to vote for directors of the corporation. Finally, the owner must obtain permission from the corporation before selling the leased unit, renting it, or remodeling it.

Partnerships

A partnership is an agreement between two or more individuals to do something, such as invest in real estate. **Limited partnerships,** as described in the previous chapter, consist of an agreement between the general partner, who has invest-

ment expertise, and the limited partners, who supply most of the funds and want to earn a profit. More will be said about limited partnerships shortly.

Stockholders

Investors can be **stockholders** in companies that specialize in real estate investments or that own large amounts of real estate. We will say more about companies later in this chapter.

Debt Holders

Investors can hold the mortgages. The relatively high yields make then an attractive investment for those who want income. Sometimes it is necessary for homeowners to hold all or part of the mortgage loan on the dwelling that they are selling in order to induce the buyer to buy it. In addition, there are **unit investment trusts,** which are million-dollar pools of government-guaranteed mortgages broken down into smaller units and sold to private investors. Although these do not represent ownership, they are one method of investing in real estate.

Each form of ownership has different economic features and **tax benefits.** Some of the major features of each are listed in Table 17-1. No explanation is needed for some of the items listed in the table. For example, an investor can use property that he or she owns, it may appreciate in value, and so on. However, the terms **financial leverage** and **equity buildup** do require an explanation, as do the tax benefits.

Financial Leverage

As used here, the term *financial leverage* refers to the use of borrowed funds to acquire real estate. If a real estate investment that appreciates in value is sold, the leverage will magnify the investor's gain. Conversely, if an investment is sold at a loss, the investor's loss will be magnified. The following example illustrates leverage.

Suppose that Linda Lane has the opportunity to buy a house for $100,000. Because it is located in an area where real estate is appreciating rapidly, she estimates that it will be worth $130,000 in two years, at which time she will sell it. Linda can pay cash for the property, or she can invest $10,000 of her own funds and borrow the remainder. Let us examine the consequences of each course of action. As shown in Table 17-2, Linda's gain before taxes is $30,000. If she pays cash for the house, the return on the funds she has invested is 30 percent. However, if she invests only $10,000 and borrows the remainder, the return is 300 percent! Interest expense on borrowed funds will reduce her return.

What happens if Linda is wrong, and the property declines $30,000 in value at the end of the third year? If Linda wants to sell the property then, she will lose $30,000. Without leverage, the loss is $30,000 of the original $100,000 investment. With leverage, the entire $10,000 investment is lost and an additional

TABLE 17-1   Methods, Economic Features, and Tax Benefits of Real Estate Investments

Methods of Investing	Economic Features	Tax Features
Direct Ownership Home	• Use of property • Appreciation potential • Low leverage • Equity buildup	• Interest expense is tax-deductible on home and another dwelling • One-time $125,000 exclusion for persons 55 years or older on the sale of their home
Investments	• Appreciation potential • Income potential • Equity buildup • Leverage varies • Management responsibility	• Income is taxable • Depreciation and interest are tax-deductible • Operating expense • Tax credits
Limited Partnership	• Appreciation potential • Income potential • Limited risk • Leverage varies • Cost of partnership units varies • Master limited partnerships are marketable	• Income is taxable • Depreciation and interest are tax deductible
Stockholder	• Appreciation potential • Income potential • Marketable security	• Dividend income is taxable
Debt Holder	• Income • Some debt securities are marketable	• Income is taxable

$20,000 investment is required to repay the loan. Leverage magnifies both returns and losses relative to the investment.

Equity

The total **equity** in a real estate venture has three components: the down payment, equity buildup, and appreciation.

Down Payment

Suppose that Bob and Betty Marshall buy a rental house for $75,000. The lender requires them to make a down payment of $15,000 and will lend them $60,000 at 14 percent interest for 25 years. The Marshalls' equity in the house at this point is $15,000.

TABLE 17-2   Rate of Return on Real Estate Investments

	Without Leverage	**With Leverage**
Selling price	$130,000	$130,000
— Loan repayment	0	90,000
— Cash investment	100,000	10,000
= Gross profit	$30,000	$30,000
Rate of return = $\dfrac{\text{gross profit}}{\text{cash investment}}$ =	$\dfrac{\$30,000}{\$100,000} = 30\%$	$\dfrac{\$30,000}{\$10,000} = 300\%$

Equity Buildup

Equity buildup, or **amortization,** is the reduction in the principal amount of the loan that results from mortgage payments. The Marshalls' payment is $722.26. As shown in the mortgage amortization schedule (Table 17-3), most of the monthly payment is for interest on the loan. Only $22.26 of the first payment is for principal. A careful examination of the table reveals that each month an increasing part of the payment goes to principal and the loan balance is reduced. In the first year the loan balance is reduced $284.94 — the equity buildup. By the end of the fourth year, the loan balance is reduced to $58,578.58, and the equity buildup is $1421.42. Most of the monthly payment in the early years is for interest on the debt.

Appreciation

If the Marshalls' rental house is in a good location and other factors are in their favor, the house may appreciate in value. On the other hand, if they are not fortunate, it may decline in value. A decline might occur if a change in zoning laws permitted a garbage dump to be located next door, or a major highway was to be built in their backyard. Let us assume that Bob and Betty are fortunate and that the property value and **cash flow** before taxes increase 12 percent per year. After making their mortgage payments and paying for the operating expenses, their before-tax cash flow in the first year was $1000. (Cash flow is income less operating expenses and mortgage payments.)

Return on Investment and Equity

Now let us put together all of the facts we have about the Marshalls' investment and examine their **return on investment** and their **return on equity.** The information is summarized in Table 17-4. The return on investment is the before-tax cash flow divided by their investment. The cash flow is increasing 12 percent per year, and their total investment consists of the down payment plus the equity

TABLE 17-3   Mortgage Amortization

Mortgage amount = $60,000
Interest rate   = 14%
Number of years   = 25
Monthly payments = $722.26

Month	Principal	Interest	Balance
1	$22.26	$700.00	$59,977.74
2	22.52	699.74	59,955.22
3	22.78	699.48	59,932.44
4	23.05	699.21	59,909.39
5	23.32	698.94	59,886.07
6	23.59	698.67	59,862.48
7	23.86	698.40	59,838.62
8	24.14	698.12	59,814.48
9	24.42	697.84	59,790.06
10	24.71	697.55	59,765.35
11	25.00	697.26	59,740.35
12	25.29	696.97	59,715.06
37	$33.80	$688.46	$58,977.37
38	34.19	688.07	58,943.18
39	34.59	687.67	58,908.59
40	34.99	687.27	58,873.60
41	35.40	686.86	58,838.20
42	35.81	686.45	58,802.39
43	36.23	686.03	58,766.16
44	36.65	685.61	58,729.51
45	37.08	685.18	58,692.44
46	37.51	684.75	58,654.92
47	37.95	684.31	58,616.97
48	38.40	683.86	58,578.58

buildup. The return on investment increased from 6.5 to 8.6 percent during the period shown.

The return on equity is the most important measure from the investor's point of view because one objective of investing is to maximize wealth; i.e., equity. The difference between the investment (down payment plus equity buildup) and total equity is appreciation. Recall that the property value is increasing 12 percent per year. Accordingly, the Marshalls' return on equity declined from 4.1 to 2.4 percent. If the Marshalls can earn higher returns on equity in other investments, they should consider selling this one.

This example illustrates a common problem in real estate and other types of investments. Investors frequently do not take advantage of increases in their equity positions. In this case the Marshalls could borrow against the higher appraised value of their rental property and try to invest the funds profitably

TABLE 17-4 Returns on Investment and Equity

	Year of Investment				
	0	**1**	**2**	**3**	**4**
Return on Investment					
Before-tax cash flow	$ 0	$ 1,000	$ 1,120	$ 1,254	$ 1,405
Investment	15,000	15,284	15,611	15,987	16,386
Return on investment	—	6.5%	7.2%	7.8%	8.6%
Return on Equity					
Before-tax cash flow	$ 0	$ 1,000	$ 1,120	$ 1,254	$ 1,405
Property value	75,000	84,000	94,080	105,370	118,014
Balance of loan	60,000	59,715	59,388	59,011	58,578
Total equity	15,000	24,285	34,692	46,369	59,446
Return on equity	—	4.1%	3.2%	2.7%	2.4%

Assumptions

1. $60,000 is borrowed at 14% for 25 years.
2. Investment is the down payment plus equity buildup.
3. Cash flow and property value increase 12% per year.
4. Total equity is beginning equity plus the increase in property value and equity buildup.
5. Values shown are those at year-end.

elsewhere. As explained in Chapter 16, there are limitations on the deductible interest expenses from the additional borrowing.

LIMITED PARTNERSHIPS

The concepts of a limited partnership were explained in Chapter 16 in connection with oil and gas tax shelters. Those same concepts apply here, but the partnerships invest in real estate instead of oil and gas properties. The basic idea is to permit investors to pool their funds and have limited risks while investing in a professionally managed real estate portfolio. It is almost like a mutual fund that specializes in real estate, and the limited partners get certain tax benefits in addition to the potential income.

Costs

The price of limited partnership interests varies from $500 to $100,000 or more. The large **public programs** generally cost less ($500 to $5000) than the **private programs** in order to attract investors. Both public and private programs are sold by stockbrokerage firms and others. These programs give stockbrokers a wider range of products to offer their customers, as well as a nice commission. For example, consider the McNeil Real Estate Fund IX, Ltd. All the information

---

BOX 17-1

THE COST OF FINANCING A HOME

How much does it cost to finance a $60,000 mortgage? The answer depends on the interest rate charged on the mortgage loan and the number of years to maturity. Would you believe that a $60,000 mortgage loan can cost more than a quarter million dollars?

Maturity	Total Cost at 10% Interest	Total Cost at 14% Interest
20 years	$138,960	$179,136
25 years	163,620	216,720
30 years	189,648	255,960

The total cost is determined by multiplying the mortgage payment per $1000 loan for each interest rate by the size of the loan and the number of months. As shown in the following table, for example, the monthly mortgage payment for a $1000 loan at 14 percent for 20 years is $12.44. Therefore, the total cost of a $60,000 loan is $12.44 × 60 × 240 months = $179,136. The information in the table can be used to determine monthly payments and total costs for various sizes of mortgage loans.

Monthly Mortgage Payment

	Years to Maturity				
Interest Rate (%)	10	15	20	25	30
6%	$11.10	$ 8.44	$ 7.16	$ 6.44	$ 6.00
8	12.13	9.56	8.36	7.72	7.34
10	13.22	10.75	9.65	9.09	8.78
12	14.35	12.00	11.01	10.53	10.29
14	15.35	13.32	12.44	12.04	11.85
16	16.76	14.69	13.92	13.59	13.45

---

presented here was taken from the **prospectus** that all investors received and should read *before* investing.

The minimum investment in McNeil Real Estate Fund IX was $5000. Of that amount, the stockbrokers who sold the fund to the limited partners received an underwriting fee of $400, and the general partners of the fund received $79.80, or 1.6 percent. Therefore, the cost of buying into the fund was 9.6 percent ($479.80/$5000 = 9.6%).

The general partners' "sales commission" of 1.6 percent amounts to $798,000. This exceeds the general partners' $96,000 investment in the fund by $702,000! In other words, the general partners have no funds of their own invested in the project. For them it is all gain and minimal risk. Additional gains to the general partners come from fees for organizing, operating, and liquidating real estate. Here are some examples.

- For evaluating and selecting real estate for the partnership, the general partners get 6 percent of the total loans and cash attributable to all partnership properties acquired by the partnership and of 18 percent of the gross proceeds.
- For property management, they get 5 percent of the gross revenues of the properties managed by the agent.
- For managing the affairs of the partnership, they get 5 percent of adjusted cash from operations.
- Real estate commissions for buying and selling partnership properties amount to half of the acquisition fee (the first item in this listing).
- A subordinated incentive for managing the partnership is equal to 10 percent of cash from sales or refinancing remaining after unit holders have received their original capital plus a reasonable return.
- The general partner gets 5 percent of the net income or loss.

After examining these costs, it should be clear that the general partner will make money, even if the limited partners make nothing.

Partnership Investments

Limited partnerships invest in virtually every type of real estate. Some limited partnerships invest primarily in hotel property, multifamily property, or commercial property. Some invest in all three types.

One limited partnership specializes in new multifamily property located in medium-sized towns located in the Sunbelt. Another specializes in existing multifamily units. The risk in the latter type is less because the units are already constructed and rented before the limited partnerships buy them. They do not have to worry about cost overruns, labor strikes, and so on. However, they may have to pay premium prices to buy the existing properties instead of building them at a relatively low cost.

The point is that selecting a suitable partnership may entail considerable research costs. Each real estate fund is unique, and each investor must decide what type of investments are suitable and the degree of risk he or she is willing to assume.

Risks

To some extent the risk depends on the type of investments that the fund makes as well as its management. The maximum risk is probably limited to the investor's

investment. However, the McNeil Fund prospectus makes it clear that the principles of law concerning the limitation of liabilities in a limited partnership have not been authoritatively established for partnerships that are organized under the laws of one state but are doing business and have partners in other states. To minimize the risk, McNeil maintains adequate insurance coverage against liabilities for personal injury and property damage.

There is also a tax risk. This risk is due to disagreements between the Internal Revenue Service and the limited partnerships over various accounting practices. In addition, tax laws and rulings change, which may have an adverse effect on investors.

Other risks include the economic risks of investing in real estate, potential conflicts of interest of the general partner, and the fact that no public market exists for most partnership units.

As a result of these risks, real estate limited partnerships, as well as oil and gas limited partnerships, are most suitable for those who already have substantial wealth. Some of the typical requirements for investors in such programs are

- A net worth (exclusive of home and automobiles) of $50,000 or more, and income over the next two years that will be taxable in at least the 39-percent income tax bracket.
- A net worth (exclusive of home and automobile) of at least $200,000.

Expected Returns

Investing in real estate limited partnerships is usually a relatively long-term proposition. There is no secondary market for most limited partnerships. This means that you cannot sell them once you make your investment, or if in the few situations where you are able to sell them, there will be a substantial discount. For example, Equitec Real Estate Investment Fund 18, originally offered at $500 per unit in 1987, could be sold for $60 per unit in 1990.[1] Therefore most investors are committed to the limited partnerships for the duration, however long that may be.

If the partnership is successful, investors should expect tax losses in the early years of operation. The amount of tax loss depends in part on the method of depreciation used and financial leverage. Partnerships that use maximum financial leverage will generate more passive tax losses than those that use little or no financial leverage. However, maximum financial leverage means increased financial risks for the partnership.

In the third or fourth year, many partnerships begin to sell their properties. The holding period to liquidate all properties may be seven years or longer. The sales are expected to provide gains.

Sometimes limited partnerships help finance the sale of their properties by taking promissory notes secured by those properties. These notes may have a maturity of five years or longer. Now the investors in the limited partnership have altered their position from "owners" to "holders of debt securities."

[1] Karen Nickel, "Yes You Can Unload a Limited Partnership," *Fortune*, June 4, 1990, 48.

When all of the properties are sold and the mortgage loans and promissory notes are paid off, the partnership may be liquidated. The remaining equity and profits, if any, may be returned to the limited and general partners.

COMMON STOCKS

Buying common stocks in companies that invest in or own substantial amounts of real estate is another way of participating in the real estate market. The major advantages of this method are the liquidity afforded by the stock market and the access to information on publicly held companies. On the other side of the coin, there are no tax losses resulting from interest and depreciation. However, tax losses may result if the securities are sold at a loss. In the following sections we will examine several types of real estate stocks.

Real Estate Investment Trusts

Real Estate Investment Trusts (REITs) are analogous to closed-end investment companies for those who wish to invest in real estate. The principal difference between the two is that REITs make extensive use of borrowed funds, while investment companies are not permitted to do so. REITs are organized as business trusts to provide real estate portfolio management for investors who lack sufficient funds to invest in large-scale projects, who lack expertise and interest in managing real properties, and who want liquidity. REITs were very popular in the late 1960s and early 1970s. However, the 1974–1975 recession resulted in the collapse of many REITs that were unable to cover the costs of their borrowed funds when the demand for real estate slackened. Since then, the survivors in that industry have reduced their financial leverage and are attempting to restructure their growth on a sounder basis. Some of the REITs are listed on the New York Stock Exchange. This list includes MONY Real Estate, Americana, and Wells Fargo Mortgage.

Real Estate Stocks

In addition to REITs, there are other actively traded companies that deal in real estate. Koger Properties owns and manages office buildings. Rouse Company is a major owner and developer of shopping centers. Del Webb owns and develops retirement communities and other housing projects. There are other real estate stocks as well.

MORTGAGE-BACKED INVESTMENTS

Unit Investment Trusts

Some investors who want the high income from mortgage loans but do not want to take the risks of being a mortgage lender or bill collector should consider a unit

investment trust that invests in government-backed mortgage loans. A unit investment trust is a special type of investment company that sells "units" — a fractional undivided interest in the fund — to investors. For example, the Government Securities Income Fund invests primarily in Government National Mortgage Association (**GNMA or Ginny Mae**) mortgage-backed securities.[2] These securities consist of "pools" of mortgages that are guaranteed by GNMA, an agency of the federal government. The **mortgage pools** go by various names, including **GNMA Pass-Through Certificates** and **REMICs,** which stands for Real Estate Mortgage Investment Conduit, and **Collateralized Mortgage Obligations (CMOs).**

Mortgage pools differ from bonds in several respects. First, investors receive monthly payments that include both interest and amortization of mortgages. Second, monthly payments also include prepayments of mortgages when the properties they are financing are sold or refinanced.

One advantage of such unit trusts is that their sponsors make them available to investors in affordable denominations such as $1000. Other advantages include payments that are guaranteed by GNMA, and limited liquidity of the unit trusts.

Second Mortgages

Homeowners and owners of other types of real estate may have to take a **second mortgage** to help finance the property they are selling. A second mortgage on a parcel of real estate has an inferior claim to taxes and the first mortgage if the real estate is foreclosed. A second mortgage created for the purpose of helping to finance the sale of real estate is sometimes called a **purchase-money mortgage.** This type of mortgage is commonly used to finance land and real estate developments. Second mortgages may also be used to finance business ventures or education or may be put to other uses.

Government-Backed Mortgages

You are already familiar with Ginnie Mae, but do you know Fannie Mae, Freddie Mac, and Sonny Mac? These are acronyms for the Federal National Mortgage Association (FNMA), the Federal Home Loan Mortgage Corporation, and the State of New York Mortgage Agency. They sell mortgages packaged in a variety of ways. For example, Freddie Mac sells collateralized mortgage obligations (CMOs), which are mortgage-backed securities issued by a government agency. These securities have denominations ranging from $1000 to $25,000, and the maturities range from 3 to 20 years.

Several mutual funds specialize in government-backed mortgages, thereby offering investors another way to invest in real estate. The Vanguard Fixed Income GNMA Portfolio and the Lexington GNMA Income Fund are two examples of such funds.

---

[2] For a listing of unit trusts or government securities funds, refer to *Wiesenberger Investment Company Services,* New York, Warren, Gorham & Lamont, published annually.

CONCLUSION

This chapter explains the different ways of investing in real estate. Many people unintentionally became real estate investors when their homes appreciated in value. Some borrowed against the increased equity to make investments elsewhere, others sold their homes at a profit and moved to other areas, but most did nothing and stayed where they were.

Intentional investors, however, use a variety of techniques to invest in real estate. These techniques range from direct ownership to investing in stocks and mortgages. Each method has its own advantages and disadvantages that must be weighed carefully before investing. Some investors prefer direct ownership because they like to manage their own properties. Others do not like being called out in the middle of the night because the toilet in a rental unit is overflowing, and they prefer some form of absentee ownership.

The major benefits of owning real estate include potential appreciation, income, and tax shelters. While it is true that real estate was an excellent investment in the 1970s and early 1980s, it is not clear that real estate in general will be a good investment thereafter. Each parcel of real estate is unique and must be considered on its own merits. As a general rule, the three most important rules in selecting real estate are (1) location, (2) location, and (3) location. Two identical buildings located in different places may have substantially different values and investment potential.

IMPORTANT CONCEPTS

Amortization
Cash flow
Collateralized Mortgage Obligations (CMOs)
Condominium
Cooperative
Down payment
Equity buildup
Financial leverage
GNMA Pass-Through Certificates
Government National Mortgage Association (GNMA or Ginny Mae)
Limited partnership

Mortgage pool
Ownership
Partnership
Public and private programs (partnerships)
Purchase-money mortgage
Real estate
Real Estate Investment Trust (REIT)
Real Estate Mortgage Conduit (REMIC)
Return on equity
Return on investment
Second mortgage
Unit Investment Trust

QUESTIONS AND EXERCISES

1. Cite five methods of owning and investing in real estate.
2. Real estate investors often use financial leverage to help them acquire property. What risks do you foresee with such highly leveraged investments?

3. Describe the three components of the investor's equity in a real estate investment.

4. Park View Towers is a high-rise rental building that is owned by a group of investors. The gross rental income is $500,000 per year. Annual mortgage payments are $210,000, and annual operating expenses (excluding taxes) are $58,000. The owners' total investment is $1 million and their equity is $2.5 million. Calculate what the investors can expect to receive in terms of (a) return on investment and (b) return on equity. Disregard taxes.

5. If you had the opportunity, would you invest in Park View Towers? Explain.

6. Many homeowners could borrow against the equity in their homes to make additional investments. What do you think of this idea?

7. Mark and Lisa are considering the purchase of a new, three-bedroom home. The total purchase price is $150,000, and the best financing terms are a 25-year mortgage at 12 percent with a 20 percent down payment. Using the monthly mortgage information in this chapter, how much will it cost them (total) to finance this home?

8. Check with local mortgage lenders (such as banks, savings and loan associations, mortgage companies) and find the following:
   a. What information do they require on loan applications?
   b. Can a prospective homebuyer save money by shopping for a mortgage? Compare the current rates on a $100,000 mortgage.
   c. How do terms and conditions vary for homeowners or investors (rental property) for a $100,000 mortgage?

9. What are the advantages and disadvantages of limited partnership investments in real estate?

10. How do REITs differ from mutual funds?

11. Examine the portfolios of several real estate stocks (listing can be found in *Value Line*). Explain their similarities and differences.

12. What is a Unit Investment Trust?

13. Explain the concept of a mortgage pool.

14. What are the benefits of government-backed mortgage pools?

15. Determine what a good real estate investment in your area would be if you had $500,000 to invest. Explain your decision and estimate your returns.

CHAPTER 18

ANTIQUES, GEMS, AND OTHER INVESTMENTS

ANTIQUES AND ART	The Diamond Market
Components of Value	**OTHER INVESTMENTS**
Fraud?	Gold
Suggestions for Investors	Silver
GEMS	**CONCLUSION**
Caveat Emptor	**IMPORTANT CONCEPTS**
How to Buy Gems	**QUESTIONS AND**
The Four-C Grading Standard	**EXERCISES**

nvestments take many forms, including stocks, bonds, real estate, antiques, art, gems, gold, and other assets. Besides the obvious advantage of diversifying in different types of assets, antiques, art, gems, and some forms of gold are a highly visible form of wealth. Antiques can be used, art can be seen, and gems and gold can be worn. If you are fortunate, they may appreciate in value and be profitable investments. But don't count on it. As explained in the following sections, dealing in antiques, art, and gems is a risky form of investment.

ANTIQUES AND ART

The executive director of an auction gallery was invited to a convent located in Yonkers, New York, to appraise a collection of paintings. While dining there, he noted a sugar bowl that had been lovingly repainted by the sisters. On closer inspection, the bowl had the letter "F" on its bottom. The "F" stood for Firenze, which is Italian for Florence. The bowl had been crafted in the sixteenth century for the Medici family. The sisters' bowl was sold at auction for $180,000.

A Scarsdale, New York, businessman brought a copper and sheephorn dagger to Sotheby's for an appraisal on one of their "Heirloom Discovery Days." **Sotheby Parke Bernet Inc.** (the *t* in Bernet is pronounced) is a London-based auction house. The businessman's grandfather was a fur trader and had given the dagger to him. The dagger turned out to be a relic of the Tlingit Indian tribe of the Pacific Northwest, and it brought $72,000 at an auction.

A St. Louis paperweight sold at **Christie's,** another London-based auction house, for $106,510. And a decoy of a Canada goose fetched $12,500 at Sotheby's New York outlet. A Chippendale carved cherrywood block-front, bonnet-top, chest-on-chest, dated 1760–1790, sold for $45,000; and a Pilgrim Century carved and painted pine and oak chest, dated 1685, sold for $18,000.

A long-lost painting was discovered at a home for delinquent boys in Manchester, England, where it had been for more than 100 years. The painting was a 9-by-6-foot oil titled *Icebergs* by Frederic Edwin Church. In an auction at Sotheby's that lasted less than four minutes, the Church painting sold for $2.5 million. In a different auction at Sotheby's New York, Van Gogh's painting "Paysage au Soleil Levant" sold for $9.9 million, and Toulouse-Lautrec's "La Clownesse Cha-U-Kao" sold for $5.3 million.

At Christie's $82.5 million was paid for Van Gogh's "Portrait of Dr. Gachet," and $78 million for Renoir's "Au Moulin de la Galette." Picasso, Monet, Degas, and Chagall are examples of other well-known artists whose works command high prices.

These examples highlight the fact that investors and collectors are willing to pay large sums for a wide variety of items ranging from daggers and duck decoys to paintings. Some of these items were discovered by accident by someone who recognized their true value. The dream of finding such "gold mines" lures many people to garage sales, flea markets, and auctions, and to collect everything from barbed wire to weather vanes. Perhaps you are already a collector, or you are interested in *objets d'art*. Although each *objet* is unique (or at least you hope so), the following guidelines may help you determine their value.

Components of Value

Investing in works of art is different from investing in stocks and bonds. One difference is the uniqueness of art. There is only one version of a Renoir but millions of stock certificates of IBM. Another difference is that art is a long-term investment, to be held five years or longer, whereas many stockholders buy shares in the morning and sell them before lunch. A third difference concerns the marketability of each. Although Church's *Icebergs* sold in less than four minutes, there is a limited market for most works. Finally, there is no analytical framework for analyzing the relative merits of different types of art. Therefore, there may be a wide range of values on the same object. For example, the executrix of an estate called an appraiser to appraise a number of items, including one painting. The appraiser valued the painting at $1000. The executrix sold it to a dealer for $1200, who, in turn sold it to another dealer for $2500. The second dealer took it to Parke Bernet (before the merger with Sotheby), which sold it for $34,000[1]

Although there is no analytical framework, here are some guidelines offered by Robert Schonfeld, head of Institutional Services at Sotheby Parke Bernet.[2]

---

[1] Gigi Mahon, "Investing in Art," *Barron's,* July 16, 1979, 4.
[2] Forum: "Investing in Art," *American Artist,* February 1980.

Because each object is unique, it must be considered on its own merits. According to Schonfeld, the four basic **components of value** of any work of art are

- The quality of the object
- The physical condition it is in
- The historical importance, including its origin and ownership
- Its rarity

Paul Revere's invoice to the Continental Congress for his ride from Boston to New York when he announced the Boston Tea Party, a filthy four-inch square scrap of paper, sold for $70,000 at auction. It commanded that price because of its rarity and historical importance.

In addition to the four basic components of value, four other components must be considered:

- Aesthetic value—its beauty.
- Intrinsic value—its material value; i.e., gold, jewels, and so on.
- Fair market value: what you can sell the object for on the open market. Fair market value is used for estate tax purposes.
- Replacement value: the cost to replace the object if it is stolen or destroyed. Replacement value is frequently used for insurance purposes.

Although investing in works of art is different than investing in stocks and bonds or real estate, all investments have one thing in common—their values go up and down. After artist Andy Warhol died in 1987, the value of his "Black Marilyn" prints soared from $6,000 to $70,000! However, the prints of Marilyn Monroe were not unique—there were 2,500 copies—and the value had fallen to $12,000 in 1990. That still represents a good return if one bought a print at $6,000, but a big loss for those who bought them at high prices.

The financial returns on art have been low. According to a study by Bruno Frey, a professor at the University of Zurich who examined the sales of 1,200 works of art from 1635 to 1987, the annual return, adjusted for inflation, was 1 to 3 percent.[3] The best investment was a 26-percent annual return on a painting that was held for 28 years and sold in 1913. The worst return was on John Singer Sargent's "San Virgilio," bought for $35,280, held 27 years, and sold in 1952 for $294. Gilbert Edelson, counsel for the Art Dealers Association of America, claims that 99 percent of all art works decline in value.

Fraud?

Knowing the components of value and being able to recognize true works of art are two different things. Many reproductions of art are sold as "originals," and many "limited editions" turn out to be numerous. In an effort to curb abuses in art, New York State enacted a law in 1981 requiring art dealers offering prints for more than $100 (exclusive of frames) to identify the artist, the medium (litho-

[3] Christie Brown, "Welcome, Suckers!," *Forbes*, June 25, 1990, 282–285.

graph, etching, and so on), and the number of prints in the limited edition. If the print is signed by the artist, the signature must be validated. If the print is not signed, the dealers are required to reveal whether the artist was alive when the print was made and whether the artist approved of the print.

Nevertheless, fakes do exist. The director of an art gallery that specializes in Miró lithographs has run into fakes and forgeries.[4] He has seen unsigned prints acquire "signatures." In addition, he has seen certificates describing prints as being "signed Miró," which is not the same as saying signed *by* Miró.

Some "Picasso prints" add to the confusion between originals and reproductions.[5] Some limited-edition Picasso prints (500 in each edition) are printed from master plates created by artists working from photographs of Picasso's works that are owned by Marina Picasso, the artist's granddaughter. On each print, Marina writes in pencil, "Collection of Marina Picasso." Each print is priced from $800 to $1500.

The lesson to be learned is that a good artist's works will be copied and duplicated and fakes will be sold. There are countless other artists, including Rembrandt, Chagall, and others, whose fakes and forgeries are bought and sold by art dealers and collectors.[6]

Finally, some limited-edition prints cause confusion because an artist may sign a limited number of prints, say 500, and then produce a larger number of unsigned prints.

Because it is possible to forge and misrepresent works of art, Sotheby's is very cautious in describing what it is selling. The rule is that items are "As Is," and potential buyers can handle the items for sale so they can make their own assessment of their authenticity and value. However, Sotheby's will take back items within five years if they are not what they are represented to be. Even Church's *Icebergs* was listed in the catalogue as "ascribed" to Church. Sotheby's did not say that it "is" a Church.

Buying stolen and damaged antiques and art works are additional considerations. In 1967 a New York couple purchased Marc Chagall's "Le Marchand de Bestiaux" from an art dealer for $17,000. They did not know that the painting had been stolen from the Guggenheim Museum. In fact, the Guggenheim did not know it was missing until it took inventory in 1970. In 1986, the Guggenheim discovered who had the painting and demanded its return. The wrongful owner refused and the Guggenheim is suing for it. Meanwhile the wrongful owner is suing the art dealer, who in turn is suing the dealer from whom he bought the stolen work.

Actor Sylvester Stallone paid $1.7 million for "Pietà" by William Bouguereau, plus an $85,000 fee to an art consultant who advised him that it was an excellent investment. He bought the painting sight unseen. Needless to say, Sly was un-

---

[4] Cynthia Saltzman, "Abuses in Art Prints Stir Effort to Ensure that Collectors Get What They Paid For," *The Wall Street Journal,* August 10, 1981, 19.

[5] *Ibid.*

[6] Daniel Grant, "Collecting Art? Beware the Wrinkles," *The New York Times,* November 29, 1987, F9.

happy to discover that the painting had been extensively damaged—there were slashes on the surface—and that it had been partially restored. He sued the consultant for $35 million. Look before you leap!

Suggestions for Investors

By now it should be clear that investing in antiques or *objets d'art* requires a lot of specialized knowledge, skill, and luck. This should not, however, discourage "small investors" from investing in such items. Interestingly, about 84 percent of the items sold at Sotheby's went for under $1000. Therefore, small investors are an important factor in the market for antiques, art, and collectibles.

Reputable Dealers

In order to avoid some of the pitfalls that have been mentioned, investors should use reputable dealers. Although there are thousands of reputable dealers, two firms stand out because of their history, size, and international reputations—Sotheby Parke Bernet and Christie's. Sotheby's was founded in London in 1744 and now has a network of auction centers in 19 countries. Today it is the world's largest auction house, dealing in everything from antiques to real estate. For example, it sold Hollywood director Dino De Laurentiis' Beverly Hills estate, "The Knoll," to singer Kenny Rogers for $14.5 million.

James Christie opened his establishment in London in 1766, next door to Thomas Gainsborough, the artist. Although there were at least 60 auction houses in London at that time, Christie's survived and prospered over the years. Today it is the second-largest auction house in the world.

There are other dealers of equal quality, but because of their relatively small size or limited specialization they do not get the same press coverage as those that handle "headline-grabbing" sales, such as a Velázquez for $5.5. million (Christie's) or a Turner for $6.4 million (Sotheby's). Finding reputable dealers is worth the effort you will have to put into it.

Recognize Risks

You may have the impression that all antiques and works of art are appreciating in value. That impression is wrong. The art market has ups and downs just like the stock market. One reason prices go down is that things go out of style. For example, eighteenth-century portraits of English lords and their ladies are not as popular today as in times past.

Speculative excesses in markets is another reason for price declines. The boom and bust of Surrealist art is one example. Works such as "Beer Cans in Bronze" by Jasper Johns sold for $1000 in 1960 and $90,000 in 1972. By the late 1970s, prices in the Surrealist market were declining, and "Beer Cans" was worth about $45,000.

Changes in economic activity can also affect prices. Antique and art dealers usually finance most of their inventories. When interest rates reached 18 percent

---

BOX 18-1

MARIA'S POTS

Maria Martinez of San Ildefonso, New Mexico, was a leading American Indian potter. She was best known for her black bowls and plates, some of which sold for thousands of dollars. Having a "Maria" is a must for any collector of Indian pots.

A collector of Indian pots visited the Studio of Indian Arts in the San Ildefonso pueblo where selected pieces of Maria's pottery were on display and for sale. There he learned that Maria stopped her potting some years ago because of her age. Shortly after this visit, he went to an art gallery in Albuquerque, New Mexico. Hoping to find a bargain, he asked a clerk if the gallery had any interesting pots. She pointed to four black pots on the shelf and told him that they were "Marias." She went on to say that she had watched Maria making the pots less than two weeks ago. He asked the price of the pots and was told that they were about $400 each. Knowing that they were frauds, he told the clerk that he would think about buying them and would return tomorrow. After he left the store, he called the police. The next morning he returned with two plainclothes detectives who heard the same story from the clerk.

Several months later, the pottery ring that sold unsuspecting junk pots at high prices was closed down by the law. Investors in *objets d'art* do not have the same degree of protection from fraud as investors in the stock market.

---

and higher in the early 1980s, dealers were willing to reduce prices to sell their wares. Buyers, on the other hand, could invest their funds at high rates and get virtually risk-free returns. Accordingly, they were willing to part with their liquidity only if the prices on the tangible assets were right—low.

There are a few common mistakes that novice investors make:

- They pay too much for second-rate works of first-rate artists. For example, tennis star John McEnroe paid $205,000 for Picasso's "Maison à Juan-Les-Pins" at a Sotheby auction in 1988. The painting was one of Picasso's minor works. It had reportedly been on sale at a local gallery for $125,000 shortly before the auction.

- Know what you are buying. Buyers of American furniture, for example, should know that the Hepplewhite period was from 1785–1805, the Sheraton Period was from 1805–1820, and so on. They should know whether dovetail joints were made by hand or machine. Much of the furniture made during and after the American Empire Period (1820–1840) was machine-

made. Similarly, prospective buyers should know the characteristics, ornamentation, motifs, hardware, and other aspects of the furniture before they buy. Acquiring such knowledge takes time and effort. It cannot be acquired the first time one goes to an auction.

- The atmosphere of an auction is designed to create excitement and to induce buyers to make higher bids. Some buyers go into bidding frenzies and bid the ante up when they should have stopped. Finally, items are commonly sold as is, with no guarantees. Examine the items before the auction and deal only with reputable firms.

How Much to Invest?

Some financial advisors suggest investing 10 percent of an investment portfolio in tangible assets such as antiques, art, gold, and jewels. If an investment portfolio is worth $150,000, about $15,000 could be invested in tangible assets. But $15,000 does not buy very much today and eliminates most major works — unless they are discovered like Church's *Icebergs*.

Limited budgets restrict investors to relatively low-cost investments such as prints, Eskimo carvings, Indian pottery, and bronzes. Such investments or collections can be seen and enjoyed, which is one of their benefits.

GEMS

For thousands of years, precious stones have been used as a store of wealth. They are sought after because of their beauty, scarcity, durability, and size; moreover, they are marketable throughout the world. Because most precious stones are relatively small and easy to transport, they are a favorite of owners who want to move their wealth on short notice and attract a minimum of attention. Thus, investors who live in politically unstable countries may prefer diamonds to shares of stock or real estate.

In recent years diamonds and colored stones, such as rubies and emeralds, have become an increasingly popular form of investment. To a large extent, the demand for diamonds stems from an extensive marketing campaign by **De Beers Consolidated Mines, Ltd.**, the world's principal miner and marketer of diamonds. Essentially, the campaign spread notions that every bride should have a diamond, that the size of the diamond reflects the degree of the giver's love and wealth, and that diamonds are a girl's best friend. In the 1960s and 1970s, it was fashionable to wear gems with casual dress, even jeans. Between 1970 and 1980, the wholesale price of a one-carat **D flawless** (these terms will be explained shortly) diamond increased from $1800 to $53,000! By 1982, however, the price had declined to $14,000.

Colored stones received increased attention when Geraldine Rockefeller Dodge auctioned nine rubies for $690,000. In 1979 a 4.12-carat pigeon's blood Burmese ruby sold for over $400,000 at a Christie's auction in Geneva. That

TABLE 18-1   Rarity of Selected Gems[a]

Gems	Color	Scale
Ruby	Red	10
Emerald	Green	9
Sapphire	Blue	9
Black opal	Black	8
Cat's eye chrysoberyl	Honey	8
Tsavorite	Green	6
Blue topaz	Blue	4

[a] 1 to 10 scale; 10 is the rarest.

amounts to $100,639 per carat. (A carat is a unit of weight used for precious stones and is equal to 200 milligrams.)

The demand for other colored stones also increased. The color and rarity of selected types of gems are listed in Table 18-1. Rubies are the most rare and blue topaz the least rare of the gems listed. Some experts argue that blue topaz is not sufficiently rare to be considered an investment. In addition, the market was flooded with "treated" topaz. A chalky white topaz is irradiated with gamma rays and heated. This process produces a brilliant blue topaz — until the color fades.

Caveat Emptor

Caveat emptor is Latin for "let the buyer beware." Doctoring gems, using synthetics, and selling inferior-quality stones are widespread practices. For example, almost all aquamarines are heated to remove the greenish color and intensify the blue color. The heat treatment is also applied to sapphires to darken their blue color. In this modern age of technology, lasers are used to "heal" certain internal flaws in diamonds. Such doctoring can usually be spotted by a qualified gemologist with a spectroscope. However, even experts can be fooled.

Consider the case of Abe Nassi, an internationally known expert on rubies.[7] While in Thailand, Nassi bought three rough ruby crystals that allegedly had been smuggled across the border from Burma, the source of the world's best rubies. Nassi sold the rubies to a dealer from London for a 25-percent profit. Shortly thereafter, the smugglers contacted Nassi and told him that they had a fourth ruby for sale. Nassi became suspicious after he saw the stone and called the **Gemological Institute of America (GIA)** in New York to confirm his doubts. GIA has a laboratory that is internationally recognized for certification of gems. Although the first three stones were genuine, the fourth was a fake. It was a Kashan ruby, a synthetic made in Texas for under $100 per carat. Had Nassi not checked with GIA, he might have lost $210,000 on that transaction. Others have not been so fortunate and have bought rubies made from red automobile taillights.

[7] Paul Gibson, "A Tsavorite for your Christmas List?" *Forbes,* December 8, 1980, 121–130.

Most investors do not go around the world like Nassi looking for gems. Frequently they get advertisements in the mail or telephone calls telling them of the advantages of investing in diamonds and colored stones. For example, they may be offered three carats of emeralds for $10 if they buy now because supplies are limited. The emeralds are genuine, but emerald chips sell for about $.045 per carat. Against this background of con artists and ripoffs, how can investors buy gems intelligently?

How to Buy Gems

The first rule in buying gems is the same as the first rule in buying art works—use a reputable dealer. The better the dealer's reputation, the better off you are. Some experts suggest that investments should be purchased in major cities, such as New York and Chicago, where there are firms that handle such investments on a regular basis.

Second, deal only with firms that have a buyback policy. Many firms will buy back the stone at about the purchase price for a reasonable period of time after the purchase. For example, assume that a retailer pays $4000 for a diamond and sells it to a customer for $6000. After five years, the diamond appreciates to $12,000 at the wholesale price. The dealer can buy the diamond back from the customer at, say, $10,000, and they both make a nice profit. The dealer, of course, can sell the gem again.

Third, have the stones, especially diamonds, certified by a laboratory. GIA operates the principal grading laboratory. Certificates from other laboratories and dealers may penalize the price of a stone by as much as 20 percent.

Some European laboratories seal stones in plastic containers after they are inspected, and they will not stand behind their certification if the seal is broken. They claim that the stone could have been switched. While there is some validity to their claim, investors can have a laser print made. A laser print for a diamond, for example, is unique, just like a fingerprint.

Fourth, buy the best quality stone you can acquire at the price you are willing to pay. Most investors favor diamonds because a uniform grading scale exists for them. (We will discuss the grading scale shortly.) There is no uniform grading scale for colored stones. Basically, the redder the ruby or the greener the emerald the better. The presence of other hues reduces their value. Another advantage of colored stones is that their prices held or increased in 1981, while diamond prices declined sharply. But not all diamonds perform the same. The price of a one-carat D flawless declined by about one third, while the price of half-carat stones of the same quality scarcely declined at all.

The Four-C Grading Standard

The quality of diamonds is determined by four grade areas, each of which has variations. The grade areas in order of their importance are **carat weight, cut, color,** and **clarity**—the **four Cs.**

Carat Weight

The carat (200 milligrams) is the unit of measure used to weigh diamonds. Each carat contains 100 points of weight, in the same way that each dollar contains 100 cents. A one-carat diamond can range in weight from 97 to 105 points. However, investors pay for each point they purchase.

It takes about a four-carat rough diamond crystal to produce a one-carat finished diamond. Approximately 90 percent of the diamonds mined weigh less than one carat in the rough state. This is why large diamonds are so rare. Although most diamonds come from South Africa, diamonds have been found near Murfreesboro, Arkansas. The largest diamond found there was 40.23 carats. Tourists, who pay the State of Arkansas for digging there, have found several other large diamonds and many smaller ones.

The value of diamonds increases sharply with their weight. If a one-half-carat diamond costs, say $10,000, then a one-carat diamond of the same grade might cost $50,000. Diamonds used in jewelry usually weigh less than one carat and have color and clarity below investment grade.

Cut

The object in cutting a diamond is to place each of the flat polished surfaces, called **facets**, so that most of the light that strikes the diamond is reflected back to the eye in a wide range of colors. The cut gives a diamond its brilliance and fire. If the diamond is not cut to maximize its optical qualities, light will pass out of the bottom of the stone instead of being reflected back to the eye. (See Figure 18-1.)

Sometimes optical quality is sacrificed in order to gain weight and size. Weight is one of the primary determinants of a diamond's value, but cut is even more

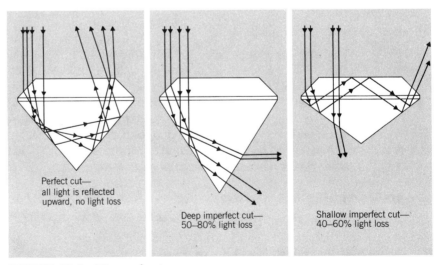

Perfect cut—
all light is reflected
upward, no light loss

Deep imperfect cut—
50–80% light loss

Shallow imperfect cut—
40–60% light loss

FIGURE 18-1   Diamond cuts.

TABLE 18-2 Diamond Color and Clarity Grading Scales

Color Grading Scale		Clarity Grading Scale	
Colorless	D E F	Flawless Internally flawless	F IF
Near colorless	G H I J	Very very slight inclusions	VVS$_1$ VVS$_2$
Faint yellow	K L M		
Very slight yellow	N O P Q R S	Very slight inclusions Slight inclusions	VS$_1$ VS$_2$ SI$_1$ SI$_2$
Light yellow	T U V W X Y Z	Imperfect	I$_1$ I$_2$ I$_3$
Fancy yellow			

important. There are mathematical formulas to determine the weight a diamond would be if it were recut to proper proportions to gain maximum optical quality. This reduced weight is called the **appraised base weight** or **adjusted weight**, which is less than the diamond's weight on weighing scales. Investors should be concerned with both the scale weight and the adjusted weight.

Color

The color of a diamond must be determined under laboratory conditions and classified into one of 24 separate categories. The Gemological Institute of America has specified procedures for color grading and uses the scale shown in Table 18-2.

The color grades run from D, which is colorless, to the end of the alphabet, where there is an increasing amount of yellow. The best quality diamond has no color at all. However, most diamonds have some yellow. In fact, nature sometimes produces brightly colored "fancy yellow" diamonds, which are valued very highly. Because color is in vogue, some dealers are irradating off-color diamonds to produce fancy colors. Although such stones are salable as jewelry, they are not

suitable as investments. Investment grades usually end at H, which appears white under the naked eye, but has some yellow according to the GIA color-grading scale.

Color is very important. A one-carat D flawless might sell for $44,000, while a one-carat F flawless might sell for $24,000. Proper certification is important to investors, because only an expert can tell the difference between a D and an F.

Clarity

Clarity deals with the imperfections, or inclusions, found in diamonds and are determined under a 10-power microscope. Some of the imperfections are caused by nature, and others include nicks and cracks. As shown in Table 18-2, the grades run from flawless F to imperfect I_3 The lowest investment grade is VS_2, which means a very slight inclusion.

Clarity affects the value of a diamond less than cut and color because most flaws do not reduce a diamond's brilliance and fire.

The Diamond Market

The major source of diamonds is the Republic of South Africa, although diamonds are found in some other African nations and in the U.S.S.R. DeBeers Consolidated Mines, Ltd., a South African company whose stock is traded over the counter, controls about 90 percent of the diamond market. A subsidiary of DeBeers, **Central Selling Organization**, attempts to control the price of diamonds by limiting the supply and establishing prices. The Central Selling Organization's sales are made by the **Diamond Trading Company,** another subsidiary located in London. The diamond trading corporation sells to about 250 clients who are required to buy all of the diamonds offered to them. Those who are not members of this select group must purchase diamonds from the members, at a higher price, or from some other source that does not market their diamonds through the Diamond Trading Company.

The Diamond Trading Company has about 10 offerings, known as **sights,** each year. The clients purchase an assortment of rough stones, known as a **series,** at the Trading Company's prices. The series takes into account the clients' needs.

The Diamond Trading Company increased the price of diamonds about twice a year until 1980, when diamond prices fell sharply. The basic reason was that high interest rates made it impractical for dealers to hold large inventories that had to be financed, and investors who could get high, risk-free returns in securities were reluctant to buy diamonds and other tangible assets. The result was lower diamond prices.

Political instability in the Republic of South Africa may also affect diamond prices in the future. Although DeBeers' near monopoly on the market has resulted in higher prices to date, there is no assurance that economic and political conditions in the future will permit the continuance of an orderly diamond market.

Finally, the Diamond Trading Company sells most of the diamonds to cutters and dealers in New York, who in turn sell to jewelry wholesalers and retailers.

| BOX 18-2 |

WANT TO BUY IT? HAVE I GOT A DEAL FOR YOU!

Not very long ago, Larry, a close friend, walked into my office to show me the Civil War belt buckle he had just bought. It was a large oval brass buckle with "U.S." stamped on the face. The back was filled with lead and had several fastening devices to attach it to the belt. The buckle was good-looking, and I decided that I wanted one for myself. After searching through various antique stores and antique shows, I discovered a Confederate sword belt buckle. It too was made of brass, but it was round and had some intricate designs and the letters "CS," standing for Confederate States, on it. The buckle cost $11 and I bought it. Soon after that Larry and I went to an antique show where I met the dealer who had sold Larry his U.S. buckle. I described the buckle I had bought and the dealer's eyes grew large and round. He said, "Do you know what that buckle is worth?" I replied, "Sure, I just paid $11 for it." He walked over to his booth and looked in a book called *Accoutrement Plates North and South 1861 – 1865 with Comparative Values* by William Gavin. After a moment he showed me a picture of the buckle I had just bought and said, "Is that it?" It was, and the book listed the value of the buckle at $250! I immediately offered to sell him the buckle because I knew where there were more buckles just like mine. However, he declined the offer, even at the substantially reduced price I generously offered him. Afterward I talked to other collectors who pointed out that the value in the book did not reflect the "true" value of the buckle for a variety of reasons. In fact, they said I would be lucky if I could sell it to anyone for the $11 I paid for it because there was a very limited market in such things. For all practical purposes, there is no market in used Civil War belt buckles. They make interesting conversation pieces, but very few people are willing to pay what the book says they are worth.

The prices of diamonds may vary considerably among the various levels in the diamond market and even at the same level. Investors offering to sell their gems to advertised jewelry dealers may get widely diverging price offers.

OTHER INVESTMENTS

There is no limit to the range of investment opportunities available. The major constraints facing most investors are usually the amount of funds available for investment and the time and knowledge required to acquire the investment. Of course, you can always hire an agent to do the investing for you.

Many investors began as collectors of stamps, coins, and other tangibles, and over the years their collections appreciated in value. Today, the older collections can be sold or traded and provide the owners with handsome returns. Would you believe that a two-cent Hawaiian "missionary" stamp sold for $230,000 and an 1892-S silver dollar is worth more than $13,000?

All that is well and good, but what about investors who are starting today with investment funds, but not very much experience? Frequently, these and other investors are caught up in the speculative booms that ultimately go bust. By way of illustration, consider gold and silver investments in recent years.

Gold

The average price of gold increased from $36.41 per ounce in 1970 to $307.50 per ounce in 1979. In 1980 it soared to $850 per ounce, and many hopeful speculators were forecasting that it would reach $1000. Part of the demand for gold came from oil-rich Middle Eastern nations. Middle Eastern investors, benefiting from rising oil prices, put part of their wealth into gold. But when oil prices fell, high interest rates made the cost of financing gold prohibitive, and a worldwide recession reduced consumer purchases of gold items, gold prices fell sharply. In 1982 the price of gold fell to $350 per ounce, and fell below $300 per ounce in 1985. Those who bought gold at the lofty prices in 1980 and did not sell it had large paper losses. Some hoped that gold would "come back." It recovered to about $380 per ounce in 1990. Investors can invest in gold in several ways.

Gold Bullion

Gold bullion is available in bars of 0.995 fine gold. Each ingot weighs 32.15 ounces (1 kilogram) and is referred to as a **kilobar.** Investors who want a smaller amount can purchase 1 gram or 1 ounce. The manufacturers of gold bars usually certify the weight and purity of the gold by imprinting their stamp on it. Buying gold in this form requires a safe place for storage and weight and purity certification when it is sold.

Coins

Buying coins that contain gold is another popular form of investment. Each of the South African gold **Krugerrands** weighs 1.07 troy ounces and contains exactly 1 ounce of gold. The $\frac{1}{2}$ Krugerrand contains $\frac{1}{2}$ ounce of gold; the $\frac{1}{4}$ Krugerrand contains $\frac{1}{4}$ ounce; and the $\frac{1}{10}$ contains $\frac{1}{10}$ ounce of gold. These three coins look like the 1-ounce Krugerrands except for the inclusion of $\frac{1}{2}$, $\frac{1}{4}$, or $\frac{1}{10}$ ounce markings. Since the coins contain known amounts of gold, it is easy to determine their values, which are listed daily in some newspapers.

Other coins that contain gold are the South African gold 2-Rand (0.2354 troy ounces of gold), the Austrian gold 100 Corona (0.9802 troy ounces of gold), the Mexican gold 50 Peso (1.2056 troy ounces of gold), the Canadian gold $50 Maple Leaf (1 troy ounce of gold), and the U.S. Eagle (1 troy ounce of gold, as well as $\frac{1}{2}$, $\frac{1}{4}$, and $\frac{1}{10}$ ounce).

Gold coins usually sell at a **premium** above their metal content. The premiums may vary from 0 to 33 percent. When a coin sells for less than the value of its metal content, it is trading at a **discount.** The prices of gold coins are published in *Barron's.*

Stocks

Buying shares of gold mining companies is another way to participate in the gold market. For example, Driefontein Consolidated Ltd. is the world's richest gold mine and lowest cost producer in South Africa. Free State is another South African gold producer. South African mining stocks are traded over the counter. Gold mines are also located in the United States and Canada. Homestake Mining and Hecla Mining are two examples. Both are traded on the New York Stock Exchange.

Futures Contracts

Gold is traded like other commodities in the futures market. Investors buy and sell contracts for future delivery (called futures contracts) of the various commodities. Commodities are explained in Chapter 21.

Precious Metals Funds

Some mutual funds specialize in investing in precious metals. Lexington Gold Fund, Bull Bear Group's Gold Investments Fund, and others offer investors a managed portfolio of investments in gold and other metals. There is less hassle investing in such funds than in buying gold or futures.

Silver

The price of silver increased from $9 per ounce in July 1979 to $50 per ounce in January 1980, and then came tumbling down to $10.80 per ounce two months later. In 1985 it traded for about $6 per ounce. The reason for the boom in silver prices was that Texas billionaires William and Bunker Hunt, together with several Saudi Arabian investors, tried to **corner** the silver market. "Corner" means to control the supply of a commodity in order to force the price up. The Hunts and their Arab partners had acquired more than 200 million ounces of silver, more than anyone else in the world, except for a few national treasuries. At $50 per ounce, their holdings were worth more than $1 billion.

The corner did not work because the high prices brought silver from places the Hunts never considered. Americans stood in long lines to sell their silverware, jewelry, and coins containing silver. The increased supply and other factors, including **margin calls** from their brokers (see Chapter 6 for a discussion of margin), broke the corner. Do not feel sorry for the Hunts. Although they lost heavily in the silver crash, they are still rich.

Investors who are interested in silver have the same avenues of investment open to them as they have in the gold market.

The boom and bust in the silver market illustrates another hazard faced by investors. Greed, fraud, and changing economic conditions contribute to speculative excesses in real estate, art, and commodities. The lesson to be learned here is that there is no such thing as a perfectly safe investment in real assets.

CONCLUSION

While writing this chapter I received an advertisement in the mail to buy original hand-colored lithographs from the First Royal Octavo Edition of John James Audubon. Audubon is best known for his wildlife paintings of birds made during the mid-1800s. The advertisement said the prints were on sale unframed for $135 each ($175 framed) and could be ordered by calling a toll-free number and charging the purchase on a major credit card or by sending a check. The gallery would select the print for the buyer.

Suspecting a rip-off, I called the toll-free number and asked several questions about the prints and the gallery. The prints had to be purchased sight unseen, and the gallery was less than a year old. Then I asked a local museum about Audubon prints and about the gallery. The response was that the gallery is a legitimate operation. The First Royal Octavo Edition of *Birds of America* contains about 500 lithographs and is worth about $10,000 at auction. The gallery is selling the lithographs at $135 each, which amounts to $67,500. The prints were designed to be in the book, not to be sold separately. Are they worth $135 each from the book? You be the judge.

IMPORTANT CONCEPTS

Adjusted weight (diamonds)
Appraised base weight (diamonds)
Carat weight
Caveat emptor
Central Selling Organization
Christie's
Clarity (diamonds)
Color (diamonds)
Components of value
Corner
Cut (diamonds)
DeBeers Consolidated Mines, Ltd.
D flawless (diamonds)

Diamond Trading Company
Discount (coins)
Facet (diamonds)
Four Cs (grading standard)
Gemological Institute of America
Kilobar
Krugerrand
Margin call
Premium (coins)
Series (diamonds)
Sights (diamonds)
Sotheby Parke Bernet

QUESTIONS AND EXERCISES

1. Define the terms "antique" and "antiquity" (check with local antique dealers and a dictionary).

2. How does investing in artwork and antiques differ from investing in stocks?

3. List basic components of value that must be considered when investing in any work of art or antiques.

4. Visit a local antique dealer who carries a varied stock and find out the following information:
   a. How do collectors' perspectives differ from those of investors?
   b. What items does the dealer recommend for investment purposes?
   c. What terms and conditions of sale does the dealer offer? For example, is there a buy-back policy?

5. What techniques would you use to spot frauds among investments in tangible assets?

6. A recent advertisement showed a photograph of 12-carat aquamarine valued at $5,000 and a 12-carat natural (not synthetic) blue topaz valued at $196. Both looked the same. Which would you buy? Why?

7. What do the terms "carat" and "point" mean when applied to precious stones?

8. As an investor, which would you prefer, a ruby or a sapphire of equal weight? Explain.

9. Cite four rules for buying gems.

10. Explain what is meant by the "four C" grading standard for diamonds.

11. Check with a local diamond dealer. What is the current price of a 1-carat D flawless diamond? What was it last year at this time? How stable is that market?

12. Describe how the diamond market is controlled by DeBeers Consolidated Mines.

13. Why do gold coins sell for more than the value of the gold they contain?

14. Is it possible to "corner" the silver market? Explain.

15. Given the current economic outlook, would you prefer to hold real assets or securities? Specify which you would buy now.

PART FIVE

SPECIAL SITUATIONS

High Flyers
Speculative Investments

O nce I attended a lecture given by a man who was selling commodities options. He opened the lecture by stating: "Happiness will not buy money; if you are greedy and want to make a lot of money, speculate in commodities options." Shortly after that speech the firm he represented was indicted on several counts of fraud and went out of business. Nevertheless, his message of greed, speculation, and the possibility of making a lot of money entices many investors to trade in puts and calls, convertible securities, and commodities. This part of the book deals with those topics. Chapter 19 describes put and call options and shows how they can be used as a speculative or conservative investment medium. Chapter 20 focuses on convertible securities, including warrants and rights, and Chapter 21 is about commodities, which have great speculative appeal.

STOCK AND INDEX OPTIONS

O ptions trading is one of the most interesting areas of investment and speculation. Options have long been associated with speculation. For example, Aristotle, in his *Politics,* criticized Thales and his use of options. Thales was a man of moderate means who gained control of (cornered) the olive presses of Miletus. Thales believed that the next olive harvest would be a big one, and he secured options for the use of the presses at harvest time. When his forecast proved to be correct, he rented the presses at a substantial profit. In more recent history, a number of better known speculators on Wall Street, such as Commodore Vanderbilt, Daniel Drew, and Jay Gould, made use of options. In one instance Commodore Vanderbilt sold Daniel Drew, Jim Fisk, and Jay Gould a four-month option on 50,000 shares of the Boston, Hartford, and Erie Railroad at $70 per share for a $1 million premium. This sale was one phase of the colorful raids on the Erie stock.

Today options on stocks, Treasury securities, foreign currencies, stock market indexes, and bonds are traded on stock exchanges in the United States and in foreign markets. Trading is so widespread that options covering the same underlying interest (i.e., stock), and with the same contractual terms may be traded in more than one market at the same time. These are called **multiply traded options.**

BASIC TERMS

There are differences between options on stocks and options on debt securities, currencies, and stock indexes. In this chapter we focus primarily on options on stocks. In addition, there are differences between **American-style options** and **European-style options.** European-style refers to "internationally traded" options. Since most readers of this book will deal in options traded in the United States, we concentrate on American-style options. Two types of options are used to buy and sell stocks—calls and puts. As in any transaction, there are buyers and sellers. The buyers of options are called **option holders,** and the sellers are called **option writers.**

Call Options

A **call option** is a contract to buy a specified number of shares of stock at a predetermined price (exercise or strike price) on or before a stated date (expiration date). Options are generally for 100 shares of the underlying stock. The contract conveys the *right* to the option holder to exercise the option if it is to their advantage to do so. If the option is exercised, the option writer is *obligated* to sell stock to the holder at the agreed price. An example would be an investor who buys a call option on 100 shares of Lincoln Company at $40 per share for 90 days. The call option gives the holder the right to buy 100 shares of Lincoln Company at $40 per share at any time until the option expires. If the stock is selling for more than $40 per share, it is advantageous for the holder to exercise the option or sell it, as will be explained shortly.

Expiration Dates

The Options Clearing Corporation, which establishes rules for trading options, has three standardized expiration month cycles:

January, April, July, October

February, May, August, November

March, June, September, December

American-style options on stocks expire on the Saturday immediately following the third Friday of the expiration month. This should not be confused with the earlier **exercise cut-off time,** which is the business day preceding the **expiration date.** This means that brokers wanting to exercise an option must advise the exchange where the option is traded no later than the third Friday of the expiration month. The option expires the next day—Saturday.

American-style options may be exercised by the holder any time before it expires. **European-style** options may be exercised only during a specified period, which may be the business day before the option expires.

Trading in options of a particular expiration month normally begins about nine months earlier, so that at any given time there are options traded that have at least

three different expiration months. Option buyers and writers can choose among the expiration dates and select a maturity that matches their needs. For example, in December a buyer who wants a six-month option would buy one that expires in July.

Exercise Price

The **exercise price,** commonly called the **strike price,** is the price at which the option may be exercised. Most options are written so that the exercise price is close to the current value of the stock. The exercise price is generally set at 5- or 10-point intervals, depending on the price of the underlying stock. By way of illustration, if a stock underlying an option is selling for $34 per share when trading begins in the new expiration month, the exercise price will be fixed at $35. Other options on the same stock, but with different expiration dates, have exercise prices of $20, $25, and $30. For higher priced shares, the exercise price may be set at 10-point intervals, such as $150, $160, and $170.

Adjustments

Most options are written for 100 shares of stock. However, the number of shares covered by the option and the exercise price may be adjusted in the case of stock dividends, stock distributions, and stock splits. By way of illustration, suppose that an investor holds an option of a stock at an exercise price of $70 per share, and the stock is going to split 2 for 1. After the adjustment, the holder would have two options of 100 shares each on the stock at an exercise price of $35 per share. Special adjustments are made in the case of mergers and tender offers.

Cash Dividends

No adjustments to the terms of the option are usually made for *ordinary* cash dividends or distributions of less than 10 percent of the market value of the underlying stock. Adjustments may be made for larger cash distributions.

If the option is exercised prior to the ex-dividend date, the holder of the option receives the value of all dividends and rights to be distributed. For example, let us say that Lincoln Company declared a $0.50 cash dividend—an ordinary cash dividend—and that the stock went ex-dividend during the contract period covered by the option. However, holders who exercise options after the ex-dividend date are not entitled to receive it. In stock market jargon, the **payout is unprotected.**

Intrinsic Value and Time Value

The value of an option can be divided into two components, intrinsic value and time value. **Intrinsic value** is the difference between the *exercise price of the option* and the *market value of the underlying stock.* For example, suppose that the exercise price of an option is $50 per share and the market price of the underlying stock is $55 per share. The intrinsic value is $5 per share ($55 − $50 = $5). A stock option

with an intrinsic value is said to be **in the money.** In the previous example the option is $5 per share in the money.

Suppose the market price of the stock declines to $50 per share, which also happens to be the exercise price. Now the option has no intrinsic value; it is selling **at the money.** If the market price of the stock declines to, say, $47 per share, which is $3 per share less than the exercise price, the option will be $3 per share **out of the money.**

Time value is the value an option has in addition to its intrinsic value. Time value reflects the volatility of the underlying asset, whether the option is in the money or out of the money, and the length of time remaining until it expires. (The relationship between these variables and option premiums is explained in Appendix 19A, which examines the Black-Scholes Option Pricing Model.)

By way of illustration, suppose that a call option is trading at $1 per share, the exercise price of the option is $25, and the market price of the underlying stock is $25. There is no intrinsic value because the option is trading at the money. The $1 per share is entirely time value. The $1 per share time value reflects investors' expectations that the price of the underlying stock will increase sufficiently for them to make a profit.

Premium

A **premium** is the fee or price that an option buyer pays an option writer for the rights conveyed by the option. It does not include the commission paid to the broker for handling the transaction. It is not refundable, and it does not represent a down payment on the stock.

Stock premiums are expressed in dollar amounts such as $200 per option contract, which amounts to $2 per share. Premiums on other types of options may be expressed in basis points, yield to maturity, or in some other fashion. Stock premiums are determined by supply and demand for that option, the price of the underlying stock, its riskiness, and the maturity of the option. For example, Lincoln Company stock is selling for $40 per share. The premium for a three-month call option on Lincoln Company at $40 per share is $250, or $2.50 per share, while the premium on a six-month option is $400. Premiums for at-the-money options may range from 3 to 15 percent or more, depending on the factors mentioned previously. Premiums for in-the-money options may be substantially higher. For example, suppose the strike price of an option is $30 per share, the market value of the stock is $34, and the option is selling for $6.75. The premium, reflecting both intrinsic value and time value, is almost 20 percent.

Some of the concepts explained previously are illustrated in Figure 19-1. The figure shows profit or loss on the vertical scale and the price of the underlying stock on the horizontal scale. The strike price of a call option is shown as a dashed line and the prices of the option are solid lines. If the price of the stock is below the strike price of the call option, the price of that option is out of the money. The price of the option (i.e., the premium) is the most the holder of the option can lose. If the price of the stock and the strike price are the same, the option is at the money. If

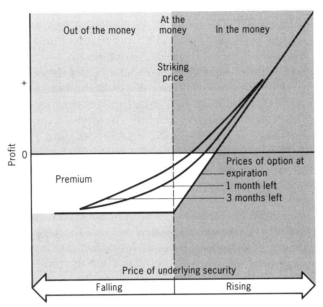

FIGURE 19-1   Time decay of call option.

the price of the stock is more than the strike price, the option is in the money. However, there is no profit until the price of the option appreciates above the price paid for the option plus commissions, which are not shown. The figure also shows three time-decay lines. Regardless of the expiration date, time value is the greatest when the option is at the money. Time value decays as the option approaches expiration. Thus, the price of the option with three months to expiration is higher than those with one month or less to expiration.

Three Courses of Action

Investors have three courses of action they can take with listed options — options that are traded on exchanges. If the underlying stock appreciates in value, the value of the call option will increase by a like amount. Suppose that the exercise price of Lincoln Company is $45 and the stock is currently selling for $50 per share. The option will be worth $5 per share, or $500 for 100 shares. The option holder can

1. Sell the option for $500. The option holder's broker can sell (or buy) options just like he or she sells stocks.
2. Exercise the option and then sell the stock for $5000. The option holder instructs the broker to exercise the option and then sell the stock. The option holder pays a commission to the broker for the services rendered.
3. Let the option expire and give up $500, which does not make sense when the option is in the money. If the option were out of the money (e.g., the market price is $30 per share), letting the option expire is the appropriate thing to do.

Call Option Quotations

Listed option quotations appear in many financial publications. By way of illustration, consider a typical listing for call options on Boeing (aircraft). In mid-September, Boeing is selling for $46\frac{7}{8}$ per share. Notice the relationships between the market price of the stock and the price of the options. The September options expire in about six trading days. The call options with a strike price of $40 sold for $7\frac{1}{4}$ (or $725 per 100 share stock option). These options are in the money, and they have an intrinsic value of $6\frac{7}{8}$ ($46\frac{7}{8}$ − $40 = $6\frac{7}{8}$) and a time value of $\frac{3}{8}$ ($7\frac{1}{4}$ − $6\frac{7}{8}$ = $\frac{3}{8}$). The call options with a strike price of $45 sold for $2\frac{1}{2}$. They too are in the money and have an intrinsic value of $1\frac{7}{8}$ and a time value of $\frac{5}{8}$. In contrast, the September options with a strike price of $55 are out of the money and sold for $\frac{1}{16}$.

Finally, observe how the time value of options decreases as the expiration date approaches. For example, at a strike price of $45, the price of the nearby September option is $2\frac{1}{2}$ and the distant November option is $4\frac{1}{2}$. In the case of the November option the time value is $2\frac{5}{8}$, while the time value of the September option is $\frac{5}{8}$.

Strike Price	Sep.	Oct.	Nov.
40	$7\frac{1}{4}$	r	$8\frac{1}{4}$
45	$2\frac{1}{2}$	$3\frac{7}{8}$	$4\frac{1}{2}$
50	$\frac{1}{4}$	$1\frac{1}{4}$	$1\frac{7}{8}$
55	$\frac{1}{16}$	$\frac{5}{16}$	$\frac{3}{4}$
60	r	s	$\frac{1}{2}$

r = Option not traded; s = no option offered.

Puts and Combinations of Options

A **put option** is a contract to sell 100 shares of stock at an exercise price on or before the expiration date. A put conveys the *right* of the option holder to sell stock to the writer. The difference between a put and a call is that a put is an option to sell and a call is an option to buy.

Buying or writing a put and a call on the same stock, with the same exercise price and same expiration date, is called a **straddle.** Suppose that the outcome of a lawsuit will either triple the value of a company or cause it to go bankrupt. An investor could buy a straddle and hope to make a profit from the outcome of the case. However, since litigation can go on for years, the options may not be a profitable investment.

Another combination that involves taking a current position in more than one option on the same stock is called a spread. A **spread** involves being *both* the buyer and the writer on put *or* call options on the same stock, with the options having different exercise prices and/or expiration dates. For example, one can *sell*

a January call on Monsanto and *buy* a February call on the same stock. The purpose of **spreading** — the purchase of a call (put) and the sale of another call (put) — is that the investor expects the price relationships between the two to change so that subsequent offsetting sales and purchases will result in a profit. Some examples of spreading will be given shortly.

Index Options

Index options are options on an index such as the Standard & Poor's 500 (S&P 500) stock index, and the New York Stock Exchange Composite Index. Stock indexes were explained in Chapter 8. One lesson from that chapter was that there are substantial differences in the underlying securities of the various indexes and the way the indexes are calculated. Therefore, it pays to know your stock index before you invest in one. Indexes are also used to measure the value of debt securities, foreign currencies, futures contracts, and portfolios of selected groups of stocks such as oils and utilities.

Although various indexes are calculated in different ways, the following explanation gives a general idea of how they work. Suppose that the total market value of the stocks in the index is $100 billion, and the index is given an arbitrary base value of 100. If the value of the underlying stocks in the index increases 10 percent, to $110 billion, the index will increase to 110 (110 percent of the base value).

Index options differ from puts and calls in three ways. The underlying asset is an index that represents a broad group of securities or assets instead of the stock of one company. Second, when an index option is exercised, the settlement is made in *cash* instead of stock. The methods for calculating cash settlement values vary from index to index. Third, the exercise price is usually multiplied by a multiplier, such as $100. The multiplier determines the market value of each point in the difference between the current level of the index and the exercise price of an in-the-money option. A multiplier of $100 means that a one-point difference between the current level of the index and the in-the-money option is worth $100 cash settlement.

Index options give investors a way to invest in "the market," or some segment of it without deciding which individual stocks are going to go up or down. Bob Johnston believes that the stock market is going to rally. In January the New York Stock Exchange (NYSE) Index was at 150 and a March call with an exercise price of 150 could be bought for $5 ($500). Johnston bought a call and the market rallied to 162 (8%) before the option expired. Johnston exercised the option at 150 and received the cash difference between the index close (162) and the call exercise price (150) times the $100 multiplied.

$$
\begin{array}{l}
162 \text{ NYSE Index close} \\
\underline{-150} \text{ Call exercise price} \\
12 \times \$100 = \$1200 \text{ cash settlement}
\end{array}
$$

Since Johnston paid a premium of $500, his profit on the call option is $700 ($1200 − $500 = $700). In this example Johnston made a 40-percent return

($700/$500 premium $= 1.40$) on an 8-percent move in the market index. This demonstrates **leverage** in connection with options. More will be said about index options in Chapter 21.

USES OF OPTIONS

Three parties are involved in every option transaction: (1) a buyer, (2) a seller, and (3) the brokers and dealers who bring the buyer and seller together on an exchange where options are traded. This section examines the general uses of options from both the buyers' and sellers' points of view and presents various option strategies.

Buyers

Options are investment tools. Buyers can use them in either a speculative or conservative fashion. Let us examine the speculative use of options first.

Speculation

For the past three weeks the financial press has been reporting that the Lincoln Company is trying to acquire another company. If Lincoln does acquire the other company, it will triple the assets of the firm. On the basis of the news stories, the stock price has risen $20 in the past few weeks. It is currently selling for $40 per share.

Buy Calls.   In this situation, a speculator can use options in several ways. If the speculator believes the stock is going to increase in value, two courses of action can be followed. The speculator can buy 100 shares of stock or a call option on 100 shares of stock.[1] The price of a 95-day call is $250. If the stock increases in value to $50 per share, the speculator can exercise the option to buy the stock at $40 per share, then sell it at $50 per share. If commissions and taxes are ignored, the speculator's profit is $750 on a $250 investment ($5000 − $4000 − $250 = $750). Alternatively, the investor could sell the option for $1000, which would provide the same profit ($1000 − $250 = $750). Notice that the value of both the underlying stock and the option changed by the same amount. This is why most investors sell the option for $1000 rather than exercising it and selling the stock.

If the stock declines in value, the speculator's losses are limited to the $250 premium that was paid for the option. For the speculator, the option accomplished the following:

1. The speculator controlled 100 shares of Lincoln for 95 days without investing $4000; only $250 was invested.

---

[1] Another alternative not discussed here is the use of a stop order. The speculator could place a buy-stop order at, say, $44 per share. If the stock advances that far the order will be executed. The assumption is that the stock will continue to advance in price.

2. The speculator limited the maximum loss to the premium, $250.
3. The speculator gained leverage. For a small investment of $250, $4000 of someone else's money was tied up. Moreover, the potential profits amount to a 300-percent return on investment ($750/$250 = 300 percent) in 95 days or less.

If the speculator believes the acquisition is not going to be successful and the price of the stock will decline in value, two other courses of action can be followed. First, the stock can be sold short at the current market price. If the stock price does decline, the speculator will make a profit. On the other hand, if the stock price appreciates, the short sale will have to be covered at a loss.

Buy Puts.   The second course of action is to buy a put option. If the stock price declines, the speculator will make money as long as the cost of the premium is covered. Let us say that the premium cost $175 for a 95-day put at a strike price of $40 per share. If Lincoln Company declined to $35 per share, the speculator would have a paper profit of $325 ($4000 − $3500 − $175 = $325). If the stock declined to $25 per share, the speculator's profit would be $1325 — a 757-percent return on the investment. Again, the maximum loss was limited to the cost of the premium paid for the option.

Buy Straddles.   If the speculator does not know whether the stock is going to go up or down but is reasonably certain that it will not stay where it is, the speculator can buy a straddle. The straddle consists of two options, a put and a call, and the premium is the sum of the premiums that would be paid for both options. In this case, the premium for the straddle would amount to $425 ($250 + $175 = $425). If the stock only appreciates, it would have to increase more than $4\frac{1}{4}$ points per share before the speculator would make a profit. However, it is conceivable that the stock could increase in value enough to profit from the call; then the stock could decline in value enough to profit from the put. Thus, if the stock were sufficiently volatile, the speculator could use both options.

Conservative Investing

Not all buyers of options are speculators. Options can be used to protect existing profits, like an insurance policy, and to maintain control over a stock.

Buy Puts for Insurance.   Jean owns 300 shares of the Lincoln Company and is concerned about the price of its shares. She is planning to go to Europe on a three-month vacation and does not want to sell the stock as long as the price is advancing. On the other hand, she does not want to return in three months and find it selling at half its current value. Jean can buy a 95-day put option for $175. In this case, the put option should be considered as a 95-day insurance policy. If the stock appreciates in value, the option will not be exercised, and Jean will have

spent $175 for temporary protection. Some investors consider this a loss. However, it is no more of a loss than paying a fire insurance premium when no fire occurs. A service was rendered, and the investor paid for it.

Buy Calls to Protect Positions.   Paco has 100 shares of Lincoln. He owns a kennel and needs funds for expansion. Paco can either borrow from the bank or sell his 100 shares of Lincoln. He already has a large bank loan outstanding and is reluctant to borrow more, even though the bank is willing to extend the credit. Moreover, he believes that the stock of Lincoln Company is going to double in the next few months after the acquisition is announced. Paco's stockbroker explains that he can sell the stock and, at the same time, buy a call option on it. In this way Paco has the use of the funds that were invested in the stock and can still profit if the stock price increases.

Sellers

Investors sell or *write* options to make money. However, the option writer must give up the opportunity to make large gains in a stock for the opportunity to make continuous smaller gains. The option writer is analogous to a banker making loans to business concerns. The business concerns use the borrowed funds to make large profits, and the banker is satisfied to get back the funds that were lent plus interest.

Another way to think about option writing is to answer the following questions: Do you think the stock of Lincoln Company is a good buy at $40 per share? Would you be willing to buy it for $37.50 per share? The difference between the current price and the reduced price is the premium that would be received for writing an option. Now comes the crucial question. If you purchased the stock at $40 per share, would you be willing to sell it for $42.50 per share within the next 95 days?

Would you be willing to sell at $42.50 per share?

Would you be willing to sell at the current market price of $40.00 per share?

Would you be willing to buy at $37.50 per share?

Those who are not willing to limit their gains probably should not write options.

Writing Covered Calls.   In the previous examples the buyers of a 95-day call option on Lincoln Company at $40 per share paid a $250 premium. Let us ignore brokerage commissions and say that the entire premium went to the option writer. Further, let us assume that the option writer bought (went long) 100 shares of Lincoln Company in order to write the option. This is referred to as writing a *covered call* option. The option writer can buy the stock on margin. If the margin requirement is 30 percent, the total cash investment (margin less premium) amounts to $950.

Purchased 100 shares at $40 per share		$4000
Margin (30%)	$1200	
Less premium	-250	
Equals: Total cash investment	$ 950	

If the option is exercised (the stock is called at $40), return on the investment can be determined by dividing the premium by the total cash investment, which comes to 26 percent ($250/$950 = 26%). Keep in mind that this return does not take into account commissions, interest, or taxes. Once these are accounted for, the return may be 10 percent on a 95-day investment. In addition, remember that the option writer keeps the premium income regardless of the disposition of the option. From the option writer's point of view, the two best things that can happen are (1) to have the option expire just below the contract price (at $39\frac{7}{8}$) so another option can be written on the same stock, or (2) to have the option exercised as soon as possible so that more stock can be purchased and another option can be written. The worst thing that can happen is for the price of the stock to decline below cost. The option writer's cost is the purchase price of the stock ($40 per share) less the per-share amount of the premium ($2.50) or $37.50 per share ($40.00 − $2.50 = $37.50).

Writing Uncovered Calls.   Option writers can speculate by writing **naked options.** The term *naked,* or *uncovered,* means that the option writer does not own the stock the option is being written for. In other words, the writer will be short the stock if the option is exercised. If the option writer believes the stock is going to decline in value, a naked call option can be written against the stock. However, the option writer will probably have to put up some predetermined amount of margin. Let us use the 95-day option on the Lincoln Company as an example. If the call is written naked, and if the stock declines in value, the option writer's return would be $250 without purchasing the shares. On the other hand, if the stock appreciates in value and the option is exercised, the option writer must buy the stock at a loss and deliver it to the option holder (cover the short position). A strategy involving writing some covered options and some naked ones is called **ratio writing.** Writing naked options is a risky business and should not be undertaken by novice investors or those who cannot use tax losses.

Writers of index options have a special problem. Even if they hold all of the components of the index in the correct proportions and sell a call option on the industry index, they might not be covered exactly because these options are settled in cash and not by the delivery of the component stocks.

The initial margin requirements that apply to writers of index options differ from those that apply to writing other kinds of options. The margin requirements for writing regular listed stock options is 30 percent of the market value of the equivalent number of shares of the underlying security, adjusted for in-the-money and out-of-the-money positions. This margin requirement is set by the

Federal Reserve System (Regulations T, U, and G). However, margin requirements of index options are set by the various exchanges that trade options, subject
to the approval of the Securities and Exchange Commission. Each exchange can
set different requirements, which are generally lower than those that apply to
regular options. For example, the margin requirement to write an option may be
equal to 10 percent of the value of the underlying index. In other words, if the
securities represented by the index option had a value of $20,000, the writer
would be required to have an initial margin of $2000 on that option. This does *not*
mean that you can write $20,000 worth of options for $2000. Most brokers require
a minimum equity of $10,000 or more in the option writer's account. Check with
your broker before dealing in these options.

Writing Puts.   If an option writer thinks a stock is going to appreciate in value, or
if the writer wants to buy a stock below the current market price, the thing to do is
write a put. The premium for a 95-day put option on Lincoln at $40 is $175. If the
stock appreciates, the put will not be exercised, and the writer will have earned
$175 without buying the stock.

   If the stock declines in value, the option writer will have purchased the stock at
$38.25 per share ($40.00 − $1.75 = $38.25).

The Key to Writing Options

Option writers should keep several suggestions in mind:

1.   Never write a call option on a stock that you are not willing to hold in your
     portfolio for a long period of time. Sometimes stock prices decline or the
     demand for options diminishes, and you may be unable to write profitable
     options on a particular stock.
2.   Write options only on stocks that have a large volume of open activity.
3.   Monitor options daily.
4.   Sometimes it is wise to take a little loss now to avoid a big loss later. Stop-loss
     orders on stock positions are useful for this purpose.

Strategies

A short-hand method called **vector notation** is used here to illustrate various
option strategies.[2] Vector notation shows how an investor is affected by stock
price changes. A plus sign (+) indicates a gain, a minus sign (−) indicates a loss,
and zero (0) indicates that the investor is unaffected. The top sign indicates the
effect when the stock price goes up; the bottom sign shows the effect when the
price goes down. The term *bought* put or call designates an option that has been
purchased, and *sold* put or call designates one that has been written.

---

[2] Vector notation was first used to describe options by Richard J. Kruizenga, *Put and Call Options: A
Theoretical and Market Analysis,* doctoral dissertation, Massachusetts Institute of Technology, 1958.

Six basic strategies can be combined in various ways to develop other strategies:

Strategies	Effect of Stock Price Changes on Investors
1. Bought call	$\begin{pmatrix} +1 \\ 0 \end{pmatrix}$
2. Sold call	$\begin{pmatrix} -1 \\ 0 \end{pmatrix}$
3. Bought put	$\begin{pmatrix} 0 \\ +1 \end{pmatrix}$
4. Sold put	$\begin{pmatrix} 0 \\ -1 \end{pmatrix}$
5. Long position	$\begin{pmatrix} +1 \\ -1 \end{pmatrix}$
6. Short position	$\begin{pmatrix} -1 \\ +1 \end{pmatrix}$

These strategies can then be combined to equal other strategies. For example, a bought call and a bought put equal a bought straddle. All of these examples assume that the options are on the same stock with the same expiration dates and strike prices.

7. Bought straddle $= \begin{pmatrix} +1 \\ 0 \end{pmatrix} + \begin{pmatrix} 0 \\ +1 \end{pmatrix} = \begin{pmatrix} +1 \\ +1 \end{pmatrix}$

A sold call and a sold put equal a sold straddle.

8. Sold straddle $= \begin{pmatrix} -1 \\ 0 \end{pmatrix} + \begin{pmatrix} 0 \\ -1 \end{pmatrix} = \begin{pmatrix} -1 \\ -1 \end{pmatrix}$

A bought call used to protect a short position equals a bought put.

9. Bought call covering short position $= \begin{pmatrix} +1 \\ 0 \end{pmatrix} + \begin{pmatrix} -1 \\ +1 \end{pmatrix} = \begin{pmatrix} 0 \\ +1 \end{pmatrix}$

A bought put used to protect a long position equals a bought call.

10. Bought put protecting long position $= \begin{pmatrix} 0 \\ +1 \end{pmatrix} + \begin{pmatrix} +1 \\ -1 \end{pmatrix} = \begin{pmatrix} +1 \\ 0 \end{pmatrix}$

A bought call and a sold put equal a long position.

11. Long stock $= \begin{pmatrix} +1 \\ 0 \end{pmatrix} + \begin{pmatrix} 0 \\ -1 \end{pmatrix} = \begin{pmatrix} +1 \\ -1 \end{pmatrix}$

Conversion

As shown in the following example, call options can be **converted** into put options, and put options can be converted into call options. An investor who has a bought call can sell the same stock short and effectively convert the call into a put.

---

12. Bought call + short position = bought put

$$\begin{pmatrix} +1 \\ 0 \end{pmatrix} + \begin{pmatrix} -1 \\ +1 \end{pmatrix} = \begin{pmatrix} 0 \\ +1 \end{pmatrix}$$

Similarly, an investor who has a bought put can buy the same stock (go long) and convert the put into a call.

---

13. Bought put + long position = bought call

$$\begin{pmatrix} 0 \\ +1 \end{pmatrix} + \begin{pmatrix} +1 \\ -1 \end{pmatrix} = \begin{pmatrix} +1 \\ 0 \end{pmatrix}$$

Conversion is also known as **synthetics** because we are duplicating the behavior of one security by using combinations of other securities. We duplicated the behavior of a bought put by having a long position in an underlying stock and a bought call. Although this list of strategies is not exhaustive, it is sufficiently large to show that a large number of combinations of puts and calls can be worked out through the use of vector notation.

It should also be noted that sold options carry a minus sign, indicating a loss, although a loss has not always occurred. For example, an investor may have bought a stock at $10 per share and sold a call option after it had appreciated to $30 per share. The investor would have had a paper profit of $20 per share before the option contract was sold.

Vector notation demonstrates how various types of options can be combined, but it does not show the profitability of different option strategies. Figure 19-2 shows three option strategies. The first is to buy a call. If the stock price at expiration exceeds the strike price, the option will be profitable for the buyer. The seller, of course, receives the premium. If the seller is *long,* the stock there is an opportunity loss. If the seller is *naked,* the option will have to be covered at a loss.

The second strategy is to sell a put. In this case, the option is profitable to the buyer while the stock price is declining. The seller of the option must buy the stock at the strike price. The seller can be protected from a loss by going short or by buying a call to offset a put. Recall from vector notation that a sold put plus a short position or a sold put plus a bought call offset each other.

The final strategy is to buy a straddle, a combination of a put and a call. The option can be profitable to the buyer if the stock price rises or falls sufficiently. The seller gets the premium and, as shown previously, can be protected from losses by using offsetting strategies.

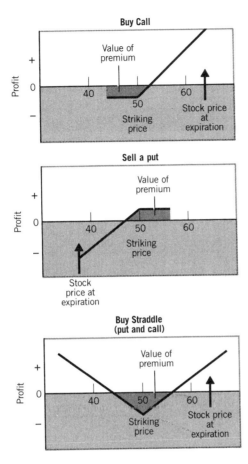

FIGURE 19-2 Profit and loss chart for option strategies.

Spreading

A **spread** consists of the simultaneous purchase of one option contract (going long) and the sale of another (going short) on the same stock, but at different strike prices or maturities. If we use vector notation, it appears that such a transaction would not be profitable, but we shall see that this is not the case because of the different strike prices.

$$\text{Bought call} + \text{sold call} = \text{no position}$$

$$\begin{pmatrix} +1 \\ 0 \end{pmatrix} \quad + \quad \begin{pmatrix} -1 \\ 0 \end{pmatrix} \quad = \quad \begin{pmatrix} 0 \\ 0 \end{pmatrix}$$

The primary purpose of a spread is to reduce the risk of being long or short. The reduction in risk can be accomplished by using any one of a variety of spreads. For example, a **vertical spread** is where both options have the same expiration month but different exercise prices (strike prices). A **time spread** is where both options have the same exercise price but different expiration months. There are also

spreads with exotic names like "Butterfly spread" and "Domino spread." The following examples of a vertical call spread illustrate some of the concepts used in spreading.

Bullish Vertical Call Spread

Suppose that ABC stock is currently selling for $52 per share, and Chris Winger believes it is going to appreciate in value. It is October, and Chris can buy January call options with an exercise price of $50 per share for $600 (for 100 shares). If he is correct, he can make a lot of money. However, if he is wrong, he can lose $600.

Option Series	Option Price	Stock Price
ABC Jan. $50 (buy)	$600	$52
ABC Jan. $60 (sell)	$300	$52

Chris is willing to forego some potential profit in order to reduce his risk below $600. To do this, he simultaneously buys the January $50 option for $600 and sells the January $60 option for $300. The $300 that he receives from the sale of the option reduces his cash outlay to $300 ($600 − $300 = $300).

Chris used the worksheet shown in Figure 19-3 to determine his risk and potential profit. The worksheet does not include transaction costs or tax consequences. Furthermore, it is only to be used for a bullish vertical spread—expectations that the stock will rise in price.

The worksheet shows that the maximum loss or risk is the difference between the prices of the two options, or $300. The maximum profit is the difference

	Option price	Stock price
Buy ABC 50's	6	52
Sell ABC 60's	3	52

(A) Price of option bought =   6 (A)

(B) Price of option sold =   3 (B)

(C) Risk = (A)   Less (B) =   3 (C)

(D) Maximum profit = Difference in exercise prices 10 Less (C) 3 =   7 (D)

(E) Risk/Reward = (C) 3 /(D) 7 =   3/7 (E)

(F) Break-even point = (C) 3 Plus exercise price of option bought 50 =   53 (F)

(G) % move in underlying stock needed to reach break-even point = (F) 53 Less stock price 52 = 1 ÷ Stock price 52   2% = (G)

FIGURE 19-3 Bullish vertical call spread worksheet.

between the exercise prices of the two options ($60 − $50 = $10/per share), less the risk ($300), which amounts to $700. The risk/reward ratio means that Chris is risking $300 to make $700.

If the stock price advances $1 per share to $53, Chris will at least break even on the transaction.

Over the next few weeks, the price of ABC stock increased from $52 to $60 per share. Accordingly, the value of the January $50 option that Chris bought for $600 increased to $1050. The difference in price reflects the difference between the exercise price of the option and the current market price of the stock, plus an additional premium for the remaining time value. Similarly, the value of the January $60 option changed. In this case, the exercise price and the current market price are the same, so only the premium for the remaining time value exists.

Option Series	Option Price	Stock Price
ABC Jan. $50 (sell)	$1050	$60
ABC Jan. $60 (buy)	$ 50	$60

If Chris closes out his positions (sells the January $50s and buys January $60s), his profit before taxes will be $700. The computations for the spread are summarized in the following example:

Jan. $50 Options		Jan. $60 Options		Profit/(Loss)
Bought	$ 600	Sold	$300	($300)
Sold	$1050	Bought	$ 50	$1000
Profit	$ 450	Profit	$250	$ 700

At this point you may wonder why Chris would want to go through all of this when he could have bought the stock at $52 and sold it at $60, making a nice profit of $800. If he had had perfect knowledge of what the price of the stock was going to do when he entered the transactions he would have done that. But like most of us, we do not know what the future holds. The spread limits the profit and the risk.

Another risk that was not mentioned is that the option on the short side of the spread can be exercised (called), which destroys the spread. The exercise can be met by delivering stock already owned, buying stock in the open market for delivery, borrowing stock for delivery and remaining short, or exercising the call option.

Bearish Vertical Call Spread

A bearish vertical call spread is used when a stock is expected to decline in value. In this case, the option with the lower exercise price is sold, and the option with the higher exercise price is purchased. For example, assume that Ann Johnson

	Option price	Stock price
Sell DEF 80's	13	91
Buy DEF 90's	6	91

(A) Price of option sold =	13 (A)
(B) Price of option bought =	6 (B)
(C) Maximum profit = (A) 13 Less (B) 6 =	7 (C)
(D) Risk = Difference in exercise Prices 10 Less (C) 7	= 3 (D)
(E) Risk/Reward = (D) 3 /(C) 7	=3/7 (E)

(F) Break-even point = (C) 7   Plus
    exercise price of option
    sold 80 =
	87 (F)

(G) % move in underlying stock
    needed to reach break-even
    point = Stock price 91 Less
    (F) 87 = 3 ÷ Stock price 91
	=3% (G)

FIGURE 19-4 Bearish vertical call spread worksheet.

believes that the price of DEF is going to decline. The stock is currently selling for $91 per share. The January options with an exercise price of $80 per share are selling for $1300 (for 100 shares), and the January options with an exercise price of 90 are selling for $600.

Option Series	Option Price	Stock Price
DEF Jan. $80 (sell)	$1300	$91
DEF Jan. $90 (buy)	$ 600	$91

Ann sells the January $80s for $1300 and buys the January $90s for $600. As shown in the worksheet in Figure 19-4, the maximum loss is $300 and the maximum profit is $700. The maximum profit can occur only if DEF is trading below $80 per share when the options expire. The $1300 received from the sale of the January $80s less the $600 cost of the January $90s is $700.

These examples of spreading show another way of using options. It also shows that this process should be used *only* by investors who are well versed in options and are willing to spend the time and energy necessary to use them correctly.

TRADING OPTIONS

Options are traded on the Chicago Board Options Exchange (CBOE), the American Stock Exchange, the New York Stock Exchange, the Philadelphia Stock Exchange, and the Pacific Stock Exchange. The CBOE was the first exchange to provide a marketplace for trading securities options. The impetus for the formation of the CBOE came from dissatisfaction with having to use the over-the-

counter market for options trading—a cumbersome and inefficient process. In that market, prospective option buyers contacted option dealers who either directly or indirectly through stockbrokers scoured the country trying to find someone to write the option. Sometimes the dealers themselves wrote options. Thus, there was no continuous options market and no secondary market where existing option contracts could be bought or sold. The CBOE was formed to provide a continuous and orderly market for the buying and selling of options. The CBOE standardized certain features of option trading to achieve an orderly market. The standardized expiration dates and striking prices were discussed previously.

Secondary Market

Existing option contracts can be bought or sold on the CBOE or other option exchanges. Thus, an investor who buys a call option on a stock listed on the CBOE can sell that option at any time until the expiration date because continuous trading is provided in that option. The market price of the option will reflect the market value of the underlying security and the amount of time remaining on the option. For example, assume that an investor buys a call option that expires seven months from now. The option is on Andrew Industries at $50 per share, and the premium is $6 per share. Within two months after the option was purchased, the value of the underlying stock increased to $53 per share, and the option is now selling for $9 per share. The investor can sell the call option and realize a 3-point profit above the 6-point premium that was paid for the option. Note that if the investor wishes to do so, he or she can still exercise the option and buy the stock.

Similarly, option writers can buy options to cover their naked option positions or to close out option contracts. For example, let us say that an October call option is written on Jeremy Corporation at a strike price of $80 per share. When the option has three months remaining, the stock is selling at $82. The writer can buy an October call option, thereby closing out the position:

$$\text{Sold call} + \text{bought call} = \text{no position}$$

$$\begin{pmatrix} +1 \\ 0 \end{pmatrix} + \begin{pmatrix} -1 \\ 0 \end{pmatrix} = \begin{pmatrix} 0 \\ 0 \end{pmatrix}$$

Now the writer is free to write on other stocks. Alternatively, the writer could buy a January call option to close out the earlier option. If that option is not exercised, the writer would still have a three-month bought call on Jeremy Corporation. Thus, a secondary option market expands the number of strategies available to option writers and buyers. Equally important, the secondary market creates liquidity.

CONCLUSION

Trading in stock options is riskier than straightforward purchases of securities and thus is not suitable for many investors. Nevertheless, investors who know what they are doing and are willing to assume the risks can make money in options.

There are two basic types of options. The call option purchases the right to buy a certain number of shares of a stock at a specific price during the time the option is in effect. The put option guarantees the right to sell a certain number of shares of a stock at a specific price for the duration of the option. Various combinations of puts and calls offer investors and speculators a number of choices in their dealings. Vector notation, with its plus and minus shorthand indications, gives investors a way of determining how a particular combination will affect them.

The buyer can use options as a means of speculation, hoping to make a large profit, or as an additional tool in conservative investment practices. Sellers of options, although they can speculate by writing calls naked (writing call options on stocks they do not own), must usually be satisfied with the relatively small profits to be made on option premiums received from those who buy options.

Since 1973, the Chicago Board Options Exchange has offered a continuous, orderly, and efficient market for options trading. It also offers a secondary market in which the options themselves can be bought and sold. Options are also traded on the American, New York, Philadelphia, and Pacific stock exchanges.

IMPORTANT CONCEPTS

American-style options
At-the-money option
Black-Scholes Option Pricing Model
Call option
Chicago Board Options Exchange
   (CBOE)
Conversion
Covered option writing
European-style options
Exercise cut-off time
Exercise price
Expiration dates
Index option
In-the-money option
Intrinsic value (of options)

Multiply traded options
Naked option writing
Option holder
Option writer
Out-of-the-money option
Payout is unprotected
Premium
Put option
Spread, spreading (vertical, time, etc.)
Straddle
Synthetic
Time value (of options)
Uncovered option writing
Vector notation

QUESTIONS AND EXERCISES

1. Define the terms "put options" and "call options."
2. How are American-style and European-style options different?
3. What adjustments are made to options in the case of a stock split?
4. What does "payout unprotected" mean?
5. How is the intrinsic value of an option determined?

6. Discuss the difference between index options and regular options.

7. Explain how options can be used to speculate when you believe that the price of the stock is going to decline.

8. Explain how options can be used to speculate when you believe that the price of the stock is going to increase.

9. Explain how options can be used to lock in existing gains. How does this differ from using "sell stop orders?"

10. Is writing naked options a good idea? Explain.

11. How do investors do "spreading" in options?

12. Where are options traded?

13. Refer to the options page of *The Wall Street Journal.* How much are near-term and distant put and call options on IBM selling for at this time? Would you buy or sell distant call options now?

14. Continuing with *The Wall Street Journal,* what options look like good buys now for long-term investors? Why?

15. Using IBM options, explain how to do a vertical bear call spread.

APPENDIX 19A:
THE BLACK-SCHOLES OPTION PRICING MODEL

Fischer Black and Myron Scholes developed a model to determine the value of an option based on the volatility of a stock, the price of the stock, the maturity of the option and its exercise price, and the short-term interest rate.[3] Although their model assumed that options could be exercised only at maturity, stocks paid no cash dividends, and the variance of their returns (volatility) was constant, it still provides us with the equilibrium value of an option that can be used by academics and investors alike.

The Black-Scholes model to determine the value of an option is presented in Table 19A-1. Although the model appears formidable (because it is), it is relatively easy to work with because most of the information required to use it is available in *The Wall Street Journal.* These items are (1) the current market price of the stock, (2) the exercise price of the option, (3) short-term interest rates, such as the Treasury bill rate, and (4) the maturity of the option. The remaining item, the volatility of the stock, measured by the standard deviation of the stock's annual return, continuously compounded, must be determined by using historical data or estimates of future volatility.

[3] Fischer Black and Myron Scholes, "The Pricing of Options and Corporate Liabilities," *Journal of Political Economy,* 81 (1973), 637–654. Also see Robert C. Merton, "The Theory of Rational Option Pricing," *Bell Journal of Economics and Management Science,* 4 (1973), 141–183.

TABLE 19A-1   The Black-Scholes Option Pricing Model

$$\text{Value of option} = P_0 N(d_1) - \frac{E}{e^{rt}} N(d_2) \qquad (19A\text{-}1)$$

where

P_0 = current market price of the stock
E = exercise (strike) price of the option
e = 2.7183
r = short-term rate of interest, continuously compounded (use a rate that corresponds to the option's term to expiration)
t = time in years, to expiration of option (3 months = 0.25 years)
$N(d)$ = the value of a cumulative normal probability density function, as defined below

$$d_1 = \frac{\ln(P_0/E) + (r + 0.5\sigma^2)t}{\sigma\sqrt{t}}$$

$$d_2 = \frac{\ln(P_0/E) + (r - 0.5\sigma^2)t}{\sigma\sqrt{t}}$$

ln = natural logarithm
σ = the standard deviation of the annual rate of return on the underlying stock, continuously compounded

To illustrate the use of the option pricing model, let us assume that the standard deviation of a stock's returns is 0.30 and the remaining terms were taken from the financial press:

Current market price of stock, P_0 = $20 per share
Exercise price of the option, E = $17
Short-term annual rate of interest,
    continuously compounded, r = 0.10
Time to expiration of option, t = 0.25 years (3 months)

The first step is to solve d_1 and d_2:

$$d_1 = \frac{\ln(\$20/\$17) + [0.10 + 0.5(0.30)^2]0.25}{(0.30)\sqrt{0.25}} = \frac{0.1988}{0.15} = 1.3251$$

$$d_2 = \frac{\ln(\$20/\$17) - [0.10 - 0.5(0.30)^2]0.25}{(0.30)\sqrt{0.25}} = \frac{0.1763}{0.15} = 1.1751$$

The terms d_1 and d_2 represent standard deviations (Z values) in a normal curve, such as that shown in Figure 19A-1. The terms $N(d_1)$ and $N(d_2)$ in the option pricing model represent a random variable with a value less than those of d_1 and d_2. For example, d_1 represents a standard deviation (Z value) of 1.3251. The Z values and areas under a normal curve are shown in Figure 19A.1 and in Appendix 19B. The value for d_1 falls between a Z of 1.4 and 1.3. Therefore, it is necessary to

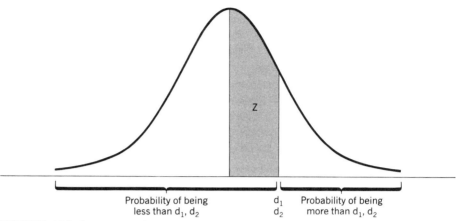

Probability of being
less than d_1, d_2

d_1
d_2

Probability of being
more than d_1, d_2

FIGURE 19A-1 Area under normal curve.

interpolate the numbers to determine the exact probability of being *greater* than d_1.

$$0.0968 - \frac{0.0251}{0.1000}(0.0968 - 0.0808) = 0.09278$$

But we want to know the probability of being *less* than d_1 for the model; therefore, we subtract 0.09278 from 1. Thus, the probability of being less than d_1, or $N(d_1)$, is $1 - 0.09278 = 0.9072$.[4] Similarly, the value of $N(d_2)$ is 0.8798.

The term $N(d_1)$ can also be interpreted to mean that a 1 percent change in the stock price will be accompanied by a 0.9072 change in the option price. Knowing that, an option writer could hedge by buying 91 shares of stock for each option contract (100 shares) that is written.

Finally, we can use the values of $N(d_1)$ and $N(d_2)$, along with the data from the newspaper and the variability of the stock price to determine the value of the option. Using equation 19A-1, the value of the option is

$$\text{Value of option} = \$20(0.9072) - \frac{\$17}{e^{(0.10)(0.25)}}(0.8798) = \$3.56$$

In conclusion, the option pricing model has a variety of uses. Only two were shown here. The most important is, of course, to determine the value of an option. Keep in mind that the model makes certain limiting assumptions. Nevertheless, it can be modified to relax those assumptions. The second use demonstrated was to develop a *hedge ratio*, the amount of stock that should be purchased by option writers to hedge their positions.

---

[4] Where d_1 has negative values, it is not necessary to subtract its value from one.

APPENDIX 19B:
AREAS UNDER NORMAL CURVE

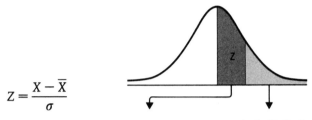

$$Z = \frac{X - \overline{X}}{\sigma}$$

Standard Deviations (Z) from Mean	Area of Z	Area Outside Z on Same Side
0.0	0.0000	0.0000
0.1	0.0398	0.4602
0.2	0.0793	0.4207
0.3	0.1179	0.3821
0.4	0.1554	0.3446
0.5	0.1915	0.3085
0.6	0.2257	0.2743
0.7	0.2580	0.2420
0.8	0.2881	0.2119
0.9	0.3159	0.1841
1.0	0.3413	0.1587
1.1	0.3643	0.1357
1.2	0.3849	0.1151
1.3	0.4032	0.0968
1.4	0.4192	0.0808
1.5	0.4332	0.0668
1.6	0.4452	0.0548
1.7	0.4554	0.0446
1.8	0.4641	0.0359
1.9	0.4713	0.0287
2.0	0.4772	0.0228
2.1	0.4821	0.0179
2.2	0.4861	0.0139
2.3	0.4893	0.0107
2.4	0.4918	0.0082
2.5	0.4938	0.0062
2.6	0.4953	0.0047
2.7	0.4965	0.0035
2.8	0.4974	0.0026
2.9	0.4981	0.0019
3.0	0.4987	0.0013

CHAPTER 20

CONVERTIBLE SECURITIES, WARRANTS, AND RIGHTS

CONVERTIBLE BONDS AND PREFERREDS
Characteristics of Convertibles
A Theory of Convertibles
Reasons for Issuing Convertibles
WARRANTS
Warrants Defined
Value of Warrants

RIGHTS
Terms of the Offering
Value of Rights
CONCLUSION
IMPORTANT CONCEPTS
QUESTIONS AND EXERCISES

C onvertible bonds and convertible preferred stock give investors the opportunity to invest in securities that have the capital gains potential of common stock and a considerable degree of safety. In other words, investors can have their cake and eat it too. This chapter examines convertible bonds and convertible preferred stock and two other types of convertible securities that have speculative appeal — warrants and rights.

CONVERTIBLE BONDS AND PREFERREDS

A convertible security is one that can be exchanged for another security, usually the common stock of the company that issued the convertible. Two types of convertible securities are debenture bonds and preferred stock. The first type is generally called a **convertible bond** and the second **convertible preferred.**

Hundreds of convertible securities are traded on stock exchanges and in the over-the-counter market.[1] Table 20-1 lists some of the companies that have convertible securities. Although the list is not complete, it is sufficiently long to reveal that some of the nation's largest companies issue convertibles. In some cases company names have been changed because of mergers or for other reasons. The names listed in the table are those of the original issuers.

[1] For a complete listing, see *Moody's Industrial Manual* (published annually).

TABLE 20-1   Selected Companies with
Convertible Securities

Convertible Bonds
  Atlantic Richfield
  Cetus Corp.
  Cummins Engine
  Equimark
  Hercules Inc.
  Johnson Controls
  Navistar International
  Ogden Corp.
  Union Carbide
  Zenith Electronics
Convertible Preferreds
  Baxter International
  B.F. Goodrich
  Household International
  Integrated Resources
  International Minerals and Chemicals
  ITT Corp.
  National Semiconductor
  Talley Industries
  Textron Inc.
  Wickes Companies Inc.

Characteristics of Convertibles

Some basic terms must be defined before the mechanics of convertibles can be discussed. Since both convertible bonds and preferreds have many of the same characteristics, the following discussion concentrates on convertible bonds.

Conversion Price

The **conversion price** is the dollar amount of **par value** of the bond that is exchangeable for one share of common stock. Recall that most bonds have a par value of $1000. Accordingly, a conversion price of $50 per share is equivalent to a **conversion rate** of 20. Similarly, a conversion price of $25 per share is equivalent to a conversion rate of 40. Conversion rates and prices can be determined using the following equation:

$$\frac{\text{Par value of bond}}{\text{Conversion price}} = \text{conversion rate} \qquad (20\text{-}1)$$

This equation was used to generate the following conversion rates for a par value of $1000:

Conversion Price	Conversion Rate
$100	10
50	20
25	40
10	100

Sometimes the conversion rate or conversion price can change over time. For example, a $1000 bond may have a conversion price of $25 for the first five years, $30 for the next five years, and $40 for the remaining life of the bond.

Conversion prices are also adjusted to take into account stock splits or stock dividends that occur during the life of the bond. Therefore, if a stock split were two for one the conversion price would be halved.

Conversion Value

The **conversion value** is the current market value of the number of shares into which the security can be converted. Suppose that a $1000 par value bond has a conversion rate of 40 and the stock into which it is convertible has a current price of $30 per share. The conversion value is determined by multiplying the conversion rate by the current price of a share of stock. In this example, the conversion value of the bond is $1200 (40 × $30 = $1200).

$$\text{Conversion value} = \text{conversion rate} \times \text{current stock price}$$

$$CV \quad = \quad R \quad \times \quad P_0$$

(20-2)

The conversion value is the theoretical value of the bond. The actual market price of the bond may or may not be the same as the theoretical value. When the market price and the theoretical value are the same, the convertible is selling at **parity.** If the market price exceeds the conversion value, the bond is selling at a **premium,** or above parity. Conversely, a **discount** is when a convertible bond sells for less than the conversion value.

Conversion Premium

Unfortunately, the terminology used in investments is confusing at times, and this is one of those times. The terms *premium* and *discount* have two meanings with respect to bonds. They refer to the relationship between the market price and the par value of a bond. A bond that has a par value of $1000 and a market price of $1400 is selling at a premium, and if the market price is $600, it is at a **deep discount.** The terms are also used in connection with convertible bonds selling above or below parity — where the market price is the same as the conversion value. We will call the latter the **conversion premium** or **discount** to distinguish between the two usages of the term.

The following examples illustrate a conversion premium. Consider a bond

with a current market price of $1100 and a conversion rate of 40.[2] The current market price of the stock into which it is convertible is $26 per share. Using Equation 20-2, we find that the conversion value of the bond is $1040:

$$CV = R \times P_0$$

$$\$1040 = 40 \times \$26$$

The dollar amount of the conversion premium or discount is the difference between the current market price of the bond and its conversion value. The dollar amount of the conversion premium in this example is $60.

$$P_m - CV = \$1100 - \$1040 = \$60$$

where

$$P_m = \text{current market price of the bond}$$

The conversion premium P^* is usually expressed as a percentage over the conversion value. It is determined by dividing the difference between the market price of the bond and the conversion value ($P_m - CV$) by the conversion value CV. In the example, the conversion premium is 5.77 percent.

$$P^* = \frac{P_m - CV}{CV}$$

$$= \frac{\$1100 - \$1040}{\$1040} \tag{20-3}$$

$$= 5.77\%$$

where

$$P^* = \text{conversion premium based on market value}$$
$$P_m = \text{current market price of the bond}$$
$$CV = \text{conversion value}$$

In the previous example the premium was based on the conversion value of a bond. Another method of determining the conversion premium or discount is based on investment value. The **investment value** is the price at which a bond will sell if it has no conversion feature. Such values are estimated by investment advisory services such as Moody's. Let us assume that the bond used in the example has an investment value I of $950. When we use this method, the conversion premium P^{**} is determined by dividing the differences between the conversion value of the bond and the investment value ($CV - I$) by the investment value.

---

[2] For simplicity, the examples disregard the fact that bond prices are quoted at the market price plus accumulated interest.

$$P^{**} = \frac{CV - I}{I}$$

$$= \frac{\$1040 - \$950}{\$950} \qquad (20\text{-}4)$$

$$= 9.47\%$$

where

P^{**} = conversion premium based on investment value
I = investment value
CV = conversion value

The relationships between investment value, market price, and premiums are depicted in Figure 20-1. If the stock sells at $26 per share, the conversion value will be $1040. However, as shown in the figure, the market price of the bond is $1100. The difference between the market price and the conversion value is the first conversion premium that was explained ($P^* = 5.77\%$). The difference between the market price and the investment value is the second type of conversion premium ($P^{**} = 9.47\%$).

Figure 20-1 also indicates that if the market value of the stock falls to $15 per share, the conversion value of the bond will be $600. Nevertheless, the bond may still sell at a premium over both the conversion value and the investment value, or

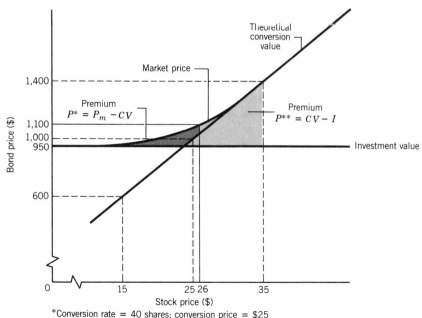

FIGURE 20-I Convertible bond model.

at about $980, as shown in the figure. The reason for the premium is that investors are willing to pay for the conversion feature of the bond in addition to the bond's investment value. Although the stock is selling at $15 today, tomorrow it may be appreciably higher. Therefore, the conversion feature can be thought of as a long-term **call option** on the stock. Consequently, the premium paid for the bond is similar to the premium paid to buy a call option.

Notice that the two conversion premiums are shown in the figure as dollar amounts: the difference between the market price of the bond and the conversion value, and the difference between conversion value and the investment value. Thus, conversion premiums can be expressed as dollar amounts or percentages. The shaded area to the right of the conversion value line is the dollar equivalent of P^{**}, and the shaded area to the left of the line is the dollar equivalent of P^*.

A careful examination of the shaded area to the left of the conversion value line shows that the P^* diminishes as the stock price increases. When the stock price is $35 per share, there is no premium over the theoretical value of the bond. However, the premium between the market price of the bond and the investment value of the bond becomes larger as the stock price increases. This is the shaded area to the right of the conversion value line. Therefore, higher stock and bond prices imply greater risk for investors who are interested in the investment value of the bond (because it is selling above its investment value), and greater returns for those who bought the bonds for capital gains.

Special Features

Some convertible securities have special features. For example, **exchangeable convertibles** are issues that may be exchanged for stocks with names other than that of the issuer. Ford Motor Credit 4.875%, 1998s are convertible into Ford Motor Company stock. Similarly, United Telecommunications 9.75%, 2010 are convertible into Southern New England Telephone. Another type of exchangeable convertible issues are those that, at the option of the company, may be exchanged for another convertible security. A convertible preferred stock may be exchanged for a convertible bond. Baxter Travenol Labs, Diamond Shamrock, and USX Corporation had such securities. Some exchanges are taxable events.

Selected convertible securities have **"put"** features. In other words, the bondholder has a put option to sell the bond back to the issuer.

Limited rights of redemption in selected convertible issues restrict bondholders' ability to convert their issues. This usually occurs in small issues of $25 million or less. The bondholder must request the redemption in writing. Beginning on the put date, the company may redeem a limited number of such requests each year on a first-come, first-served basis. If the requests for redemption exceed the limit for that year, they will be held for consideration the following year or years.

Some convertibles have **resets,** which means that the interest rate paid on the securities can be changed periodically. For example, if the price of United Artist Communications 6.375%, 2002 bonds was less than 101 during a certain period in 1990, the interest rate was reset to bring the price back up to 101.

Finally, some convertibles have **call protection.** This means that the issue cannot be redeemed before a certain date, or it can be called only if certain conditions are met.

A Theory of Convertibles

Convertible bonds have some characteristics of both bonds and common stocks. Therefore, a valuation model for convertible bonds contains some elements of the bond and stock valuation theories that were developed in Chapters 2 and 3. The market value of a straight (nonconvertible) bond with annual interest payments can be determined by the following equation:

$$P_b = \sum_{t=1}^{n} \frac{C}{(1+r)^t} + \frac{F}{(1+r)^n} \tag{20-5}$$

where

P_b = current market price of the bond
C = annual coupon income (\$) from the bond
F = face value of the bond at maturity (\$)
r = current rate of interest on newly issued straight bonds with similar characteristics. It is also the yield to maturity (%)
n = number of years to maturity

If the bonds are converted, they will not be held until maturity. Therefore, Equation 20-5 can be modified to take into account the conversion of the bond. The revised equation is

$$P_b = \sum_{t=1}^{n} \frac{C}{(1+r_c)^t} + \frac{CV}{(1+r_c)^N} \tag{20-6}$$

where

CV = conversion value of the bond
r_c = expected rate of return on convertible bonds
    ($r_c \geq$ coupon interest rate on the convertible)
N = number of years until conversion ($N \leq n$)

From the previous discussion, it is known that the conversion value of a bond is related to the price of the stock into which it is convertible. If the current stock price is P_0, then increases in the stock prices over time can be expressed by

$$P_t = P_0(1+g')^t \tag{20-7}$$

where

P_0 = current price of the stock
P_t = stock price at the end of period t
g' = expected rate of growth of the stock price

Therefore, the conversion value CV is equal to the expected stock price P_t times the conversion rate R, which is the number of shares received upon conversion. Stated otherwise,

$$CV = P_0(1 + g')^t R$$
$$= P_t R \qquad (20\text{-}8)$$

For example, suppose that a bond has a conversion rate R of 40 shares (which is the same as saying the conversion price is $25 per share), the current market price of the stock P_0 is $26 per share, and the price of the stock is expected to increase 10 percent per year for five years. The conversion value is $1675:

$$CV = P_0(1 + g')^t R$$
$$= \$26(1.10)^5(40)$$
$$= \$1675$$

Now assume that the bond pays $90 annual interest C and that investors expect an 8-percent return r_c on their investment. Using Equation 20-6, we find that the bond has a market price of $1500:

$$P_0 = \sum_{t=1}^{5} \frac{\$90}{(1 + .08)^5} + \frac{\$1675}{(1.08)^5} = \$1500$$

Reasons for Issuing Convertibles

Issuing convertible securities is really a form of deferred common stock financing, because the issuer and investors assume that the bond will be converted before maturity. In order to assume that the conversion takes place, the **conversion terms** (conversion rate and price) must be set so that they can be attained; otherwise investors will not buy the bonds. Moreover, most convertible bonds contain a **call provision.** If the market price of the bonds becomes sufficiently high, the company can force investors to convert by exercising the call provision. By way of illustration, let us say that the bond used in the previous example is called at 104($1040). Since the current market price of the bond is $1500, investors will convert their bonds into stock rather than turning the bonds back to the company for $1040.

Another reason for issuing convertible bonds is that market conditions may not be right for issuing common stock even if the company wanted to do so. In addition, convertible bonds generally have lower interest rates than comparable nonconvertible bonds because the conversion feature acts as an incentive to investors who, in turn, are willing to accept a slight reduction in interest payments.

In summary, convertible bonds are a form of deferred equity financing. They provide the issuing company with increased leverage until the bonds are converted. In addition, the interest charges on convertibles are somewhat lower than those for comparable straight bond issues. On the other hand, when the bonds are

converted, the earnings per share will be diluted. That is, total earnings after taxes will have to be distributed over a greater number of shares of common stock. If investors believe that a large number of bonds are about to be converted into common stock, it may have a depressing effect on share prices. Investors know that when such **overhanging issues** are converted, earnings per share are diluted and an increased number of shares of stock will be traded. If all other things were held constant, the increased supply of stock would result in lower stock prices. If the bonds are *not* converted the firm may have to continue servicing the debt and may find additional borrowing more difficult.

WARRANTS

Warrants have great speculative appeal. A $500 investment in R.K.O. warranties in 1942 would have been worth $104,000 in 1945! But glittering opportunities may prove to be fool's gold. A $500 investment in Atlantic Richfield Oil warrants in 1969 would have been worth only $15.47 three years later!

Warrants Defined

A warrant is a call option to buy a stated number of shares of stock at a specified price, on or before a predetermined date. Most warrants have a life of 5 to 10 years, but some are perpetual. Tri-Continental Corporation has **perpetual warrants** that entitle the holder to buy 8.81 shares of Tri-Continental common stock at $2.55 per share. The perpetual warrant means that there is no expiration date. In contrast, Safeway Stores Inc. has warrants that expire in 1996. They entitle the holder to purchase one share of stock at $2 per share until the expiration date.

The holder of the warrant can buy the stock of the issuing corporation by paying cash and, in some cases, by surrendering bonds (usually at par value) in lieu of the cash exercise price. Several companies that have warrants are listed in Table 20-2.

TABLE 20-2 Selected Companies with Stock Purchase Warrants

Commonwealth Oil Refining Co. Inc
Dr. Pepper/Seven-up Companies, Inc.
Eli Lilly & Co.
Gulf Resources & Chemical Corp.
Magma Cooper Company
Mattel Inc.
Orion Pictures Corp.
Parker Drilling Company
Safeway Stores, Inc.
Wurlitzer Co., The

Value of Warrants

The theoretical value of a warrant can be determined by the following equation:

$$\text{Value} = \left(\begin{array}{c} \text{Market price of} \\ \text{common stock} \end{array} - \begin{array}{c} \text{exercise} \\ \text{price} \end{array} \right) \times \begin{array}{c} \text{number of shares} \\ \text{that can be purchased} \\ \text{with each warrant} \end{array} \quad (20\text{-}9)$$

To illustrate the use of this equation, let us examine the Tri-Continental Corporation warrants. Each warrant entitles the holder to buy 6.37 shares of Tri-Continental common stock at $3.53 per share. If the stock is selling at $20 per share, each warrant is worth $104.91.

$$\text{Value} = (\$20.00 - \$3.53) \times (6.37) = \$104.91$$

This equation is applicable only when the market price of the stock is greater than the exercise price. When the market price of the stock is less than the exercise price, the warrant may still sell for a few cents. If the stock has any growth potential, that is a small price to pay for a long-term call option. Therefore, like convertible bonds, warrants can sell at a premium above the investment value.

Warrants are terrific investments when the price of the underlying stock is rising, but watch out when the stock price falls. If the share of Tri-Continental declined from $20 to $10 per share (a decrease of 50 percent), the value of the warrants would fall from $104.91 to $41.21, a reduction of 60.7 percent.

RIGHTS

Companies may offer new stock issues to their existing stockholders instead of offering them to the public. The primary reason for this type of offering is to allow existing stockholders to maintain their proportionate share of ownership in the corporation. Stockholders are said to have a **preemptive right** to purchase their **pro rata share** of new stock issues. Although the concept of preemptive rights is being questioned in the courts, so-called **privileged subscriptions,** or rights offerings, are commonplace.

Terms of the Offering

Normally, each stockholder receives one right for each share of stock that is owned. The issuing company informs its stockholders of how many **rights** are required to subscribe to each additional share at a **subscription price.** The subscription price must be lower than the current market price in order to induce stockholders to take advantage of the rights offering. Finally, the rights offerings are generally limited to 30 days or less. In essence, a right is like a short-term warrant. Both are call options on the stock.

Value of Rights

Stockholders receiving rights have three courses of action: (1) exercise the rights (subscribe to the stock), (2) sell the rights, or (3) let the rights expire. The rights have monetary value, so most investors exercise the rights or sell them.

Stocks can be traded with rights (**cum rights**) or without rights (**ex-rights**). The difference between cum rights and ex-rights centers around the date of record for the rights, which is established by the Board of Directors of the issuing company. Stockholders listed on the books of the corporation as of the date of record are entitled to receive rights. Stockholders who buy the stock and are not able to have their names listed on the corporation's books by the date of record are not entitled to receive the rights. The stock trades ex-rights three business days before the date of record because it takes four days to transfer names to the record books.

Until the rights are mailed to the stockholders, they are traded on a **when issued (W.I.) basis**. Trading W.I. rights usually begins the day the stock goes ex-rights and can last from several days to several weeks. As soon as the rights are mailed to stockholders, trading begins on a regular way basis.

Value Cum Rights

When a stock sells cum (with) rights, the theoretical value of one right can be determined from the following equation:

$$V_1 = \frac{P_0 - S}{N + 1} \qquad (20\text{-}10)$$

where

$V_1 =$ value of one right when stock is cum rights
$P_0 =$ market price of a share of stock
$S =$ subscription prices for a share of the new stock
$N =$ number of rights required to purchase a share of the new stock

For purposes of illustration, assume that the Brush Company has a rights offering. The stock is selling at \$40 per share, and four rights are required to buy a new share at the subscription price of \$38. When the rights are still attached to the stock, each has a theoretical value of \$0.40.

$$V_1 = \frac{P_0 - S}{N + 1} = \frac{\$40 - \$38}{4 + 1} = \$0.40$$

Rights, like warrants, are highly leveraged. For example, if the stock price increased 10 percent to \$44 per share, the rights would increase 300 percent to \$1.20:

$$V_1 = \frac{P_0 - S}{N + 1} = \frac{\$44 - \$38}{4 + 1} = \$1.20$$

If the stock price fell below the subscription price to $37 per share, theoretically the rights would have no value. Investors would buy the stock at the current market price ($37) instead of at the higher subscription price ($38). In reality, the rights still might sell for a few cents each. This premium is attributable to speculators who think that the stock will increase in value before the rights expire. In addition, the investment banking firm that underwrote the issue might buy the rights if there is a **standby underwriting agreement** in which the underwriter agrees to buy the unsold portion of the rights offering. The underwriter then exercises the rights and sells the stock to the public.

Value Ex-Rights

In theory, when a stock sells ex-rights, the market price of a share declines by an amount equal to the value of a right. In other words, the market value of a share of stock that is selling ex-rights is equal to the market value cum rights (P_0) less the value of a right (V_1) and the subscription price (S). Therefore, when a stock is selling ex-rights, the theoretical value of a right (V_2) can be determined as follows:

$$V_2 = \frac{P_0 - V_1 - S}{N}$$

$$= \frac{(\$40 - \$0.40 - \$38)}{4} \qquad (20\text{-}11)$$

$$= \$0.40$$

where

V_2 = the value of one right when the stock is ex-rights

The value of the rights is the same when the stock sells cum rights or ex-rights.

CONCLUSION

Convertible securities can be in the form of bonds or preferred stock. These securities are attractive to investors because of their yields and security and because they offer the opportunity of converting to common stock at a later time. In effect, they act like call options on common stock.

Convertible bonds can be converted to common stock during an established period ending before the maturity date of the bond. The conversion rate and the price per share are also established. The bond's theoretical value is related to the market price of the shares it can be converted into. Convertible bonds may sell at a premium because investors are willing to pay more for convertibility and safety.

For the issuing company, convertible bonds are a form of deferred equity financing. If market conditions are not right for issuing common stock, it may be possible to issue convertible bonds successfully. In addition, interest rates on convertibles are usually lower than on straight bonds.

Warrants and rights also act as call options on common stock. A warrant is an option to buy a certain number of shares of stock at a set price on or before a specific date, although some warrants are perpetual. Warrants can be attached to bonds to make the bond issue more attractive. The value of a warrant is determined by the relationship of the market value of the stock to the stock price set by the warrant. If the stock falls below the warrant's set price, the warrant may still have some value if the company has growth potential.

One effect of convertible bonds, convertible preferreds, and warrants is to increase the number of common shares outstanding—and often to dilute earnings per share and depress share prices. Rights have a somewhat different effect on individual stockholders. Rights are options to purchase stock offered to existing stockholders so that they can maintain the same proportion of ownership in the company. The price of stock purchased through rights is somewhat less than the market price. Rights have a value of their own, and stocks can be traded cum rights (with rights) or ex-rights (without rights).

Both rights and warrants are highly leveraged. A small increase in stock prices will cause a large percentage increase in the value of rights and warrants.

Call options are contracts to buy stock, and they are interesting vehicles for speculation and investment. Since convertibles, warrants, and rights contain option features, the holders of these securities have in effect bought calls.

IMPORTANT CONCEPTS

Call option
Call protection
Call provision
Conversion premium
Conversion price
Conversion rate
Conversion terms
Conversion value
Convertible bond
Convertible preferred
Cum rights
Deep discount
Discount
Exchangeable convertibles
Ex-rights
Investment value

Limited rights of redemption
Overhanging issue
Parity
Par value
Perpetual warrant
Preemptive rights
Premium
Privileged subscription
Pro rata share
"Put" feature
Resets
Rights
Standby underwriting agreement
Subscription price
Warrant
When issued (W.I.) basis

QUESTIONS AND EXERCISES

1. In what respects are convertible bonds similar to call options?
2. In what respects are warrants and rights similar to call options?

3. If a $1000 corporate bond has a conversion rate of 60, what is the conversion price?

4. Suppose that a convertible bond has a conversion rate of 50 and a conversion price of $20. If the underlying stock is selling for $30 per share, what should be the price of the bond?

5. What are the principal advantages of owning a convertible bond?

6. What is meant by the term "conversion premium?"

7. When is a convertible bond likely to have a conversion premium?

8. Refer to *The Wall Street Journal* and list five companies that have convertible bonds. Use the *Standard and Poor's Stock Guide* to find five companies with warrants.

9. Use *Moody's* or *Standard and Poor's* to determine the call provisions (not to be confused with conversion) of the five bonds from the previous question.

10. Examine the prices of the five bonds. Explain why they are selling at their current prices (premiums or discounts).

11. Some warrants can be purchased for only a few cents. Why might warrants be selling at such a low price?

12. In theory, what should happen to the market value of a share of common stock when it goes ex-rights?

13. In a recent rights offering, the market value of the stock was $75 per share, the subscription price was $60 per share, and 11 rights were required to subscribe to 1 share. What is the value of a right (ex-rights)?

14. If the market value of the stock in question 13 increased by 20 percent, what would be the percentage increase in the value of the rights?

15. If the market price of the stock in question 13 were to decline to $58, what would be the value of the rights?

COMMODITIES

S peculators who have the proper temperament and sufficient risk capital may find the commodities futures market an attractive investment medium. Two features that make commodities futures attractive are low margin requirements—frequently less than 10 percent of the value of commodities contracts—and prices that fluctuate. The high leverage gained from the low margins and the price swings make it possible for those who are skillful and lucky to make large profits. Those who are less fortunate incur large losses. This chapter examines some basic elements of commodity trading.

Most commodities traded in the futures markets are agricultural products, so our discussion is limited to such commodities. Nevertheless, the same principles apply to forestry products, metal, mortgages, Treasury bills, currencies, and other "commodities" traded in futures markets. In addition, futures are traded on stock market indexes such as the S&P 500 Stock Index.

TRADING FUTURES

The term **futures** refers to contracts to buy and receive, or sell and deliver, a commodity at some future date. Each commodity that is traded in the futures market has unique contract specifications. Figure 21-1 shows the contract specifications for the soybean futures, 1000-ounce silver futures, and U.S. Treasury bond futures, all of which are traded on the Chicago Board of Trade (CBOT). A close examination of the specifications reveals significant differences between the deliverable grades, price quotations, contract months, and other terms for the three commodities.

	Soybean Futures	1,000-ounce Silver Futures	U.S. Treasury Bond Futures
Trading unit	5,000 bushels	1,000 troy ounces	$100,000 face value
Deliverable grade	No. 2 Yellow at par and substitutions at differentials established by the exchange	Refined silver, assaying not less than 999 fineness and made up of one or more brands and markings officially listed by the exchange, in bars cast in basic weights of 1,000 troy ounces (each bar may vary not more than 12% more or less)	U.S. Treasury bonds maturing at least 15 years from the first day of the delivery month, if not callable; if callable, not so for at least 15 years from the first day of the delivery month. Coupon based on an 8% standard
Delivery method		By vault receipt drawn on deposits made in exchange-approved vaults in Chicago	Federal Reserve book-entry wire transfer system
Price quotation	Cents and quarter cents per bushel	In dollars and cents to the last 1/10 of one cent per troy ounce	In points ($1,000) and thirty-seconds of a point; for example, 80-16 equals 80 $\frac{16}{32}$
Tick size	One-quarter ($\frac{1}{4}$) cent per bushel ($12.50 per contract)	10/100 of a cent per troy ounce ($1 per contract)	One thirty-second of a point, or $31.25 (one tick) per contract
Daily price limit	30 cents per bushel ($1,500 per contract) above or below the previous day's settlement price	$1 per ounce above or below the previous day's settlement price	3 points ($3,000) per contract above or below the previous day's settlement price
Contract months	January, March, May, July, August, September, November		
Contract year	Starts in September and ends in August		
Trading hours	9:30 A.M. to 1:15 P.M. (Chicago time), except on the last trading day of an expiring contract, when trading closes at noon		

Last trading day — Seven business days before the last business day of the month

Last delivery day — Last business day of the delivery month

Ticker symbol — S

Contract months — Current month and the next two calendar months and February, April, June, August, October, and December

Trading hours — 7:25 A.M. to 1:25 P.M. (Chicago time), Monday through Friday

Last trading day — No trades in 1,000-ounce silver futures deliverable in the current month shall be made during the last three business days of that month

Ticker symbol — AG

Contract months — March, June, September, and December

Trading hours — 7:20 A.M. to 2:00 P.M. (Chicago time), Monday through Friday

Evening trading hours are from 5:00 to 8:30 P.M. (Central Standard time), or 6:00 to 9:30 P.M. (Central Daylight Saving time), Sunday through Thursday

Last trading day — Seven business days prior to the last business day of the delivery month

Last delivery day — Last business day of the delivery month

Ticker symbol — US

FIGURE 21-1 Selected contract specifications. *Source:* Chicago Board of Trade.

Futures contracts and contracts to buy or sell for cash differ in several important respects:

1. Futures contracts specify *standardized quantities and qualities* while cash contracts can be for any quantity or quality of a commodity. For example, soybean futures are traded in 5000-bushel units and the deliverable grade is No. 2 Yellow at par, or some other grade at differential prices established by the exchange. Similarly, the trading units for silver and the deliverable grade must be not less than 999 fineness. However, the weight of the 1000 troy ounce silver bars may vary up to 12 percent. U.S. Treasury bonds are traded in $100,000 face value units. The deliverable securities are specified in terms of a U.S. Treasury bond with at least 15 years to maturity or to the call date, and an 8 percent coupon. Because there are large numbers of U.S. Treasury bonds with other maturities and coupons, the CBOT publishes *conversion factors* to adjust the futures price for the actual coupon and maturity of the delivered bond.

2. Futures contracts specify *future months for delivery* while delivery can be in any month for cash contracts. The delivery months for agricultural commodities are commonly associated with harvest seasons, volume of trading, and other considerations. In the case of soybeans, for example, the delivery months are January, March, May, July, August, September, and November. Other factors relevant to the metals and financial markets determine their delivery months.

3. Futures contracts are *traded on organized commodities exchanges.* In many respects, commodity exchanges are analogous to stock exchanges. Both provide a place where members can make purchases and sales. To carry the analogy further, the cash market is an over-the-counter market.

4. Futures contracts can be **offset** — long positions can be liquidated through the sale of an equal number of contracts for the same delivery month. Similarly, short positions can be covered with an equal number of contracts for the same delivery month. Fewer than 3 percent of all futures contracts result in the delivery of the physical commodity.

The Futures Market

Price Risk Management

One economic function of the futures market is shifting the risk of changes in commodity prices from those who do not want it (hedgers) to those who do want it (speculators). Hedgers include processors and commercial producers and users of agricultural, financial, and other commodities. For example, a wheat-flour miller has a contract to deliver 10,000 pounds of flour to a bakery at a fixed price six months from now. The miller has not bought the wheat yet because of lack of storage space, and is concerned that the price of wheat will rise in the interim. Therefore the miller wants to "hedge" or "lock in" the existing price of wheat. In other words, the miller wants to transfer the risk that the price will change to someone else — a speculator.

Price Discovery, Stabilization, and Liquidity

Speculators are traders who attempt to anticipate commodity price changes and try to make a profit by trading in commodity futures or the physical commodity. In this case the speculator hopes that the price of wheat does change. Speculators and other traders in the commodities markets each have certain market information that they believe will affect commodities prices. For example, suppose that there is currently a bountiful supply of wheat and that wheat prices are relatively low, but a private forecast for the coming season indicates that the crop will be small and that prices will rise. The speculators who have access to this forecast believe that wheat prices are going to rise in the future and will take advantage of the current low prices and buy large amounts of wheat. In effect, they are withholding wheat from current consumption in order to sell it in the future, thereby adding to the supply at that time.

This example illustrates another economic function of the futures market and the role of the speculators. The other economic function of the market is **price discovery.** That is, the information that speculators, hedgers, and others bring to the market is reflected in the fair market prices of the commodities they trade. The result is that there is a link between commodity prices and the underlying cash market prices throughout the life of the contract. Thus, the prices of futures contracts provide some information about the cash price movements of commodities in the months ahead.

Second, the fact that speculators withheld wheat from current consumption and will add to the supply in the future has a **stabilizing** effect on prices. This is so because the purchases now tend to hold the price up, and the sale of the wheat in the future tends to keep it from rising as high as it might have gone. Therefore, if the speculators are functioning properly, they will stabilize both the supply and the price of commodities over a period of time.

Finally, speculators provide **liquidity** for the hedgers' transactions. There is a market with a large number of willing buyers and sellers who are able to trade large quantities with small price changes.

Hedging

Hedging is the initiation of a position in the futures market that is intended as a temporary substitute for the purchase or sale of a physical commodity. To elaborate on this definition, let us say that hedging consists of taking an equal but opposite position (long or short) in both the cash and futures market at the same time. Strict adherence to these conditions for hedging are not necessary, but they facilitate the explanation of the process. To explain how a hedge works, we make the following simplifying assumptions:

1. Commodity price changes occur in the same direction in both the cash and the futures markets. If prices increase in the cash market, they will increase in the futures market too.
2. Prices change by the same amount in both markets.

3. Profits (or losses) from the cash market offset losses (or profits) from the futures market.

4. There are no transaction costs.

To illustrate a hedge, suppose that a producer of food products has promised to deliver 1,120,000 pounds of sugar at $0.22/lb. in July. The producer is short the sugar. A contract for sugar is 112,000 pounds. To hedge, the producer goes long 10 July contracts of sugar in the futures market at $0.26/lb. If the price of sugar declines 3 cents, the producer will make a profit in the cash market by covering the short position. The profit will exactly offset the loss incurred in the futures market by closing out (selling) the long position below cost. These transactions can be summarized as follows:

Cash Market	Futures Market
1. Short 1,120,000 lbs. @ $0.22/lb.	Long 10 July contracts @ $0.26/lb.
2. Price declines $0.03/lb.	Price declines $0.03/lb.
3. Cover short at $0.19/lb.	Sell contracts at $0.23/lb.
4. Profit = $0.03/lb.	Loss = $0.03/lb.
5. Total profit = $33,600 ($0.03 × 1,120,000 lbs.)	Total loss = $33,600 ($0.03 × 1,120,000 lbs.)

Had sugar prices increased instead, the profit made from the long position in the futures market would have offset the loss from the short position in the cash market.

The reason for hedging is to protect against a potential loss from a change in the cash price of a commodity. Farmers, manufacturers, and others use several types of hedging transactions to transfer price risk to speculators.

Hedging can also be used to make profits because of basis fluctuations. The term **basis** refers to the arithmetic difference between the cash price of a commodity and the futures price. When the difference between the two prices is small, the basis is said to be strong. A wide difference in prices gives rise to a weak basis. The strength or weakness of a basis depends primarily on the supply and demand for that cash commodity. Generally, a weak basis indicates an oversupply of the cash commodity.

Selling Hedge

A selling hedge involves selling a futures contract to protect the value of existing inventories. For example, in September Farmer Jones owns 10,000 bushels of wheat, and the cash price at the local market is $3 per bushel. Jones wants to receive that amount in order to cover his costs and make a modest profit. He believes that the price of wheat will decline by December, when he has a contract

to deliver the wheat to a miller. Nevertheless, futures contracts for wheat to be delivered in December are selling for $3.10 per bushel. In order to ensure that he receives $3 per bushel, Jones hedges. He sells a contract to deliver 10,000 bushels of wheat in December at $3.10 per bushel. Now Jones is **long** the wheat because he owns the crop, and he is **short** in the futures market. Because of the $0.10 basis ($3.10 − $3.00 = $0.10), he can protect his $3 cash price. This is possible because cash prices and futures prices are affected by the same factors, and they generally move together and change by the same amount.

Let us say that the price of wheat in both the cash and futures markets declines by $0.05 in December. The farmer's loss of $0.05 in the cash market was offset by his gain of $0.05 in the futures market. Therefore, the net gain was zero, and Jones received the $3 per bushel that he desired.

Cash Market	**Futures Market**
September 1	**September 1**
Owns 10,000 bushels of wheat; price is $3.00 per bushel at local market (long position)	Sells a contract for 10,000 bushels of December wheat at Chicago Board of Trade for $3.10 per bushel (short position)
December 1	**December 1**
Sells 10,000 bushels at local market for $2.95 per bushel	Buys a contract for 10,000 bushels of December wheat at Chicago Board of Trade for $3.05 per bushel.
Loss $0.05 per bushel	Gain $0.05 per bushel
Net gain = 0	

If both the cash price and futures price had risen by the same amount, the net gain would still be zero. The gain in the cash market would have exactly offset the loss in the futures market.

At times the cash price and futures price do not change by the same amount. The result can be a profit or a loss, depending upon the direction and extent of price movements. More will be said about this in connection with basis trading.

Buying Hedge

Those who buy commodities (grain elevator operators, processors, manufacturers, and exporters) may use a buying hedge to reduce the risk of price changes. With this type of hedge, a futures contract is purchased (long on futures) to protect against price changes for inventories that are yet to be acquired (short on cash markets). For example, suppose that a manufacturer of breakfast cereal receives an order to deliver 5000 bushels of processed oats three months from now. The manufacturer sets his price based on the current (April) price of $1.50

per bushel, even though the oats will not be purchased until a week before the delivery date in July. In essence, the manufacturer is short 5000 bushels at $1.50 per bushel. In order to protect against a price rise, which would result in a loss, the manufacturer buys a futures contract that exactly offsets the short cash position. In this example, July oats are selling for $1.48 per bushel. In July, the manufacturer closes out both the short and long positions. The loss from the short position exactly offsets the gain from the long position, so the manufacturer was perfectly hedged.

Cash Market	Futures Market
April 1	**April 1**
Sells 5000 bushels of oats at $1.50 per bushel for delivery to supermarket in processed form in July (short position)	Buys a contract for 5000 bushels of July oats at $1.48 per bushel (long position)
July 1	**July 1**
Buys 5000 bushels of oats at $1.51 per bushel	Sells a contract for 5000 bushels of July oats at $1.49 per bushel
Loss = $0.01 per bushel	Gain = $0.01 per bushel
Net gain = 0	

Basis Trading

Basis trading focuses mainly on the difference between the cash and futures prices because the basis is generally more stable and predictable than the price level of commodities. In the examples used to illustrate selling and buying hedges, the price level of the commodities changed but the basis remained stable. In basis trading, the cash price is said to be *over* or *under* the *futures price*. If the cash price for beet sugar was $0.59 per pound in January and the March futures price was $0.61 per pound, then the basis would have been $0.02 under. Stated otherwise: the cash price was $0.02 under the futures price.

The following example shows how basis trading works. Jane Lafarge, an elevator operator, buys soybeans at $4.50 per bushel, which is $0.10 under the November futures price. In order to hedge, she sells November soybean futures at $4.60. She is long the cash soybeans and short the futures, and her buying basis is *$0.10 off November.* The amount of money that she can make depends on the price at which she can sell the soybeans. She has to sell the soybeans at something less than $0.10 off November in order to make a profit. Let us say that a manufacturer agrees to pay Lafarge $0.02 off November for the soybeans. The transaction is not completed until the long and short positions are closed out. When this occurs, Lafarge has a profit of at least $0.08 per bushel.

Cash Market	Futures Market
Buy soybeans at $4.50 per bushel or $0.10 off November future (long position)	Sell November futures at $4.60 per bushel (short position)
Sell soybeans at $0.02 off November futures	Buy back November futures
Gain = $0.08 plus whatever change occurs in November futures	Gain = whatever change occurs in November futures

Spread Trading

The terms **spread** and **straddle** are used interchangeably in commodities trading. A spread is the simultaneous purchase of one futures contract and the sale of another contract for the same commodity, but with a different delivery month. A spread also refers to the purchase of one commodity and the sale of another related commodity on the same or a different market. For example, a trader may be short on March pork belly contracts and long on August contracts. Similarly, a trader may be long on wheat and short on oats. The idea behind spread trading is that a trader believes that a profit can be made because the difference between prices in various contract months (or in related commodities) will change in his or her favor.

Commodities Options

Traders can deal in puts, calls, and double options (a put and call) that are backed by commodities instead of stocks. Such commodities include corn, cotton, sugar, gold, silver, other commodities, and stock index futures.

Financial Futures

Financial futures contracts are similar to grain futures contracts, except that the underlying asset consists of Treasury securities, commercial paper, or some other type of security, including common stock and stock indexes. Consider U.S. Treasury bond futures. The basic trading unit of U.S. bonds has a face value at maturity of $100,000 and an interest rate of 8 percent. Prices are quoted as a percentage of par; accordingly, 100 – 100 means 100 percent of par. A price of 98 – 16 means 98 and 16/32 percent of par. Each 1/32 of a point is worth $31.25 per contract ($100,000 ÷ 100 ÷ 32 = $31.25). The prices of these futures contracts reflect current and expected levels of interest rates. Recall that the prices of outstanding bonds and the current level of interest rates are inversely related. That is, if interest rates are high, bond prices will be low. Investors expecting interest rates to rise (bond prices to fall) can protect their positions by hedging in the interest rate futures market.

Stock Indexes

Futures contracts are traded on stock market indexes such as the S&P 500 Stock Index, the NYSE Composite Stock Index, the Value Line Index, and others. Investors dealing in these futures should be familiar with the characteristics of the underlying stock index. The major stock indexes were examined in Chapter 8.

MECHANICS OF TRADING

Commodities are traded in the same manner as stocks and bonds. There are exchanges where trading takes place, clearinghouses, various types of orders to buy and sell stocks, margins, and other similar features. Because these topics have been discussed elsewhere in the text, only those aspects that are significantly different from stock transactions are discussed here.

Exchanges

There are more than a dozen commodities exchanges in the United States and elsewhere, with trading in more than 175 commodities. The major exchanges in the United States are in Chicago, New York, and Kansas City. Each exchange generally deals in a variety of commodities. For example, the Chicago Mercantile Exchange deals in frozen pork bellies, live cattle, shell eggs, nest-run eggs, live hogs, lumber, potatoes, milo, feeder cattle, frozen boneless beef, frozen hams, frozen eggs, turkeys, and butter. In addition, the International Monetary Market of the Chicago Mercantile Exchange specializes in trading international currency futures. This list of commodities traded on one exchange gives some idea of the variety of commodities that are actively traded. Table 21-1 presents a partial list of actively traded commodities and the exchanges where they are traded. In some cases the same commodity is traded on several different exchanges. Wheat, for example, is traded on the Chicago Board of Trade, the Kansas City Board of Trade, and the Minneapolis Grain Exchange.

Commodities exchanges in other countries are accessible through a variety of agreements between U.S. and foreign exchanges. **GLOBEX,** for example, is a joint venture between the Chicago Mercantile Exchange, Reuters Holdings, PLC, and commodities exchanges in Europe, Asia, and elsewhere. It is an electronic trading system for futures and options that creates a market that is available almost 24 hours a day because of its worldwide scope. When it is midnight, central standard time, in Chicago, trading is going on in Tokyo (3 P.M.), and the markets in London (6 A.M.) and Paris (7 A.M.) will open shortly. The exchanges that participate in GLOBEX are linked together through Reuters' Digital Equipment Corporation computers and terminals. Reuters, specializing in financial news and information, has more than 165,000 terminals in 118 countries around the world.

The Chicago Board of Trade, in an effort to participate more actively in global markets, trades long-term Japanese government bond futures, Tokyo stock price index futures and options, and Japanese yen futures (on its affiliate, the Mid-

TABLE 21-1   U.S. Exchanges and Selected Commodities

Exchange/Commodity	Contracts
Chicago Board of Trade	
Wheat	5000 bushels
Corn	5000 bushels
Oats	5000 bushels
U.S. Treasury bonds	$100,000
U.S. Treasury notes	$100,000
GNMA (mortgages)	$100,000
Stock index (Amex)	$100 ($250) × Index
Bonds, muni	$1000 × Index
NASDAQ 100 Index	$250 × Index
Silver	1000 troy ounces
Gold	1 kilogram
MidAmerica Commodity Exchange	
Wheat	1000 bushels
Corn	1000 bushels
Oats	1000 bushels
U.S. Treasury bonds	$50,000
U.S. Treasury bills	$50,000
Hogs, live	15,000 pounds
Cattle, live	20,000 pounds
Silver	1000 troy ounces
Platinum	25 troy ounces
Copper	12,500 pounds
Dollars, Canadian	50,000
Francs, Swiss	62,500
Marks, Deutsche	62,500
Pound sterling	12,500
Yen, Japanese	6,250,000
Kansas City Board of Trade	
Wheat	5000 bushels
Stock index, Value Line	$500 (100) × Index
Minneapolis Grain Exchange	
Wheat	5000 bushels
Chicago Rice and Cotton Exchange	
Cotton	100 bales
Rice	200,000 pounds
Chicago Mercantile Exchange and International Monetary Market	
Hogs, live	30,000 pounds
Pork bellies	38,000 pounds
Cattle, live	40,000 pounds
Gold	100 troy ounces

TABLE 21-1 U.S. Exchanges and Selected Commodities
(*continued*)

Exchange/Commodity	Contracts
Treasury bills	$1,000,000
Dollars, Canadian	100,000
Francs, French	250,000
Francs, Swiss	125,000
Pesos, Mexico	1,000,000
Pounds sterling	25,000
Yen, Japanese	12,500,000
Certificate of deposits, 90-day	$1,000,000
Eurodollars, 3-month	$1,000,000
Stock index (S&P 500)	$500 × Index
Stock index (S&P) OTC 250	$250 × Index
European Currency Unit	125,000
New York Mercantile Exchange	
Heating oil	42,000 gallons
Potatoes (Maine)	50,000 pounds
Palladium	100 troy ounces
Gasoline	42,000 gallons
New York Cotton Exchange and Associates	
Cotton	50,000 pounds
Orange juice	15,000 pounds
Dollar index	$500 × Index
European Currency Unit	100,000
Coffee, Sugar, and Cocoa Exchange	
Cocoa	10 metric tons
Sugar	112,000 pounds
Coffee	37,500 pounds
Index, CPI	$1000 × Index
Commodities Exchange	
Silver	5000 troy ounces
Copper	25,000 pounds
Gold	100 troy ounces
Aluminum	40,000 pounds
New York Futures Exchange	
Stock index (NYSE)	$500 × Index
Commodity Research Bureau Index	$500 × Index
Philadelphia Board of Trade	
Francs, Swiss	125,000
Marks, Deutsche	125,000
Pounds sterling	25,000
Yen, Japanese	12,500,000
Stock index, XOC	125,000

Source: Commodity Futures Trading Commission.

America Commodity Exchange). The CBOT has expanded trading hours, from 6 P.M. to 8:15 P.M., central standard time, to coincide with the Tokyo Stock Exchange's morning trading session. These are just a few examples of the increased globalization of financial and commodities markets.

Figure 21-2 shows the trading floor of the Chicago Board of Trade. Trading activity takes place in octagonal areas known as **pits.** The traders stand in designated areas of the pits according to the delivery month in which they wish to trade. The trading is done by the "auction" method, and traders use the hand signals shown in Figures 21-3 and 21-4 to conduct their business. A trader whose hand is facing inward wants to buy. Conversely, a hand facing outward means that the trader wants to sell. Each finger held vertically indicates the quantity to be bought or sold. And fingers extended horizontally indicate the price at which the trader will buy or sell.

Most of the commodities exchanges in the United States are voluntary associations of member firms whose principal business is the production or marketing of commodities traded on the exchange. Commodities exchanges in the United States are regulated by the **Commodity Futures Trading Commission (CFTC),** which was created by Congress in 1974 to regulate commodity futures and

FIGURE 21-2 Trading on the Chicago Board of Trade.

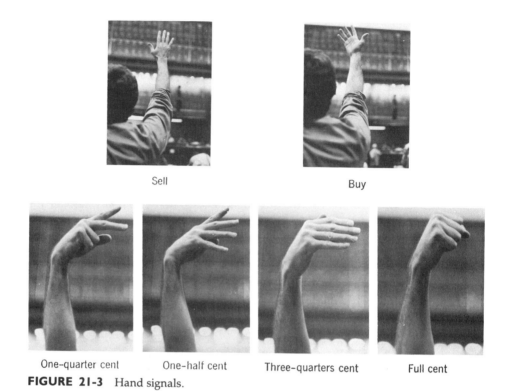

Sell   Buy

One-quarter cent   One-half cent   Three-quarters cent   Full cent

FIGURE 21-3   Hand signals.

FIGURE 21-4   Traders using hand signals.

related trading activity in the United States. The Commission consists of five members appointed by the President and confirmed by Congress. The CFTC has exclusive jurisdiction over all futures trading on contract markets, which means that federal and state agencies cannot regulate futures trading on contract markets. The Futures Trading Act of 1978 authorized a "sunset" provision for the CFTC, which means that Congress must renew its charter on a periodic basis or the CFTC will go out of existence. In addition to federal regulation, there is an industry-wide, self-regulatory organization, the **National Futures Association (NFA),** that is under the oversight of the CFTC.

Margin

The fact that commodities trading is traditionally done on small **margins** attracts speculators. The margin deposit is really a form of bond that is deposited with the commodity broker to indicate the speculator's good faith or willingness and ability to pay. In contrast, margin in stock transactions represents a down payment in a credit transaction.

Each commodities exchange sets its own minimum margin requirements. Commodities brokers can impose higher margin requirements on their customers if they wish to do so. Margin requirements are usually specified in dollar amounts. For example, the margin requirement for a contract of soybeans is $1250. Some typical margins are as follows:

Commodity	Margin per Contract
Wheat	$1,000
Oats	500
Corn	500
S&P 500 futures	$15,000 Speculators / $10,000 Hedgers

Suppose that wheat is selling for $3 per bushel. A wheat contract consists of 5000 bushels and is worth $15,000. The initial margin requirement is only $1000, which is 6.6 percent of the total value involved. In the case of a spread between two different delivery months, the margin requirement may be as low as $500. Because the margins are low, generally 5 to 20 percent, small price changes can result in large profits or losses to the investor.

Price Changes

At this point it may be useful to clarify a popular misconception about commodities prices. In general, commodities prices are less volatile than common stock prices. The wide fluctuations in returns made by speculators are attributable largely to the high degree of leverage that comes from the low margin requirements. One reason commodities prices are less volatile than stock prices is that

TABLE 21-2 Selected Daily Limits and Trading Ranges

Commodity	Daily Limit	Maximum Daily Range
Broilers, iced	$0.02	$0.04
Copper	$0.03	$0.06
Corn	$0.10	$0.20
Deutsche mark	Subject to change	None
Gold	$10	$20
Industrial oil	$2	$4
Japanese yen	Subject to change	None
90-Day Treasury bills	Subject to change	None
Oats	$0.06	$0.12
1-Year Treasury bills	50 Basis points	—
Plywood, softwood	$7	$14
Rubber	$0.02	$0.04
Rye	$0.15	$0.30
S&P 500 futures	30 Basis points	—
Silver coins, U.S.	$150	$300
Soybean meal	$10	$20
Soybean oil	$0.01	$0.02
Sugar	$0.02	$0.04
Wheat (Chicago Board of Trade)	$0.20	$0.40

there are two limitations on price changes. The **daily limit** restricts the amount that a price can change from the previous day's settling (closing) price. The **maximum daily range** limits the amount the price can change during the day. Sometimes the daily limit and the maximum daily range are the same, which in the case of frozen concentrate orange juice is three cents. Typically, the maximum range is twice the daily limit, as Table 21-2 shows.

In addition to the maximum limits on price changes, there are minimum limits on price changes. This limitation is similar to that for common stocks where the **minimum price change** is $\frac{1}{8}$ of a point or 12.5 cents per share. The minimum price change in a commodities transaction is called a **tick.** Prices of futures contracts must change by some multiple of the minimum tick. When the price of soybean meal changes by a minimum tick of $0.05 per ton, the value of a 100-ton contract traded on the Chicago Board of Trade changes **$5.** Generally, commodities traders refer to price changes as **points,** with a point equal to $0.01. Because grains, such as wheat, fluctuate in $\frac{1}{4}$-cent ticks, the prices are quoted in dollars and cents per bushel. A $\frac{1}{4}$-cent change amounts to $12.50 on a contract for 5000 bushels of wheat. Oats are traded in $\frac{1}{8}$-cent ticks, which amount to $6.25 on a 5000 bushel contract.

Reading Commodities Quotations

Reading commodities quotations is similar to reading stock quotations. There are two types of commodities quotations: **future prices** and **cash prices.** The futures

prices reflect what commodities traders think the commodities prices will be at some future date, while cash prices reflect current market conditions. The quotations for futures prices shown in Figure 21-5 list the following information for numerous commodities.

1. *The open:*
   the price at which the first transaction of the day transpired.

2. *The high and the low:*
   the highest and lowest prices at which a contract was traded during the trading day.

3. *The settle:*
   the final price at which contracts traded during the trading session. Sometimes two prices are shown to indicate the range of prices that was being traded at the time of the close.

4. *The change:*
   the difference between the closing price shown in the paper and the closing price for the previous trading session.

5. *The lifetime high and low:*
   the highest and lowest prices at which contracts traded during the duration of those contracts.

6. *The open interest:*
   contracts outstanding.

Now let us examine several commodities quotations. Corn futures, traded on the Chicago Board of Trade (CBOT), are the first commodity listed under the heading *Grains and Oilseeds.* The size of a contract is 5000 bushels of corn and the price is stated in cents per bushel. In Figure 21-5, the opening price of the December contract was 227, or $2.27 per bushel. The March 1991 contract opened at 236, or $2.36 per bushel. The cash price, shown in the right-hand column, for No. 2 yellow corn was $2.17 per bushel. Thus, the futures price is higher than the cash price. A glance at the distant futures prices of corn suggests that the price of corn is expected to rise.

The figure also shows the lifetime high and low prices for the contracts. The lifetime range for the December contract was $296\frac{1}{2}$ to $221\frac{1}{2}$. The open interest is the number of contracts outstanding—125,938.

An examination of other commodities reveals that despite the problems in Iraq in the summer of 1990, crude oil, heating oil, and gasoline prices were expected to decline.

FUTURES VERSUS OPTIONS

Figure 21-6 illustrates the profitability of futures contracts and call options when the price of the underlying asset changes. The two top panels show that the buyer of futures contracts gain as the price of the contract rises. In contrast, the seller of futures contracts gains as the price of the contract falls. This is so because the seller

COMMODITY FUTURES PRICES

Wednesday, September 26, 1990

Open Interest Reflects Previous Trading Day.

	Open	High	Low	Settle	Change	Lifetime High	Lifetime Low	Open Interest
–GRAINS AND OILSEEDS–								
CORN (CBT) 5,000 bu.; cents per bu.								
Dec	227	229	226	228¼	+ ½	296½	221½	125,938
Mr91	236	238½	235¾	237¾	+ ½	302½	230¾	39,925
May	241½	244	241½	243¾	+ ½	306½	237½	16,399
July	246	247¼	245¼	247	....	308½	242½	15,873
Sept	244	244	242¼	243¼	– 1¼	287½	241¼	1,900
Dec	245	245¼	243½	244¾	– ¾	275	242½	8,293
Est vol 34,000; vol Tues 32,613; open int 208,452, –487.								
OATS (CBT) 5,000 bu.; cents per bu.								
Dec	114¼	115½	112½	114¼	– ¼	194¼	110	10,224
Mr91	124½	126	122¾	124¾	– ¼	201	120½	2,299
May	130	133	130	132½	....	183¾	129	517
July	....	....	....	139¼	....	145	135½	111
Est vol 1,250; vol Tues 923; open int 13,153, –87.								
SOYBEANS (CBT) 5,000 bu.; cents per bu.								
Nov	616	618¾	612½	615½	– 2	682	564½	60,037
Ja91	631	633	627	630	– 2	692	587	14,010
Mar	643½	645½	640	642¼	– 2½	703	608	10,615
May	653	654¾	649	651¼	– 2¼	711	614½	5,796
July	659¾	661¼	655	658¼	– 2¾	718	625	4,086
Aug	655	656½	655	654	– 3	695	628	630
Sept	....	....	....	633	– 2	670	629	569
Nov	626	627	624	624¾	– 2	674	612½	3,750
Est vol 35,000; vol Tues 30,569; open int 99,465, +733.								
SOYBEAN MEAL (CBT) 100 tons; $ per ton.								
Oct	175.80	177.20	175.20	176.50	....	200.00	168.00	9,755
Dec	181.00	182.30	180.10	181.80	+ .30	205.50	170.50	29,758
Ja91	183.30	184.10	182.20	183.60	+ .10	204.00	171.50	7,734
Mar	186.50	187.00	185.50	186.70	....	212.00	174.50	4,509
May	187.30	188.00	186.80	188.00	....	208.00	175.80	2,651
July	189.50	190.00	188.30	190.00	+ .50	209.00	177.50	2,093
Aug	188.50	189.50	188.50	189.00	+ .50	199.00	176.50	1,383
Sept	188.00	189.00	188.00	188.70	– .30	193.50	175.50	628
Oct	....	....	....	187.70	+ 1.20	190.00	184.00	196
Dec	187.00	188.50	187.00	188.50	+ 2.00	189.80	182.00	207
Est vol 17,000; vol Tues 21,491; open int 58,914, –163.								
SOYBEAN OIL (CBT) 60,000 lbs.; cents per lb.								
Oct	23.57	23.65	23.46	23.46	– .13	25.56	19.65	10,147
Dec	23.75	23.91	23.68	23.75	– .03	25.55	19.75	34,095
Ja91	23.95	24.15	23.95	24.00	....	25.55	19.81	11,620
Mar	24.23	24.40	24.23	24.27	– .01	25.61	19.85	7,395
May	24.43	24.50	24.40	24.47	+ .02	25.65	20.25	3,721
July	24.50	24.55	24.50	24.55	+ .05	25.70	20.90	2,565
Aug	24.50	24.50	24.40	24.40	+ .05	25.50	24.15	508
Sept	24.10	24.10	24.10	24.10	– .10	25.10	23.85	308
Oct	....	....	....	23.75	– .23	24.90	23.76	149
Dec	23.40	23.60	23.40	23.60	– .10	24.75	23.40	112
Est vol 18,000; vol Tues 14,290; open int 70,620, –1,680.								
WHEAT (CBT) 5,000 bu.; cents per bu.								
Dec	273¾	278¾	273¼	276½	+ 1¾	380	267¾	35,470
Mr91	288½	292½	287½	290½	+ 1	382½	282½	15,614
May	295	300½	295	297¾	+ 1¾	373	291	5,079
July	301½	304½	301	303	+ 1¾	355	296½	2,899
Sept	309	310	307	307	+ 1¼	326	302	108
Est vol 12,000; vol Tues 9,128; open int 59,182, –186.								
WHEAT (KC) 5,000 bu.; cents per bu.								
Dec	275½	279	274½	278½	+ 2¼	388	269½	16,497
Mr91	287	290	286	289¾	+ 2½	386½	281½	7,454
May	295	297½	294	297	+ 2	371	288¾	2,595
July	299	302	298½	301¾	+ 2½	320½	293½	868
Est vol 3,643; vol Tues 3,802; open int 27,414, +59.								
WHEAT (MPLS) 5,000 bu.; cents per bu.								
Dec	267	269¾	266½	268¼	+ ½	386½	262	8,521
Mr91	279½	281¾	278½	280½	+ ¾	379¼	275	2,908
May	286	289	286	288¾	+ ¼	308	282	737
July	....	....	....	294	....	306	289	238
Est vol 1,689; vol Tues 2,019; open int 12,432, +332.								
BARLEY (WPG) 20 metric tons; Can. $ per ton								
Oct	80.10	81.50	79.80	81.50	+ 1.10	122.50	78.90	3,137
Mar	56.90	56.90	55.55	56.22	– .40	62.95	49.20	827
May	57.25	57.55	56.15	57.15	– .25	63.35	49.50	301
Est vol 3,108; vol Tues 2,168; open int 5,796, –68.								
–FOOD & FIBER–								
COCOA (CSCE)–10 metric tons; $ per ton.								
Dec	1,278	1,285	1,271	1,274	– 14	1,558	965	17,810
Mr91	1,318	1,325	1,315	1,315	– 15	1,581	985	9,531
May	1,345	1,350	1,345	1,346	– 17	1,572	1,000	4,552
July	1,378	1,378	1,378	1,378	– 15	1,590	1,060	7,308
Sept	1,413	1,413	1,413	1,409	– 15	1,515	1,264	3,473
Dec	....	....	....	1,442	– 15	1,535	1,325	5,606
Est vol 3,541; vol Tues 3,237; open int 48,280, +322.								
COFFEE (CSCE)–37,500 lbs.; cents per lb.								
Dec	94.70	95.30	94.10	94.35	– .30	109.50	81.00	24,672
Mr91	97.90	98.25	97.20	97.30	– .40	112.00	85.00	9,700
May	100.10	100.25	99.50	99.50	– .45	113.00	91.25	1,804
July	102.00	102.25	101.30	101.55	– .30	111.50	94.00	603
Sept	104.00	104.00	103.50	103.55	– .85	113.50	97.50	250
Est vol 2,883; vol Tues 4,673; open int 37,071, –208.								
SUGAR–WORLD (CSCE)–112,000 lbs.; cents per lb.								
Oct	10.98	11.05	10.81	10.82	– .26	15.93	9.78	11,686
Mr91	10.75	10.82	10.57	10.58	– .27	15.08	9.72	63,908
May	10.75	10.82	10.59	10.60	– .25	14.91	9.80	17,595
July	10.76	10.77	10.59	10.60	– .24	14.70	9.88	9,382
Oct	10.78	10.82	10.76	10.66	– .23	14.40	9.87	3,302
Est vol 22,746; vol Tues 22,506; open int 105,873, –4,179.								
SUGAR–DOMESTIC (CSCE)–112,000 lbs.; cents per lb.								
Nov	23.31	23.35	23.31	23.35	+ .04	23.84	21.80	2,040
Ja91	23.13	23.13	23.13	23.13	....	23.30	22.50	3,592
Mar	23.08	23.09	23.05	23.05	– .03	23.31	22.51	1,186
May	23.16	23.18	23.16	23.18	+ .06	23.30	22.76	1,517
July	23.16	23.20	23.16	23.20	+ .08	23.30	22.77	1,963
Sept	23.14	23.18	23.14	23.18	+ .04	23.35	22.78	778
Nov	22.90	22.90	22.85	22.85	– .05	23.05	22.55	396
Est vol 692; vol Tues 412; open int 11,472, –102.								
COTTON (CTN)–50,000 lbs.; cents per lb.								
Oct	73.60	74.00	73.55	73.70	– .30	82.05	63.95	546
Dec	71.73	72.30	71.50	72.28	+ .46	77.00	62.70	17,942
Mr91	72.85	73.40	72.56	73.40	+ .54	77.70	63.82	7,581
May	73.55	73.90	73.10	73.90	+ .32	77.40	64.40	6,272
July	74.00	74.15	73.60	74.07	+ .47	78.38	65.67	2,342
Oct	69.90	69.90	69.90	69.60	– .15	72.85	67.70	277
Dec	67.80	67.85	67.80	67.85	– .03	69.10	66.40	1,131
Est vol 5,000; vol Tues 8,218; open int 36,091, +71.								
ORANGE JUICE (CTN)–15,000 lbs.; cents per lb.								
Nov	135.05	136.70	135.05	136.70	+ 1.60	199.50	126.25	3,652
Ja91	130.90	132.40	130.90	132.40	+ 1.80	196.75	125.50	1,862
Mar	131.90	133.00	131.00	132.40	+ .90	190.50	130.50	784
May	....	....	....	132.10	+ 1.10	190.00	131.00	168
Est vol 600; vol Tues 343; open int 6,702, +88.								
–METALS & PETROLEUM–								
COPPER-HIGH (CMX)–25,000 lbs.; cents per lb.								
Sept	129.50	135.00	129.50	133.80	+ 4.60	138.40	92.50	1,617
Oct	124.30	125.00	123.00	124.90	+ 1.40	136.00	94.50	1,937
Nov	....	....	....	121.00	+ .80	127.80	94.50	369
Dec	117.80	118.80	115.50	117.60	+ .10	131.20	91.50	19,023
Ja91	115.00	115.00	114.20	115.60	....	126.40	94.00	506
Mar	112.60	113.20	110.70	112.20	– .10	122.60	92.30	3,591
May	110.50	110.00	109.50	109.80	....	117.80	97.00	1,308
July	108.10	108.10	106.50	107.40	....	113.50	96.50	1,138
Sept	105.20	105.80	103.70	105.00	....	110.50	95.50	1,354
Dec	103.30	103.30	100.80	102.00	– .50	108.50	94.50	747
Dec	532.0	532.5	530.0	531.9	– 3.8	623.5	525.0	1,450
Mr92	....	....	....	543.6	– 3.8	613.0	537.5	513
May	....	....	....	551.7	– 3.8	....	....	189
Est vol 21,000; vol Tues 16,564; open int 92,379, –1,052.								
SILVER (CBT)–1,000 troy oz.; cents per troy oz.								
Oct	480.0	480.0	476.0	480.0	– 3.0	632.0	471.0	822
Dec	489.0	489.0	481.0	488.0	– 3.2	645.0	478.0	10,454
Fb91	497.0	497.0	490.0	495.5	– 4.5	647.0	487.0	188
Apr	505.0	505.0	500.0	503.0	– 4.0	603.0	496.0	146
June	511.0	511.0	510.5	510.5	– 3.5	579.0	504.0	398
Est vol 500; vol Tues 406; open int 12,076, +89.								
CRUDE OIL, Light Sweet (NYM) 1,000 bbls.; $ per bbl.								
Nov	36.70	39.05	36.48	38.67	+ 1.14	39.20	17.30	75,644
Dec	35.35	37.45	35.10	37.13	+ 1.06	37.45	17.78	36,585
Ja91	33.90	35.80	33.75	35.54	+ .79	35.80	17.86	27,446
Feb	32.60	34.30	32.60	34.14	+ .64	34.55	18.15	16,272
Mar	31.50	33.00	31.45	32.84	+ .49	33.25	18.40	14,660
Apr	30.30	31.80	30.25	31.66	+ .41	31.80	18.03	11,218
May	29.60	30.70	29.60	30.61	+ .36	30.80	18.03	12,737
June	28.75	29.75	28.75	29.64	+ .26	29.80	18.30	12,079
July	27.65	28.80	27.65	28.84	+ .21	28.80	18.31	6,756
Aug	27.08	28.30	27.08	28.19	+ .16	28.30	19.05	5,325
Sept	26.50	27.50	26.70	27.70	+ .12	27.78	19.10	6,731
Oct	26.70	27.00	26.60	27.28	+ .08	27.20	19.63	5,023
Nov	26.15	26.40	26.15	26.95	+ .05	26.95	19.10	3,433
Dec	25.85	26.50	25.80	26.69	+ .03	27.00	19.45	7,855
Ja92	25.90	26.00	25.90	26.44	+ .01	26.80	20.90	4,769
Feb	25.71	25.71	25.71	26.21	– .01	26.18	21.20	4,362
Mar	25.40	25.40	25.40	25.99	– .03	25.75	22.40	6,640
Apr	25.60	25.60	25.60	25.78	– .05	25.75	24.95	1,600
Est vol 123,054; vol Tues 117,126; open int 259,135, +5,042.								
HEATING OIL NO. 2 (NYM) 42,000 gal.; $ per gal.								
Oct	.9870	1.0400	.9850	1.0257	+.0137	1.0725	.5005	13,199
Nov	.9950	1.0490	.9925	1.0372	+.0195	1.0490	.5130	20,549
Dec	.9960	1.0520	.9960	1.0477	+.0248	1.0579	.5327	19,043
Ja91	.9860	1.0375	.9860	1.0326	+.0214	1.0478	.5295	12,631
Feb	.9390	.9900	.9390	.9811	+.0169	.9925	.5260	8,123
Mar	.8900	.9340	.8950	.9311	+.0129	.9400	.5070	4,571
Apr	.8512	.8825	.8512	.8836	+.0104	.8950	.4930	2,647
May	.8300	.8460	.8300	.8486	+.0104	.8475	.4840	2,631
June	.7950	.8230	.7950	.8236	+.0084	.8318	.4840	9,403
July	.7850	.8100	.7850	.8116	+.0074	.8258	.4855	3,479
Aug	....	....	....	.8166	+.0074	.8300	.5350	588
Sept	....	....	....	.8286	+.0074	.8428	.6785	100
Est vol 36,151; vol Tues 34,470; open int 96,964, –1,329.								
GASOLINE, Unleaded (NYM) 42,000 gal.; $ per gal.								
Oct	.9925	1.0180	.9870	1.0010	–.0195	1.0630	.4870	8,151
Nov	.9425	.9830	.9385	.9760	+.0075	1.0025	.4775	13,188
Dec	.9125	.9585	.9125	.9491	+.0090	.9680	.4895	14,301
Ja91	.8910	.9360	.8910	.9258	+.0145	.9370	.4910	6,412
Feb	.8700	.9180	.8700	.9075	+.0134	.9180	.4985	10,531
Mar	.8800	.9175	.8775	.9100	+.0125	.9200	.5065	3,867
Apr	.9390	.9500	.9390	.9450	+.0100	.9500	.5490	2,428
May	.9230	.9380	.9230	.9375	+.0100	.9425	.5545	1,448
June	....	....	....	.9225	+.0100	.9270	.5490	1,186
Aug	....	....	....	.8975	+.0100	.7476	.5350	80
Est vol 26,635; vol Tues 22,414; open int 61,692, +1,701.								
NATURAL GAS, (NYM) 10,000 MMBtu.; $ per MMBtu's								
Nov	1.876	1.945	1.876	1.945	+ .015	1.965	1.700	1,338
Dec	2.300	2.380	2.300	2.365	+ .030	2.380	1.800	1,913
Ja91	2.510	2.585	2.510	2.585	+ .042	2.585	1.950	2,518
Feb	2.330	2.380	2.330	2.370	+ .020	2.380	1.958	2,024
Mar	1.830	1.885	1.830	1.880	+ .016	1.910	1.650	1,254
Apr	1.725	1.740	1.720	1.725	+ .005	1.785	1.580	847
May	1.720	1.725	1.720	1.725	....	1.780	1.550	666
June	1.725	1.725	1.72	1.725	+ .010	1.780	1.625	701
July	....	....	....	1.730	+ .005	1.765	1.630	312
Aug	1.730	1.740	1.730	1.740	– .005	1.790	1.645	253
Sept	1.745	1.745	1.745	1.745	....	1.760	1.665	242

EXCHANGE ABBREVIATIONS
(for commodity futures and futures options)

CBT-Chicago Board of Trade; CME-Chicago Mercantile Exchange; CMX-Commodity Exchange, New York; CRCE-Chicago Rice & Cotton Exchange; CTN-New York Cotton Exchange; CSCE-Coffee, Sugar & Cocoa Exchange, New York; IPE-International Petroleum Exchange; KC-Kansas City Board of Trade; MCE-MidAmerica Commodity Exchange; MPLS-Minneapolis Grain Exchange; NYM-New York Mercantile Exchange; PBOT-Philadelphia Board of Trade; WPG-Winnipeg Commodity Exchange.

CASH PRICES

Wednesday, September 26, 1990.
(Closing Market Quotations)

	Wed	Tues	Yr.Ago
GRAINS AND FEEDS			
Barley, top-quality Mpls., bu	n2.20-.40	2.20-.40	3.47½
Bran, wheat middlings, KC ton	81.00	83.00	82.00
Corn, No. 2 yel. Cent-Ill. bu	bp2.17	2.18	2.15½
Corn Gluten Feed, Midwest, ton	75.-100.	75.-100.	102.50
Cottonseed Meal, Clksdle,Miss. ton	170.-175.	175.00	187.50
Hominy Feed, Cent-Ill. ton	83.00	83.00	80.00
Meat-Bonemeal, 50% pro. Ill. ton.	210.-215.	210.00	240.00
Oats, No. 2 milling, Mpls., bu	n1.20-.22	1.22-.23	1.58½
Sorghum, (Milo) No. 2 Gulf cwt	4.46	4.45	4.63
Soybean Meal, Decatur, Illinois ton	169½-172½	1.69½-72½	208.50
Soybeans, No. 1 yel Cent.-Ill. bu	bp5.98½	5.99	5.48½
Wheat, Spring 14%-pro Mpls. bu	2.83¼	2.82¾	4.07
Wheat, No. 2 sft red, St.Lou. bu	bp2.61½	2.61½	4.06
Wheat, No. 2 hard KC, bu	2.83	2.80¾	4.15¼
Wheat, sft wht, del Portland Ore.	3.09	3.10	4.57
FOODS			
Beef, Carcass, Equiv.Index Value, choice 1-3,550-700lbs.	117.75	117.90	n.a.
Beef, Carcass, Equiv.Index Value, select 1-3,550-700lbs.	111.20	111.30	n.a.
Broilers, Dressed "A" NY lb	x.5481	.5481	.5774
Butter, AA, Chgo., lb.	1.03¼	1.03¼	1.25½
Cocoa, Ivory Coast, $metric ton	[illegible]	[illegible]	1,318
Coffee, Brazilian, NY lb.	[illegible]	.86	.78
Coffee, Colombian, NY lb.	n.97½	[illegible]	n.a.
Eggs, Lge white, Chgo doz.	[illegible]	[illegible]	.76½
Flour, hard winter KC cwt	7.30	7.30	10.10
Hams, 17-20 lbs, Mid-US lb fob	.98-.98½	1.08-.09	.75
Hogs, Iowa-S.Minn. avg. cwt	58.75	60.00	46.50
Hogs, Omaha avg cwt	58.50	60.00	45.50
Pork Bellies, 12-14 lbs Mid-US lb	.60	.58-.60	.38
Pork Loins, 14-18 lbs. Mid-US lb	1.09-.18½	1.19-.21	1.07
Steers, Tex.-Okla. ch avg cwt	79.00	79.75	70.00
Steers, Feeder, Okl Cty, av cwt	96.50	97.75	88.65
Sugar, cane, raw, world, lb. fob	.1092	.1115	.1480
FATS AND OILS			
Coconut Oil, crd, N. Orleans lb.	xxn.14⅛	.14¼	.26
Corn Oil, crd wet mill, Chgo. lb.	.27¾	.28	.20
Corn Oil, crd dry mill, Chgo. lb.	n.28½	.28½	.21
Cottonseed Oil, crd Miss Vly lb.	a.24¾	.24½	.19½
Grease, choice white, Chgo lb.	n.11¼	.11¼	.12½
Lard, Chgo lb.	.13¾	.13½	.14¼

FIGURE 21-5 Commodity quotations. *Source: The Wall Street Journal*, September 26, 1990, reprinted by permission, © Dow Jones & Co., Inc., all rights reserved.

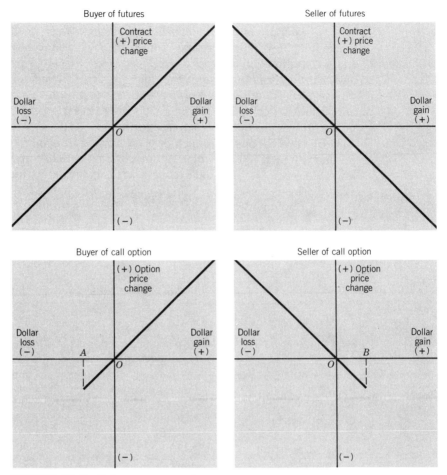

FIGURE 21-6 Futures versus options.

can cover the short position at a profit. The buyer incurs losses if the price of the contract falls and the seller incurs losses if the price of the contract increases.

The two lower panels concern call options. The buyer of a call option profits if the price of the underlying stock option increases. The maximum loss (OA) is limited to the amount of the premium paid by the buyer if the price of the stock declines. The seller's maximum profit on this transaction (OB) is the amount of the premium received from the buyer, excluding transaction costs. In a sense, the seller loses if the price of the stock and option increases. In reality, the seller loses only if he or she is holding the stock when the option expires and it is worth less than the cost. For example, assume that an option writer buys 100 shares of stock at $50 per share and sells a call option for $400 at that price. The seller gets $400 no matter what happens to the stock. However, if the stock is worth less than $46 per share ($50 − $4 = $46) when the option expires, the seller has a loss.

Options and futures contracts can be used together in various trading strategies. For example, suppose you believe that stock prices are going to rise and you take a long S&P 500 futures position. If stock prices increase, the value of your futures position will increase as well. Let us say that stock prices have increased and that they *may* increase further, but you are not confident about it. You can buy an S&P put option and protect your existing profit. The put provides insurance against a decline in stock prices. If stock prices continue to increase, the value of the futures position will increase further.

Let us consider one more example. Stock prices are expected to decline, and you sell short an S&P 500 December futures contract at 183.00 and hope to profit from lower stock prices. Prices did decline, and the value of the futures contract is now 175.00. This represents an 8.00 profit (8.00 × $500 = $4000). You can protect this profit by buying a December 175 S&P call option for 2.10 ($1050). At this

	S&P 500 Stock Index Futures	Options on S&P 500 Stock Index Futures
Ticker	SP	Calls: CS Puts: PS
Size	S&P 500 Index × $500	One S&P 500 Futures contract[a]
Value	Futures price × $500	Option Premium × $500
Contract months	Mar, Jun Sep, Dec	All 12 calendar months[b]
Strike prices	N.A.	5.00 point intervals
Minimum price fluctuation	.05 = $25	.05[c] = $25
Trading hours (Chicago time)	8:30 A.M.–3:15 P.M.	8:30 A.M.–3:15 P.M.
Last day of trading	Thursday prior to the 3rd Friday of contract month	Mar, Jun, Sep, Dec: Thursday prior to the 3rd Friday; other 8 months: 3rd Friday

[a] Exercise procedure. Long puts or calls may be exercised on any trading day. Any short put or call position open at the end of a trading day may be assigned by a random process. Exercised long calls and assigned short puts result in long futures positions, executed at the strike price. Exercise of long puts and assignment of short calls result in short futures positions, executed at the strike price. Check with your brokerage firm for details of exercise procedure.

[b] The three monthly expirations within a quarter are all exercisable into the quarter end futures contract (e.g., the December futures underlies the October, November, and December options).

[c] Trades can occur at a nominal price (.002 = $1) if the transaction results in liquidation for both parties of deep out-of-the-money option positions.

FIGURE 21-7 Standard & Poor's stock index futures and options. *Source:* Chicago Mercantile Exchange.

Following S&P 500 Futures and Options Prices

Price activity can be monitored daily in the business pages of most major newspapers. The displays reproduced below are examples of the way these prices are shown in *The Wall Street Journal*. To convert the quotations below to dollar value, simply multiply the quote by $500.

FUTURES PRICES

Prices represent the open, high, low, and settlement (or closing) prices for the previous day.

One day's change in the settlement price.

High and low prices over the life of the contract.

The number of contracts still in effect at the end of the previous day's trading session. Each unit represents a buyer *and* a seller who still have a contract position.

Contract delivery months that are most actively traded.

S&P 500 INDEX (CME) $500 times index

	Open	High	Low	Settle	Change	Lifetime High	Low	Open Interest
June	301.20	304.25	299.60	304.15	+4.35	304.25	228.90	87,265
Sept	303.00	306.00	301.30	305.90	+4.45	306.00	229.90	1,043
Dec	303.20	307.60	302.80	307.00	+4.25	307.60	243.20	89

Est vol 78,924; vol Fri 94,834; open int 138,455, +4,452.
Index (prelim.) High 301.17; Low 297.50; Close 301.16 −2.99

The number of contracts traded in the previous two trading sessions.

The actual index open, high, low, close and change.

The total of the right column, and the change from the prior trading day.

FUTURES OPTIONS

Expiration months.

S&P 500 STOCK INDEX (CME) $500 times premium

Strike Price	Calls – Settle			Puts – Settle		
	Jun-c	Jul-c	Aug-c	Jun-p	Jul-p	Aug-p
295	12.90	16.80	18.95	3.80	6.05	8.20
300	9.80	13.85	16.10	5.65	8.00	10.30
305	7.20	11.20	13.55	8.05	10.30	12.65
310	5.10	8.95	11.30	10.95	13.00	. . .
315	3.50	7.00	9.30	. . .	. . .	. . .
320	2.35	5.40	. . .	. . .	. . .	. . .

Est. vol. 8,209; Fri vol. 7,565 calls; 4,727 puts
Open interest Fri; 31,335 calls; 14,300 puts

Most active strike prices.

Closing prices in each option.

Volume of options traded in the previous two trading sessions.

The number of options contracts (each unit represents *both* the buyer and the writer) that were still open at the end of the previous day's trading session.

FIGURE 21-8   Standard & Poor's price activity.

point your profit is $2950. It is the least you can earn. If the index declines to, say, 160, the net profit will be $10,450 (23.00 × $500 = $11,500 − $1050 = $10,450).

Figure 21-7 gives the contract specifications for the S&P 500 Stock Index futures and the options on those futures. Figure 21-8 shows how to interpret information both on contracts in the newspapers.

PROGRAM TRADING AND STOCK INDEX FUTURES
Index Arbitrage

Now that you have a better understanding of futures contracts, let us see how program trading and stock index futures, such as the S&P 500, are used by large investors and institutions. Some large investors track the prices of the securities underlying the S&P 500 or other stock index futures. When the market value of the underlying securities is different from the value of the index futures, the investors arbitrage. **Arbitrage** is the simultaneous purchase of one commodity against the sale of another in order to profit from differences between their prices. An **index arbitrage** is where the two commodities are stock index futures and the stocks underlying that index. Because of the large number of stocks involved, the purchase and sale of thousands of shares worth millions of dollars is done almost instantaneously with the aid of computers. The large volume, computer-assisted transactions are referred to as **programmed trading.**

By way of illustration, consider the S&P 500 futures contract. If the market value of the 500 stocks is less than the value of the S&P 500 futures, arbitrageurs will buy stocks and sell an equivalent amount of futures. Their profit is the difference between the two values, less transaction costs and taxes if they apply. Pension plans do not pay income taxes, for example. Because of the large volume of trading, transaction costs may be as low as $0.30 for every $1000 traded. If stocks are valued higher than futures, arbitrageurs will sell stocks and buy futures. Programmed trades to such arbitrages amount to millions of dollars.

Portfolio Insurance

Portfolio insurance is the name given to hedging a stock portfolio with stock index futures. Suppose that a pension plan manager believes that stock prices are going to decline and she wants to protect existing profits. To do this, she sells put options on the stock index futures. The put options are used for "insurance" — to lock in the profit. If stock prices decline, the put options can be sold or exercised at a profit. If stock prices increase, the cost of the insurance was the premium paid for the put options.

Unfortunately, portfolio insurance is no guarantee of success. Moreover, programmed trading and index arbitrage "significantly accelerated and exacerbated the market decline" that occurred in October 1989, according to a U.S. Govern-

ment Accounting Office study.[1] Friday the 13th is considered bad luck by some, and it certainly was bad for investors in October 1989. Quoting from the GAO study:

> On Friday, October 13, 1989, the Nation's securities and futures markets experienced extraordinary price volatility, dropping $190 billion in value, $160 billion of which was lost in the last 90 minutes of the trading day. At 2:40 p.m., on Friday, the New York Stock Exchange (NYSE) halted trading in the stock of UAL (the parent company of United Air Lines). At 2:55 p.m., the wire service reported that financing for the proposed buyout of UAL was in doubt. The Standard & Poor's 500 futures contract fell to its 12-point price limit at 3:07 p.m. at the Chicago Mercantile Exchange (CME). At 3:16 p.m. The Chicago Board Options Exchange (CBOE) stopped stock index options trading for the day. At 3:30 p.m. CME lifted the limit on stock index futures trading, but prices quickly fell further and at 3:45 p.m. prices reached CME's 30-point price limit. By the close of trading the Dow Jones Industrial Average declined by 191 points. The decline continued into the opening of the markets on Monday, October 16, 1989, when the Dow fell an additional 63 points before rebounding and closing up 88 points. The price volatility was accompanied by hourly trading volume levels that rivaled the 1987 market crash.

CONCLUSION

Originally, the futures markets were limited to trading grains. Today, the futures markets include a variety of commodities ranging from chickens to yen. In general, futures are used by hedgers to transfer price risk to speculators. The speculators are in the market to make money, but they generally lose instead.

In recent years trading in financial futures, including stock indexes, has received widespread public attention, especially after the stock market declines in October 1987, 1989, and 1990. Most of this trading is done by financial institutions. As a result of their trading activity in the stock and futures markets, both the volume and volatility of trading has increased, making it especially risky for small speculators. Before you speculate, read the following trading rules:

1. Speculators should have the following personal characteristics:
   a. They should have risk capital. Speculators should limit investments to funds they can afford to lose.
   b. They should have the temperament and willingness to take a loss.
   c. They should have the time to appraise both the fundamental and technical analysis of the commodity or stock.

---

[1] U.S. Government Accounting Office, *Securities and Futures Markets: Assessment of SEC and CFTC Studies of October 1989 Market Volatilities*, GAO/GGD-90-108BR, July 1990, 1–2.

2. If you are losing money, take a small loss to avoid a bigger one at a later date.

3. Let the profits grow. Stick with the winners. Commodity traders often use charts to determine support and resistance levels where they will sell or buy.

4. Limit your trading to the commodities you know best. It is impossible to keep track of all of the commodities, so restricting your activities to a small handful will increase your chances for success.

5. When in doubt, stay out of the market! If you do not like the way the market is behaving or you do not think that this is the time to be in the market, stay out of it.

6. Do not over-invest. If you know that you can afford to deal and lose in only two contracts, do not speculate in five contracts.

7. Know your broker. All brokers are not created equal. Some brokers are clearly better than others, so pick a good one.

IMPORTANT CONCEPTS

Arbitrage
Cash price
Commodities Futures Trading Commission (CFTC)
Daily limit
Futures
Futures price
GLOBEX
Hedging
Index arbitrage
Long
Margin
Maximum daily range
Minimum price change

National Futures Association (NFA)
Offset
Open interest
Pits
Points
Portfolio insurance
Price discovery
Programmed trading
Short
Speculators
Spread
Stabilization
Straddle
Tick

QUESTIONS AND EXERCISES

1. The term "commodities" is applied loosely to the futures market. What types of commodities are traded in the futures market?

2. Who are the major participants in the commodities markets?

3. Select five companies that are listed on the New York Stock Exchange. List the commodities they might use on a day-to-day basis.

4. How are commodities futures similar to call options?

5. What economic function is served by the futures market?

6. Assume that last year was an excellent year for growing wheat. The weather conditions were perfect, resulting in a bumper crop. What impact did this have on the price of wheat? Explain.

7. What is the idea behind a selling hedge?

8. The Fresch Bakery has received an order to deliver 750 dozen cookies three months from now. Explain what the bakery can do today in the commodities market to assure making a profit on this order.

9. If the price of U.S. Treasury bond futures were quoted at 97-24 yesterday and 97-26 today, how much is this change worth? Explain what information this provides about current interest rates.

10. Do commodity prices fluctuate more than stock prices? Explain.

11. Explain the meaning of an index arbitrage.

12. What is portfolio insurance?

13. Why is dealing in commodities considered riskier than dealing in common stocks?

14. Some investors consider gold a safe investment becase it is a hedge against inflation. What do you think of it? Explain.

15. Your friend has the urge to speculate in commodities but does not know the difference between rapeseed and flaxseed. His broker told him to buy one of them, but he cannot remember which one it was. What advice do you have for your friend?

PRESENT VALUE OF ONE DOLLAR

The value today of $1 to be received at the end of two years, discounted at 10 percent, is $0.826.

YR	1.00%	2.00%	3.00%	4.00%	5.00%	6.00%	7.00%	8.00%	9.00%	10.00%
1	.990	.980	.971	.962	.952	.943	.935	.926	.917	.909
2	.980	.961	.943	.926	.907	.890	.873	.857	.842	.826
3	.971	.942	.915	.889	.864	.840	.816	.794	.772	.751
4	.961	.924	.888	.855	.823	.792	.763	.735	.708	.683
5	.951	.906	.863	.822	.784	.747	.713	.681	.650	.621
6	.942	.888	.837	.790	.746	.705	.666	.630	.596	.564
7	.933	.871	.813	.760	.711	.665	.623	.583	.547	.513
8	.923	.853	.789	.731	.677	.627	.582	.540	.502	.467
9	.914	.837	.766	.703	.645	.592	.544	.500	.460	.424
10	.905	.820	.744	.676	.614	.558	.508	.463	.422	.386
11	.896	.804	.722	.650	.585	.527	.475	.429	.388	.350
12	.887	.789	.701	.625	.557	.497	.444	.397	.356	.319
13	.879	.773	.681	.601	.530	.469	.415	.368	.326	.290
14	.870	.758	.661	.577	.505	.442	.388	.340	.299	.263
15	.861	.743	.642	.555	.481	.417	.362	.315	.275	.239
16	.853	.728	.623	.534	.458	.394	.339	.292	.252	.218
17	.844	.714	.605	.513	.436	.371	.317	.270	.231	.198
18	.836	.700	.587	.494	.416	.350	.296	.250	.212	.180
19	.828	.686	.570	.475	.396	.331	.277	.232	.194	.164
20	.820	.673	.554	.456	.377	.312	.258	.215	.178	.149
21	.811	.660	.538	.439	.359	.294	.242	.199	.164	.135
22	.803	.647	.522	.422	.342	.278	.226	.184	.150	.123
23	.795	.634	.507	.406	.326	.262	.211	.170	.138	.112
24	.788	.622	.492	.390	.310	.247	.197	.158	.126	.102
25	.780	.610	.478	.375	.295	.233	.184	.146	.116	.092
30	.742	.552	.412	.308	.231	.174	.131	.099	.075	.057
35	.706	.500	.355	.253	.181	.130	.094	.068	.049	.036
40	.672	.453	.307	.208	.142	.097	.067	.046	.032	.022
45	.639	.410	.264	.171	.111	.073	.048	.031	.021	.014
50	.608	.372	.228	.141	.087	.054	.034	.021	.013	.009

YR	11.00%	12.00%	13.00%	14.00%	15.00%	16.00%	17.00%	18.00%	19.00%	20.00%
1	.901	.893	.885	.877	.870	.862	.855	.847	.840	.833
2	.812	.797	.783	.769	.756	.743	.731	.718	.706	.694
3	.731	.712	.693	.675	.658	.641	.624	.609	.593	.579
4	.659	.636	.613	.592	.572	.552	.534	.516	.499	.482
5	.593	.567	.543	.519	.497	.476	.456	.437	.419	.402
6	.535	.507	.480	.456	.432	.410	.390	.370	.352	.335
7	.482	.452	.425	.400	.376	.354	.333	.314	.296	.279
8	.434	.404	.376	.351	.327	.305	.285	.266	.249	.233
9	.391	.361	.333	.308	.284	.263	.243	.225	.209	.194
10	.352	.322	.295	.270	.247	.227	.208	.191	.176	.162
11	.317	.287	.261	.237	.215	.195	.178	.162	.148	.135
12	.286	.257	.231	.208	.187	.168	.152	.137	.124	.112
13	.258	.229	.204	.182	.163	.145	.130	.116	.104	.093
14	.232	.205	.181	.160	.141	.125	.111	.099	.088	.078
15	.209	.183	.160	.140	.123	.108	.095	.084	.074	.065
16	.188	.163	.141	.123	.107	.093	.081	.071	.062	.054
17	.170	.146	.125	.108	.093	.080	.069	.060	.052	.045
18	.153	.130	.111	.095	.081	.069	.059	.051	.044	.038
19	.138	.116	.098	.083	.070	.060	.051	.043	.037	.031
20	.124	.104	.087	.073	.061	.051	.043	.037	.031	.026
21	.112	.093	.077	.064	.053	.044	.037	.031	.026	.022
22	.101	.083	.068	.056	.046	.038	.032	.026	.022	.018
23	.091	.074	.060	.049	.040	.033	.027	.022	.018	.015
24	.082	.066	.053	.043	.035	.028	.023	.019	.015	.013
25	.074	.059	.047	.038	.030	.024	.020	.016	.013	.010
30	.044	.033	.026	.020	.015	.012	.009	.007	.005	.004
35	.026	.019	.014	.010	.008	.006	.004	.003	.002	.002
40	.015	.011	.008	.005	.004	.003	.002	.001	.001	.001
45	.009	.006	.004	.003	.002	.001	.001	.001	.000	.000
50	.005	.003	.002	.001	.001	.001	.000	.000	.000	.000

PRESENT VALUE OF AN ANNUITY ($1)

The present value of $1.00 received per year for the next 25 years, discounted at 10 percent, is $9.07 ($1.00 × 9.0770 = $9.07).

n	1%	2%	3%	4%	5%	6%	7%	8%	9%	10%
1	0.9901	0.9804	0.9709	0.9615	0.9524	0.9434	0.9346	0.9259	0.9174	0.9091
2	1.9704	1.9416	1.9135	1.8861	1.8594	1.8334	1.8080	1.7833	1.7591	1.7355
3	2.9410	2.8839	2.8286	2.7751	2.7233	2.6730	2.6243	2.5771	2.5313	2.4868
4	3.9020	3.8077	3.7171	3.6299	3.5459	3.4651	3.3872	3.3121	3.2397	3.1699
5	4.8535	4.7134	4.5797	4.4518	4.3295	4.2123	4.1002	3.9927	3.8896	3.7908
6	5.7955	5.6014	5.4172	5.2421	5.0757	4.9173	4.7665	4.6229	4.4859	4.3553
7	6.7282	6.4720	6.2302	6.0020	5.7863	5.5824	5.3893	5.2064	5.0329	4.8684
8	7.6517	7.3254	7.0196	6.7327	6.4632	6.2098	5.9713	5.7466	5.5348	5.3349
9	8.5661	8.1622	7.7861	7.4353	7.1078	6.8017	6.5152	6.2469	5.9852	5.7590
10	9.4714	8.9825	8.7302	8.1109	7.7217	7.3601	7.0236	6.7101	6.4176	6.1446
11	10.3677	9.7868	9.2526	8.7604	8.3064	7.8868	7.4987	7.1389	6.8052	6.4951
12	11.2552	10.5753	9.9539	9.3850	8.8632	8.3838	7.9427	7.6361	7.1607	6.8137
13	12.1338	11.3483	10.6349	9.9856	9.3935	8.8527	8.3576	7.9038	7.4869	7.1034
14	13.0038	12.1062	11.2960	10.5631	9.8986	9.2950	8.7454	8.2442	7.7861	7.3667
15	13.8651	12.8492	11.9379	11.1183	10.3796	9.7122	9.1079	8.5595	8.0607	7.6061
16	14.7180	13.5777	12.5610	11.6522	10.8377	10.1059	9.4466	8.8514	8.3125	7.8237
17	15.5624	14.2918	13.1660	12.1656	11.2740	10.4772	9.7632	9.1216	8.5436	8.0215
18	16.3984	14.9920	13.7534	12.6592	11.6895	10.8276	10.0591	9.3719	8.7556	8.2014
19	17.2261	15.2684	14.3237	13.1339	12.0853	11.1581	10.3356	9.6036	8.9501	8.3649
20	18.0457	16.3514	14.8774	13.5903	12.4622	11.4699	10.5940	9.8181	9.1285	8.5136
21	18.8571	17.0111	15.4149	14.0291	12.8211	11.7640	10.8355	10.0168	9.2922	8.6487
22	19.6605	17.6581	15.9368	14.4511	13.1630	12.0416	11.0612	10.2007	9.4424	8.7715
23	20.4559	18.2921	16.4435	14.8568	13.4885	12.3033	11.2722	10.3710	9.5802	8.8832
24	21.2435	18.9139	16.9355	15.2469	13.7986	12.5503	11.4693	10.5287	9.7066	8.9847
25	22.0233	19.5234	17.4131	15.6220	14.0939	12.7833	11.6536	10.6748	9.8226	9.0770

n	11%	12%	13%	14%	15%	16%	17%	18%	19%	20%
1	0.9009	0.8929	0.8850	0.8772	0.8696	0.8621	0.8547	0.8475	0.8403	0.8333
2	1.7125	1.6901	1.6681	1.6467	1.6257	1.6052	1.5852	1.5656	1.5465	1.5278
3	2.4437	2.4018	2.3612	2.3216	2.2832	2.2459	2.2096	2.1743	2.1399	2.1065
4	3.1024	3.0374	2.9745	2.9137	2.8550	2.7982	2.7432	2.6901	2.6386	2.5887
5	3.6959	3.6048	3.5172	3.4331	3.3522	3.2743	3.1993	3.1272	3.0576	2.9906
6	4.2305	4.1114	3.9976	3.8887	3.7845	3.6847	3.5892	3.4976	3.4098	3.3255
7	4.7122	4.5638	4.4226	4.2883	4.1604	4.0386	3.9224	3.8115	3.7057	3.6046
8	5.1461	4.9676	4.7988	4.6389	4.4873	4.3436	4.2072	4.0776	3.9544	3.8372
9	5.5370	5.3282	5.1317	4.9464	4.7716	4.6065	4.4506	4.3030	4.1633	4.0310
10	5.8892	5.6502	5.4262	5.2161	5.0188	4.8332	4.6586	4.4941	4.3389	4.1925
11	6.2065	5.9377	5.6869	5.4527	5.2337	5.0286	4.8364	4.6560	4.4865	4.3271
12	6.4924	6.1944	5.9176	5.6603	5.4206	5.1971	4.9884	4.7932	4.6105	4.4392
13	6.7499	6.4235	6.1218	5.8424	5.5831	5.3423	5.1183	4.9095	4.7147	4.5327
14	6.9819	6.6282	6.3025	6.0021	5.7245	5.4675	5.2293	5.0081	4.8023	4.6106
15	7.1909	6.8109	6.4624	6.1422	5.8474	5.5755	5.3242	5.0916	4.8759	4.6755
16	7.3792	6.9740	6.6039	6.2651	5.9542	5.6685	5.4053	5.1624	4.9377	4.7296
17	7.5488	7.1196	6.7291	6.3729	6.0472	5.7487	5.4746	5.2223	4.9897	4.7746
18	7.7016	7.2497	6.8399	6.4674	6.1280	5.8178	5.5339	5.2732	5.0333	4.8122
19	7.8393	7.3650	6.9380	6.5504	6.1982	5.8775	5.5845	5.3176	5.0700	4.8435
20	7.9633	7.4694	7.0248	6.6231	6.2593	5.9288	5.6278	5.3527	5.1009	4.8696
21	8.0751	7.5620	7.1016	6.6870	6.3125	5.9731	5.6648	5.3837	5.1268	4.8913
22	8.1757	7.6446	7.1695	6.7429	6.3587	6.0113	5.6964	5.4099	5.1486	4.9094
23	8.2664	7.7184	7.2297	6.7921	6.3988	6.0442	5.7234	5.4321	5.1668	4.9245
24	8.3481	7.7843	7.2829	6.8351	6.4338	6.0726	5.7465	5.4509	5.1822	4.9371
25	8.4217	7.8431	7.3300	6.8729	6.4641	6.0971	5.7662	5.4669	5.1951	4.9476

(*Continued*)

n	21%	22%	23%	24%	25%	26%	27%	28%	29%	30%
1	0.8264	0.8197	0.8130	0.8065	0.8000	0.7937	0.7874	0.7813	0.7752	0.7692
2	1.5095	1.4915	1.4740	1.4568	1.4400	1.4235	1.4074	1.3916	1.3761	1.3609
3	2.0739	2.0422	2.0114	1.9813	1.9520	1.9234	1.8956	1.8684	1.8420	1.8161
4	2.5404	2.4936	2.4483	2.4043	2.3616	2.3202	2.2800	2.2410	2.2031	2.1662
5	2.9260	2.8636	2.8035	2.7454	2.6893	2.6351	2.5827	2.5320	2.4830	2.4356
6	3.2446	3.1669	3.0923	3.0205	2.9514	2.8850	2.8210	2.7594	2.7000	2.6427
7	3.5079	3.4155	3.3270	3.2423	3.1611	3.0833	3.0087	2.9370	2.8682	2.8021
8	3.7256	3.6193	3.5179	3.4212	3.3289	3.2407	3.1564	3.0758	2.9986	2.9247
9	3.9054	3.7863	3.6731	3.5655	3.4631	3.3657	3.2728	3.1842	3.0997	3.0190
10	4.0541	3.9232	3.7993	3.6819	3.5705	3.4648	3.3644	3.2689	3.1781	3.0915
11	4.1769	4.0354	3.0918	3.7757	3.6564	3.5435	3.4365	3.3351	3.2388	3.1473
12	4.2785	4.1274	3.9852	3.8514	3.7251	3.6060	3.4933	3.3868	3.2850	3.1903
13	4.3624	4.2028	4.0530	3.9124	3.7601	3.6555	3.6381	3.4272	3.3224	3.2233
14	4.4317	4.2646	4.1082	3.9616	3.8241	3.6949	3.5733	3.4587	3.3507	3.2487
15	4.4890	4.3152	4.1530	4.0013	3.8593	3.7261	3.6010	3.4834	3.3726	3.2682
16	4.5364	4.3567	4.1894	4.0333	3.8874	3.7509	3.6228	3.5026	3.3896	3.2832
17	4.5755	4.3908	4.2890	4.0591	3.9099	3.7705	3.6400	3.5177	3.4028	3.2948
18	4.6079	4.4187	4.2431	4.0799	3.9279	3.7861	3.6536	3.5294	3.4130	3.3037
19	4.6345	4.4415	4.2627	4.0967	3.9424	3.7985	3.6642	3.5386	3.4210	3.3105
20	4.6567	4.4603	4.2786	4.1103	3.9539	3.8083	3.6726	3.5458	3.4271	3.3158
21	4.6750	4.4756	4.2916	4.1212	3.9631	3.8161	3.6792	3.5514	3.4319	3.3198
22	4.6900	4.4882	4.3021	4.1300	3.9705	3.8223	3.6844	3.5553	3.4356	3.3230
23	4.7025	4.4985	4.3106	4.1371	3.9764	3.8273	3.6885	3.5592	3.4384	3.3254
24	4.7128	4.5070	4.3176	4.1428	3.9811	3.8312	3.6981	3.5619	3.4406	3.3272
25	4.7213	4.5139	4.3232	4.1474	3.9849	3.8342	3.6943	3.5640	3.4423	3.3286

APPENDIX C

USEFUL EQUATIONS

Equation

Dividend valuation

$$P_0 = \frac{D_1}{k - g}$$

(2-3)

Preemptive rights (cum rights)

$$V_1 = \frac{P_0 - S}{N + 1}$$

(2-4)

Current yield

$$\text{Current yield} = \frac{C}{P_0}$$

(3-1)

Yield to maturity

$$YTM = \frac{C + [(F - P_0)/n]}{(F + P_0)/2}$$

(3-2)

Yield to call

$$YTC = \frac{C + [(F_c - P_0)/n]}{(F_c + P_0)/2}$$

(3-4)

Tax-free equivalent

$$TFE = \frac{\text{Tax-exempt yield}}{1 - \text{Income tax bracket}}$$

(3-5)

Treasury bill discount

$$C = \frac{A}{360} \times B$$

$$P = \$100 - C$$

(3-6)

Bond equivalent basis

$$Y = \frac{C}{P} \times \frac{365}{A} \times 100$$

(3-7)

Ride yield curve

$$Y = \frac{S - P}{P} \times \frac{365}{D} \times 100$$

(3-8)

Holding period return (stock)

$$HPR = \frac{D_1 + P_1}{P_0}$$ (4-1)

Duration

$$D = \frac{C\,[n - (1 + r)\mathrm{PVAIF}_{r,n}]}{P_0 \times r}$$

Holding period return (bond)

$$HPR = \frac{I_1 + P_1}{P_0}$$ (4-1)

Margin equity

$$\text{Equity} = V - D$$ (6-1)

Margin

$$\text{Margin} = \frac{V - D}{V}$$ (6-2)

Buying power

$$\text{Excess} = \text{Profit} \times \text{Initial margin requirement}$$
$$\text{Buying power} = (\text{Excess} \times 100\%)/\text{Margin requirement}$$ (6-3)

Profit

$$\text{Profit} = (V - D) - \text{Original investment}$$ (6-4)

Earnings per share

Table 13.2

$$\text{Net income/Average number of shares}$$ (1)

Payout ratio

$$\text{Dividends per share/Earnings per share}$$ (2)

Profit margin

$$\text{Net income/Net sales}$$ (3)

Return on assets

$$\text{Net income/Average total assets}$$ (4)

Return on equity

$$\text{Net income/Average total equity}$$ (5)

Net working capital

$$\text{Current assets} - \text{current liabilities}$$ (6)

Current ratio

$$\frac{\text{Current assets}}{\text{Current liabilities}} \tag{7}$$

Acid-test ratio

$$\frac{\text{Cash} + \text{Marketable securities} + \text{Receivables}}{\text{Current liabilities}} \tag{8}$$

Inventory turnover ratio

$$\frac{\text{Cost of goods sold}}{\text{Average inventory}} \tag{9}$$

Average collection period

$$\frac{\dfrac{\text{Net sales}}{360}}{\dfrac{\text{Average accounts receivable}}{\text{Sales per day}}} \tag{10}$$

Fixed-asset turnover

$$\frac{\text{Net sales}}{\text{Total average assets}} \tag{11}$$

Long-term debt as percentage of total capital

$$\frac{\text{Long-term debt}}{\text{Total capital}} \tag{12}$$

Debt coverage

$$\frac{\text{Operating profit}}{\text{Interest expense}} \tag{13}$$

Cost of long-term debt

$$\frac{\text{Interest expense}}{\text{Average long-term debt}} \tag{14}$$

Dividend valuation (variable growth rate)

Equation

$$P_0 = \sum_{t=1}^{n} \frac{D_0(1 + g_x)^t}{(1 + k)^t} + \frac{D_{n+1}}{k - g_y}\left[\frac{1}{(1 + k)^n}\right] \tag{13-3}$$

Capital asset pricing model

$$k = R_f + b(k_m - R_f) \tag{13-4}$$

Characteristic line

$$k = a + bk_m + e \tag{13-5}$$

Price/earnings ratio

$$P/E = \frac{D/E}{k - g} \tag{13-6}$$

Market value exchange ratio

$$\frac{\text{Market value of benefits offered to seller}}{\text{Market value of benefits offered to buyer}} \tag{13-7}$$

Tax shelter

$$TI = CFBT + A - D \tag{16-1}$$

Conversion rate

$$R = \text{Par value of bond/conversion price} \tag{20-1}$$

Conversion value

$$CV = R \times P_0 \tag{20-2}$$

Conversion premium

$$P^* = \frac{P_m - CV}{CV} \tag{20-3}$$

Conversion premium

$$P^{**} = \frac{CV - I}{I} \tag{20-4}$$

Bond value

$$P_b = \sum_{t=1}^{n} \frac{C}{(1 + r)^t} + \frac{F}{(1 + r)^n} \tag{20-5}$$

Convertible bond value

$$P_b = \sum_{t=1}^{n} \frac{C}{(1 + r_c)^t} + \frac{CV}{(1 + r_c)^N} \tag{20-6}$$

Warrants

$$\text{Value} = \left(\begin{array}{c} \text{Market price of} \\ \text{common stock} \end{array} - \begin{array}{c} \text{Excessive} \\ \text{price} \end{array} \right) \times \begin{array}{c} \text{Number of shares} \\ \text{that can be purchased} \\ \text{with each warrant} \end{array} \tag{20-9}$$

Preemptive rights (cum rights)

$$V_1 = \frac{P_0 - S}{N + 1} \tag{20-10}$$

Preemptive rights (ex rights)

$$V_2 = \frac{P_0 - V_1 - S}{N} \tag{20-11}$$

GLOSSARY

This glossary contains many terms that are used by investors. Words that are *italicized* are explained elsewhere in this section.

Accrual Accounting   A system of accounting whereby expenses are recognized when a cost is incurred in the creation of revenue, not when a disbursement is made. Revenue is recognized at the time services are performed or goods are delivered to customers, not when cash is received.

Acid-test Ratio   A "narrow" measure of *liquidity* derived by dividing cash, marketable securities, and accounts receivable by current liabilities.

American Depository Receipts (ADRs)   ADRs are negotiable receipts of a domestic bank representing title to foreign shares.

Annuity   A series of periodic payments that are usually made in equal amounts for a specified period of time. Interest payments on bonds are one example of an annuity.

Arbitrage   The simultaneous purchase and sale of equivalent assets at different prices in order to profit from the difference. For example, XYZ stock is selling for $30 per share in the United States and $31 per share in Great Britain. An arbitrageur will simultaneously buy XYZ in the United States and sell it in Great Britain, thereby earning $1 per share.

Arrears   A *preferred stock* is said to be in arrears when the company fails to pay its preferred stock dividend.

Asked price   See *Spread.*

Asset Allocation   This term refers to proportion of stocks, bonds, and other assets held in portfolios. It is also used in connection with *program*

trading, or dynamic asset allocation and tactical asset allocation. The latter commonly refers to the timing of purchases and sales.

At-the-Money   A *put or call option* with an *exercise price* equal to the underlying *futures* price. See *In-the-money* and *Out-of-the-money.*

Basis Points   One basis point is one hundredth of a percentage point   (0.01% or 0.0001) and is used in quoting bond and other prices.

Best Efforts   A type of *underwriting* in which *investment bankers* use their best efforts to sell a new security issue, but they do not buy it from the issuer. Hence, the investment banker has less risk.

Beta   An index of volatility in the return on an asset relative to the return of a market *portfolio* of assets. It is a measure of *systemic risk.*

Bid Price   See *Spread.*

Black Monday   Monday, October 19, 1987, the Dow Jones Industrial Average plunged 508 points (22.6 percent) and 604 million shares were traded. This was worse than "Black Monday," October 28, 1929, when the average plunged 12.8 percent.

Block of Stock   A block consists of 10,000 shares or more, or stock with value of $200,000, whichever is less.

Blue Chip   This refers to a company with a national reputation for quality products or services and a sound financial condition.

Bond   A long-term debt that has a stated interest

rate and fixed dates on which the interest and principal are to be paid. The specific features of the bond, including *collateral, restrictive covenants,* and call features, are written in the bond's *indenture,* or contract.

Bond Ratings   Bonds are rated by agencies such as Moody's and Standard & Poor's according to their investment quality. The highest quality bonds are called gilt edge and are rated Aaa by Moody's and AAA by S & P. Not all bonds are rated, which should not reflect their quality.

Book Value   The original cost of the asset less accumulated *depreciation.* The book value of a stock is the assets per dollar of common stockholders' equity.

Business Risk   *Risk* is inherent in a business, such as when sales decline because of increased competition. It is reflected in the variability of earning before interest and taxes. Business risk plus *financial risk* equals *total risk.*

Call Option   The holder of the option can buy a specified number of shares of stock, or a commodity, at a predetermined price on or before a certain date. Options on stock are also called equity options and options on commodities are also called nonequity options. Nonequity options include stock market indexes, foreign currencies, and other commodities.

Call Protection (Bonds)   This feature on bonds prohibits a *bond* from being called (redeemed) by the issuing *corporation* for a certain number of years (i.e., five years). It affords investors who bought bonds with high yields some measure of protection from having the bond called if interest rates decline and the issuer wants to refinance the bond. If the bond is called, investors generally receive a "premium" over the face value of the bond, depending on how long it has been outstanding.

Capital Asset Pricing Model (CAPM)   The CAPM relates risk and return of assets such as *common stocks.* It indicates that the required rate of return for any common stock is equal to the *risk-free rate of return* plus a *risk premium.* See also *Security Market Line.*

Capital Gains (Losses)   Capital gains (losses) arise from the sale of certain assets that have a useful life of more than one year and that are not normally bought or sold in the oridinary course of business. The sale of such assets is classified as short-term if they are held for less than one year and long-term if held for more than one year.

Capitalization Rate   Capitalization rate and discount rate, interchangeable terms, mean the interest rate used in various calculations such as determining the present value of a stream of income or the required rate of return on an investment.

Capital Market   Long-term debt and *equity* securities are traded in the capital market. It includes financial intermediates, government, business concerns, and individual investors who buy and sell stocks, bonds, and other securities. See also *Primary Market,* and *Secondary Market.*

Capital Stock   The permanently invested *equity* capital of a *corporation* is called the capital stock.

Capital Structure   The permanent long-term financing that is represented by long-term debt, *preferred stock, common stock,* and retained earnings. Financial leases may also be included.

Cash Flow   The statement of cash flows in corporate annual reports provides information about corporate cash flows from operations, financing, and investing activities. The term may also be used to refer to certain dollar amounts from particular investments. For example, the periodic payments of interest and the payment of principal are the cash flows from bonds. Similarly, it is commonly defined as net income plus depreciation. Because the term "cash flow" is widely used and has many different meanings, it must be used and interpreted with caution.

Certificates of Deposit (CDs)   Negotiable marketable receipts for funds deposited in a financial

intermediary for a specified period of time and at a specified rate of interest. They have denominations of $100,000. CDs of less than that amount are not negotiable.

Collateral Trust Bonds Bonds that are secured by stocks and bonds owned by the issuing *corporation.* The securities are held by a trustee for the benefit of the bondholders.

Commercial Paper Unsecured short-term promissory notes of the leading industrial companies, finance companies, and bank holding companies.

Commodities Futures Trading Commission (CFTC) An independent federal agency responsible for regulating commodity *futures* and related trading in the United States.

Common Stock Common stock represents ownership of a *corporation.* The common stockholder is a residual claimant—the last one to receive assets if the firm is liquidated. However, they can benefit from growth through appreciation of shares and increased cash *dividends.*

Compound Interest Interest computed on the accumulated interest as well as the original principal amount.

Condominium A form of real estate ownership by which certain property is jointly owned by the residents—a roof, a parking lot, and so on. The residents share in the upkeep for the jointly owned property.

Conglomerate A conglomerate *merger* consists of the combination of essentially unrelated firms. According to the Federal Trade Commission, conglomerate mergers are classified as product extension or market extension. Product extension means that the companies are functionally related but do not compete (toothpaste and floor cleaners). Market extension occurs when companies manufacture the same product but in different markets.

Consol Perpetual (they never mature) *bonds* that were issued by the British during the Napoleonic wars. They pay a fixed coupon rate forever, or until they are retired.

Consolidated Tape A ticker system for reporting securities transactions on participating stock exchanges and *over-the-counter* markets.

Consolidation A consolidation occurs when two or more companies combine to form a new company and the original companies cease to exist. For example, North Central and Southern Airlines combined to form Republic Airlines.

Continuous Market A continuous market for securities has five attributes: frequency of sales, narrow *spread,* minimum price changes, prompt execution, and *liquidity.*

Conversion Price (Rate) The dollar amount of *par value* of a bond that is exchangeable for one share of *common stock.* For example, if a bond has a par value of $1000 and a conversion price of $50, it can be exchanged for 20 shares of common stock. The conversion rate is 20.

Conversion Value The current market value of the number of shares into which a convertible security may be converted. It is equal to the *conversion rate* times the current market price of the stock. If a bond has a conversion rate of 20 and the current market price of the stock is $80 per share, the conversion value is $1600.

Convertible Securities Convertible *bonds* and *preferred stocks* can be converted or exchanged for another type of security, typically *common stock* of the issuing *corporation.* The terms of the exchange are described in the *indenture.*

Cooperative A form of real estate ownership by which each owner owns a proportionate share of a nonprofit *corporation* that holds legal title to a building. The owner of the cooperative leases his or her unit from the cooperative and pays monthly fees for common services.

Corporation A legal organization chartered by the state to conduct business. It is an artificial entity existing only in contemplation of law. Corporations are owned by investors who hold

shares in it. Generally, the common shareholders have the right to vote to elect directors and to decide other important issues. Some shareholders have a preference (preferred) over others for the distribution of income and assets if the firm is dissolved.

Cumulative Voting The system of voting entitles shareholders to have as many votes (for each share held) as there are directors to be elected. By using this method, minority shareholders have an easier time gaining representation on the Board of Directors of a *corporation*.

Curb Exchange The "Curb" is the former name of the American Stock Exchange, derived from its origin on a street in downtown New York City.

Current Ratio A "broad" measure of *liquidity* derived by dividing current assets by current liabilities.

Current Yield The dollar return (dividend or coupon) divided by the current market price of a security.

Date Declared The date on which the directors of a company declare that a *dividend* (or *rights*) is going to be paid. They also establish a date of record, which means that only those stockholders whose names are on the company's books on that date are entitled to receive the dividend. It takes about four business days from the time a person buys stock until it is properly recorded on the company's books. Hence, the date called the ex-dividend date is established to let potential buyers know who is eligible to receive the dividends. The date payable is the date upon which the dividend is paid.

Dealer See *Stockbroker*.

Debenture A corporate bond that is backed by faith and credit in the issuing *corporation*. There is no specific collateral.

Deep Discount *Bonds* that are selling at a deep discount have a market price that is far below their face value. For example, a bond that is selling for $400 that has a face value of $1000 is said to be a deep discount bond.

Depreciation A variety of accounting methods may be used to allocate the cost of an asset over its useful life.

Directors Shareholders elect directors to represent them in establishing corporate policies, including hiring officers, declaring dividends, and other important issues.

Discount See *Capitalization Rate, Parity,* and *Par Value*.

Diversification Diversification refers to a combination of assets in a *portfolio* that have returns that are not perfectly correlated. That is, the returns do not increase or decrease in exactly the same fashion.

Dividend Dividends may be in the form of cash, stock, or tangible property. Cash dividends are declared by the directors of a *corporation* and are usually paid from corporate earnings. Cash dividends are the only return that most investors receive until they sell their stock.

Dividend Reinvestment Plan Some companies allow their shareholders to buy additional shares of newly issued stock instead of taking cash dividends. No brokerage fees are charged, and sometimes the new shares are offered at a discount from the market value to encourage participation.

Dollar Cost Averaging See *Formula Plans*.

Dow Theory A method of predicting stock prices based on the performance of the Dow Jones industrial and transportation averages. According to the theory, the market is in an upward (bull) trend when one of these averages surpasses a previous high, and it is followed by the other average. Conversely, declines in both averages can signal a declining (bear) market.

Efficient Capital Markets The term efficient markets implies that a large number of investors

have access to all relevant information and that they act on that information as soon as possible. Therefore, security prices fully reflect all available information. The extent to which this occurs may vary. The weak form of the efficient market hypothesis states that stock prices follow a *random walk*. The semistrong form incorporates a wider range of information. The strong form incorporates all information.

Equity The residual value of a business concern once the liabilities have been discharged. It represents ownership. The equity portion of a balance sheet includes stock, retained earnings, and certain reserves and surplus accounts.

Eurodollars Short-term deposits that are denominated in dollars and placed in banks outside the United States. They generally carry higher rates of interest than domestic deposits.

Ex-Dividend See *Date Declared*.

Exercise Price Exercise price or striking price is the price at which an option may be exercised. The exercise cutoff time is 5:30 P.M. Eastern Standard Time on the business day preceding the date when the option expires. Options must be exercised by that time.

Ex-Rights A stock selling without *rights* (from a rights offering) attached is said to be selling ex-rights. If the rights are still attached, it is selling cum rights. The difference between the two centers on the transfer process necessary to transfer the stockholder's name on the company books. Only those whose names are on the books are entitled to the rights. See also *Date Declared*.

Federal Funds Rate See *LIBOR*.

Financial Leverage The relationship between borrowed funds and shareholders' equity. Some analysts consider *preferred stock* in the same category as debt-borrowed funds. Firms with a high proportion of debt to equity are said to be highly leveraged. Financial *leverage* increases the volatility of earnings and the *financial risk* of the firm.

Financial Risk The *risk* that a firm might not be able to meet its financial obligations. Firms that have a high proportion of debt to equity face greater financial risk than firms with a low ratio. Financial risk plus *business risk* equal *total risk*.

First Mortgage Bond See *Mortgage Bonds*.

Formula Plans A mechanistic way of determining when to buy and sell securities, formula plans are based on price changes or on periodic investments without regard to price.

Four C Grading Scale The quality of diamonds is determined by carat weight, cut, color, and clarity.

Futures Contracts To buy or sell financial instruments or physical commodities for future delivery on a commodity exchange.

General Mortgage Bond See *Mortgage Bonds*.

Gilt-Edged Bonds that are highly rated and issued by companies with the proven ability to meet their financial obligations.

Globalization This refers to the increased linkages between financial markets throughout the world. See *GLOBEX*.

GLOBEX The GLOBEX commodity trading system is computerized information/trading system that links the Chicago Mercantile Exchange to European and Asian locations. See *Globalization*.

Gordon Model This theoretical model, developed by Myron Gordon, can be used to determine the theoretical value of a stock by discounting expected cash *dividends* by the rate of return required by *equity* investors.

Hedging When used in connection with commodities, hedging is a means of transferring the *risk* of price fluctuations to speculators who are willing to take that risk in the hope of making a profit. It means taking an opposite but equal position in the cash and futures market.

Holding Period Return A measure of returns during a given period of time; derived by summing the cash dividend and the price at the end of the period, then dividing that amount by the price of the security at the beginning of the period.

Horizontal Merger A horizontal merger occurs when companies are acquired in the same line of business—for example, one food store buying another. See also *Conglomerate*.

In-the-Money The market price of a *futures contract* is higher than the *exercise price* of a *call option* or lower than the exercise price of a *put option*. See *At-the-Money*; and *Out-of-the-Money*.

Income Bonds A hybrid type of *bond* developed out of reorganizations of railroads and other types of business. Interest on these bonds is paid only if it is earned, and interest payments will accumulate until there is sufficient income to pay them.

Indenture The contract portion of a *bond* that specifies all of the terms and obligations of the debtor.

Interest Rate Futures Market This market is organized to trade in financial "futures contracts" in the same way that commodities are traded in the commodities markets. Futures contracts are traded on various government securities, currencies, and *commercial paper*. See also *Hedging*.

Intrinsic Value That portion of an option premium representing the dollar amount the option is *in-the-money*. See *Investment Value*.

Investment Bankers Intermediaries between business concerns that need capital and investors who have funds to invest. To serve these two groups, investment bankers *underwrite* security issues and provide other services for the issuing company and investors.

Investment Company A financial intermediary that pools the funds of investors and invests

them in securities such as stocks and bonds. *Money market funds* are a specialized type of pool that invests in short-term securities. Generally, investors can write checks against their money market funds, which makes them equivalent to interest-bearing checking accounts.

Investment Value (1) The theoretical price of a *bond* without a conversion feature. It is the present value of the coupon payments and principal amount discounted by the current market rate of interest for an equivalent bond. (2) The investment value of a share of *common stock* is its theoretical value. Such values can be determined by the *Gordon Model* or by some other means. Sometimes the investment value is called the intrinsic value. The investment value can differ from the market value of a security.

Leverage Refers to the magnifying effect that changes in sales can have on earnings as a result of fixed expenses and payments. See also *Financial Leverage*.

LIBOR The acronym for **London Interbank Offering Rate**, the interest rate charged on short-term money in the *Eurodollar* market between banks. It is analogous to the federal funds rate, the rate at which banks lend excess reserves to each other.

Life Cycles An analytical tool used to evaluate products, companies, and industries as they evolve through four phases (pioneering, expansion, stabilization, and decline) of development.

Limited Partnerships Limited partners in oil and real estate investments put up most of the money and get some of the return. They also have limited liability and take no part in management. The general partner puts up a relatively small amount of money and manages the investment. The general partner receives a fee for these services and a share of the earnings. The general partner is liable.

Liquidity (1) The ability of a firm to meet its current financial obligations. (2) The ability of

investors to sell assets on short notice, with little or no loss from the current market value of the asset, is also known as liquidity.

Listed Stock The stock of a company that is traded regularly on a securities exchange.

Load The commission charge on an open-end mutual fund. The commission usually costs 8 percent or more and, in most cases, is charged only when the shares are purchased.

Margin (1) Credit extended by stockbrokers or banks to investors to buy securities. (2) Margin, used with commodities, is a good-faith deposit, not credit.

Mark-to-Market The daily adjustment of open futures positions to reflect profits or losses.

Member Firm A member firm is a member of an organized *stock exchange,* such as the *New York Stock Exchange.*

Merger A combination of two or more firms where only one firm survives and retains its identity — for example, Pizza Hut merged into Pepsico, which is the surviving company.

Money Market Funds *Investment companies* pool the monies of investors and invest in short-term financial obligations. Money market funds provide relatively high yields, and drafts can be written against current holdings. Thus, they are like interest-bearing checking accounts.

Mortgage Bonds A corporate bond that is backed by a mortgage on specific real estate. A first mortgage bond is backed by the first mortgage on that real estate. A second mortgage bond is backed by the second mortgage. A general mortgage bond is backed by a third or some other mortgage on that same real estate.

Naked Options The term *naked* or *uncovered* means that the seller of the *call option* does not own the underlying stock.

National Association of Securities Dealers The **NASD** is an association of brokers and dealers in *over-the-counter* securities organized for self-regulation.

Net Worth See *Equity.*

New York Stock Exchange (NYSE) The largest organized securities exchange in the United States. About 1500 different companies have their securities traded on the exchange. They include the major companies in the United States. Only stockbrokerage firms that are members of the exchange can trade securities there. However, nonmember firms may utilize the services of member firms (called correspondent firms) for a fee to have securities traded and for other services.

Options See *Call Option* and *Put Option.*

Ordinary Voting Shareholders are entitled to one vote for each share held when voting for directors of a *corporation* and on other issues. See also *Cumulative Voting.*

Original Issue Discount (OID) A bond that is issued at a price less than the face amount. The OID, the difference between the initial offering price and the face amount, is considered a form of taxable interest as it accrues over time.

Out-of-the-Money The market price of a *futures contract* is below the *exercise price* of a *call option* and above the exercise price of a *put option.* See *In-the-Money* and *At-the-Money.*

Over-the-Counter (OTC) The OTC market is a securities market consisting of brokers and dealers throughout the world who are linked together by telephone, telegraph, and other means of communication to execute transactions. Securities that are not traded on exchanges are traded in the OTC. See *National Association of Securities Dealers.*

Overvalued See *Undervalued.*

Parity When a convertible *bond* is selling for its *conversion value,* it is at parity. If the market price exceeds the conversion value, it is selling for a premium. Conversely, if it is selling below its

conversion value, it is selling at a discount. See *Par Value* for other uses of premium and discount.

Par Value   (1) The stated value of the bond in the *indenture*, typically $1000. If the market price of the bond is above par value, it is selling at a premium. Conversely, if the market price is below par value, it is selling at a discount. Premium and discount are also used in connection with *parity*. (2) *Common* and *preferred stocks* also have par values or stated values on the face of the stock certificates. Generally, these values have little to do with the market value of the stock. However, in the case of liquidation, the par value of preferred stock may be important.

Payout Ratio   The percentage of earnings paid to common shareholders in the form of cash *dividends*.

Portfolio   A combination of assets. For example, all stock listed on the *New York Stock Exchange* comprises a portfolio.

Preferred Stock   One class of ownership in a *corporation*. *Common stock* is another class. The preferred stocks usually have fixed *dividends*. Some are convertible, and some participate in earnings over and above the fixed dividends. Preferred stock may have voting rights. See also *Arrears, Common Stock,* and *Corporation*.

Premium   See *Parity* and *Par Value*.

Price Earnings (P/E) Ratio   The number of times earnings that investors are willing to pay for a stock. It is determined by dividing the market price of a stock by its earnings. Growth stocks tend to have higher price earnings ratios than stocks that are growing at a slower pace.

Primary Market   The first time newly issued securities are sold to investors by *investment bankers*. The securities can be placed directly with financial intermediaries such as insurance companies or be sold to the public. The primary market provides business concerns with an important source of funds — the investor's money.

Profit Margin   A measure of profitability derived by dividing net income by net sales. It is the percentage of profit earned for each dollar of sales.

Program Trading   Computer-assisted purchase and sale of large numbers — both amounts and issues — of securities. It is frequently used in connection with *futures contracts* on stock indexes and *arbitrage*.

Prospectus   A legal document required by the Securities and Exchange Commission in connection with the issuance of certain new securities. It is supposed to provide prospective investors with sufficient information so that they can make intelligent decisions about buying the securities.

Put Option   The holder of the option can sell a specified number of shares of a stock, or a commodity, at a predetermined price on or before a certain date. See also *Call Option*.

Random Walk   Stock prices are said to follow a random walk. This means that stock prices in the previous periods cannot be used to predict stock prices in future periods because changes in stock prices are random.

Red Herring   A preliminary *prospectus* issued to investors is called a red herring because some statements on the front page are printed in red ink to warn investors that the prospectus is incomplete — the price is missing.

Restrictive Covenants   Bond contracts — *indentures* — contain clauses that prohibit the debtor from taking certain actions in order to protect the creditor. For example, payment of *dividends* may be limited to current earnings.

Returns   The total return on a security includes both income and price changes. See *Holding Period Return*.

Reverse Split   Stock splits are used to increase the number of shares outstanding. However, a reverse split is used to reduce the number of shares outstanding. A 2 for 1 reverse split means

that a stockholder will hold one share after the split for every two shares held before the split. See also *Stock Dividend.*

Rights Companies selling additional *common stock* may give their stockholders rights to buy their pro rata share of the new issue. Rights are actually a short-term *call option* to buy a certain number of shares at a predetermined price. The rights have market value and can be traded. Rights are also called preemptive rights or a privileged subscription.

Risk The probability that the actual returns will deviate from expected returns. The standard deviation is one commonly used measure of deviation from expected returns.

Risk-free Rate of Return Considered to be the return on default-free Treasury securities.

Risk Premium The increased return over the *risk-free rate* that investors require to invest in a risky asset is called the risk premium.

Secondary Distribution The sale of a large *block* of stock (i.e., 300,000 shares) at a reduced price. If the block, which is held by investors, were sold directly on the market, the price of the stock might be depressed. The secondary distribution minimizes the depressing effect of selling the stock.

Secondary Market In the secondary market, investors who bought new issues in the *primary market* can sell them to other investors. The secondary market provided *liquidity* for investors. Without the existence of a secondary market, investors would require higher returns because of the inconvenience of not being able to sell securities and the higher risk of holding them over time.

Securities Exchange Commission (SEC) The SEC was established by Congress to help protect investors, primarily by regulating the issuance and trading of certain securities.

Securities Investor Protection Corporation

(SIPC) The SIPC is a nonprofit membership corporation created by Congress to insure certain customer accounts if member securities firms fail.

Security Market Line (SML) The relationships between expected rates of return for assets and their respective *systemic risks* measured by *beta.* See also *Capital Asset Pricing Model.*

Short Sale The sale of a borrowed security or commodity at a high price in anticipation of buying it back at a lower price is a short sale. The difference between the high selling price and the low buying price is profit. The borrowed stock is returned when the security is purchased.

Sinking Fund Provides for the periodic retirement of certain portions of a *bond* issued through periodic payments made by the *corporation.* The payments are made to a trustee who can purchase the bonds, call them, or let the funds accumulate.

Spin Off A *dividend* consisting of assets, such as stock held by a *corporation,* is distributed to its shareholders. For example, in 1962, shareholders of E.I. du Pont DeNemours and Company were given shares of General Motors as a result of antitrust litigation.

Spot Rate The cash price for immediate delivery of a commodity.

Spread (1) The difference between the price at which an investor can sell a security (bid price) and the price at which it can be bought (asked price). For example, a stock is quoted at $15 bid – $16 asked, meaning that an investor can sell it at $15 per share or buy it at $16 per share. The spread is $1. Spread also refers to the difference between yields of *bonds* with different degrees of *risk.* (2) In connection with options or commodities, spread is the simultaneous purchase of one contract (going long) and the sale of another (going short) on the same stock, but with different striking prices or maturities.

Stand-by Underwriting A company with a *rights* offering may employ an *investment banker*

to stand by to buy all rights that are not exercised by investors. The *underwriter* buys them and provides the firm with the funds it needs, for a fee.

Stock Dividend   Most stock dividends are for 25 percent or less. When a company issues the additional stock to its shareholders, the increase in capital stock is offset by a reduction in retained earnings by a like amount. In the case of a stock split, the split represents an increase in the number of shares outstanding but there is no accounting adjustment to retained earnings. Most splits are 2 for 1, which means that the stockholder gets one additional share for each one held. It is like a 100-percent stock dividend from the stockholder's point of view.

Stock Exchange   The physical place existing for the benefit of its members who buy and sell securities. The largest stock exchange in the United States is the *New York Stock Exchange*, followed by the Midwest and American Stock Exchanges.

Stock Splits   See *Stock Dividend.*

Stockbroker   Stockbrokerage firms act as both brokers and dealers. As brokers in the *secondary market*, they are agents for their customers, receiving a commission for their services. As dealers, they trade for their own accounts and are principals in the transactions, hoping to make a profit from the difference between the buying and selling price.

Straddle   A combination of a put and *call* option.

Striking Price   See *Exercise Price.*

Synthetics   The duplication of the behavior of one security by using combinations of other securities is usually accomplished with the use of *put and call options.*

Systemic Risk   Risk that is common to all assets and cannot be eliminated by *diversification.* It is measured by *beta.*

Tax-exempt Bonds   *Bonds* issued by state and local governments. Interest payments are exempt from federal income taxes.

Tax Shelter   A means of deferring income tax until the future or reducing current income tax payments. Oil and real estate investments are typical tax shelters because they provide large noncash tax deductions in the form of *depreciation.*

Tender Offer   An offer to buy stock from shareholders at a predetermined price for a certain amount of time. The tender offer is generally limited to a certain number of shares (i.e., 1 million). It is used by companies that wish to acquire the stocks of other companies.

Total Risk   Equal to *systemic risk* plus *unsystematic risk.*

Uncovered Options   See *Naked Options.*

Undervalued   The difference between the *investment value* of an asset and its market value. If a stock has an investment value of $50 per share and a market value of $40 per share, it is said to be undervalued—it is worth more than the current market price. Conversely, if the stock were selling at $60 per share, it would be overvalued.

Underwrite   *Investment bankers* underwrite securities, which means that they buy a security from a company and sell it to investors. The investment banker receives the difference between the buying and selling price, which is called flotation cost. The flotation costs include legal fees and other expenses associated with the new issue.

Unsystematic Risk   Risk that is unique to a particular asset and can be eliminated by *diversification.*

Vertical Spread   See *Spread.*

Warrant   A *call option* to buy a stated number of shares of stock at a stated price on or before a

predetermined date. Warrants are attached to other securities, such as *bonds,* when the bonds are issued in order to make them more attractive to the investor. Sometime thereafter, the warrants are detached and trade on their own.

When Issued Securities may be traded on a "when and as if issued basis" when a stock goes *ex-rights.* The trading in *rights* will be on a when issued basis until the rights are mailed to the stockholders. Then they will be traded on the "regular way."

White Knight A *merger* partner of a company's own choosing. A company make seek a white knight to keep an unwanted suitor away.

Yield Curve The relationship between interest rates *(yield to maturity)* and the maturity of a security. The shape of the yield curve can be used to evaluate the future course of interest rates.

Yield to Maturity The weighted average return on a debt security, taking into account the income provided by interest payments as well as *capital gains* or *losses* until the security matures.

INDEX